Vaughan Williams

1. Ralph Vaughan Williams, *c.* 1920

VAUGHAN WILLIAMS

by

A. E. F. DICKINSON

FABER AND FABER

24 Russell Square

London

First published in mcmlxiii
by Faber and Faber Limited
24 Russell Square London W.C.1
Printed in Great Britain
by Spottiswoode, Ballantyne and Co. Ltd.
London and Colchester

Contents

7

Illustrations

Acknowledgments

1. GENERAL

I have pleasure in making certain acknowledgments: to the retail and hire sections of the Oxford University Press Music Department for generous loans of music, and various special information; similarly, on a smaller scale, to Messrs. Curwen and Sons Limited, Stainer and Bell Limited, and Boosey and Hawkes Limited; to the Council of the Durham Colleges in the University of Durham for the granting of a term's leave for the necessary study, and for travel assistance at various times, and to the Durham University Library staff for constant help in obtaining the loan of accessory works; to the gramophone record library of the B.B.C., for access to old records, and to the recordings department of the B.B.C. for similar access to recorded radio music; to the music library of the B.B.C. for access to certain music; to Mr. Hans Keller for information about recordings, and to Mr. John Huntley of the National Film Institute for information and access to film-music; to Mr. O. W. Neighbour for valuable corrections and suggestions; and, not least, to my wife and son for help in rendering my handwriting into typescript.

2. MUSIC EXAMPLES

I wish to thank Mrs. Vaughan Williams for permission to quote the tune and words of the folk-song, 'Our captain calls all hands' (Ex. 8), and music from the film, *Scott of the Antarctic* (Ex. 68). I wish also to thank Sir Adrian Boult and the university authority concerned for permission to quote from his copy of the corrected original version of the *London Symphony*, which he has placed on permanent loan in the library of the music department of Liverpool University (Ex. 21*a*, 21*b*, 22). (See p. 499, however.)

I wish to acknowledge the kind permission of the publishers to quote music as listed below:

ACKNOWLEDGMENTS

Publisher	Music Example	Work
Boosey & Hawkes Ltd.	12, 13	*On Wenlock Edge*
	19*b*	Ireland: *London Overture*
Breitkopf & Härtel, Wiesbaden	11	*Willow Wood*
J. B. Cramer & Co.	5*h*	Folk-tune: 'My Johnny was a shoemaker'
J. Curwen & Sons	7*g*	'Ca' the yowes'
	6*c*, 6*d*, 7*a*, 7*b*, 25, 26	*Pastoral Symphony*
	7*e*, 29, 30	*Sancta Civitas*
	6*a*	Overture, *The Wasps*
Durand et Cie	2*c*, 2*d*, 2*e*	Debussy: *Reflets dans l'eau*
	2*b*, 2*f*	Ravel: Sonatina for piano
Hinrichsen Edition Limited	1*e*	Strauss: *Till Eulenspiegel*
Novello & Co. Ltd.	1*b*	Elgar: *Enigma Variations*
	1*c*	Elgar: *The Dream of Gerontius*
	1*d*	Elgar: Symphony 2 in E flat
	5*e*	Folk-tune: 'Searching for lambs'
	5*f*	Folk-tune: 'The sign of the Bonny Blue Bell'
	5*i*	Folk tune: 'A bold young farmer'
Oxford University Press Music Department	69	*Ten Blake Songs*
	66	*Coastal Command*, suite
	60, 61, 62	Concerto for piano and orchestra
	63	*Concerto Grosso*
	27	*Dona nobis pacem*
	28	*Flos Campi*
	48–53	*Hodie* (*This Day*)
	14, 15	*In the Fen Country*
	47	*Job, a Masque for Dancing*
	64, 65	*Partita* for double string orchestra
	33	*Poisoned Kiss, The*
	34–37	*Riders to the Sea*
	54, 55	*Sinfonia antartica*
	6*e*, 31, 32	*Sir John in Love*
	67	*Story of a Flemish Farm*, suite
		Symphonies:
	7*d*, 38–40	4 in F minor
	41	5 in D
	42–46	[6] in E minor
	56	8 in D minor
	57–59	9 in E minor

ACKNOWLEDGMENTS

Publisher	Music Example	Work
Schott & Co. Ltd.	2a	Ravel: *Pavane pour une Infante défunte*
Stainer & Bell Ltd.	7c, 7f, 18, 19a, 20, 21c, 21d, 23, 24	*London Symphony*
	6b, 16	*Sea Symphony*
Universal Edition (London) Ltd.	5a, 4g	Two Hungarian folk-tunes (Kodály: *Mátra Pictures*)

3. ILLUSTRATIONS

Acknowledgments are due to the Oxford University Press for reproduction of pages of the MSS of *Riders to the Sea*, the *Romance for Harmonica*, and the ninth symphony; to Mrs. Vaughan Williams for reproduction of a page of the sketch for the *Sea Symphony*; to the Radio Times Hulton Picture Library for reproduction of the photograph of Vaughan Williams taken by Mr. Charles Hewitt; to the Central Office of Information for reproduction of the photograph of Vaughan Williams that appeared in the *Year's Work in Music*, 1947; to the Librarian of Charterhouse and Mr. David Paton, A.R.P.S., for reproduction of a group photograph with Vaughan Williams in it; and to Mr. Allan Chappelow, M.A., F.R.S.A., for reproduction of his photograph of Vaughan Williams at the 'White Gates', Dorking.

ABBREVIATIONS USED IN THE MUSIC EXAMPLES*

orch.	orchestra
str.	strings
v. (v. I, v. II)	violin (1st, 2nd)
va.	viola
vc.	violoncello
d.b.	double bass
picc.	piccolo
fl.	flute
ob.	oboe
c.a.	cor anglais
cl.	clarinet
b. cl.	bass clarinet
sax.	saxophone
bn.	bassoon
d. bn.	double bassoon
br.	brass
tr.	trumpet
ct.	cornet
flüg.	flügelhorn
hn.	horn
trb.	trombone
ta.	tuba
perc.	percussion
timp.	timpani
s.d.	side drum
k.d.	kettle drum
t.d.	tenor drum
b.d.	bass drum
d.-r.	drum-roll
cymb.	cymbals
vibraph.	vibraphone
hp.	harp
pf.	piano
org.	organ
ch.	chorus
S. (sop.)	soprano
A.	alto
T. (ten.)	tenor
B.	bass
con sord.	con sordino
pizz.	pizzicato
stacc.	staccato
trem.	tremolando

* See also footnote on p. 165. For the abbreviation of melodies and harmonic sequences by means of figures, see p. 122*n* and p. 180*n*.

14

I

A Cultivated Response

The development of music in the last two centuries has been conspicuous for the establishment of a growing number of national styles, which have both shaped and been shaped by many great composers, and many more of lesser stature. The foundation of the operas of Handel and Mozart in the craft of Italian composers, the similar debt of Bach's church and keyboard music to later musical Lutheranism, as well as to cosmopolitan Italian fashions, and the common symphonic background of the work of Schubert and Beethoven, Wagner and Strauss, are now well known to have gone beyond considerations of language. Their individualities have, indeed, risen independently to an increasing extent, while manifesting a broad genre of clue-theme, exhaustive treatment, and emotional release. In every case, this national or regional art has penetrated or side-stepped the barriers of language and custom, thanks to some impresario or performer or missionary influence. In this way, Italian, French and German opera and German instrumental music have been accepted in this country as the staple diet for the greater part of the last hundred years. But while homage to foreign personalities, especially conductors, has had its place in converting fresh and widening audiences to a taste for this music, it may still be assumed that its strength has depended on having suited or overcome a local situation in the past.

The patriot who seeks to adorn this narrative by a recital of English conquests in the wider world finds himself baffled by the fugitive attempt of English-bred composers to meet the deeper needs of national music. The stage songs and dances of Purcell and Arne, Handelian Old Testament drama, the pastework of *The Beggar's Opera*, the thin stream of church anthems, the blend of sentimentality and farce in

15

Balfe, did not add up to a distinctive native style, compared with the dominant influences of the time. Nor is anything but cold comfort to be discovered in the occasionally greater poetic intensity of the English and Irish songs, the choral works and operas of Parry and Stanford, of which scarcely a handful remains in any repertory at national level in England, and nothing abroad. The cultivation of the orchestra by Elgar, both in oratorio and in symphonic works, exhibiting various strains of national pride and poetical fervour, but also resplendently cosmopolitan in its pursuit of clue-theme on a symphonic scale, seems at first to be a recognized exception. For many English choral societies, orchestras and audiences, the Elgarian mode is a living tradition, even if its former recognition in Germany, thanks to Richter and others, has largely receded, while elsewhere it hardly counts. Yet there are severe limitations about the wider orbit of this development.

The vocabulary of Elgar's music springs from terms that have ceased to be compelling. All his confident melodies and magical transformations cannot conceal the diminishing impact of the once powerful symbolism of a melodic and harmonic texture that is in decline. Quite apart from the gaping void in any tradition of native opera, the need for fresh sources of expression had become imperative. Otherwise English music, having so eloquently and triumphantly asserted itself, would return to the rehearsal stage of family celebrations, in oratorio or in a symphonic style long rendered obsolete. To speak (as the institutionally minded did) of a 'successor' to Elgar as leading composer was altogether to under-estimate the call for independence, not continuity.

In the discovery at this juncture of fresh national idioms and other necessary stimuli, the art of Ralph Vaughan Williams has been at once the leading English influence and the most enduring in itself. In a comparatively small major output, he has disclosed a steady growth of personality in characteristic music, choral, dramatic and symphonic. Downright from the start, his moods and methods had become recognizable by 1914. But since his craft has singularly kept pace with his art, he has never been openly indebted to his earlier works at any period. He has had no compulsion to excel himself in any symphony, for example, since each is distinctive; and he remained unpredictable to the end.

Encounter with his fifty years of musical output, all at first new music, will accordingly trace a distinct pattern for each age group. Enthusiasts of 1910 could hardly be aware of more than a vigorous, probing musical personality, who did not take symphony for granted, or, incidentally, the strings; or, again, congregational hymnody. A joyful return in 1919 to a world of tempered and widening opportunity confirmed this sense of adventure for critical musicians and added a pioneer orchestral symphony, the *London*, that combined earthy contacts and a classical sense of pattern with flights of fancy; but few listeners could have forecast any subsequent turn of events. Audiences, however, who had been in touch with the composer's main work up to 1925 were aware of a refinement of his methods of appeal in the *Pastoral Symphony* and *Sancta Civitas*, along with the much broader and largely post-dated *Hugh the Drover*, and a fresh concern for the hymn-tune repertory in *Songs of Praise*. By 1936, the more or less recent novelties, *Job*, the fourth symphony, *Magnificat* and *Five Tudor Portraits*, had each shown a fresh pressure of ideas and basic material, the symphony being conspicuously arresting. Once again, *Sir John in Love* pointed almost retrospectively to the composer's wider, rather than to his 'contemporary' leanings. But *Riders to the Sea*, just published and not yet performed, although in fact a work of the late 'twenties, was as uncompromising as any work, except in the avoidance of any overt violence of statement. The main emergent impression was that the meditative obsessions of the 'twenties were not forgotten but were being held in tight reserve, along with the earlier exuberance of melody and declamation. To hear back ten or fifteen years was becoming an effort of self-rarefication.

By 1951 it had become clear that while the fourth symphony had marked a turning point, there were other routes of progress. More than ever, the stage product of the time, *The Pilgrim's Progress*, showed far more confirmation of earlier styles than the establishment of any fresh features; and, less surprisingly, of the new and vigorous film-music only *Scott of the Antarctic* pointed forward at all. Moreover, if the fifth and sixth symphonies were the later models, now they promoted a return to the third and fourth. Then came three more symphonies of notable contrast, none predictable, with a compact 'Three Choirs' work, *Hodie*, between the seventh and the later symphonies. If in the final movements of *Hodie* and the eighth symphony the elation of the *Job* Galliard seemed, to questioning ears, too easily revived, in its initial recollection of the titles-music of *Scott*, as a recurrent feature, the *Sinfonia Antartica* had made an impressive start to the new stage; a stage of informal and arbitrary development, not of intense argument. At this point the fourth symphony might seem too concentrated, the

London Symphony too seriously comprehensive, and the sixth symphony decidedly lacking in humour. Such distances of time and genre remain musically considerable, whether covered forwards or backwards. No such problem of style separates *The Kingdom* from *Gerontius*, or *Falstaff* and the Elgar symphonies from the oratorios, *mutatis mutandis*. The main question there is of structural validity; of the integrity of component movements and works.

In whatever order of period or preference for an individual listener, the music of Vaughan Williams has made a nation-wide appeal, from the exuberance of *Hugh* and *Sir John* and, in another sphere, *Benedicite*, to the startling range of *Job* and the monumental progress through the symphonies. Some works, such as *Sancta Civitas* and the piano concerto, have not been so recognized, but that has probably been a matter of chance and failure in promotion. In this emancipation from the past, for an important part of his career, Vaughan Williams had Holst closely by his side, and a new generation was to follow. If the stern impressiveness of *Savitri* (1908) and the choral hymns from the *Rig Veda* was still barely recognized in 1919, without question *The Planets* broke down any prejudice that lavish and exact orchestral characterization had ended with Strauss; the *Hymn of Jesus* established a new and thrilling absorption in the musical moment, to match a veiled *Communion* ritual; the *Ode to Death*, *First Choral Symphony* and the *Choral Fantasia* followed, with *Egdon Heath* pointing to a fresh, unfulfilled specialization of mood, and the operas to an uncouth relaxation. Nor could the composer of the *Mass of Life* and *Sea Drift*, enjoying the special support of Thomas Beecham, fail to convey to English audiences the potentialities of a new musical impressionism. Nevertheless, the musical half-century in England may be described, if anything, as the age of Vaughan Williams, not of Holst or Delius. It is the free-speaking age in which the art of composers so unlike as Walton and Rubbra, Tippett and Britten, has been brought to light. On any valuation, Vaughan Williams has remained at the front as an outspoken artist, not merely the longest surviving figure in a group. Nationalist trends and political restrictions have prevented any definite spread of his music abroad, except to the United States. Nevertheless, its impact beyond its national frontiers is growing, and where it has penetrated, critics have recognized its hard core of experience.

As a leading figure of a genuine English revival, and as a fearless, veracious artist, of commanding appeal in his time, Vaughan Williams is assured of a place in the nation's memories and records. Meanwhile, his art claims a more practical recognition. The accession of the *Tallis Fantasia* to popularity, after years of sporadic appearance, is a reminder that a time-lag can be diminished by persistent performance and personal advocacy. It remains to close certain gaps on similar lines, and to keep the symphonies in regular circulation, without that obsession for one or two, from which Beethoven has suffered in the past. The recording of the nine, and of the *Job* music, is a firm start for the home listener, but in the sphere of live performance hardly any choral work is sure of the regular attention of choral societies, the piano concerto has not properly arrived, and one cannot be sure of the future of any stage work, apart from *Job*.

A spontaneous circulation of his general output is the first claim which a composer of more than national standing can make on immediate posterity. This will be the concern of conductors, executives and committees. Meanwhile the individual has his own account to settle, and by his informed interest in, and particular demand for, the composer's works may hope to influence musical society, whether he starts as a believer or as a sceptic.

It is a large undertaking. There are wide differences between one period and another, and wherever a listener happens first to have struck Vaughan Williams, he has to extend his receptiveness in quality as well as quantity of material. Then there are different genres and levels, choral, orchestral and dramatic, each appealing to different types of listener, and in the choral-orchestral works ranging from the repertory of struggling village choirs and their conductors, working towards competition and combined performance at the end of a season's grind, to the more agile accomplishment of the regional festival choir. There is also a certain amount of chamber-music, solo-songs and pieces for intimate vocal ensemble. In all this exploration, a sense of direction and a selection of characteristic examples are expedient.

This, briefly, is the objective, material problem of investigating the music to some profit. But underlying it all is the challenge of expanding styles, as expressed in changing textures, in the structures which give them meaning, and sometimes in the texts that explain why the music is there at all. In an art grounded on the perception of relationships in physical and psychological time, *what* takes place from section to section, and from movement to movement, is not often immediately obvious, and the characteristic *how* is frequently elusive, except to practised ears. In consequence, a fresh development of style can be baffling. Moreover, in Vaughan Williams's music, as in that of many other creators, a duality of expressive medium soon makes itself felt, and leads to further subdivisions. Bluntly, there are the downright melody-maker, rhythmic and rough, influenced by folk-song in choice of melodic pattern, and the 'dreamy' pursuer of harmonic and instrumental texture, capricious in appearance at first, but on acquaintance showing definitely automatic stages of expansion. One can discern, analogously, the sociable composer, transforming common sounds into things of quality, and the unworldly composer, moving in a region of remote contemplation and ecstasy. Later, there appears a third composer, positive but thriving on contradictions of degree in an implied scale, and harmonically incisive, but now, it sometimes seems, in passionate social denunciation or arousal, not in mere contemplation. These different strains may be observed within the orbit of a single work or movement. Presumably the harmonically trenchant has cost the composer the most thought. Yet he evidently attaches the first importance to a directly melodic appeal of a solid kind, depending on some spontaneous movement of the voice or on the casual modification of a degree in an established stretch of melody. For the sophisticated listener, the apparent drop in tension is sometimes baffling. But at least the alternation of appeal must be recognized. The keen observer has to arrive at the composer's inner dynamic at a given period, or in a particular work, from a nice balance of what dominating influences his ears identify as integral.

A composer writes a work to be performed, not studied, on the assumption that if it will not please now, it will please some day, that is, after an interval for repeated hearings. On some such grounds, no doubt, Vaughan Williams declared more than once that if a composition needed any explanation beyond itself, it had failed. Yet this is no more than half the truth about reception. There are many ways of taking a piece of music, not all of them strictly relevant, and the immediate apprehension of the bare structure is often a precarious stage. Moreover, not many listeners can give the proper time for a special reception of every piece that is new to them. Thus, sheer repetition, even with a score as guide, is frequently, for listeners as for performers, the hard way to understanding. A preliminary sizing-up of the order of events, and of the salient features of appeal, is a patent economy of effort. Further, modern art, the heritage of centuries of experience and changing method, is not merely to be intuitively experienced. It is to be sifted, and that means discussing it with another observer, comparing facts noted and the values set upon them. Performance, with all its sweat in the effort of co-ordinating mind and muscle, has a receiving side, in which listeners of intelligence will not refuse to play their special and far from passive part. If they can be players or singers too, so much the better. But such participation, even the conductor's comprehensive enactment of the music, is not the same thing as the listener's observant and concentrated reception of it into his awareness, with any apt comparisons of precedent style and of present and remembered fact.

Such a comparison of sheer 'fact' is offered by the process recently demonstrated by Mr. Hans Keller and termed functional analysis. This works by way of analytic preludes and postludes to a performance, demonstrating by didactic juxtaposition the essentially similar or related melodic features, which then spring into place, mentally, as functional elements. This method, which is not altogether new in the spoken and illustrated side of educational practice of the last half-century, is a convenient approach to a tightly packed, economic quartet-movement whose general structural trends and basic phrase-lengths can well be taken for granted. It would be laborious for any part of a work that is prodigal in material and development, such as an extended symphonic movement or act; and *a fortiori* for a work of studied variety and complexity. On paper, it would involve lavish quotation, and at the end only the primary connecting factors of a certain, mainly melodic, type would have become apparent. Rhythmically answered or unanswered phrases, or passages, the general lay-out of material and, above all, relative significance, would be left with the barest indication. Literary comment must attempt at least to summarize the order of events in such wider aspects, with as much functional analysis as quotation and indication of its later relevance may provide, leaving it to the reader's faculty of observation, memory, or deduction to supply what is not quoted. Whatever its abuses, literary suggestion has its own powers of functional distinction. A working compromise is needed. In every developed composition there are, to clarify to oneself, first, a proposition, a sequence of general assertions of relationship, and secondly a supporting or underlying argument or contrast of ideas and impressions.

There is no 'practical' limit here to the number of major works which call for this clarification. It is, broadly, not true that a work is less worth examination because it was written around 1910 or 1935 or 1955 or even 1905; nor, again, because it was written for only two players, or for the specially exclusive or equalitarian conditions of a festival, organized for a particular purpose or on an ambitiously national level. All the operas and choral works find their own peculiar shape, according to the text, and even the symphonies observe little in common, apart

21

from a series of four movements, some of which end while others reach a condition of finish. It would be safe to assume that most readers bring to the enlargement of their experience of Vaughan Williams a gapped series of verified impressions of particular works. There is no work whose total impact is familiar enough to be left with a bare mention; not even the *Tallis Fantasia*, apart from its tune and its sonorities. Moreover, even the plays of Shakespeare continue to be discussed at a high level, not only in terms of salient imagery, characterization and metrical treatment, but of elementary shape. No account of a musical work here can lightly take its lay-out for granted; and discussions of detail cannot proceed except in reference to a pattern laid down, apart from references to numbered bars and rehearsal marks in the printed text of a given movement, the availability of which cannot be generally assumed.

In seeking to identify the nature of a work or movement, it is possible to forecast certain alternatives. First, a work will contain a certain number of declared movements, or, where these are too numerous, of a more palatable number of unofficial groupings of movements, which may be patent to the ear, or such as a reasonable synthesis suggests. The number will not be significant, but the validity of a balanced variety will be. As Hegel observed, music, like architecture, has an abstract quantitative relation, as distinct from its inward and emotional quality. What is paramount in the sequence known as symphony must be sought in other genres. Textual divisions and dramatic scenes and incidents often prompt a sense of pattern, but the tempo-contrast of movements is the main and patent phenomenon presented at this level. Each movement may similarly show obvious subdivisions of successive and, to some degree, contrasted mood or tempo, in terms of which various features attract notice. To distinguish the main stages of the finale of *A Sea Symphony*, for example, is an inevitable preliminary to the understanding of its symphonic validity; and the same question arises over the composition of the longer of the *Tudor Portraits*. Among the more typical and formally organized movements, the scherzo is conspicuous for its elementary definition of the main mood by sheer contrast with one or more interludes or diversions midway, and other movements are occasionally framed in this way.

Alternatively, the design of a movement is not founded on such a contrast but on that synthesis of distinct ideas in which music excels. Two methods recur: the extended strophe, repeated with significant modifications, and the 'sonata' pattern of exposition, development, restatement, and coda, which may perhaps be of a special kind, commonly termed epilogue. In each of these, a firm core of perceptible features, whether interpreted in a strophe or associated in a wider deployment of motives and connecting formulae, makes itself felt initially. Later variations of such cardinal features derive their meaning, for alert ears, as fresh amplifications of the structural part concerned. Each method may be used on a more perfunctory scale, in recurring clue-phrases, and in thematic development that becomes side-tracked. The principle of consistent imagery remains.

All such musical argument may be characteristically promoted by the progressive stages of a poem in its various stanzas or, as in a sonnet, sections, or by the varied encounter of a succession of poems, taken from one source or many; or it may treat the poetry as the mere stimulus and connecting substance for a free musical assertion. In any case, there is set up some relation between the musical balance and the original one, to recognize or perhaps to ignore. A salient entry in opera, ballet or the mind's concert-drama similarly initiates a fresh turn of expression, whether it corresponds closely or marks an altogether novel stage of development. A vocal soloist or chorus also evokes a working relation of text, singing matter and orchestral theme on the lines of declamatory recitative, arioso, cantabile, or sheer vocal exploration, propelled by an intermittent orchestral rhythm or, at least, harmonic progression. Any of these may qualify, or alternate with, the strophical pull already mentioned.

As a final underlying synthesis, the revelations of character and the dramatic and symbolic objectives of each act or textual part will guide, if not determine, the musical course of a stage work, or of a concert-work whose imaginative programme points to some stage of emotional conversion, from provisional, uncritical acceptance to intense concern. The didactic urge, the stimulating and discomforting call to more than lip-service, informs the whole music, as in a true hymn-tune. It is no use treating *Hodie* as a refined set of Christmas decorations, or *The Pilgrim's Progress* as a collection of picturesque incidents. In the latter, the decision to go forward, the later delays and advances, the hazardous and thrilling arrival at the summit of endeavour, are deliberately chosen points of suspense in a quest assumed to be the business of every maturing spectator. In *Hodie*, the most familiar narrative of all is unfolded once more in a growing essay to lead men ecstatically back to a sense of rare delights, but also to universal, tremendous tasks of co-existence, the key-word being the *then* of an ideal future. There are also certain works with only titles or quotations, or even without titles, which may be judged to be romantic or didactic in principle by a probing listener. This controversial reception will be discussed when it arises.

In this connection, it will be understood that some works are, by their encounter with historic phases or personal features in other arts, complicated or confused in their literary or dramatic associations, out of proportion to their abiding artistic interest. It is none the less expedient that these should be exposed and sifted as such, in order that a proper estimate may be arrived at. It is not practicable always to confine literary space here according to the importance of its musical content. Indeed, the most pronounced works may be the least noteworthy. On the more pedestrian levels, the listener may find investigation tedious, but if there are opposing pulls or awkward twists of contrary or even incompatible imagery, they should be recognized for what distraction they may be worth. It has been my endeavour not to gloss over such underlying problems of multiple style, as they may occur to a well-balanced listener, nor to grudge a wider concern for any non-musical development that may seem to converge in, or radiate from, a particular musical work. This is particularly urgent with a work that absorbs (or should absorb) a compilation of texts, whether similar in style or united only in theme. Nor can a pivotal period of artistic achievement, such as Blake's developed symbolism, or Anglo-Irish drama in the first decade of the century, be taken for granted in interpreting Vaughan Williams's absorption of these communications. The composer travelled in many realms.

Such are the main dispositions of works and movements, which call for definition. We come to the difficult question of component and evocative texture, rhythmic, harmonic, melodic, instrumental and vocal, and all its corroborative detail. Sooner or later it becomes confusing to be vague about the roots of Vaughan Williams's working contrasts and plenary changes of style; the relation of his melodic lines to the modes of folk-song and the normal major and minor scales, and the recurrent melodic formulae that arise; the turn towards manifold and scalically oscillating melody, three or four notes deep, and a counterpoint of different manifolds; the exploitation of contradictions of degree,[1] sharp

---

[1] Where the context admits, this term is used to denote a step in a scale established by creative use, usually numbered with reference to the seven different degrees of the octave long taken as the minimum. (I have occasionally left to the reader to it recognize movement in *two* octaves, since the ascent or

or flat, and the crystallization of certain associations of what, isolated, may sound self-contradictory in a fresh and staple texture; the resulting equivocal cadences, which yet still punctuate the designs; the capricious dependence, in movements or works, on a sense of tonality, that is, the establishment of pivotal centres of intonation in a fluid relation to one primary and ultimate keynote, or less commonly to the classical hierarchy of main, neighbouring and distant orders of pitch; and the employment of instrumental-group rejoinder to define fresh entries, to stress tonal contrasts and to qualify symmetrical assertions.

There is nothing involved about the modes, as didactic classifications of a characteristic development of three or four similar but distinct orders of interval, with fixed and oscillating degrees. A working acquaintance with these period traits is an indispensable clue to the understanding of Vaughan Williams's individuality of style. I have therefore sprinkled my narrative with recollections of mode by name or in terms of degree-patterns. The auralization of such detail may not come at once, but the visual aid to the perception of a very recurrent underlying reversion of style remains to be consulted.

Harmony is more elusive. Yet it is not textbook knowledge that is necessary to the interpretation of the composer's advances from his near-classical start. A reader may take his time to relate a basic 'flattened third falling to the keynote' to an instant experience of the actual progression. But he can play the 1-3-5 chords of E flat and C major or minor on the piano—for wider understanding, I shall indicate chords not, as in common instructive parlance, in descending order of interval, but upwards, from a given note, counting the latter as 1—and he can permute these with the inversions of either, 1-3-6, 1-4-6, by altering the bass. When he is advised of the recurrence in a new work of the cadence as previously cited, he may recall the latter more distinctly than he anticipated, or refresh his memory by further rehearsal. Anyhow, the persistence of style or mannerism is there, to hold in solution some more astringent turn of thought. Such systematizations of once contingent and expedient arrangements of harmonic colour are constantly noticeable.

The same urgency of alert perception applies to changes of key.

descent concerned will be patent, and a degree has the same harmonic or tonic-ward bearing, whatever the octave.) The current textbook terms, 'dominant', 'mediant' and the rest, do not show the overt and mutual interval-relation of different degrees, and they are founded on the nature of the later scales, or, as in the case of 'dominant', mean one thing for the modes and another for the classical period. For degree abbreviations, see p. 122n and p. 180n.

'G–E–D♭–B♭', etc., may not at first register as an aural impact of rousing transitory changes in the centre of melodic gravity, but these form the material clue to the sense of expanding vision which the 'Pavane of the Sons of the Morning' (*Job*) evokes, and to the formal resemblance of the broad close of the *Scott* film-music. Further, it may be doubted whether listeners can claim direct acquaintance, unless they have held in their ears the conflicts of bitonality, which occur from *Wenlock Edge* onwards, and the atonality, or denial of a primary degree, of the flattened fifth and second, such as haunts the fourth symphony as a chord and the ninth symphony as a melodic orbit. And no inquiring listener can remain incurious about the typical note in the fourth symphony which, according to the composer, looks wrong and sounds wrong, but is right.

The blends and contrasts of instrument are much more familiar ground to the concert-goer, but certain orchestral mannerisms and vocal uses attract attention and will be noted as they occur. It is not possible to give more than a hint of the composer's scoring.

The composer's method of communication may thus combine distinguishable aspects with a background of more elusive features. In setting out to assimilate the structural and textural facts of representative works, the listener will soon become aware of two opposite and alternating ways of artistic expression: the assertion of a fresh thought and the more or less automatic reverberation of an earlier one. The persuasiveness of music depends on the satisfactory balance of these two processes of appeal. This applies also to the balance of traditional and individual elements, as formerly to that of 'classical' and 'romantic'. It applies also, with discretion, to a previous composer's work in the same field of literary or dramatic or didactic encounter, or the purely musical grouping of instruments. In such a comparison the anticipation may be remote or unrecognized, but to the informed listener any previous approved attempt with given material, by another composer or by the same composer, conditions the impact of a new one. The process may continue further, when a present step forward is challenged by a later advance in the same direction, or on the same ground, dramatic, literary or whatever.

Thus, the first enquiry about Vaughan Williams's progress must be to discover what precedents he had to follow. No composer can start from an artistic blank. Tradition is indispensable for any understanding with an audience. A preliminary question is to compare the English composer's opportunities with those of a Continental composer of the past who was also seeking to liberate his country's music from the domination of a foreign style, Italian, French, or, later, German.

Folk-song was a latent and influential part of Vaughan Williams's tradition, and an estimate of his debt to it, not to mention its debt to him as an assiduous collector, claims half a chapter to itself, the other half being given to his emancipation from folk-song. It is not commonly realized, for instance, that the oscillation of a given degree, so often noticeable in his texture, is a recognizable by-product of the earlier folk-song, as it emerged from the five-degree stage. Up to a certain point, Vaughan Williams's absorption of folk-idiom became automatic—sometimes much too automatic, it may be thought—but he did not leave it at that. In this context the discussion of folk-song arrangements readily follows.

From this topic it is natural to pass to the editorial hymnody by which the composer, twice and monumentally, exercised his judgement of a good strophical and congregational tune, afraid neither to let a tune have its head nor to reshape what he found uncouth, and never taking an 'old favourite' for granted. He exercised equally his sense of fitness of a tune to a hymn. Apart from some facile adaptations, his general collocation of tunes brings together timely reverberations of tradition, while the mainly editorial harmony conveys, on the other hand, its refreshing touches. Vaughan Williams's own tunes seem to arise by the same method, as good given material, riveted into shape and firmly disposed in a sweeping or intimate harmonic rhythm. From them, and from some of their companions, one can obtain a strong sense of the composer's dynamic in one direction, which continued to operate spontaneously throughout his life, over against fresher impulses. While, then, this review of *The English Hymnal* and *Songs of Praise* and the rest will inevitably be concerned with a comparison of the tunes in varied circulation in the churches of the various denominations, the musical orbit of this research into the higher potential of strophical and communal melody goes much further than the parish pew or institutional piano or organ where it primarily belongs.

In turning to the composer's original works, the listener may prefer to exercise his musical intelligence as he goes—and accordingly pass now to the next chapter—but, as a forecast of the shape of this inquiry, the burden of criticism which this addition to the Vaughan Williams literature proposes to face may be summarized here. In the early works, one becomes first aware of the main song-poets, Gabriel Rossetti and A. E. Housman. It is necessary to consider more closely than is usually done the relation of the songs to the poetic movements represented by these two names, and in particular to the sonnets and stanzaic designs that the songs, necessarily enough, supersede. The whole composition of *On Wenlock Edge* is fascinating and needs fresh probing. Next, the mention of a folk-song rhapsody raises the question of orchestral arrangements of folk-tunes, including Continental precedents, and whether these are ever justified. Among other orchestral works one finds the prophetic and little known symphonic movement *In the Fen Country*, the familiar and most unsymphonic *Tallis Fantasia*, and *The Lark Ascending*, modal and typical. Significantly, the *Wasps* music represents the stage, with minor and forgotten incidental music. Among choral works, *Toward the Unknown Region*, still current where *Willow Wood* is, somewhat regrettably, past history, takes pride of place. Its treatment of its text will commend its interest to more than performing librarians, as practising musicologists are apt to become.

So far the musical genres handled have been treated as they arose, as early experiments in each line. With the accumulation of more mature work, it becomes necessary to adopt a method of grouping. By period or by genre? The symphonies must be considered in sequence, as cumulatively the prime accession to the established repertory of the nineteenth century, parallel with Sibelius's. To assemble three works at a time is arbitrary but convenient. The first three represent three periods, early, transitional and later (once 'third'), but the next three symphonies are much more contemporary in style, and the last three make a tolerable conflation. The choral works of the middle period hang together more loosely, as development of a fresh idiom of expression at various levels. The structural integrity of these heterogeneous meditations and evocations calls, indeed, for close scrutiny in each case. Sometimes it needs some intense functional analysis to make coherent sense of the whole, and sometimes even that leaves the listener critical of the parts. *Flos Campi*, with its wordless chorus, advanced idiom, and mystifying sequence of short movements with text-titles, offers its peculiar problems, not least of final structure. However pertinently shaped, the total impression must be weighed for significance, whatever its size or period.

More symmetrically, the first three symphonies each offer the listener their propositions and problems. The *Sea Symphony* raises the questions of the relation of the music to the associated poems, of the musical sufficiency of each movement, and of the justice of the choral intrusions throughout the symphony; the extended finale, especially, calls for some explanation of its position as the concluding movement. The long and originally longer *London Symphony*, with its symphonic eccentricities of style, needs, perhaps, a searching acquaintance and strong powers of synthesis before it yields the persuasive appeal of each movement, especially the first and last, and of an all-absorbent epilogue. The anomalies of melodic character must somehow be straightened out. In any structural check, the drastic compression of the original (1914) third and fourth movements, and the abbreviation of the second, for the first publication (1920), must be brought to light. This has been done here, almost for the first time, together with a notice of further compressions for the later 'revised' edition. As the first purely orchestral symphony, this is eminently a step that counts, and the achievement grows as the different pattern of each movement exercises its cumulative force on one's sense of classical propriety.

The *Pastoral Symphony* marks the advent of a new technique of rhythmically wayward phrases, strange polyphony, and, rarely, a brisk tempo. The shape of each movement, so conditioned, needs definition. Except in the Scherzo, the impact of restatement, and the consequent relaxation of pressure on the ear, is elusive, and the low dynamic relief of much of the symphony makes distinction of feature a strain. This 'study in grey' cannot be lightly embraced, nor can it be lightly dismissed as a symphonic solecism. The advance in texture, the stronger for the restrained rhetoric, must be probed, and the resultant effect estimated.

Opera thrives most on fresh experiment, but it will be convenient to take the four secular operas together, since only one branches out with an utterly fresh musical style. The first opera, *Hugh the Drover*, with its Cotswold romance, its broad, melodious appeal and its reactionary texture, calls for a fresh response to its two-act appeal, powers of characterization and varying strands of expression. Here again, there must be a comparison of the definitive 1924 vocal score with the new issue for the 1933 production, and of a succession of amendments listed in 1956 and implemented in the 1960 score. Recognition of the folk-songs and other quasi-national features raises the thorny question of Russian and Bohemian precedent. The final issue is how far an admirer of *Flos Campi* can possibly go with Hugh the boxer and his masterful ways, as frequently expressed in direct, strophical music with a vernacular tinge. *Sir John in Love*, which invites comparison with *The Merry Wives* (Shakespeare) and with the *Falstaff* of Boito-Verdi, to go no further, blends vernacular elements with a rich thematic development and a wide variety of dramatic level. The total assessment may be a subtle balance of solid worth with a commoner mintage. *The Poisoned Kiss* is an unabashed Number Opera, and so exuberantly tuneful as to raise doubts about its musical intentions, based as it is on a farcically rationalist fairy-tale. It offers a new problem of semi-serious sportiveness.

There can be no mistaking the strained and tortuous course, up to the last stage of unequivocal release, of *Riders to the Sea* as set to music by Vaughan Williams, literally following Henri Rabaud at almost every turn, yet scarcely ever betraying a derivative touch. Nevertheless, a full recognition of the few clue-themes and their growth illuminates the persistent and coherent imagery by which the later composer enriches Synge's terse and bare dialogue. It also clarifies the basic relationship between the probing music, so apt for the Galway women's struggle with the bare necessities and inexorables of life, and the more fanciful, emotional suite of *Flos Campi*.

From these four stage examples, the impossibility of registering a substantive Vaughan Williams operatic style, apart from certain similarities in the first two, becomes apparent. All that can be said, summarily, is that a release of talent in the service of national opera may have its own appeal, but it is no precedent for the astringent quality of the Synge setting.

By contrast, a methodical return to symphony (4, 5, 6) involves what have since been the most performed works. The compressed utterance of the fourth symphony leaves us much to understand about the translations of theme which qualify the riveting structure of the movements, and in the last movement drive home the modern analogy with sonata-form with a transcendent and diabolical 'epilogue'. The fifth symphony is easier on the ear, both harmonically and in dynamic balance, but there are many motives, most of them following a certain type of pitch-order and barely characteristic in themselves, and no movement observes a traditional pattern. The return to a more contemplative mood has its own method. In a broad sense, the first three movements of the sixth symphony are more bluntly shaped, but there are some subtle transformations of theme in the first and third movements, and delicate transitions, as well as a trenchant climax in the second. Then there is the fugal finale, dynamically a solecism (*sempre pianissimo*) and cumulatively an unprecedented cultivation of loneliness, whose appalling and prophetic tone commands notice from classical and romantic listener alike. There are many other contrapuntal threads to unravel, the

Scherzo being something of a fugal *tour de force*. The difficult synthesis of these heterogeneous impressions, functionally analysed, conditions a clear valuation.

What proved to be the final symphonic stage cannot yet be beyond comment. The unorthodox *Sinfonia antartica*, attempting to renovate film-music without the film; the innovatory trend of every movement of the eighth symphony—even the third, when its wide tonality is recognized; the complicated movements of the ninth—all these call in turn for some kind of ancillary presentation. For the composer's entertaining-to-a-fault programme notes provide a limited coverage, usually purely melodic in reference and inevitably unquestioning about the validity of structure or texture, on which there seems to be no lack of conflicting second opinions. It need hardly be said that in this sketch of very wide ground only a few typical points of criticism, in the strict sense, have been cited.

Between the last two symphonic groups I have placed together *Job*, *The Pilgrim's Progress*, and *Hodie*, as pronounced affirmations of belief. As the composer's main ballet-music, *Job* has been reserved for this purpose, instead of being considered with the contemporary secular operas. The Morality, *The Pilgrim's Progress*, then falls into its normal place chronologically, and its detachment from the secular operas, in more than title, needs no explanation. *Hodie*, actually appearing between the seventh and eighth symphonies, follows naturally here, if didactic purpose means anything. Linked by their sense of dedication, these three works provide a measure of the composer's range of expression in the second half of his career, as well as of his special interest in didactic themes. The relation of the *Job* music to the biblical story-and-poem and to the Blake engravings, especially the latter, has been newly investigated, the debt to Blake being discounted somewhat by the degree to which, contrary to public belief, Blake's design has been ignored. The fresh stages of Vaughan Williams's most familiar master-work have thus been reconsidered to some purpose.

The music for *Pilgrim's Progress* is plain to the ear at almost every turn, but, since it is rarely performed, a summary of the main scenes must precede a general estimate of the work, as an augmentation of Bunyan and of the composer's art, anticipated almost literally, in the eighth scene, by the miniature opera of 1922. Finally, the nominally sixteen separate movements of *Hodie* demand clarification, by reduction to broader stages of illustrated narrative, with some distinction of musical genres and patterns in the interludes which brush past the ear usually in concentrated measure. From this enhanced sense of the general pattern must come any response to the final and conclusive return to Milton and a vision of a just world. A comparison of Bach's resourceful treatment of the almost identical Gospel text is inviting.

There remain, to sort out into their component genres, the concertos and miscellaneous orchestral and chamber music, songs and film-music. The distinctive quality of certain of these works still leaves symphony and the choral-orchestral pursuit of a text as the composer's main pre-occupations, but a treatment of the critical problems of compositions for a particular literary, dramatic or instrumental occasion is needed to complete the estimate.

Finally, in Appendix C, I have tried to indicate the extraordinary range, as records of artistic refinement, of the manuscripts recently presented to the British Museum.

As a preliminary, Vaughan Williams's musical career will be sketched, showing the appearance of his compositions against a background of folk-song and hymn-tune collecting, conducting and organizing the Dorking Festival, the absolute gap of 1914–18, subsequent academic service, and numberless social contacts in the quest for the better condition of musical society—Parry, Stanford, Sharp, H. P. Allen, Holst, Boult, Percy Dearmer and the rest. Mrs. Vaughan Williams is writing an account of the composer in association with Mr. Michael Kennedy. I have therefore made no attempt to obtain special access to essential recorded comment and correspondence, which might throw light on expressed intentions and preferences, since this will be forth-coming from an authoritative source. I prefer not to be involved with any 'official' account of creative schemes, and thus to preserve my independent views, concerning what is already public knowledge, for what they may be worth.

Such is the range and magnitude of Vaughan Williams's fifty-odd sizeable works, from song-suite to full-blown opera, as matter for present discussion and elucidation, in terms of performance but not absolutely taking it for granted, and not depending in any given case on reference to the text of the score, or on any programme-note. This material discrimination precedes evaluation, without compelling it, but the further task has not, I hope, been shirked here.

Certain objections to the musical treatment may at once be anti-cipated. It may be suggested, first, that the method of observation and comparison has been visual rather than aural; that many things which a score-reader has time to notice consciously would and should pass unidentified in actual listening. That might be true of early hearings; but the richer experience is only a question of time, and the score, after all, represents as far as possible what the composer had in mind, or, if a 'piano score', a reduction or abstraction of this. When it comes to practical details, indeed, a score is the surest check on what is intended, in so far as it can be auralized. It would be ridiculous, in the long run, to refuse to be thus better informed, and rely on a casual recollection of the music.

A broader objection might be to reject the principle of discussing works in turn except as technical matter, of concern only to composers, when what is generally needed is, rather, a selection of works with the enumeration of a few characteristic touches and judicial comments, leaving the rest to the individual's intuition to find their shape and texture. The time has passed for such an arbitrary selection and ephemeral comment. In support of the present treatment, one could cite the many thorough and detailed books on the works of so familiar a figure as Beethoven, in which all the symphonies continue to be appraised, often movement by movement. The foregoing pages indicate that most of the works of Vaughan Williams, characteristic yet never alike as wholes, assert many broader and many smaller relationships, which, if not wholly unpredictable, are not at once obvious in isolated performances. The later works show shifts of texture, forwards and also backwards, that defy quick perception.

Bluntly, the 'intuitive' approach, which must indeed be the ultimate ideal when enriched by the necessary clarifications, yields very considerable enjoyment and exaltation, but sooner or later the gaps cause annoyance. It is, indeed, common experience to be carried away at first and then wonder what was the cause. My first quest, then, is to determine the composer's material intentions by probing into his freshly gained relationships, work by work, between complete hearings, in order to *save* the listener's energy for a much more continuous and balanced perception of the composer's ultimate state of mind at a later hearing. While most of this book has been written on the basis of musical memory, referring to the scores only for precise details, I have found that a fresh recollection and verification of Vaughan Williams's works, in conjunction, has both clarified and enhanced considerably my previous acquaintance with his styles and periods of expression.

The final objection will be that, even if informative at times, the criticism is too subjective; that a weight of aural and literary observation should not be used to reinforce an account determined by a necessarily capricious bias and reaction. But such 'caprice' is either inevitable and, in principle, healthy, or it is a conclusion from stated evidence. Music is an assertion of values, to be weighed by the receiver, not merely accepted. In this process any keen listener will sometimes accept the composer's mintage, but he will also reject it, if he has any critical nerve. This is particularly true of a composer so pronounced in his delivery as Vaughan Williams; so many-sided, also, and so doctrinal about certain controversial methods of appeal. His art, its clear imagery and often declared background, form a challenge to be equally uncompromising, to be so downright in response as to discountenance different interpretations on the same ground. On this account, incidentally, his output does not lend itself to the symposium treatment which might at first glance seem to be called for. A multiplicity of estimates, however well-informed, will never form a consistent critique. It follows that it is best for a single mind to venture its judgement here.

This situation will be accepted by many readers, in the name of tolerance, yet they will be reluctant to believe that approval so selective and exclusive can carry any conviction. But the sympathy which discovers the best in every work, but the composer's standards in no particular direction; which avoids issues in evasive comment on this and that aspect of a work, such as its Englishness or other grateful touches, but never stresses musical and, where relevant, literary and dramatic considerations— this kind of admiration is so lacking in critical thrust that it gives no lead in any direction. Certainly, in the spoken and written word alike, I have found criticism of the fearless but not necessarily iconoclastic type both the most stimulating and the most steadying, whether I agreed with particular findings or not. As an example, admittedly rare in a book on a modern English composer, I may cite the study of Holst's music by Miss Imogen Holst, who refuses to be cautious because her judgements might be taken to have special authority. How much more forcible her admiration is for her recognition of impoverished or mistaken technique where it strikes her as such! How much more vivid *The Hymn of Jesus* becomes in performance, apprehended through her musical intelligence as a demonstrably perilous translation of ultimate experience into choral antiphony, fresh progressions and the rest. How awkward it will be for future writers on Holst to shirk the problems of style.

Accordingly, in writing candidly both of Vaughan Williams's music and of earlier criticism of it, I have started out with no particular axe to grind except to appraise the composer's standards in the light of classical achievement in the broadest sense. Not that Beethoven and his peers were never known to nod. But they certainly reduced rawness of accomplishment to a fine limit that can be specified, where lesser composers have left enough queries in their trail to face the uncertain reception of posterity in each generation. No undue respect need be paid to the recurrent urchin critic who persistently saves his admiration for the continental composer, but one is aware of the wide reverence formerly paid to Parry, and of its subsequent exposure as a tribute to him as a leading and outstandingly disinterested educative musician rather than as a supreme composer. (I refuse to take literally Vaughan Williams's late exaltation of *Blest Pair of Sirens* as quoted in *Heirs and Rebels*, 97.) The unparalleled esteem in which Vaughan Williams has been held in England and in some North American States, as a platform and committee personality, has by no means been directly reflected in a generous promotion of his newer music at any time. I should be inclined to judge, then, that an attention to the art of Vaughan Williams will be a serious question to future generations, if not also to the generation that remembers him at the height of his reputation. It would certainly be bold to predict otherwise, and, if so, futile to assume that (in Arnold's fine phrase) 'he is free'.

Not that the reputation of Shakespeare himself is entirely free from reconsideration. But, in all the flow of analysis of Shakespearian texture and structure which passes as criticism, it would be difficult to find an uncompromising 'speech for the opposition' calculated to prejudice the revival of a single play. In the English concert world the omnipotence of Beethoven is even more exclusively established. His work is still the safest choice for the programme of any pianist, quartet or orchestra with soloists, from London to Sydney. In their various ways Grove (as promoter and annotator of the Crystal Palace concerts), Wood, Hadow and Tovey contributed to this certitude, and this was confirmed (1926) in a bold minority-cultivating policy in B.B.C. music. (It might have been Tchaikovsky or nobody.) The list might be extended and modernized to a handful of other names in opera, oratorio and other separate clientèles. However this may be welcomed or deplored in typical cases, the recognized facts of unconfined and exclusive modern promotion, through the rise of printed music and powerfully organized performance, bring home the very different situation that may arise with any composer outside the upper ten in our somewhat authoritarian, somewhat demagogic, musical republic.

I am prepared to assume this typically sceptical concert choice as regards Vaughan Williams. I have not shut my ears to questionable elements, where they seem exposed by their context. Nor have I shirked the constant intimation that the composer is intransigent more often than not, where he cuts deepest; that the struggles for expression, rather than the releases, are what matter in the *London Symphony* and its successors, and that for all its narrower scope the trenchant *Riders to the Sea* may wear better than the melodious *Sir John*. Nor, however, can anyone dream of ignoring the value that the composer attaches to the uninhibited melody of tradition or his own invention, or the varying persuasiveness of this method.

With this approach, as dateless as possible and without any leanings to any period or genre, beyond what the composer has made of it, I have taken aim. My target is not so much an authoritative tone as an inner circle of accurate estimates, compounded of an assembly of ventured opinions, following the cumulative output of the composer to the end of the schedule adopted. With music of so wide a range of subject, mood and intensity, there is still considerable scope for different accounts of Vaughan Williams's art. Few composers have so demonstrably widened their sphere and revised their methods as Vaughan Williams did between *Wenlock Edge* and the last symphony.

The present attempt to clear and control the area of potential communication existing between composer and listener is designed to carry beyond the compendium stage a watching brief that began, unconsciously, over forty years ago and has never—well, hardly ever—faltered since, from lack of compulsive deliverances from the ear. The growth of this from case to cause has, meanwhile, faithfully survived the pursuits of other problems of sound-relationship and the promotion of musical theses as remote as the progress of J. S. Bach or of the pre-classical symphony. Whatever the genre or period, it has always become irksome to be vague about a characteristic Vaughan Williams work, and examination has usually brought an enhanced perception of content. Now that the record is well-nigh complete, manuscripts and all—there was a thorough turning out of drawers in 1930, and since then any desired publication has been near-automatic—it has become more practicable to parcel up, and label the significance of the output in each genre. But the main clue has been the singularly personal quality of successive works and periods. The romantic touch, rather than the classical mastery of ideas, has been the chief conscious attraction. Ultimately, there is no telling anyone why these assertions of value may well remain an indispensable and central reference in a difficult but not unenlightened world. But after unforgettable experiences of the German classics, and a working knowledge of Berlioz, the Russian revival and Bartók, and a not inconsiderable acquaintance with loneliness and its ecstasies, as well as the infectiousness of performances in rapport with audiences, I make a certain claim to *know* what I like and dislike in music, without being continually conscious of a personal preference or abhorrence.

If one considers the wide literary, dramatic and structural interest of Vaughan Williams's output, it is surprising how little has been written on his fifty years and more of productivity. An intermittent flow of critical notice has since 1945 reached greater profusion, too considerable to detail here, after Edwin Evans's crusading but well-documented trio of articles in the *Musical Times* (61:1920), and H. C. Colles's occasional and penetrating weekly articles, between the wars, in *The Times*, some of them included in his *Essays and Lectures*. Most articles have been on specific works or aspects. Mr. Scott Goddard's comprehensive essay on the composer, for *British Music of our Time* (ed. A. L. Bacharach, 1946), gives a balanced summary of the music up to the fifth symphony, distinguishing the various genres and indicating the changes of texture with no little skill. The same writer's contribution to *The Symphony* (ed. Ralph Hill) analyses the first six symphonies, with liberal illustration of basic motive, and stresses the constant discipline which the composer's developing fancies demanded and received. The structural finesse of each work, however, is very much taken for granted. Among more recent writers, Mr. Hugh Ottaway's reflections on the symphonies in *Musical Opinion* have been noticeable, but there has been almost nothing about the choral works, apart from reviews of performances.

As I write, there have been, in English, four complete studies and one comprehensive compendium of analytical notes. The late Hubert Foss's enthusiastic, yet lightly written monograph is somewhat obsessed with the native background of the music, fancifully referred not only to English literature but to the English way of life. The book in consequence does more justice to the vocal works, of whose fitness to their text Foss often shows an acute appraisal, than to the instrumental works, on which he has been content to leave stray subjective impressions, rather than informative comment. Vaughan Williams's personal contribution to this volume, of a slice of his early life, reveals, in the course of its 'simplified' narrative, much about his influences. In his subsequent book on the composer, more comprehensively indexed,

Dr. Percy Young, too, is inclined to exploit literary analogy, or some other kind of external programme, in the interpretation of musical works, and to hunt for a 'positive symbolism' in purely symphonic contexts. There are sporadic and perceptive allusions to the *initial* texture of a work, with full harmonic citations, but the treatment of structural problems (e.g. the alleged faltering invention in the finale of the *London Symphony*) is inclined to be evasive. There is a chapter on style, entirely literary, apart from the quotation of a fugue subject. The author seems often to have in mind a musical tourist constantly on the move, rather than a reader absorbed in a particular work, and judgements of works are correspondingly elusive. There are some informative accounts of the original reception of early works, and some readers will find the stream of literary comparisons stimulating to the survey of genres.

Mr. Frank Howes's volume of analytical comment is an extension of two earlier brochures, which are served up again here much as they were. A steady account, work by work, of the main melodic events and tempo-contrasts, with liberal quotation of top-line thematic entry, is combined with an indication of the emotional components of each work, as determined by the accompanying text, or, as in most of the symphonies, as inferred by the writer. Inevitably, this seldom points to a properly critical estimate, but, as the most comprehensive and balanced material survey of the composer's works, the book offers itself as the most useful reference for functional analysis, with the possibility of a cumulative sense of disagreement which need not be misinterpreted. Mrs. Simona Pakenham's book on the composer is a candid and refreshing account of her reactions, deliberately and avowedly avoiding technical analysis (chiefly as regards harmonic and key distinction and the use of obsolete textbook terms for structure), but offering plenty of another sort, including sharper critical comment, on literary issues and poetic justice in general, than appears elsewhere. In her somewhat subjective manner, Mrs. Pakenham communicates the inner elation of her impressions in a way that will challenge the sceptical reader, besides confirming the fundamentalists. However, the book remains an interesting pilgrimage rather than either a definite guide book or a scrutiny of the composer's work.[1]

[1] The titles of these four books are as follows: Foss, *Ralph Vaughan Williams, A Study* (1950); Young, *Vaughan Williams* (1953); Howes, *The Music of Ralph Vaughan Williams* (1954); and Pakenham, *Vaughan Williams, A Discovery of His Music* (1957). Mr. V. Konen's brochure (Moscow, 1958) stresses the

These rough and ready impressions of the earlier full journeys may convey the openings left for a fresh account. Every comprehensive book on the subject is bound to repeat for each work the common knowledge about its sources and occasion, with suitable quotations from the composer's increasingly jaunty programme notes; but after that the narrative will diverge in the direction of structural or textural estimates, literary comparisons, and revelations of evocative and sometimes communal mood, or of a more subjective response. To do material justice, there should be found sooner or later a gradual exposure, first, of changing texture, from the Debussy-Ravel period of 1905 to the Vaughan Williams period of 1955, from modal folk-song to the neo-modal and utterly unmodal; and, secondly, of the promotion of different and juxtaposed textures in symphonic movement, choral cantata and stage works. For this is how a composer works. He does not decide to write an aria, or a movement in sonata-form. He cultivates variety as it comes into his mind, and then disposes it in a plain strophical or ternary shape, or in the closer knit imagery of sonata-form, or in free correspondence with a given text, or lines sketched earlier. Mere 'score-reading' on the part of an exponent, reciting the order of themes —i.e. identifying a quotation or description of a as a, of b as b, and so on, as in a programme note—with stated qualifications of literary or emotional association or instrumental entry, may condition the ear for the pattern of theme or mood, but it does not bring the composer's thought any nearer, any more than a list of characters and scenes, and a sketch of the plot, will reveal a dramatist's intentions. Mr. Howes is well aware, of course, of this need to correlate the assertions of sound-relationship with the implications of the material, or with some inner dynamic, to which a text may give a clue. He has, however, limited the scope of his exposition by keeping usually to the top line of the music.

No account has yet stressed the changing repertory of typical sound-relationships, which marks and in part unites the work of each period, or the creative reaction to these in modified structures or fresh provenances. Nor has the singular 'blend' of the modal and the spasmodically semi-tonal received enough attention. This is not more complicated, basically, than the definition of the seven scale-degrees concerned, with their

composer's vernacular contacts. Mr. James Day's book was published after the present volume was in the press. His hundred-odd pages on the music form a direct and critical account of works, moods and motives. Harmonic texture is under-stressed.

variants, and the working harmonic texture, if any. The composer's pursuit of tonality to the end depends on the modified key sense of these modal and other motives, modified to the extent that not every melodic line with a minor third, or every line with a major, can be set down as being as good as composed in the minor or major key of classical music, as Mr. Howes seems constantly to imply.

The assessment of works on the basis of this correlation of constructional assertion with a developing texture or text, as against a more partial survey of musical events, or the barely explained subjective impression, is the ultimate claim to attention of the present volume, not only for its broad conclusions but for its method. It means risking the explanation of what may be apparent, or of the inexplicable, for the sake of more alert listening—not as a slur on the composer's efficiency, as he himself was inclined to regard all introductory comment. The alternative is a blunter dogmatism, based on a hazardous perception of shape and timbre, which may or may not touch firmer ground later. The reader may not be willing to give the time to so deliberate a study of some twenty-five major works and twenty of varying sort and size. He would do best in that case to select his works, not to remain inveterately vague and half-conscious. The short cut of the unqualified intuitive approach is always an available alternative for the symphonies and other recorded and much performed works, if it is preferred. Meanwhile, here are logs and soundings for the longer journey. It is not more rewarding for being more arduous and thorough—that is the great lie of traditional education—but it may ensure a firmer critical concern for quality in music than the hit-or-miss method. For, in spite of all that conductors and other performers can do, it is a live musical public, urged on by the pressure of conflicting aesthetic interests and opinions, that composers of the recent past need. Indeed, an art becomes stilted and immobile unless it is stimulated and scrutinized by a working body of critical perception. When—as notices of works by Stravinsky, Schoenberg and Berg seem to imply more and more, after a long period of violent disapprobation—receptiveness has lost its sting and declined to a passive admiration, one can be sure that the next swing of the dogmatic pendulum will be to a point of indifference towards the composers concerned.

For Englishmen of today, if for no others, a monumental chapter is now closed, and it remains to achieve and preserve a sense of proportion about it, neither taking the great things for granted nor exalting unduly the works of good intention but questionable achievement. Such is the call to the receptive listener to extend and consolidate his conquests of the Vaughan Williams territory, from the partial stage to a broad acquaintance with the whole, not grudging repeated attempts, nor losing his temper every time he finds that the ground, which he had previously regarded as fruitful, is here downgraded. He is welcome to maintain his opinion, but not to say that he was not warned! However, such judicial classification is only one of the objectives in what is intended to be a creative schedule. In this context, the companion volumes of Mrs. Vaughan Williams and Mr. Michael Kennedy rouse expectation. In the meantime, Mrs. Vaughan Williams has, through her splendid gift to the British Museum, made possible full access to a superbly representative collection of the composer's manuscripts, comprising over fifty scores (full, vocal or piano) of main works and several of smaller pieces, with many extra scores of movements and a plenitude of 'notebooks' and sketches. There has not been time or opportunity to discuss these scripts in the main text, but an interim account will be found in Appendix C, which may convey the exceptional nature of this accession for the imaginative listener. Stray references, in the main text, to sketches and early or 'original' versions may be taken to be based on a scrutiny of the manuscripts now in the British Museum.

II

The Musical Career

Vaughan Williams's musical career has had more sides than one. He must have been known to thousands, at varying levels, as the guiding spirit of regular and organized music-making at Dorking and elsewhere, as conductor of his own works in many places, as lecturer and university examiner, and as a vigorous and often combative figure on the committees of the English Folk Dance and Song Society. That, in spite of these calls upon his time and interest, his life remained simple, and concentrated upon composition, is an obvious testimony to his industry, grasp of proportion and moral fibre, but also to his sense of dedication. Once he had made his name at the Leeds Festival with the production of *A Sea Symphony* in 1910, following that of *Toward the Unknown Region* (1907), he became a musical personality to reckon with, amongst those who were at all in touch with native music.

The rest of his career has been a matter, chiefly, of the gradual expansion of creative impulses, with moderate but dependable audiences after the War of 1914–18, gradually growing to an unnumbered crowd, from the production of *Job* in 1930, and of the fourth symphony in 1935, to the bold but significant inclusion of the eighth symphony in the last of the 1957 Henry Wood Promenade Concerts. Inevitably, the infectiousness, brilliance or quiet interpretative competence of certain of the earlier conductors and soloists, some still happily at large, have so promoted the reception of certain works as to make them seem indispensable. In the last twenty-five years of Vaughan Williams's career, the appearance of new works was comparatively uneventful, and less hazardous. Publication, when desired, of full or 'vocal' score, with orchestral parts on hire,[1] was automatic by this time.

[1] This hire-only system, for orchestral parts, is a regrettable feature of modern musical life, due to the competition of lending libraries. How often one would

42

ART WITHOUT DISTRACTIONS

The composer's most publicized production was probably *The Pilgrim's Progress* at Covent Garden—part of the Festival of Britain—in 1951. This somewhat paradoxical statement, about so restrained and unoperatic a conception, indicates that to gain contact with a wider public has been a constant issue in the background of creative activity; and, for that, composition and test performances in public were essential. Occasionally, revivals were of paramount interest, as when in 1958 the composer broke hospital leave in order to attend a performance of *Sir John in Love* at Sadler's Wells. Latterly recordings, too, became a concern, that of the ninth symphony occupying the composer's chief attention in what proved to be the last weeks of his life.

Apart, then, from the unforgettable war years, 1914–18, in which he served as an orderly in the Territorial R.A.M.C. in Macedonia, and as an Artillery officer on the French front, Vaughan Williams's tangible career can be fairly summarized, with some notice of his steady choral conducting and occasional lecturing and literary writing, in terms of his main compositions, as that of a man who, like Blake, 'was so seldom there' but always leaving for that 'other country' beyond his study. This is not to imply that he led the life of a self-regarding musician: few composers ever showed a more keen interest in the work and efforts of other living composers, from Gustav Holst down to the young man by whom Vaughan Williams was consulted on the day before he died. But it does imply a life undistracted by considerations of national position or institutional appointment, or, once past the preliminary period, of institutional or other public approval. Any observation of the composer's contacts with society must be set in this context, as the background of a progress that can be tabulated succinctly as a catalogue of titles. The preliminaries of how and where Vaughan Williams became a composer of his stature are of less interest. But they may now be summarized.[1]

have liked to purchase a dozen parts of a work, to take out and try with casual performers at home or in educational centres! But this is only possible with the voice-parts of vocal works, accepting a piano reduction for accompaniment.

[1] Vaughan Williams contributed a short and selective sketch of his career to Foss's book on the composer. He also contributed an article, 'Carthusian Music in the 'Eighties', to *The Carthusian* (21. 1 (December, 1952)), on the occasion of his eightieth birthday. Mr. J. W. Wilson, of Charterhouse School, who drew my attention to this article, summarized Vaughan Williams's Charterhouse contacts (1887–90, 1950) in a tribute in the same magazine (22. 9 (December, 1958)).

Among the many personal recollections and tributes which appeared in magazines in 1958–9, particular mention must be made of the Vaughan Williams

43

A son of the vicar in the village of Down Ampney in Gloucestershire, Vaughan Williams was brought up at his mother's home, Leith Hill Place, Dorking, Surrey. He had private lessons in harmony, piano and violin, which continued at Rottingdean (Sussex) Preparatory School. The violin lessons, under an Irish fiddler, W. M. Quirke, were of lasting value, and prompted the pupil, fifty years later, to break into Raff's *Cavatina* at an informal moment in the Gloucester Festival week. What is more important, this early acquaintance with the violin and its myriad textures guided his hand in the definition of special strings for a given violin melody. Of the bigger things in music, piano duets—at that time the common home contact with music on the grand scale—included Handel choruses and Haydn symphonies, Handel being the accepted great composer, Bach the interesting figure. A 'Bach Album' (Berthold Tours) revealed that that figure stood for something more than a variation of the Handel type.

In January, 1887, Vaughan Williams followed his elder brother (H. W.) to Charterhouse School, where he stayed three years. He was at first placed in Saunderites, the headmaster's house, but when he became a monitor, two years later, he moved into Robinites, whose housemaster, G. H. Robinson, the school organist, was 'a sensitive musician and a kind-hearted man'. A Robinite house photograph of the time, still extant (*see* Plate 2), shows one boy with the same masterful, far-seeing and candid expression as in later years. Musical experience (viola) included regular orchestral work, *Judas Maccabaeus* (a warning against dull writing for string amateurs?), and a rough but genial acquaintance with Italian concerti grossi. There were also some notable performances on the piano and organ (Bach fugue in E flat), including those of H. V. Hamilton, later a professional. More signicantly, in 1888 a miscellaneous programme was given in the School Hall by Hamilton and his fellow-musician, including a composition by Hamilton and trio in G by his colleague, played by four players, the violin part being doubled in Household Music style. It was attended by several of the masters and their wives 'and even some of the boys'.

number of the *R.C.M. Magazine* (55. 1), which ranges from distinguished contemporaries, performers and musical collaborators in Britain, Canada and the United States to personal encounters in many walks of life, rural, professional and military.

Heirs and Rebels, edited by Ursula Vaughan Williams and Imogen Holst (1959), assembles some forty letters exchanged between Ralph Vaughan Williams and Gustav Holst with some articles and lectures. There is a full list of all works referred to by name or by implication.

Best of all, the mathematics master, Mr. James Noon, a power in the land, pronounced as his *quod erit demonstrandum*, 'Williams, you must go on'; an encouragement so rarely given later that the recipient developed a rare resource for the encouraging phrase when it came to his turn to judge. (Strauss dedicated a school setting of choruses from Sophocles' *Electra* to the master who advised him *not* to take up music.)

As far as one can tell, the school curriculum at Charterhouse was steadily and thoroughly classical, apt for a boy who had shown a marked proficiency at irregular Greek verbs at Rottingdean. Forty years on (or rather less) he was quoting the *Phaedo* (114D) as a firm justification for *Sancta Civitas* as such. Then there was the French Debating Society, at which R. V. Williams spoke stalwartly in support of compulsory games. It may be added here that in 1950 Vaughan Williams wrote the music for the final scene of the *Charterhouse Masque*, adapting himself punctiliously to the demands of the text and the musical material available, and boldly re-introducing the disused school *Carmen* (William Horsley) in a typical crusading, latitudinarian spirit.

How far the inevitably philistine influences, and lack of any musically cultivated school life, bore on a boy who cared intensely about music, can only be guessed. But Vaughan Williams emerged with many qualities: a strong social conscience; a firm critical sense and nerve to reject; a devotion to music that was disinterested enough to be free from any awkward intensity; a willingness to submit to the discipline of musical thinking; and a buoyant temperament, which contained its trenchant side but little bitterness. In the lack of evidence to the contrary, one may assume that the impress of the Charterhouse groove was more stimulating than restricting.

The career, it seems, was fixed. Vaughan Williams went up to the Royal College of Music, passed on to Cambridge, and after that (1895) back to the Royal College. This brought him into touch with some of the finest teachers that England has known: Parry, Charles Wood and Stanford for composition or accessory study, and for the organ the redoubtable Walter Parratt, many of whose pupils now enjoy national repute. These four men shared, each in his own way, an artistic conscience.

Of the composer-tutors, Parry appeared sympathetic and informative, but one cannot help wondering what, apart from his wide and discerning memory of musical history, he had to impart technically, unless it was in the direction of choosing expressive, non-popular texts, and setting them with some respect for English rhythms, and with a lively awareness of a call to liberalism in all things. 'That healthy beefsteak optimism of Parry is a delusion that blinds one to the real difficulties in the way', wrote Holst in a letter of 1903. Parry's personal nobility of character is universally attested, not least by Vaughan Williams himself, but this did not prevent him from being conservative by nature. His queer reference to 'impertinences' in the *Sea Symphony*, in a private note later on, does not suggest the accent of a progressive leader; and his steady renunciation of anything approaching sheer orchestral rhetoric, as a kind of despicable confidence-trick, was almost pathological. However, Parry may have communicated some of his spasmodic creative impulses, and his keen sense of a time-spirit in art. Charles Wood, a competent general coach, proved an unfaltering expositor of technical tricks, of finding available means, under the guidance of top-level precedent, to pursue plausible structural ends, balancing key by key and texture by texture. Whatever control of fugue he inculcated, it did not go much further with his pupil than an occasional inclination for a fugal episode or coda. Wood confessed later that he had had no hope for him as a composer (*R.C.M. Magazine*, 55. 1, p. 14).

Vaughan Williams's most formidable teacher was Stanford, an accomplished composer and, in his own limited way, a methodical teacher, who knew what he liked and disliked. What he liked to observe in a contemporary was a neo-classical, post-Brahmsian style, clear in outline and free from vagueness, but certainly not uncompromisingly modern, however coherent. Downright novelty of speech he could not stomach. I have good reason to believe that, in his final contact with Vaughan Williams's developed art, Stanford deplored the 'decline' from the *Sea Symphony*, which he championed wholeheartedly, to the *Pastoral Symphony*, which was doubtless too much *sui generis* for him. As a composer, in spite of his devotion to Wagner (but not to the abandoned sensuality of Strauss), Stanford excelled in a light touch, in the neat and practical solution to some problem of text-setting, or of the unobtrusive renewal of texture or theme. He admired the craftsmanship of light French and Viennese music. He himself made the contingencies of variation, concerto, choral ballad and operatic scene his creative opportunity. In extended works, the lack of a major structural impulse is often apparent, in spite of his steady, unaffected address to the common listener. It is significant that the best songs, such as *Loughareema*, are masterly miniatures, formed from the proliferation of one strophe with variant detail.

As a teacher, Stanford inculcated basic 'technique', by which he meant, primarily, the much tempered modal harmony of late sixteenth-century counterpoint. His reputed consultation of Rockstro, a dogmatic and far from scholarly theorist, over the modal proprieties for the exquisite finish of his *Stabat Mater*, suggests an extraordinary faith in the expressiveness of a bygone method of appeal, even at second hand. It was also a peculiarly disarming procedure, in a serious exponent of the period in question, confirmed somewhat by legends of the same exercise appearing again after a short interval and being judged as fresh work. Apart from this contrapuntal grind, modelling pieces closely on the lines of an early Beethoven movement, and orchestrating the piano transcription of a Mozart symphony to compare with the original, were typical exercises.

The rest was a mass of practical comments and brusque judgements. For Stanford 'practical' included, by common consent, an unerring sense of 'padding' or other such weakness, and a remarkably wide command of apt precedent for handling any given situation. Texturally to pass muster, a score had to be not only economical but fool-proof in the parsimonious conditions of musical Britain as then known. No 'extra' instrument, however right, was allowed, or any balance so delicate that it needed, as Debussy did, 'too much rehearsal'. Judgement meant good, blunt words on pretentious, 'journalistic' craftsmanship, at whatever level. But it also meant an equally impatient and brusque 'It won't do, m'boy' for choices of texture and text that seemed patently arbitrary. There was no chance of reprieve from this sentence. Any pupil of individuality was liable to turn merely sullen, or be driven into secret rebellion. Paradoxically, Stanford's lasting influence may well have been in the qualities of which he was least conscious.[1]

This cool appraisal of Stanford's art and didactic skill may astonish some readers. But it is necessary to distinguish the man's strong personal influence on growing and on grown musical minds from his authority to speak as the composer of the moment, and again from his capacity to sort out, from a general curriculum of token creative experience for non-committed students—such as the pianist of the future, Harold Samuel—a special training for a genuinely creative writer. (Stanford's *Musical Composition* moves at incredibly varying levels of address, from composer-student to provincial teacher.) That apart from his comprehensive scale of classical references and first-hand

---

[1] See the revealing composite tribute, 'Charles Villiers Stanford—by some of his pupils' (*Music and Letters*, 5. 3 (July, 1924)). Also, *Heirs and Rebels* (21) for Holst's reactions to Stanford's 'moods'.

experience of composing for English ears, Stanford's *methods* were not of great concern to them, appears to be the unanimous testimony of his many loyal pupils. It thus appears that Vaughan Williams is making more than allowances when he writes, in the course of a recollection of Stanford's teaching (Hubert Foss, *Ralph Vaughan Williams*, p. 27), 'Stanford was a great teacher, but I believe I was unteachable. I made the great mistake of trying to fight my teacher. The way to get the best out of instruction is to put oneself entirely in the hands of one's instructor, and try to find out all about his method regardless of one's own personality, keeping, of course, a secret *eppur si muove* up one's sleeve.' For he continues a few lines later, 'The details of my work annoyed Stanford so much that we seldom got beyond these to the broader issues . . . there was no time left for any constructive criticism'.

It must plainly be inferred that Vaughan Williams obtained from Stanford the stimulus of a watching brief for the neo-Brahms interests, but very little real guidance, for he himself had no need, as some over-ambitious composers have, for an outside mentor to insist upon integrity of outlook. Indeed, he must often have found these lessons a sheer hindrance and waste of time. In other words, he accepted the rigorous and uninviting challenge of the Stanford curriculum as a kind of discipline. To some readers it will have seemed obvious from the start of this discussion that instruction is bound to be unimportant and negligible to a man of genius, or to any independent thinker about musical issues. Yet musical creativity does admit of some conscious consideration of the kind of textural appeals chosen in a given instance, and of the structural assertion devised to give them meaning and poise with or without reference to any outside medium of words or actions or mime. Also, a student may gain an acquaintance with established alternative routes, though not necessarily after a grinding assimilation of the renaissance, baroque and classical styles.

At this level, I judge that Vaughan Williams chiefly taught himself, probably slower than he might have done under a more progressive mentor. That he was able to advance by the mimetic method— developing one's own themes on the plan of a classical model—is no tribute at all to the method, cordially as he himself recommends it. He would have worked out his line of progress by another route just as surely. Perhaps, after all, Parry was on a sounder track than he realized when he enjoined his most distinguished pupil 'to write choral music as befits an Englishman and a democrat'. For one of the clues to the ideal music of the milling and artistically bewildering industrial classes rising round his own was, as Parry prophetically remarked in an address in 1899, folk-song. And here lay a hidden power of more consequence than he ever dreamt.

It is no surprise, then, that subsequent lessons that Vaughan Williams took, at Berlin, with Max Bruch (disregarding Stanford's illiberal advice not to have any lessons) roused him to work hard, but left him vague about the value of the teaching given. Round 1900, he asked Elgar to give him lessons. He received a note of polite refusal from Lady Elgar, suggesting Bantock instead. He therefore took the lessons *in absentia*, by an examination of the scores of *Enigma* and *Gerontius*, as later of the symphonies. A recollection of this rebuff, in a tribute to Elgar in a composite radio hour to celebrate the centenary of his birth (1957), indicates a more than passing indignation. A further encounter was also mentioned then. Elgar greeted Vaughan Williams with forced surprise on his appearance at a performance of the violoncello concerto. This reception was based on the hasty assumption that he was behind E. J. Dent's trenchant criticism of himself, recently republished in the revised edition of Adler's *Handbuch der Musikgeschichte* (1930). Elgar here had altogether disregarded the younger composer's constant attendances at his oratorios and other major works for years. In any case, Vaughan Williams had had to learn scoring mainly by trial and error and ransacked precedent, and he remembered this solitary journey to the end. The Palmer Patron's Fund, to provide for public orchestral rehearsals of the work of past and present R.C.M. students, was not endowed till 1903.

In 1908 Vaughan Williams decided that he must go to Paris to acquire a superior technical ease without too cramping a course. He told Edwin Evans, who was considered a specialist in modern music, that he had thought of going to Vincent d'Indy. (A strange choice—a very eclectic craftsman, whose gospel was the progressiveness of Franck.) But Evans consulted his highly knowledgeable friend M. D. Calvocoressi, who maintained that a less theoretical (and less self-contradictory) tutor was called for, and shrewdly suggested Ravel, with whose teaching methods he was well acquainted through the composer Maurice Delage. After further talk, this was agreed upon. Calvocoressi approached Ravel and gained his assent. Vaughan Williams found it necessary to resist outright Ravel's attempts to apply the mimetic method ('next time a minuet in the style of Mozart, please!'), but he learnt new values in orchestration, prompted by piano experiment—by the Ravel way, in fact—and he acquired a certain cult of simplicity and nonchalance, in

D   49

contrast to Germanic complexity and seriousness. 'Ravel', he wrote to Calvocoressi, 'is exactly the man I was looking for. As far as I know my own faults, he hit on them exactly, and is telling me to do exactly what I half felt in my mind I ought to do'.[1] A generous tribute.

Long before this, certain enduring contacts had been made. While at Trinity College, Cambridge, Vaughan Williams struck up an acquaintance with H. P. Allen, organ scholar at Christ's, and a leading figure of the University Music Club; initially, as a promoter of Brahms! Allen himself was drawing musical society to wider horizons than they had ever conceived. This included organizing, probably in the teeth of public taste, a performance (and, when this flopped, an encore) of a quartet for men's voices by his younger contemporary. This defiant and prophetic association reverberated later in performances of *A Sea Symphony* at Oxford and in London, after a sticky reception at Leeds, with memorable repeats at Oxford in 1919 and 1922, and *Sancta Civitas* in 1926. Rarely insistent upon detail, except for rhetorical purposes, Allen represented the Busoni type of interpreter, who could find a true satisfaction in anything, from Schütz to Holst, which he considered worth his trouble. As a conductor he was supremely capable of conveying the central and component moods that he divined in a work to a barely awakened chorus, orchestra and audience. His rendering of *A Sea Symphony* may have been at times too brisk and noisy for the composer, but it certainly quickened the spirits of those present, not least because, like Parry, Allen was a man who relished the sea, not as a mere aesthete, but as a practical seaman, who, twenty years later, rowed a lifeboat-load of land-lubbers to safety from a liner sinking off Australia.

It was Allen, too, who, as the new director, invited Vaughan Williams to come to the R.C.M. Somewhat later promoters—Henry Wood, Albert Coates, Dan Godfrey of Bournemouth, Adrian Boult—long remained exceptional in an extended period of virtuoso conductors, foreign and native.

While at Cambridge, Vaughan Williams conducted a small choral society, in which he found useful experience of amateur limitations and scope. He continued this line, with an orchestral society and some organ recitals, as organist for three years of St. Barnabas, South Lambeth, London. His organ appointment does not seem to have produced any fondness for the medium, which he reserved for emblems

---

[1] M. D. Calvocoressi, *Musicians' Gallery*, p. 285. Calvocoressi's declared personal admiration for d'Indy's analytical skill and genial personality confirms the integrity of his judgement in proposing Ravel instead.

of blasphemy and defeatism, in *Job*, *Joanna Godden* and the *Sinfonia antartica*. As 'chapel-master', he learnt, once and for all, about good and bad church music, and the social appeal of either.

The composer's memorable fellow-students at the R.C.M., a lively and voluble crowd, included Holst and Ireland. Holst became not only a lifelong companion, but a constant partner in a testing process, mutual criticism of the other's latest composition. Vaughan Williams declares that he found Holst's integrity 'terrifying'; terrifying in its insistence on a greater reduction to essentials, in texture, as in the case of *Job*. One suspects that he was, in fact, well able to take care of himself. But Holst was a steady stimulus, with his bursts of genius, restless, cosmopolitan eclecticism, and his strong strain of originality, enhanced, it seemed, by a study of Sanskrit writings. Presumably John Ireland, too, was companionable, with his fastidious literary approach and his cultivation of chamber-music and the piano. With the future pianists, Evelyn Howard-Jones, and Herbert Fryer, H. C. Colles, destined for *The Times*, Nicholas Gatty, Martin Shaw and a number of others, these made a genial coterie of Davidites, in permanent session in 1896–7 as the R.C.M. Literary and Debating Society. Weekly meetings included debates on 'Has music reached its Zenith?', the motion, 'That the moderate man is contemptible', proposed by R. V. W., and a paper from the same source on didactic art, which marked the last meeting. It is of some passing interest to note that Thomas Dunhill, recalling the Society's proceedings in 1908, mentioned three names as *literary* lights of this latter day. 'Vaughan Williams is well known as a lecturer ... Colles ... Gatty ... ?'[1] A few years later, he may perhaps have smiled at his miscalculation.

We turn now to the music heard or studied by Vaughan Williams at this formative period and later. Inevitably there were the greater and lesser works of Bach, noted and admired, and of Beethoven, noted but not so admired, as well as Palestrina, Purcell, Handel, Haydn and others. But two new experiences must be cited. On holiday at Munich in 1890, Vaughan Williams, characteristically missing his supper in a wild rush to be in time, heard *Die Walküre*, and at once found in it echoes of his own mind. In the sophisticated declamation, dramatic

---

[1] Thomas F. Dunhill in *R.C.M. Magazine*, 5. 1 (Christmas Term, 1908); reprinted, *Ib*. 54. 3 (Christmas Term, 1958). (By a coincidence: obviously this 'Fifty years ago' reprint was passed for publication well before the editor found himself starting the opening page with some deeply commemorative words signed 'Adrian C. Boult'. The full tribute followed in the next number, as already cited.)

touches and vivid orchestral development he perceived, we may say, basic assertions, the counterpart and true derivation of the fundamental human encounter; the mutual need of an unhappy, childless wife and a romantic, solitary stranger; the nagging conscience over the marriage bond and the wilful schemer's longing for compromise and face-saving; and the primitive, emotional Brünnhilde. Before Vaughan Williams could hear from Parry of the liberating influence of Wagner and his clue-themes, here was positive proof of the power of national tradition to place music on a fresh but firm basis, at once folky in spirit and true to the nascent force of the orchestra, and so reaching over the frontiers in a general assertion of flowing music. *Tristan* at Covent Garden in 1892 proved equally impressive.

Early encounter with folk-songs and folk-dance tunes—'Dives and Lazarus', 'Bushes and Briars' and the rest—had a more pertinent effect. Here, too, was something essential, demonstrably arising out of a need for something to 'say and sing', strophically, from corny tales of courting, seduction and occasionally marriage to elaborate ballads. Further, as the best folk-tunes and versions accumulated and sorted themselves out from the jejune airs and variants, by the emergence of the fittest, their fascination and significance for questing English composers grew. This was something which not only belonged as their birthright, but had an unmistakably fresh quality about its primary curves, quite unlike those of German or of Russian music. Following Baring-Gould, Frank Kidson and others, Vaughan Williams interested himself in 'collecting' a number of songs, and in 'setting', i.e. harmonizing in varied texture, many more. He wrote a number of rhapsodies, fantasias and variation-sets on folk-tunes later. But the chief fruits were unconscious, in the recognition of an inner necessity which must somehow be re-discovered in English art-music, or, nearer the surface, in the formation of certain melodic mannerisms.

Collecting implied a rigorous censorship. The Folk Song Society (1898–1931), which Vaughan Williams joined in 1904, existed partly to keep the new repertory clear from confusion with the anonymous but sophisticated airs of national tradition (such as 'Tom Bowling') or some Vauxhall occasion. Melodic trends, variants and concordances were examined at leisure as they came into view. Then Cecil Sharp strode upon the scene. In 1899, a disappointed composer, he had begun a new lease of life when, from his window at Headington, Oxford, he observed eight men dancing to the concertina-playing of William Kimber, later a dancer of national fame.

Sharp noted five tunes from Kimber at the time. He had no idea what to do with them except 'set' them; but professionally perplexed by the need of genuine English songs for the boys whom he was teaching at the time at Ludgrove Preparatory School, he dipped into William Chappell's *Popular Music of the Olden Time* and other sources. In 1902 he produced *A Book of British Song for Home and School*, with a sprinkling of genuine folk-songs. But he observed that Chappell had confined himself to literary sources, and left unsifted the songs to be *heard* in the country. In 1903, then, Sharp began seriously to hunt for such songs in the parish, Hambridge in Somerset, of his friend from earlier days, Charles Marson. This anglican clergyman was not popular with his superiors. Had he not roundly declared, to the assembled diocese, that the Church's need was not the 'gentlemen-ordinands' advocated by Dr. Warre of Eton but 'bounders like Peter and Paul'? Such a commited equalitarian was more than a good companion for Sharp, as he moved into the untrodden, classless ways of the folk-singer.

One afternoon, in the hearing of Sharp and Mattie Kay, a singer whose voice he had helped to develop, Marson's gardener, John England (*sic*), came out with 'The seeds of love', as he was mowing the lawn. By the same evening Sharp was accompanying Mattie in his setting of the song, at a choir supper, to the delight of the audience, except for John, a true Briton, who cast a very proper doubt upon the 'evening dress' (i.e. piano accompaniment) in which his normally unadorned utterance had been clothed. From there Sharp never looked back. By 1907 he had collected, in school holidays, fifteen hundred songs. He had realized from the start that a much more determined effort to preserve the vanishing songs was necessary than that shown by the Folk Song Society with its hundred songs in five years. (See a letter to the *Morning Post*, February 2, 1904.) The five volumes of *Folk Songs from Somerset*, a hundred and thirty songs in all, were published in 1904–9.

What was more, in 1907 Sharp himself published *English Folk-Song: Some Conclusions*, a documented challenge to the equivocal attitude which he had found alike in the Board of Education's 'recommendation to teachers' (1906), an utter confusion of national and folk-songs, and in the Folk Song Society's support of the Board. In his thesis, Sharp showed the revising process through which a true song of the people may pass, and concluded by looking forward to the time when, through the general singing of folk-song, a national and current musical idiom would arise, to be at the service of the English composer of the future, as it had served Austrian and Bohemian and other national 'schools' in the past. A notable anticipation of Kodály's educational aims.

Much more of folk-song material reached Sharp's pen and the printer. In 1907 appeared the first *Morris Book*, compiled for the Esperance Girls' Club, St. Pancras, London. It was the beginning of another large project of collection and documentation, eventually backed by its own organization, the English Folk Dance Society (1911–32), to be finally amalgamated with the Folk-Song Society in 1932. Vaughan Williams was on the committee of the E.F.D.S. from the start. In 1922 he wrote *Old King Cole* for the Cambridge Branch. Sharp died in 1924. In 1929 was laid the foundation-stone of a memorial central building in Regent's Park Road, London, to be, as Margaret Bondfield well expressed it, 'not a museum but a home of joy'. It was inscribed, 'In memory of Cecil Sharp who restored to the English people the songs and dances of their country'. In 1930 H. A. L. Fisher, Warden of New College, Oxford, and a lifelong educationalist, declared Cecil Sharp House open. In a tribute to Vaughan Williams in December, 1958, Maud Karpeles, one of the pioneers of the folk-song movement, wrote, after a reference to the chance and separate encounter of Vaughan Williams and Sharp with living folk-song in 1903 and 1904: 'During the next twenty years they stood side by side in the fight for the recognition of English folk music' (*Journal of the English Folk Dance and Song Society*, 8. 3).

This apparent digression has been undertaken for various reasons. It is not easy, at this distance of time, to appreciate the many vital, but not always musical, strands of thought and work behind the active discovery and promulgation of English folk-song and folk-dance. There have been the various collectors as such, with varying motives. There have been the purists, anxious to preserve any original version of a tune. There have been the popularisers, some purist at heart, some not at all. There have been the antiquaries and anthropologists, probing the concordances of racy, obscure or obscene metaphors. There have been, on a trail laid by Carl Engel,[1] the idealists, determined to find the artist in everyone round them, and so levelling *up* society to a dignified equality of experience. Above all, there have been the musical visionaries, who perceived the new potentialities of an English society familiar with native folk-song, just as an acquaintance with the ballads of Bishop Percy's *Reliques*, embellished as they are, had prepared for Wordsworth.

[1] *An Introduction to the Study of National Music* (1866), p. 173.

In Sharp, it must bluntly be said, these responses to folk-song met and became dynamic, so that in those twenty industrious years he redeemed the neglect of a century, and expressed, indeed, the good intentions of many fellow-workers of weaker aims.

Vaughan Williams was soon united in spirit with Sharp. He shared his quest and his scholarship, and he supported him firmly against the Board of Education in the matter already mentioned. He also turned a sympathetic ear to his accompaniments, because—apart from their manifest expediency for promoting the tunes to a harmony-bound generation—he maintained that, even when they look wrong and feel awkward, they make the tune sound right. (A subtle argument.)

Socially, Vaughan Williams was prepared to give his firm and steady support in turn to the Folk Song and Folk Dance Societies, while declining to be their standard-bearer; joining issue with committees and directives when he thought fit. But having collected folk-songs in at least six different counties himself, he did not allow this pursuit to gain a major hold, by driving him to sort out, regionally and technically, the now endless material, as happened to Kodály and, in part, Bartók. As a composer, he recognized the movement as more than timely; he set many songs, and, as will appear below, adapted others. But he took no more than he wanted. Yet it cannot have been easy to resist the fascinations of the inner body of this constructive, scholarly and tremendously enthusiastic group, and of the accumulating treasure-trove. 'Stand and deliver' was the slogan when Sharp was about; you had to be on one side or the other over folk-song. Vaughan Williams admitted later that Sharp's uncompromising assumption of the historical importance of English folk-song had helped him to crystallize his own perceptions; but while its promotion was becoming Sharp's life, for the composer it must only be a start.

These folk-song contacts provided some fresh material, and plenty of stimulus, for Vaughan Williams's first main achievement: the music for the *English Hymnal* (1906). This compilation took him two years, and it might appear to some readers as two years wasted, or at least scarcely worth recalling here. But the selection of over six hundred strophical tunes, to nearly as many hymns, was much more than a matter of selecting alternatives and checking sources. It involved the constant constructive effort of re-fashioning a tune until it could present a coherent strophe suitable for the repeated use of a musically untrained and perhaps unawakened congregation. The new tune-repertory was to be at once as authentic as possible, of an uncompromising standard not yet found elsewhere, and adventurous in range. (Vaughan Williams recalled these aims to the Hymn Society, at the Jubilee of the *Hymnal*.)

The tunes came from psalm-tune and hymn-tune collections of many periods and sects, but also from English folk-song sources. The recognition and reconstruction, where expedient, of such a multitude of tunes, with an equal or even greater multitude of rejections, was a creative process almost as valid as the constructive effort which attended a number of original tunes, cited here as anonymous but since identified as the music editor's. After using the *Hymnal*, at first hand, or, as in later editions of Nonconformist books, at the next remove in many cardinal points, no one could doubt whether tunes matter, either for themselves or for their power to give fresh meaning to the declamation of a text.

Nor could the composer have any doubt that tunes, in the right place or in a reasonable place, mattered. Folk-song discovery was prompting him in the same direction. Thirty-five years later, he was promising film studios some tunes, if they would take them. Meanwhile, with Martin Shaw, he had found the music for the seven hundred hymns of a more literary and modernist collection, *Songs of Praise* (1925; enlarged 1931), and for the fine anthology, for general use, the *Oxford Book of Carols* (1928), and had extended and revised the musical range of the *English Hymnal* (1933). He thus showed his continued concern for congregational music, and his willingness to submit to the discipline of a plain strophical setting for this purpose, which has, in the case of *Songs of Praise*, been widely identified with school needs, *inter alia*. In this way, Vaughan Williams established a contact of abiding significance with the common and habitual singer of all ages, and more consciously with the workaday music-promoter in parish and school, by his standard of melodic and harmonic sufficiency and of word-matching aptitude. If hymns were 'the poor man's poetry' in the past, the hymn-tunes of the collections cited remain one of the most pertinent and persistent challenges to the flood of melodic and harmonic banality which pours into the ears of poor and rich today. These hymns have been the stand-by of many a musical chaplain, as one of them testified in 1958. The close bearing of a hymn-tune critique on composition will be considered in Chapter V.

In 1905 Vaughan Williams started the Leith Hill competition-festival at Dorking, Surrey, where he lived for half a century. It began as a 'village' event, defying predictions of flying too high above popular taste, and, when it had become an institutional four-days of competition, combined rehearsal, and performance with 'symphony' orchestra by ascending choir-groupings, it remained unpretentious through the director's downright manner. Increasingly and impressively familiar as a resident personality, 'Uncle Ralph' to most, he regimented a rural assembly of varying musical accomplishment, with shrewd alternations of fiery intolerance for half-hearted efforts and heartening comment, and a fund of genial, mischievous allusions and recollections. There was infinite evocation, but very little sign of education, as then understood, apart from expert directions. By these means Vaughan Williams discovered a new potential for extended choral music on an amateur foundation of varying levels, which remains one of the chief sources of production in this country. He wrote works for each choir-division for the 1930 festival, of which the strongest, *Benedicite*, far from being relegated to a strictly provincial rank, appeared at the Queen's Hall, London, in 1931, as the final and conclusive event of the annual display of modern music by the International Society for Contemporary Music. It would not have seemed to all listeners the 'return to common-sense' that it appeared to be to some English listeners, in the *avant garde* context, but it exemplified a new choral standard in terms of a local achievement not necessarily confined to one place.

In 1953 Vaughan Williams ceased to be the conductor of the Leith Hill Festival. He remained president, and in 1955 was able to congratulate the choirs on the soundness of their tradition of half a century, defying the earlier pessimists. Vaughan Williams also conducted annually at Dorking, up to the last, his own selection of Bach's *St. Matthew Passion*, in a rendering more romantic than scholarly. To judge by a performance elsewhere, what mattered to him was not verisimilitude of production, but the impact of the central experience, of the life of God breaking into human life, in terms which it is the function of music to quicken to resolute thought.[1]

The vital repercussions upon the average singer of this extended period of adventurous activity in the Dorking area—defeating the

---

[1] This impression is based on my recollections of a moving performance given by the Bach Choir. It is entirely corroborated by recent references to 'tremendous dramatic excitement, a sense of acute personal involvement in the action . . . a stirring reflection of R. V. W.'s own massive splendour of thought . . . a fierce, angry, sorrowful, joyous and triumphant performance' as the differentia of Vaughan Williams's approach. (See an article by E. M. Webster in *Musical Opinion*, 968 (May, 1958)).

apathy of those committee-members who were fearful of change and obstinate about works they did not care about—must have prepared many people for the better reception of the composer's more advanced music, besides infecting their taste with a pungent antiseptic flavour.

During this long career, Vaughan Williams succeeded Allen as conductor of the Bach Choir (London) for a short period (1920–6). Here he released his Bach enthusiasms, in a somewhat magisterial style, combined with a sometimes obscure beat, but he secured notable performances of *Sancta Civitas* and Holst's *Ode to Death*. However, he did not write anything for the Bach Choir.

Vaughan Williams took his doctorate in music at Cambridge in 1899. His Exercise consisted of an *Offertorium* for full orchestra, a *Credo* (the largest section) and *Hosanna* for double chorus and full orchestra, divided by a *Sanctus* for double chorus, brass, drums and organ, and a *Benedictus* for four soloists and small orchestra.[1] But this output was neither a prelude to choral development nor a patent fulfilment of earlier attempts. Composition was gradual. Songs for voice and piano began to appear towards the turn of the century. In 1903 came the D. G. Rossetti sonnet-set, more selection than cycle, *The House of Life*, followed at intervals by the two *Songs of Travel* groups, the A. E. Housman set, *On Wenlock Edge* (1909), and the Herbert set, with orchestra and chorus, the *Five Mystical Songs* (1911). After that, song-writing became sporadic. A further setting of Rossetti sonnets for women's voices, *Willow Wood* (1903), was succeeded by a pronounced adoption of Walt Whitman. *Toward the Unknown Region* appeared in 1907; *A Sea Symphony*, for which the composer began to select texts in 1903, was performed in 1910; both at the Leeds Triennial Festival. The symphony was repeated in 1911, by the Oxford Bach Choir under Allen in March, and by the C.U.M.S. under the composer in June. In its notice of the latter performance, the *Cambridge Review* reported a 'tremendous ovation', and very surprisingly

---

[1] The *Credo* in G major is a continuous, concise setting in Stanford style, with a long, versatile *Amen* fugue. The *Offertorium* in G (cf. pp. 24, 32), exhibits sonata form with a Schubertian second theme. A formal *Sanctus* and vociferous *Hosanna* (D), with a cantabile *Benedictus* (G), achieve brevity. An incalculable expense of spirit.

For Mus. B. (1894) there was a setting (ch. str. org.) of *Vexilla Regis* (5 vv.). No. 1, in B♭, seasons its cheerful outer strophes with astringent canonic development in G minor. No. 2 achieves, with one break, a voluble fugue in D. No. 3, in G (sop. cantabile), leads into No. 4, an extended five-part fugue in declamatory style. Method is paramount, with close imitation favoured.

noted that the Scherzo had been re-written for orchestra alone, as an alternative version.[1]

In spite of the difficulties, for the chorus especially, of wry intonation and shifting metre, which resulted in a dubious performance of the symphony, it must have stirred a profound sense of liberation, in its contemplation of the heroes of the sea, its inexhaustible energy and its further significance as the sign of endless voyages. There was enough musical substance to remember, in clue-themes, swinging tunes and altogether striking textures, to establish Vaughan Williams as a composer with a sense of purpose and a technique of his own. At the Queen's Hall, too, in 1909, under Thomas Beecham, observant listeners might have noted, besides the manifest gravity and contemplative tone on which official comment fastened, the more steadily absorbed and homogeneous style of an extended *Fantasia* for strings on Tallis's 'Phrygian' third tune in Parker's *Psalter*, following the equally long-drawn *In the Fen Country*, based on original melodies, which had been given in 1907 under the same conductor. There was also the first *Norfolk Rhapsody*. (Numbers two and three have been withdrawn.)

This assured impact of a fresh note in English music should have been reinforced by the completion, in 1914, of a boxing-match opera for Covent Garden, long projected and now well in hand. In the event, *Hugh the Drover* was finished after the War of 1914–18, and successfully produced in 1924 at the R.C.M., and then at His Majesty's Theatre by the British National Opera Company. After all, Covent Garden has still to see that boxing-match. Even with the time-lag, and perhaps aided by it, the opera widened the composer's range from purely poetic figures to the more commonplace and solid characters of a Cotswold town under duress of Napoleonic threats and local disturbances. It was typical of the frail national or municipal basis of the newly formed opera company that it gave little encouragement to an English composer to build Bayreuth in Covent Garden or in any social centre whatever, as in August, 1914, Rutland Boughton had, economically, formed his clientèle in Glastonbury, Somerset. *Hugh the Drover* promised the composer very little future. Certainly no rewarding commission: there were no reserve funds. Hence, his further operas were sporadic, with one more normal example, *Sir John in Love*.

Meanwhile *A London Symphony*, the alleged expansion of a symphonic

---

[1] I cannot trace any performance of this version. The *Yorkshire Post* notice of the symphony (October 13, 1910), quoted by Young, states clearly that the Scherzo was conspicuous for the 'virtuosity in choral singing'.

poem (in response to a challenge from George Butterworth to write a symphony, it is related) had one fleeting performance under Geoffrey Toye in 1914, and another under Dan Godfrey at Bournemouth in 1915.[1] Its revival after the War under Albert Coates, in a reduced and otherwise reconstructed version, capped a 1918 performance under Boult. It formed a rallying point for the newly formed British Music Society, and for individual promoters like Boult, Coates and Wood. The work showed, once and for all, that Vaughan Williams was not dependent upon any text or programme, though going into the common walks of life for some of his basic material. *London City* (as Parry described it in his diary) showed, too, that with all its renewed moods of quiet absorption, a V. W. symphony was not an extended *Tallis Fantasia* or County-Rhapsody. At the same time, the plan of making a symphony seem not only to rise from, but to return to, the indefinite sound of London's traffic-hum, was original, and the fading end, repudiating all sonorous climax, remained a characteristic and defiant trait in symphonies 3, 5, 6 and 7, as also in *Sancta Civitas*.

Moreover, the extravagantly contemplative third symphony, the *Pastoral* (1922), was baffling to most listeners. It was manifestly a fresh release for the composer, but its dispensation with the usual contrasts of mood and tempo, in favour of a special pursuit of sonorities of various kinds, hinted at an idiosyncrasy, which the suite *Flos Campi* (viola solo; 1928) confirmed, and perhaps also the wayward procession of images in *Sancta Civitas* (1925). Otherwise, *Sancta Civitas* established Vaughan Williams as a dedicated composer in his own right, rejecting oratorio in nearly every sense but conveying all the more an authentic awareness of a crisis in experience; its echo of the *Revelation* text was not merely a display of craftsmanship. We shall return to the vexed question of structure in due course, and meanwhile may set down the work as neglected to this day.

Job (1930), nonetheless, exhibited many fresh turns in a ballet which presents, on the basis of some of Blake's illustrations, the apotheosis of the disciplined will, after a Miltonic struggle with corrupting influences in the soul. Thanks to a felicitous scenario, ballet was jerked out of

---

[1] This information has been supplied by Mr. D. Morris, librarian of the Bournemouth Symphony Orchestra, from the programmes of the Municipal Orchestra. Apart from the composer's final allusion, in his programme-note, to the March, 1914, performance, his reference to alternations of tempo in the finale makes it clear that he is writing of the original version. See Chapter 7.

Godfrey gave the symphony fifteen times in all, the last being in 1932. Surely a record promotional effort in the time, in one English town.

a rather madcap trend without too obvious moral pressure, and the dramatic impetus stirred the composer, too, out of certain grooves. The dreams of Job and Elihu are developed and haunting fantasies, but the resourceful trenchancy of the challenges of Satan and the comfortless comforters, and equally the melodic force of the firm assertions of world-order, leave the uppermost impression. It was reinforced by the uncompromising tone of the piano concerto. This work, however, was given too little chance of making a proper impact, even at home. Thus, the fourth symphony (1935) not only seemed to seize English audiences by the ears, but was the first work since *Flos Campi* to be sufficiently 'contemporary' to challenge foreign music on its own ground by a national style, broadened and toughened into something cosmopolitan.

Two choral-orchestral works followed, both appearing by chance in one week: *Five Tudor Portraits*, to verses by Skelton, and *Dona nobis pacem*, to a mingling of biblical and other fragments with the central appeal from the depths of a Christian social conscience in the later nineteen-thirties. Between them, these deliverances met the needs of a provincial festival (Norwich) and of the historical moment. Their total expressive range was remarkable, whatever remains to be said about the parts of each whole. More committed in harmonic texture and dramatic concentration, *Riders to the Sea*, a musical setting of Synge's play, was published about the same time (1936). Together, these additions to the *Pastoral Symphony* group left in no doubt the vivacity of the composer's invention, or his freedom from any restriction to a single method of appeal.

Not that Vaughan Williams ever seemed to bother about his reputation. He was quite devoid of the self-pity which afflicted Elgar in his correspondence with his friends, his grievance being a lack of proper recognition by the public. Vaughan Williams could count, indeed, on the plenary interest of the music critic of *The Times* (H. C. Colles, d. 1943), A. H. Fox-Strangways of the *Observer*, and others, whenever he was launching a new work of any consequence. He received plenty of candid criticism from their pens. The composer counted on their integrity, not on their favour. In the orchestral arena itself, he had Henry Wood to thank for many early performances and later renewals, both in London and the provinces, and Boult for a large number of first performances from about 1920 onwards. Sargent launched *Hugh the Drover*. (Barbirolli became associated with Vaughan Williams performances nearly thirty years later.)

With his established position as the leader of English music, it was unfortunate that a celebration of the composer's seventieth birthday fell due in 1942. Tributes were paid, amongst others, by Hubert Foss with a patriotic speech on the B.B.C., summarizing the composer's profoundly national position along lines which the speaker developed in his subsequent book; the music critic of *The Times* had some pertinent things to say about the snares of a self-conscious nationality (October 12); and the B.B.C. offered a programme or two of Vaughan Williams.

The real creative event, however, took place in 1943, when the fifth symphony was played for the first time, under the composer, at the Royal Albert Hall (relayed through the B.B.C.'s Home Service), the Queen's Hall having by this time been destroyed. What could follow now, if 1935 had produced the F minor? Contrary to expectation, the symphony proved to be, if anything, a positive rejoinder to no. 4, a conservation of images of thought and contemplation that no rule of violence could keep out of music. The prevailing tranquillity of utterance, both in melodic texture and in dynamic level, vindicated earlier trends with a fresh melodic distinctiveness. The symphony so far balanced its predecessor, as Brahms's second had matched his first, and at the same time left further symphonic turns an exciting issue. (Would the next symphony be tremendous or just 'deep'?) Henceforward, apart from opera, in which nearly every native product is a serious risk to this day, every major work of Vaughan Williams was assured of public performance as soon as it was made available.

Meanwhile, Vaughan Williams concerned himself with the musical welfare and common local necessities of his Dorking neighbourhood. After major sewage fatigues in Salonica (1916), he made short work of any 'salvage' collecting which he considered it his duty to undertake. He was equally helpful to distressed composers and other musicians, some foreign or utterly without country.[1] For the musicians he wrote *Household Music*, a setting of three Welsh hymn-tunes for string quartet or wind alternative.

Vaughan Williams first became interested in film-music in 1941, with the film *Forty-ninth Parallel*, one of a documentary-patriotic series to which he was assigned the music by agreement. Far from being cynical over the limitations of action and spectacle in motion, and over the restrictions of a clientèle of dubious listening quality, he entered with

---

[1] In 1938, his music had been banned in Germany because he had asked that his Hamburg prize-money should be given to a fund for refugee Jews.

zest and efficiency into the proposition of writing musical snippets that were capable of a multitude of abbreviations and extensions. He surprised film-producers (who thought themselves efficient men, moving in a world of hustlers) by the speed with which he furnished, complete, what he was asked for, with every modification that might be desired. He also found in this hit-or-miss genre a fresh opportunity for cultivating tuneful music, not merely strophical in shape but depending on a growing tune or theme. He ended by strongly recommending film work to students as a cure for loose ends and *longueurs*. The fulfilment of this line was *Scott of the Antarctic* (1948), of which the seventh symphony embodied a free extension.

Vaughan Williams also wrote music for various B.B.C. sound programmes, of which the chief were 'See the Vacant Sea' (the music was taken from the film-score, *Coastal Command*), 'Richard II', the four-episode 'The Pilgrim's Progress' (1946) and 'The Mayor of Caster-bridge', a serial.

The end of the War of 1939–45 was marked, musically, by the broadcast of a piece prepared for the occasion, Vaughan Williams's *Thanksgiving for Victory*. Designed for a difficult moment of confused purposes and contrasted reactions, of simple thankfulness and bitter memories, this short but sonorous choral piece contrived to convey a timeless, unquenchable message of Christian conviction and national dedication in the direct manner which had long been second nature to the composer, and with a spontaneity which avoided any impression of superior attitude. The last point may claim discussion later; but one cannot miss the personal concern behind this restrained uplifting of the human spirit above the deadly struggle. It was thus consistent that the by no means exultant sixth symphony (1948) reflected, if anything, a tormented awareness of the world's old anger, as well as a philosophic calm (or exhaustion). A 'heroic' symphony, first entrusted to John Barbirolli and the Hallé Orchestra, came later (1953). But it was founded on recollections, not of recent history, but of Captain Scott and his men, and derived from the film-music already mentioned. The purely musical symphonies, 8 (1956) and 9 (1958), followed. Meanwhile, two important works had shown a clear relation to a didactic text: the long pondered Morality, *The Pilgrim's Progress* (Covent Garden), a contribution to the Festival of Britain, 1951; and *Hodie* (Worcester, 1954), a fresh dedication to truth and justice against a background of Christmas celebration, spontaneous but strenuous.

The humanist and deeper references must not be overstated, but they cannot be ignored, as elements in a fresh stage of composition, and as growing links with listening audiences at large. The appearances of the composer at these premières and repeats could not fail to confirm the presence of a wise, unpretentious, stalwart figure, ageing but far from *passé*; a grand presence, whom every audience rejoiced to have seen as well as experienced artistically. At Dorking, as president of the Festival, Vaughan Williams was the guiding spirit to the end, as one who in his own work was steadily in training, whether for the simpler local needs of church and cinema, or the sophisticated demands of cosmopolitan concert-hall, or for the service of some special prophetic purpose, arising from some recognized contingency or maturing gradually in experience from new verifications of central references.

He made a similar impression on the orchestras with whom he rehearsed his symphonies, for concert-performance or for recording. Mr. Bernard Shore recalled, in a broadcast tribute, that at a dead stop during a rehearsal of the fourth, he rallied a confused orchestra by declaring 'Heaven only knows where *I* am!' He misled no one by that disclaimer! To an observer in the audience, his leads to the orchestra sometimes seemed too late to be of any use. Yet his stick, we are told, was 'quite clear enough to give us complete confidence . . . the sheer power of that rugged personality invariably produced a fine performance' (*R.C.M. Magazine*, 55. 1, p. 35). Actually, he was sometimes nervous. Referring to the sixth symphony, he once said, 'I'm a bit worried about my 'tune' at Gloucester next week . . . Oh, you chaps [L.S.O.] are all right, you know it. But I've never conducted it before' (*Ib.* p. 44). In the last years he had to rely much on a deaf-aid, or on Mr. Roy Douglas, for discerning necessary adjustments of balance at orchestral rehearsals, and in the last months he could not hear properly. Yet to the end he enjoyed the general confidence. The artistic impact and the personal influence vibrated in tune. Of the disciplinarian, it is sufficient to mention the simple-minded fury with which he greeted the trumpeter who came in late after the interval; or, equally, his habit at the Dorking concerts of putting down his stick after a few bars, confident in the alertness of his choir of 200–300. (*Ib.*, pp. 10, 39.)

Vaughan Williams led a considerable side-life as a critic in various directions. He summarized his experience of folk-song as the dry-witted Mary Flexner Lecturer at Bryn Mawr College, Pennsylvania, in 1932. The nine lectures, later published as *National Music*, pursue the main contention of Sharp's *English Folk-song*, but are probing where

2. The composer as a boy at Charterhouse School, 1889

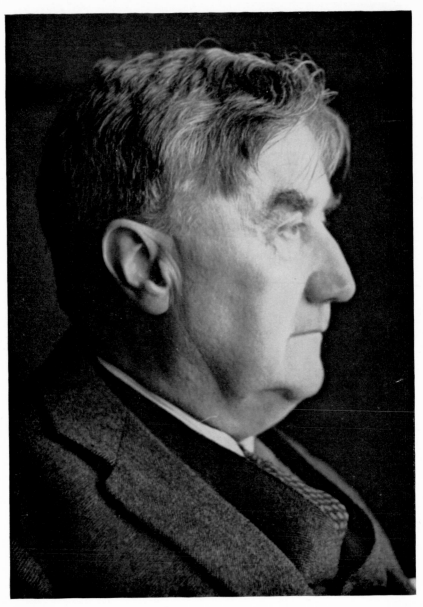

3. Ralph Vaughan Williams, *c.* 1947

Sharp was tentative. More recently, Vaughan Williams published a collection of essays, articles and notes on Beethoven's *Choral Symphony*, Holst, Bach and other miscellaneous topics, with the racy self-portrait written for Foss's book. These reveal Vaughan Williams as an outspoken and therefore stimulating observer, sometimes more provocative than convincing in attack. The lectures given at Cornell University, published as *The Making of Music*, are almost extravagant in the promotion of paradox in cold print, but evidently their delivery, with their impromptu phrases and spontaneous, unscheduled piano illustrations, made an attractive, unforgettable experience for the large audience who had come to hear, some from a great distance.

As commentator on the *Choral Symphony*, Vaughan Williams displays the mock reverence for the analytical-descriptive programme-note of English tradition (Grove, Rosa Newmarch & Co.), which he increasingly showed in notes on his own works. These (e.g. that for the *Pastoral Symphony*, January, 1922, as given at a Philharmonic Society concert) at first confined themselves to a citation of melodic themes and the barest suggestion of the order of events, and from the sixth symphony onwards indulged in an almost continuous parody of the Method, in loquacious references to 'fussy little themes', and to mock-pleas of Haydn precedent for defaulting patterns which would worry no listener after the age of Parry. In other words, while the mischievous tone will have intrigued some readers, as impishness often does elsewhere, the music quotations remain the chief 'authentic source', so far as they go. The occasional recurrence in modern programmes of the tiresome verbal paraphrase of sound-relationship, mingled with features of conventional and uncomprehending technical allusion to structure and texture, does not, in fact, invalidate the uses of intelligent annotation. In this sphere Vaughan Williams appears commonly to have released his irritation with critics in general, as representatives of a trend that is actually almost past history. To his passing reference, in a late preface to a book not by himself, to 'our bat-eyed musicologists', the only reply can be: We note the new term of opprobrium.

As a lecturer, Vaughan Williams was admirable. He had a gift for reducing technical distinctions to the plainest speech, his choice of analogy and diction was stimulating as well as entertaining, and he always led his audience towards a more musical experience. He once lectured with ease and eloquence, in my hearing, to a boys' school (Leighton Park, Reading), on internationalism in music. Afterwards, he confessed that the notes which he had apparently been consulting were for another lecture. But no one would have guessed. As an adjudicator at competitions, he was equally successful. His probing ear, clear expression and genial corrections made his pronouncements conducive to a choir's better performance, next year or at the combined rehearsal to follow.

As a composition teacher, he worked best, no doubt, with pupils advanced enough to profit from his blunt comment and technical advice. At this level he little resembled Stanford, except in practical questions. His rejections were uncompromising, but he was always concerned that a struggling composer should find his own style, without sharing Parry's habitual response to any variant that might pass as characteristic. Even unimaginative and incompetent pupils were made aware of the logic of music, of an ideal answer to whatever question their theme propounded. Some such recognition must have prompted Allen, as one of his first acts after his appointment as director of the R.C.M., to invite Vaughan Williams to give the College one day a week, stilling the fears of the reluctant composer with the broad injunction, 'Come up to London and be yourself'. So Allen described this step, however romantically, in the last conversation that I had with him; and in many lessons Vaughan Williams certainly appeared as counsellor and fellow-artist rather than judicial authority. 'His pupils continued to go back to him for criticism and advice', recalls Miss Elizabeth Maconchy, and adds, 'I always found, when I thought it over, that what he said was right, even if I did not like it at first'. Miss Grace Williams uses similar phrases. They and Dr. Gordon Jacob agree that their teacher had a rooted distrust of technical skill, but Dr. Jacob testifies that subsequently pupils were 'made to do their stodge', and E. J. Dent found him a 'strict' examiner on the technical side (*R.C.M. Magazine*, 55. 1).

To turn to the amateur world on whose voluntary effort this country is particularly dependent: as a committee-man, Vaughan Williams was, perhaps, inclined to be on the provocative side, as a period of cautious, punctilious committeemanship is apt to goad men of individuality into being. He appears to have been conservative by nature, radical in intention, and thus unpredictable but open-minded. He supported Sharp's impatient attitude towards the Folk Song Society's complacent standards both of output and of promulgation, and it was he who paved the way, on solid realistic grounds, for the amalgamation of that Society and the English Folk Dance Society. He remained a genial supporter of the E.F.D.S.S., and, as president for twelve years, contributed personally to the Society's *Journal* for the Jubilee and Diamond Jubilee of the Folk Song Society (Numbers 5. 3 and 8. 3). The latter retrospect appeared in December, 1958, as part of a celebration inevitably mingled with fervent recollections of the late president. In a short tribute, Maud Karpeles enlarged on the composer's steady services to the E.F.D.S.S. and its predecessors over half a century. He had also been president of the International Folk Music Council, formed in 1947 for the comparative study of folk-music of different nations and to promote friendship through a common interest.

From the start, English folk-song, once encountered, struck a deep chord in his musical consciousness and social conscience, and for him it remained a good cause, for what it had promoted, even when the battle for the recognition of national music was as good as won. First a stimulus to him as a composer, it became a reserve force on which he might at any time draw, and also the natural meeting-point of all classes of listener, which none could consider redundant in its place. Manifestly, many E.F.D.S.S. members responded by meeting him more than half way as a composer.

In 1935, Vaughan Williams was awarded the Order of Merit by King George V, in company with John Masefield and Frederick Gowland Hopkins, well-known for his work on vitamins. Evidently that was the only Order he was prepared to accept. He shared Holst's views on official distictions, though he was not a conscious follower of the *Bhagavad Gîtâ*. He accepted an honorary doctorate of music at Oxford in 1919, at Trinity College, Dublin, in 1939, and at Bristol in 1951.

In 1897 Vaughan Williams married Adeline Fisher, member of a large and distinguished family, of which another member, H. A. L. Fisher, historian and educational leader in many spheres, has left an account (*An Unfinished Autobiography*). A singularly united family, with a strong sense of common purpose, as they made their way in the worlds of university teaching, the fighting services and business, it took them a little time to accept young, silent, unsociable Ralph Vaughan Williams, who had no proper profession, even if he was a Wedgwood on one side and a Darwin on another. But if their future brother-in-law was to be this austere musician, it was confidently expected that he would turn out to be good at his job. As it happened, another sister, Emmeline, married a kindred spirit, R. O. Morris (1886–1948), composer, writer and academic teacher of the best kind.

Adeline Fisher was a pianist of some accomplishment, and there were later family memories of a grand concerted invasion of Wagner prior to an excursion to Bayreuth. As Mrs. Vaughan Williams, she acted as copyist and more, taking scores and revised scores in her stride, and ferreting out texts to set. She became a victim of arthritis. When she could no longer go out, she listened to all the broadcasts of her husband's works, and reported on any that he had not heard. Increasingly immobile, she continued, by her command of inner élan, to make her home the centre of artistic comings and goings, as well as of family reunions and wartime guests. Such 'unlimited goodness' in a private home remained for many a refreshing experience, and, indeed, an inspiration in itself. Severe discipline at his mother's old home had done something to inculcate the spontaneous and unfailing considerateness which the composer showed to people in every walk of life. (*R.C.M. Magazine*, 55. 1, pp. 19, 25). An ingrained fantasy that he was a redundant amateur among brilliant know-alls, and a habit of asking advice, or of giving it with every nominal permission to ignore, helped, no doubt, to give his visitors a sense of security in consultation. But behind it all was a positive sense of a centre of reference, of a life to be lived responsibly and to the full, in and beyond the nation, in answer to present needs but equally to a clear perception of a wider world beyond sense.

Adeline Vaughan Williams died in 1951. In 1953 the composer married a friend of hers, who had been his amanuensis, Ursula, daughter of Major-General Sir Robert Lock, and widow of Lt.-Col. J. M. J. Forrester Wood. 'Ursula Wood' had supplied the long and unusual text for *The Sons of Light*, and now joined the noble throng of word-makers in *Hodie*. Her constant identification with her husband's work in the last years will no doubt appear in her book, and I shall not try to anticipate this final chapter and commentary.

During this period the Vaughan Williamses settled in London, and he went about more than before. He became a conspicuous figure at the Cheltenham Festival, amongst other gatherings, as an early comer at the rehearsals of the new music. His presence must have made the labour of preparation joyfully spent for any modest composer. It was characteristic that, working unobtrusively to the end, he was advising a young musician on the day before he died. (Let that man stay anonymous, for he represented a great company, any one of whom might have been that privileged person.) There recollection may leave the composer, talking, relevant and concerned, giving old age a new vitality, Ben Ezra without the smugness.

Some clues to his purpose in life are unmistakable. First, a belief in music as a necessity, and in English music of the future. Second, a supremely imaginative conception of the occasions for which music should be found, not only in affirmations of belief, or first-aid at a critical point of world-sickness, but in answer to a deep need for music on a more popular basis than previously experienced with art-music. Third, an assumption that to produce music at the bidding of genius or craft-exercise was not enough. Music must be aimed at those who did not think they wanted it, beginning with the most indigenous sort, folk-song, and not stopping, chorally, at competition snippets. For some, lectures were desirable; for students, regular coaching, and examinations as musically probing as they could be made. For the luxuries (e.g. discords) of today's music may become the necessities of tomorrow's. Every occasion demands its style of promotion. As major texts change from Whitman selections to a *Job* scenario, so the music for them shifts, not only in its texture but in its provenance and, indeed, in its audience. The common elements in pronounced achievements are not only experience and logical working out, but what Aristoxenus, dismissing mathematical conceptions of music, called perception (*aesthesis*). The purpose of the remainder of this volume will be to observe the workings of this discriminating activity, as it moves from symphony to cantata or opera and back, usually without falling into grooves or, on the contrary, pursuing a course so eclectic as to be un-identifiable from work to work.

III

Victorian and Edwardian Tradition

A creative artist is not concerned with history, but only with practical problems of communication. History begins later. Yet a composer cannot project his work into a void. He must choose his ideal audience: local, provincial or metropolitan centre, general public or trained and responsive gatherings. He must also choose his ideal performers and *venue*: orchestral forces, or an ensemble of soloists, or piano solo, each with or without singers of similar range; and concert, or opera, or ballet. In addition, if an English composer at the turn of the century could make up his mind where there was any audience for him, it was not so easy to decide whether new music was wanted at all. If he found encouraging opportunity, it is history's business to trace it to its source; and if, on the contrary, he had to create an audience for his art, his pioneer quality should be mentioned from the start. Not that a pioneer is necessarily a great artist, or vice versa. But precedent must be shown, where it is apparent, and its lack exposed.

The need for a national tradition in music may be questioned by some observers, who hold that nationalist music is music forced into a non-musical groove, and point to the many contemporary signs—the more recent output of Stravinsky, for example—that nationalism is now done with. A later turn on the part of a controversial composer, however, is not a binding argument, and an assumption that national tradition is artistically irrelevant is a flat repudiation of the evidence of the nineteenth century and of earlier periods. It cannot be denied that the art of Schubert and Weber, of Wagner and Brahms—leaders of once irreconcilable parties—is fundamentally German, in one way or another, as the art of Dvorák is Bohemian, and of Borodin, Russian. If the impact of these artists has since broken comfortably over many frontiers, this has been partly due to the strength of their national flavour. Moreover, this assertion of national character was a reaction from the Italian and French styles that had become well-nigh universal in contemporary music, through distinctive manners of speech, rather than from any specific concern for a national way of development. The conclusion is irresistible that, for its renewal, music had to go through this stage, to establish new currencies.

NATIONAL MUSIC THROUGH LITERATURE

Three focal points of this process were literary contacts, opera and folk-song. The first of these hardly calls for much explanation. One need only reflect how much characteristic German music, still pertinent, owes a debt to Goethe (not to name Heine and the rest) for its primary stimulus and spontaneous reception, sometimes inexplicable but often in direct contact with the many singers and singers' pianists waiting for material in German middle-class homes. Select publication, with often felicitous translations, in time found English audiences scarcely less responsive to the fusion of word and tone. On the same lines, aided by recordings, Mussorgsky's songs are just on the way in. Similarly, through de Nerval's translation of Goethe, and Latourneur's of Shakespeare, supported by the performances of Kemble's company (and by the romanticist influences which liquidated the recent post-Waterloo distaste for Shakespeare as an 'aide-de-camp of Wellington'), Berlioz's *Faust* and *Roméo et Juliette* revived French music-drama in the concert-room, on the basis of an accepted literary contact. Boito's *Mefistofele* overrode national reactions at its second production after a riotous reception at its first. In time, rounding a circle, the musical *Faust* became the stand-by of English choral societies. Dr. Faustus, once at home in a blaze of Elizabethan poetry, had returned 'in evening dress' as a leading solo in a dramatic score. The republic of letters has often thus supplied a ready passport to a musical work on its travels.

Later, the audacity of *Till Eulenspiegel*, and of other hubristic and ultra-assertive natures, formed the terms of reference of Strauss's extravagant orchestral appeal, which unmistakably succeeded Wagner's historic invasion of all the senses. The Strauss conquest was achieved without a word sung or spoken. An earlier attempt, Raff's, to write a patriotic symphony by the simple expedient of providing academic titles for the movements, failed from a lack of musical material to corroborate the claim. A liberal sprinkling, again, of Shakespearian quotations (in German) in the score of Pierson's symphonic poem *Macbeth*, with marches of the opposing armies, although suggesting a reaction from the Leipzig style of Bennett, did not amount to an underground movement in the country of Pierson's adoption. (His sometimes lively *Faust* music is also a setting of the original German.)

Parallel to Strauss, however, a new series of symphonies was connected with the setting or suggestion of poems, in one movement or another, from the equalitarian level of the *Knabenhorn* to the redemptive ardour, not without pomposity, of the *Faust* finale, succeeding an immense setting of an otherwise established text, *Veni Sancte Spiritus*. Programme music, with regional basis, was thus openly reasserted by Mahler, in symphonies 2–4 and 8, with a certain systematic flourish, along with folkish traits and many personal features. In contrast, Brahms, coming to the symphony proper in full maturity, was able to dispense with the textual links on which, with a corresponding call for choral declamation and fugue, he had leant in his 'Requiem'. Yet the restless, Faust-like struggle for mastery in the first symphony—the comparison is Hanslick's—was partly conditioned by the typical conflicting moods of lyrical drama. The process continued, in psychological reverse, in the ebbing energy of the third symphony. In his second symphony, in all movements but one a serenade in spirit, Brahms relies on the capacity of his themes to fill sonata-patterns of mounting insistence. This cumulative touch, as against the lighter finale of the serenade type in most eighteenth-century symphonies, may without strain of evidence be associated with Beethoven and the German symphonic method of appeal, as adopted in due course by Dvořák, Tchaikovsky, Franck and others, but most comfortably revived by Brahms. This, to speak broadly, is the structural opposite of the English symphony up to Elgar, of which Stanford's resort to national tunes in the finale of the *Irish Symphony* is symptomatic.

NATIONAL OPERA

The opera-house has provided steady evidence of national movements towards self-culture. A long period of preparation, a kind of resistance movement in enemy-occupied territory, marked out Handel and Mozart, in turn, as composers of Italian opera who were different from the rest, not only because of their command of haunting melody but also their greater cultivation of the orchestra. This absorption in orchestral periods, shaping with a deepening mood an otherwise feckless plot, remained more characteristic of Mozart's experiments with German opera than any native elements of singspiel style or ceremonial incident. The same is true of Beethoven and Schubert, in the wake of whose impetuous but also lyrical operatic movements Weber found a German setting for stage-music propelled by orchestral development, in the naturalism and magic of *Freischütz*; with similarly romantic material on a grander scale in *Euryanthe*. Meanwhile Berlioz, with a new command of texture, enriched the dynamics of French music-drama with a startling precision of orchestral expression, visibly triumphant in *Les Troyens*.

Wagner went much further. Aided, eventually, by far greater fortune in his lifetime, and by an often fanatic and hysterical national enthusiasm since, his steady pursuit of German or German-biased saga, super-men and exalted but anthropomorphic gods, supported by an unparalleled grasp of proliferating clue-theme, established, on the fantastic scale of Bayreuth, a proud tradition of self-revealing music. National states, marshalled with increasing intensity towards a sense of a common and nationalist objective, found their mission here. This search for the national self involved the absorption of all possible discoveries of Liszt, virtuoso pianist, improviser, and nominally descriptive writer, as well as the exploration of new orchestral groupings. Strauss brilliantly short-circuited the process in his series of orchestral 'tone-poems' on stated subjects, which, without using vocal elements, clearly reflected remembered personalities of German literary tradition, past and present.

Meanwhile Italian opera had been re-born, in a trenchant *verismo*, sometimes a product of the *risorgimento*, and in Verdi, in a penetrating humanity to which Wagner never aspired. Musically, a still dominant vocalized impulse was being buttressed by the growing orchestral interest of a developing act, without the organizational drive of Wagner. French opera remained bourgeois in general, relieved by the piquant ballets of Thomas and Délibes.

Composers of Bohemian and Russian opera worked from these increasingly sophisticated lines towards a fresh style of speech-song, distinctive in melodic curve and harmony, on the realistic side, and detached from a symphonic context, although, under the spell of Berlioz and others, orchestrally striking and characteristic. These features matched the resort to novel and indigenous texts and legends. In Dvorák, the new procedures radiated from operatic production to symphony and chamber music that rendered the German sonata tradition with a decidedly new accent and a less discursive manner. Russian music, with a theatre history from 1790, made its greatest discoveries on the stage, with one notable exception. Tchaikovsky's output shows, in spite of a professed aversion to Beethoven, distinct German or cosmopolitan features in symphony and concerto. The 'Hungarian' music of Liszt and Brahms remained at best a vogue, not truly indigenous. The creator of Hungarian style in opera was Ferenc Erkel, who used his position, as director of the national theatre at Pest, to voice national aspirations in the stalwart measures of *Hunyadi László* (1844), blending czardas and oratorio (cf. Act 2 *fin.*, in *Elijah* style), and *Bánk Ban*, since a hardy annual. The free speech-song of *Brankovics György* (1874) points forward to the work of Mussorgsky. It was Erkel to whom Berlioz dedicated the famous March that left Faust's wanderings in Hungary connected for ever with an appropriately militant song.

A SEARCH FOR ENGLISH MUSIC

To understand the barren English situation, it is necessary to delve further back into the past. During the mastery of the London musical public by Handel and other Italian-trained dealers in opera, the Englishman's awareness of the national potential almost stopped ticking. Purcell was forgotten, the grey dawn of an unaccomplished day; he lacked, indeed, any firm grip on a structural method capable of handling a full-scale music-drama above the pastework level. There was no national future in Handel's treatment of Italian opera. English ballad-opera was too thin and patchy to lead further. Oratorio was not much better. As with *Zauberflöte*, *mutatis mutandis*, the resort to the Old Testament and a vernacular text still left the Italian-German style in command, except for the adaptation of music-drama and epic story to concert conditions, and a noticeable emphasis, not to be taken too seriously, on choral declamation and fugue in a lightly woven texture and wayward structure. Even the recitatives suppress more English rhythm than they articulate. Nor did the exceptional *Messiah* exercise a different influence on any potentially English taste. On the contrary, its sacrosanct perpetuation, with a reverence for its most hazardous qualities, as number succeeds number, has until recently been matched by the clumsiest possible defiance of the original plastic texture, in festival hall and Gothic cathedral, since the performance at the Three Choirs Festival in 1759. More than any other master-work, *Messiah* has promoted the acceptance of monumental compositions, in however foreign a style and however blunt the rendering, as one of the necessities of our musical life.

Yet the frail talent of Arne could not bring the masque, such as *Alfred* with its grand empire-building finale to Thomson's words, or the Italian sinfonia behind some of his overtures, to new stature. Arne's move to Italian opera, with a setting of his translation of a Metastasio text, *Artaxerxes* (1762), coincided symbolically and almost fatally with the adoption by a minor composer, T. A. Erskine (Lord Kelly), of the 'Mannheim' symphony. However expedient as respective modish steps towards a more coherent and organized musical appeal, these changes of style prepared the way for a later stage of Italian opera in London, in which Signor Pasticcio (alias Sacchini) was the leading composer. Salomon's organizational initiative brought two sets of Haydn symphonies before a London public with equally fatal results to native talent. (Yet Salomon has his monument in Westminster Abbey!) All this music was exotic and irrational in one sense or another. The opera moved in a stilted dream-world, more tied to favourite singers' rhetorical skill than to the vague classical and other plots chosen; with aria-pattern limited to a few repeat formulae, any wider sense of structure is likely to be an accident of compilation. In the realm of pure music, the satisfying orderliness of Haydn's movement-construction was based on needs that had first arisen in a society which had learnt to take the symphonic habit for granted, quite apart from the echoes of local folk-song, now judged to be German, not Czech.

ENGLISH OPERA

If observation now leaps a hundred years from Haydn's last symphonies of 1795, one may discern a sense of occasion stirring in England, but it is not a revolutionary one. Current opera is now basically Italian, French or German. That is, those who could afford it expected to be served with opera from abroad; Italy for plain, strong drama, France for a more subtle, quasi-lyrical style, Germany for heavy weather of all sorts. It is unnecessary to go into details. The main exceptions were Sullivan and early Stanford. Sullivan's operettas revived the English language, in the intonation of a pungent patter and with a certain range of congenial and often thick sentiment. In dramatic tone, Sullivan (or Gilbert) followed Vincent Wallace, with his condemned noblemen having their fate bewailed by creditors (as in *Maritana*), down the road of British compromise with serious opera. But the new régime deflated grand opera, with its steady descent to the prosaic in and outside the sung portions, while introducing (a perpetual attraction to participants at all social levels) plenty of pompous or egregiously fantastic scenes in the course of the capricious and sometimes inhuman plots contrived, mainly, by W. S. Gilbert. The flow of song is punctuated by flashes of orchestral humour, along with many all too expected brass or *tutti* entries, but never by anything approaching symphonic development, even in the first finale. Nor is the harmonic norm of Sullivan perceptibly ahead of Schubert; which unconsciously delights his reactionary admirers, but none the less has to be taken into account in assessing the positive gains of the Savoy series, compared with other native stage works.

Ivanhoe, which might conceivably have led Sullivan to a more sustained expression, with its weightier literary ballast, only succeeded in sounding 'slow'. The cult of light orchestration, with the sung word as paramount, defeated its object. Once more the orchestra is not taken seriously enough to carry Julian Sturgis's Tennysonian thoughts on to a wider plane, or to a deeper characterization; voices cannot do this unaided. There is a lack of creative will-power.

Sullivan has been flattered by his imitators, but he cannot now be considered more than an adventurer. Still less can his vast clientèle of today be reckoned as vanguard material for more developed English opera. On the contrary, the steady feature of a Sullivan public's opera-scheme is—yet more Sullivan.

C. V. STANFORD

It is not easy, in face of such a nation-wide establishment, to canvas the claim of a composer so rarely heard on the stage as Stanford. His early operas can hardly be reconsidered now. It is sufficient to record that *The Veiled Prophet* (Moore-Barclay Squire) was produced at Hanover in 1881, and in London in 1893, on the last night of the Season. In April, 1884, *Savonarola* and *The Canterbury Pilgrims* appeared at Hamburg and Drury Lane. The former began well but missed its mark, owing to intrigue and some frivolity over production, in the London season of German opera in the same year. Carl Rosa filled Drury Lane for four performances of *The Pilgrims*, and then fatally abandoned the work. With such lively and familiar company on the stage, and 'Sumer is i-cumen in' as the theme-song among more questionable Old English features, and some pertinent revisions, the opera might well have caught on in time. Earlier, *Faust*, a very doubtful starter in London, would never have gone further, had not the fighting manager of Her Majesty's Theatre, Colonel Mapleson, kept on and organized his public until they had accepted the opera as suitable for home consumption; and there must have been many similar instances of successfully insistent premières or revivals.

It should be added that in 1875 the Duke of Edinburgh laid the first stone of the superstructure of a national opera-house on the New Embankment (opposite what is now South Bank), for which Mapleson had secured the land, reclaimed from the river, and had the foundations built at a cost of £33,000. After spending another £70,000, he only needed £10,000 more, for roofing, to secure a mortgage. The roof was never built. But an address presented to the Duke on his visit outlined plans for Italian opera in the spring and summer, and English opera by English composers, singers and orchestra for the rest of the year, in association with the R.A.M. and kindred institutions, encouraged by training facilities.

Thus Stanford's hopes were dashed, leaving another composer to reap the Chaucer field. Nearly half a century later, Dyson, nothing if not practical, made his *Pilgrims* an extended and sociable choral suite, structurally in the new short-oratorio tradition. Thirty years later still, Vaughan Williams exploited both the seasonal quality and the modernity of the famous Round, as a focal number in his *Folk-songs of the Four Seasons*. Another casualty of the 'nineties, Goring Thomas's *Esmeralda* (from Hugo), was almost in the Bizet tradition. The sense of characterization promised more, had the composer lived longer. Yet there is little sign of a distinctive national style here.

In 1895 Stanford's *Shamus O'Brien* was produced at the Opera Comique (London). Widely welcomed at the time—with some protests against the ridiculing of the English army—as a sentimental but tolerable exaltation of a lovable protagonist of 'ould Erin' (1798), it became, two decades later, by the war of 1916, an awkward period-piece; and there are too many man-hunting police states nowadays. Structurally, the work keeps closely to the serial sing-and-speak style of light opera, and many musical numbers are purely strophical. The whole impact seems too scrappy, in perusal, to be worth remembering. Stiffly formal songs are joined by perfunctory choral matter (e.g. no. 6, the arousal of the mountain rebels). In the finale of Act 1, the collapse of Nora's artificially strained allusion to the Banshee, directly Father O'Flynn enjoins her to dance her troubles away, is arrant stage-Irish, where the laughing finale, for example, of either *Falstaff* (Verdi, Vaughan Williams) is persuasive in its context.

Much Ado about Nothing (1901) is another story. Its two performances at Covent Garden were as cruel treatment as the four for *Benvenuto Cellini* (1838). The ubiquitous Sturgis here contrived, while economizing in characters, to amplify the Shakespeare version, especially the Claudio-Hero elements, but to preserve the major and the minor conspiracies, with the piquant Beatrice-Benedick theme duly stressed and integrated, and Dogberry and Company at hand for further relief from sentiment. Stanford's four acts are effectively shaped towards successive turns of plot: the growth of the minor 'conspiracy', the destruction of Claudio's idyllic confidence in Hero, his repudiation of her as a bride, and the chain of counter-measures that keep the last act on the move; Benedick and Beatrice supplying the main linking episodes. This virtual guarantee of 'good stage', without restriction to Shakespeare's dramatic pattern, was obviously a tremendous stimulus to the composer's mastery of varied means, and for the spectator the general continuity of occasions for music is at once striking. There are some points of stagnation: the strophical habit still haunts too many situations, and its recrudescence for the final duet is almost fatal; the repeated rising sixth for the lovers' mutual devotion is a too patent symbol, and soon wears thin; and Stanford's jejune music for the church service is odd in a leading church composer. But these hitches are overridden by many felicities. The opera holds together, is manifestly an English opera, and is seriously comic, not farcical. It was revived at the R.C.M. in 1935, and by the Oxford University Opera Club in 1949. On each occasion the respiration process was far from strained.

The Travelling Companion (Anderson-Newbolt) became part of the Sadler's Wells repertory (where I encountered it) in 1925, after the composer's death, although published in 1919. It may be summarized as a moral-magic opera; the message being the power of the resolute spirit to conquer all obstacles, including a proud woman's capricious and ultimately regressive irresolution before a suitor; the magic resting in the operations of a dead man's spirit, as companion to a desolate young man, and of a wizard influence in false protection of the girl. The impact thus oscillates between the ethical note, which shows its bare teeth in the Companion's exhortations ('Go forth!' etc.) at the finales of Acts 1 and 3, and the whimsical tone of king and folk, which prepares for the downright symbolism of the wizard's-cave scene in Act 3. Bound by the text, the two styles coalesce uneasily, from a lack of musical flow; this is apparent when the Companion starts echoing, correctively and canonically, the princess's fanciful phrases. The longest musical interlude, the lead into the wizard scene, is a restless, barely integrated, transition; and so is the princess's dance. The penultimate sense of release, when John produces the head-goblin's head and all the previous victims of the princess's fatal guess-my-riddle-or-else test return to life, recalls *Hänsel und Gretel*, with its softer sentiment but greater spontaneity. It cannot have been easy for the impresario concerned to be confident about admitting this genial opera into the repertory of the irreverent 'twenties.

Any one who appreciates the place of opera in national music elsewhere will agree to the pertinence of this bland inquiry into the forgotten and not very positive stage side of Vaughan Williams's background. It is the most vital question, *a priori*, not to be side-tracked by talk of choral cantatas, still less of the comely and often perennial miniatures of church and concert-hall, to which Stanfordites constantly refer. That it has been expedient to enumerate, and even more to indicate the clear dramatic scope of the chief operas concerned, tells its own story. It remains to suggest that even Stanford, with his versatile pen, did not go far in establishing a distinct national style. One may dwell, indeed, upon the exaltation of the chorus, on the wider possibilities of settings of Shakespeare and others, and on the fitness of English for dialogue. No claim, however, can be seriously admitted for any advance towards a new kind of music. Any relevant stimulus must be sought elsewhere, with a corresponding burden on the next composer. This dismissal is made with full appreciation of Stanford's critical perception of the importance of having, as in Italy, a standing operatic repertory as an objective for trained musicians, rather than training the musicians first and then looking round for a non-existent opening, as was being done. Parry had no such sympathies. A Wagnerite ahead of his time, he still could not dissociate opera from an elaborate tissue of pretence and mere rhetoric, alien to his musical nature.

On the same lines, Parry publicly welcomed English folk-song (with the glimmerings of a twinkle) as an escape from the hereditary taints and general misanthropic impulses which worried his generation; as a bond of union between the heads that direct and the hands that ply, as a spontaneous appeal which all could admire. In the same spirit, two decades later, he himself supplied the song which, above all other English songs, continues to unite men and women of resolution along the road that goes upward all the way. Yet of English folk-song, as a body of native music, he can have had little knowledge. It seems that he called his third symphony the *English* merely because its independent spirit reflected the mental breeziness that he associated with folk-song. Stanford had, perhaps, a fairly wide knowledge of Irish song, with a corresponding impulse to publish books devoted to it; but, apart from a few direct allusions, as in the finale of the *Irish Symphony*, and some modal curves in the songs of Shamus and the like, it did not affect his style. He rejected Vaughan Williams's flattened sevenths *a priori*. How, following others, Vaughan Williams began collecting and arranging folk-songs from various English counties, and how Cecil Sharp, in twenty years' hard work of collection, comparison and promotion, redressed the neglect of a century, has already been told. It remains to define more closely the artistic orbit of English folk-song.

ENGLISH FOLK-SONG

To limit the field, we may conveniently set aside at once such ballad-tunes as 'John Dory' and 'Greensleeves' (to take two set by our composer), and all the other English tunes of uncertain origin, of which written settings recur, sometimes with instrumental variations, in the sociable three-men song-books, lute-books, virginal books, Playford dance-sets and Netherlands collections of the seventeenth century. Such tunes had long passed beyond their singers, and had shown sophisticated variants by Playford's time. They comprise the substance of William Chappell's *Popular Music of the Olden Time* (1859). But numberless tunes were retained in the memories of singers, as Carl Engel conjectured when, in his comparative study of national music, he found himself baffled on English territory (see p. 54). The course of such memories persisted, but might vary from one singer to another, and a variant might be selected, as in the flight of birds. Thus these tunes, as now assembled and assorted regionally, show many tunes with a history, through changes of melodic detail and text, and many that are solitary and apparently unique; some well formed but many ill; many beginning life in one 'ancient' mode or another, but becoming sophisticated major or minor, and with fifthward modulation, later.

So with metre. All are strophical; that is, calculated, in the stronger examples, not only to stand but to need the wear and tear of six to ten verses for their full expression. All were remembered in close association with one text or another, whether as the original tune or one transferred or adapted to a fresh text. Their date is thus elusive and almost irrelevant. The main feature is the concentration on line, relying on certain commonplaces of statement and development to support more positive intonation—so that different tunes may sometimes acknowledge a common stem—and using recurrent patterns ($a\ b\ b\ c$, $a\ a^1\ b\ a^2$) to point the order of phrase.

But this bare summary of method conveys little how sharply certain noted examples of English folk-song struck Vaughan Williams's awareness, and continued to do so throughout his career. Here was something efficient for its declared purpose of offering a slice of life, basically concise and unsensational, comparatively fresh in its melodic idiom, and, in a number of features which could be analysed, English. It is not correct to deduce that from this experience Vaughan Williams developed a folk-song style, in any literal sense. It may, however, be said that, since he never ceased to be nostalgic in this direction, it was here that he acquired, first and foremost, a belief in the power of melody, and of melodic concentration. He also observed, then or later, the debt of great German composers—Beethoven and Wagner, as well as the more obvious Haydn and Schubert—to folk-song for the raw material of their racy rhythms, characteristic melodic turns, and sometimes a whole sequence of phrases. He would have agreed with Sharp's wild surmise, the main constructive proposal of his summary of his life's work, *English Folk-song: Some Conclusions*, that when every English school-child knew his folk-song, the composer of the future would have a national musical idiom ready to hand, if he wanted it. The German melodic accent had long ceased to be provincial, and had become aggressively cosmopolitan, overwhelming Parry and Stanford amongst others. (The similar vogue of Russian music was a matter of time.) There was no inherent ground for supposing that genuine English folk-idiom had a narrower potential.

ENGLISH ORATORIO

The German-speaking composers, then, had had a recognized literature, opera and peasant craftsmanship behind them; and, it should be added, strong habits of making music, and being unable to do without it, both in public and in the home. We turn to Victorian substitutes for opera. The chief of these was oratorio, as revived under the shadow of Handel, Mendelssohn and Gounod, in the context of an amateur chorus at established festivals, solo singers experienced in the genre, and some kind of orchestra. Outspoken comment, led by *The Musical Times*, considered Macfarren's *Joseph* (1877) as 'daring', but not too daring, in its use of clue-theme, while Cowen, in *St. Ursula*, had fallen a prey to 'the advanced school' (Wagner). Of Parry's three oratorios, it will be sufficient to recall here the shortest and latest, *Job* (1892), which shows at least a titular precedent to a more distinguished setting. The familiar narrative of Job's trials and schooling is enclosed in four more or less dramatic scenes of prologue, plague, lament and philosophy; the first two functional and exuberantly descriptive, the third an extended *arioso* excursion, the last a rambling criticism of man in choral terms, which at last comes to a brief, serene finish, not unworthy of Bach's 'Truly this was the son of God'. There are other thrilling and exalted moments, but Satan's unfaltering buoyancy is a severe lapse, Job's melancholy is half-hearted and sentimental, and the divine voice too literary to be coherent. (This comment springs to mind even after participation in the work under Parry's most sympathetic interpreter, H. P. Allen.) Parry's imagination did not embrace religious narrative.

Stanford's *Eden* (1891) was stimulated by Bridges's text, with its extended visions of heaven, hell and a redeemed earth, which the composer seeks to link by means of a few very plain clue-themes. Bluntly, however, Stanford had taken on more than he could absorb in these twenty-eight numbers: too much text, and a stage (since Bridges calls them three acts) that he could not match with consistency. 'We on the orbit of the wandering spheres' is a good angelic summary of the wayward Act 1; Satan's company will needle no sinner, and the declamation descends to incredible depths at the unison arpeggio for 'Ours shall man be'; the music for the redeeming presence may be what Walker, as a historian, terms 'very solemn and tender', but to my ears it is quite unpersuasive; and the main clue-themes are stilted and unevocative. (This estimate is restricted to the vocal score.) *Stabat Mater* is shorter, and spasmodically more impressive, and the close is a distinct precedent for a *niente* (fading) finish; but, especially at the end, the work is altogether too much contrived (on Verdi lines) to be memorable. The composer's final simple faith in the texture of one of the old modes is disarming. I might add that I find the repetitive end of Honegger's *King David* as jejunely contemplative.

CANTATAS

Parry's first notable work was not an oratorio, but a setting from *Prometheus Unbound* in five scenes (1880). But for its traditional harmonic idiom, this was almost a signal departure, in its grasp of dramatic lyric in gratefully choral terms, its unity of mood, after so many sprawling oratorios, its creative use of English poetic rhythm—in contrast, for example, to Barnett's *Ancient Mariner*—and its steady and dramatic evocation of the first free-thinker. It promised more, and was followed by the compact but less distinctive *Blest Pair of Sirens*, a thoughtful and genial Victorian setting with a rather pompous concluding fugue, and by the later (i.e. post-1900) *Pied Piper*, a shapeless but exuberant narrative. Subsequent works—*War and Peace, Voces clamantium, The Love that Casteth out Fear*, amongst others—revealed an increasing and obsessional concern for ethical affirmation, backed by the recurrences of clue-themes (or rather clue-intonations like a rising fifth) that wear as poorly as the comradely and high-flown phrases which drop in with incredible facility. ('Hands together, and face the coming years!') The listener cannot miss a profound decline in style, in the Parry sense of finding means to crystallize expressive ends at which the texts hint. It was partly due to other preoccupations, but chiefly to the lack of a central impulse. The shorter *Nativity Ode* (1912) is altogether a happier, but not a pivotal, work. The expectations after *Prometheus* were not fulfilled. It was, indeed, mainly a *Prometheus* of the 'Leipzig' school of Schumann and Bennett, English only in its fresh grasp of Shelley's rhythms.

Meanwhile Stanford had brought out his choral ballads, of which *Phaudrig Crohoore* is the most compact and congenial, while *The Revenge* aspires to epic. These found their limited, mainly amateur, level, and started the search for further texts.

Symphonic works include Parry's stalwart *Symphonic Variations*, his overture 'to an unwritten tragedy', and the conventionally moulded *Cambridge* and *English* symphonies (nos. 2 in F, 3 in C) of the 'eighties. The symphonies are dogged by vigorous commonplace first subjects and facile, chic, clarinettish second subjects, and, in no. 3, by a weak resort to a variation-finale, which is paralleled by Stanford and Walton. No. 4 in E minor is no better, and its revision, with ethical titles (1910), negligible. A similarly titled symphonic fantasia followed it to an unregrettable oblivion.

Stanford's fourth symphony, in F minor (the *Irish*), is today the most played of his symphonies. It has a more or less conventional opening, a scherzo movement, a slight, nostalgic andante, and a finale that calls on traditional tunes both for first subject and for a coda in the major. Structurally, it is far from impressive.

ENGLISH SONG: PARRY AND STANFORD

We may return, accordingly, to the strong literary contacts, of which most may be expected, as such, in songs for voice and piano. Here Stanford and Parry were fortunate to have eloquent advocates, with a new mastery of style, in Harry Plunket Greene and Leonard Borwick. Their song-recitals were historical in their intimate musical ensemble and in their free choice of programme, replacing the royalty-ballad by songs of Schubert and other classics in English. In time—which expression must until further notice be taken to embrace an often incredible lag of response—other singers and players, and their audiences, took the cue and found certain English songs good company, not just drawing-room or smoking-concert accessories to be relished and forgotten. Greene has also written eloquently of his interpretations of Stanford's songs (*Music and Letters*, 2. 96 (1921)).

Yet these songs have severe limitations. Whether in narrative ballad, whimsy or lyrical style, Stanford is remarkably content with a strophical scheme, or occasionally the *Bar* of two strophes and an aftermath. His best songs, *Loughareema* and *Cuttin' rushes*, are no more than that: a 'reading' of the first verse which relies upon fresh contingent detail to implement the others, the whole soaked well with a nostalgia, localized or gerontic. This soon cloys as it is sampled in song after song. Later songs pursue the quaintly or quietly characteristic with equal agility. Greene emphasizes the speed of composition in proof of technical mastery. In proof, too, of a limited objective, including the choice of text, with a positive weakness for the undeveloped or pitiful figures in the human scene.

Parry was much more searching and particular in this sphere. The first six of his twelve books of *English Lyrics*, with some songs in the posthumous Books 11 and 12, cover the period 1886–1903, and may be placed together here. They show example after example of what H. C. Colles well styles 'good reading vocalized'. A good reading, too, of good poems, more often than not, and therefore interesting to pursue to the end but difficult to set. The range is from Shakespeare to Meredith, with the recurring Sturgis—too lightly chosen for his congenial aspiring themes. Tuneful strophes, or a *Bar*, or a convenient *a b a* scheme, may suffice here ('When lovers meet again', 'A lover's garland', 'Crabbed age and youth' with its felicitous coda, 'Lay a garland on my hearse', 'Rosaline'). The listener is left with 'a saturated solution of poetry in music' (to quote further from Colles's full account in *Essays and Lectures*). Moreover, from Book 7 onwards Parry was moving to a more thorough-going setting, while preserving unity of imagery in the piano part. 'What part of dread eternity?' (Book 11), with its emergent refrain, was the most developed and logical specimen of this method, maintaining the close and penetrating reading of the earlier songs. With this and 'On a time the amorous Silvy' (for contrast) in mind, one need not worry about well-meaning and almost repellent songs like the prophetic 'Whence?' (Sturgis). The concluding impression of Parry's songs is of a 'youthful' composer, always experimenting with melody, declamation and piano figure; in contrast to the stagnant choral-orchestral works of the present century. Some (not all) of the choral *Songs of Farewell* mark another revival of spontaneity. But they are, again, miniatures, and it is no service to Parry's larger aims to treat them as if they were major works.

It is not easy to do justice to the art of Parry and Stanford today. At first hearing they prompt quick dismissal as past history. All too lightly have they been regarded as the beginning of a renascence of English music. Fabulous tributes to their worth can be read in English accounts of the period. (See, for example, W. H. Hadow's tribute to Parry after his death, in *Collected Essays*.) On reconsideration, the two composers emerge as very limited pioneers in various directions, with Stanford as usually the more resourcefully equipped and Parry as the more critical at his best. As practising educationalists, they stood together under the aegis of a musical conscience, as the sole ultimate criterion in musical issues. Parry's College lectures and Stanford's direction of the R.C.M. orchestra along partly untrodden ways, were working examples of a dynamic and missionary activity, following Grove's steady training of audiences at the orchestral concerts at the Crystal Palace. They could not do much to immobilize the 'royalty-ballad' and other profitable misuses. Socially, they had to accept that for the general public there was one English composer: Sullivan.[1]

[1] Late in life Parry expressed without bitterness his regret that the English could only accommodate one composer at a time. First, Sullivan; then Elgar. Some years later, Ivor Gurney, wandering in dockland, was arrested as a spy. He produced a letter from Sir Charles Stanford. 'Stanford? Never heard of him,' stormed the policeman. Nor, indeed, had he heard of the other two correspondents, R. Bridges and J. Masefield, whose signatures were produced.

But these two leaders and others made audiences and students aware that there was another way out of Vanity Fair. Inevitably, forced into an isolated position, and both conservative by nature, especially Stanford, they struck attitudes, which Shaw could not resist caricaturing in his notices of London music. And yet their stimulus continued.

German Classics in England

There remained, however, a dearth of masterpieces, and these had to be imported. In this context, besides *Messiah*, such works as *The Ring* (in German) and Bach's *St. Matthew Passion* and *B minor Mass* were given special performances in London, around 1880, with full support from Parry and Stanford. The latter was also instrumental in encouraging Joachim and Richter to enter English musical circles as necessary instruments of personal advocacy. Meanwhile, the comprehensive programmes of the Crystal Palace concerts were preparing for the start of the Promenade Concerts under Henry Wood and Robert Newman in 1895. The national tradition of German music, with a dash of Russian, was being absorbed at the second remove, as supranational and, for all practical purposes, increasingly English. The acceptance of this situation was finally confirmed in its continuation during the first German War. Most of the public, indeed, had for many generations accepted an endless exotic parade as the normal music routine. Nor, in another sphere, were Good Friday congregations much concerned whether Stainer's *The Crucifixion* was in a different class from Bach's Passion music.

Enter Elgar

In this confused state of opinion, there appeared, towards the end of the century, the music of an English composer different in breed from Parry and Stanford; self-taught, unpredictable, neither an opera nor an oratorio composer, and altogether careless of the texts that he set. Yet he disclosed a vitality of theme and texture never heard in native music before. Thus *King Olaf* and *Caractacus* impressed choirs and their audiences, in spite of their glaring ideological confusion, wavering between sheer violence and spiritual resistance, between non-violence and sheer defeatism, between the illusion of power and the confident exercise of it. 'Freedom is lost, but peace and rest are ours!', cry the British captives; and, in grotesquely ominous confirmation of a hollow peace, the clue-theme for the Arch-Druid's blasphemous false prophecy of success provides the main material for the final, Victorian exaltation of Britain's mission amongst the nations in 1897. Word-tone associations could not have been more heedlessly jumbled. Here was a new voice, wayward in quality, but powerful.

A set of variations for orchestra and a strikingly 'unorthodox' oratorio, replacing the genial 'scraps' of Old Testament stories by a deeply personal experience of last things, established Elgar's position amongst the musically intelligent. *Gerontius* may have missed its deserts at its first performance (a matter which continues to cause Elgarians an odd concern to discover the true reasons), but a proper grasp of its meaning was chiefly a question of patience and discrimination. In time, the oratorio became one of the very few modern works which could safely fill an evening for a choral society, especially one for the Three Choirs Festival. The *Variations* similarly proved a document in variation in the most accomplished orchestral sense, as well as a series of witty personal allusions. Nor were these illusory flashes of talent. Two full-size oratorios, two symphonies, a violin and later a violoncello concerto, two overtures and a tremendous fantasia, *Falstaff*, followed in due course.

The Dream of Gerontius, as selected by Elgar, is an unceasing journey of the imagination from this life into the next, in two stages, each continuous. Periods of soliloquy and dialogue, part symbolic and part human, are punctuated and carried further by choral movements of varying dimensions, and constantly linked by clue-themes on the Wagnerian system. In the second part, the emergence, after a chorus of devils, of an expanding and apparently final vision of the life of God breaking into the world, from the cross of Christ, is later revealed as only a preparation for the supreme moment, of coming before the throne of judgement. A quiet, mystic epilogue forms a conclusion, after an agonizing transition.

The pattern of Newman's journey is thus matched by a stream of musical *arioso* and choral phrase in a widening context in the symphonic manner, in place of the conventional limits of aria and chorus. The literary contact, to use our formal term for what must have shaken Elgar to the depths, has produced not only new themes but an original design, sufficient to resuscitate oratorio as a substitute for opera, as happened in Handel's day, but without any reliance on established narrative. If the use of proliferating clue-themes is acknowledged as general current idiom, this is still English oratorio, didactic in its plain speech-song, but absorbed by choral periods, and reinforced by a brilliance and nervousness of orchestral texture that can no longer be regarded as a German or Russian prerogative. The selected scenes from the Gospels and the *Acts*, which, with many pious and sometimes confusing recollections of the Old Testament, make up *The Apostles* and *The Kingdom*, are comparatively fragmentary, and a faltering clue-theme craftsmanship, of capricious rather than creative patterning of succeeding phrases, dogs the forbiddingly familiar main text. Yet these works considerably extend the revived genre. *For the Fallen* (1916) proved a memorable appendix to this significant augmentation of the choral-orchestral repertory.

Elgar's symphonic works may seem burdened with an excess of material and gorgeous texture, and to betray an uncertain control of contrasted levels of expression, but they leave the comparable products of Parry and Stanford far behind in sheer dynamic quality. To be just, Parry was not slow in promoting the *Variations* and other works, nor was Stanford, as conductor of the Leeds Festival, silent about the need to produce *Gerontius*, and to ignore the timidity of those who 'did not care for' the work. There can be no doubt about the renascence of creative power here, nor of something like a national response, amongst professional orchestras and amateur choirs alike, though discouragingly less immediate than Elgar expected. Eventually, the promotion of Elgar's art took on such an aggressive character as to become quite irrational towards any gesture of reconsideration, such as from time to time becomes expedient.[1]

Yet no special reaction to the coverage and opulent style of Elgar's recognized output is needed to perceive that materially his music is rooted in the nineteenth century, no less than that of Parry and Stanford. Much more than Mahler, on the whole, Elgar has left his personal signature on his chosen idioms: on his melodic curves, on his sequences

---

[1] Indications of this are headed by the almost hysterical tone with which the re-publication in Adler's *Handbuch* of E. J. Dent's strictures on the Elgarian quality ('For English ears . . . too emotional and not quite free from vulgarity. . . . His orchestral works . . . animated in colour, but pompous in style and of a too deliberate nobility of expression') were countered, in a collective letter headed by Shaw. There was, moreover, Elgar's own and hasty assumption that Vaughan Williams, a friend of Dent, must be numbered amongst his personal detractors (see p. 49). I might also cite a personal and quasi-patriotic attack made by the late George Sampson, of which I was unaware at the time. In a rejoinder to an article on the conflicting elements in Elgar, the writer rose with indignation at my incidental suggestion that, in the internationalist world of post-1918, Elgar's nationalism had dated (*Music and Letters*, 1942).

(on which see an article by Mary Dann in *Music and Letters*, 19. 3 (1938)), and many other points of texture. His basic idiom is none the less, like Mahler's, heavily shared with Liszt and Strauss. His instrumental music, in particular, must be regarded, in any wide survey, as an appendix to the German tradition as broadened by Brahms, intensified or lightened by Tchaikovsky, made extravagant by Strauss, and thematically ubiquitous by Wagner. His 'cosmopolitan' style was thus acclaimed by the Amsterdam *Telegraaf* in 1919 (Nov. 21).

From this fresh review of past and present reputations, of acknowledged and forgotten works in the English repertory, we may be in a surer position to come down to the basic facts of organized communication between a composer and his audience round 1900. For the rising composer, there was an inhospitable opera-house, some oratorio centres, the odd chance of one hearing for a new work at an orchestral concert, and a few progressive recitalists; but no encouragement, in the form of a substantial agreement with audiences, for an English composer to be himself. To speak of a crisis at a given period, claiming scrutiny, is becoming a commonplace of modern criticism. Nevertheless, a crisis lay here, and the test of a composer of quality was to realize it.

THE HIERARCHY OF THE SCALES

Certain formulae of musical approach had accumulated. After the sixteenth century the conflation of the old modes in the exclusive alternatives of the major and minor scale became the established thing, with a consequent stabilization of the fifth degree as the dominant or tonic controlling degree within the scale. *Per contra*, in the eighteenth century, the circular chain of twenty-four possible keys, in relation to a given tonic, was coming into the general orbit of musical thinking, with a corresponding extension of melodic and chordal vocabulary, as well as a consequent hierarchy of tonic and dominant and dominant's dominant, stretching in disciplinary and steadily maintained order on one side of the circle, and of that order, reversed, beckoning to underfifth or subdominant, and subdominant's subdominant, on the other side. In the nineteenth century, the chain of command was adapted to numberless leaps from one pivotal degree to another, or to a degree previously considered irrelevant, especially in the brilliant quasi-improvisatory style of Liszt, and in the dramatic application of his harmonic repertory and typical transforming theme by Wagner and then Strauss. Nevertheless, the traditional sense of bass-movement, gravitating to a given tonic from its dominant, or being pulled up to the tonic from the subdominant, remained at hand, to punctuate the rambling progression and to give a firm assurance of finality. The following cadences, referred to one key for convenient comparison, illustrate the semitonal colour typical of the penultimate moment and audaciously applied to the final chord in one instance. But the major scale, semitonally extended, is none the less triumphant. At this stage of convergence, from the most diverse paths, it is not certain whether melody and harmony, derived from the twelve-note major or minor scales, have any future but a purely decadent one.

Wagner: *The Flying Dutchman*, 1843

Ex. 1*a*

Elgar: *Enigma Variations*, 1899

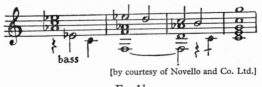

[by courtesy of Novello and Co. Ltd.]

Ex. 1*b*

Elgar: *Gerontius*, 1900

[by courtesy of Novello and Co. Ltd.]

Ex. 1*c*

Elgar: Second Symphony, 1910

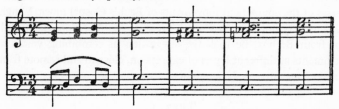

[by courtesy of Novello and Co. Ltd.]

Ex. 1*d*

Richard Strauss: *Till Eulenspiegel,* 1895

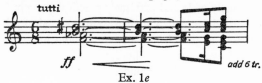

Ex. 1*e*

TRADITIONS

It does not seem that either Parry or Stanford was aware of the difficulty of adding to the cultural inheritance of 1890. In these circumstances, it may be assumed that Vaughan Williams went his own way, taking from a wider past what was of general validity. He certainly assimilated, in principle, the varied contrapuntal styles of Palestrina and the Elizabethan composers; that is, the interweaving of something like speech-rhythm in each part, the blending of vocal textures *per se*, and the binding of these in a regular but not absolute metre, by means of a disposition of more or less unanimous long *versus* short notes, and of accented chords arising from discordant delaying notes (suspensions). The presence of this background makes itself steadily felt in numberless episodes, both of choral expression and of instrumental analogies. Vaughan Williams could also affect the regimented and harmonically more well-defined counterpoint of J. S. Bach, where required. One has only to turn to the *English Hymnal* to be aware of Bach's style of chorale treatment, in many settings not by Bach. Of fugue, in a full structural sense, there happens to be only occasional evidence; but plenty of echoes of Bach's inexhaustible control of varied means of changing a basic progression by a shrewd economy of thematic development in a contrapuntal context. The method of exploiting manifold texture is retained, but not the hierarchy of key, which usually conditions Bach's

91

patterning. Again, for the cut and dried, symmetrical and predictable courses of the component movements of Bach's Gospel music Vaughan Williams may not have had much present use. Yet from Bach, rather than from Berlioz, he took the suggestion of combining voices and instruments at different levels of expression, close to and remote from a point in a narrative or lyric moment.

<h2 style="text-align:center">TEXTURE</h2>

His control of sheer declamatory choral harmony came, perhaps, from Handel via Parry; of declamatory melody from Purcell, whose *Welcome Songs* he edited. His general experience of the choral potential at many levels, was unusually wide and extremely practical (see pp. 50, 57). It is unnecessary to document Vaughan Williams's absorption of the harmonic repertory of the nineteenth century, but his free use of the sharpened sixth, moving to a *tonic* chord, as the focus of the penultimate stage of *A Sea Symphony*, is a reminder. (A curious precedent for this progression is contained in the opening of Franck's violin sonata.) It is also certain that Vaughan Williams was early acquainted with the French musical impressionists' method of drawing melodic lines three or four notes deep, replacing a syntactical harmonic progression by liquescent chordal movement, in which a unit might be the combination, at a given melodic point, of third and fifth degree above the bass, with sixth, seventh or ninth in free association, without the obligation to resolve discords, as in classical music. The English composer's course under Ravel has been mentioned (see p. 49). He remained independent, but not, I think, unaware of Ravel's system of improvisation.

Ravel: *Pavane pour une Infante défunte*, 1899

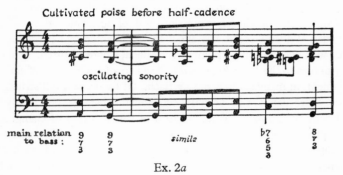

Ex. 2*a*

Ravel: Sonatina for piano, 1905

Ex. 2*b*

Debussy: *Reflets dans l'eau*, 1905

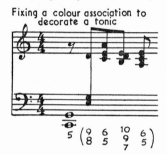

Ex. 2*c*

Debussy: *Reflets dans l'eau*

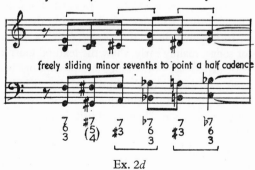

Ex. 2*d*

Debussy: *Reflets dans l'eau*

Ex. 2e

Ravel: Sonatina for piano

Ex. 2f

The piano seldom interested him as a solo instrument. Not, of course, from any unawareness of past history, but from a perception that the solo-sonata is severely exhausted as a mode of expression, and also from a lack of the executant's craftsmanship that was to prompt Ireland's pen in his own distinctive pieces. On the other hand, the various sets of songs, mainly early, show the textural grasp of a pianist, as well as a wide experience of the range and promptings of an intimate voice-and-piano ensemble, as demonstrated by Schubert and his successors. The neglect of the string quartet is surprising in a violinist, with the popular concerts of chamber-music in process at St. James' Hall, up to 1898, and, for all classes, at the meeting-house of the South Place Ethical Society, Moorgate, from 1887 to 1927, continuing else-where, in substance, to this day. The Joachim Quartet were playing in

England from 1900. Debussy's string quartet (Paris, 1897) was played at an early date at the R.C.M. (One of Parry's many liberalizing acts, undertaken on principle, rather than from musical conviction.)

Once again, one must conjecture some distrust of string rhetoric for its own sake, for which there is some evidence in the trenchant criticism of the profuse and, for the writer, nugatory coloratura in the variations of Beethoven's ninth symphony. We shall consider the string-writing of the stray chamber-music output later, but it was obviously not the composer's favourite medium. He professes to have learnt orchestration from studying Elgar scores, both in private and in performance. This would certainly not have excluded writing for strings. From the general absence of Berlioz's open-air scoring, it may be inferred that that pioneer's art came to Vaughan Williams's knowledge late. In his melodic emphasis, however, and his imaginative sense of the occasion, Berlioz must be regarded as at least an unrecognized predecessor, and should have been a stimulating influence. Wagner, we have seen, was an early impression. I recall that at a composition class Vaughan Williams was a little startled at the general unfamiliarity of the *Ring* motives to those present. He would have been more confounded if he had tried to discuss the nature of the thematic development, with which he was manifestly acquainted as a result of due attendance and study.

INFLUENCE OF BEETHOVEN

Vaughan Williams professed an early reaction to the art of Beethoven. Nevertheless, it was certainly not without a wide knowledge of Beethoven that he developed an early concern for structure, for the total effect and the abiding effect; and he recommended the sedulous imitation of Beethoven movements as structural practice for students. His tunefulness in extended works has seldom the confident cantabile of the Viennese masters, who juxtapose phrase on phrase until the expression is complete; but his concentration and downrightness of mood, alike in quiet and in high-pitched moments, in sudden climax and in sustained epilogue, echo Beethoven more than any other classical composer. Equally, his declared determination to bring art to people in general, not neglecting the sounds of common day, reflects the reforming quality of Beethoven far more than that of the neo-romantic Brahms, who was Stanford's hero. In this context no equalitarian can resist the sheer communicating zeal of the *Choral Symphony*'s finale and the *Mass in D*, even if he questions the strain placed on pivotal themes. The modern composer's reaction, shared by Ireland (see a 'speech for the opposition' in the Beethoven number of *Music and Letters*, 8. 2 (1927)), was, presumably, away from the basically French pomposity which attends the Beethoven emphasis.

There will be later occasion to observe Vaughan Williams's retreat from grand restatement. Yet one reflects how much of the flow of the Beethoven scherzo movements seeps into modern music. Again, Beethoven, surrounded by no Stanford or Holst to steady or rouse his craftsmanship, was the first composer not to consider writing symphonies in sixes and threes. He gave himself time to go on where he, or a predecessor, had left off, discarded the first draft of the fifth symphony because its finale (since totally replaced) was below standard, and left, in his gradual attack on no. 9, a document in symphonies, which the ample documentation of the symphony no. 9, 1958, strikingly matches, or rather transcends.[1]

In short, it was Beethoven, first and foremost, who combined a rousing spirit of formal abandonment with an equally influential guiding integrity. To Beethoven, too, must be attributed the general conception of the cumulative symphony, not relaxing in the finale; to be confirmed by Brahms, Tchaikovsky, Mahler and in part Elgar, as by Wagner in music-drama. Between the Beethoven coda, to formulate the whole trend of a movement or even of a symphony, and the Vaughan Williams *niente* epilogue, steering solitarily for the deep waters long after the close of *A Sea Symphony* was past history, there is little similarity of manner, but a discernible identity of principle.

Whether Vaughan Williams was influenced at all by Mahler's steady pursuit of successive 'worlds' of self-revelation, in the latter's partial return to symphonies in series (2–4, 5–7), the first three with literary associations, is doubtful, in view of his references to Mahler's 'interminable codas' and so on; and Mahler's choral symphony (8), of two movements with ostensibly unconnected texts, although completed earlier, appeared too near in time to *A Sea Symphony* to admit of any relation in composition. Yet the daring association of these texts, from remote church tradition and Goethe, in a flowing profession of conviction and mystic longing, remained a firm precedent for another significant use of the chorus with orchestra, with a bold range of text, in later Vaughan Williams works.

How meagre were the incentives to write a well-developed English opera has been amply indicated earlier in the chapter. So far as textual

[1] See Appendix C.

trends can have counted, Holst's unperformed *Sita*, a dramatization of a Sanskrit legend with which Vaughan Williams was certainly acquainted, has never been published, but one may guess its quality from the clear account of the music provided by the composer's daughter (I. Holst, *The Music of Gustav Holst*). *Hugh the Drover* appears to have been a reaction from a dangerously extravagant symbolism in the direction of *The Canterbury Pilgrims*.

Before Vaughan Williams, then, was a narrow outlet for fresh public communication. Behind him was the guidance of the past in certain limited aspects of texture, with some firm standards of structural unity in large-scale works, but an overpowering sense of exhausted melodic method, with the harmonic vocabulary equally in decline. Across the English Channel, a reaction from Wagnerism was in process. The general course of the future was very uncertain. There were advantages to be drawn from the weakness of immediate tradition. There was little danger of formalism or archaism, if initiative were exercised, and less likelihood of awkward comparisons. If a personal style could be discovered, there was every prospect of a serious contribution to the wider cosmopolitan life, which a civilized continent, of countries in living contact but remaining true to their developed customs and institutions, is capable of enjoying through music.

A Cue for Audiences

There is a time-spirit about artistic, as about political, developments. The growth in the eighteenth century of freedom of action and speech, and of parliamentarian habits with plenty of sting if they were threatened, was, once again, congenial to Beethoven, although his upbringing had been unencumbered by foreign verbs, science, history or Current Events, and although he responded directly to English liberators with nothing more musically advanced than *Wellington's Victory*.

What is more important, the concentration on music in the German states in the same period was of such intensity and wide range that, in Spengler's trenchant summary, its artistic life 'today is hardly a memory'. The doctrine of evolution which in turn enthralled the last century, and was respected (especially in Erda's influence) in *The Ring* with all its trappings, was almost reversed in the fundamentalism of Elgar's patriotic and religious approach. There was virtually a vacuum in this region, waiting to be filled by some attempt at a musical

G 97

tribute to a fitter culture-hero than the Duke of Plaza-Toro, or Caractacus, or Drake, or St. Peter.

Even if it were filled, it would not be much use unless more people
than this country had yet known found time for serious music. The
Birmingham and Leeds triennial festivals could be put beside London
and West-country organizations. The London and provincial colleges
of music, and not merely foreign conservatoires, were beginning
to send out men and women with more than a hobby in music. In a
very few schools and in some universities, general, non-specialist
interest was beginning to stride forward. If this could be focused
towards a sense of musical future and not merely to the glorious past,
something might happen. Otherwise, English music would present one
more example of a time-lag between a rising composer and the musical
receptiveness of a dependable audience.

AUDIENCE INITIATIVE

The assumed period of this elementary state of national culture in
music is round 1905. The multiplication of a citizen's resources two
decades later, moreover, while immeasurably extending the number of
homes into which music of all sorts was beginning to pour, and also the
variety of programme available, irrespective of locality, did not of
itself improve the receptiveness of audiences. On the contrary. The
B.B.C. were fortunate to gain, in Sir John Reith, a director-general
of courage and vision, who was quite prepared to regard the cultural
needs of a minority as a first consideration in determining the running
establishment and the types of programme for general service, and to
keep the non-cultural demands of the majority within bounds. Yet
there was still immense pressure to give satisfaction to the *greatest
possible* minority, which meant opulent renderings of the classics and
popular favourites, but not the enterprising programmes which Henry
Wood and others had contrived to insert into more general schemes.
Still less were the gramophone companies disposed to engage in
hazardous enterprise on behalf of the modern or unknown composer.
They were, in the main, quite content to supply existing demand for
reputable recordings of classical symphonies, *Messiah*, Wagner,
Mozart and so on. Both of these new music agencies were living on the
net successes of years of earlier and determined personal advocacy in
the concert-hall; of inducing orchestral audiences to take Mozart and
Brahms and Elgar for granted as well as Tchaikovsky. If today the

position is sometimes reversed, and audiences assemble to hear in the concert-hall what they have previously accepted on the machines, the listening may be more sophisticated, but the programmes are hardly less classical than they were. Back, then, to 1905, when concerts are, to modern observation, desperately few and far between, and confined to established centres, but public taste is in process of re-formation, and responsible concert-givers are not unknown. Orchestral concerts are a financial strain, on whatever scale, but the growing compromise of providing for a smaller orchestra than intended, by a system of cued-in parts, is better than nothing.

MAN IN MUSIC

In this elusive assurance of audience interest, it may be observed that Vaughan Williams took his dramatic cue from Parry and *Prometheus*, if anything. His characteristic figure was first the pioneer, as in the Whitman settings, later to become the pious Pilgrim to the heavenly city, but also the dauntless spirit of the Antarctic heroes who did not come back. As a variant, there was the proud Vagabond, to become the liberating, money-despising character on the fringe of a Cotswold town; or, later, Falstaff and the kindred companions of the Rector of Diss (*Tudor Portraits*). Most striking of all, Job ceased to be merely a much tried man, fit only for learning a higher wisdom and consolation, and became, as partly suggested by Blake's illustrations, a representation of divinely inspired resolution, master of all the savage and disintegrating elements that plague man and mankind. An earlier step could be noted in the stoics of *Wenlock Edge*.

From there the way was open, as in the past, to purely instrumental tokens of man confronted by discords and barriers, sometimes haunted by a sense of present violence or imminent disaster. Thus history, it may seem to some listeners, found her match in the series from the fourth symphony to the seventh. But if this is true, it is partly because the musical imagination was at the height of activity. The sheer affirmation of nos. 2, 3, 8, 9 is no less expressive because these works betray no overt sense of the event. Meanwhile, as verbally articulate as the chosen texts could make it, appeared the integrity of man 'in the spirit', seeing visions of power behind a declining imperial civilization (*Sancta Civitas*), or in a world rescued from war and dedicated to justice in various degrees of Christian emphasis (*Dona nobis pacem*, *Song of Thanksgiving*, *Hodie*). Folk-song fantasias and suites and film-music, with many practical settings for similar purposes, provided warm and characteristic reminders of the racy past, and of the long forgotten singers of ballads and other things. But here was a musician who thought most of the critical future.

The pertinent and significant criticism of life in the period, in a widening sense, is not the main purpose of art, which must find its own unquestionable justification. Yet this background of times freshly and profoundly observed, without being a distracting obsession, as it certainly became with Parry, forms a steady and original thread in the evolution of Vaughan Williams's musical personality. His lack of pomp, beyond the sound of distant choirs or of Christmas bells, is reassuring. His dispensation with a visible stage is historic, and must be regarded as a foundation of the new English music, vaguely in continuation of *Gerontius*. Unfashionable to-day, the music retains its quality.

The problem of method remains untouched, and in the next chapter a start at probing sources will be examined.

IV

Folk-Song

'The English people are obviously most voracious of music which is not their own, and only of their own music when it is imitated from that of some other nation.... It represents their really energetic cosmopolitanism.' In this sharp satire (from his Oxford lectures round 1900, as transcribed in *Style in Musical Art*), Parry shows some awareness of the impasse for which his period was heading, for all its native literary contacts. It may serve as a background to the subsequent exploration of English folk-song, in which Vaughan Williams, like Holst, found not only a liberating influence but a formative substance of melodic style which proved permanent.

This influence may be traced in its various aspects of text, structure, rhythm, curve and mode. These features of a folk-song were determined by a cumulative process which must not be exaggerated, as such, but does frequently include a principal and initiating effort, capricious variants which lose their creases in time and tend to cancel out, and a perceptible and more critical activity, represented by Böhme's felicitous observation, 'changing what they do not like'. This stage of adaptation and revision serves to blur many customary distinctions of place and period. When a tune is known to stem from the time of Elizabeth I, it cannot be pronounced eighteenth century, whatever the suggestions of that period. Nor is a modal tune necessarily early. The idiom sturdily persisted, regardless of parallel harmonic developments in art-music. Folk-songs found in one county may similarly bear clear relations to songs heard in another. Elasticity in terms of reference is essential here. The effective qualities of native folk-song must be sought in other ways.

It is now generally realized that the printed versions of folk-song

101

words are rarely unedited, and are often romantic substitutions for the uninhibited narrative or symbolism, the latter intrusive at the decadent stage, of the original words sung. Specimens of the genuine product may be seen in James Reeves's *The Idiom of the People*, based on the Sharp scripts. The texts may be classed as rural or urban; the city class bearing a more witty, sophisticated and commercial flavour, merging into the published broadsheet. But a light and almost comic touch is a recurrent feature of these renderings of the trials and successes of mainly amorous encounter, and distress is rarely tragic. In his settings, for voice and piano, of folk-songs from the Eastern Counties and from Sussex, which he contributed to the series *The Folk Songs of England* round 1908, Vaughan Williams has followed Sharp, and every other music editor that matters, in altering, without misplaced qualms, what he does not like in a text. He has contrived to preserve a vein of delicate sentiment, founded on the constancy of one party or the other, and his main interest in the text is not Mr. Reeves's robust anthropological ardour but a respect for any underlying sincerity that may be found. It was thus not necessarily an impossible leap from 'Our Captain calls', and many other tales of longing, to their use as hymn-tunes. Of this, more will be said later. Where the editing has taken the form of cutting out verses, the general appeal of a recurrent and continuing strophe is preserved, along with all the cliché allusions of chance walking out, right month, sympathetic Nature, and the other features of vernacular narrative.

PATTERN AND RHYTHM

We come to the musical intonation. The four-phase pattern of 'Searching for lambs' is very common, with a distinct balance of pairs of phases ($a\ b$—$c\ d$ or $a\ a^1$—$b\ c$). The asymmetrical $a\ b$—$b^1\ c$ of 'A bold young farmer' has parallels but we shall note later Vaughan Williams's significant reconstruction of 'Our Captain calls'. The unbalanced a—$b\ c\ b\ c$ of 'Through bushes and through briars' is romantic and acceptable. The main thing is the compactness and economy of the swinging phrases. One note to a syllable is usual, and more than two exceptional. 'Say and sing' is a practical reality; a standard for ordered declamation and cantabile.

Mention of rhythm is a reminder of the dance-impulse behind these songs, such as breaks out more specially in folk-dance tunes. Here, again, the economy of delivery is often impressive (see Ex. 5 below).

The high potential of many of Vaughan Williams's own tunes reflects his early encounters with folk-singers.[1] Sometimes, as in 'Searching for lambs', the metre is slightly reducible (5–5 balanced by 5–3 beats in each half), with a more subtle balance in the Cambridgeshire 'As I walked' (3–3 to 2–3, twice). In contrast comes the longer span of the folk-dances, in which an almost primitive 'step' may possess a tune, as in the tremendous vigour of 'Haste to the wedding'. This six-beat recurs in *Sir John in Love*, and is implicit in some symphonic scherzos, where the jiggety nine of Stanford's symphony no. 4 is more self-conscious. It may surprise some readers to learn that there was once a wide craze for the 'sharper sensations of the folk-dance' amongst those who were tired of the quiet lilt of folk-music. It caused serious comment in January, 1914, in an article by Ernest Walker on 'the tyranny of the dance' (quoted in *Free Thought and the Musician*). A decade later, there was a similar outcry against 'the tyranny of the bar-line' in music since 1700. It would not be hard to confirm Walker's misgivings by listening to a folk-dance festival and observing the exaggerations of rhythm; but the strong current remains. The emotional precision that marks an individual folk-tune may thus be confined to a closed pattern or call for free expansion.

THE MODES

Thus accentuated, the most distinctive element in a folk-song is its melodic curve. In a multitude of tunes, vocal movement takes a given pitch-location, shapes it in a certain way, and widens the resultant curve, or balances it, with some sense of ultimate or early climax. In this shaping, certain successions of mainly broad intervals recur again and again. Their common ground may loosely be described as an extension of the gapped five-note 'scales' of the most elementary Western music—as typified on the piano by the white-note paradigm D F G A C , F G A C D, etc.—to various types of seven-note scale, termed modes, and represented on the piano by white-note scales from D, E, F, G, or, where more convenient for vocal register, a fourth below these, while preserving D, E, etc., as centres of reference. Such a modal scale, however, is a frivolous abstraction, if it implies that the order of interval is the chief difference from the major or minor scale.

---

[1] Cf. the impact of the 'dynamic potency' of Bartók's rhythms, as related to the stimulus of folk-music (J. S. Weissmann in *Monthly Musical Record*, 87, p. 981 (May–June, 1957)).

Distinction of mode is not a peculiar theory of intonation but a regularization of recent past achievement. It must be understood in terms of the pentatonic stage from which it developed empirically. Modal melody arose as a calculated blend of opposed phrases, chosen for their contrasting, often contradictory, pitch-location and vocal register. What matters first, then, in an observation of typical vocal movement, is on what degrees the main burden of intonation falls, by repeated use and by rhythmic emphasis, with a corresponding neglect, omission or possibly variation of other degrees.

THE DORIAN MODE

(1) The commonest type of collected folk-song may in this sense be said to lie within the orbit of the following familiar extension of the five-note group, D F G A C, exposed in an *imaginary* continuous ascent from the final or gravitational note, which, for the sake of its commoner use today, may here be prematurely termed the keynote or tonic. This was also a standard for one kind of plainsong psalmody.[1]

Ex. 3

This Dorian octave falls readily into two sections, 1–5 and 5–8 or 1–4 and 4–8. These may be pitted against each other as they stand, or with 5–8/4–8 sung in the octave below. But the practical melodist is free to choose which degrees to make pivotal by constant use or rhythmic stress. In English and many foreign folk-songs of this genre, the first and fifth degrees are primary, both in frequency and in metrical

[1] This representative octave, which seems constantly to have been in Vaughan Williams's consciousness as an *a priori* pattern of melodic expression, has been recognized from medieval times as the 'Dorian' mode. The tribal names of this and other modes were taken over from comparable but far from identical classes of vocal movement in Greek music of the fifth and fourth centuries B.C.; an utter confusion of substance, with the irrationalities of which we are not here concerned. It is chiefly necessary to warn readers of the *Republic*, etc., that the Damon theory of mode-*ethos* has to be steadily re-named before it can be applied at all to the modes of modern plainsong and folk-song. Thus, whereas the original 'Mixolydian' or Dorian-Lydian mode was a blend of two idioms, the 'Mixolydian' mode of today has no such connection with the 'Dorian' or 'Lydian' mode of today. But the plain musical connotation of each is clear.

emphasis. After them come the seventh, fourth and third; then, the second; finally but not invariably, the sixth. The frequency of the seventh ('flattened' in the modern sense) will be noted. Folk melody juxtaposes arbitrary sections of the above imaginary scale with the bias stated.

THE AEOLIAN MODE

Some melodies show a flattened sixth, B flat. This may be quite incidental. If it is felt to be organic, the tune may be referred to the more modern, post-Gregorian mode, the Aeolian (the white note A–A^1, or, as here, a transposition of it up or down so many degrees). The identity of this mode's descending octave with that of the commonest minor scale marks it as one transition to the classical period (1700–1900), but the cultivation of the Aeolian mode in its own right has not differed from the Dorian in its favouring of fourth and seventh, and not sixth, as secondary pivots. It should so far be regarded as an interim variant of the Dorian mode. (In many tunes classified by collectors as Aeolian, with B flat put in the key-signature, owing to an isolated B flat, the differences from Dorian tunes are quite trifling. Other such tunes, without any sixth, are not Aeolian at all.)

THE MIXOLYDIAN MODE

(2) A common extension of the five-notes, G A C D F, intones the accessory third at B, thus reaching the Mixolydian mode, which appears as follows with D as keynote:

Ex. 4

English tunes in this genre again take the first and fifth degrees as primary, fourth and seventh as pivotal. But the third commonly 'lies low', hinting at the modern major third but not concerned with its closer harmonic relation to the keynote, which has since popularized and finally vulgarized the major scale.

LYDIAN AND PHRYGIAN MODES

(3) Another five-tone group, F G A C D, plus B and E—D E F ♯ G♯ A B C in D—makes the Lydian mode, an occasional basis of song.

Here the major third is more pronounced in appearance, and the seventh and 'sharpened' fourth negligible. Similarly, and about as rarely, D F G A C plus E flat and B flat makes the Phrygian mode, a kind of doubly relaxed Dorian, still with little of the second or sixth degree.

(4) On the borderline between a singer's confused memory and sophisticated modifications lie tunes which do not keep to one mode. An example is 'As I walked out' (second tune in Sharp's *School Song* series), with major thirds which flatten later to minor. The contradiction, being vocally explicable (as the termini of minimum and therefore preferable (1) descents from the fifth, (2) ascents from the keynote), is implicit and not pointed. A more essentially Dorian example of double-mode is 'The jolly thresherman', collected by Vaughan Williams himself, along with a demonstration of Dorian tunes with the *sixth* slipping flat ('The Sheffield apprentice').

The 1–2–4–5–7 melodic pattern of the above examples is thus common to multitudes of folk-songs, the varieties of 3 and 6 being incidental.

(5) Some tunes show the major scale. Here the absence of seventh, and prominence of the sixth, may be noticed in tunes of the transitional stage. (Britten appears to take cognisance of this in the formulation of a racy curtain-tune for *Let's Make an Opera*.) Although the transition is to the use of the full major scale, where the balancing groups of mode reach vanishing point, the earlier stage has proved an abiding melodic influence.

National Music in Folk-song

Such are the distinctive formalities of English modal song of the past, along with many recurrent trends, such as the cadences. They mark regional emancipation from the restrictions of earlier and more primitive formulae. A similar process took shape, earlier or later, in other countries, and is now on record in print or on tape. It is tempting but hazardous to pick out native features. To avoid hasty inferences, let us compare the styles of a miscellaneous group of tunes, disregarding any signs of national trend that may be perceptible in the subject, tone and rhythm of the texts. Limitations of space prevent the inclusion of the sophisticated tunes of English and French vaudeville, Hungarian *verbunkos* or Swiss yodelling, as 'control' instances, and also, on the other side, of English songs that are melodically closer to the Hungarian songs but less expansive, and so far less representative, in outline. For the sake of easier comparison, the examples have all been quoted with D as keynote, ignoring the vocal disadvantages. The use, however, of modern key-signatures with perpetual accidentals, suggesting a major or minor key manqué, has been rejected here.

pitch location   pentatonic to dorian

Ex. 5

Ex. 5a

aeolian

repeat endlessly

Ex. 5b

hexatonic

Ex. 5c

pentatonic

Ex. 5d

('Searching for lambs')

hexatonic

[by courtesy of Novello and Co. Ltd.]

Ex. 5e

('The sign of the Bonny Blue Bell' (coll. and arr. by C. J. Sharp))

aeolian

[by courtesy of Novello and Co. Ltd.]

Ex. 5f

dorian

Ex. 5g

('My Johnny was a shoemaker')

Fine

hexatonic

Ex. 5h

D.C.

108

('A bold young farmer')

[by courtesy of Novello and Co. Ltd.]

Ex. 5*i*

The actual origins are as follows: Ex. 5*a* is Hungarian, and used by Kodály in his song-suite, *Mátra Pictures*; 5*b*, 5*c*, 5*d* are Russian, 5*b* being a Bilina or epic chant used in the opera *Sadko* and 5*c* a Russian folk-song, but 5*d* is a motive in the first of Mussorgsky's *Tableaux d'une Exposition*; 5*e* and 5*f* are from Somerset; 5*g* is Hungarian (*Ib.*); 5*h* and 5*i* are English. The extraneous specimen (5*d*) betrays its modernity by its too brisk changes in pitch-location. It is, in fact a demonstration of the 'modo russico' (*sic*) by way of suggestion for a street-scene, and terminates eventually in F. It is inserted as an early reminder that not everything pentatonic is solid earth.

It remains to estimate how far the appeal of English folk-song is exclusive. The melodic classification shown makes it clear that a hexatonic-to-Dorian strain is common to all the national styles cited. Of the Russian examples, 5*b* shows the early origins of the 'circular' tune, discernible in the first melodic theme of the *Wasps* overture, with a chance anticipation of the Aeolian mode, traceable to Oriental sources, and, cumulatively, the 'Russian' fall of a fourth. 'The Legend of Kiev' shows an almost complementary 3–4 | 5 4 3 | 2 1 curve.[1] In 5*c* the repetitive impulse takes shape in a plain pattern of unexpansive, obsessional phrases, easily paralleled in the motives of modern Russian music, from Glinka to Shostakovich, and almost parodied in advance in the finale of the vaudeville *L'Union des deux opéras* (*c.* 1690).[2] The three-bar pattern has analogies in Polish song and in the third of Chopin's *Polish Songs* (op. 74).

[1] See an arrangement by A. D. Kastalsky, showing the traditional counterpoint (Dorian mode). Ed. K. Schindler, 1925. For degree abbreviations, see p. 122*n*.
[2] *Musical Quarterly*, 27(4), p. 523.

The Hungarian and English songs are an interesting comparison. The general proportion of recurrent melodic degrees (which could be abundantly confirmed in other examples) is similar. Degrees 1 and 5 predominate, cumulatively—not in the direct harmonic association to be noted later—and these are also the degrees most frequently stressed; then come 7, 4 and 3, with Hungary favouring 4; then 2, followed by 6 as regards frequency, while 2 and 6 are equally unstressed. Indigenous traits (or, possibly, period traits) may be sought, in the various components of 5, in the Hungarian seventh-degree emphasis of 5*a*, and in the didactic insistence on the opening formula in 5*g*; in the 'English' handling, in 5*e*, of a curve and speech-metre established, developed and returning to basic location in a compact structure; in the no less English steady, almost dancing movement of 5*f* down the octave and, more urgently but with equal grace, up to the climax and down to the keynote, with the pathos of the flattened sixth; in the hexatonic and more primitively poignant ascents of 5*h*, and its leaps of voice; and, more firmly, in the intimacies of 5*i*, with the more genial major third (standing in, or near, a simple 5:4 acoustic relation to the keynote), but still bearing on degrees 4, 7 and here 6. As will shortly be apparent, it is important to accept the mode of the last song as a variant of the Dorian mode, not 'our' major scale with a flattened seventh. Almost peculiar to English folk-song,[1] it is significant for the present narrative. Yet the chief qualities of English folk-melody

---

[1] In an early collection of Russian folk-songs by V. F. Trutovsky (1782), the second is in the Mixolydian mode, while leaning on the fourth degree, and the eleventh, here harmonized as in C major, gravitates to G in a Mixomixolydian manner (B C G G). But as Mixolydian intonations both of these go their own way, to English ears, by not showing a firm fifth degree. They are not a true anticipation! I have not observed any Mixolydian tunes in the later collections of Balakirev and Rimsky-Korsakov, or in their folk-song rhapsodies (overtures, sinfonietta), but in a careful survey Alfred Swan declares the Mixolydian mode to be a highly popular basis, citing the collections of Melgunov (1885) and Glière (*Fifty Songs, Musical Quarterly*, 29, p. 505; October, 1943).

Irish folk-music was comparatively late in the provision of handwritten sources but, with the collection of the shapely tunes of the harper, Carolan, in *c.* 1721, early in publication on a perceptible scale, as Mr. Donald O'Sullivan has made clear in his recent book on Carolan, with full illustrations of the music. Carolan's tunes that are not major (e.g. the 'Lament for Sir Ulick Burke') tend to a hexatonic minor (no sixth) with a compass of a twelfth or more, but 'Carolan's Cap' is Mixolydian, with a stress on the fourth degree, and there are more normal Mixolydian outlines in 'What news' (Petrie collection) and 'Castle Tirowen' (Goodman collection), both in the manuscript library of Dublin University (Trinity College).

So far 'almost peculiar to English' may be of doubtful validity; but the characteristic quality of English Mixolydian song remains unchallenged.

are its elasticity of phrase, less isorhythmic than the Hungarian type, and its melodic agility, transcending the mere balance of phrase, breathing emancipation after a period of near slave-song, and keeping in contact with the unfailing briskness of a rhythmic stanza, repeating a line where the musical strophe requires it. All this, without drawing upon the major or minor scales.

So much for the positive nature of the folk-song influence which was gaining ground in England at the start of the century, as earlier elsewhere. It was not so much a forgotten and now stimulatingly novel order of interval in a hexatonic scale, but rather a creative extension of answering pitch-locations, developing into melody that did not require harmonic support, and was not, indeed, concerned with the harmonic implications of its favoured degrees. There is usually a dominant or leading recital note, and invariably a point of gravitation, but the sense of key is not strong enough to stand the suggestion of a fresh key on its own terms.

THE FOLK-SONG IDIOM

If one now turns to another group, again reduced to the same key each time, one becomes sharply aware of what folk-song is not. Here, at first hearing, is comparable music, springing from some plain strophical text. On closer observation, the motives have not the same independence or the same capacity to circulate. They need harmony. At certain points they spell out harmony, which calls for underlining punctuation or qualifying accompaniment. In 6a (overture, *The Wasps*), the first

Ex. 6a

three bars pick out 153 or the major chord of 1; in the fourth bar 2 and 5 suggest a plainer chord of 5. This is a conceivable fanfare on a trumpet, but it will not make a motive. Harmonic support is essential. Further, 6a is not the stuff of a tune that calls for simple and serial repetition, but of a component in a wider scheme of preparatory and supplementary motives, with fresh and restorative keys for the theme itself. Properly disposed, it will be right in a symphonic overture, while the national tunes in Stanford's *Irish Symphony* remain intruders. It may detach itself later, as this tune does, as an avowed song in the heart of patriotic worthies (disguised as wasps), but never as an independent strophe.

The spontaneity of 6b (*Sea Symphony*) is deceptive. It marks the end of a long period of experiment and re-casting, as the sketches show. Melodically it appears to be more 'traditional' than 6a, but bars 2 and 4 are too stationary, bars 5–6 twist too much, and bar 9 bears too heavily on the third degree for a purely melodic statement. The text points to an apocryphal Genesis, to introduce the Adam and Eve of

Ex. 6b

Ex. 6c

Ex. 6d

Whitman's *Passage to India*. As folk-melody the tune is correspondingly and suitably unauthentic, but acceptable enough as an extended melodic line, harmonized, from which arises an imitational stage in the symphonic scheme of the finale of *A Sea Symphony*. In 6c (*Pastoral Symphony*), similarly, the rise to and retreat from the fifth degree is mannered and harmonically suggestive. It demands harmonic support and an answering development of phrase; later, perhaps, a variant mode, inconceivable in a single version of a folk-song. Thus this motive, springing from a pentatonic milieu, acquires symphonic status in the

Pastoral Symphony. Ex. 6*d*, from the same symphony, has the deceptive lilt of a folk-tune but the deepening harmonic association of degrees 1 and 5 again postulates a bass, and the spasmodic climb to and fall from 7, in bars 6–7, must be justified by some informative bass. A racy exterior thus blossoms into symmetrical, harmonically pointed melody, to start the main interlude in the scherzo of the same symphony. Ex. 6*e* (*Sir John in Love*) is the most strophical line of the group, but the close succession of fourths (i.e. inversions of fifths, e.g. 5 and *upper* 1, the latter being the true basic note) reveals the harmonic texture of the conception.

※ harmonic bass or note of reference

Ex. 6*e*

The composer once drily remarked on a debated tune in a work of his, 'It has not been collected yet'. While in a number of recognized fantasias and variations, and in the course of his first two operas, Vaughan Williams pertinently introduced folk-material whole, the careless assumption, tedious to repeat, that specific echoes of folk-song are a patent feature of his development, must be repudiated once and for all. It will be clear from the above examples how judicious is the criticism that cannot distinguish harmonized themes with a modal tinge or aphoristic rhythmic pattern from unilinear song *per se*. But, as has already been suggested, it is true that Vaughan Williams's melodic idiom takes for granted the *working pivots* of English and other folk-song, and thus distinguishes itself at once from, say, Elgar or Ireland or even Holst, whose music has its folky cachets.

Folk-song is the best clue to Vaughan Williams's gradual renunciation of the later nineteenth century. He reverted to the post-pentatonic stage of pure melody, not (as is again vulgarly stated) as a 'melting pot' period of modes marked for a liquefaction into the rounded symmetry of the major scale and the compromises of the

minor, but, on the contrary, as a period of firm and admired crystallization of certain genres of pertinent and creative melody. These fell
out of use in the first growth of harmonic texture, in which cadences and
pivotal progressions were groomed so as to break the impact of any
mode. Properly, modal melody and harmony thus became obsolete by
1600. But the abandoned technique now continued underground, and
embraced fresh potential melodic types, not so much in any literal
recovery of one or two modes, but in a reconsideration of melodic
procedure, and in framing harmony, not just in 'faithful' corroboration—as in the many folk-song settings of Sharp and of Vaughan
Williams himself—but rather in a creative relation to the new current
of melodic resistance.

Products of Early Influence

On such lines the composer went forward from this early response
to his discoveries of English folk-song, to which he continued to testify
on the surface throughout his career by numberless settings and
scattered interpolations. It was a kind of Pre-Raphaelite cult in music,
backed by the same sort of reaction against a decadent rhetoric as had
animated one side of the Pre-Raphaelite Brotherhood itself, but without
any medievalist obsessions.

Some passing indications may now be given of how the revival of the
five-to-seven-degree style worked out, without confining a melodic
curve to the old restrictions of balancing pitch-locations, which were
now past experience. Some lines are freely rhapsodic. Others are precisely rhythmic. Others, again, begin almost pentatonically but then
slip away where no pseudo-Greek tribe could round them up; or
alternatively, begin out-of-mode and slide by a semitone into the orbit
of a recognizable pentatone. Such composite fragments of melodic
drive gain a touch of spontaneity from the old and now refreshing
magic. I shall reserve for Chapter VI a demonstration of the crucial
transition in *On Wenlock Edge*. It will be noted that it was only after
considerable preliminaries, including the *Sea Symphony*, that this early
tradition began to pull its weight.

The first and primary example, from the finale of the *Pastoral
Symphony*, has a precedent in the *Wasps* music (prelude to the prayer
to Apollo, with a similar vibrant bass, again just a drum), but it is
more striking as the opening of such a finale, being a 'jubilation' for
wordless voice. It is almost non-harmonic in its overtones, except

114

that the drum-roll accompaniment again makes A, the tonic, the pre-vailing term of reference. It is thus a well-nigh complete reversion to the sheer pitch-locating of the post-pentatonic stage, and its formal purpose is to give nothing away. In 7*b* the theme is shown on its return, pitched round E, a fifth higher, but now acutely harmonized by reference to a dissonant chord. The monotony has been turned into a virtue,

distant soprano or tenor solo (or clarinet)

senza misura

drum roll

Ex. 7*a*

str.,wood wind

Tr.

Ex. 7*b*

2nd. time

Ist. time

3rd. time

Ex. 7*c*

as of a trenchant committedness in controversy, for the chord is there first. Ex. 7*c* is a plain example of modal idiom in a modal atmosphere but symphonic design, the Scherzo of *A London Symphony*. It thus recurs in various keys, but its final *modal* change, from hexatonic minor to Mixolydian major, has its precedent in the regional variants of a folk-song. Actually, the 'first time' version was an after-thought, not found in the original piano score, which has only the 'second time' version, except at the end.

Ex. 7*d* uses mode in a very different scherzo, that of the fourth symphony, where its fundamentalism counters the prevailing semitonal thrust. Once again its obsessional quality, as of a Bilina chant, contributes its sense of enslavement to the stress of the moment, where a more modern theme would have counted less. Ex. 7*e* (*Sancta Civitas*, cf. Ex. 5*d*) is one of the modal features, by which, harmonized, the composer wishes to convey the sense of a new but fundamental world, impinging on imaginative experience (*Revelation*, 21. 23). The tune is hexatonic, but the harmony makes it Dorian. Finally in 7*f* (*London*

Ex. 7*d*

Ex. 7*e*

Ex. 7*f*

Symphony) an old mode suffers the wind of change in tonality, with corresponding effects in the oscillating multiple harmony.

Lest the reader suspect that this celebration of precedent is unnecessary fuss over the origins of the composer's early work, one may add that this line of discernment could be followed right up to the *Blake Songs* (1957). That the traditional element is, more often than not, absorbed in a richer appeal, is a strong incentive to the gaining of clarity about its various forms. It is so far incumbent to discriminate between the Dorian, Aeolian, Mixolydian and the rarer modes, and neo-modal lines not yet specified, and it is thus expedient, for any efficient scrutiny, to be aurally familiar with the plain variants of the degree-pattern denoted by these obsolete but accepted terms of distinction.

FOLK-SONG SETTINGS

The steady postulate here of a harmonic setting, in ready amplification of, or manifest tension with, the given melodic line, exposes in its true quality any harmonic setting of a folk-song. For folk-song, abjuring culture in a degree without parallel, needs no accompaniment. Mode is not a mere question of scalic interval but of pivotal degrees in vivid and self-contained relation. The keynote drone of 7a, underlining what recurs most, is tolerable, and so may be any complete chords of key-note, fifth and other prevalent degrees. But even these are apt to tie down the expression in a tiresome fashion. Even the main melody of the solemn and mystifying thanksgiving-after-sickness movement of Beethoven's quartet, op. 132—a *soi-disant* antique 'tone' with the degrees of the Lydian mode, but with a cultivation of the seventh degree quite alien to the usual turns of Lydian plainsong—sounds awkward and ceremonially over-clothed in its apparently 'period' harmony, let alone some utterly non-period sevenths. Much less will a true folk-song benefit by being 'pushed around' by a busy thorough-bass and figurated harmony, including even modulation, though not in Vaughan Williams's settings. In particular, a tune which, like Ex. 5h, has no sixth in its orbit, is likely to be romanticized by a minor sixth in its harmony, making the fourth-degree chord minor in the tradition of numberless cadences of the late nineteenth century. Similarly, a tune that has no definitive third, may be wished a minor third, in order to preserve that sense of the human struggle typical of the last century.

This must be said in frank criticism of Vaughan Williams's support of Sharp's general compromise with the harmony-addict, as somehow the right thing, not a mere sociable gesture which in time would become as redundant as Mozart's harmonic embellishments of *Messiah*. One may greet with the same severity the folk-song settings of Vaughan Williams himself for voice and piano, or for chorus. They must be taken, like Mozart's *Messiah*, as at best interesting glosses on their musical text, however beguiling the additional texture. Howes makes the bold suggestion (p. 196 and elsewhere) that, whereas some ingenious or capricious settings merely use the tune for their own ends, the Vaughan

Williams settings are so peculiarly sympathetic that they enhance the native quality of the tune. While the first part of the statement can be well supported, the conclusion is a false inference from a truism of experience, that if a setting is truly and consistently personal, its integrity makes an over-riding impression. The fact remains that solo-melody belongs, however datelessly, to one era, harmonized melody to another. The past may be re-created in the art of the future, but, if it has fulfilled its purpose, it does not need that extrinsic touch to complete it. The folk-tunes of the Lutheran repertory did not call for Bach's regimentation, except where the actual tune is inadequate. This is true enough of a folk-song like 'Innsbruck'. It merely suited Bach's purpose to take 'Innsbruck' (less its secular jubilations) and give it a solemn eighteenth-century character in keeping with the prevailing harmonic texture of his Passion commentary.

In folk-song, the tune relies on its text for development and serial pattern. With the added pomp and circumstance of solo voice and a gracefully manifold-declamatory S.A.T.B., with the tune passing from top to inner voice and back, discreet neo-modal cadences to replace the punctuating turns of modulation, and a contrived prolongation or postponement of the last cadence, a setting is apt to become a predictable ritual. There seems to have been something froward about the persistence with which Vaughan Williams, followed by Holst, absorbed folk-songs in odd sociable moments, however much competition festival promoters and other educationalists may welcome them for their steady and accomplished part-writing and fresh harmonic touches, including the novelty of uncompromisingly modal cadences.

An unusual place was found for 'an old carol-tune', hexatonic in texture (a congener, indeed, of 'The truth sent from above'), as the motto-theme for music for a serial broadcast of Hardy's *The Mayor of Casterbridge* (1951). It is known generally as the tune sung by South Staffordshire colliers to an hour-long carol beginning 'On Christmas night the joy-bells ring' (*Journal of the Folk Song Society*, 2. 126); but also as the tune for an eighteenth-century ballad on the first convict fleet for Australia (Mr. Owen Reed of the B.B.C.). Certainly its message here is admonitory, not exultant: '''Tis Doom, I reckon', as Mr. Reed concluded at the end of the series.

Orchestral strophes of this tune, with snatches of incidental music, supplied the prologue, interlude and epilogue of this fall of a man from a social pinnacle. The 'bold' prologue-music moves comfortably from string promulgation to clarinet undertones and a brass climax. The 'sad' epilogue betrays a now familiar disturbance of tonality (C and E flat minor in an orbit of A minor) and a quasi-pathetic obsession with the sixth-degree chord, adumbrated in the prologue. In 1960 the music was used for *Great Expectations*. There let it rest. The routine treatment carries the tune no further, besides being superfluous. What is more, the composer's art is not advanced in the least. That is the constant danger of a rhetorical appeal to the past. It may work all right in severe isolation. In wayward overflow, it may make the listener forget that the composer is capable of more. That recurrent background music cannot easily progress beyond variation-form does not weaken the truth of this statement.

Ex. 7*g* ('Ca' the yowes')

On a subtle question of harmonic interpretation, one may query the setting of the rare tune, 'Ca' the yowes' (tenor solo and chorus). In the second verse, the first note of the tune is pegged down as the keynote of a Dorian tune in E, instead of the last note, B, emerging as the keynote of a pentatonic tune in B, making the first note the fourth degree. The cadential fall of the bass from 2 to 1 (Ex. A above) seems forced, where a fall from 5 to 1 (Ex. B) is more compulsive. In verse 4, indeed, the harmony seems to be gravitating to B minor, and might well stay there, but B proves once more to be the fifth. However, it is an intimate setting—if there has to be one.

THE FOLK-SONG FANTASIA

The association of folk-songs in an orchestral or choral-orchestral suite or fantasia is now a familiar extension. Texturally, it is bound to involve the same arbitrary and artificial treatment, song by song. It also raises the question of the propriety of mixed periods; tunes in the major being often so much later as to lose all relation with the post-pentatonic stage. Of such juxtapositions the *Folk-song Suite* for military band (1923) is the bluntest, having no texts to implement in the successive strophes. It is just a matter of reed or brass or both. And what has 'Seventeen come Sunday' to do with 'Dives'? But in general one must expect a prevailing sense of raw material, of imported characters that are dressed up and then set to confront others, as like or unlike, in a routine ternary or rondo pattern. A sense of design will then have to be sought in some central idea of the text, such as the revival of the Christmas revelation which unites the *Fantasia on Christmas Carols* (1912) and the folk-dance ballet, *On Christmas Night* (1921),[1] and forms the converging point of the procession of tunes that carries along *Folk Songs of the Four Seasons* (1950) in four clear, naturalistic stages, with a background of folk-lore. The rest of the construction lies in the maintenance of obvious rhetorical sequences.

The *Fantasia* thus sets a blend of folk-singer and baritone-solo intimacy in a context of choral humming, preparatory to choral verses of varying genres of grouping and harmonic texture. Parallel disposi-tions of violoncello solo and orchestral blend support the working

[1] Written to a scenario by Adolf Bolm (see p. 337), *On Christmas Night* was produced by Bolm at Chicago in 1926. In 1935 the work was revived with fresh choreography at Cecil Sharp House by Mr. Douglas Kennedy, who had been director of the English Folk Dance Society after Sharp's death and continued in a similar capacity in the E.F.D.S.S. Imogen Holst conducted.

repartee. Rhythmically, a free five-beat and a light six-beat metre give place to a stamping tread of two beats of increasing urgency. There is a gravitation of key from A in the Dorian mode to E Mixolydian major, G major and E Mixolydian major again. The intermittent strophical routine is pointed by textural and dynamic means, with some capricious passing conflations of song or song-phrase, sung or (tuba, *Nowell*) played. Very deftly, the main threads are sorted out and interwoven without losing the essential disturbing impact of the songs of a transformed family life for human society.

The ballet, shaped as the dream of Scrooge, adds its dramatic, contemplative, and *The Seasons* its descriptive, legendary and dramatic, touches to similarly planned successions of tunes, in the latter case on a larger scale. These works have a plainly romantic objective; to provide stirring renewals of the Christian spirit at Christmas and of other seasonal messages, traditional or imaginative. Every revival of each work takes this background for granted. The occasion is familiar, the effort to rise to it is, or should be, new every time. These communal stirrings readily acknowledged, the musical appeal is still of an intelligent arrangement of song-settings which are in themselves mainly superfluous to their subject. They may so far be compared with Bach's chorale-movements, of which the plainest and most extended assembly can be observed in the four chorale-numbers that frame cantata 95, *Christus der ist mein Leben*, as assurances of an untroubled journey through death. The second and fourth are plain settings, but in the first and third (whose tunes were conceived in harmony from the start) the successive phrases of the tunes are summoned by or evoke independent orchestral motives. None of the Vaughan Williams settings call for the tune in the same way. The introductions merely anticipate it with a statement of phrase or indication of rhythms. With the slight exception of 'The lark in the morning', there is no confirming reverberation of orchestral motive.

In the *Norfolk Rhapsody*, the first and surviving one of three, one is not so conscious of the serial setting, here of naval ballads, but rather of the use of traditional material in a broad stroke of the imagination. On this ground the piece will fall for consideration in Chapter VI. The withdrawal of the other rhapsodies is significant. The spell of the ancient mariner cannot last. Perhaps Holst's *Somerset Rhapsody*, a too well-meaning and affectionate blend of folk-tunes, made his friend more aware of the snags.

Later in his career, Vaughan Williams drew on folk-song for the music of two films, *The People's Land* and *Dim Little Island*. These will be considered in their place, along with the orchestral variations on 'Dives and Lazarus'.

Enough has been said to establish folk-song as a constant inner voice to Vaughan Williams's exploration of method; as a pronounced directive towards a forgotten type of vocal movement; as the basis of musical material in general, and as a conspicuous source of diversion into broad and sociable avenues. The discipline of the spare strophical variant counted here, along with seventh degrees that rise a tone to the tonic or fall back to the fifth. The serious student need not study the accidents of mode in this connection, but he will be better for having sung enough folk-songs to take for granted the variable third, sixth and sometimes second degree of the modal style, and also the constant sense of inescapable rejoinder, independent of any harmonic punctuation that may accrue. This was the kind of material which hovered in Vaughan Williams's mind as he set out, and continued to be there steadily as he considered one turn of style and another.

Almost as early came the call to edit the music of a new hymn-book supplement. The observance of a strophical pattern, and a search for tunes which soon became a problem of disposition of the 'new' and deposition of the old, proved so absorbing a task that the supplement became a complete book. The examination of this monumental challenge to *Hymns Ancient and Modern* (1904) claims a fresh chapter, but it will not be surprising if folk-tune finds an entrance into these exclusive precincts.

NOTE ON ABBREVIATIONS OF DEGREES OF SCALE: Groups of figures have been used throughout the book as abbreviations of melodies (or note sequences) and harmonic sequences—and sometimes of chords, too. It will be clear from the context what is being abbreviated. Vertical lines denote rhythmical shape, and when found in conjunction with these, hyphens denote a divided beat. Elsewhere hyphens merely indicate a close connection between notes or chords.

V

Hymnody

THE ENGLISH HYMNAL

The *English Hymnal* (1906) made hymnodic history far beyond the original intention. The role of supplement soon forgotten in the pressure of fresh material and growing ideas of reform, there now appeared a whole new hymn-and-tune book for the use of the Church of England, which became a liberating influence in the musical and other counsels of the various Nonconformist churches, and in time of church bodies in Canada and the United States. Later came *Songs of Praise*, musically the virtual extension of the *English Hymnal* repertory, apart from a small number of modern examples. The *Oxford Book of Carols*, which followed, broke plenty of new ground, and remains quite unchallenged as an annotated collection of carols in English with tunes, nearly all obtainable separately. Finally, the *English Hymnal* was revised so as to include a large number of tunes introduced in *Songs of Praise*, as well as fresh material.

Whether general or supplementary, the true purpose of a hymnal with tunes is to promote a growing corporate personality in church life by a pronounced and discriminating choice of material, fortifying accepted tradition, but stimulating a gradual extension of repertory, limited only by the amount of regular effort that a minister and his congregation will make to improve their musical condition and, failing a melody edition, to enlarge their musical memory. In the long run, congregations and churches gain the hymns and tunes that they deserve, according as they demand, for this part of their worship, the austere, the grand, the intensely subjective, the congregational, or nothing in particular, which means the stalely derivative. But there will be a stage at which a choice of good and wide material can be a tremendous stimulus.

The *English Hymnal* was started by Percy Dearmer (vicar of St. Mary's, Primrose Hill, London) and his friends, as a small supplement to the 1904 edition of *Hymns Ancient and Modern* (henceforward *H.A.M.*), which still seemed a poor provision for any congregation. At the suggestion of Cecil Sharp and Canon Scott Holland, Dearmer called on Vaughan Williams, asked him to edit the music for the proposed Supplement, which he estimated at two months' work, and offered £50 for expenses. He agreed. By 1905 so many good hymns had been collected that a whole hymn-book was decided upon. It took the music editor two years to complete his work, with expenses at £250; his research matching the enlargement of Dearmer's range.

The clear corporate intention of the *Hymnal* is to provide a companion to the Book of Common Prayer. It seeks to observe with a new precision, in some respects apt only for Anglo-Catholic practice, but systematic in its approach, the events of the Christian year; but also to provide for odd processional occasions and an abundance of general occasions, celebrating the Church as rouser of the public conscience, or missionary band, wherever men and women are united in a genuine sense of purpose. This extension of the Anglican hymn book, as planned by Bishop Heber and furthered in *H.A.M.* (1861), retains much that is of questionable level, but also introduces, besides a much purer text, many new and fiery grains of Christian truth. 'The most challenging and catholic book the Church of England had yet seen' is Dr. Erik Routley's summing-up of the hymnal as such (*Music of Christian Hymnody*, p. 138). This estimate is based on a thorough historical survey, and comes from a musician and practising minister whose warm response to the *Hymnal* is apparent up and down *Congregational Praise*, of which he has been music editor.

Here, then, were over six hundred and fifty hymns to be furnished with tunes, suitable for strophical rendering by an incalculable parish congregation, and combining the already familiar with fine additions that might be implemented in time, according to the progressive energy and musical interest of minister and congregation. Apart from the established occasions, round the year, for the principal services, there remained a wide margin of general and recurring situations for enthusiastic singing, as distinctive points in any meeting for worship, from a short and informal assembly to some special act of dedication or devotion.

Such was the challenge which Vaughan Williams met, not with the darkened counsel of the professional amongst amateurs, but with imaginative resource, with signal results now known far and wide, and by no means confined to high-church or anglican circles. For he realized that here was an opportunity, not yet properly used, of leading a multitude of assemblies, regularly gathered with some sense of common ideals, towards a condition of musical fulfilment in their chosen context.

THE NEED OF REFORM

That meant one or two decisions, which must not be under-estimated because they seem simpler now. First, hymns are to be sung by the man or woman in the pew. But an editor has an obligation to bring out the best in a congregation, and not to countenance what he believes to be a bad tune because it has been popular for some vague period since 1861. Secondly, choice must be adventurous in any comprehensive hymnal. The centuries must be freshly gleaned on the lines previously pursued, broadly by *H.A.M.*, and selectively, in the revival of certain classics of hymnody, by G. R. Woodward in *Songs of Sion* and by Robert Bridges in the *Yattendon Hymnal*, as earlier by the editors of the *Chorale Book for England* (1863). Any hymnal worth compiling must assume some kind of local progress from a given starting point to a healthy catholicity of taste. On a very moderate scale, *H.A.M.* might have led the way, from the communal, semi-secular style of Genevan and Lutheran tunes, and of their later British and Roman Catholic derivatives, to the intimacy of Gibbons and Vulpius; or from the jaunty exaltation of the eighteenth century to the gracious fervour of the nineteenth—or vice versa. But the lead was not given, and there was every scope for tapping these sources more thoroughly, and for exploring others.

FRESH SOURCES

Three lines of expansion may be cited:

(1) In the field of Roman Catholic hymnody, an enlargement of the French repertory of diocesan and parish melodies (e.g. *Deus tuorum militum*) was matched by a similar extension of German melody, of which *Lasst uns erfreuen* has proved the prime example.

(2) Welsh tunes, traditional, adapted and individual, now appear in force.

125

(3) More controversially, as it proved, adaptations of English and other folk-songs were introduced. Few later hymnodic editors would have dared to take the initiative in this field. Actually, however, there had been a long strain of precedent association between rustic, wordless jubilation, and then folk-song and folk-dance, and dedicated song. The connection has been demonstrated in a recent study by Father George Chambers, *Folk-song —Plainsong,* to which Vaughan Williams wrote a welcoming introduction. First a practical matter of seeking out basic expression; the use of secular material became the focus of a growing policy of 'robbing the Devil' of his best tunes, most pertinent in Luther's adaptation of 'Innsbruck, ich muss dich lassen' (shorn of the final melisma) and of many other songs, whose familiar associations he was prepared to swallow whole for the sake of a widening and more racy congregational future.

Similarly, even the inhibited Calvin, dangerously Nonconformist, appears to have accepted, *per se* rather than in all innocence, the popular tunes to which the poet Marot's early versifications of the psalms (biblical and hence unassailable) were sung round 1540. He ended by approving the many virile settings compiled and adapted by the Genevan cantor Louis Bourgeois. These became the musical foundation of the earliest English and many later Scottish psalters, as well as of the French and English psalters at Geneva. This was the kind of tune sung by 'five thousand' at Paul's Cross (London) round 1560, 'after the Geneva fashion, *all the congregation together*' (my italics). One might have been *Mon Dieu prête-moi l'oreille* (Psalm 86), an obvious ballad tune; another, *Psalm 42*, later *Freue dich,* as rendered in a vernacular finish to many a Bach cantata. Both tunes survived in the Scottish Psalter down to 1635. Under Moravian influence, John Wesley widened the range, including the carol-like *Savannah* and cheerful *Hanover* in the 'Foundery' Collection (1742), the first Methodist tunebook, with the solemnization of an ultra-jaunty street air (now *Helmsley*), for 'Lo, he comes', to follow. The 'shaking' Quakers, too, who landed in America in 1774, based their worship music on folk-song and folk-dance). Earlier, the Moravians had brought their music (Handel, Haydn, Pichl) to Salem.[1]

---

[1] Hymn-tunes cited are identified by their usually established titles, here given in italics. They can be traced from the list of tunes to be found at the end of the *English Hymnal*, 1933, and very frequently from other hymn-tune books. It is beyond the scope of this book to trace variations in hymnal collocation.

In the new assault on secular and possibly satanic territory, Vaughan Williams could, in fact, claim the support of signal congregational experience, not to mention St. Francis and many a bold *joculator Dei*.

PROBLEMS OF COMPILATION

Routley (*op. cit.*) shows how Bourgeois altered some of the angular tunes of the earlier Strasbourg psalter to a smoother, more symmetrical and so more congregational pattern. Most of the folk-songs which Vaughan Williams adopted here were already parcelled up enough for parish use. But in the now most familiar case he exercised his creative faculty by re-fashioning an unbalanced and slightly awkward song which he had taken from the lips of Mrs. Verrall of Monksgate, Sussex. For

Ex. 8

congregational purposes, it was necessary, or at least expedient: (1) to strengthen the too light anacrusis of each phrase; (2) to iron out the distracting crease of the five-beat bar (another version of the folk-song maintains a metre of 4–5–4 beats, but this would be equally impracticable); (3) to replace the 'period' fall to the sixth degree in bar 3 by the more civilized seventh. Above all, the *a–b b–c* pattern is wrong, and *a a—b c* sounds right. So to *Monksgate* in readiness for making a hymn out of Pilgrim's poem, or rather out of a more parochial version of it, since it was never intended for a hymn.[1] (In eliminating hobgoblins, however, the reviser has taken refuge in a jingling platitude that calls for re-editing.) With a local summons thus transformed into a universal appeal, and the partly harmonic thrust of the first phrase (1–3–5 6 5 5–1 in a clear major) pressed home in the repeat, a harmonic setting may be justified by its enhancement of the initial ascent of 5 6 with a bass of 5 (not 1) 4, its absorption of the otherwise raw penultimate 7 of three phrases in a 2 4 5 7 chord, and its sally into the nearest minor

Catholische Kirchen Gesang, 1625

Lasst uns er-frew - en herz-lich sehr, Al - le - lu - ia, - ia
Ma - ri - a seuffzt und weit nicht mehr.

Ver-schwun-den al - le Ne - bel sein, Al - le - lu - ia,
Jetzt scheint der lie - ben Son-nen-schein,

Al - le - lu - ia, Al - le - lu - ia,

Ex. 9

key to distinguish the third phrase. The revised tune was, in fact, composed for harmony. It has ceased to be unilinear. The upshot is certainly compulsive, given a steady organist and no facilities for self-righteous pomp at the end. Tune and setting make one unrelenting whole.

This refining process has been followed in detail because it is typical of critical hymn-tune compilation, on the melodic side. The exasperatingly unmusical condition and equipment (tune-book) of the average worshipper imposes a discipline that means giving him some assistance. The idea that hymn-tunes fall like rays from heaven is purely romantic. One other example may be given, however, of a tune from an old hymn-book (to be found in the British Museum), which is almost fit as it is for general use. Here all that was needed was to equalize the bars,

[1] Bunyan's text appeared in E. Paxton Hood's *Our Hymn Book* (Brighton, 1862), without tune.

so as to preserve a uniform triple metre. Another early version joins the first two phrases shown, and then repeats them. (The *Westminster Hymnal* follows this.) But the location of the melodic movement first in the lower half of the octave, twice, and then in the upper half, twice, makes a better strophe than seesawing twice. It remains to add the momentum of a pulsating harmonic bass, to reinforce the lift and downward pull of the voice.

Such, in brief, is the reality of 'editing', when a musician bears the responsibility and exercises the initiative. Without Vaughan Williams it may be said, there would have been no *Monksgate*, no *Lasst uns erfreuen*, nor many other tunes in firm English use today, to rouse the young of all ages and to carry reminders, wherever the tunes are sung, of issues faced and still to be faced.

TUNES BY THE EDITOR

There remained, as typical material, a few modern tunes by Somervell, Holst and the editor. The last were printed as anonymous in 1906, but it was a matter of time before it became clear that *Sine nomine* and the rest could only be by the editor himself, however much he may have sponsored one-tune composers like Shrubsole, composer of *Miles Lane*. *Sine nomine*, like *Jerusalem*, should be reserved for special occasions, but the tune has stood the wear and tear of constant use well enough. The gradual descent, in the first half, from upper to lower fifth degree is countered by a quick return, more trumpet-like than vocal, to the high note, sealed by the rise of one more degree for the final 'jubilation'. This powerful strophe, betraying no raw places in repetition, has carried Bishop How's worthy but not impressive text to many compulsive uses, as one of the affirmations of the year.[1] *Randolph* is more declamatory, but none the less firm in shape. The refrain of *Salve festa dies* has a spare melodic line, interesting to compare with the more exultant *Sine nomine*; with its varied verses, this looks an artificial tune, but its coherence improves with acquaintance. *Down*

[1] Let two examples be recorded here. On an All Saints' Day after a bad air-raid in the last war, the headmistress of a big London school faced an assembly of exhausted faces, but no one was missing. There was little doubt what had united them after the night's terrors.

An earlier and altogether historical occasion, nationally, at which the tune was still new enough to provoke a protest (in favour of Barnby) from King George V, who was present, was the Commemoration of the First Seven Divisions at the Royal Albert Hall in 1917. Allen conducted. *Toward the Unknown Region* was also introduced (to most of those present) in this context.

Ampney is by widening consent the quintessential V. W. in harmonized melody. One may notice, once more, the antithesis, in each half of the tune, of the ascent and descent to the fifth and sixth degrees, and of the opposite trends in the second phrase, and then the unity of the third and sixth phrases. But for the integrity of this composition no category can properly be given.

Let us assume that the first stage is complete, and that some seven hundred selected tunes have been placed on the assembly-line, waiting for an exact assignment. They will include some odd transferences, taken from *H.A.M.* Here, for example, is the serviceable but regrettable reduction, by W. H. Havergal and others, of freely flowing German tunes, down to the workaday measures of *Dix, Franconia, Mannheim, Ravenshaw, St. Flavian, Winchester New* and (W. H. Monk's good deed) *Crüger,* with the deplorable *Angelus* and *Rockingham.* There is also, of course, W. H. Cummings's fantastic adaptation of a section of the jubilant second chorus (male voices and brass) of Mendelssohn's festal cantata in celebration of Gutenberg, inventor of printing, to promote Charles Wesley's Christmas hymn (de-universalized: see the previous hymn). A century of fervent association cannot make this pompous refrain (so apt for Schiller, and conceivable, as the composer thought, for some general jollification) suitable for such a 'Methodist' outburst.[1]

CREDITS AND DEBITS

There are also some appalling things like *Redhead 47* and *76*; the debilities of *St. Oswald* and the glib *Hursley*, neither relegated to the appendix till the 1933 revision; and the retention of the incredible *Leominster* seems downright cynicism. After these, it hardly seems consistent to rail off, in an appendix, what the editor used to call his Chamber of Horrors. By this device he curiously retains a number of tunes under magisterial disapproval as 'not entering into the general scheme of the book', but with a tolerant assent to deviations for the weaker-minded organist or other musical executive; languishing things like Barnby's *St. Chrysostom* and *For all the Saints*, and the singularly named hospital hymn, *Requiem*, along with *St. Cross, Northrop* and various higher settings of approved tunes. But there are steady rejec-

---

[1] For the originals of *Dix* and the rest, see Dearmer and Jacob, *Songs of Praise Discussed*, or similar companions to the revised Nonconformist hymn-tune books. Routley's *Music of Christian Hymnody* is based on references to the *English Hymnal*, which an index shows to concern nine tunes in ten, but it is not a tune-by-tune commentary.

tions, 'old favourites' (since 1861) not excepted, as a matter of religious obligation, moral decision and sheer artistic distaste. Routley has neatly summarized one of *H.A.M.*'s fatal retentions in his enumeration (Ex. 160) of a prolific family of congeners in triple metre, of which *Pentecost* ('Fight the good fight') and *Cloisters* ('Lord of our life') are the best known. Of the two in the *Hymnal*, *St. Chrysostom* was relegated at once, and *St. Crispin* became a Horror in 1933. (The refiner's fire kindles gradually when the hymnodic habits of decades are involved.)

In place of these and numberless other decadent or purely nugatory tunes one finds, as one turns the pages of the *English Hymnal*, for a planned year of congregational music, tune after tune with 'the moral atmosphere implied by a fine melody'. The mental effort may often be grudged, and many tunes may for a practical or even no reason remain unused. But it is not the hymnal that is on trial. Let the musical reader who is willing to discover the melodic material, if the titles are unfamiliar, consider how much Church life was, or might be, braced by a repertory drawn from the following typical tunes for daily or special occasions; and then compare with *H.A.M.* (1904, well meaning in places but somehow ineffective, in practice, in reforming capacity) and its musical derivatives, on the one hand, and with the somewhat exotic and antiquarian note, on the other hand, of *Songs of Sion* and the fabulously produced *Yattendon Hymnal*. The revised *H.A.M.* (1950) groups itself with the *Oxford Hymn Book* (1908) as anglican aftermaths, with the specific qualities of which this narrative is not concerned.[1]

A CROSS-SECTION

1. PSALM TUNES FOR HYMNS

(a) *French and English Psalters (Geneva and Strasbourg)*. Psalm 68 (Old 113th), Donne secours, Rendez à Dieu, O Seigneur (Old 122nd), Psalm 42, Old 120th, 124th, 134th.

(b) *English, Scottish and Welsh Psalters* (to 1700). London New, York, St. Mary, Windsor, Winchester Old, Martyrs, Bristol, Cheshire, Old 104th, Songs 1 and 46, Illsley, St. James.

(c) *English after 1700*. St. Matthew, Croft's 136th, Bedford (Weale), Wareham, Bangor, Epsom, Darwall's 148th, Duke Street, St. Thomas (S.M.), University.

---

[1] On the weaknesses of the 1875–1889 revision of *H.A.M.*, see *Hymn Society Bulletin* 94. On the betrayals of the *E.H. Service Book* (1962), see *Bull.* 96.

2. HYMN TUNES

(a) *English*:

    (i) *Eighteenth Century*. Easter Hymn (plain or decorated), David's Harp, Uffingham, Yorkshire, Truro, Veni Sancte Spiritus.

    (ii) *Later*. Affection, Martyrdom, Westminster, Nicaea, St. Fulbert, Irby, Sandys, Christchurch (Steggall), St. George, Regent Square, Benson, Universal Praise, Langdale, Kendal, Cathcart, Cranham, Sheen.

(b) *Folk-songs*. Anima Christi, Capel, Forest Green, Gosterwood, King's Lynn, Monksgate, Picardy (source?), Sussex.

(c) *Welsh*. Ffigysbren, Gwalchmai, Hyfrydol, Llanfair, Llansannan, St. Denio.

(d) *French*. Annue Christe, Coelites plaudant, Iste Confessor (Rouen), Regnator orbis.

(e) *German*:

    (i) *Early*. Divinum mysterium, Laus tibi Christe, Quem pastores, Es ist ein Ros'.

    (ii) *Lutheran*. Ein' feste Burg, Innsbruck, Christus der ist mein Leben, Hasst du denn Jesu (Lobe den Herrn), Es ist kein Tag, Das Leiden des Herrn.

    (iii) *Roman Catholic*. Ave Virgo, Culbach, Lasst uns erfreuen, Omni die.

    (iv) *Eighteenth Century*. Ellacombe, Gott sei Dank, O Jesu, warum legst du mir.

    (v) *Nineteenth Century*. Capetown, Wir pflügen.

(f) *Plainsong*. Adoro te (late), Aeterna Christi munera (late), Pange lingua, Veni Creator.

Some of these tunes have either found the right hymn once and for all, or are a reasonable collocation for a given hymn. Most of the tunes are sufficient in themselves to call for the 'right' hymn, or an alternative hymn, to point their meaning. Today their variety and strength are taken for granted by anyone who cares about church music, apart from those obsessed with a particular period. But it must be recalled that fifty-five years ago chorale and long tunes generally were overwhelming innovations, new tunes were an attack on tradition, enthusiasm and informality were seldom welcome, and structural logic equally not in demand. The daring of placing such a conglomeration before the parishes of England must shine brightly in any rehearsal of hymn-tune reform.

The general provenance of each tune is briefly but clearly stated, for the first time in a general hymnal. It is less interesting to discover what information has since been superseded than to start listing the sources in some sort of chronological and organizational order. This will bring home the vast and vivid pattern of growing congregational tradition behind this magnificent collection: folky and plainsong, Lutheran and Roman Catholic, Anglican and Nonconformist, Oxford Movement and evangelical, liturgical and artistic, recovered-old and personally distinctive. These sources have been explored and assessed, and, where gathered, set down with a proper historical sense. Not that the precise date of publication often matters much; but once a period sense is cultivated, it becomes irksome not to know the source of tune and hymn, and the editor was singularly thorough in tracing and naming his sources.

VERSIONS OF TUNES

In choosing the version of a traditional tune, Vaughan Williams's principle is to seek out the best for the situation; not necessarily the earliest, still less the easiest, and not always any particular version literally, if it is too variable rhythmically. *Old 137th*, for example, appears in a tough regularization, in a nearly steady four-beat rhythm, of an originally plastic balance of 7–6 beats and the like. *Epsom* is reduced, for an unfaltering delivery of Blake's *Credo*, to a uniform six-beats from a more subtle 6–6–6–3 series (twice), less the syncopation of bars 2 and 7. Today a freer rhythm is more conceivable; but the editor was obviously trying to meet congregations halfway by a firm rhythm; organists being erratic enough in many cases, and not only in village churches. Earlier, we observed the equalization of the wayward phrases of *Lasst uns erfreuen*, manifestly expedient for use by the large bodies of singers intended. So with *Ave Virgo*. Lutheran tunes are put into a rigid rhythmic mould, as in Bach's settings. So also are later Roman Catholic tunes of similar content. Even more regularized is the fourteenth-century *Laus tibi Christe* (German, Scottish, German again, in turn), audaciously demodalized from A in the Dorian mode to an exultant D major. The free rhythm of the Genevan Psalter has in general been restored. Listen to *Rendez à Dieu* as in *H.A.M.*, and then as here. On the other hand, *Sandys* is a tune almost picked out of nowhere and then shaped. All these melodic details had to be decided freshly; for *H.A.M.*, which had never been in the control of a music editor, rarely gave any lead. On one congregational point the editor of the *Hymnal* is insistent: tunes are pitched for men to sing as well as women; an accommodation still often overlooked by organists, some of whom are reluctant to admit that a tune is improved by being made generally singable.

CHARACTER IN HARMONIZATION

Few features, however, identify the *English Hymnal* more nearly, in its time, than the harmonizations. It is a plain question of structural and textural grasp. The often stodgy spacing of *H.A.M.* is replaced by a lighter tenor and bass, no longer sinking into despond; the bass is a vocal effort, not a mere pedal excursion; and judicious non-harmonic notes on the beat give the harmonic rhythm a jog. Take, for example, the settings of *Vom Himmel hoch* (or *Erfurt*). In *H.A.M.* (1904: a distinct improvement on the shapelessness of earlier editions), the bass capers irrationally in the first half, the modulations are spasmodic creases rather than structural features in the harmonic pattern, and the chordal texture is almost entirely undecorative, and monotonously average in spacing. The *Hymnal* setting comes from the *Christmas Oratorio* (Part 1), put down a tone. Decorative notes keep the polyphony alive throughout, and the chordal texture is plastic. The bassline is shaped steadily towards various related points, with leaps balancing conjunct movement, and passing modulations in a clear relation; sharpwards and back, flatwards and back. Non-harmonic notes, passing or suspended from the previous chord, strengthen the harmonic rhythm. The result is a meaningful articulation of the original melodic curve, even if it is sometimes confined to the organ because the choir cannot spare the time to learn their detail.

For the Lutheran tunes, then, one of Bach's settings is usually sufficient to shape the tune in the desired metre and coherent pattern of key. Similar treatment is applied, somewhat bluntly, to non-Lutheran tunes, such as the Bohemian Brethren's *Mit Freuden zart*, or the much earlier *Laus tibi Christe*, now a confident major, with calculated modulations to minor keys. The process is extended to the Genevan repertory and its English derivatives, such as *Psalm 68* and *Old 137th*, to *Lasst uns erfreuen* and *Ave Virgo* and other late Roman Catholic tunes, to some Welsh tunes, and even to the folk-song adaptations; all originally single-line music. That this accommodation of material from varying periods to a harmony-bound generation has been performed with a rare, indeed expert, discretion, is a further reminder of the editor's musicianship. Imperceptibly, a congregation that tries out these fresh strains of corporate expression will discover their unique structural strength. So they pass from *Old 120th* or *Hyfrydol* to *Iste Confessor*, set alternatively in modal and modern minor styles; or from the reformed *Monksgate*, now clarified by the key-crease in the third phrase, to the sterling free bass which, with riveting harmonic progressions, makes *Lasst uns erfreuen* the most overwhelming of the traditional tunes in modern use today. Round these group themselves pertinent settings of Tallis, Gibbons, Croft, Filitz, Goss. After them follow the few modern tunes furnished by composers of standing. If the choice of tunes is vital, the quality of their harmonization is equally bracing. In some cases it is the most bracing feature.

COLLOCATIONS

Whatever the accompaniment, these pulsating melodies were never intended for anything except to be sung to a text, to bring them down to earth in the general mind, and to call for their repetition in an unfolding strain of narrative, reflection, communal concern or deepening affirmation. In assigning hymns to tunes, the general editor naturally accepted some of *H.A.M.*'s persuasive collocations. For the rest, some practical distinctions may be made.

(1) A tune in common, double common, short, long (or other prevailing) measure, will be distributed to a corresponding hymn or hymns as may best be arranged, and accepted fitness here is largely a matter of association. This group includes the shorter psalm-tune, beginning with the *Old 100th*.[1]

(2) The longer Genevan psalm-tunes and Lutheran hymn-tunes called for fresh texts. Notable solutions include the revival of Mason's neglected and early hymn, 'How shall I sing' for *Old 137th*, Lacey's *ad hoc* 'O Faith of England' for *Psalm 68*, Heber's 'Bread of the world' for *Rendez à Dieu*, 'Praise to the Lord' (tr.

---

[1] The congregational survival since 1560 of tune and text (as opposed to Psalm 100 in the New Version of 1696, to the new tune later current, *Illsley*) is a record of association which made the *Old 100th* an obvious choice in 1953, as the first hymn to be sung congregationally, as well as in the ears and eyes of millions outside, at an English Coronation Service. (Vaughan Williams provided a special arrangement for this.) But there is no need to exalt Kethe's stilted re-translation as a creative achievement, or *Old 100th* as specially jubilant. It is a well-made tune, not to be oversung.

Winkworth) for *Hasst du denn Jesu* (or *Lobe den Herrn*). 'When morning gilds the skies' is *not* good enough for *O Seigneur*, and Laurence Housman's 'Lord God of hosts' deserved better than *Falkland* (Lawes).

(3) The Roman Catholic tunes made a like demand. *Iste Confessor* (Rouen) slips readily over 'Lord of our life'; Riley's 'Ye watchers' was expressly intended for a triumphantly processional *Lasst uns erfreuen*; Dearmer's translation of 'Nocte surgentes' is serviceable for *Christe Sanctorum*.

(4) Of the Welsh tunes, *Ffigysbren* takes good care of the corporate longings of 'O thou, who at thy Eucharist', *Llanfair* of 'Hail the day' (toned down), *Llansannan* of How's 'Who is this so weak?'. 'Immortal, invisible' for the orderly adaptation, *St. Denio* (Holst's discovery), 'King of glory' for *Gwalchmai*, and Lowell's 'Once to every man' for *Hyfrydol*, are remarkably felicitous choices.

(5) Of folk-songs, the adaptation of *Our Captain Calls* for Bunyan's 'Who would true valour see' (adapted) has been discussed; the ballad-tune stiffened into *King's Lynn* adds the right vernacular touch to Chesterton's 'O God of earth and altar', *Capel* will do for 'The church of God', and so on; but to assign *Hambridge* to 'In Paradise reposing' was extraordinary, and *Langport*, impishly disguising 'Lord Rendal', makes a queer tune for 'The story of the cross'.

(6) Of miscellaneous tunes, *David's Harp* seems made for 'Come, O thou traveller', and surprisingly apt, too, for 'We saw thee not'; *Universal Praise* and *Benson*, on the other hand, are respectively the earliest, and by no means the least, of many express settings of 'Let all the world' and 'God is working his purpose out', and their replacement by *High Road* and *Purpose* in the main body of the 1933 edition is no obvious improvement. Moreover, specially composed tunes, 'that bane of many a hymnal' (the music editor), manifestly includes his own. For better or worse, there can now be no alternative hymn for *Sine nomine*. Littledale's rendering of Bianco's *Discendi, Amor Santo* (*The People's Hymnal*, 1867), despite 'loathing' (v. 3), is the right, as well as the intended, collocation for *Down Ampney*.

This cross-section is indication enough of unparalleled care in fitting hymn to tune, tune to hymn. Although he restored the original texts to good purpose, the 'undergrowth of Victorian stupor' left Dearmer and his colleagues with a great deal of embarrassing material to sort out *vis à vis* the numerous, too numerous, fine tunes already available, and many good tunes are thus collocated with hymns of remote appeal or rare use. Yet tunes are doing even less good in the archives of the Hymn Society of Great Britain and Ireland! It is not easy to overstate the immense and penetrating influence of this repertory, as a collection of tunes, of which enough are in regular use, firmly grasping their texts in a musical clasp, while abundant fresh interest lies ahead on untried pages. There is hardly a devotional series in which Vaughan Williams's craftsmanship and integrity are not making themselves felt in the music, from Westminster Abbey to the most elementary assembly.

INFLUENCE ON NONCONFORMIST HYMNARIES

For slowly, or rather by fits and starts, his stand against the enervating tune, and on behalf of intelligent research, made its impression on the revising hymn-book committees of non-Anglican churches. From the *Church Hymnary*, 1927, to *Congregational Praise*, 1951, Nonconformist music, too, has in varying degrees taken an upward turn. In the trail of these revisions have appeared companions to each book—hymn by hymn and tune by tune—to be read as promotional prefaces to intelligent use, deepening the historical basis of changing versions and exposing the grotesque arrangements as such. These were monumentally anticipated, indeed, by the *Historical Edition* of *H.A.M.* (1909). The influence of the *Hymnal* has spread to the hymnals of the churches in America and Canada, although, again, this does not guarantee a regular resort to the 'new' tunes. A cross-section of tune-content in leading hymnals of the century will be found in Appendix A.

SONGS OF PRAISE

Meanwhile, although seemingly heavily engaged already, Vaughan Williams was not inactive in the hymnodic field. With Martin Shaw as co-editor, he produced the music of the seven hundred tunes for *Songs of Praise* (1925; enlarged 1931). The collaboration of Percy Dearmer, as sole editor of the words, ensured continuity of purpose. The compilation of *Songs of Praise* combined the catholic and partly liturgical aims of the *Hymnal* with a desire to make a national collection of hymns for gatherings of all sorts and ages. Culturally, it was resolved to replace the Watts-and-after repertory, from which most hymns had been taken, by a move 'to enter into the heritage of noble religious verse which is ours', and, it is clear, to do more justice to the growing social conscience of the time; an offshoot, in a sense, of the League of the Arts for National and Civic Ceremony. Newly exposed exploitations and injustices, challenging Christian thought and action, needed fresh hymns, and new tunes, it seems, were still crowding in. Dearmer set himself to fill the gaps, not least by his fluent pen. His growing idiosyncrasies (he abhorred references to blood, I understand) involved a certain amount of theological relaxation, which has alienated the exclusively orthodox set who govern taste in many churches. How far doctrine should be sung is a matter of taste.[1] Yet the general literary quality was now vastly improved, and in schools, especially, these hymns have silenced earlier complaints of sentimentality and pious doggerel.

Certainly Vaughan Williams did not grudge the time to furnish the book, at the height of his career, with a fine new repertory of tunes to encourage this broader sense of dedication, uniting all men and women of good will. About a third of the tunes are not found in the *Hymnal* (1906). In this sense, there are new or new additional tunes to well-known hymns: for example, *Alberta* (1931), *Bromsgrove, Marching, Thornbury* (1898) and *Vision*, and *Prince Rupert*, defiantly, to supplant Sullivan's *St. Gertrude*. (It is odd that the most fluent *joculator* of Victorian music became laboured and formal, at best, in his hymn-tunes.) There are new tunes for, or supplied with, new hymns: the traditional-adapted *Caerlleon* and *Slane*, and the otherwise composed and here adapted *Repton* and *Chilswell*, but also the splendidly precise *Risby* for Hankey's 'Lord of the strong' and *Love Unknown* for Crossman. If numerous good tunes remain in abeyance, partly owing to their hymn-collocation, they are not less to the music editor's credit. But there are also some good new assignments; in the increasingly pertinent 'Turn back, O man', *Old 124th* emerges at last from obscurity, while *King's Lynn* for 'O God of earth' (*Hymnal*, 1906) now finds itself in fit company. *Remember the Poor* is right for Kingsley's 'The day of the Lord is at hand'. *Lasst uns erfreuen* is restored to its Resurrection setting, with St. Francis-Draper, 'All creatures', as an alternative on another page. The weak point of the collection, leaving the Nonconformists to fill the gap, is the small proportion of modern tunes.

Vaughan Williams's new settings include the gracious *Magda*, the

---

[1] See the Introduction to Dearmer and Jacob, *Songs of Praise Discussed*, p. 20, for an apposite citation from Lord Selborne's *Book of Praise* (1867).

stalwart *Guildford*, the magnificently cumulative and modal *King's Weston*, and *Famous Men*, a unison anthem whose insertion here shows a characteristic assumption of a tune-rehearsing congregation for progressive church life. The inclusion of *Marathon*, a spirited unison song in the *Wasps* music, seems a strained effort not to let a jolly tune die out. Not all that dances is hymn-worthy. It must be admitted that the whole tune-repertory of *Songs of Praise* is rather overwhelming in practice; as when 'Praise to the holiest' is paired off with *First Mode Melody* (Tallis), and *Abinger* (R. V. W.) is wasted on 'I vow to thee, my country'. However, a tremendous variety of poetic singing material has been furnished with a practical vehicle for communal affirmation. That was a historical achievement, although musically on the conservative side. A new standard of literary range and musical experiment was held up to any revising committee.

THE OXFORD BOOK OF CAROLS

The Oxford Book of Carols, with the same editors, is of equal importance, as the first critical collection of carols in English on a large scale, with music. A wide range of occasions is matched by the variety of style, with a considerable cross-section of foreign carol-tunes. Of Vaughan Williams's own contributions 'Sleep, baby, sleep' (Blake) is the strongest, but the chief feature of the book is the perennial freshness of its infectious tunes. No 'horrors' here.

THE REVISED ENGLISH HYMNAL

In 1933 the *English Hymnal*, revised, appeared. The change consists of an enlargement of the tune repertory to seven hundred and fifty-odd by the addition of extra tunes, or by the substitution of a new tune for one which now swells an enlarged appendix or is found elsewhere. A large proportion of the new tunes come from *Songs of Praise*, so that musically *E. H. Rev.* is an amalgamation of two periods of research. The remainder range from *Michael*, used by the Bohemian Brethren (1531), to the cumulatively rousing *Corona*. The gains from *Songs of Praise* are numerous (for example, *Birmingham* instead of *All Souls* for 'Lift up your hearts'), and they include *Magda* and *King's Weston* in place of *Ellers* and *Laus tibi Christe*, which retains its other hymn from 1906. It is impossible to avoid the impression, however, that numerous hymns are saddled with new tunes more for the sake of comprehensiveness than for any superior fitness to the context. Indeed, something has been lost by this grim determination to force so much material into the six hundred and fifty pigeon-holes available, with the questionable slogan, 'Nothing sacrificed in this revision'.

When a revision of the *English Hymnal* is on the way, the tune repertory may well call for some reduction as well as extension, since the musical condition of a church congregation still limits the number of hymn-tunes that they can hope to command in a reasonable period of self-help and progress. However, there must be additions, including, possibly, new genres, and less of the old. Versions, settings and all adaptations, none of which were substantially recast in 1933, apart from settings of the plainsong tunes, must similarly be reconsidered, and some source-detail needs correction. Possibly, also, the specific needs of a meticulous cultivation of the Christian Year may be reviewed. Observers of that year, for example, will find that of the hymns for Lent, two in three have tunes in the minor; an undue promotion of 'deeply wailing'.

Nevertheless, the revisers will be hard put to it to maintain the inner dynamic of the *English Hymnal*, with its firm call to united worship in a liberal and expansive musical spirit, good for bounders like Peter and Paul as well as the more exclusive participants from the colleges of music. It extends from a spare Scottish psalm-tune to the deeper rhythm of the later hymn tunes, with a harmonic support that carries the whole strophe with it and, if need be, stands up to the wear of recurring verses. What was right in particulars in 1906 may be wrong today, but the new particulars must be equally right, not just the product of a magnified, whimsical iconoclasm and equally whimsical taste. Readers will have gathered from the second chapter that Vaughan Williams combined with an exceptional educational ardour, typical of his generation, an extraordinary interest in people for their own sake, much more irrespective of class than most clergymen of his day. It may seriously be conjectured that something of like quality guided the width of the *English Hymnal*. Such virtue will not easily be cultivated or maintained by a new directive. It implies the freedom of the disciplined character.

A similar line of thought is suggested by any prospect of revising *Songs of Praise*. As the commonest book in use in schools, it is of special importance that it keep pace with the fresh contributions of estimable hymn-tune writers, and also with the changing tastes of the rising generation. The much more even literary challenge of *Songs of Praise* is a further stimulus to tune reform. But again the unity of a collection with a minimum of specially provided tunes and settings, as opposed to a book burdened with the contributions of the editor and his friends, should not lightly be disregarded. If some of the earnest tunes by Martin and Geoffrey Shaw and other respected church musicians seem now, after ample trial, to betray a lack of spontaneous construction, it must be asked how long will the newer and lighter sort last out a decade of promotion. The plain historical fact is that Vaughan Williams has stood almost alone amongst composers of his calibre in his habit of responding to a situation with an integral tune, apt for voices more often than not. The others were either minor specialists in the strophical métier, or improvising composers of more standing. The latter do not now trouble themselves with tune writing. The field has narrowed, and an editor must look further for the filling of gaps.

Twice, then, from 1904 and round 1924, Vaughan Williams had a period of congregational tune-compilation. Close examination reveals each as a searching and monumental test, melodically, harmonically and to some extent in the relation of text and tune, in addition to the labour of sifting and comparing sources. Whatever the practical interest of the reader in these tunes and settings, a strong, almost obstinate, grasp of the strophical pattern may be assumed, primarily melodic in appeal, though distinctive also in harmonic impact, and ready to summarize a situation, or fix a moment, in a wider context. Without undue credulity the composer's statement may be accepted that in the first period the proving of so many good and bad tunes was well worth the loss of time, which might have been spent on more creative musical effort.

On that account the musical proposition, which the editing of a hymn-tune book involves, has been examined in detail. It needs only time, the trouble to identify a melodic setting from its name, and some sifting of other editors' work on similar material, to enter into the exacting process of tune-testing and harmony-testing involved. Vaughan Williams brought much to his early compositions from this course, and later, as past experiences to a mature period. It is largely non-semitonal harmony in the major and minor scales, with occasional bursts of mode from the older periods. There is little that could not have been written in 1850. Parallel to all this lay the unilinear impact of folk-song, harmonized by custom but not of necessity. Both sources were connected with a text. The text or the tune might change or be replaced, but a firm association was assumed at each point. Larger or more elaborate vocal compositions must still preserve this sense of structure and literary contact.

The hymnals are our first considered example of a body of work which is bound up with a text of dedicated purpose. One must beware of false artistic standards. The fulfilment of a deep social or individual need does not make a piece of music better or more intelligible; and it has been shown that the association of tunes with given hymns is frequently arbitrary and changeable. The main test must be an aural one. However much associations with a text, or with an event in a year of worship and assembly, may help to bring a tune home, it must be a fine and characteristic tune before it can be truly memorable. The critical quality of the hymnody now discussed lies primarily in a perception of the musical structure and texture that an alert ear accepts as right for each other. Where the text appeals to the singer, as theology or humanism or for its own sake, the right tune will enhance it. In other cases, the text may be of pedestrian quality, but still sing (and play) well. Yet every one of these tunes, as here presented, has been set to a hymn, not as an exercise in style, but as a skilled contribution to the special circle in which men and women seek a fundamental and enlightened response to the demands of living. Composers who write preludes on these tunes as sheer musical material ignore all this congregational history. This is not true of the most accomplished chorale-preludes of J. S. Bach, or of Parry.

VI

Early Works

EARLY SONGS

It is not possible to place all Vaughan Williams's works in a strict chronological order. A date of publication may give only an approximate idea of the period of composition, and in some cases an entirely false and post-dated one. On the question of a proposed bibliography, the composer wrote to me in 1928, 'I fear I cannot help you as to dates as I have forgotten', and twenty years later he was saying the same to Foss.[1] However, there is no doubt at all that, round 1900 and after, Vaughan Williams wrote a number of songs, of which *The House of Life* (1903) is the most substantive collection, with *Songs of Travel* (*c.* 1904) to follow on broader lines, and *On Wenlock Edge* (1909) to show a complete maturity of style. He thus began song-writing before the major encounters with folk-song and hymn-tune discussed in the previous chapters. Yet what has been said about such strophical settings, folk-song in particular, has some bearing here.

---

[1] See *The Dominant*, 1. 9 (July, 1928). In *The Music Student*, 12. 9 (June, 1920), Miss Katherine E. Eggar introduced a warm-hearted survey of Vaughan Williams's work up to the *London* symphony with a 'complete list kindly revised by the composer', giving dates of composition and publication, and publisher, for each piece, with a few minor gaps in the first date column. Apart from folk-song arrangements, this list is nearly complete. (It omits *How can the Tree but Wither?*.) It may be regarded as the most authentic source for early dates so far published. However, the divergences of date in the list of works in Foss's book, reproduced in *Grove's Dictionary* (1954), do not exceed a year or two, apart from a transference of four isolated songs from 1903–5 to *c.* 1894–8. Hence, no serious problem arises about dates here. Nor is there any dispute about the date of the first performance of works after 1920. There are a few questions of inception, such as that of the fourth symphony, but they are rarely significant.

143

Blackmore by the Stour, *Whither Must I Wander* and *Linden Lea*
are all plain examples of this strophical method, applied to solo-
voice and piano. The texts of the first and third, 'Dorset songs' in profession but not origin, are by Barnes, and they declare in three verses
the abiding charms of the local girls and of an unworldly corner in a
certain exquisite orchard. The second, by Stevenson, is the earliest of
many 'vagabond' songs. The poem is sub-titled 'To the tune of Wandering Willie', about which it is needless to speculate, except that it
shows that Stevenson, at least, regarded his 'songs of travel' as singable.
This poem is highly nostalgic, and seemed out of place when it was
included recently in a complete recital of the *Songs of Travel* (see later).
The tunes respectively assigned to the songs, to carry the singer through
three verses, are all symmetrical four-phrase constructions, guided into
two halves by the *a a b b/c* rhyme-scheme, and binding the intonation
further by some repetition of the first phrase in the Barnes songs, of the
second in the Stevenson. A recurrent flattened seventh, following a
spontaneous use of the normal seventh in the accompaniment, gives a
dash of Old Mode to the first song's major-key feeling, and ultimately
to the second song's minor, while the absence of seventh in the tune of the
third song recalls a more elementary stage of major.

Those are the limits of the traditional element here. The organization
of the melody itself is too harmonic and too chic to rouse any serious
suspicion of uncollected folk-song. The actual harmonization is
noticeably freshened in each case, pianistically, in the second or third
verse. This confirms the harmonic conception: the piano settings of the
folk-songs remain a framework. The vernacular touch, of assumed
simplicity of measure, suits the Barnes lilt, and does well enough for
the Stevenson cult of the open road. Yet such is the slender evidence of
Vaughan Williams's 'folky' style, or of any 'hovering between art song
and folk-song' (Young and others). It is high time that criticism
recognized the true quality of this kind of musical tourism, which is
disposed to identify everything miniature or handmade as folk-craft,
and cannot distinguish a harmonically conditioned melodic course from
sheer melodic declamation, on account of the spare phrases and
recurrent commonplaces that find their way into the former.

Shorn of such false associations, the three songs are almost equally
singable and unpretentious. *Whither Must I Wander*, with its faltering
tonality and trite modulation in the third phrase, is too commonplace to
be worth remembering. *Blackmore* has the most rhythmic interest.
Melodically it is limited, but its recurring modulation flatward, to the

144

fourth degree as tonic, affords a certain stoic support for the country-man's simple admiration. *Linden Lea* has the most organically developed strophe, with modulations in the middle phrases to the fifth and second degrees, sharpward and flatward, to shape the vocal move-ment in each stanza. Its widely acclaimed geniality, however, cannot be justified by any suggestion of special integrity, or of superior texture, unless smoothness is a virtue. Incidentally, *L'Amour de Moy*, an arrangement of an old song, has a good tune, but it is not, as sometimes stated, a folk-tune. It is too sophisticated.

Another song of this period was for some reason not published until 1934: *How can the Tree but Wither?*, to a text by Lord Vaux. It is taken from the *Oxford Book of English Madrigal Verse*, having been already set by or for William Barley in his lute-book of 1596, as an *air de court* to be sung, perhaps, by a London wait at a tilt or masque, as a simple strophical 'reading'. The modern composer also disposes the graceful pessimism of this early Tudor lyric in plain strophical terms, using the piano's initial descent down the octave to underline the concluding 'Is this a life?...' of each stanza. In the third verse the ironic relaxation of the tonality to major keys before turning back to the inevitable refrain makes this the 'after-song' of a shapely *Bar* (see p. 152), not too rigidly symmetrical. However, this too is a poetic intonation, rather than a song. These four settings remain elementary exercises in the handling of words, with *Linden Lea* as the most spontaneous. The discipline of a more exacting text and poem-structure was needed to ensure a growth of idiom.

THE HOUSE OF LIFE

An attack on six, and then four, of Gabriel Rossetti's *House of Life* sonnets was an evident response to this impasse. In his selection of typical moments in Rossetti's poetic consciousness, the composer was dealing with an imagery at once derivative and individual. Its mythology and metaphors come from Dante's *Vita Nuova*, but they are used for the exotic expression, less of a transforming love, than of the erotic reverie of an unsatisfied love. There is a correspondingly fragile relation between the contemplative ideal and the sensational and all too human aspects of a protracted but confined encounter that thinly conceals the poet's relations with the woman who became his wife for two years. To recognize glibly the official and provocatively exclusive genre, 'Pre-Raphaelite', or the rich contradictions of the Brotherhood that the nominal pursuit of pre-decadent Raphael called into being, is not to explain away the throwback to which his reading of medieval Italian lyric inclined Rossetti, coincidentally with Tennyson. The discriminating listener to any recital of these sonnets must be prepared, not only for the imagery of religious ritual to suggest earthly love, but for the use of such fictions at one remove from Dante's original conception; so that worship has its altar and its voluntary in contexts of mundane passion. On the other hand, this steeping of the self in its own complicated emotions was a stimulating change of ground for the song-writer, after the conventional programme of nostalgia, naturalism or the dry humour of Have-you-ever-been-in-love-my-boy. Any settings of these sonnets must release new springs or give up any pretence to literary sensibility. A corresponding structural problem arose from the partly fixed pattern of the 'moment's monument' that Rossetti found in the sonnet. The broad 8–6 symmetry must either be exploited in a wider context or re-moulded according to a fresh and musical sense of proportion.

Vaughan Williams left bolder spirits to grapple with Dante-Rossetti's confused idealization of his relationship with his dead wife (*The Blessed Damozel*)[1]; which poem Rossetti often deplored later. The composer here took six sonnets (4, 19, 9, 22, 48, 59) of the *House of Life* cycle from the fifty-nine which comprise the first part of the set. (It was eventually extended from the fifty-six sonnets in the *Poems* of 1870—including 4, 9, 48 above—to the hundred and one in the *Ballads and Sonnets*, 1881.) This first part is called 'Youth and change' (originally 'Love and change', according to W. M. Rossetti's introduction to the sequence) and the second part 'Change and fate'; the simple suggestion being that youth (love), change and fate are elements in that horoscopic state of becoming, life. Since, however, the original sequence is demonstrably an accumulation, not a cohesive experience, the composer was free to make his own selection. He avoided equally the hyper-erotic and the hyper-mystic, without being provincially 'reasonable' about it. He changed the title of the third sonnet from 'Passion and Worship' to 'Love's Minstrels'; from two assumed stages of love-making to their musical personifications.

But Vaughan Williams must have recognized in the now neglected Rossetti a fund of critical initiative and medievalist influence, whose

---

[1] Debussy also almost completed a setting of *Willow Wood*, but only one page has survived. See Edward Lockspeiser, *Debussy et Edgar Poe* (Paris, 1962), where the page (No. 4) is reproduced. *La Saulaie* remained 'in process'.

orbit stretched not only from Dante to William Morris, Pugin and a ubiquitous Gothic revival, but also to many works of 'literary' art, beginning with the paintings of Rossetti himself, supported by Ruskin and going on to Whistler's 'Harmonies in grey', to challenge the overt impressionism of Gautier's 'Symphonie en Blanc Majeur'. The bland dismissal of Rossetti is said to be decreasing today, but it remains general. Here, it takes the form of sympathizing with Vaughan Williams for bothering with Rossetti at all. 'Captures all too successfully the lilies and languors, the stained-glass airlessness' (Pakenham) is typical modern comment. Hence the present attempt to recreate more precisely the rich and complicated associations which any contact with Rossetti was likely to evoke for any educated listener of 1903, as well as the peculiar fusion of an almost wantonly revivalist imagery with contemporary passion. The capricious disregard by singers of all but one of the six settings, today, is more due to a lost literary sympathy than to any positive musical consideration. Long since abandoned, their texture still contains some clues to the composer's first emancipation, and the structural handling, while open to discussion, is distinctive enough to be examined here.

It will be convenient to group the songs according to their use of the piano to complete or modify the balance of octet and sestet. The more pointed the latter is, the more fragmentary musically.

(1) Songs 1 and 5, 'Love-sight' and 'Death in love', balance two associate quatrains with the sestet, split into convenient sections. The octet is couched in symmetrical phrases of cantabile and piano figuration. The sestet adopts a freer speech-song, in the first song with suggestions of returning cantabile. A piano refrain, echoing the opening, amplifies the vocal ending of the first song, somewhat transparently, while the ominous final twist of the fifth song is similarly attached to the main framework, by means of the piano motive, devitalized. The steady 'lovesight', and the characteristic foreboding of death in love, serve to justify these reverberations. The later song presents, too, a dramatic picture of Change, so orchestral as to sound pompous on the piano, and in lines 4 and 8 so *nobilmente* as to be suspect.

(2) In songs 2 and 4, 'Silent noon' and 'Heart's haven', each standing for a 'close-companioned inarticulate hour', the opening cantabile returns, with key restored, briefly but comfortably; so comfortably, indeed, in the first case that the love-song of twofold silence seems to slip too easily to its close. The fourth song has impressionist reserves to implement its 'roundelay' after a stilted interlude. 'Silent noon'

extends effectively from its initial absorption, resembling 'Sapphische Ode' (Brahms) in style. A fresh descriptiveness (*più mosso*) reaches a point of suspense at the observation, in speech-rhythm, of the 'blue thread' hanging in the sunlight. From there the initial impulse is easily recovered for 'So this winged hour is dropt to us', by means of a calculated harmonic progression from the chord of suspense (basically a movement from the second degree to the fifth (held), with cadence on the first). But this return is too assured, or the sense of completion comes too early, to be persuasive. A Plunket Greene of today may conceal the baldness of the detail, but there are still seventeen bars to go. Also, the texture of the Più mosso is thin.

(3) The last song, 'Love's last gift', presents love's various gifts in a tree-leaf imagery. Accordingly, the sestet begins and ends with a return of the 'gift' motive, so absorbing the contrasting glances, pointed by fresh keys and tempi, at 'strange secret grasses' and the sharpness of autumn. The second return, maintained by a singular repetition of text (the other is in 'Silent noon'), is more insistent, and is completed by the piano, as in the first song. The melodic line is trite here. The start of a broad processional hymn-tune (*Sine nomine*) is one thing; the salient curve in an intimate song is another. Its definite harmonic trend—to absorb the fifth, third and first degrees in a single chord—shares a certain fixity with the inverse operative phrase in *Linden Lea*. 'Love's last gift' fails to add more than a vernacular swing to the simple imagery.

(4) The third song, 'Love's Minstrels', is a record of psychological conflict. The dispute between passion and worship occupies the octet, with conflicting accompanying motives, forecast in the piano prelude. In the sestet the rhapsodic passionate motive acquires vocal force, but it gives place to the motive of worship, whose signally repetitive chord-on-its-head (5 instead of 1 in the bass) makes an evocative substitute for a normal cadence, and overflows into a postlude. Thus the eventual collocation of the harmonically memorable worship motive with the pale gleam of wan water in a wan moon informs this exaltation of a psychological stage. The motive is composed to ask a question and then, more crystallized, to answer it: the conflation of contrasting themes is clear enough. The critical issue is whether the themes are compatible or even comparable, and whether the second is pianistic at all. It must be added that the latter is not plainsong but a species of secular jubilation, as Father Chambers has re-defined the term (see p. 126). This does not make it more in place here. It is hardly an acceptable symbol of

'rapturous tone', as is, say, the jubilation of *Flos Campi* (oboe and viola). This declaration of faulty texture is not, however, ground enough for dismissing the song as just 'weak'.

The formal interest of this passion-censoring setting remains the trenchant harmonic impressionism contrived to match the commended love-impulse, compensating for the monotony of key-centre. Similar pivotal sequences recur rather later. There may be parallels in contemporary music, but none so aptly placed as this, for those who take the trouble to interpret text and music together.

Ex. 10

In this cycle, then, the composer has handled a series of limited, richly charged, near-monotonous, Dante-esque poems with resource, exploiting the sonnet structure and using his discretion with the imagery. Song 1 reflects the poet's absorption in a cantabile style, broken only in lines 9–11. Song 2 is more firmly enclosed in a musical pattern of contrast and recovery. Song 3 lets the prickly dialogue take its course before drawing the musical threads tight. Song 4 sings itself into elementary melodic shape and piano colour, in growing intimation of the 'chiming spirits' of the last line, with modified texture for lines 9–12. Song 5 exploits the piano to glorify the mysterious figure of love before the portentous, precisely annotated sequel. Song 6 shapes love's bounty into a miniature rondo and facile cantabile returns. It cannot be doubted that the composer attacked his selection both with full intelligence and with a close reading of his 'model'. If the 'easy' settings (1 and 4) are the most satisfactory wholes, the set remains unparalleled, in its time, in its general enlargement of musical range and in its shrewd response to difficult but individual poetry.

WILLOW WOOD

From there Vaughan Williams went on, somewhat surprisingly, to a setting of the four *House of Life* sonnets called *Willow Wood* (49–52), in a single composition for baritone, women's chorus and orchestra (1903; first performed, 1909). A clear design absorbs this tense and

involved account of parted lovers. The first sonnet is set in a broad
pattern of partly recurring motives and speech-song, for solo voice or
accompaniment, on lines already anticipated. Here the interlude (lines

Ex. 11*a*

6–11), originally in unbroken vocal continuity with the opening, also
has its themes, and their development, amplified by the chorus in a
blend of sheer sonority (to 'ah') and declamation, links the otherwise

Ex. 11*b*

wayward and keyless delivery of the second sonnet with the opening.
The chorus-and-solo recital of the third sonnet recalls directly the first,
with an extension of the second musical phrase for the sestet. This
leaves room for further development of the first phrase as the basis of
the last sonnet.

Ex. 11*c*

The whole composition is compact and economical. The general
texture blends a hexatonic minor scale (no sixth) with the free use of the
modern minor scale elsewhere, and with plenty of semitonal movement,
rhapsodic or more pivotal. The upshot is a distinctive small work, whose

long and complete abandonment is a loss to choral life. The 'depressing' text (for most women's choirs and their audiences) opened certain doors in the composer's mind (Ex. 11*b* is especially prophetic) and kept him off facile cantabile, unless this be found in the lapse into the major for the final sestet. In a retrospect of 1922 (in *The Chesterian*, 21, quoted by Young), H. C. Colles conjectures that the composer was 'not quite happy' with his scheme of harmony and tone-colour (wordless voices), but he does not explain details, and I do not find any uncertainty of touch. Nor can I agree with Young that the composer's insistence on 'real' (i.e. integral) bass parts makes for 'heaviness'. It is a question of depth, here deliberate and appropriate.

SONGS OF TRAVEL

Willow Wood exhausted interest in Rossetti. The next choice was Stevenson, whose *Songs of Travel* were now explored further. Vaughan Williams chose eight more poems, it seems, of the forty-six: nos. 1 3, 4, 6, 9, 11, 15, 23. He issued seven of these in two Parts, published separately (1903, 1905): nos. 1, 15, 11 and nos. 9, 3, 4, 6. Neither of these has much claim to be sung as a suite, or in a continuous series. It may just be said that 'The Vagabond' (no. 1) defines the poetic range, and 'Youth and Love: 2' (no. 3) returns to the highway. But after the composer's death Mrs. Vaughan Williams found the missing song, 'I have Trod the Upward and the Downward Slope' (no. 23), a kind of epilogue to the series. This was broadcast on the Home Service (May 20, 1960), as the closing number of *nine* songs—the ninth being the earlier 'Whither Must I Wander?' (no. 17)—in the poem-order: nos. 1, 3, 4, 6, 9, 11, 17, 15, 23. The publication, however, of this extra song (no. 17) in 1912 makes no reference to the *Songs of Travel*, and the revised order shows no special point except the direct sequence 1–3, the reservation of 'Bright is the Ring of Words' (no. 15) and the concluding note of no. 23. For the rest, the songs may be taken in their two Parts and epilogue.

'The Vagabond' has never been credited with folky contacts, in spite of the pentatonic surface of its salient 1–3–5–7–5–4–5 curve (see Ex. 3). Its bold and calculated ramblings of key, with an unconventional texture of fixated basses in random succession, keep the main strophe fresh and securely constructed, and apt for the proud, moody wanderer. One may contrast Walford Davies's blithe and exuberant portrait (1931), in the major and with a recurrent rising sixth from 5 to 3 to typify the *laughing* philosopher indicated by the titular *Allegro giocoso*, and with an irrepressible flow of two-bar phrases. Following the balance of the text by repeating verse 2 after verse 3, it provides an interesting demonstration of how far one can, and how far one cannot, go with heroics without any stoic stamp. No doubt, Walford Davies took Vaughan Williams's reading as already known. However, the present song goes no further than a broad, succinct recital of its 'More fresh air!' text, in the spirit of the writer's modest collocation in the sub-title, 'To an air by Schubert'. 'The Vagabond' would never have been popularized without its stoic message of virtuous renunciation, possibly more persuasive when delivered from the moral foundations of a white (or coloured) shirt, emblem of the civilization so heartily abandoned. The song is not inferior for this, but it does raise the question of musical *versus* ethical appeal.

'Bright is the Ring of Words' is a thoughtful reading, with nice variants in the second verse, but scarcely a substantive song. 'The Roadside Fire' (composer's title) is a *Bar*, in the broad sense of German minstrelsy, which has no English equivalent: two strophes are succeeded by an 'after-song', here with a recovery of the initial impulse at the last moment. The impressionist sparkle makes an original background to the tune. The texture of the subsequent release of feeling is of a commonplace, neo-romantic sort; a stimulus, one may think, to make more of the *Bar* pattern with a better text than this. The song was a manifest enhancement of any song-recital of the time, but one suspects that the problems of interpretation made Greene and others unduly favourable to its inclusion.

In the second Part, the composer sets his texts more precisely, all except the first being through-composed. Harmonically the second, 'Youth and love', begins and ends where 'Love's Minstrels' left off, but in calm adumbration of the progress of a junior vagabond with a song in his heart, pressing on to his 'nobler fate', rejecting life's glitter and *a fortiori* anything wan. (There is some anticipation of 'Clun' in the close here.) The sheer exuberance of the intrusive 'song' (high piano octaves)—a greeting to the girl at the gate—nearly wrecks a delicate, monotonous, atmospheric setting. Moreover, the tune is that of 'The Roadside Fire', vulgarized by fresh treatment; an uncomfortable sensation. The melancholy of 'In Dreams' (reduced from twelve lines to six) is semitonal, sophisticated and impersonal, and I do not find 'The Infinite Shining Heavens' truly evocative.

In 1960, as related earlier, there appeared what was described as an

epilogue to the whole series, newly come to light: 'I have Trod the Upward and the Downward Slope.' This followed a new conflation of the
two Parts and another song, changing the order of succession to the
following: 1a, 2a, 1c, 2b, 2c, 2d, 'Whither Must I Wander', 1b, 3. The
final song at once introduces a clue-phrase of 'The Vagabond', with
a suggestion of 'Bright is the Ring of Words' for the epilogue touch.
Altogether a raw finish to an uneven cycle.

These songs, some still familiar enough household sounds, carried
the composer's craft into circles that welcomed the sparing, almost
Scottish treatment, as well as the absence of a stale Orientalism, or of
the heavy sentiment hovering behind such subtle titles as 'Because' and
'Until'. Yet such slender net achievement held no future prospects for
the method chosen. Harmonic style is too much tied down to a succession of orderly progressions in a liquescent tonality. If it holds the
semitonal and other obsessions of Wolf and his successors at a proper
distance, the moment has come to seek another tradition.

On Wenlock Edge

Folk-song, of the downright post-pentatonic sort noted in Chapter IV,
appears to have given the composer the clue that he needed. A. E.
Housman supplied the point of approach. This I consider the more
likely order than that Housman's downright sketches of rural character
prompted the composer to probe folk-song sources. However it arose,
the craftsmanship of the cycle, *On Wenlock Edge* (1909, published 1911),
for tenor solo, string quartet and piano, with an alternative reduction
to piano alone,[1] is startling. It is well known that Housman abhorred the
very idea of a musical setting of his poems. He has the sympathy of
poetic natures who have had some experience of the average musician's
lack of comprehension and cheerful cultivation of the vernacular, as
well as of all those who do not care to risk seeing their pet schemes
being promoted in what is inevitably a translation of mood, meaning
and emphasis. Certainly Housman did not release his thought in a
calculated sequence of wiry stanzas in order to have it unravelled and
re-wound in fresh colours and patterns. Yet even he might have admitted (he did not, of course) that Vaughan Williams had penetrated

---

[1] An orchestral version, first given in 1924, was repeated in 1957 at the
composer's 85th-birthday concert, presumably to please him. The orchestra,
full, without trombones and including a harp, introduces glockenspiel and
celesta (and cymbals) into 'Bredon Hill'.

with unparalleled sympathy the resolute, insouciant and serenely desperate moods of his 'Shropshire' characters, besides respecting the ballad lilt and disciplined phrase of the text.

What is more, Vaughan Williams used Housman's stark rural figures as a ramp for a series of highly charged tone-poems, almost every one fresh in texture and all pressing home their impact in resourceful turns of strophical expansion and musical development. The musical world has long treasured the ballads, scenes and mood-pictures which Goethe and others drew from Schubert, Wolf and the rest. Specially remembered are Schubert's transfigurations of the lonely, unfortunate and defiantly free-thinking, and Wolf's pressurized studies of more tortured minds, in resolutely taut semitonal progressions, piquant arpeggio and a balance of pervasive tuneful phrase or paragraph with something near speech-rhythm. In a disillusioned and apprehensive age the defiant tones of the young and discontented are the most prevailing mode. But Schubert accepted the harmonic vocabulary of *opera seria* and reinforced it with the increasingly mobile sonorities of the piano as Beethoven left it. Wolf similarly followed Liszt. Both song-composers are harmony-bound. Even Schubert never writes a tune for its own sake.

Vaughan Williams, after Housman, pursues the lonely, uncharted road in more respectable, stoic company than the Romantics' self-regarding, self-pitying culture-heroes and sheer unfortunates. He brings to these still refreshing etchings of sentient existence a style of expression that takes harmonic progression for granted, as a working method of amplifying a melodic line, but does not depend upon it, and cultivates, rather, a train of sonorities, or a radically opposed basic line, over against a coherent vocal intonation. He thus, with an extrinsic appeal that was less obviously timely to Edwardian ears, transcends the most 'qualitative' indignation of today in a blend of neo-primitive utterance and an advanced accompaniment that frequently 'looks wrong and sounds wrong' as a purely harmonic conception. This early clashing of basic semitones, in vicinity or in candid simultaneity, has proved so prophetic that to the informed ear it now seems about as classical, as the *modus vivendi* in the fourth symphony and after, as the semitonal cadence to the third pause-note in Beethoven's fifth symphony becomes for a new Promenader. It is so far necessary to recollect the pioneer character of the cycle in its original context.

The distribution of the accompaniment between piano and strings, with the piano alone as an expedient in reserve, warns the listener not to expect any conventional metrical setting. The violin accompaniment of the eight Housman songs written in the next decade points in the same direction. The presence of a tenor solo also makes it clear that passion and anguish are to be at full stretch. There can be no 'Bredon Hill' in E, as a concession to high baritones.

The composer has chosen nos. 31, 32, 27, 18, 20 and 50 from the historical collection of 1896. One suspects that of these six he picked nos. 1, 3 and 5 for the main material, linked them with slighter pieces, and then, having ended no. 5 in extreme intimacy, tacked on no. 6, which I find almost superfluous. Certainly it is nos. 1, 3 and 5 which give the cycle its main shape; no. 1 ('On Wenlock Edge') sets a new standard of mood-concentration, no. 3 ('Is My Team Ploughing?') is a tense dialogue, and no. 5 ('Bredon Hill') is, obliquely, a scene in itself. In some such proportions the six songs congregate, cumulative and wayward, answering stabs of experience but hardly a coherent musical cycle.

It is interesting to observe, again, the different ways in which the steady, sometimes unrelenting, stanzaic succession is steered into musical patterns without any noticeable repetition of phrase. In song 3, a recurring musical strophe carries the three selected pairs of verses to a tense, jagged finish, tempered by the return of the original motive. Song 4 ('Oh, When I was in Love with You') repeats the process with an agility suitable to its light humour. Song 2 ('From Far, from Eve and Morning') contrasts the impersonality of the first verse with the human cry of the next six lines, compactly enough to leave ample space for the return of the opening progression for the remaining two lines. In songs 1 and 5, the most developed pieces, the fertile imagery is still placed on a strophical basis. In song 1, with fresh declamation for verses 3–5, the pianist's left hand supplies a returning strophe. In 'Bredon Hill', after considerable development of line and figure a reverberating but distorted strophe gives place, as in song 3, to the pervasive sonority of the opening instrumental motive. Song 6, 'Clun', moves from a strophical start to a portentous epilogue.

Thus, as against the halting sestet of the Rossetti sonnets, or the glib after-song of 'The Roadside Fire', *On Wenlock Edge* exploits the forward movement of equal stanzas with a creative blend of the inevitable and the unexpected, giving vocal movement its head but presenting the musical texture in a new role of expression on a related but different plane.

A subtle and fructifying relation, then, to what looks like a binding, unyielding verse-rhythm, with a crusty, truculent thought in each stanza, widens into a succession of pithy musical structures, interspersed (2 and 4) with more commensurate renderings. It is expedient to realize from the start this versatile synthesis of verse, voice and instrumental phrase in a musical cycle whose underlying texture is provocative and problematic.

The challenge to the alert ear can be precisely stated. Any feeling of root-scale is distracted. Song 2 is reasonably settled as Mixolydian with a variable second and third degree. Its solemn procession of piano chords, alternating with a more supple string harmony, is a persuasive illustration of a haunting, elusive figure. The satirical song 4, in which a fixed chordal movement parallel (not intersecting) with the melodic line rouses attention, gives a new twist to its Aeolian mode; at the half cadence on the sharpened third degree that pinpoints the onset of virtue, and in verse 2 at the atonal descent in whole tones (at four adjacent levels), to mark the immediate passing of virtuous fancy. The piquant symmetry of the two balancing ten-bar phrases is corroborated by quick steps of a fourth, whose persistence, upward or downward, at once abolishes any thought of folk-song. These binding elements accentuate the mutable features in this witty portrait of Mr. Insouciant Mode.

Song 3 dramatizes the voices from two worlds by a pronounced and indeed somewhat facile contrast of vocal period. The first is Dorian and speechified, with a background of fluid sonority that cannot be called harmony. The second voice, which takes its cue from the violoncello, is beyond both mode and minor key, and gravitates to an unexpected pivot, the fourth degree sharpened—the harmonic opposite of the keynote—but its phrase is cast in taut four-bar divisions by a harmonic nexus. A confirming strophe breaks Housman's ploughing and football, girl and friend, symmetry by cutting out football. The third and last strophe raises the pitch-location quasi-antiphonally and then piquantly lifts the tonic three semitones for more in the hieratic style. The haunting doubt having been thus ritually but temperamentally posed, the answer is intensified by its altitude, repeated 'Yes, lad' (a liberty taken only once later) and compression to three beats from four (technically, as Elgar forces a demure 'Enigma' into a brusque 'W.M.B.'). An 'automatic' succession of declining but hard, 'scaly' chords reaches reluctantly the sharpened-fourth chord, which identifies the living man's girl with the dead man's. The narration is complete, but music cannot break off so abruptly. A hectic return (difficult to bring off) to the initial murmur restores a sense of key and basic plane of utterance; a structurally right and poetically pardonable amplification. While the trenchant violoncello knows no terminus, a modal phrase is always sure of its tonic. The old style thus puts the new in its place, leaving the departed spirit to his grief.

In this scheme, the football verses had to go. A third confirming strophe, or two climactic ones, would have been an equally disastrous pull against the momentum of passion, quite apart from the embarrassment of singing intensely about football and goal-keeper, as the composer pointed out for the consolation of the enraged poet. The three strophes left make an upstanding *Bar*, unfaltering and yet trenchant to the end.

The close relation of present and Roman times of storm and torment similarly dictated the structure of the first song. Now and Then are equated in direct strophical antiphony. A plainer and more didactic intonation presses home the continuing analogies of verses 3 and 4. In a final verse, burying storm and Roman in oblivion, a reduced, subdued strophe (piano) shapes the decline of disturbance, compressed to the minimum imagery in the coda. For this polarization of the broadly recurrent historical-geographical moment and the biting gale of a more present awareness, the composer once and for all challenges tonality to a point that nicely and significantly holds bitonality in solution, within reach but not spilling over the borderline.

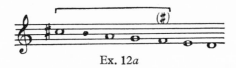

Ex. 12*a*

For a melodic start, he screws up the Dorian mode so that in descent it falls four whole-tones running (*a*). In this mode, the ensemble strikes

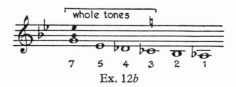

Ex. 12*b*

up what we will call 'Wenlock Edge in A flat' (*b*), dropping bluntly to G, round which the voice moves formally in pentatonic steps (*c*), while

Ex. 12c

the piano sets a bundle of these degrees in vibration, as the primary background (chord of *d* less bass). A phrase later, an A flat bass line

Ex. 12d

attaches itself to the same chord, and the key seems to be twisting towards A flat (*d*, *e*), ready for verse 2. (It is not made clear whether

Ex. 12e

E flat, the final pivotal chord here, is fifth-degree in A flat major or the tonic of a Mixolydian E flat, but there is a firm sense of transition and suspense.) Verse 3 contrasts Then and Now in a plain antiphony of dry, ritual intonation and vibrant semitones, which serves also for verse 4. Meanwhile the key of A flat (or E flat) is retained, despite a multitude of

Ex. 12f

variants and counter-variants (*f*). Verse 5, thus concerned with restoring G, as the remembered past recedes, uses the ambivalent 12d as a

Ex. 12g

convenient link (*g*). With only two lines to go, it is left to the piano to recover a sense of the original pentatonic strophe. This time the voice finishes, not on the familiar chord of E flat (a now pointless cue) but on a more trenchant chord. (This is the 'French' sharpened sixth or 1 3 ♮4 ♯6, based here on the third degree, making the tonic the forced-up

Ex. 12*h*

note.) So to a critical, halting conclusion. Hence, when the harmony relaxes to the E flat chord once more, it is countered by the suggestion of a dissonant A mode. In a penultimate recrudescence of A flat, against the G mode restored, the bitonality of the whole movement converges before submitting to resolution (*h*).

Whether the listener responds intuitively or by a close comparison of phrases, he can hardly miss the composer's mastery of his material at this crucial point. After conflating mode with a twelve-note group (in any order), harnessing modes a semitone apart, and developing as primary chords what had been previously considered as discords, he has still in reserve an almost Hindemithian progression, of calculated declining stress, to convey a sense of arduously recovered poise. In consequence, the critical listener continues the cycle with a strong sense of confidence that his powers of assimilating a manifestly elastic tonality are being exploited in a good cause, quite apart from any perception that here Housman has met more than his match in the trenchant phrase and driving pattern of words.

In 'Bredon Hill' Vaughan Williams moved from the charged dialogue of song 3 into a vivid reminiscence of the past. He has developed this renowned church-bell poem into an almost virtuoso display of bell-like figures, in turn sonorous, tuneful, persistent, dissonant, monotonous, tuneful in the wrong key, sonorous again, and significantly vocal. All these arise from the fifth and first degrees located at once in a dense antiphony of strings and piano. They propel a comparatively straightforward pair of strophes in near-speech rhythm, jubilant declamation for verses 3 and 4, near-plainsong for verses 5 and 6, and a final strophe, disturbed and then melting into the opening sonorities. Indeed, as in

'Die junge Nonne' (Schubert), the flood of physical imagery threatens to submerge the human struggle.

But the texture of the 'automatic' sections thus set in motion is skilfully varied. In the prologue, the free but paralysing 'harmony' of independent oscillations in strings and piano, with each note sounding a manifold of four notes a third apart, gives place to a recurrent curve in descending sequence, supported by piano harmony. This prepares for

Ex. 13

a vocal strophe in G-Mixolydian, slipping later to a Dorian minor third (B flat) to characterize the last phrase. The purpose of this rhetorical turn will appear later.

Verses 3 and 4 (13, *x*, in piano), explore key waywardly enough to make the return to G pinpoint expectation. Defeat of this is readily conveyed by the persistent A flats (as in song 1), extended to other notes of the rare Locrian mode (white-note scale of B) in G, for the funereal verses 5 and 6.[1] The plain speech-rhythm facilitates the neo-modal idiom, and the perceptible funeral pomp of verse 6 maintains with blunt effectiveness what A flat continues to repudiate. The fatal occasion thus disposed of, the music is free to add its bitter gloss on the returning G major strophe, chiefly an A natural against a pivotal E flat chord, comparable to the G sharp and D in song 3, and curiously prophetic of a piquant moment in the *Pastoral Symphony* (Ex. 25*d*). This is a spasmodic repudiation of the returning, unbearable bells. On the same E flat basis, the last phrase of the strophe (with the B flat) follows at once, reduced to essentials, for 'I will come'. In this impasse—for

---

[1] A significant musical precedent is the opening of the Temple of Vesta scene in Berlioz's *Les Troyens*, in which Cassandra's fanatic band of resisters prepare for voluntary death, in order to cheat the conquerors of their prey. The 'Locrian' harmony strikes a chord of settled acceptance of a desperate course. Berlioz, however, betrays the mode, and eventually treats G as the seventh degree, rising to A flat.

renunciation is not the keynote of the poem—a return to the automatic and now relentless sonorities by which Bredon church was first signalized is inevitable.

In this deepening miasma the song might have ended, faithful to its text. But from another point of view the last word has not been said. 'I will come' may spell, not a meek conformity but forty days of resistance to despair, or at least a desperate gamble on finding peace of mind. With entire simplicity, the phrase is re-affirmed, free from any ritual gesture, yet a decisive *Credo*, answering the call to church. The accomplished strophical rhetoric is caught up in a new train of thought, and the song translated, for one moment, from a common tale of deprivation to a stroke of affirmation. (Assuredly an anxious moment, in actual recital, challenging the singer's command of *tessitura*, as well as his imaginative quality.) For Housman, the bells prevail. For Vaughan Williams, the last word is a man's response to them at the difficult minute.

After these heart searchings, the extension of 'Clun' from a strophical start in a wayward mood to an after-song that assumes the nature of a broad, fading epilogue offers no problems. The strophe being in a confused mode and key (A or E), the epilogue is in a positive, though modifiable, A major. The descending 1 3 2 5 vocal phrase here is on the trite side, but the basic movement of the piano in whole tones right down the octave, at three levels, is a noticeable token of a receding horizon along which Roman, ploughman and other forgotten lovers and sufferers appear to converge in a processional march in a confident, aspiring, un-Housmanesque mood. There is little else to make 'Clun' more than the last number of a rich cycle of vignettes. It seems scarcely in place. The opening of doors that Housman merely named here seems intrusive.

It cannot be doubted that work on these texts roused the composer to fresh and characteristic strains of expression, transcending a vivid reading in a more dramatic and romantic conception. How much Vaughan Williams went beyond the still current pursuit of a strophical method may be realized by listening to other renderings. In his setting of all eight verses of 'Is my team ploughing?' (1911), George Butterworth is content with four symmetrical strophes of wayward harmony but melodious declamation, with a second half set off by louder tone, increased speed and a lower pitch-location, heightened for the final 'Whose'; all within the compass of a baritone octave in an ambiguously keyed mode. Ivor Gurney (1926), also setting the whole poem without apprehensions about the football lads, provides more inflections for each stanza, and separates the third pair of verses by means of tonality and a resort to speech-rhythm. The fourth pair restores the normal strophe, except for a slightly more intense sense of modulation. Pursuing a similar path in a more tenor register, C. W. Orr (1927) contrives a wayward first half of low tessitura with which to contrast a shriller second half. Again the third musical verse is different and pathetically flatward, but the fourth verse reverses the former tessitura, so that high, *mezza voce* colour, slipping from major to modal-minor, is answered by low-pitched grimness. Homogeneity is preserved. In the two strophes of 'Oh, When I was in Love' Orr uses a pianistic after-phrase to bring the fit of good behaviour and the reaction from it under one category, and thus to balance a capricious melodic line in the neo-Dorian manner.

'Bredon Hill' has attracted many musical aspirants. In his *Shropshire Lad* cycle (1904), Somervell fits two of Housman's verses to a longish, tranquil strophe, with modifications for verses 5 and 6, but with a bland return to verse 7, the 'local trouble' now past history. Butterworth's sevenfold intonation, tuneful in a commonplace way, restlessly moves semitonally upwards for new verses, and from major to minor, before recovering the original key, there to startle the ear by a comparative explosion in the last line. All these betray the inveterate English hypothesis that a row of stanzas is to be treated strophically, with just enough disturbance of the common round to make its restoration meaningful; especially when the poet writes directly enough of plain folk to recall folk-song to blunt perceptions, even if his lyrical quality is quite his own. (An offshoot of the English romantic movement that accepts feeling as prior to form, so long as this is not taken too far ?) Even Ireland, most accomplished of setters, not least of Housman, seems to have had difficulty in shaking off this routine, the Hardy settings (1923) being almost the other extreme.

By never relying on reverberations of strophe, except where amplification is expedient, if only to promote later diversions, Vaughan Williams gives, for the analytical observer of his craftsmanship, a clue to its altogether different orbit. None of his successors here, nor Somervell before him, had the motive-power or the resources to emulate him by carrying Housman on his shoulder. The limitations of these near-vernacular readings of the poems—for the harmonic colours have faded—must not be glossed over with the false and often repeated claim that they have 'respected the poet's structure'. Literary stanzas are written to carry a general momentum, but also to succeed and vary in their own right; not to have their corners knocked off by musical regimentation. (Folk-song stanzas, on the contrary, appear to be written to carry just enough variety and continuity to call for a basic recital-tune.) Yet, as Schumann, most sympathetic of poem-setters, remarked (apropos of settings of *Wilhelm Meister* by Joseph Klein), a composer must not shrink from taking a poem in his grasp, as if he might do it an injury. On the contrary, a poem 'should lie like a bride in the minstrel's arm'. This attitude contains a good deal more truth than the caution of the literary musician. The aesthetic impact of language and its forms must be duly weighed, but a song must absorb its poem, come what may. It is no more a compromise than a purely instrumental piece.

If work at the *English Hymnal* was worth many symphonic drafts to the music editor, this cycle alone was worth all its harmonic momentum as an effective jolt out of the classical rut, pointing to new paths in a degree without parallel. For, apart from some Gallic pellucidity of texture, it was not through Ravel's influence that the present situation was growing fruitful, though a musical tourist might have described the *engloutie* touch of 'Bredon Hill' as 'just like Debussy'. The main lines of emancipation have been indicated. The connoisseur of a certain type may resist such meticulous annotation of what he has already known 'by heart'. He may partly be answered by the rejoinder of Sibelius, when he heard that, at a rehearsal of one of his symphonies, an orchestra had complained of being instructed in what they 'knew by heart': 'Yes, perhaps they know it by heart—but not according to the book' (Simon Parmet, *The Symphonies of Sibelius*, p. 55). I for one cannot remember when these songs did not strike me by their fresh texture and absorbed moods. Yet I have found that a fresh rehearsal of salient detail has clarified the radical nature of the advance in style. The mere top-line observer will miss the clash of key, the two-plane harmony, and the interplay between mode and semitonal scale, which mark the encounter with Housman. Without some such clue, he leaves *On Wenlock Edge* unaware of its historic position in the composer's progress, as a remarkably early link with third-decade workmanship. One may well respond to these later works without seeking for precedent; but the precedent is there.

MYSTICAL SONGS

The *Five Mystical Songs* (1911), for baritone, chorus and orchestra—reducible to baritone and piano—add little to the general experience of

Vaughan Williams's musical nature, as so far observed. These songs owe much of their welcome to their collocation with Herbert's homely mysticism. Each is a straightforward juxtaposition of strophes or balancing sections, followed or divided by new matter, and the texture is too reactionary to be distinctive. Harmony derived from various modes in turn (the chief feature of the much sung 'The Call'), a restless but steadily pegged tonality, and a firm turn to the major by way of epilogue, musically unpersuasive, and a weak text, are prevailing features. 'Let All the World' maintains an inner exuberance without going much further.

Four Hymns for tenor, viola and piano (for the Worcester Festival, 1914, and hence performed after the War)—there is also a setting for viola and strings—is in a similar vein, with a different poet each time. The modal is once again assumed to be the good, finally pressed home by a recurrent and Holstian (or Purcellian) descending scale and repeated strophes, in a setting of Bridges's version from the Greek of the time-honoured 'lamplighting' hymn to Christ. It would not be hard to discover the modal elasticity, textural flow and declamatory freedom which separates this song from the Mixolydian *Blackmore by the Stour*. Yet the reliance on mode is ominous. The Dorian basis of 'Lord! Come Away!' similarly limits the degree with which the return of the *Hosanna* refrain to the central key makes the cry of the stones in the mind's transformed temple not only articulate but ecstatic. So with the frail Phrygian finish, in the next song (Watts's 'Who is this Fair One?'), to the passionate and indeed fantastic emanations of a communal conscience, couched, as Howes notes, in the manner of the *Song of Solomon*. The sliding chords of 'Come, Love' (Crashaw) are more significant, and even more so their organic role. The set as a whole betrays too much raw material to achieve the intensity claimed for it.

So much for the first stimulus of texts, apart from fully choral works. It is obvious that the problems of fitting music to literary moods and structures engaged the composer as he developed his early style. Two early orchestral pieces, *In the Fen Country* and the first *Norfolk Rhapsody*, must now be mentioned, fortified by the knowledge that the composer found it worth while to re-orchestrate them in 1935 and 1925 respectively. The *Rhapsody* bears a direct relation to the composer's collecting expeditions of 1905. The other piece is stated by the composer, in his note at the end of the score, to have been composed in

IN THE FEN COUNTRY

April, 1904 (revised 1905, 1907). Reported lost in 1920, it re-appeared later.

IN THE FEN COUNTRY

While, then, its title evokes a-wandering in Norfolk, *In the Fen Country* may be assumed to have preceded the Norfolk journeys, and to constitute the composer's first developed piece. It takes a quarter of an hour to play, and is on the elaborate side. Its texture[1] has a contrapuntal air, with quasi-fugal entries of the main theme, and at the same time readily passes to liquescent sonorities in an equally melting tonality, enhanced by the interplay of a wind band of twenty-one and strings frequently in nine parts. The structure also is subtle. A link between the first fugato, a transitional phrase in the wind (recalling 'Bushes and Briars', second phrase) and a faster but dignified cadential feature, is

Ex. 14

confirmed in conditions of a receding tonality; a theme in the oboe, initially but not otherwise related to the first theme, leads to new matter in an often dense texture, now contrapuntal, now impressionist; restatement is clear but oscillating, both in tonality and in a capricious background of tremulous strings, and the brass theme, cadential in a new sense, is absorbed in a slow ding-dong gravitation down the whole-tone scale, countered by the ascent of violins to an acoustic vanishing-point. In consonance with this feeling of levitation, the music dissolves gradually (as such), as the first theme, unilinear once more, is heard on the violas, diminishing from twelve to one player, and the intonation (Dorian mode) is left to reach silence on the fifth degree, not the first.

---

[1] In the indication of relative octave in the statement of an orchestral line or progression, 8 (ft., as for an organ pipe) will designate the passage *at the pitch quoted*; 16, 32, 64, one, two, three octaves lower; 4, 2, 1, $\frac{1}{2}$, one, two, three, four octaves higher. The duplication may or may not be literal, but will be substantial enough to constitute a perceptible second or third range of colour, the lowest octave being usually the pivotal octave, with the higher ones sharpening its edges, in so far as they are of the same quality. (See Ex. 15.)

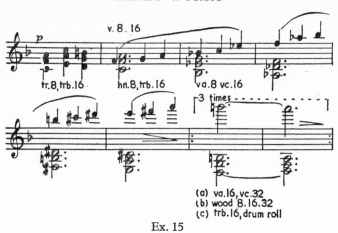

(a) va.16, vc.32
(b) wood 8.16.32
(c) trb.16, drum roll

Ex. 15

It is quite conceivable that the 're-orchestration' of 1935 may have covered extensions such as Ex. 15 and after. But, considered as 1904 music, the pivotal use of the chord of the minor third degree in a turn to the tonic major (or, if you prefer, the conflation of 1–3 in the Phrygian mode with 3–5 in the Mixolydian) is noticeable, and even more the characterization of a theme by this means. This feature is much more characteristic of the third decade. Again, the anticipation above of passages such as the prelude to the last movement of the *Pastoral Symphony* places this piece as progressive. It will always sound fresh, and has been neglected. I could not say in what sense Pakenham finds it 'a truthful impression of that flat wind-swept East coast', or why the composer encouraged her to 'dig' that coast for origins. Not even the opening Dorian motive is folky. If he had called it 'Mist over Russell Square', it would not have sounded less characteristic. If it comes to the tang of modal idiom, there is no more monopoly in Norfolk than in Transylvania. The very folk-songs of a county have a way of turning up six counties away. But possibly the writer has orchestral colour in mind.

NORFOLK RHAPSODY

How should the people's songs be given back to the people? Principally, as Sharp and Vaughan Williams agreed, by providing tune and text with a piano accompaniment or vocal setting. But there might be something, too, for the Queen's Hall orchestra and their audiences. Hence the three *Norfolk Rhapsodies*, planned like a folk-song symphony.[1] The second and third have been withdrawn; and one, indeed, is enough. The first, now scored for full orchestra, introduces three tunes from King's Lynn, more seaport than Norfolk; originally there were five. The tunes succeed and combine as follows (x represents free development, and arabic numerals the verses):

(Read from left to right)	Tune I	$x\ 1\ 2\ x\ \ 3\ x$		4	x
	II	1	$\left.\begin{array}{l}x\end{array}\right.$		
	III		$1\ 2\ 3\ \left\{\begin{array}{l}x\\ x\end{array}\right.$	x	

[1] Formal precedents include Glinka's *Karaminskaya* (two tunes), Balakirev's *Overture on Three Russian Themes* and, more important and sadly unknown, his delightful *Russia*—nominally a documentary display of three periods of national history but of firm musical substance and structure—and Rimsky-Korsakov's sinfonietta (op.31), which with three movements (Scherzo-finale) and eight tunes must now (see below) hold the all-comers record for quantity and size. Even the last of these works, apart from its conventional and stylized contrasts of tempi, goes little further with its potpourri of tunes than a skilful succession of changing backgrounds. The tunes are all major, minor, or more minor than modal. They impart little of the freshness that Vaughan Williams's *Rhapsody* draws from the underlining of the individual degrees to which his pentatonic tunes gravitate. This, at least, must be said. It is clear from Rimsky-Korsakov's disingenuous comments on the concoction of traditional songs that he regarded folk-song as material to absorb, not to release as a catalyst.

As originally planned, the first *Norfolk Rhapsody* presented something like the first movement of a symphony, with an Adagio prelude leading to an Allegro. The second rhapsody compounded a slow movement with a scherzo-like interlude. The third rhapsody was a quick march with interlude. The first rhapsody contained five tunes, two in the Adagio, and three in the Allegro. The second and third rhapsodies contained three and four tunes. Evidently performance exposed the weaknesses of the tune-abundance and three-fold sequence. 'Vociferous applause' (*Musical Times,*? October, 1907, quoted in Young, 33) and the swing of 'Ward the pirate' could not redeem the perfunctory touch of the third rhapsody and like the second it was withdrawn. Then, the surviving rhapsody must have been re-shaped. 'A basket of eggs' (see *The Penguin Book of English Folk Songs*, edited by Vaughan Williams and A. L. Lloyd) was dropped from the Adagio, and 'Ward the pirate' from the Allegro. 'The captain's apprentice' became the principal theme, and 'On board a ninety-eight' an interlude, possibly extended. Presumably the reverberation of the Adagio now followed as a matter of course. Thus the ample disposition of the tunes, as now known, was actually the result of elimination of basic material.

The *Fantasia on English Folk-Songs* compounded an Allegro, a slow movement and a Finale that ultimately included *allegro* features. It bore the sub-title, *Studies for an English Ballad Opera*. Whether this contained a presage of certain elements in *Hugh the Drover*, it is futile to conjecture. But it shows a pre-occupation that might have become fatal, and did not end with *Hugh*. (See the account of these works in Edwin Evans's second article, in the *Musical Times*, 61, p. 304 (May, 1920), which appears to be based on first-hand information.)

It is unnecessary to repeat previous comment on the harmonization of folk-songs, and on the use of folk-tunes in repetition without any justifying text (see p. 117). Here, fresh instrumentation must be regarded as a means to continued 'reification', in the absence of a text. Let us consider the musical consequences of using the folk material, apart from cutting up the music into sections. The first tune ('The captain's apprentice') has a plastic measure of mainly three beats. A firm *a b b* pattern invites orchestral antiphony. Melodically, it may be summarized as post-pentatonic. In degree-emphasis, it has a firmly shaped 5 7 5 1 curve. The *x* sections (clarinet, sepulchral bass) derive from this. The opening thus prepares for the tune, as, more subtly, an adumbration in the first movement prepares for the later emergence of 'The Peacock' in Bartók's first quartet. It is left to the harmonization to move from a primitive background to sophisticated colouring, including the minor chord of the fourth degree and later a final interrupted cadence. The second tune ('A bold young sailor'), a steadily triple measure, simply repeats one phrase, and is thus handy for interpolation. Its main curve is 1 3 8 5 4 1 with the barest trace of an Aeolian minor sixth. The third tune ('On board a ninety-eight') has the closest construction, a confident four-square *a b b a*, and a clear antiphony of 8 7 5 and 4 3 1 in its main phrase. It is the most suitable material for the wear and tear of changing semitones, tonality and orchestral entry.

The musical interest thus lies in the free impact of these unyielding patterns and primitive intonations, distinguished, as the figures imply, by changing shapes within a common pentatone rather than by any more positive melodic trend. Certainly, it does not sound in the least like 'Down among the dead men' (Stanford). In 1905 this seaport piece must have come like a breath of Atlantic air in Regent Street. But the total impact remains sectional, derivative and lacking in any occasion except the imagined secrets of a Norfolk harbour. Manifestly the unhappy captain and the rollicking veteran of the two main songs have no connection. As a clue to the composer's direction, the *Rhapsody* is revealing but inconclusive. The fruits are to be found in *On Wenlock Edge* and elsewhere. It is superfluous to pursue conjecture on the similarly liberating but limited scope of 'Ward the pirate' and the other material which made up the second and third *Norfolk Rhapsodies* of 1907 and the *Fantasia* (not *Suite*) *on English Folk-songs*, performed in the Promenade Concerts, 1910, and queerly hinting at 'an English Ballad Opera'. Two pieces, *Harnham Down* and *Boldre Wood*, Adagio and Scherzo, followed the rhapsodies to oblivion (Young 33, 124).

THE WASPS

If Dorian blood is found in the men of Shropshire, what may not be expected of the veterans in the music for *The Wasps* (Cambridge, 1909)[1]? However, in the sparkling overture which has for too long represented Vaughan Williams to most orchestral audiences, mode is not at once apparent. The litigiousness of the Athenians (assumed in Aristophanes's title) is portrayed by a pertinent motto-theme, a contentious flattened fifth and an uncontrolled trill or whirl; bustling officialdom stumbles into a circle of dapper whole tones, conveniently reduced to a normal major phrase later. Only in the third and more familiar violin-horn theme can one detect a reliance on mode for a celebration of the distinctively old-fashioned ways that are represented by Philocleon and his patriotic zealots. It can be recalled in Ex. 6*a*, in which context its intrinsic rejection of unilinear movement is explained. It remains a rigid, unyielding march-tune, so that even when it is finally interrupted by intrusive officialdom, one knows that it will pick up the step nine paces later.

Consequently, the midway arrival of the serene tenor theme, destined to lyricize the mellowing of Philocleon under his son's tutelage but here absolutely adventitious, has something of the pastework touch of the lighter operatic overture. Its later combination (full wind and harp *v.* strings) with the release of a current of officialdom, in the loose contrapuntal manner of Berlioz (*Herminie*, *Roméo*: Romeo at the ball), may have gone down at Cambridge, after Parry's *Clouds*, but it is too contrived to stand repeated renderings in the concert hall. One must not suppose that it only takes good tunes to bring a symphonic movement home. The overture is a sharp-witted tribute to a buoyant, truculent and historic democracy, in which puissant nations of every constitution would be glad to find themselves. With the constant demand for a short, small-orchestra overture of professional quality, this incidental piece has had a fortunate reception, somewhat out of proportion to its abiding quality.

The style of the dozen-odd developed movements in the incidental music that follows is equally erratic. One may contrast the modal hymn to Apollo (the brooding introduction to this has been mentioned as a precedent for Ex. 7*a*) and the experimental and much more striking opening of the choral Parabasis (12), which can draw upon *L'Après-midi d'un faune* for a clue-theme to the quest of 'something new'

---

[1] The autograph scores are in the Fitzwilliam Museum, Cambridge.

without losing all sense of style. Then, there are the hearty, equalitarian processional chorus (which survives as *Marathon* in *Songs of Praise*, in search of a widening world-conscience), and the final set of dances.[1] In the last, one may detect preliminaries for the folk-dance ballet, *Old King Cole*, written for the Cambridge branch of the E.F.D.S. (1923). The latter was regarded by Sharp as something of a culmination of modern folk-dance practice, the antithesis of mime, but musically it is a medley of old and mock-old. In *The Wasps*, in short, the composer responded readily to different interludes with different levels of appeal, and left them to adjust themselves.

He did, however, authorize an orchestral suite of four detachable movements. The first, called Entracte, was originally an introduction to Act 2 in the Cambridge version, recalling the self-pitying ditty of the old men in Act 1. It has a piquant lilt and more, with its processing of a rise of a minor third (5–7 in the Dorian mode) in manifold style, with a nice piece of steadying counter-melody to freshen the restatement; an apt apéritif before the solemn address to Apollo. The march of the pots-and-pans witnesses, from the mock-trial scene, stresses the puppetry in a pleasant exploitation of a falling minor third in the bass, and of a Phrygian 2–7–1 as cadential pattern, for a perky and compact tune.[2] The trumpet (muted, of course) and supporting piccolo, two octaves up, are nicely balanced by violins and wood. The march here has an interlude, not in the vocal score or any autograph version. It is derived from the song at the end of Act 2, in which the chorus celebrate their waspishness *per se* ('pollachou skopountes'). It is a square tune of 8–8 bars, bluntly repeated (8–8 8), as was carefully avoided in the original setting. It assumes the pulsation of a folk-dance, and is overpowering for its context. Surely an impulse from this episode jogged the composer when he wrote the queer interlude for the Scherzo of his eighth symphony.

In the second Entracte, intended for a prelude to the feast in Act 3, the hollow pomp of assembly is severely exposed by the much more characteristic and suggestive middle section, not found elsewhere. The latter contains the germ, perhaps, of more incisive later episodes, such as the alto-oboe entry at the beginning of the development of the *Pastoral*

---

[1] Introduced by four topical numbers (full score).

[2] Presumably it was during this march that an orchestral player at Cambridge was directed 'to shake a bag full of broken china ... Wedgwood, of course' (the composer informed his Wedgwood cousin), 'it is the only china which would make the right sound!' (*R.C.M. Magazine*, 55. 18).

Symphony finale. As it is, this movement fits in awkwardly. Its functional tone is heavy for a minuet and weak for a final solid movement before the closing ballet. The last movement is a compression of the closing music, without the invocations to the dance: the dances of the first son of Carcinus (nine unit beats to the bar, wavering Mixolydian mode in C), of the second son (fifteen beats, G major with Lydian touches), of all three sons (six beats, Mixolydian in C), and the general version of the third son's dance (three beats, neo-modal in C). The music is thus, in a compression of the original stage detail, economically individualized. In the final sequence, the cumulative energy and oscillating tones of the bass may recall the obsessions of Byrd's variation-set, *The Bells*. Hearing it as a purely orchestral piece, one is conscious of square dance-measures and of repeated figures, without the dancing to make them persuasive, and without the vocal impulse to give them meaning. Yet there seems no place for it in the dance-room, and so the compromise has to be accepted, or else oblivion.

As a parallel to *A Sea Symphony*, the overture and suite form a reminder of the less studied music in the composer's mind at this time, more racy and less tied to a text, matching the splendours of a sea-girt existence with the insouciance of an earlier and historic defiance of the invader from the East. It must be admitted, however, that the comparative popularity of this suite is rather odd. Its reflection of the original illustrative music, never now heard as such, is missed, and the conflation of entractes and finale inevitably lacks shape.

Vaughan Williams's music for the Cambridge production of *The Wasps* was preceded by that of Tertius Noble (1897), which is true to its Victorian period. The light but symmetrical first subject of the overture, and the fervent second subject, have much in common with the craftsmanship of Edward German. Noble's jaunty B flat setting, in nine-metre, of the chorus, 'Long ago we were sturdy in the dance' (Act 2), bestriding a rising 5 1 3 5 curve and back, makes a good foil for the harmonically romantic colour of the later rendering in a Mixolydian E. On the other hand, when it comes to the old contemptibles' celebration of their part in past battles, it is chiefly the hardiness of *Marathon* which places it above Noble's 'early-major' tune, incidentally with a V. W. triplet for '*O . . . spec*-tators' that sounds prophetic. It was a start. Of later parallels, Bantock's overture to *The Frogs* (1935), one of his many overtures for Athenian plays of the same period, has vigour but an uncertain style. Its croaking sounds are more extra-musical than the buzzing agitation of *The Wasps*, which maintains a flattened fifth (#4–8) as the provocative but coherent start of a piece whose major-key assertions suffer distraction and oscillation to creative purpose.

In 1913 Vaughan Williams wrote incidental music for five plays at the Stratford-on-Avon festival, at which Frank Benson was producer. (Benson was moving in the trail of Kean and Irving, who had brought composers from Sullivan to Elgar into the theatre.) Lady Benson later presented the music that had come into her possession to the Memorial Theatre Library: autograph scores of music for the normal orchestra, and a few numbers for the stage, with some voice-parts.[1] The plays were *Richard II, Henry IV: Part 2, Richard III, Henry V* and *The Devil's Disciple*. The music for the last consisted merely of three arrangements: the march from *Judas Maccabaeus* and a verse of 'Yankee Doodle', divided by 'The British Grenadiers', prescribed but not scored. (What 'Corno di basetto'—G.B.S. as music critic in the 'nineties—thought about this is not, I think, recorded.) The *Henry V* music, apparently a full-dress affair, survives in two songs: 'J'aimons les filles' (for Act 3. 7) and the Agincourt song. Their numbering (20, 21) points to much other material, not found here and probably destroyed.

The *Richard II* set (four wood, three brass, strings and percussion) accounts for fifty of the eighty pages of the main score, but most of its thirty-two numbers, for orchestra or for performers on or off stage, are entrance-music or fanfares (cornet) of a few bars, and there is no attempt at any portraiture of character, or even of any tragic mood. Of the ten integral numbers, three are fresh, though scarcely original music: a simple march for the King's entrance, consisting of a square tune with an equally square interlude in the minor (key, sixth-degree); a two-verse *Agnus Dei* refrain (soprano solo and organ), presumably for the sentenced men (3. 1 *fin*), in an old-hymn style, reminiscent of *Iste confessor* (Rouen) in line and tonality; and a short ominous prelude to Act 5, whose blunt oscillating fourths chance to prepare for *Vanity Fair* (1951). The remaining seven numbers are all settings of traditional melodies: folk-song and folk-dance tunes, a carol-like rendering of a Mixolydian plainsong (*English Hymnal*, 176) and the Requiem plainsong. The main interest is thus purely genetic since the selection of

[1] Mr. Patrick Donnell, manager of the Memorial Theatre, drew my attention to the existence of this music, and Miss Robinson, assistant librarian, furnished me with some corroborative details and with the information about the Jonson masque, below.

source has no particular dramatic significance. For here, in turn, are many now familiar figures: 'Greensleeves', (entrance of queen and followers); 'Princess Royal' (later in *Sea Songs* for military band) for Bolingbroke's entry (3. 3); 'The springtime of the year' (later adopted in *Five English Folk Songs* and the *Six Studies for Violoncello*), with 'Bonny sweet Robin', presumably for the queen's entrance (3. 4); 'I'll go and enlist' (see below), translated into a military march for Bolingbroke's 'Lords, prepare yourselves' (before his coronation); two verses of the tuneful 'Jamaica' (used in the ballet, *On Christmas Night*) for the music in the penultimate scene, apparently for wordless voice and violin with quasi-lute accompaniment; the cheerful tune, to 'Exultet orbis gaudia', which runs to three choral-unison verses for Bolingbroke's final entry; and the traditional Requiem for Richard II.

The natural conclusion is that Vaughan Williams was here already in his mood of 'If folk-song won't save the situation . . .', which will be observed in *Sir John in Love*; and it is interesting to observe that 'Greensleeves' is already associated with the descant to the closing bars found in the opera ($\flat$3–4 5–4|$\natural$3–2 1).[1] The play is left to gather into its flow these stray spurts of melody. Vaughan Williams was later to give *Richard II* a thorough and consistent treatment, though equally spare, number by number (see p. 459). There the material is original throughout, and themes are closely linked with characters, so that the musical conclusion is based on the initial premises.

Of the six main numbers of the nine in the *Henry IV* set, the first and fourth are Elizabethan or Jacobean: an anonymous Alman (*Fitzwilliam Virginal Book*, 14) for the Music at the 'Boar's Head' (2. 4. 240), and Dowland's *Lacrimae Pavan* (strings) for Henry IV lying sick. The finale is the tune (less five bars) of the old carol, 'Angelus ad Virginem', sung to the last verse in a free adaptation more suited to national thanksgiving,[2] for Henry V's final entry, superseding Falstaff's promise to rescue Doll, with an orchestral verse to make a curtain-tune. The other three numbers are settings of: 'Half Hannikin' for the 'merry song' at the 'Boar's Head', another forecast of *Sir John*; 'Princess Royal', now transferred bodily from Bolingbroke to Prince Hal and later to Henry V (five strophes in all); and 'Lady in the dark' for the entrance of Doll (presumably 5. 4). The last was to reappear a decade

[1] See p. 180 for note on use of accidentals in degree-shapes.
[2] 'Gloria tibi, Domine, qui pacem reddidisti
Angelis hominibusque bonae voluntatis
Uno Trinoque Domino sit sempiterna gloria
In saeculorum saecula, Alleluia.'

later, for the affectionate encounter of Doll and Jack (observed by Prince Hal and Poins), as one of the forty folk-tunes of Holst's Falstaff opera, *At the Boar's Head* (see p. 260). 'I'll go and enlist' (*Richard II*) appears earlier in the same work, as the chief motive of Falstaff's blustering challenge to the Prince, mainly as a jaunty morris but for one moment with the Bolingbroke solemnity. Here there is no sign of Falstaff. A prophetic gap.

The *Richard III* music, on the contrary, reveals a queer debt to Holst, for the first appreciable number is the Hampshire 'Dargason' which had appeared, ultimately combined with 'Greensleeves', in the finale of Holst's second military band suite (1911), before its revival in the *St. Paul's Suite* (1913). This is followed by the Requiem as in *Richard II* (here, voices only), now anticipating Edward IV's demise, and a short and amazingly insouciant march for the King's baleful entrance in Act 4. 4; finally, a perfunctory 'repeat-ad-lib.' blend of cornet fanfare and hectic harmony for the horseless monarch. The stark harmony here of B flat–A minor (1–4–6 position) is less horrific than the comparably C–A minor progression at the climax of the sixth symphony, second movement, but the sense of antinomy and the syncopated-tutti gesture are the same. It is a sobering thought that while the first sequence accompanied the angry flight of the common oppressor from the world which he finds unanimously against him, the second is considered by some observers to betoken the imaginative world-citizen's equally disturbed contemplation of a fresh defiance of the rule of law, eloquently summarized by Mr. Adlai Stevenson in December, 1961.

The interest, then, is in the continued cult of native tunes, but also, critically, in the disarming assumption that such tunes are the chief need of drama in music. Altogether there is a singularly faint relation to the composer of the *Sea Symphony*, or even *The Wasps*. But *Hugh the Drover* was round the corner; almost as if Richard III's desperate cry, now amplified in a musically tense but brief moment, had, by a fresh twist of the wheel, called into existence the national opera which the nation needed unconsciously. Less fancifully, the stage contact that had begun at Stratford with folky-traditional music (two folk-tunes, a pavan and a galliard) for Jonson's masque, *Pan's Anniversary* (1905), and had developed at Cambridge and now at Stratford again, was, we may assume, pressing on the composer's imagination, inviting him to take charge. We shall resume our observation of this process in Chapter IX.

FANTASIA ON A THEME BY THOMAS TALLIS

Two works completed the purely orchestral output of what we may now call the early stage: the *Tallis Fantasia* and *The Lark Ascending*. The solemn fantasia on one of Tallis's nine settings for Parker's Psalter, for *tutti* string orchestra, one-desk string orchestra and solo quartet (1910, shortened by revisions in 1913 and 1919 prior to publication in 1920) has taken a firm and peculiar hold on public taste in the past decade, and was thus the inevitable choice for Barbirolli and his orchestra to play *extempore* at the Promenade Concert on the night of the composer's death. The piece absorbs the sixteenth century and the Phrygian mode. But it is also a convergence of earlier Vaughan Williams trends that reverberates into the works of the third decade. It would be a mistake, however, to regard it as more than one side of the composer's development, and its preponderant revival has been a doubtful service to the composer's reputation.

Once again, a strophical process is applied to a textless tune. It is not strictly a theme. It is a setting by Tallis for the doggerel of Parker's Psalm 2, with the caption—in a pretended characterization of each tune that appears in an introductory poem—'doth rage and roughly brayeth'. The characteristic ascent to the keynote was meant for 'The kings arise', and the message is one of denunciation. But in the *Fantasia* the tune is anything but a song of agitation, and it is generally accepted as an intimation of rare quality.

There are three principal features: (1) The whole tune, old-modal in its deliberately rising and falling vocal curve but with harmonic implications developed at once, closely following Tallis's four-part setting of the tenor tune (see Maurice Frost, *English and Scottish Psalm and Hymn Tunes*); (2) the fresh lilt of the ascent in the ninth bar of the tune (identifiable in *English Hymnal*, 92), treated as a unit in a rhapsodic or contrapuntal thread; (3) a derivative oscillating sonority, cadential from the start, with other quasi-automatic progressions into strange tonalities which arise later. The somewhat odd shape of the music is clearly determined by the extended development of the second feature in a fresh tempo, between the second and third of the three strophes which form the framework. Originally there were four.[1]

Stray phrases are linked by means of free chordal movement, with some reference to pivotal keys (mainly of the sixth and fourth degrees

---

[1] The revised score (R.A.M. Lib.) shows, with slight reductions at E, F4 and Y5, the supersession of a whole verse at T7–U3.

175

of the basic Phrygian-minor scale), prompted by the uncommon anti-phony or polyphony of *tutti*, intimate orchestra and solo ensemble (Great, Choir, and Solo organ, so to speak); for example, the transcendent intimacy of the last strophe (violin tune, viola bravura, harmony of tremulous strings on the fingerboard, plucked bass). For the subtle phrase-development, as well as for the modal texture, Palestrina's *Stabat Mater* is a precedent and a likely model, as Fox Strangways pointed out, with special reference to the variants of *Stabat Mater* in *Fac ut ardeat*, *Paradisi gloria* and elsewhere (*Music and Letters*, 1. 2 (April, 1920)). But there are wayward places, in the latter part of the development and in the academic 7–4–1 cadence, which I find too 'churchy' and static.

The abiding interest and the true importance of this *Fantasia* are in the struggle for expression. There is no specially noble quality in Tallis's plodding tune. Nor is there any ground for assuming that the composer's absorption in the given material is more than musical; that it is 'mystical' in approach. The breathless hush that attends certain moments of suspense (the first viola solo, the aftermath of its plenary affirmation) is breathless, indeed, without necessarily suggesting 'the immediacy of the mystic's vision' (Scott Goddard). Strengthened by the *Pilgrim's Progress* associations of the fifth symphony, the cathedral atmosphere (Gloucester, originally) seems to have hung heavily about the work. That does not make the invocation of the modal idiom more, or less, persuasive. As a striking transitional work, resourceful in method, the *Fantasia* claims full study and hearing. Its hold over audiences is an incident of promotional history which will find its due level in the future.

THE LARK ASCENDING

The Lark Ascending, a short piece for violin and small orchestra, is referred in a quotation in the score to Meredith's lark that makes 'our valley his golden cup'; which, incidentally, admits a melodic line in flowing fifths, etc., in the solo, but not the percussive harmony of multiple stopping. The prolonged carolling of the violin floats into and over quasi-rustic strains, plainly harmonized. The connecting link is the fall from the seventh to the fifth degree in the Dorian mode, thus echoing the *Norfolk Rhapsody* in a fresh exploration of familiar melodic ground. It is therefore expedient that the middle Allegretto should sound 'the key of his wild note of truthful' in a more adventurous mood. It does not. If its playful 1–3–4–5 ascent, with a tinkling triangle, instils 'love of earth', so much the worse; the skilfully delayed violin rendering is more an incentive to restatement than anything else. The recovery of the opening tune and cadenza is spontaneous but uneventful, apart from an exquisite final canon in the orchestra. With such a nugatory central section, the much admired violin rapture has more to carry than is commonly admitted, if 'expression, not description' is the professed aim. This 'Romance' is a document in instrumental jubilation of the highest order (a single violin) but also in the limitations of neo-modal music. It was toccata stuff, to store for coming necessity, not to pursue at the moment. It seems now to have been a preliminary study for the viola rhapsody of *Flos Campi*, rather than a pronounced addition to the violin *concertante* repertoire.

Quartet in G Minor

In chamber music, two early quintets (piano, 1904; horn, ?), since withdrawn, were followed by the string quartet in G minor (1908; lost, *c*.1920; revised and published, 1924), written after the course with Ravel. The latter, in four normal movements with a 'minuet' second, is an uneven work but far from negligible. The unevenness lies in a comparison between the considerable outer movements and the weaker inner ones. The first movement, which Young singles out as the 'finest' as opposed to the 'significant' finale, begins in a leisurely, Dorian, 'As I went out' style, and the somewhat prim isolation of the viola tune, as of other melodic interests throughout the quartet, by a 'solo . . . normal' mark in the part, hints at a stilted manner. A second group in E modal major (not quite Mixolydian) and in a slower tempo also makes for preciosity, confirmed in a secondary phrase to be played on the fingerboard—that is, with inhibited resonance—and marked *misterioso*. In the event, all these elements find fresh life in a more animated context of quickening rhythm or vivid harmony. The Sibelius-like transformation of the finger-board phrase at the end of the development is especially piquant. Thus, the ample restatement and clear dénouement in G major is more than a conventional finish. The Minuet is slight throughout and its key of E Mixolydian major an odd turn of tonality, anticipated in the Allegro as an auxiliary of G minor. The slow movement, called 'Romance'—an equivocal title—is hardly justified by its five-beat *cantabile* start or the three-beat and ultimately intense sequel.

The long finale soon takes shape unmistakably in the Rondo capriccioso of its title, with its pronounced, lilting theme, vernacular in trend but not in detail, and auxiliary phrases which would defy anything in the nature of a supplementary subject-group. Hence the question becomes one of balanced episodes and renewed theme. The use of a fresh mode of G major takes care of the latter, and an unpretentious second-episode refrain (viola, violins), adumbrated ethereally on the finger-board in multiple texture, returns later as the prelude to a long coda. There the imitational development of one of the auxiliary phrases of the main theme acquires enough contrapuntal heat to make a unison statement of the G major version of the theme, with harmonic insistence on its special modal features (chords of 2–♯4–6 and ♮7–2–♮4), a stimulating climax.

The detachment of this coda, despite its organic features, makes it almost an epilogue. Young detects anticipations of sixth symphony harmony in the fugue section, and of the fourth symphony melodic stretches in a later procession of fourths. But there is more than echoing fourths in the tortuous motive of 1935. Altogether, this movement has as much constructional ardour as the finale of the later quartet lacks. Admitting, then, the weaker elements, one is surprised that this quartet, whose elasticity and independence were recognized soon after publication (for example, in E. C. Rose's 'appreciation' of the composer in *The Sackbut*, July, 1926), never caught on much, and its total neglect today is a pity.

PHANTASY QUINTET

The *Phantasy Quintet* (1914, published 1921) was designed as an entry for a W. W. Cobbett chamber-music prize, which prescribes a continuous work. Again a viola leads off, now in a formal ascent of quasi-pentatonic 'plainsong' (5 ♮7 1 2 4 5), answered with plain descent, (8 7 5 4 2) by high violin. The impact of this decidedly pentatonic revival, on an ensemble gathered for harmonic progression or directive sonority at selected levels, makes a positive 'Prelude', but the essential curves persist in fresh and salient contributory or intrusive figures. A developed and capriciously polymodal Scherzo in seven-time is followed by a slight Lento interlude (barely twenty different bars) and then a playful finale, in which the violoncello resumes the humorous role begun in the Scherzo, and the pentatone is bandied freely about. Meanwhile the tonality has moved on a path which can be summarized as F modal–D modal minor and major–F modal minor–D modal minor. Thus the cyclic or recurrent-theme pattern of the typical Cobbett prize product was given some fresh stimulus from the modal period, without the burden of any strophe. The degree-figures that have been cited from time to time may remind the calculating listener that the relation to the parallel orchestral works is one of general melodic bias, not of specific curve. In itself, the quintet is stronger for not attempting to cover the ground of four developed movements, although the Scherzo is much the best section.

Toward the Unknown Region

Meanwhile, in a harmonically more conservative vein, Vaughan Williams had produced the work which most led him to broader symphonic trails, besides making the general public aware of a new spirit in music. In 1907 *Toward the Unknown Region* appeared at the Leeds Festival, with Stanford's *Stabat Mater*. Whitman's text, from *Whispers of Heavenly Death*, is so elementary as to sound pompous in declamation. But its restraint invites music, and the composer welcomes the challenge with a succession of appropriate themes for solitary, unprecedented exploration and a firm advance on the great inaccessible. So, rather easily, to a grand epilogue: 'Then we burst forth'. The now familiar bounce from the fifth degree to the tonic and back is made the pivotal curve in most of the remaining entries, and as a means of expression this is severely tested. Here, after the taut quality of a subversive bass on flattened seventh and sixth, cutting the ground below the tonic and other pivots, to enhance 'equipt *at last*', the bald orchestral return just before 'Them to fulfil' sends a spasm of raw experience to mingle with the final and acceptable spiritual and material fanfare.

The texture of this work, with its drifting sevenths from the start, marks the beginning of a new era. It is fresh but tentative, without any radical renunciation of the major and minor scales in the related key-system. That, in spite of this, it served, where Parry's aspiring prophetic cantatas had failed, to evoke and conserve assurances of a vague call to a new, inaccessible life, cannot be referred to Whitman's superior vocability. As the humblest choirmaster discovers, in unison, polyphony and accessory colour, the writing for each voice is compulsive, and the integrity of the whole is greater than the incidents of the moment. It was the beginning of an impression on the English musical world, later summarized by Fox Strangways, 'Whose music do we want on the great occasions of life except this?'.

Ten years later, when it came to remembering those in the First Seven Divisions who had marched, not to distant vistas, but into the blackness of Flanders, the performance of *Toward the Unknown Region* assumed a new meaning for the Service-men, relatives and others who were present for the fresh reception of this strange experimental music in the Royal Albert Hall. For some, no doubt, it was too modern. For others, Fox Strangways might have spoken: and there was much to follow of the same universal character, yet individual and unpredictable in the best sense. The composer made a short, entirely fresh, unison choral setting later (see p. 478).

From this cantata for Leeds, Vaughan Williams turned back, we may suppose, to his sketches of settings of what he at first called 'Whitman Sea Songs'. He ended by writing, not a cycle but four developed movements, which turned into a *Sea Symphony*. The sense of communal ethical affirmation, which Whitman had aroused, persisted, supported by the same kind of conservative liberalism as regards harmonic methods. It would not be inappropriate to consider the symphony in this context, as the major achievement of seven years (1903–10). But for the sake of its symphonic quality, it will be reserved for the next chapter, to be compared with the two symphonies which similarly summarize, between them, the next seven years of musical output (1910–14, 1919–22).

NOTE: In the indications of degree-shape, ♮3 = *major* third (unless it follows ♯3, when it means *minor* third) and ♮7 = *minor* seventh. ♯3, ♯6, and ♯7 refer to the major intervals, and ♭3, ♭6, and ♭7 refer to the minor intervals, except in certain places where it is clear that they refer to augmented and diminished intervals respectively.

VII

Three Symphonies

A symphony is not a mould to be filled. It is a matter of widening context, by means of which a given motive finds its true nature in its different impact in a more splendid setting or after an alien feature; and correspondingly a movement seeks another two or three, as foil or broad extension of mood, to satisfy a composer's major impulse. When the operatic overture had been pruned of sonorous rhetoric and the divertimento of superfluous episodes, the characteristic themes of Haydn and the textual control of Mozart established, for the symphonic habitués at the courts of Vienna and Mannheim and at the Hanover Square Rooms, London, the *sinfonia* of three movements with room for another middle movement. In turn, the wider range of Beethoven and the extended thematic output of Brahms, and the cyclic plan of themes continuing from one movement to another, preserved the four-movement pattern. A substantial opening Allegro, a simple or more extended meditative sequel, a capriciously tuneful or liquescent interlude, converged in a finale that tended to carry the burden of the whole symphony on its shoulders before reaching a sense of fulfilment. In 1910 Elgar was still pointing in the same direction with his first symphony, with an exceptional emphasis on thematic setting as the way of evolution.

Meanwhile this calculated glorification of dance-rhythms, subject to the propulsions of logical development or a convenient substitute, had faced its limitations creatively in the romantic, dedicated finale of Beethoven's ninth symphony. Berlioz, in direct succession, equipped his third symphony (*Roméo et Juliette*) with a choral interpretative role,

181

a familiar dramatic story in the background and a final message of reconciliation. Choral prologue and epilogue thus attend more normal symphonic movements. *La Damnation de Faust* went much further with singers and an anticipated story, but the symphonic spirit persists in the rounded experience and converging moral of each Part. Fascinatingly admonitory, the work became popular with English choral societies. Seldom had such an unredeemable character appeared on the concert stage. A decade later, Brahms, adopting scriptural music in a commemorative context, joined chorus to orchestra in the symmetrical stages of his early *Requiem*, a choral suite with many symphonic thrusts behind its homiletic tone.

Mahler, after resorting to vocal interpolations in earlier symphonies (2–4), took the redemption of Faust as the chief theme of his eighth symphony (1907, performed 1910). An altogether monumental movement around the Faust finale is introduced by a spacious prelude on a romantically congener text, 'Veni Sancte Spiritus'. Of these two exclusive movements, the first is in the nature of a choral Allegro; the second develops new material with the old in a succession of different tempi, without fully establishing (as is commonly stated) slow and scherzo sections, and proceeds to an epilogue to end all epilogues. This thorough-going choral symphony is the work of a composer who, while master of many orchestral styles, was inclined to regard a symphony as a stage in a vision of life which might at any moment call for textual declamation to interpret it in a more succinct manner. In the eighth symphony, Mahler packed into one symphony what he had previously spread over three or four symphonies, and he was more concerned with carrying out his chosen programme to its just and resounding climax than with any underlying apotheosis of the dance on the Beethoven model.

Meanwhile, in *Gerontius* Elgar had harnessed a chorus and solo-singers to the full symphony orchestra in relays of communal experience, soliloquy, song and orchestral link, matching stages of a dream-transition from death to another life in music dominated by *idées fixes*. Without being positively symphonic, the oratorio drew audiences towards a sustained expression only paralleled by Wagner.

Such was the dubious precedent and outer stimulus for Vaughan Williams's approach to choral symphony as such, whatever practical motives, such as the demands of the Leeds Festival Chorus, may have led him in that direction. A chorus and soloists cannot be treated just as an extra band. Their capacity to utter human thoughts, as well as natural sounds, gives them a paramount position. On the other hand, a choir cannot usually be regarded as a professional body on a par with an orchestra. Their limitations and their quick reactions to what is intelligibly singable must both be respected.

Vaughan Williams, like Mahler, believed in music with a meaning, and he even followed him in one respect by developing one Whitman setting in another and larger. Any extensive selection of Whitman is likely to be engaged, first, with his characteristic 'chant of personality', such as he found in the 'divine average' of humanity and its 'untold latencies', especially in the way of comradeship; secondly, with the projection (as in *Toward the Unknown Region*) of this 'song of myself' into a 'song of the universal' by a combination of vision and bold exploration, with the imperative question-answer ('What are you doing, young man?') firmly disposed in the background.

Vaughan Williams's first decision was to choose from one jubilant song and another those poems or stanzas which most consistently and evocatively lead from common experience at sea to the boundless vistas of every pioneer. He took three poems from the group in *Leaves of Grass* called *Sea Drift*, for the first three movements,[1] adding an odd but convenient stanza from part 8 of the patriotic exhibition-piece, *Song of the Exposition*, to begin the symphony with a broad salute to seamen and to avoid an otherwise intimate start. (He thus left intact the first poem, 'Out of the Cradle', which Delius had set and entitled *Sea Drift*.) For concluding movement he drew upon *Passage to India* (parts 5, 8, 9), a document in symbolic recital of restless exploration, finding at the critical point a true sense of purpose on trackless seas. For this last stage he did not spare himself the structural problems of an expansive, effusive text. Yet it may be presumed that he adopted it with at least some inkling of what he would do with it eventually.

So far, then, the composer was committed to (1) a joyous celebration of the mariner's life and the universal flag of heroism ('A Song for all Seas, all Ships'); (2) meditation on the tremendous, binding unity of all men and nations ('On the Beach at Night Alone'); (3) observation of the panorama of waves in the wake of a great ship ('After the Sea-Ship', here entitled 'The Waves'); (4) a journey of the mind through the universe, from Eden to the unlimited-unknown (here called 'The Explorers'). The resort to Largo and Scherzo between the two outer movements was plain, but not any other symphonic procedure.

For the first movement, the composer accepts a boisterous flow of

---

[1] A sequel, 'Aboard at a ship's helm', was set but discarded. Echoes of this appear in the finale (K9).

imagery and declamation, choral and solo, propelled by orchestral motives as convenient. Primary themes and colours (the initial fanfare and striking ♭6–1 harmonic progression) merge into more incidental ones without any suggestion of the bi-focal curve of sonata-form, or, indeed, a coherent first subject, except that it is in the orbit of D major. Accordingly, the late appearance of a clear melodic line,

Ex. 16

restoring D—previously and casually released, in distracting conditions of key, as a background of the initial port scene—is memorable, quite apart from its evocative context. The climax of the poem explains: 'Token of all brave sailors. . . .' This must be the central point of the movement. (Perhaps more demonstrably so after the history of the half century since. Certainly a rehearsal after the news of the sinking of the *Titanic* drove the idea home to one Oxford choir, as I was informed.) The rest—development of the new theme on the widest lines, overwhelming *più mosso* rhetoric, a subdued return to the opening imagery with closing fade-out—is a matter of applied method. This *tema eroica* thus appears as the primary afterthought of development in a free-and-easy pattern of statement and restatement in D major, not otherwise symphonic in manner. We may pause here to recall one point and anticipate another. The modal-minded listener is bound to notice the rise to the sharpened seventh in the new D major tune, not less firmly instilled on account of the accompanying harmonic sevenths that save it from banality. The more romantic listener, taking his cue from the 'recitative' and 'chant' of the first stanza and the orchestral lead for the second, will consider this as a step towards the later quiet and aphoristic celebration of named and unnamed heroes in the *Scott* and *Coastal Command* film-music. A listener thus committed, responsive to

4. *Sea Symphony*: first page of an early draft of the vocal score (autograph)

5. *Riders to the Sea*: a page from the full score (autograph)

the pioneer call of the symphony, may be a little indulgent towards the rawness of 'a pennant universal', as representing the click of restatement, and he will accept as a finish the simply receding vision of the coda: 'all men, all ships.' For the rest, this recovery may seem inexplicably casual, the termination frail. Yet peroration would have been fatal.

The second movement moves from desultory *arioso* (the absence of strophe is perceptible here) to a choral interlude with a sudden, declamatory climax, leaving it to the orchestra to recover the opening solitary move without vocal prompting. The initial pondering ♭6–1 progression may as such recall the exhilarating opening of the previous movement to analytical ears, though the penultimate restatement of the motto, heralding the coda, was different (♮7–1). Moreover, the later spondee-anapaest motive of the horn actually reflects the rhythm, though not the mode, of the baritone's 'rude, brief recitative', now absorbed in calmly flowing harmony. These and other features help to keep the movement going, with a lingering return of the horn theme to round off the orchestra's near-automatic simulation of the 'husky song'. Otherwise this movement drags somewhat before and after the moment of vision. The harmony is too compromising, and the horn motive cannot stand the exposure of reduced speed. A similarly raw falling third degree marks a corresponding theme in the next symphony, but there only as a background. The seismic message of unity remains.

In 'The Waves', Whitman indulged his reportage in surging lines that a cynic might regard as ideal material for the amplification of a naval panorama when there is a gap in scheduled events. The final 'following the stately and rapid ship' almost asks to be submerged in orchestral boisterousness, as here. This, then, is the sea as the tourist finds it, ceaseless but conducive and stimulating, the Cunarder's dream. There is no moral under the surface. Vaughan Williams goes for a sonata-form of clear features and unassailable broad detail: a minor movement with a strongly rhythmic first subject and a delayed, but unmistakable, tuneful second subject in the major key of the third degree, and later of the first degree in impatient repetition.[1] This does

[1] Apart from its clear and traditional keys of 'relative' and tonic major, the whole context of this subject determines its entry as belated but ultimately complementary—as melodic and freshly cadential after the first subject's rhythmic and scattered phrases and the transitional matter's impressionism, but not different in genre from the opening. Howes's 'Trio' or interlude (followed by Pakenham), implying diversion instead of completion, is quite unacceptable, and his 'Begins in G minor' (the first *chord* chancing to be of this description) an utter disregard of the whole context. The simple Trio in G was soon re-cast.

not prevent him from indulging in all sorts of semitonal and whole-tonal features. In 1910 the first impression on choirs, and potentially on audiences, was the extreme difficulty and wryness of the mere notes. (For the last two bars there are now parts for the wind 'only when there is no chorus'.[1]) Today, the whirl of natural declamation and orchestral bravura, brief lyrical exultation, 'motley procession' of whole-tone scales, meeting from extremes in the cumulative fragmentation of slowing movement, and final choral abandonment (in the glorious trail of the whirling close of the Gloria of the *Mass in D*), is not altogether convincing, owing to the oscillations of melodic style.

The exultant major tune, congener of 'Then we burst forth' (*Unknown Region*), is even supported by orchestral snatches of a Norfolk folk-song 'The bold Princess Royal', *tutti*. This triumphant but fleeting collocation of folk-tune fragments, where no folk are, seems a strange intrusion, in so far as it is recognizable. It never re-appears. So with earlier fragments of 'The Golden Vanity'. May one detect the influence of Purcell's *Welcome Song*, 1686 (edited by Vaughan Williams), in which a folk-dance appears?

On the whole, the salty vigour of this Scherzo in G balances the absorption of the slow movement. Its sweeping interest in a vivid, trenchant relationship of voice and voice, chorus and orchestra, classical tonality and the stimulus of other pitch-sets, makes a well-timed prelude to an urgent but wandering finale.

'The Explorers' is occasionally performed separately. This is actually authorized for each movement, as a concession to choral societies who cannot cope with the whole work in performance. The nominal appeal to divine intervention (part 5) apparently secured the movement one hearing, at least, at the Three Choirs Festival, where its independent impression was considerable. Nor does this movement further the first in any obvious turn of mood, theme or structure. Its very key, E flat, is an absolute repudiation of D, an almost prophetic relationship.

The mysterious exposition unfolds *de novo* in the contemplation of

---

[1] When the choral entry is considered too uncertain. The report of the first Cambridge performance, under the composer (*Cambridge Review*, June 8, 1911), mentions that the third movement 'has been re-written for orchestra alone'. I have not been able to trace such a version. The late C. Armstrong Gibbs, who was up at Cambridge at the time, told me (in 1960) that he could not remember any such occurrence. The account in *The Yorkshire Post*, October 13, 1910, quoted by Young, makes it clear that at Leeds the Scherzo 'was a piece of virtuosity in choral singing'.

marine expanse and the focussing on man's primeval and restless wanderings, chased by blank inner misgivings (distant SSAA choir). (The composer's cheerful ascription of his first theme to a motive in the fifth vocal bar of *Gerontius* need not be taken seriously; nor the much greater chance resemblance to the march tune in the *Wasps* overture.) The modal-minded will feel more at home in the exodus from Eden, the non-modal aspects of which were, however, demonstrated in Chapter IV (Ex. 6*b*). The antique flavour is piquant enough, furthered by the distant choir's sliding harmonic fourths, to add splendour to the triumphant return of the main theme, conclusive if it were not in a fresh key (G), with attendant fugal polyphony and a tremendous cadence, 'The true son of God shall come'; an extravagant phrase, though it should not sound so here. But to what does this lead?

Musically, two things in quick succession. First, a joyous suggestion of the initial choral motive of the first movement. This may seem very far-fetched, but the composer certainly intended this motive to be remembered, and he has repeated it longingly at the end of the first movement. Then follows a modulation back to E flat for a second start. Thus, the connection with the heroic 'Song for all Seas' is laid down for further confirmation and a second departure from E flat, which remains the keynote, inaugurated.

The composer's problem is to keep this fresh development adventurous and at the same time symphonic. No one can miss the direct appeal, true to Whitman (parts 8 and 9) yet much more lyrical, of that prolonged but rhapsodic duet, solemn self-committal, and the scattered sally forth (the sole literary contact with Delius's third 'Song of Farewell') in a pungent atmosphere of salt water and uninhibited, unenslaved sea-chant. The choral imperative, 'Steer forth', prepares for the final quiet establishment of unresting oars. But the real triumph of this movement is that, quite apart from the thematic contact with the first, the initial outburst of the baritone is capable, in a refined orchestral statement in the context of the same motto-theme, of framing an epilogue to the whole symphony. It can be interpreted by the sense of infinite drift to which the dream-journey has at last come, but it still reverberates in its own right, as persuasively as the first subject of Mozart's symphony in E flat (K.543).[1] The historically minded will observe the

---

[1] The impact of first-movement and baritone themes is renewed intermediately in the fifty-six 'optional' bars that prepare for the final self-committal. These now seem superfluous. In an articulate performance the stanza beginning

final bearing on the sixth and fifth degrees, as in early major folk-tunes. Development and episode are stretched to the upper limit of the symphonic style, but, like the compulsive tune that emerges in the finale of Beethoven's *Choral Symphony*, the 'O we can wait no longer' motive vindicates itself as both the fulfilment of the 'O vast rondure' section (when completed) and the clue to the last stage. 'Passage to more than India!', as Whitman observes to introduce the concluding stage of his fervent venture.

To the Mahlerite may come luxuriant recollections of the final synthesis, in the eighth symphony, of 'das ewig weibliche zieht uns hinan', and adumbrations of 'Veni Sancte Spiritus'; of solo-singers representing every degree of the spiritual scale; of massed and counter-massed choirs, super-orchestra, brass band and organ, with tam-tam and organ for the final touches. For ears so conditioned, the understatement of *A Sea Symphony* must appear a devastating renunciation. The unprejudiced listener notes the absence of the grand peroration possible in *Toward the Unknown Region* but precluded by the text here, and presumes that in accepting it, the composer knew that he could replace the note of triumphal affirmation with a compensating absorption of mood. He may also observe that this sustained recession of tone and incessant cadence, by way of finish—*niente* in later scores—became more than a mannerism with Vaughan Williams. Here it is the final turn in a flood of personal expression. It is this, not mere structural ingenuity or any *tour de force* of meditation, which continues to satisfy listeners that the symphonic purpose of the work has been fulfilled. Those who find it a mere semantic travelogue, somewhat pretentiously prolonged to four movements, miss the basic integrity. So do those who expect the ample flow of clue-theme of *Gerontius*. Convergence, not saturation, is the method of total appeal.

The tentative harmonic style is a more serious consideration, and must, even in the second decade, have irked those who had assumed that mode was leading the composer out of his bondage to classical tonality. The eventfulness of the first and third movements, and the growing tension of style in the last, releases creative energy; the second movement is more tentative. I might add that when the idea of a short introduction to his music was mentioned to Vaughan Williams in 1926 —to which he acceded reluctantly—he made it clear that he wished

'O thou transcendent' is more than dispensable, on top of 'Bathe me, O God, in thee . . . '. The optional cut, inevitably not taken in the Boult recording, eliminates this dubious transition.

A Sea Symphony to receive little or no attention in comparison with the next two symphonies. It was, he thought, a stage that he had passed. The symphony remains his largest work with chorus, and nothing has demonstrably superseded it as such.

What did succeed it, in its genre, was the work enthusiastically entitled *First Choral Symphony* (Leeds 1925), to poems by Keats, with the *Grecian Urn* for slow movement. Of this I must briefly and bluntly suggest that the magnificent virtuosity of the choral and instrumental writing is certainly the first impression, rather than any cumulative sense of symphonic thought. Holst's music too often seems to move at a tangent to its text, as in the slow movement, or, as in the finale, is so engaged by the flow of the poem that it loses its grasp of the total impact.[1]

A LONDON SYMPHONY

A Sea Symphony must have awakened the composer to his symphonic potential not without some struggle. He had used the exigencies of a chosen text to guide his hand and to promote constructive solutions of fresh problems, but these were not indispensable. What next? Something or someone suggested London. (One cannot take literally the composer's now much-quoted statement, in a tribute to George Butterworth, to whose memory the symphony is dedicated, that he owed the idea of a symphony 'entirely to him'. Symphonies originate in themes not blueprints. In so far as the first association of the subject is grey and grim, the idea was, incidentally, true to Whitman's principles: to write plainly on a subject; 'to hammer beauty out of ugliness, not to go where beauty was and leave ugliness to take care of itself' (Fox Strangways). But it also accorded with the composer's own growing prejudices against a too cosmopolitan style in favour of handling matter nearer home. (These were set forth in an article in the *R.C.M. Magazine*, 9. 1 (1912), which Foss put into his book.) This pursuit of local colour has a doubtful appeal, unless the colour is fully integrated.

But musically 'London' is not just a matter of metropolitan lore. It stands for a tremendous community, inarticulate but not unconscious of purpose. Vaughan Williams had no need to worry, as he did a little after early performances, about the limitations of the title.[2] On the

---

[1] Miss Holst, too, regards the symphony as a misconception of text and general design, in spite of its great moments, and the finale as the weakest stage. (*The Music of Gustav Holst*, pp. 76–85.)

[2] He then seemed to prefer 'Symphony by a Londoner', as declared in his own note for the Bournemouth performance on February 11, 1915, and anticipated by Edwin Evans in *The Outlook*, April 4, 1914. I take this phrase to

contrary, it has grown with history, as the epitome of a free community, gorgeous and vulgar but also with latent powers of resistance in all weathers. It was so recognized in performances in the autumn of 1940 at Boston, New York, Cleveland, San Francisco and Cincinnati, undoubted gestures of firm encouragement from a neutral nation. Moreover, during the most forcible and sustained attack that has ever been made upon Britain, the recorded chimes of Westminster, as daily signals of radio identity, conveyed hopes of an emancipated world to stalwart resister-listeners in conquered states. The passing appearances of Big Ben's second and third quarters will continue to strike chords of memory, not only in every visitor, but in citizens of many lands, and a modicum of respect in those who find most reason to curse London.

The imaginative appeal to the stalls and gallery of a widening theatre may be assumed, then, without implying that the symphony is merely picturesque, or that the movements have any concrete programme (the *Cockaigne Overture* has more). This assurance is necessary for a preliminary artistic balance. The formal precedent is Beethoven's third symphony, a token of the mental states of human leadership without descriptive incident, and not the sixth, which observes Knecht's programme in more than the title, in spite of the composer's later attempt to conceal his lapses in the notoriously unconvincing protest, 'more expression than painting'.

The symphony was first performed in March, 1914, and revised considerably before its first publication, in the Carnegie collection of British music, in 1920. A further and slight compression or simplification was published after 1935. There was, at first, a considerable struggle for expression, which is now past, though interesting, history, as may appear later.

An essential clue for symphony, it has been said, is widening context. A *London Symphony* may be expected to stretch the process romantically—the listener is so far committed to appreciation, and indeed

mean, not literally 'by a resident' (Howes), but 'by a man who, native or stranger, knows London life, its richness, vitality and inner strength'. In other words, the change of title would have been trifling. I do not understand the comment of Mr. Olin Downes, of the *New York Times*, on the timely performance of the symphony in New York in November, 1940; 'the lack of any programmatic explanation deprived the symphony of much of its meaning for the audience assembled' (quoted in the *Music Review*, 2. 2. 182). 'London' is clue enough. The clock chimes are unmistakable as such, and no listener will lose any thread from not identifying the 'Lavender' cry, hansom bells, etc. 'In no sense descriptive' was the phrase used by the composer in the early programme note.

promotion, of London's story—but design is paramount. Of the four classically disposed movements, as now performed, the Allegro emerges, and later derives vital matter, from an obviously preludial and independent movement, to be answered at the very end by an Epilogue (so named in the score) of similarly misty-monolithic texture. This Allegro is the most developed structure, and shows an almost classical balance of fertile exposition, imaginative development and a restatement compressed, expansive and increasingly sonorous. The slow movement begins with an intense absorption of mood, which can hold episode and rhapsody and local touches in its orbit and then return to consciousness. The 'Scherzo (Nocturne)' maintains a clear association of subdued themes as the recurrent feature of a diversionary movement. The finale provides a march-like Maestoso, which is strong enough to supersede an intrusive Allegro (originally there was much more of this), but it acquires a subversive mood which spends itself; hence the next Westminster quarter can usher in the Epilogue, forming a sixth movement. Thus each movement covers wide ground in a different way, and a motto theme links the movements unobtrusively and forms a conclusion to the whole symphony just when the finale is breaking up.

In every movement there is a definite gravitation to the opening matter of the main movement, the finale's restatement being only temporary in relation to the Epilogue. There is little sense of late-emerging motive, as in the *Sea Symphony*. The principle is: the wider the emotional orbit, the more essential it is to bring it firmly back to the starting impulse, or to a more thorough-going restatement; to season the fresh with the familiar. With this steady and unmistakable sense of musical relationship, the passing suggestions of London, awakening from dawn to the noise and street-calls of garish day, showing a subdued but lively face at night and pondering to the 'tune' of

> 'Come the three corners of the world in arms
> And we shall shock them'

before settling back to London *per se*—these fall readily into their place in an orchestral symphony. It is not necessary, in fact, to have been a Londoner to understand the composer's full concern here, though there are intimations of things that only Londoners know. This is not a 'riddle' symphony; even less so than Beethoven's *Pastoral*, where the listener might be baffled by the clarinet's *Nachtigall* jubilations in the Adagio.

191

It remains to consider the different impact of each movement. The prologue reveals a line (two tetrachords) that invites extension to a pentatonic pattern and meanwhile to a harmonic epitome of the whole.

Ex. 17

The main Allegro explodes, with an almost transatlantic bark, from this deep 'Westminster Bridge' calm. Apart from obvious assaults on the ear, some perhaps once topical, 'the key of E flat minor is reached by way of G major', as the composer might have described, in his later manner of self-annotation, the conflation of a liquescent G harmony and E flat bass. A somewhat dubious establishment of 'G minor' by the tenors of each group, in what happens to be neo-Phrygian style, with a lapse of whole tones, provides just enough solid ground to render what follows as transitional, although it maintains contact with the primary 1–2–5 ascent of the motto-curve. A massing of wind begins the procession of incidents which may conventionally be termed second subject. As in the Scherzo of *A Sea Symphony*, the orthodox major key of the third degree is installed, and here it lasts up to the climax. The material may be compared before the connection dissolves, not unremembered.

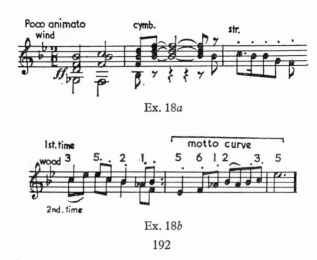

Ex. 18a

Ex. 18b

Ex. 18c

Ex. 18d

Of these, *a* seems to begin 'by establishing G flat by way of B flat'; but here the tables are turned, and it is G flat that gives ground. Meanwhile, the pivotal chord is confirmed as a link, and the now uni-linear melodic thread proceeds pentatonically and perhaps hieratically but with a humorous nonchalance which it is difficult to accept. Sequel *b* lapses into A flat and a rhythmic spasm that so-called critics continue to describe as folk-song style. Actually, the 'melody' is unvocal, consciously pentatonic major and harmonic, piquantly harmonized (staccato wind, plucked strings, later with glockenspiel) and not even symmetrical. It calls not for answering phrase but answering key, shifting further from B flat. This occurs another tone down. B flat is recovered by a jaunty repercussion of the motto (jubilation for cornet and side-drum), extended by an obvious suggestion of the last phrase of a popular song, hexatonic and lacking the crucial sharp 7 of the truly banausic[1] but not without the bass slide to and from the flat 6; another raw moment, to be accepted as a passing token of London's solidarity, for the sake of what it may bring (*c*). *d* quickly restores dignity for the growing pyramid of tone, before a fresh start. But the listener goes forward with some uncertainty about what is to be taken seriously.

In accordance with the earliest symphonic procedure the second part of the Allegro begins like the first, but in the new key. Thus B flat major becomes a medium for G flat minor. After the second subject (Ex. 18*a*), one is dubious whether B flat will be the one to go, but it is. Soon all is flux, maintained by the motto and by stray pentatonic phrases (one might be a congener of 'Searching for Lambs'—Ex. 5*e*) in a

---

[1] Cf. Parry, *Style in Musical Art*, 116–118, for illustrations from 'various low-class tunes . . . popular a few years ago'.

casually contrapuntal weave. The strings are muted and tremulous, while the key lapses waywardly from F, to linger round F sharp. During this increasingly automatic and obsessional phase appears a notable progression, played by a string octet, reinforced by string *tutti*, all unmuted, somewhat in the manner of the *Tallis Fantasia*. It may be compared now with a similar type of intimation of London's dreamers in Ireland's *London Overture* (1936). The more recondite

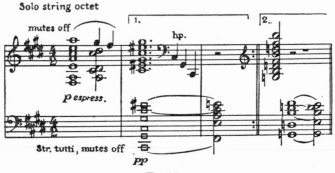

Ex. 19*a*

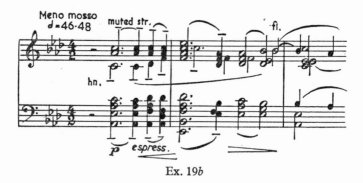

Ex. 19*b*

texture of the older composer is a striking contrast. (The barring has been halved in either case.) Early transitional figures (the 1–2–5 ascent, etc.) carry the music to an affectionate lingering cadence; by which time, if not earlier, one has become aware that free fantasy has reached the limit.

An obvious structural problem now arises. The initial onslaught has expended its force as the dénouement of Ex. 18*d*, and has no meaning here. But the stimulus of arriving at E flat minor by way of a sliding

G major is still effective, even in a subdued muffle; and if at a further stage the skid from G major is sanded up, the listener begins to suspect that E flat is giving ground—an obvious cue for the second subject to arrive (over E flat) in G, most orthodox of keys. The wind is confined to the brass, but the glitter now induced by soft *unmuted* lip-reeds is piquant and magical.

This all happens in so deprecatory a manner as to glorify the art of concealment. (The composer correctively informed me in 1929 that he regarded the movement as falling into *two* parts—the second beginning *fff*, as indicated above—not three, so that he must have intended to convey only the shadow of recapitulation here.) But, veiled as it is, recovery is in the air, and once the second subject is installed, the rest should follow. It is now expedient to avoid a too predictable course homeward by a diversion at a legitimate moment, as well as by fresh settings.

Hence 18*b*, always sure of its key, is shifted into a new relationship (E, G), and the motto-sequel is 'repressed' (minor key and *pp*). Similarly, 18*c*, previously so jaunty and vernacular, is stiffened by simultaneous delivery at normal and double speed. This, besides dispensing with what Tovey would have called the trombone joke, admits of expansion and digression (in E, etc.) from which the prologue effects a rescue of G major. Moreover, in a token bar, repeated, *c* at last recovers its impulsive unanimity, but leaping freely from key to key and jostled by the counter-impact of *b*, not with its former light flick of reedy tone and percussion but in a blaze of trombone pentatony and dry vibration. (It will be half-consciously realized that, as shown in the quotation above, *b* is a congener of the missing second phrase of *c*, of which it becomes an all-embracing substitute.) Again, when *d* returns for the climax, it has to make its way, not through a mere quiver of orchestral harmony but against a tremendous reiteration of *c* (the essential bar), now keeping steadily in G.

For the third time the blow falls (E flat bass), its force broken at once by a rhetorical *ffpp* and fugitive chain of sonority. This clears the way for a final reappearance of 18*a* in full and solemn brass and inevitably now without the light string appendage, leaving the orchestral remainder to provide a crowning touch of vibration and percussion (with bells). The plain phrase from the Scottish rhymer's celebration of a mayoral reception (1501) of a Scottish delegation comes to mind:

'London, thou art of townes A *per se*.'

Thus, both the trenchant and the convivial elements of the main matter are projected in restatement into fresh textures, now rarefied and now closer woven contrapuntally, and this justifies the often brusque, aphoristic touch of the exposition, even the ultra-vernacular *c* and its sliding trombones. What seems at first raw or 'vintage' experience acquires its true potential. The two resourcefully symmetrical courses enclose a prolonged and evocative interlude, whose undertones are, one guesses, near-documentary. Those at once cast their remote shadow over the restatement and by their quiet relief rest the ear before the bustle and clangour which must ensue. Only in the lingering harmonies here (e.g. Ex. 19*a*) are the sevenths and other such half-discords noticeable constituents. Elsewhere the harmonic texture is either basic, repetitive and near-automatic, or trenchant in the manner typified by the opening chords of the Allegro and of the second subject, and anticipated in *On Wenlock Edge*. A new compulsion supports the flow and counter-flow of melodic ideas, and brings home the triumph of an almost unique ending, not to be encountered again till the eighth symphony.

This detailed review is called for by a critical tendency, which I have encountered from time to time, to question the symphonic authenticity of this movement. Perhaps only those who have lived with it in rehearsal and repeated performance can appreciate its superlative integrity. It is also expedient at this point to become familiar with symphonic methods which recur.

The course of the slow movement is more straightforward. Stages of slow, extensively less slow and briefly slow again, enclose an eloquent and sobering contemplativeness; there are not ten whole bars of fortissimo here. In the opening, a set progression of whole tones (each to a heavy chord) establishes flux from an arbitrary point, and becomes the setting of a motive in a queer mode, reaching G by way of A flat minor, in horizontal succession (Ex. 7*f*, p. 116). A subdued, low-pitched secondary phrase, for flute and trumpet, steadily cadential in texture, establishes C. Qualified restatement (E–G sharp and C again) confirms all this. Originally (1914), after one mention of the main motive (bars 1–8), a preliminary statement moving from C to E without the wind tune, augmented the exposition. Its omission strengthens the fresh start in E, and the cadential postscript is thin and repetitive enough as it is.

In the polytonal interlude, snatches of tune and colour melt into each other pastorally; a viola-solo modal rhapsody in E, whose

5–1–5–7–4–5 curve makes it a congener of 'The captain's apprentice';
the lavender-sellers' cry (clarinet); and renderings of hansom cab bells
(jingle-bells and percussion tuned to the motto-chord (Ex. 17)).
There is a quiet and more poignant cadential phrase, of major chords
based on the fall of a flattened third to tonic and marked by contradictory thirds in successive chords. It is repeated higher, later, with
some intensity, by full wind. (In the 1914 score the prescribed emphasis
is a passionate and rather shrill *forte* each time.) This brings the interlude to a marked close before it dissolves into the Lento. (The spontaneous extension of the climax, in the thirteen bars before the Tempo
primo, replaces a more distrait twenty bars of quick dissolution and then
brief résumé of viola, hansome cab and lavender-seller motives, in the
1914 version, which also introduces the cadential progression into a
Tempo primo of very different detail.)

The 1920 version of the resumed Lento contains entries of the main
tune in A flat–C and C–E (as in the suppressed bars 9–26 of 1914),
followed by a striking semitonal progression of shimmering chords, as
an astringent setting to the aftermath of phrase before the expected
cadential one. In the final post-1935 version, there is only one first

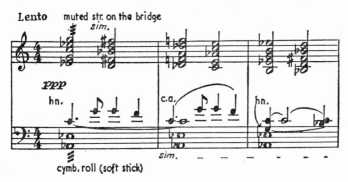

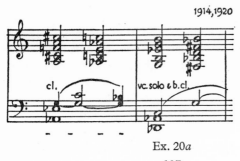

Ex. 20*a*

197

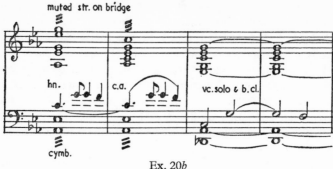

Ex. 20*b*

entry, and the texture is drastically integrated; twenty-two bars are thus reduced to a doubly spare eleven. The lost and retained progressions are worth comparing today. Having performed (without alternative) the earlier version with complete satisfaction, I for one must admit an objection to the later simplification, which sounds suspiciously like the legendary 'not wanting my stuff to sound like modern music'. In general, one must freely allow a composer to determine, and to revise, his own method and degree of exposition, restatement etc. But when he has committed to print what is in fact a consistently revised version of a major work, and lets it take root in the minds of audiences for fifteen years, then, if he revises a second time, he must somehow convince his audiences that his economy of means (as it is here) is a gain.

The cadential repeat is shadow rather than substance, and so the viola solo is able to weave in again, now a plainchant in A, but with the string harmony pointing to C via the F chord with which it ends, as in the similar chord of *A Sea Symphony*, which duly moves to its tonic. (In case this concern for final tonic seems fantastic in the present context, I might mention that at a university examination Ernest Walker, the last person to put an idle question, or to impose the conventions of the classical period where they did not apply aurally, questioned me on this very point, and, having obtained no answer, suggested C quite firmly. Lately, with due reservations for mode, E minor has been suggested. This has some support but hardly works throughout.) The hypothesis of a last moment mental change to A makes no sense to me. On any interpretation, rhapsody here reaches a new point of indeterminate finish, *niente*, and in a symphony.

In an introduction to the earlier works, long out of print, this movement was singled out as the most purely musical movement of the symphony, whose creation 'must have given the composer peculiar pleasure'. The absorption of this movement is certainly striking, and also a test of the listener's sympathy. Presumably some fear of promoting *longueurs* prompted the composer to compress, and to shape more pointedly or succintly the original draft of the movement, which now takes only ten minutes to play. There can be no criticism of the degree of restatement here. Yet the rambling, ruminating quality of this movement is symptomatic and not conventionally symphonic. Even the slow movement of the *New World Symphony*, also nostalgic and wayward, is comparatively hieratic and its fool-proof tonality keeps everything parcelled up after use.

For its more sympathetic reception this Lento shelters, perhaps, behind Whistler's 'Nocturnes'. (In the early note already cited on p. 189*n*., the composer permitted 'Bloomsbury Square on a November afternoon' to serve as a clue to, but not an explanation of, the movement. A fine distinction!) It is the Scherzo, however, which is called Nocturne in the score. The sub-title is a warning of dim lighting and probably further impressionism. ('Westminster Embankment at night' was the official tip.) The movement is laid out as if it were a rondo with two episodes, and the relic of a third in the coda. The prevailing section, lacking the piquant identity of a rondo-refrain, is more or less bifocal, and the re-shaping of its components keeps its repetition eventful. Its impetuous six-time calls up a picture of hustling, flitting figures with many folk-dances in their toes; the sword-dance, the Abbots Bromley Horn Dance, for instance.

The salient texture of the melodic line is unmistakably modal. It tends to be almost virulently hexatonic, but the insistent rising and harmony-forming thirds and the early, rapid and again harmonic woodwind 7–5–4 3–2–1 cascade (harmonized 5 4) shows how far vocal intonation has been left behind. The sixth degree is optional, and sharp or flat as in some early folk song. The upshot is that of a minor key with something different in the cadences: the unsharpened seventh, which continues to disturb many ears. However, the rising 5 1 of the motto sets its stamp on the main phrases, and a casual fall of whole tones, each a chord deep, makes its anti-modal impression, disintegrating enough to switch the key down two tones (D to B flat) for the second group of figures. The latter continues the main restless mood unconcernedly. The most noticeable feature has been quoted in Ex. 7c. The more articulate first episode, inserted after a total repeat of the foregoing matter, continues B flat minor in the same modal style, with further falling tones, but its boisterous mock chant in triple metre and unmuted sounds make a brief, defiant incident, suggestive of some established local folk-dance ceremony. In the reduced repeat of the main motives, the second key is accordingly changed to D. Here the modal tradition, in the broader sense explained earlier, is exploited in the oscillation of the third degree from major to minor, while the five degrees of the pentatone (1, 2, 4, 5, 7) remain intact.

In the second episode (a plain two-beat rhythm, and poco animato in the revised version), the incessant patter is exchanged for music at a different level. Heralded by the fanfares of a mouth-organ, the wind play a trite and eminently youthful 'whistle'-tune, in the major and making considerable play with the dominant-ninth (5–♯7–2–4–♯6) of classical harmony; an analogue of the equally perky but more darting phrases of Elgar's errand-boy. This equalitarian stroke may be in line with the old tradition of rural lays after a courtly minuet, and of 'Turkish' orchestration in the most exalted contexts, but its intrusion here is disarming and almost perverse. Melody is certainly needed, and this is a well-made 14-bar tune, both for its chosen level and for its capacity to extend just relevantly enough to invoke the rising fourth of the opening motive. Yet the duality of style is disturbing. In a perfunctory, nicely calculated recovery of the principal movement, a missed cue in the second group lets in the cornets (with triangle) in a blatant and primitive descent (♮7 4 ♭3 1) in now irrelevant keys. The motto is enlisted (as in the first movement at QQ, just before the plenary return of 18*d*) to recover key and lost subject. This is now so broadly and triumphantly major that a flattened third (with big drum) at once conveys a new concentration of mood in the return of the chief theme before the next step.

This was at first (1914) an entire episode, roughly equivalent to a hundred and fifty more bars of the present movement, and consisting of a leisurely four beats and brisker three (to observe Henry Wood's marks). The former tempo contains the features below (Exx. 21*a*, 21*b*); the latter throws up a fragment of 'My bonny boy'. A fugitive coda closed this incident on the same lines as the end of the coda now. In the new coda, faltering, unexposed reflections (*c*, *d*) of *a* and *b* (with fourth reversed to correspond with the rising 5 1 of the chief theme?) mingle with the main motive, whose ebbing energy nicely echoes fading human activity, before two deep string chords signal 'Lights out!' The thought is compressed and baffling, like life, and resolved by the inexpressible

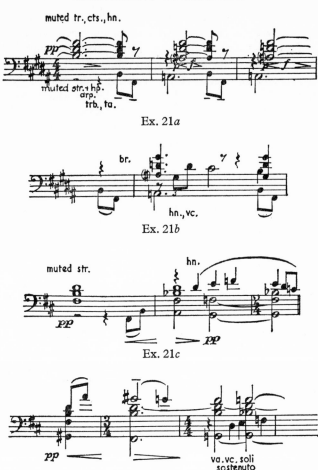

Ex. 21a

Ex. 21b

Ex. 21c

Ex. 21d

vitality of London at its darkest hour. This, at least, is a conceivable underlying imagery, and, admitting the enigmatic and surprising touch of *c*, as a penultimate stage of D minor, the listener has no difficulty in accepting the 'automatic' running-down of the final, twisting 1–3–7 1 figure in the bassoon, to which the earlier 7–3–7 1 is reduced. The obvious precedent, the end of the *Coriolan Overture*, is less spontaneous. A fresh example will be observed at the end of the fifth symphony's Scherzo.

The general listener is bound to resist any implication that the development here is a matter of juggling with variant modal degrees. The firm and curious link with the post-pentatonic period remains, as a source of revivalist and slightly spurious freshness of technique, and the capricious changes of the second group cannot better be defined than as the resourceful application of the oscillating semitones of early modal writing. No listener can miss the swaying rhythm which propels the slippery answering phrases from one point to another, or the sense of proportion with which one idea is adopted or abandoned. Yet the flight from classical tradition has left in some decidedly raw humour to absorb.

The ominous finale-introduction (Andante con moto) sprang, one would say, from some central experience, such as the memories which separated existence in January, 1919, from five years earlier and deepened the epic sense into the sternness of the opening resolution. Actually, it is all (with bars 5–6 amplified) in the 1914 version. This searching introduction must be accepted as a broad challenge, from which alone the stoic calm of the march theme could convincingly emerge. Its texture has been anticipated in principle by the opening Allegro.

Once launched, the course of the movement is downright, though far from predictable. A stately theme in G, which Young surprisingly finds too contrived, dissolves into an elusive Allegro, in which a racy and ominous motive takes possession of the full orchestra for two tremendously cumulative entries. (The *pace* must *not* be furious.) Originally this interlude was not only longer and more involved, but extended to a quite different episode. Its relation to the printed version is summarized below.

In the original scheme, the re-entry of the Andante (5) is trenchant. It is evident from his own note (see p.189) that the composer first conceived the main movement, before the epilogue, as an alternation of an 'agitated' Andante and a march movement, at first solemn and then energetic. Eventually, he made the Andante preludial, and the Allegro the main contrast with the solemn march, though on a compressed scale. Thus, in this now uniform Allegro, the second full entry of the ominous motive (7) is bound to show an *obvious* cumulative relation to the first— hence a *tone* higher—but is followed by a headlong atonal sequence, as shown. The further interlude (9) has a melody of calm intention. It is a revelation of the hazards of symphonic writing, for it is easier to understand why the composer rejected so jejune an episode than why he ever proposed it. The idea of such an interlude remained for another occasion. This symmetrical interlude demanded more contrast than

	Rehearsal letter (1920, 1936)	Number of bars		Comparative content (1914)
		1920	1914	
1	E	7	7	Allegro
2		7	7	Motive 1
3	F	7	13	Motive 2 in E, etc., with an appendage anticipating section 8, now F6–7
4	G	8	8	Development of 1
5	H	—	19	Andante(3/2), expanding the opening bars of the movement
6	H	11	11	Allegro. Development of motive 1, with allusion to 2
7		4	4	Motive 2 in F and C sharp (now F sharp and D)
8	K	21	20	Motive 2 in B flat, breaking the two-tone sequence now preserved. Relaxation of mood for —
9	M	—	28	Andantino in B (4/4). (a) Lower str.; (b) Wood (str.)
10	M	12	8	Marcia. Return to Tempo primo, modulating from B minor. Not the direct return of 1920
		77	125	

Ex. 22

the plain Marcia in itself, so the latter was recovered as an interruption which straightens itself (10); whereas after the downright entries of the one overwhelming theme the Marcia *da capo* is timely.

With the renunciation of a strong mind, then, Vaughan Williams secured the impact of the terse interlude that he left. Its brief intimation of forces not entirely under control is one of the events of symphonic music, comparable to the more organized and cumulative 'nightmare' of the second episode of the Scherzo of Elgar's second symphony. After this, the March is not very secure, and aided by the rising semitone of the Andante and an echo of the Allegro, a discordant and hubristic note

Ex. 23

reaches a climax of tone (with gong), reinforced by a blurred recollection of the discord of the first movement (muted brass, and strings with the weird truncated vibrations of the bow-hair 'on the bridge'). Once more, G major confronts a basic E flat, but not now to capitulate. Hence when the fixation is taken over by the string quartet, the three-quarter chime in G of the light harp harmonics seems to come pat on the cue, romantically consigning the chord beyond time and discord. (Originally, an intrusive echo of the Andantino—in E flat—postponed this.) With this gesture of *tempus fugit*, relaxing the tension in a brief but meaningful recollection of a familiar sound (see p. 191), the Epilogue makes a fresh start, carrying the ascending 5 1 2 of the motto (bass) into B flat minor and sundry keys against a haze of vibrating harmony, with a final subtle echo of the Andante.

The resolution of this in a clear recovery of the Prologue has been steadily reduced in size from what was originally 'a movement of some length', a definitive Epilogue, balancing the Prologue as first movement by something like a sixth, after the intervening four. Once more the stages of compression, amounting to twenty-four bars less each time, may be stated.

	Rehearsal letter (1920, 1936)	Number of bars		
		1914	1920	1936
1	T (Lento)	8	8	8
2		17	17	—
3		7	7	—
4	(W)	23	—	—
5	W	25	24	24
		80	56	32

Section 2 embodied an expansion of the Prologue's second theme (almost the subject as in Bach's fugue 33), now in counterpoint with the motto reiterated. Section 3 was at first a low-pitched half close, later

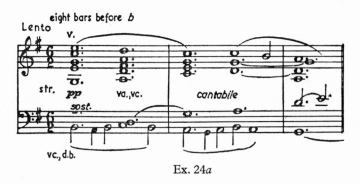

Ex. 24a

spaced out, almost prophetic of the fifth symphony's close (24a). Section 4 was a manifold, near-automatic, impressionist canon on the motto, in grave danger of making, with the opening fog of the Epilogue and sections 1, 2, 3 and 5, an imitation of 'Dvořák's five endings' (R. V. W.). One listener regrets the absence of stages 2–3, without which stage 5, a marvellous sublimation of the Andante (24*b*) and of the discord of the first movement (24*c*), seems abrupt to ears used to the more

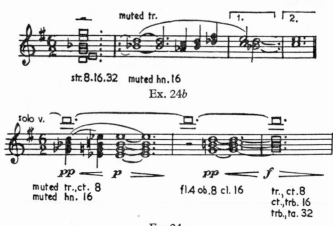

Ex. 24*b*

Ex. 24*c*

sustained transition. But this will not strike others. A sense of crisis then, in restatement has been answered by a compressed reverberation of the Prologue. This pattern of ending, of a transcendent Epilogue to the last movement, finally absorbing the dramatic encounters and vivid pattern of contrasted motives in an unfaltering contemplation, is notable for future occasions. With it appears the fading finish, the plenary but vanishing tonic chord, answering, after all, the question left open, harmonically, by the last Westminster Quarter.

The major-key texture is here convincing, after a freely modal march, which emerges from the discords of the Andante with an oscillating third, yet strong enough to try a phrase in other keys before closing in G. The interlude, also modal in certain respects, exploits key-change uncompromisingly and compulsively, and the march restores G firmly enough to be worth going as far as Ex. 23 from the key hypothesis. The unresolved discord underlying the Westminster chime is, in turn, a crux from which to extricate the music, slowly and portentously, in quest of G, and recover its true major chords, so joyously affirmed at the end of the Allegro.[1]

[1] For the gradual stages by which the composer obtained the cadence that satisfied him, see the note on the original piano score in Appendix C.

Mastery of texture thus underlies the more overt movements of theme and tempo in this finale. The discipline of working on a symphonic scale without any text has been accepted and faced at a moment —following two much looser linked movements—where a binding of threads is needed. This, briefly, is the abiding satisfaction which *A London Symphony* offers at any time. The listener can be left to decide how far this, the most characteristic work so far, is the product of thematic and textural control and how far a sheer stroke of personality and imagination. At this summary moment, one may with the composer ponder on the heterogeneous material and rejected alternatives which have so strikingly given place or converged, but the prevailing impressions will be musical. 'London' is past history, a mental stage from which the music took off before it became a symphony. Even if that stage stays in a listener's mind, as the stronghold of a pulsating community, impulsive and inconsistent, yet buoyant and free, the symphony will justify itself as an epic stroke by its musical qualities, not by its regional appeal. The controversy about title becomes trifling, provided that it does not encourage any one to regard it as a primarily descriptive work. He may begin by colouring his musical experience with distant pictures of a crowded Strand and fog and Whistler's 'Nocturnes', but as he listens a second and third time, these images will recede to where they belong. As a check on hasty descriptive renderings of motives, the listener might well recall that the contour of the motto theme here shows some reflection of the viola motive in Debussy's 'De l'aube à midi sur la mer' (*La Mer* suite). Whichever element is preferred, the spacious calm remains; and the coincidence of sustained, unresolved chords is trifling.

The first performance of the symphony (Queen's Hall, March 27, 1914) provoked a chance comparison with Ravel's *Valses nobles et sentimentales* (1912). Holst, in an immediate letter to his friend, wrote, 'You have proved the musical superiority of England to France. I wonder if you realized how futile and tawdry Ravel sounded after your Epilogue' (*Heirs and Rebels*, p. 43). That comparison cannot be pressed, especially with one of the three works which Ravel wrote first for piano and then orchestrated for use as ballets, before their appearance in their present orchestral form. Had it been the later sardonic-sweet *La Valse*, one might have understood. As it is, one wonders whether, missing unconsciously the pianistic charm and ringing appeal of the *Valses*, Holst did not react against the accomplished languor and brilliance of the orchestral version. However, no informed listener, remembering the

lessons so patiently taken with Ravel, could have doubted the pronounced and far reaching individuality of the *London Symphony* in form
and content.

The orchestra in this symphony is an assembly of (1) strings, dividing
where necessary into soli and tutti, and harmony sixteen notes deep;
(2) woodwind in threes, with piccolo, alto oboe, bass clarinet and double
basoon; (3) brass of two nominally F-trumpets (longer and wider in
bore than the modern short trumpet), two cornets, three trombones and
tuba; (4) tuned percussion of harp, glockenspiel and kettledrums; (5)
pitchless percussion of triangle, cymbals, big drum, side drum and
jingles. A cueing system makes a smaller orchestra practicable.

PASTORAL SYMPHONY

The orchestra for the *Pastoral Symphony* (1922) has no double bassoon,
cornets, side-drum or bells, and confines the pitchless percussion and an
added celesta to the third movement, but it calls for a third trumpet and
a vocal soprano, replaceable by a clarinet; a solo-violin is also noticeable
throughout. Acoustically, then, only the florid cornet tone and the
noisy rhythmic resources of the earlier symphony are out of reckoning;
cornets being a *Cockaigne* touch that, in spite of the long Paris tradition,
cannot be regarded as indispensable. But this common ground does
not ensure any similarity of address.

Once more the title, which Boult and others considered 'unwise',
caused some misunderstanding, with expectations of concrete suggestions encouraged by what Beethoven did in rural style with a programme
suggested by J. H. Knecht's symphonic *Portrait Musical de la Nature*.
Indeed, 'symphony number 3' would have been a better title, and much
more convenient in the long run, for the informed listener is bound to
concern himself with which symphony came immediately before the
fourth. In his programme note the composer stated, 'the mood of this
symphony is, as the title suggests, almost entirely quiet and contemplative; there are few fortissimos and few Allegros'. In other words, the
symphony is 'pastoral' in so far as it is restrained, not restrained because it strikes a pastoral note. In any case no titular reminder is needed
to suggest that this is a quiet and meditative work, avoiding most of the
contrasts of tempo and emphasis by which symphony has commonly
contrived to distinguish, and to widen the context of, its themes and
moods. Nor do the hard demands of the soil and farm (as in *Joanna
Godden*), or the realities of wakening spring afford the slightest clue to the

'bliss of the countryside' which is so glibly on the mouths of some exponents. That fantasy is an escaping townsman's creation, influenced by *The Task*, Wordsworth and pantheism in general. Nor do I find a recollection of the texture of the Sussex downs (Colles) a useful analogy of the thought unfolded here. In short, 'pastoral' is more hindrance than help, if it is a symbol of segregation.

Let us turn, then, to the music. In *A London Symphony* the composer chose as his staple material, as token of an abiding community, a blend of trenchant semitonal and discordant features with convivial phrases and modal lines which become freely rhapsodic at times, but preserve a constant power of quasi-vocal melody. The vernacular tinge of the brass motive at the end of the Allegro, the swing of the later march, and even the speaking intonation of what I termed the ominous motive in the centre of the finale, are reminders of a derivative quality which might at any moment expose the rawness of the texture; the repression, it may be thought, of a composer somewhat obsessed by the integrity of resourcefully strophical melody (think of the many folk-song fantasias) and, so to speak, missing his singers. In the third symphony there is every sign of an emancipation from this eclectic strain, as a handicap to development. Melodically, a pentatonic or articulately variant modal flavour recurs, and also a quite different tendency to shape a line round the common chord (1 3 5), with or without an accessory sixth or seventh—5 1 7 1 begins the pattern of a violin solo in the ninth bar—but this concerns phrases rather than themes, and the phrases may not be salient. Nor, as in the Scherzo of the *London*, does any sweeping rhythm carry the listener off his feet as his perception passes from one half-sensation to another. The new textural appeal lies in the harmonic setting of apparently formal phrases, either in interwoven lines of remarkably free scalic pattern, some three or four notes deep, or in more foursquare formation.

As a consequence, orchestral polyphony, or the calculated contrast of solo and group tone, acquires fresh importance in placing a harmonization or by its own assertion of a relationship. Harmonic setting must not be conceived as an orderly, semi-metrical procession of chords tethered to a bass, but this 'accompaniment' acquires its own formulae, especially at cadences. In particular, a progression from the minor chord of the third degree to the major of the tonic is noticeable (Ex. 25*b*). It could be argued that if the third is, by long folk-song habit, unstable (major or minor), why not the fifth? But no such casuistry is called for. A bare recollection of 'Love's Minstrels' (see Ex. 10) shows the progression to be an early established one. It is here used, now to conclude an equivocal passage, now to consolidate before one. Thus in *b* below, by the sixth bar of the music there is no doubt that G is the tonic, making the oboe motive Lydian in G, not modulating to D. Here, then, are typical features of the interplay of tonic-centres; of the strong sense of dissolving or distracting relationships which it becomes necessary to probe. (To quote isolated melodic lines is quite misleading.)

Interspersed with these are more straightforward, near-pentatonic (1 2 4 5 7) entries, such as the salient melodic feature of the second subject of the first movement (quoted in Ex. 6*c*), the flute's pirouetting against a fixated 1 2 4 5 chord in the third movement (bar 27), the trium-

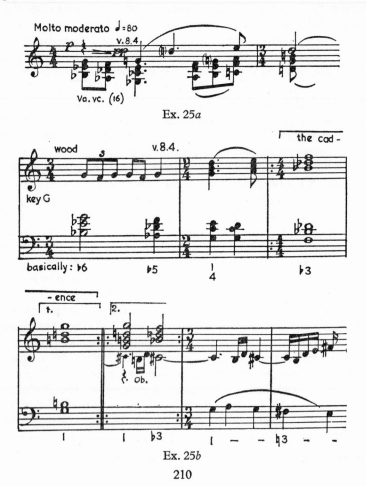

Ex. 25*a*

Ex. 25*b*

Ex. 25c

phant dance in the centre of the same movement (Ex. 6d) and the two vocal (7a) and orchestral themes of the last movement, as first introduced. Even these, however, have a decided harmonic texture, except the vocal example, and to cite the melodic shape conveys only a half-truth of experience.

One may assume that some of these typical foci of interest were plotted in the composer's mind before he began. Of these and others, we can now perceive that only four called for dynamic structural emphasis: in the first movement, the elemental 1 5 6 5 of the first 'subject' (violin line of 25a); in the second, the wayward opening 5 6 10 9 7, if sounding against a provocative and alien tonic; in the third, the opening 4 5 1 disgruntlement and brass tune (6d); and in the fourth, the revelation of the inner strength of the opening plainsong (7a). The prevailing tone must thus be unassertive. Hence, the embodiment of these impulses in a symphony showed a bold confidence in their independence of the graded emphasis and tempo by which a developed orchestral movement is expected to distinguish its themes and their fresh contexts. Thus, the composer's approach to a steadily and markedly contemplative work becomes increasingly clear.

In these circumstances, the listener is confronted with four movements entitled Molto moderato, Lento moderato, Moderato pesante, and Moderato maestoso with *lento* Prologue and Epilogue; respectively 80, 70, 80 and 72 beats to the minute. It may be assumed that the prevailing contrasts will be in low relief. It is therefore pertinent to search, as one listens, for evidence of linking structure. Except in the first movement, the balance of ideas is clear enough. In the Lento, exposition divides into motives proceeding from 5 6 (somewhat as the violin and violoncello in Brahms's A minor concerto set out in pursuit of the officially announced 8 7 5) and the trumpet cadenza, and once the returning first subject has resolved its bitonality (c above), the immediate restatement becomes unequivocal. The next movement shows a main section in the Aeolian mode (i.e. minor without cadential security),

211

joining in variable order a plain 4 5 1 figure, a wind 3 5 1 ascent, which would be commonplace if it were not three notes deep, and the flute roulades mentioned earlier. The brass tune, Mixolydian with a difference, collects enough emotional energy into one positive fresh channel, though the music is not confined to melody, and the gusto of its brief and at first more glamorous recurrence will not be missed. Once more, as in the previous symphony, a further episode appears to follow the third return to the minor. Said to be derived from a ballet of 'oafs and fairies' and alien to the prevailing gruffness, it displays a sudden fleetness of movement and quasi-fugal entry. It proves, instead, to be a wayward coda, as returning salient figures show. This time there is one final chord, but an exquisite one. In the closing movement, the Lento solo for soprano appears to be a mere prelude to the Moderato. The protracted vocal and modal texture might even be considered reactionary in this context. But when the Moderato has spent its first impulse, the preludial phrases show a surprising aptitude for symphonic development. When the basic theme emerges in a tremendous unison of strings and woodwind, as in 25d, its first-subject quality is absolutely vindicated, and after it has shown the way to what is now recognized as the second subject (Moderato), it is free to return to its plainsong origins for a coda. How far the two subjects complement each other, and how far they represent quite different levels of experience, which are approximated in the midway oscillations of tempo, is a matter of individual experience.

The shape of the first movement is more elusive. A clear enough tonality (G, A) distinguishes two groups of motives, the second showing rather more melodic quality. A pronounced second start in A becomes diversionary and expansive, so that it is not until the cadence (25b) that a sense of recovery is reached—in time for the second group. Thus, as on the larger scale of the *London Symphony*, this first movement conveys a free balance of two bi-focal stages, the second diverging from, and then converging towards, the former pattern. A blunt but resourceful coda reaches the cadence for the third time. Is this an Amen, as in a literal parallel in the contemporary *Mass*? No, the oboe is still around. But it is now alone on its circular course. With a *pax vobiscum*, consigning the oboe's Lydian deviations to oblivion, muted basses repeat the initial 1 5 6 5, summarizing the whole movement. This rising fifth recurs noticeably throughout the movement, and to some extent in later movements, but it would be absurd to regard so generic a relationship as characteristic of anything.

A classical sense of pattern, then, draws the threads of each movement together. It remains to give some attention to the specific relation of the the motives as successively presented in each movement, and correspondingly, of the movements themselves.

The first movement sets the pace in more senses than one. The recurrent phrases are characteristic only in their setting, but definite enough to make small alterations of their basic lines, such as the extension of the opening 1 5 6 5 to 1 5 6 7 at the climax of development and in the coda, count, as well as fresh orchestral nuances. The motives are all homogeneous, and in view of this, a somewhat increased pace underlines the arrival of the second group, besides the move of key to A from a re-established G. In the restatement G, just recovered after diversions, is left undisturbed as the central key, and in the second group the accent falls on mode and texture: (1) pentatonic minor (1 2 3 5 7) as before, violas and bassoon for violoncelli; (2) Mixolydian major with a bias to the minor third as well, replacing clarinet by strings two octaves apart.[1] Hence the quick projection of the opening motive into fresh keys, in the coda, is pronounced enough to call for the cadence once more. In this subtle eventfulness the movement flows continuously up to its low-pitched, subdued and unilinear finish, renouncing the garish life of a conventional symphonic metropolis and its corybantic brass for the more absorbing quality of a rich but spacious string harmony, oscillating flutes and an imperative harp.

Continuation with a Lento of mainly typical basic material in the most casual succession, with a cadenza for second subject, is a severe test of the composer's new method, and I find the exposition monotonous and unpersuasive. The opening is virtually a horn cadenza; the secondary pentatonic motive on a sluggish bass scarcely justifies the length of its treatment, and the insouciant trumpet cadenza, confined to natural harmonics (of which the seventh sounds flat to ears used to tempered-scale harmony), is a raw piece of unassimilated material, luxuriously uncalled for.[2] The fierce bitonality of the first subject, recovered in

---

[1] An early piano score shows that this G major uniformity (O to P7) replaced a symmetrical restatement of D5–F2 a tone down.

[2] In a 'natural' octave, the tone between degrees 2 and 1 is represented by a vibration-proportion of 9 to 8; between degrees 3 and 2, by 10 to 9 (a slighter interval); between degrees 8 and 7, by 8 to 7—a wider interval than the first. The piano's tempered scale equalizes these (theoretically to the proportion of the sixth root of 2 to 1). To the tempered ear, the natural tone from 8 to 7 is an unusual stretch, and so the seventh sounds flat.

A similar 'natural' effect is prescribed by Britten in the horn-solo Prologue and Epilogue of his *Serenade* for tenor, horn and strings. There the horn starts

the teeth of the last trumpet note, restores interest, and its later 'combination' with the trumpet cadenza (now on the horn), against a gradual whole-tone descent of string chords, keeps the ear in suspense before the violins reach the cadence on lines prepared by Ex. 25c and anticipated by *In the Fen Country* (and a little by *Tristan*, Act 3). An exacting movement for the listener, the Lento reflects the ruthless regularity of country life below the surface.

The Moderato to follow, a challenge to the characteristic drift of the Lento, is no Scherzo, but its prevailing stoic refrain on a stolid bass, admits the variant and elastically admissible phrases of wind-groups, moving three-deep in a kind of 'Phrygian' progression, and of flute, enlivening a single chord with rhythmic coloratura. The brass tune and its episode would make a striking appearance anywhere, but never more striking than in this symphony, for it is the first fully melodic appeal, and remains far the most pronounced one, aided by its ♭3–1 cadence, echoing that of the first movement with a difference. Its compression to less than half its original size enhances its reappearance, with the refrain, equally succinct, on its heels. A vacuum has been created for the *presto* finish. It is more postscript than conclusion, but just within the orbit of the movement, and sealed by the magic of the celesta (with the early wind phrase) and by the collapse of the tonal structure on a favourite chord. This was once a prime emblem of trouble (*On Wenlock Edge*, for instance) but becomes here an almost mechanical interruption, like the supertonic ninth in classical harmony. If this *was* a ballet once, it may be surmised that here one party, presumably the oaf group, was sent packing, like Caliban. But no visual aid is needed. The dissonant A flat chord is put on a harmonic slide (out of recognition) and G gracefully reinstated. Thus the first and third movements are linked (the fourth, in A and B flat, standing apart), and a quiet finale becomes conceivable.

Once more, the reduced speed for this finale is a plain renunciation, to be justified by the new features. The use of a voice-part without words

at 'scratch', and the recurring seventh harmonic is rather less noticeable, without any harmony. Whether the Mixolydian (or Dorian) degree below the keynote was nearer a natural or a tempered seventh, only a very experienced and sharp-eared collector, confirmed possibly by modern tape-recordings, could tell; and it is unlikely that any folk-singer would be consistent enough to establish a hypothesis either way.

The fact remains that Vaughan Williams bought an open E flat trumpet for use in this symphony. It was played at the first performance, and again at the Leeds Festival, 1927. At the latter, under Beecham, the cadenza was played off-stage, but against the composer's wishes. (*R. C. M. Magazine*, 65. 1. 34).

is first noticeable in the chorus parts of the *Fantasia on Christmas Carols* (Carol 1). But there the text is supplied by the soloist. Here the voice, soprano or tenor solo, is used for its own sake, and yet denying its main purpose. Indeed, a clarinet may be substituted.[1] The composer's object is presumably to revive melodic fundamentals in the pentatonic style, as an original substitute for some normal announcement, anticipated by the trumpet cadenza and by the freedom of line in general. Hence the 'plainsong', lacking any riveting meaning or established ritual intonation, has to find its own pattern of linked phrases in A, strong enough to be a true prelude to the dignified and tuneful Moderato in B flat (Lydian mode, relaxing later), incidentally, the first theme to be drafted, pending a proper context. This expanded, the two subjects have somehow to be brought together, partly by wilful alternation, partly by the transformation of the first into a full harmonic setting (violoncello in C sharp). Thus incorporated into the main movement, the latter can take the strain of inaugurating a plenary recapitulation. Indeed, it *must* sooner or later recover its original shape.

It remains to find the right setting for a united entry. A wordless chorus had yet to be tried, in *Flos Campi*. Hence, this must be an orchestral entry. Then, merely to amplify the initial drum-roll background by bearing on or around the given chord would be utterly jejune. Equally so, if the tonality were raised to another degree. But if a chord, resourcefully reached by thematic means, were bluntly *opposed* by the plainsong with *its* tonic, there would be matter for orchestral dynamics. So to Ex. 25*d*. The resolving of this tension, as a figure of fervent declamation dissolves into sheer imagery, makes a striking

Ex. 25*d*

[1] The late Frederick Thurston played the solo at the first performance at the R.C.M., at the instance of the composer, who had observed the clarinettist cueing in the part at early rehearsals to his complete satisfaction. So a singer was not essential to him! He only needed a vocalizer. At the close of his career, he put voice and clarinet on equal footing in his *Vocalises*.

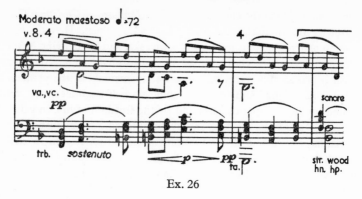

Ex. 26

setting for the entry of the second subject in the depths, in an unperturbed B flat tonality. An absolute return to the basic plainsong, now rich with other associations, is, perhaps, an inevitable finish. The renunciation of modern resources is complete.[1]

That consideration, however, concerns the liberal use of orchestral rhetoric. It does not undermine the symphonic conception of the work. Wider context does not necessarily involve pronounced changes of tempo, or a predominance of allegro. It is merely safer to have these incentives to mental enlargement. The *Pastoral Symphony* had no direct successors, but as the application of a new repertory of ideas to a symphonic framework, it occupies a pivotal position in the music of its time. Only a prejudiced listener, waiting for a symphony to show the familiar bustle and explosion, or for the established blend of trenchant progression and tuneful incident, will dismiss this symphony as a byway. On the contrary, it carried to wide fulfilment what the composer had recently begun to pursue. Mode was now mastered as a pattern of elasticity, rather than of literal melodic association, and a new type of development, based on a revolving manifold of sound, was in progress. Quote a theme at random here, and it may barely remind the reader of the symphony. Quote a setting, and its identity will be apparent, even in its proper context; and there will be no doubt about the composer.

These three symphonies thus stand together only as three stages of emancipation; the first wresting character out of an almost classical

[1] This may seem hasty comment on a hearing or two. Actually it is not. I played in the first rehearsal and heard the first performance of the symphony (1922), and also conducted a broadcast performance, in a programme of my own choice (1931). I have had every opportunity of arriving at a true focus.

tonality and a universal epic of the sea, the second extending the range of ideas immeasurably and almost forcibly, under the stress of a doctrine of modernist 'delight in simple things', and the third almost starting afresh by its independence of characteristic theme, major, modal or semitonal. It was ten years before another symphony was undertaken. That commitment was conditioned by work in non-symphonic, or not directly symphonic, fields, some continuing and some abandoning the trend of the third symphony. It was partly a matter of expanding resource, and partly of shaking off the contemplative mood of the middle decade. The third symphony contains research enough to equip ideas for other works with a fresh style. The calls of county and opera-house occupied the composer without necessarily enlarging his musical orbit perceptibly. A new discipline was needed, by Vaughan Williams's standards. It remained to discover the right stimulus of material or mood.

VIII

Middle Choral Works

Between the wars, Vaughan Williams wrote a number of substantial works for chorus and, usually, orchestra, along with more occasional pieces. Three or four of these are of considerable importance, as outstanding specimens of a genre not easily defined. The rest can be left to their occasions with a brief summary.

MASS IN G MINOR

The *Mass in G minor*, for solo quartet and double chorus (1922), available in an Anglican version, is, in its chosen limits, the earliest characteristic work of this post-war group. It is not the kind of work that one might have expected from this composer, using plainsong tones after the manner of Bach, and, more recently, of Britten, without sacrificing individual idiom. On the contrary, it depends more on harmonic progressions of a certain restricted kind than on any broad intonation on traditional lines, such as marks the *Te Deum laudamus* for the Coronation of George VI and Queen Elizabeth (1937).[1] Yet no one else could have written it. Not only does one soon become aware of juxtapositions of the Dorian and Mixolydian modes in the Kyrie, followed by freer extensions of the old modes in the G major settings which follow, as the working basis of the melodic and harmonic texture. From the Gloria onwards, the music is flecked with recurrent elementary cadential progressions; basically, for example, from minor third to tonic (here, both major chords and sometimes with the seventh or second inter-

---

[1] This setting, 'founded on traditional themes', is an incredibly derivative work, and its use of 'Dives and Lazarus' in triple metre towards the end is almost grotesque.

vening), such as punctuates the more capricious polyphony of the *Pastoral Symphony* (Ex. 25*b*), and, more exactly, the brass tune of the Scherzo of the same work. Such a cadence at once marks and stabilizes the solemn declamation of 'Et homo factus est' and 'Et sepultus est' by the united choruses. Moreover, while developing counterpoint, from a blunt two-part imitation of one choir by another to the steady fugal entries of 'Kyrie Eleison', often determines the choral impact, the harmony may at any moment change to the 'automatic', half-primitive sort, of a melodic line appearing at three or four levels of pitch, but (the modern half) with oscillating component scale-degrees. This can be observed both in such jubilations as the 'Benedicimus te' and the 'Amen' of the Gloria, and in the crucial repentant moment of 'Miserere nobis' in the same setting; all extensions of the fall from third degree to tonic. Moreover, an elastic sense of mode is allied to an elastic tonality, so that the thought has a semblance of freedom.

Nevertheless, it has been arbitrarily confined by the restriction of chords to the primary units of 1 3 5 and 3 5 8, within an almost twelve-note scale. The work is thus a demonstration of what can be done with versatile choral handling, with a plastic mode, unlimited use of the long avoided consecutive fifths, whether harmonic or colour-features, and, not least, a free hand with the harmonic metre, varying from one to eight harmonies in a bar. There is thus little reflection of sixteenth-century music, with its regularized metre and prodigal use of suspensions. 'Direct re-creation of the polyphonic style' (Foss) is wide of the mark. But what is gained? For apart from the avoidance of any elaboration of the text after the Kyrie, the expressive material is restricted to the most direct species of choral intonation, that which has for at least four centuries been regarded as non-discordant. While, then, the restrained meditations on the text—even the most lapidary sentences—may promote a sense of worship and contemplation, whether or not they are sung (as originally) as a part of worship, and while, artistically, the use of mode and a spontaneous choral antiphony crystallizes once more some refreshing and transparent moments of vocal utterance, our experience of the composer's art has not been advanced, apart from the general contact with the ritual text, which may be described as direct and suggestive, but uneventful. The economy of expression promises more than it achieves.

One cannot miss the vivid rejoinders and intimate 'chording' of a distant chorus (such as assisted the original impact from beyond the 'high altar' of Westminster's Roman Catholic Cathedral). Mystic and sceptic alike may find many suggestions of transcendent order in this fresh recital of a text that neither accepts at its face value. (I may add that I myself sang in the first rehearsal of the Kyrie, with some of Holst's 'Whitsuntide' singers, to whom the work was dedicated.) But once more a sensitive 'reading' does not in itself constitute a work of art.

This comment is appropriate also to the sparely constructed motet for Holy Week, *O vos omnes*, an interesting setting to place beside Bach's rendering of the earlier verses, 'Schauet doch' (cantata 46, first chorus). The latter, from which 'Qui tollis' (*Mass*) was condensed by a masterly stroke, represents a comparatively conventional stamp of Bach rendering, a work of character but not supreme achievement. Yet it remains a reminder of what fugue and canon and ritornello can do to enhance a sense of guilt by the cumulative repetition of predictable phrases in unpredictable creative detail. After which, the modern composer's reliance on neo-pentatonic progressions and choral antiphony seems hazardous. *O vos omnes* is in tune with its text without being memorable.

Two contemporary pieces may be mentioned. A setting of Psalm 90, *Lord, Thou hast been our Refuge* (chorus and organ or orchestra), by blending a verse of Watts's metrical paraphrase with selected verses of the Prayer Book Version, develops as a miniature fantasia of declamation and polyphony, circling round two separate and spaced-out strophes of the hymn-tune, *St. Anne*, and converging in the second. The upshot is too laboured and contrived to be worth reconsidering. *O Clap your Hands* (chorus, brass and organ) resourcefully carries a pentatonic line (1 2 4 5 7, destined for Mixolydian implementation—i.e. with a major third) into fresh contexts of oscillating sonority, wavering tonality and a sudden, penultimate gravitation to the minor third, three-deep, as cadential pivot. One retains a sense of the discovery of wider lines of expression. It proved later to be an intimation of *Thanksgiving for Victory* (1945).

LEITH HILL FESTIVAL WORKS

Sancta Civitas (1925) is of an altogether different order of construction, and full consideration of it will be left to the end of the chapter. Of the three works written for the Leith Hill Festival, 1930—one for each of three grades of choir and choir-assembly—only one shows any urgency of structural organization. *Three Choral Hymns*, for the first Division, juxtaposes fresh settings of three hymns from Coverdale's pioneer but pedestrian translation of Lutheran hymns, originally supplied with their

Lutheran tunes.[1] A consistently strophical scheme is in each case supplemented by polyphonic 'Alleluia' or 'Kyrie eleison' refrains, but in different ways according to the selected text. In the three-verse 'Christ is risen', a firm but supple Dorian strain moves, rather suddenly, to a triumphant Mixolydian major by way of the 'Alleluia' refrain, which began as Dorian. In the seven-verse 'Now blessed be thou, Christ Jesu', with stanzas 4 and 5 reversed, an adaptable, somewhat trite major tune in six-time, with a jubilant 4|5 6 4|5 curve (now familiar to the audiences of the fifth symphony), achieves, after a lapse into modal-minor for verses 3 and 4, a rousing change to full major for the rapturous 'Eternal light' of what is now the fifth verse, with a remote and con-templative sixth verse, and a resolute conclusion, freely *da capo* and aided by the return of the 'Eleison' in diminishing tone. 'Come, holy spirit', making four verses of the 1a, 2a, 3a, 1b of Coverdale's three, is a plain and meditative reading in melodically early-major style (bearing on the sixth degree), for voices only, led by tenor solo, with a steady growth of tone in the last eight bars; an odd finish. The general impression is of procedure rather than decision. The music is orderly and singable, but uneventful. Cumulatively, the strophical routine, without supporting narrative, wears thin.

The Hundredth Psalm, for the second Division (no soloist), is a steady blend of choral declamation, polyphony and cantabile in brief sections. Kethe's doxology is bluntly attached to a serene conclusion of the psalm, to make a ready climax out of a historical tune, transferred from the French to the English Genevan psalter (1561) and remembered ever since. So exposed, without much inner compulsion from the allusions to the tune in the earlier movements, this final verse lacks the disciplined phrasing of a Bach chorale-finish, which the weaker second half of the tune needs. With its light-hearted trumpet refrain (used in the congregational rendering of the last Coronation) the music gravitates

---

[1] The text of this premature 'chorale-book for England', much too contro-versial and Lutheran for Archbishop Parker and non-committal Anglicans, is in the Parker Society's edition (1846) of Coverdale's *Remains*. Only a single original copy (library of Queen's College, Oxford) survives the order to destroy the edition round 1540. The relevant Lutheran tunes accepted by Coverdale can now be readily verified as 'Christ ist erstanden', 'Gelobet seist du' and 'Komm heiliger Geist' (Maurice Frost, *English and Scottish Hymn Tunes*, c.1543–1677: 1953). The first is hexatonic and the rest major. So, in a vague way, are Vaughan Williams's three settings. But this correspondence must be sheer coincidence. Moreover, the symmetry of the composer's first tune is one more reminder that a tune can be modal and yet quite out of the modal period of melodic expression.

before its time. Compare Bach's setting of the tune in his Michaelmas cantata, no. 130, for a brilliant independent excursion that still leaves the tune absolutely 'on top'.

Benedicite was written for the Dorking town choirs. Its broad colour-scheme has been flatteringly compared to Cézanne. The long procession of adoring creation demands some scheme of arrangement, but rules out another bout of stanza. The musical motives have momentum enough of their own for the four sections into which the work falls, as choral opening, soprano with chorus, a fresh start for a text by John Austin, and summary recovery and climax, each with its own tempo and metre. Only the third section shows any strophical movement, and that is flexible enough not to be intrusive. Moreover, while the texture is basically polymodal, it is given stimulating kicks into semitonal sonorities by the naturalism of the opening verses, as well as being goaded on by sundry challenging fixations of a two-deep bass, over against the simple harmony of choral declamation or jubilation. After the opening section, however, the modal style is much more set, relieved only by the contrast of polyphony and three-deep linear movement, of cantabile and declamation. Also, the embarking, with an adventitious text, upon a second contrasted section, recovering the original keynote in a penta-tonic style, sounds as a raw contrivance to widen the orbit before confirming the starting-point. While, then, the prevailing elation of this work is unmistakable, its flow of ideas scarcely rises above the familiar tone of a full and active mind, and the design neutralizes, rather than widens, its impact. The work made a stalwart, 'reactionary' appearance, at the last concert of the 1931 festival of the International Society for Contemporary Music (Queen's Hall, London), as a blunt but foundational piece, and will, no doubt, continue in circulation, as a vigorous outburst of 'not too modern' choralism.

MAGNIFICAT

Magnificat, another non-ritual setting, for contralto, women's chorus and orchestra, is superficially a slighter work, but it is far more memorable for the retentive ear. The text has a long musical tradition, stemming from Lechner and Zielenski. From the stately choral-orchestral counterpoint of Monteverdi in D minor to the formally staged elation of J. S. Bach in D major and of C. P. E. Bach's more intimate setting, and from the somewhat blunt 'symphonic' treatment of Stanford in B flat (to which, indeed, Stanford in G is a lyrical and serene contrast) to the capable modern handling of Petrassi and John Gardner (in the last of the *Cantiones sacrae*), there has been a trend towards a jaunty celebration, in jubilant motive and a joyous or even flamboyant equalitarianism, of the revelation that came to Christ's mother before his birth. Vaughan Williams was determined to lift the text out of the smugness of the Anglican evening service (*Heirs and Rebels*, 79), but also, one gathers, to achieve a more perceptive treatment of the situation from which Mary's song sprang.

The key-sentence here is surely the second: 'God has paid due regard to my humiliation', as an unwanted girl-mother. It was in some such mood of uncertainty about explaining her intimations of a higher vocation to the husband who was proposing to divorce her, that Mary went eagerly to see her older cousin, whose prophetic greeting stirred her to song and serenity. Her words would seem to have echoed initially the lyrical outburst put in the mouth of Hannah but to have grown, with constant repetition in the critical months, into something essentially itself, blunted only by pompous or thoughtless monastic routine since.[1]

So rapturous an occasion calls for anything but a garrulous or argumentative choralism. It needs, rather, a translation of the opening dialogue in oratorio style, or an absorbed solo-setting.

Vaughan Williams combines both approaches. He encloses his rendering of *Magnificat*, for solo-voice, in the context of a spaced-out choral recital of Gabriel's familiar but signal phrases of annunciation, couched in the abstract, elusive style of a voice from an inner centre of consciousness. Hence his first concern is to establish and maintain the existence of this centre. The vocal line is insistent but unpredictable. An unusual oscillation of chord develops, and an evocative flute releases a trenchant semitonal succession that rejects all conventional relations of pitch. Only an Elgarian falling-fifth phrase (6 5 1), in the strings, hints at a calmer mood. This reappears in the final salutation stage. The soloist begins 'Magnificat' with a cry of awe, in spreading melisma, but acquires a steady rhythm with the falling interval (now 6 1) noticeably recurrent. The remainder of the setting continues to juxtapose this absorbed sense of disturbance and a serene, extending melodic expression. After Mary's hymn is over, the Gabriel motives are marshalled for confirmation. What was at first mystifying has become

[1] On the differences between the songs of Mary and Hannah, and on the interpretative overtones of 'lowliness' and 'regarded', see an article by S. A. Cawthorn in *The York Quarterly*, 8 (August, 1958).

a positive and extending horizon, in which the *Ave* of the centuries seems to find expression and, eventually, a literal place. There is no homage in such a spontaneous welcome in spirit to the mother of Christ.

Quotation of a recurrent theme or intonation would conceal the breadth of the composition. This is one of the works which do not need examining so much as patient listening. A vocal score would hasten the comprehension of the harmonic development for most listeners. The freedom of movement has benefited, no doubt, from *Flos Campi*, to which we shall return later. But this is a unique setting of a unique occasion, and it would be absurd to consider it in any other context. It stands or falls as a coherent enhancement of Mary's response to Gabriel's visit and to Elizabeth's assuring words. Its rare quality lies in its capacity for such amplification in its own terms.

FIVE TUDOR PORTRAITS

In 1936, the Norwich Festival included *Five Tudor Portraits*, for contralto, baritone, chorus and large orchestra, to texts by Skelton. This at once revealed a new current of inventiveness. The mockeries of *Job* and *Sir John in Love* had conveyed, once and for all, that the composer's literary interests were not confined to worship, but this contact with the riotous rector of Diss was an exceptional departure. By basing the *Portraits* on a heterogeneous collection of five poems, the composer committed himself to matching with music not only five very different shades of personality, but, in the first and fourth especially, a motley procession of images. Such rollicking variety called for high-powered internal organization to become functional, even if the resultant characters —squalid tavern-keeper, mysterious elusive charmer, unlamented slanderer, grief-stricken girl, and tipsy alien—simply do not add up to anything but life's circus.

Some textual questions need to be sorted out in a preliminary way. 'The Tunning of Elinor Rumming' is a setting of rather less than a third of Skelton's poem. This still leaves about two hundred lines of script, but Skelton's short and wiry lines go readily into musical phrases, and his acrobatic, offhand manner adapts itself easily to any leap over missing lines or incidents. The composer's task is to hold this ebullient narrative within the compass of a single movement, and to keep this portrait of a village character in degrading surroundings tolerable to hear about. On their side, listeners and performers must forget the man of taffeta phrases who stands behind the anthologist's favourite, 'Merry Margaret', one of the pretty compliments to young women which figure in the mellowed poet's late, conciliatory and tremendously self-satisfied compilation, *The Garland of Laurel*.[1] *Elinor* displays the real Skelton, almost in tune with *Carmina Burana* and much too boisterously vernacular to be attached to the renaissance as the humanist understood it.

The sequel, 'My proper Bess', is an utter contrast. The poem comes out of the blue in an unexpected epilogue to 'Speak, Parrot', an elaborate and veiled attack on Wolsey's foreign and educational policy. The proposed and barely explicable subject, the lament of Pamphilus for Galathea, is obviously tangential on the surface. (Prof. J. M. Berdan's conjecture that the clergy are here urged to return to Latin, in place of Wolsey's spurious Greek, under cover of the mediaeval *De arte amandi*, may be said to balance in guessmanship Mr. Edwards's discovery that 'Bess' is mankind, and the longing for her divine.[2]) So far the poem lends itself to transference to a context where it will be taken at its face value. Yet as a direct token of love-longing, as it may well appear when sung, it entirely misses the inscrutable but manifest double-talk of the original. (The third verse has been dropped.) The 'Epitaph on John Jaybeard' here retains most of its scurrilous, inexpressible, goliardic text. The abuse is loud and direct, and readily admits of a noisy male chorus and orchestra, in so far as the text may, in performance, sound a little more intelligible than, say, Berlioz's devils in *Faust*. But the setting of the hexameter verse, in the middle six-time section, with a

$$\cup \ \cup \ - \ \ - \ \ -$$

complete disregard for quantity—so that '|Carmina|cum can|nis|' sounds 'Carmina cum|*cann*is', and so forth—is discouraging to the attentive ear. Anyhow, the choice was another challenge to make the voluble tolerable.

The 'Lament for Philip Sparrow'—for Jane Scroope, the blossoming protegée[3] of Carrow Abbey to recite—is shrewdly reduced to less

---

[1] This incidental poem is also the musician's favourite, having had graceful settings (voice and piano) from Parry and Howells; Parry's, an early song, is in a thoughtfully strophic manner, in which key-quality and 'sequential' figure count more than melodic interest; Howells uses a freer rhythmic style in the Mixolydian mode, leaving the main phrases nonetheless articulate and a little tense. W. H. Mellers's less shapely unaccompanied setting is trenchant and impromptu.

[2] *Modern Language Notes*, 30. 5; H. R. L. Edwards, *John Skelton*.

[3] Since her father died in 1485 and she was not his last child, Jane, unlike most of the girls with her at Carrow Abbey, was past her 'teens in 1503, the

than a third of the main poem, cutting out the 'epitaph' stanzas and subsequent blasphemous homage to Jane, and transposing lines (e.g. 'Vengeance I ask. . . .') to screw up the emotional pitch. The elaboration of Jane's grief for her lost sparrow into a semi-goliardic Mass of the Birds has its own problem, if it is to absorb such a mock-ritual procession of grief and intercession in dignified music. This forms the most extended piece. Finally, 'Jolly Rutterkin', whose main text is to be found, anonymous, in an extended male-voice setting (with 'Hoyda' refrain to each of its changing verses) by William Cornyshe of the Chapel Royal.[1] It comprises a jape about drunken foreigners, anticipating Mrs. Page's reference to Falstaff as 'this Flemish drunkard' and probably aimed here at the Flemings who were upsetting the wool trade in Norfolk. (Riot in *The Bouge of Court* might be a preliminary sketch.) To this the composer attached part of a speech of 'Courtly Abusion', one of the infamous court characters attendant on greatness in Skelton's didactic Interlude, *Magnificence*, a daring hit at Henry VIII, his minions and advisers; 'Abusion' having entered two scenes earlier singing 'Rutterkin'. This is scarcely an adequate reason for interposing a text from a source very obscurely indicated by the content! Elinor is thus balanced by this composite gallant, whose long topicality is forgotten but whose sort is far from obsolete.

Once more, then, one may observe the composer choosing the outspoken and erratic Skelton as Norfolk's most memorable literary character, plumping for the most characteristic of the possible poems, and, like Purcell, not being balked by the tough characters or jostling images. While Berg at this period was engaged in *Lulu*, the human tragedy of a woman destroying while she is destroyed, conveyed in

earliest possible date for the poem. (She was married by 1508, which is the commonly accepted date of the poem, owing to its denigration in a work of 1509.) She was therefore not actually the nice little girl which she has been assumed to have been by Howes and others, including, it seems, the composer. See Mr. Edwards's life of Skelton. He regards a date after 1505, the year in which Jane's mother died, as psychologically inconceivable for this mock-Requiem; but three years later seems credible enough.

[1] In the Fairfax Manuscript (B.M.). It is quoted in full by Hawkins in his *History of Music*. The other settings attributed to Cornyshe in this collection are 'Mannerly Margaret' and 'Woefully arrayed'. The former is undeniably Skelton's text. The latter, almost as undeniably (not in Bale's list (1548), but mentioned in the *Garland of Laurel*). There is also a setting of this meditation on Christ's suffering by (John) Browne. (One regrets that the context precluded a V.W. setting here.) There is therefore an inconclusive argument from proximity in favour of *Rutterkin* being Skelton's work. It is odd, however, that it is not in the far from short catalogue in the *Garland*.

music of mounting strain, Vaughan Williams let himself go with the unceasing springs and eddies of low life unrepressed, with a long stretch of pathos as tributary. Even so, it was not the kind of thing expected at festivals. Dyson had produced his gallery of Canterbury Pilgrims, but they are mainly genial, and all obliquely reflected characters, not letting anybody feel their stinking breath. Like Skelton, Vaughan Williams sought (to quote from the preface of the 1718 reprint of *Elinor*), to discover Nature in the lowest Scene of Life:

'Hoc est
Vivere bis, vita posse priore frui'.

Having scanned the literary ground, we may consider what wider relationships reach experience in the concert-hall. *Elinor* falls into five unequal sections: (1) portrait of Elinor, wrinkled but gay; (2) survey of her disreputable tavern customers, with one thought in their head; (3) focus on drunken Alice; (4) further and noisier customers; (5) 'so much for Elinor Rumming'. These differences of visual level are implemented by salient themes and tempi.

(1) There are two motives for Elinor. The first, plainly rehearsed in a preliminary sketch, is mere rhythmic asseveration ('I know a woman down town . . .'). But the second, clearly announced with a new key and the entry of the triangle, has a plainly conceived rhythmic and melodic shape (8 6–2 2–6 6) and leads to a fresh and equally sweeping phrase at 'Her kirtle Bristol red'. These carry the ear past the queer turns of twisted vocal intervals, muted brass, percussion (xylophone), wobbly sonorities and sheer *tutti*, that lend Elinor's portrait depth as well as a wide surface. A broad key-relationship of A–E flat and G–C to A (covering Fit 1) holds fluid sequences together.

(2) A reduced tempo (nine-metre) enables the crowd of drinkers to become articulate through manifold choral declamation, and introduces a rollicking phrase (whose 8 5 2–6 8–6 outline might be a variant of Elinor's tune) before her chase of pig (Fit 2) is caught up by noisy neo-pentatonic canon. The key moves from B Phrygian-minor to F, and the recurring C–A relation for the return to Elinor is now a circular route to F.

(3) The music for Alice (of Fit 4, with four of Sybil's lines from Fit 7) also has its keys, D Phrygian with C major for sleep, to keep her uncontrolled but clearly noted gossip in its place. A bassoon, muted brass and sliding wind are typical background features.

(4) A new and functional phrase for 'With hey and with ho'

(borrowed from Fit 3), characterless but a convenient start and finish to fresh, trochaic, orchestral bustle, in B flat but moving sharpwards, brings bibulous clatter to a head (cymbals).

(5) The established G–A key-relation secures, with the xylophone, a triumphant end to the racy narrative. What might have been a breathless chase after motives is in practice a balanced affair of succeeding tempi, developing theme and passing illustration to the text. How memorable, after a few close hearings, the music is! Obviously Elinor aroused the composer's invention to a high pitch.

The enigmatic 'My proper Bess' is set neatly in verses for baritone, chorus and an oboe-led orchestra, developing enough to claim a repeat of the first strophe with subtle extensions, such as the last phrase in slow motion. An oscillation of key between G major and E Dorian-minor keeps the sentiment within bounds. It would spoil it to say which prevails, but this is the slightest of intermezzos, and before the informed listener has quite decided whether its sentiment is 'going steady' or not, it is over. The student may ponder whether the return, in the choral texture, to the sevenths of a much earlier period is not a raw deal. That choirs will enjoy the lingering phrases is, once more, no answer.

The 'Epitaph', the scherzo movement though called 'Burlesca', is cast by tempo changes into three parts, fast two-beats, slower six (mainly)[1] and back. These enclose the harsh blend of Skeltonics and hexameter verse. A declamatory rising fifth forms a spontaneous link and invites a subversive bass or continuation. Pedantic rejoinders for *Asinum et mulum* (a raw jest) and a final imprecatory descent from the fifth (big and side drums) keep the close wayward. This vituperative interlude, which owes something to Wagner's brooding Nibelung, is more exhilarating for the choir than for the listener, even if doggerel Latin is accepted as the natural idiom for the detraction of the departed, but it releases with orderly gusto our fond and secret disgusts over the knaves in authority who roam unscathed. The harmonic craftsmanship, centring round the sharpened fourth as a constituent feature, is resourceful.

The long and elaborate rendering of 'Philip Sparrow' for contralto and women's chorus shows three main stages: (1) Jane's lament, curse on Gib (put forward) and tender recollections; (2) summons to the winged congregation for Requiem Mass; (3) adieux.

---

[1] I.e. the two main beats, divided into three each, are slower.

(1) A violoncello solo motive sets the opening and closing tone of the initial Lento doloroso, with vengeance (chorus) and affectionate reminiscence (solo) as contrasts, set off by key (C minor–E flat minor–G, B Phrygian, E–E minor).

(2) So to the mock-serious but nowhere parodying ceremony, which Skelton defended later, in the *Garland*, on the simple plea, 'Why condemn the holy rites of a sparrow?' and whose conventual style Vaughan Williams was prepared to take seriously as a piece of unobjectionable piety.[1] Musically, it was for him a challenge, like that of Benedicite, to discover different orchestral modes to typify each contingent group, as later he did with film scenes. (A general precedent was, perhaps, Bliss's *Pastoral Elegy*.) There is no lack of invention here. After a series of individual miniatures, the rhythm gathers fresh and fierce energy for a comprehensive swan-goose turn, while the *nobil-mente*, loud-voiced peacock is here reserved for a pompous climax, representing the 'Grail' (*Graduale*). In reaction the music becomes involved with a haunting figure (violins and wood) on a fixed bass, 'Phrygian' in origin but not in melodic character, with a perpetual shimmer of harp-tone. This for the phoenix. (The expression seems to echo what was conveyed in more homely terms in the 'secret grasses' episode of the last *House of Life* song.)

(3) The token-Mass ended at last, the continuity of the choral finish, which finally echoes Jane's 'tender recollections' (strings), in G major, recalling an earlier moment, is grateful to the ear. It relies much on sevenths and a semitonal, almost 'Hear my prayer' chord (Mendelssohn) for 'evermore'—resolving, however, on the basis of a direct fall from the second degree to the first.

Listeners who, without going in for the pious anti-goliardic renunciations of 1510, find the whole conception fantastic, must not dismiss the music outright on that account, and it needs several hearings before its fragments begin to cohere. On the other hand, the music must be justified by its own assertion, not merely by any emotional or descriptive propriety or finesse. It may seem, as was claimed at once by some responsible criticism, the 'gem' of the whole suite, yet, with its dogged pursuit of illustrative phrases, obviously burdening the recital of so frail a poem, I find it uneven, restless and marred by an excess of invention. This may be a tribute to its vitality, more commonly associated

---

[1] 'I see no reason why Jane should not pray for her sparrow's soul' (note for first performance). But C. S. Lewis eloquently rejects immortality for sentient creatures (*The Problem of Pain*, ch. 9).

with the young experimentalist than with a composer of supposedly settled style.

Little need be said of 'Rutterkin' (baritone solo), offered as the misplaced 'Scherzo' of the suite. Its forthright combination of 'Hoyda' cries, strewn over a bar, and a tune for the verses, avoids a too settled feeling, as in *Benedicite*, by an uncertainty of key (D major or B minor, hexatonic). The tender seventh has become literally derisive in tone. A glockenspiel (last heard at the entry of popinjay) later translates vibrations in the gallant's fuddled brain. Two musical strophes in E flat (hexatonic, with a similarly dominating sixth degree), absorb the four verses from Courtly Abusion's soliloquy with ready solo-chorus repartee. These form one of the bluntest episodes, as such, in the composer's repertoire. A tune as interlude to a symphonic scherzo is familiar experience, though even that would not be strophical. But after an already strophical stretch, the tangential course of this episode is all too patent. However, now back to D. B. Rutterkin with greater attack and the maximum of sheer vibration (wood trills, percussion rolls and prolific arpeggios). There is nothing else for it. Obviously the aim is to avoid a plenary final session with the Tudors, but Rutterkin scarcely makes his portrait worth while. Warlock had made a neat setting for voice and piano, in piquant *chant recitatif*, in three clear stanzas.

The total experience, then, of the *Portraits* is a whirl of conflicting and uneven impressions, with a comparatively jejune finish. The sequel does not live up to the tremendous promise of 'Elinor'. Hence the work offers many problems to conductors, quite apart from the possibility of the defection of singers (or, as at first, of listeners) on non-musical grounds. All the same, without this approach to Skelton, which has no parallel in the composer's career, something vital in Vaughan Williams would not have been brought to light.

Twelve years later, as a tribute for the birth centenary of his 'master', Hubert Parry, he wrote a short 'reading', for chorus, of Skelton's *Prayer to the Father of Heaven*, an early poem in the medieval, impersonal style. The second of the two balanced strophes here is fresh, and compressed at first, in order to leave a margin for the echoing last line:

'And after this life, to see thy glorious Face.'

In a note of dedication, the composer declares his aim to be no pale reflection of style, but something that Parry would have termed characteristic. In fact, style is positively repressed, and the texture hardly recognizable, apart from the vocal concentration; yet the motet is searching enough to stir the imagination as a token of aspiration. It is surprising that the two companion poems were left unset.

DONA NOBIS PACEM

Dona nobis pacem, for soprano, baritone, chorus and orchestra, was written for the centenary of the Huddersfield Choral Society, and was first performed a week after the *Portraits*, though the latter's publication date was a year earlier. The work is evidently occasional in a deeper sense. It springs from a determination, roused by the menace of resurgent nationalisms, once more to drive home the iniquities and tragedies of war, the permanent qualities of a reconciled world, the need to put them in the forefront of human endeavour, and, first and last, the strong intimations of an immanent will, that a new earth must be created in this generation. The way to this dynamic and Christian conception of peace is sought by a certain sublimation of wartime impulses and reflections, each epitomized in a short movement, for horror and desperate need are not enough, though they recur throughout as a colouring of the basic *Dona nobis pacem* solo. No field here for any choral triumph but that of living up to the challenge of the times.

For this dedicated purpose, for which Bliss's *Morning Heroes*, an earlier Norwich-festival work, was an unbiblical precedent, Vaughan Williams has used a wide selection of texts, beginning with Agnus Dei and Whitman and ending with *Micah* and *Luke*. There are eight distinguishable movements: (1) spiritual evocation from the prayer Agnus Dei; (2) recollections of a state summoned to war; (3) an idea for realistic reconciliation on the field; (4) lament for two generations killed in battle; (5) evocation in a context of war (in the Crimea, etc.); (6) vision of a reformed world; (7) the Christmas message; (8) evocation. Extensive settings of Whitman (2–4) are thus balanced by a rather 'scrappy' visionary sequence, linked by one evocation or another but otherwise united only by a certain ethical spirit. A further cause of fragmentation is the stoic earlier style of the Dirge (4).

Of the mainly sentimental settings from Whitman's *Drum Taps*, which succeed the picture of a world on its knees, the first, 'Beat! beat! drums!', is the strongest, inconclusive as its tale of destruction inevitably is. 'Reconciliation' is serene but comparatively conventional, with its smooth modal intonation, recurring strophes and false-ringing final line, repudiated by the critic, Richard Capell, from his trench experience. The Dirge, with a stirring Dorian march tune of firmly knit phrases,

Ex. 27

and a contrasted impressionist motive for the silvery moon, makes a massive structure in its dour manner that is more incisive than Charles Wood's lyrical setting, and not appreciably less tense than Holst's blunter setting (male voices, brass, drums, 1914). But it is also a massive digression. Incidentally, the bass entry at the end ('and my heart, O my soldiers . . .') is an awkward, strained moment, too plain to absorb its text. After an evocation that can only be described as a jumble

232

of both word and tone, *Micah*, 4. 3 and the rest are absorbed in a fresh and extended melodic line, clearly paralleled in certain stanzas of Ireland's J. A. Symonds setting, *These Things Shall Be*. This is at first focused round E flat, but closes sonorously in G. Nevertheless, the leap to the angels' message to the shepherds is not consonant, for all its return to E flat and echoing phrases. This *animato* is a forced release of ubiquitous energy. As the key turns, however, to C major, the delivery becomes solemn, antiphonal (orchestra and chorus) and informally liturgical. Thus the way is plain to the recovery of the serene and positive *dona nobis pacem*, the tortured, protesting reading having fulfilled its purpose initially and later (section 5).

The general message of this cantata, from one resolute man to another, likely to be pertinent as far as thought can reach, is one which no sane listener can refuse the composer's right to deliver, as the subject of his music; or to which he can refuse his moral agreement. Yet such a composer can only plead by the combined art of poet and musician, and he cannot leap from scene to scene unless there is an underlying connection of thought or musical motive. Vaughan Williams seems to have decided that the general testimony of the ages, from Isaiah to Whitman, was what mattered, and for the rest he felt no obligation except to illuminate for its own sake each turn of the scrapbook text as it came, mentally, into his score. Paradoxically, then, the nominally ecstatic point is one of the most questionable. In spite of Bliss and Ireland, and, earlier, Parry (*War and Peace*), there is nothing quite like *Dona nobis pacem* to renew a sense of the urgency of its theme. But musical bewilderment will not be silenced by propitious incidence.

The *Serenade to Music*, a celebration of music in the familiar lines of *The Merchant of Venice*, Act 5. 1, was composed for Henry Wood's jubilee, and first performed in the Royal Albert Hall on October 5, 1938, under the deeply blackening shadow of Hitler's entry into Czechoslovakia. Designed there for sixteen singers of international repute, it is also intended for a normal chorus with four soloists. It is mellifluous but uneventful, and it adds little to the composer's real output. Its inner nonchalance is tacitly admitted in an orchestral setting. Its expert choral touch and cosy idealism will probably maintain it in the repertory, but its texture is reactionary.

FLOS CAMPI

In all these choral works, the vocal writing is consistently congenial to a singer's natural extension of register, and often striking in itself. Yet the voice is properly treated as a medium of declamation and affirmation, not of quasi-instrumental expression. In *Flos Campi*, for viola, small orchestra and small eight-part choir—first produced in 1925—the choir joins on an equal footing with the orchestra in the ensemble which forms the basis of the 'tune for Tertis', that is, a rhapsody for viola in six short movements. As in Debussy's '*Sirènes*' (Nocturne no. 3) and Ravel's *Daphnis and Chloe*, the singers hum or 'ah': they carry no privilege of expression. There is, however, a clue to the sequence of movements, some thematically linked. The suite is in some sense a reflection of certain verses of the *Song of Songs*, a work successively interpreted as a cycle for a wedding ceremony, a collection of liturgical pieces for the ancient Adonis-Tammuz celebrations, a fertility cult, or, most probably, a set of erotic poems, written possibly under their influence.[1] Stray verses from the book, in Latin and English, are placed before each movement in the score (vocal or full), and would appear in any programme note. The references and emotional associations are, briefly: 2. 2, 5 (the pains of separation); 2. 11, 12 (spring invitation); 3. 1, 5. 8, 6. 1 (further separation); 3. 7, 8*a* (heroic company); 6. 13*a*, 7. 1*a* (greeting to princess—not, however, the queen-bride of modern Syrian wedding festivities); 8. 6*a* (devotion).

The title 'Flos Campi', then, is a little obscure, but it denotes no common bloom; and it would appear extraordinary to regard the love-longing steadily delineated here as a token, on familiar 'bride of Christ' analogies, of a divine quest for the beloved community, mankind (as is Skelton's 'My proper Bess', on one reading); or of a desire for the return of the lost tribes of Israel. However this may be worked out in the book as a whole, the biblical quotations here might have been placed as an after-thought, or they reflect a very broad coincidence of a plan to elaborate the Hebrew poem in music and a decision to write a work for viola. Certainly, there is in the texts only the barest clue to the changing moods of the music, apart from the recurring 'I faint for love' and serene finish.

With this broad expectation of a group of tense and sensuous lyrics, the listener discovers that what is relatively plain and straightforward music needs no literary image to place it, and what is arresting and dissonant calls much more for line-upon-line comparison than for any 'cushion' of oriental passion or devotion. The novel interest is, of course, the intrinsic quality of the viola part, and of voices used as a

[1] Professor George W. Anderson has summarized the alternatives in his *Critical Introduction to the Old Testament*.

special reed-chorus in conjunction with solo wood and brass and incidentally a tuneful celesta. The viola had constituted a clue-texture in the scoring of *The Shepherds of the Delectable Mountains* (1922). In the third of the *Mystical Songs*, a wordless chorus had been preferred to the proper text of the tune sung. The *Pastoral Symphony* (finale) had called boldly for a wordless singer, with clarinet as alternative. But nothing so chorally uncompromising had appeared before *Flos Campi*. The text-references having been quoted, then, the work will be considered in its six movements for what they may be worth musically.

(1) *Lento*. The opening reveals the trenchant quality of the prevailing texture. The bitonality (E and F) of the oboe and viola in the initial cadenza was once made an historical exhibit of the complete repudiation of the nineteenth century.[1] Ex. 28*a* shows the immediate translation of

Ex. 28*a*

the oboe line, its basic fifth stretched in the bassoon line by a semitone to a sharpened fifth which is soon recognized as basic by the viola and confirmed later by the full orchestra at the climax of the fifth movement. The strings below meanwhile circle, in extended 1–♭3–5 chords, round E flat, the semitone on the other side of E from F. This is followed by a bare unison theme, of which the later free canonic development is quoted (28*b*). It reappears under a new tension of opposed rhythms in preparation for the climax of no. 5. A choral figure (28*c*) of oscillating sevenths and common chords, an amplification of the sharpened fifth, as the viola shows, maintains the interest and lowers the tension in favour of something more automatic. (This motive, too, recurs later, after the climax mentioned.)

[1] H. C. Colles, *Oxford History of Music*, 7 (1930). Three years earlier, in *English Music*, W. H. Hadow had quoted the third movement as his last characteristic specimen of style.

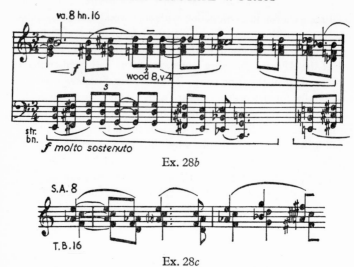

Ex. 28b

Ex. 28c

(2) *Andante con moto.* Over this now transitional music, released from an almost tortured experience, and poised on a non-committal E, steals the tonality of G major, unconventionally and indecisively, yet implicit in the broad and striking tune, too long to quote, that spreads from the viola to the voices. (Colles's invocation of the 'Londonderry Air', with its studied symmetry, is a little unfortunate. In any case, the sharpened fourth of the Lydian mode avoids any possible triteness.) The singers have to accustom themselves, here and elsewhere, to give out an impulsive vocal melody without feeling that they have lost their *raison d'être.* Thus, suave celesta sonorities (1–3–6 texture) lend piquancy to the finish. Sheer vocal shape has its limits.

(3) *Lento. Allegro moderato.* The initial falling-fifth motive, which the viola has already made its own, now pressed inwards to a diminished fifth, introduces fresh turns of choral expression, marked by revolving chords of simple texture (1–3–6, 1–3–5 in interval) but oscillating semitone. (Although this oscillation between, say, A natural and A flat in the same orbit has been known from early folk-song, language has not yet produced a better term than 'false relation' to denote this contingency of a given *degree*, which has been a commonplace of harmonic progression in the last forty years, and especially, for present readers, since the *Mass in G minor.*) After the second viola invocation, the choral line becomes more articulate but far from conclusive. 'I found him not' may help to explain this; but after the pungent dialectic of no. 1, this inter-

lude might be put down as 'so shapeless that it must have a programme behind it'.

(4) *Moderato alla marcia.* The punctuation is now exemplary. The patent and solemn march-rhythm (90, not 120 to the minute), set phrases (of 8/7, later 4/5 bars) and steadily opposed key-centres (C/E) are enhanced by the disciplined and antiphonal grouping of varied solo-ensemble and *tutti*, the astringent D flat of the C Aeolian-minor phrases, the free viola part and the striking incursion of the chorus in primitive fifth-degree consonance with the bass. The cumulative impact of these unfaltering phrases has an inexorable touch.

(5) *Andante quasi lento (largamente).* There seems to be some sugges-tion of 'Reconciliation' (*Dona nobis pacem*), eminently vocal in texture, apart from the viola bravura, which the wayward harmonic movement, slipping more than it steps forward, provokes. The opening progression is stressed. Then, a spasm of agitato, the only passage of its kind, introduces the reflections of no. 1 already mentioned. The choral oscillations now find a point of gravitation in the chord of B minor in place of E.

(6) *Moderato tranquillo.* In direct continuity, the viola begins a new theme on a leisurely gradual curve of 3–8–3 in the Aeolian mode. In the multiple reverberation of this, D soon acquires, without any argument, a position of priority, so that the tune gains the 1–6–1 shape of, say, the hymn-tune *Adoro te.* (It is now familiar through the counter-melody of the finale of the fifth symphony.) This pervasive line, with an equally typical answering 8–5 descent, is irrevocably cadential, and the sudden scouring of the texture, leaving plain major-key harmony, leaves no room for ambiguity. From this point, apart from a brief return to the opening (now opposing F natural with F sharp tonality), the music seems to move in a straight line, except for incidents of harmony, voice, and instrument (celesta, etc.) throughout its hundred and more ample bars. Once more, a reference to *Solomon* (8. 6a) may suggest to the sceptic why the music sounds as it does; and if it comes to that, it is hard to imagine why the complementary 'for love is strong as death' was left out. Yet this flow of serene corroborative melody, now imitative and manifold, now quasi-strophic, is enigmatic in its context. The rift of style, the sudden abandonment of the characteristic in favour of an epilogue which might occur anywhere, cannot escape notice. The composer seems to show some final misgivings by his elusive close on the basis of a two-plane ascent from the fifth degree of B minor to the tonic, on a receding horizon, leaving the fifth degree within hearing and an

unequivocal tonic to the imagination. Even then, there remains a choice of accepting B minor as the keynote, taking the ear back to the start of the movement, or of invoking D major as a necessary completion after so much assertion of that key. Certainly a rigid close is, as so often, avoided. The main matter is none the less unpersuasively becalmed and monotonous to my ears. 'Dynamic calm' does not mean relaxed imagery.

On the whole, this suite, of under twenty minutes, is expressive out of all proportion to its size, and has accordingly been considered in detail. In its terse style, it is an obvious companion to the *Pastoral Symphony*. It shows a similar unconcern with conventional contrasts of rhythm, a novel and uncompromising texture, an absorbed contemplative manner, and orderly enlargements of experience within its chosen limits of mood and material. Yet the free disposition of the suite into six arbitrary movements, its overt titular references to a coherent text, and its exploitation of intimate choral and instrumental sonority, place it beside the unscheduled, opportunist choral works, rather than the broader, symmetrical route of the symphony.

SANCTA CIVITAS

The nearly contemporary *Sancta Civitas—The Holy City*, a setting of verses from *Revelation* for baritone, chorus and full orchestra, is also a contemplative piece, especially in the 'new heaven' section, but its orbit is much wider than *Flos Campi*, and its organization of short movements in one striking whole is almost symphonic. The work is thus of special importance in its decade, and indeed in the composer's progress in general.

He calls it an oratorio, choosing Latin for the main title to avoid any confusion with Alfred Gaul's cantata of 1882, still described by *The Referee* in 1892 as 'that amazingly popular work'. English oratorio, of the reflective kind favoured by Parry and Stanford, can easily sink into choral aphorisms linked by solo-declamation and cantabile in an endless, pointless sequence. Parry's confinement of *Job* to five 'scenes' was a significant attempt to crispen his narrative, and (whatever Cowen may have made of *leitmotiv*) *Gerontius* showed, once and for all, the advantages of binding symphonic motives, released and reverberating in a working antiphony of solo and choral stages in a spiritual journey. One reaches the final translation of the soul with a rich reserve of accepted symbols, with a musically steady potential, of divine life and communal exercise at the highest level. *Gerontius* also illustrates the stimulus of a single thought, here divine judgement, in maintaining a central grip on the imagination.

In choosing his text from representative verses of *Revn.* 4, 7, 18, 19, 21 and 22, Vaughan Williams brings the listener from the start into the inner territory of revelation, not without familiar phrases long since revered by musicians through Handel's incandescent intonations. From there the visionary narrative moves to the terrible figure of judgement, and in the shadow of its sweeping lethal power turns back to cast a sharp light on condemned 'Babylon' (18). But on universal Babylon, not historical Babylon. Hence the sudden transition to a bold vision of the reformed and revered city (21, omitting the chapter on the cycle of judgements) is conceivable without confusion of category. It continues, with a happy interpolation from the vision of the martyrs (7. 15–17), in more resplendent imagery (22), bluntly reinforced by the Sanctus from the Communion Service. This vernacular touch, analogous to the accession of Psalm 90 in *Gerontius*, prepares for the final 'even so come Lord' of a prophet turned worshipper, ending where he began. Still, it makes a curious shifting of ground from imaginative exercise to a well-worn ritual formula. Throughout, the text has been precisely selected, mainly from the Authorized Version. (Where the 'additions from Taverner's Bible' can be found, would be hard to say.) The purge of Babylon and her vested interests is kept in its place and the note of pathetic regret amplified; and the image of the ideal city, which makes *Sancta Civitas* a pioneer work of religious imagination, is kept simple and reasonably continuous.

From the outset, then, this oratorio, for what the name is worth, ranges itself away from the common Handelian drama of national and personal conflict and a wave of religious elation towards the inner moods of *Messiah*, but without the free-and-easy range of text. Handel, accepting his librettist's lead with seeming nonchalance, first draws on *Revelation*, in his 'Hallelujah!' chorus, almost by accident; as the sudden climax of a procession of isolated prophetic verses, cast in a conventional pattern of recitative with air or chorus. While his translation of the writer's constancy in face of State-worship is truly as magnificent as his methods are simple, his achievement is hazardous, as the average pompous or perky rendering demonstrates, and even after a lifetime of happy acquaintance it would not be easy to predicate *inner* elation. Vaughan Williams's purpose is, in a sense, narrower, but it is much more positive and unmistakable. It is to affirm the truth of revelations, made to persons 'in the spirit', of an omnipotence that has judged and will judge a corrupt, godless civilization, and of an ideal kingdom that must be brought to earth by vision and resolution. An introductory quotation from the *Phaedo* of Plato (114D) finds good ground for the entry of a musician here. The belief expressed in myth, that the cycle of existence after death depends on the character of life on earth is, Socrates maintained, a gamble worth the highest stakes, and it demands evocative music. Hence the present call to exercise new sources of power, through a response to inner convictions, cries equally for imaginative music.

Such is the hazardous, dare-all spirit in which the oratorio has been written. The composer is determined to leave the listener on the right track, rejecting the urbanity of traditional English oratorio for a more experimental, impromptu manner, and realizing in its place a higher musical dialectic. We have noticed a similar but more distracted mood, confronting an urgent world-situation, in the later *Dona nobis pacem*. Between these, the ballet *Job* presented in a new medium fresh figures of resistance to the destructive forces in human nature. With these confirmations fresh in the mind, there is little question why *Sancta Civitas* has been written. The whirling imagery would be meaningless rant if it were not meant seriously. As a purely aesthetic hypothesis, the music is persuasive but baffling at certain points of both stress and relaxation. As didactic music, it 'corresponds' and coheres.

So much must be borne in mind in approaching music which, it seems, remains somewhat remote from general comprehension. A text so precisely selected and disposed calls for as much thought as the composer himself gave to its choice, and for an imaginative grasp of its content, whether new or familiar, whether incredible or a result of the mind's long discipline.

The music falls into six unequal movements: (1) *Rev.* 19. 1, 5–9: introduction (mainly *lento*); (2) 19. 11–12, 14–16: the figure on the horse (*allegro*); (3) 19. 17, 19, 21; 18. 2, 10, 9, 11, 14, 16, 18–23, 2: transition to a doomed Babylon (*lento*); (4) 21. 1–2, 11–12, 21–23, 25–26; 7. 15–17; 22. 1–2, 4–5: vision of the Holy City (*adagio* with later modifications); (5) 4. 8: vernacular response (*poco animato*); (6) 22. 7, 16, 20: unity of spirit affirmed (*lento*). The division (made by Howes and others) into only three sections, corresponding with the verses from chapters 19, 18 and the rest, does not do justice to the contrasts and distinctness of each tempo and mood. Nor is there more than a passing repetition of substantial motive until the brief epilogue. Let us face the true problems of structure, as suggested by the foregoing tabulation. A glance at the text explains why there are at least six stages, and why 2, 3, 4 and 5 cannot conform, and must be left to form their own shape, symphonic movements in miniature. It remains to observe how far continuity is maintained. Facing a similar issue in *Benedicite* yielded some misgivings midway, but alert listening is the only hope at a critical turn.

(1) *Lento*. The prologue at once makes clear that, apart from solo and choral declamation 'framed to the life of the words', texture will be of primary importance. The broadest definition here is of key, or at least key-base, leaving mode and an occasional major to assert itself as expedient. C, the basic start, is thus a clue to the roots of the music, with A flat and E to follow, A flat for the distant and holy choir of boys' voices and trumpet, E for the approach to the centre of power, made familiar to numberless English audiences by Handel's vocal thrust and un-English declamation. These two pivots, each related to C independently, form recurrent centres of repose, with C paramount. Secondly, two features of chordal colouring command attention: one, at the start,

Ex. 29: 1*a*

Ex. 29: 1*b*

intimating a mental shake-up that may become ecstasy, is cadential, and seems to begin where the slow movement of the *London Symphony* left off (1*a*, 1*b*); the other is a trenchant fixation, which may or may not

Ex. 29 : 2*a*

resolve later, such as appeared in the Allegro of the same symphony and meanwhile establishes itself as a tonic major chord with a difference (2*a*). To this may be added a general linking assertion of revolving

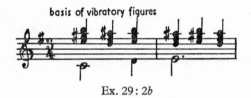

Ex. 29 : 2*b*

1–3–5 ♯5 chords, as in 2*b* and the distant-choir motive, which actually lifts the key from A flat back to C for 2*a*. A primary 1 5 6 8 9 8 phrase for 'Praise our God' fills in other gaps. This still leaves a special and tremendous cadence (and rejoinder to Handel's melodic concentration) for the ringing, Caesar-defying declaration of true omnipotence, echoing the brass motive of *In the Fen Country* (Ex. 14) with a more taut pen-ultimate chord and fresh issue.

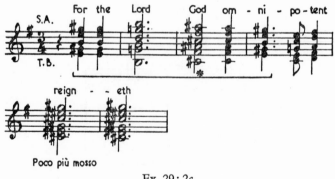

Ex. 29 : 2*c*

(2) *Allegro.* Ex. 1*b* above may be a closed circle, or, as now, a chain to cast aside. In a 'lightning' tonality, the judicial figure is present to the inner eye, though 'he doth *judge and* make war' here appears without the italicized words (to avoid replacing the preceding 'in|righ-teous-ness|' by 'in|righteous-ness-he doth'|?) The encounter is translated into whirling choral triads and octaves in a sweeping triple, soon quintuple, measure and fiercely dazzling orchestral colour. A Mixolydian strain saves the melodic trend from banality, and the non-melodic rising thirds (5 7 8) keep it free from old modality. The revelation of the divine identity is assigned to another special progression (prosaically the intonation of 1 ♮7 1 ♮3 1, threefold), reduced to bare essentials, including side-drum and brass. Thus a single fortified phrase covers what took Handel an extended series of rising plagal (4–1) cadences. The absorbing impressionist texture of movement 1 has been replaced by dynamic rhythmic movement in harmonically unpredictable directions. Hence, the final cadence is absolutely conclusive and committal, and the side-drum seems to place it in the depths of consciousness and, indeed, conscience, perceptible to the rawest intelligence.

(3) *Meno mosso—Lento.* This overwhelming advance on the faltering start of 'I was in the spirit', is followed by an equally sharp turn to the judgement of 'Babylon'. The chordal characteristic of theme 2,

movement 3

drum

Ex. 30*a*

Lento ♩=72

p

16.32
Ex. 30*b*

tightened by an extra dissonant note (Ex. 30*a*) and semitonal texture, throws a fierce light on the figure of the angel of retribution, and, by a masterly transformation (30*b*), introduces the fearful lament over the pulverized city. A variant of the upper harmony of 30*b* against a bass of E flat or G, forms a lyrical refrain for semi-chorus, to link pious head-shakings in impromptu *fugato*, the now censorious distant-choir motive in its exclusive key, and further symbols of punishment. Harmonic reminders of the wrath that came in *Wenlock Edge* are also perceptible to the retentive ear (G chord against A flat). This becomes the feature of the final fixation (cf. 29: 1*a*). 'Alas, Babylon' thus forms a practical ground for music at various levels, but threatens surfeit in the end.

(4) *Adagio* and *Meno adagio*. The leap of thought from an almost cosy decadence back to renascence, by translating an obstructive A flat into an assonant G sharp, is reasonable enough, but the problem of the barely articulate utterance, impossible at an animated speed, is con-siderable. Compensating factors are a primitive solo-violin phrase on a rising 1 2 4 5 curve, answering themes (oboe, flute and oboe) for the pearl-gates and ever-open gates, and a startling variety of mode and of scale beyond mode; the Dorian F for verse 23 (Ex. 7*e*), the Lydian F with flat seventh for 7. 15, and a consolidation in a distracting context of the E major previously inaugurated by making A flat into G sharp. The combination of a basic texture, reflecting odd curves of plainsong, with perpetual novelty of key and mode, may be said to convey, in spite of a tempo never above 80, the needed lightness of spirit after the heaviness of Babylon. There is a qualified return to E major, in itself only a contributory key at first, and another entry of the treble choir, still in A flat but renewed in detail and now extended by the full chorus. Yet there is no material sense of levitation. Gropingly, one might say, another movement has been pursued to a finish.

'Music for this noble, hazardous hypothesis!' cried Socrates. 'Less of this exuberant humanism!' echo some preachers of today. The music for these is becoming available. Once more, it depends less on any riveting structure (though it would not be hard to document the resource further) than on some personal grasp of the situation, com-municated within the terms of reference. That is probably why, at this crucial stage of formulation, reception has sometimes not been at all forthcoming. The best performances were those under the composer; and reservations will not help a conductor. But a committed interpreter can solve these problems, and audiences *can* meet him part of the way. The hazard of communication remains, and nowhere more than in this superficially ruminant Adagio. But gradually our understanding improves.

(5) *Poco animato*. There is now a considerable need to drive some-

thing home. The plain canonic entry of a new motive, in C and E, and then in broader orchestra-chorus antiphony in A flat, leading to E and back to A flat, provides an unusual contour (1 2 3 ♯4 5 ♭6 5, propelled by the chord of 2a above). Thus when, at the powerful climax of this interpolated rubric of worship, the tremors of 2b reverberate, there is an increasing sense of recovered atmosphere and confirmed textural grip. More, perhaps, than the text demands.

(6) *Lento.* A last grasp of A flat (the vanishing point of the distant choir's horizon) fades before the return of the opening progression in C. This is now the background of the tenor's striking brief entry, with ritual choral reply. The last chord of 1a becomes the receding focal point of the original bass stirrings, in the context of personal committal. The long orbit of exploration is complete, or at least it will now move in a straight line of contemplation.

The gravitation of the fourth movement, after a wayward *lento,* to a long and protracted *adagio* section, is one of the baffling features already mentioned. It would be impossible to account for the shape of this series of episodes on purely musical grounds; and the fresh start for 22.4 is so plain and pentatonic that great skill of interpretation will always be needed to avoid a raw moment. Yet as an evocation it fills its place in the scheme. When Ernest Newman confessed to a 'consuming nostalgia for dear old Babylon' after a certain performance, owing to a lack of warmth in the later movements, he seems to have forgotten the monotonous pathos and penetrating sense of vacuity in the Babylon section. On the whole, Vaughan Williams has never done better with words. He always seemed to reserve a special place for *Sancta Civitas,* in the spreading of his mature discoveries round the country; and the acceptance of the work may be regarded as a fair test of a true understanding of the composer.

Flos Campi and *Sancta Civitas* thus start together on the fringes of the third symphony, as ultra-rhapsodic works. There is a meditative trend which, allowed further licence, might end in a closed circle. *Job,* composed round 1930, begins with perpetual drift but soon pulls up. The fourth symphony admits drift only as a piece of ironic pathos. The mannerism has been checked. We shall observe later the novel trio of symphonies which thus emerged in numbers 4-6, and then the place of *Job* in the composer's later affirmations. We may now consider the secular operas, the earliest of which dates from the period of the *London Symphony,* while the largest is comfortably in the early 'thirties.

IX

Works for the Stage

A PRELIMINARY SURVEY

In surveying the composer's choral works, one is brought into contact with a remarkable variety of texts, and is conscious that he was creating the taste for his styles as he went on. The one common assumption is that a chorus is entitled to a leading part in the score of a work that may be crystallizing round a given text on an orchestral scale. The main process of composition is fitted to the text adopted. This usually begins with a general, and then a particular, choice of text, followed by a scheme of movements into which to dispose isolated settings. In turning to the operas, one pauses to consider what there was in the national tradition, which might pave the way for a certain type of stage product.

The conclusions of Chapter III on this topic were extremely negative. There was the voluble speech-song and fantastically rational plots of Gilbert and Sullivan operettas, unconcernedly bitty and unexpansive in structure, reactionary in texture, and appreciable chiefly for the disciplined, witty and often tuneful delivery of vernacular speech. At another level, there was Stanford's work on material derived from Chaucer, Shakespeare and Newbolt, of which *Much Ado about Nothing*, revived at Oxford in 1949, remains the most notable. One should not dismiss these well-nigh forgotten operas of Stanford too lightly in the present context. They asserted a belief in English opera, and cleared the ground of any rumours that it need be an imitation of other national styles, like Smyth's *Wreckers* (1909), or, if English, then incurably heavy or comic. Yet the ballad-opera tradition influenced Stanford's work considerably and left strophe and impromptu declamatory rejoinder in command, at the expense of a more expansive development.

In any case, round 1910 nothing had established native opera in serious competition with opera from abroad, whether Italian, French, German or (from 1913) Russian. Nor was there any demand for opera in the vernacular at Covent Garden, as at opera-houses in other countries. The composer of a full-blown English opera was thus, if he was any good, something of a philanthropist. If Elgar ever wanted to write an opera in his fifties, he could hardly have afforded the time as a specula-tion on the chance of having his opera accepted. There was no question of a commission. On a wave of national fashion and militant feminism, *The Wreckers* at Covent Garden (1910) earned Smyth a national reputation; but it had first been produced in Leipzig and Prague.

However, with deep early memories of *Walküre* and the gripping stage moment, and the feeling that melody might carry over many situa-tions, and that gumption would go a long way to solving fresh problems of construction, Vaughan Williams followed up *A Sea Symphony*, and incidentally the *Folk-song Fantasia*: *Studies for an English Ballad Opera* (see p. 167), with *Hugh the Drover or 'Love in the Stocks'*: *a Romantic Ballad Opera* on an imaginary incident in a Cotswold town during the war with Napoleon. Written in 1911–14, the opera was produced in 1924, considerably revised in 1933, and further revised in 1956. There are two acts, with an additional scene to commence Act 2 in the 1933 revision, which was withdrawn in the 1956 version, published in 1959. A full chorus is involved, besides more than six soloists. In 1922 appeared a short chamber-opera, *The Shepherds of the Delectable Mountains*. This was later incorporated, with a different end-ing, in the Morality-with-music of 1951, *The Pilgrim's Progress*. The composer's largest opera, *Sir John in Love*, formerly sub-titled *The Fat Knight* and closely based on the Falstaff scenes in *The Merry Wives of Windsor*, was produced in 1929 and 1930 by amateurs, but profes-sionally not till 1946. This four-act work, with a very large cast, has also been revised and augmented, chiefly by an additional scene for Act 3. A prologue, used at Bristol in 1933[1] and introducing the opera as entertainment for Queen Elizabeth I on the lines of the eighteenth-century tradition, has been withdrawn. An additional episode, for Bardolph and Co. before they enter with booty (Act 1), remains optional. A further additional interlude, formerly intended to divide the scenes in Act 2, is now placed at the start of Act 3. The near-contemporary,

---

[1] For production by the Bristol Opera School, which, under Robert Percival, had included *Hugh* (1929) in an enterprising annual repertory of national opera of many nations.

but slightly earlier, *The Poisoned Kiss*, an Extravaganza in Three Acts to a text by Evelyn Sharp, appeared in 1936, and the still earlier *Riders to the Sea*, an unembellished setting of almost the whole of Synge's one-act play, with soloists and women's chorus, was published in 1936. Finally, after decades of pondering, *The Pilgrim's Progress* was produced at the Festival of Britain, 1951, and revised before publication, chiefly in the enlargement of the 'Vanity Fair' scene.

Vaughan Williams has thus been in and out of opera for a considerable part of his career, but in different creative moods, as well as in a variety of chosen situations. *Hugh the Drover* is a normal romantic opera. *Sir John* follows Verdi and Holst in celebrating an almost historical figure with fresh gusto. *The Poisoned Kiss* is a relaxation of style, in separate numbers, but it is on a full scale. *Riders to the Sea* is a close reading of Synge. *The Pilgrim's Progress* is so much more didactic than operatic that it may be reserved for a chapter on such works. We have thus to deal here with one shorter and one full-size normal opera, one sophisticated magic-opera, and one play-setting.

HUGH THE DROVER

Hugh the Drover, then, is the first of two operas, representing the composer in the second and third decades, with some later work added, subtracted or made optional. Both are English to the roots in their dramatic atmosphere and melodic background. Their use of folk-song is, indeed, pronounced enough to recall earlier attempts to do justice to national character in the last century, which have for too long been regarded as a composite precedent in a common musical category.

Four questions arise in every opera so coloured: (1) How much there is of genuine folk-song, whatever the setting? (2) How much of imitation of a folky or national style? (3) What dramatic use is made of either? (4) How far musical interest is furthered or retarded?

The idea of introducing 'national folk music' into an otherwise cosmopolitan (that is, Italian) style of opera goes back to minor Russian composers of the eighteenth century, such as Fomin and Matinsky, liberated serfs trained in Italy, or foreign court composers like Canobbio. The popular *The Miller who was a Wizard, a Deceiver and a Marriage Broker*, a forecast of the rogue of *The Bartered Bride*, was adapted from French vaudevilles. Ablessimovich, the librettist, indicated to the composer Sokolovsky (whose work survives only in the revision by Fomin), places where the words were to be sung to folk-tunes, as solo-numbers, harmonized, not as choruses. In *The Post Drivers*, a one-act opera by A. F. Lvov, a keen folk-song collector, and Fomin, a coachman's life is freely and boldly illustrated by folk-song and dance; the then vulgarian associations of folk-music are disregarded. In *The St. Petersburg Bazaar* (1779), Matinsky, his own librettist, contrives to set another humorous exposure of business and bourgeois types in a framework of national and, in the wedding-eve scene, traditional song, although the solos are in a derivative Italian style. Matinsky's work was remodelled, again, by Vassily Pashkevich, whose version, *As you sow, so shall you reap* (1792) is alone extant.[1] In the composite *The Early Reign of Oleg* (1790) by Pashkevich, Canobbio and Sarti, Canobio brings into the third act the 'Kamarinskaya', in a rather dandified variation-setting, anticipating Glinka (see p. 167); and Sarti experiments with his idea of Greek modes. A large number of folk songs were in fact published during these years.

In this comic, 'rehearsal' atmosphere, then, vernacular music supported the historical rise of the Russian theatre at St. Petersburg and Moscow with the flavour or substance of village tunes.[2]

Glinka, a much more important composer, was first attracted to Italian opera, and his determination to write a 'Russian' opera was the product of deliberate thought about the possibilities. *A Life for the Tsar*, now commonly entitled *Ivan Sussanin*, is patriotic, or at least Tsarist: Tsar Michael is saved by the peasant Sussanin's self-sacrificing diversionary manoeuvring of the Polish enemies. *Ruslan and Ludmila*, long in completion, is gallant and full of oriental magic—spasmodically national in appeal, for Dostoevsky's interpretation of the basic libretto, Pushkin's youthful poem, *Ruslan*, as an allegory of Turkish oppression and Russian succour to the Slavs, does not bear scrutiny. The strong individual note, however, of both works, with *Ruslan* far ahead of the earlier opera musically, might be broadly and imaginatively summarized as national in character, centring round 'the old Russian heroic style' (Calvocoressi), with all its then modern touches. Yet beyond an occasional curve of Tatar melody, as in Prince Ratimir's air in *Ruslan*, Act 3, or the more positively hexatonic major tune of Finn's ballad in Act 2, or an infectious rhythmic inflection like the tumultuous

[1] For a few numbers, see A. S. Rabinovich's history, *Russian Works* (1948). The ballad types of song are all major.

[2] See. M. D. Calvocoressi, *A Survey of Russian Music*; N. F. Findeisen, 'The earliest Russian operas', *Musical Quarterly*, 19. 3 (July, 1933); Gerald Seaman, 'E. I. Fomin', *Monthly Musical Record*, 88. 21 (January–February, 1958).

'Caucasian' (but major) *Lezginka* of Act 4, there are few genuine folk-elements; and the harmonic colour of the music is utterly of its half-century. The 'Russian' element in this eclectic art consists, rather, in bursts of plain, symmetrical tune and a stalwart style, such as the patriotic chorus sung by the Moscow crowd in the Epilogue of *A Life for the Tsar*, or a similar musical incident in the finale of *Ruslan*, Act 2, forecast in the prelude. They are all wholeheartedly major or minor, some modulating. Rhythmically, they are elementary and rather square, but never with the detachment of a unilinear melody. The same applies to the mere modal colouring of the choruses in Verstovsky's *Askold's Tomb* (1835).

In Mussorgsky's quasi-epic tragedy, *Boris Godunov*, from the very start one is more aware of the actual accents and turns of Russian folk-song. The homage song in the prologue (first introduced into opera by F. X. Blyma in *Old-World Christmas*, 1799) is traditional, although modern enough to have made a substantive major interlude in the Allegretto of Beethoven's E minor quartet (op.59); the 'revolution' song and the monks' song near the close are folk-songs; the children's songs of hostess and nurse are at least folky; and (to make her more historical) Marina is labelled unmistakably Polish by the use of the rhythms of the Krakowiak, mazurka and polonaise—as in the Polish intrusions in *Ivan Sussanin*—as a build-up to her differentiation from the false Dmitri, and also to cover a certain weakness of characterization in an accessory figure; which arouses reflection, in the context of the present chapter.

Yet the folk-element in Mussorgsky (for there is more in *Khovan-shchina*) is absorbed, not exposed. Mode is not just reverted to, but exploited in a *coincidentia oppositorum* of free harmony. The national features must be sought in a peculiar, often pantomimic truthfulness of expression, improvisatory structure, versatile instrumental colour, rhythmic reiteration instead of thematic development, and the dramatization of mass-feeling. (These appeals, and limitations of appeal, may be remembered as fresh challenges to opera composers who do not rely on clue-theme and symphonic development.) Similarly, in *Prince Igor* Borodin quotes one actual tune, in Act 4. Even the Polovtsi dance-tunes are only *based*, if at all, on oriental sources. The national touch lies in the rhythmic drive, sharp colouring, and so on. Tchaikovsky used folk-song constantly but *generically*, in typical motherly-servant choruses, love-lamenting solos, ritual hymns and wild village dances (Russian for *The Voevoda*, *Snow Maiden*, Ukrainian for *Vakula*, *Mazeppa*), with many folky phrases in attendance, to broaden the passionate appeal elsewhere.[1]

Rimsky-Korsakov, a more calculating composer, and an industrious collector, uses folk-song, including the orally transmitted songs of legendary epic, to some purpose in the crowd scenes of *Sadko* and *Kitezh*, in contrast with the brilliant semitonal hues of the more fantastic tableaux. But even these lack spontaneity; and in his memoirs Rimsky-Korsakov betrays his concoctive methods by remarking in his own defence, 'Folk-songish melodies must naturally be based on the curves and motives of genuine folk-songs', and goes on to ask how they could be effective if they did not follow these curves. Such a composer is a warning to nationally minded audiences.

Cross another frontier, and one can hear *The Bartered Bride*, Smetana's second opera, to a libretto by K. Sabina, for the national Czech theatre established in 1862. It is a work of dazzling gaiety, reflecting the freedom of rural Bohemia from the darkening shadow of German interference; perceptive without being distressful. Musically, however, one finds only a background of comparatively modern popular music—scarcely folk-music—and the folk tune of the opening 'spring' chorus is as exceptional as the old Hussite chant inevitably introduced into the later 'festival picture', *Libuše*. The equally popular Furiant and Polka were added for a later version. Smetana, in fact, disapproved of counterfeiting the art of the people. He considered that national character was to be expressed 'in the thought and substance of a work'. Indeed the tremendous popular appeal of the *Bride*, as a perpetual embodiment of the national spirit for audiences for whom, doubtless, melodic authenticity or antiquity was not a prime concern, seemed to Smetana to be an obstacle to the appreciation of his later and more reflective operas, such as *Dalibor* and *The Kiss*, and he professed disdain for the *succès d'estime* that he had gained. Hence, for a methodical pursuit of folk-song, one has to move forward to Janáček; and even *Jenufa* yields no whole folk-tune.

So much, then, for the reality of 'the successful use of folk-song for dramatic purpose by the Russians and most conspicuously by Smetana in *The Bartered Bride*' commonly credited, and adduced by Howes (p. 273) as a precedent for Vaughan Williams procedure. Once more the legitimate cultivation of the rhythmic and melodic *idiom* of folk-song is not to be confused with whole quotations (harmonized), or sophisticated imitations, or the racy touches which may be mistaken for

[1] See Gerald Abraham, *Tchaikovsky*, ch. 7.

251

traditional material. Even Bach's use of chorales in his Passion music—Lutheran but none the less traditional by 1723—is not a true musical precedent. There a chorale verse is either absorbed in or accessory to a movement generated from other motives, or it is, in intention, a congregational, over-to-you moment, as any chorale incident, whether sung or played, is, obliquely, to the sympathetic observer. A native folk-tune has no such symbolic appeal to a dedicated listener. At best, it can only carry an allusion to a familiar encounter, like a classical allusion in literature or art. In the public opera-house, imprisonment, oppression and exile situations have sounded in varying degree the voice of freedom to a potentially insurrectionary or rescuing audience, as in Auber and early Verdi, but not noticeably through any recognizable song, such as *Lilliburlero*.

We must turn, then, to *Hugh the Drover* without any firm sense of precedent. The librettist was Harold Child, a London journalist and dramatic critic. Here, as in *Shamus O'Brien*, a vigorous, combative town life encourages the flow of more or less independent incident expected in a ballad-opera, in which slices of life are put together in a rich but amorphous sandwich. (Foss remarks, 'Hugh is so picturesque as to be unconvincing'.) Traditional street cries, a ballad-seller putting across one of his tunes, Morris-men with a suitable West-country dance-tune and workable counter-melody, all vigorously urbanized by harmony, supply diversionary numbers and fill gaps by quotation.

Further, there are simple strophical tunes that sound almost like national songs, such as the Showman's early patriotic song, a reflection in method of construction, of Shamus's first song. The same character's more compact and equally pro-Cotswold ballad, 'Oh! the Devil and Bonyparty', uses the Dorian mode and is not unlike a folk-song, apart from the usual fixations and harmonic associations, which are duly exploited, in a later repeat of the verses, in *changing* keys. Another derivative and equally mobile tune, first sung by the crowd to 'O the cock has had his comb cut' after John has gone down before Hugh in the fight, comes back at the end of the act to augment the sudden reversal of village feeling as Hugh is arrested as a suspected enemy agent, on the deposition of the Constable. (All these are naturally introduced by Maurice Jacobson into his choral arrangement of the opera, *A Cotswold Romance*.) Thus, blunt but shapely melody is used to build up an image of the 'gentle', but unbowed, yeomen of England, faced with Napoleon. At a more personal level arises the verse that Mary adds to the ballad-seller's sample one: 'On Tuesday morning the bells they shall ring', applied at once and tearfully to her own approaching marriage to butcher John, whom, as soon appears, she does not love. (Her entry-verse makes a singularly forced appearance on the arm of ballad-coincidence! Surely one of the most artless entrances that a prima donna ever made.)

A background, then, of rural, stalwart music (for a war-threatened English town may well reflect, musically, the heroic style of a Tsarist court) is present here. It carries the strong, civic, crowd-feeling, con-servative and defensive, and interested only in fair play at home and resistance to the Enemy everywhere. The texture is elementary. It may be reluctantly accepted (but not Mary's song) as hearty without excess. But it wears thin at the end of the act. In the second act, traditional melody makes a further, mainly picturesque, appearance—even John knows a May-day carol-tune of genuine Dorian make—but soul-states here occupy the main interest.

The main reactions lie with a faltering Mary, steel-elbowed John and the fascinating mystery-man, Hugh, rounding up horses for the war.[1] Hugh, rover and drover with gold in his pocket and unlimited confidence in his swelling head, can hardly fail to win against John, a bully and a cad, or, even in 1812, against Mary's obstinate father, the town Constable, ready to stop at nothing to put Hugh out of the way but otherwise without any real determination. Mary is soon at Hugh's feet, only waiting to be thrown out of her own house for the vagabond life that she impulsively accepts at first, in the desired company.

Structurally, a balance is struck between the somewhat stiff ballad style of Hugh's masterful overtures (first playfully ironical, then sternly lyrical), and of later exchanges between Hugh and Mary, and a wayward impromptu development, with some piquant motives to bring home Mary's repulsion from John and her realization that she has met her fate and must abandon her safe life. These include a somewhat catchpenny outline for the Drover; a major-key descent of 8 6 5 3. This is anticipated in the opening bars, and destined for more pomp and circumstance and brass than it can take. Sullivan is more canny in making a similar curve a sheer ritual formula of Mikado-worship. The fight makes lively, bustling *vive-le-sport* music in nine- and twelve-

---

[1] Late in 1918 a rather tired British officer reported to the Education officer (H. E. Mann) at Valenciennes, to organize music. He had been looking after the horses of a heavy battery. Doubtless he remembered this when he witnessed *Hugh the Drover* emerging. His narrative to Holst runs, 'Can you imagine me in charge of 200 horses!... Before I had time to find out which were horses and which were wagons I found myself in the middle of a retreat' (*Heirs and Rebels*, p. 46).

time; its dynamic quality prompted the late Tudor Davies actually to lay out his opponent at one performance.

The remaining demonstrations of crowd feeling against John, and then Hugh, are of the blunt communal type already noticed, making a blustering but unalarming close. The general texture so far is remarkably unsubtle. Even Hugh's 'Camp fires' aria is as breezy as a Song of Travel; and Mary's spirited 'Ah no! you shall not fight him' scarcely fulfils its promise. Its stanza of sixteen bars folds up too early for the immediate repetition that it gains.

There was an optional opening scene for the second act (1933), complete in itself, with plenty of songs for John and one for Aunt Jane, and hinging on a proposal to release Hugh on the condition of Mary's renunciation of him—contemptuously dismissed by a distrustful John, who is determined to gain Mary, with Hugh safely under close arrest. This scene was withdrawn in the later revision, possibly because there was too much of 1930 about it, or too much argument—or it just would not go in production. The scene moves at a vivid level of speech-song, regularized in strophes from time to time, and certainly adds body to John's possessive character, but Mary's willingness to surrender to John's lust (by marriage) to save Hugh's life must have been difficult to make persuasive.[1]

As it now is, the second act at once discloses love in the stocks. Hugh, undaunted as Egmont by condemnation without hearing, returns blithely to strophic song for his 'Gaily I go to die'. Piquant harmonic

---

[1] Mr. Maurice Jacobson informs me that the composer withdrew the new scene for Act 2 because he thought that it did not serve dramatic factors, to which better justice could be done by some changes made in the final version. Mrs. Vaughan Williams adds that the composer scrapped the scene because he considered it dramatically redundant. The main interest of these statements is that the composer regarded dramatic considerations as paramount. For these he was prepared to jettison forty pages of vocal score. Certainly this scene must have blunted the impact of the following scene, with Hugh in the stocks being baited by John but always believing in Mary's fidelity, which she confirms later at considerable length.

Musically, amongst other things this revision sacrifices one more G major tune, quoted *con amore* by Howes. It had the equivocal role of intimating, both in the voice part and in the orchestra, that Mary is still true to Hugh, while she sings the *words* of betrayal. But if *Mary* sings the tune, who is the audience to believe? Thus, the musical implementation of this shocking, though two-faced, declaration, was not really satisfactory, either as a dramatic incident or as revealing music.

The composer anticipates the cut by his note, in the 1933 score, that this first scene may be omitted from Act 2, 'if the Opera is thought too long'. But he developed rather an obsession about his works being too long.

texture makes more of the A flat song of release, though it is equally strophical. This follows a serene dialogue, involving a solo-violin's top-string cantabile in G. From this point, the structure of the act was considerably altered in 1933, with some further revisions in 1956.

(1) The duet, in which Hugh's gentle admonitions and more passionate declarations soothe Mary's reluctance away, is postponed till after Hugh's confident 'Now she is mine'.

(2) The false-alarm-of-escape episode is cut out, and the ensuing escapist dialogue re-cast, but (1956) Mary's final 'My father will disown me', etc., has been withdrawn in favour of 'Do all I say . . . into the stocks again . . .' (1924). This leads as before to the ponderous recovery of the motive of Hugh's first song for Mary's arioso, 'Sweet little home, in my lover's arm'. After this, two Maying carols (John, the girls) and, after the discovery of the pair in the stocks, another extended but plain strophic song, now worded, 'Here queen uncrowned', from an *entêté* Mary, relax the interest.

The last song is extended by Aunt Jane (1956), Constable and John in a singularly imperturbable manner, considering that Mary is throwing herself at the head of a condemned spy with disgusting publicity. However, this is to enhance the later recovery. Accompanied by technically prophetic blobs of uncontrolled, capricious four-deep harmony, the Constable 'disowns' Mary and leaves her, penniless, to John, who spurns her. The arrival of the sergeant to collect his prisoner soon redresses the balance: Hugh is identified as the thoroughly sound Englishman that his supporters thought him (link with Act 1) and John is marched off as a recruit. The only question about Mary's marriage now is one of terms, in which neither Hugh nor Mary have professed interest. Apart from past insults, Hugh has never been in such a favourable position. The drama has therefore reached a pitch of no-resistance, where plot and music must shake themselves or move in a straight line. Here the revisions are of importance and may be further detailed.

(3) The 1924 sequel was quite different: there, after a moment of awestruck silence, marked only by the drum-taps of the retreating soldiers, the Constable begins pompous overtures to Hugh (fresh link with Act 1), supported by the rest; Hugh responds, after a firm glance at Mary ('A free heart and a bold heart . . .') in the unconcealed tones of an angry young man in a small-minded community. This diatribe, more speech than song, was plausible but ineffective; reduced to a short recitative in the 1933 version, it was replaced altogether in 1956. Instead, the crowd march off with the soldiers, singing a semi-patriotic song of

two verses, 'March away, John', musically ditty-ish and nugatory, but reducing the tension. Hugh then proceeds to the stanzaic 'Now she is mine' (shortened) in Shamus O'Brien style and without fear of contra-diction.

(4) It remains to reassure Mary, and here the postponed and extended duet, less Hugh's original taunt that Mary will be safe in John's strong arms, is perhaps equal to the occasion.

(5) New matter follows: a brief chorus of cheerful protest (for chorus' sake) and didactic monologue (Hugh), intolerably superior but received by the crowd with meek, modal resignation. The latter was replaced in 1956 by a short air from Aunt Jane and Hugh's 'A free heart' (in a fresh key, F sharp).

(6) The music leaps from this to the confident penultimate B flat (fourth degree of F) of 'Life calls us', the after-song of Hugh's camp-fire air, leading to the couple's gallant departure for the open road in F. (The orchestra's chord on the third beat here has been altered to a plain B flat minor from a mixture of this with F.)

(7) Aunt Jane and the Constable now make the merest gesture of protest, and a D major and minor interlude ('Life calls these lovers out to wilder ways') is omitted. So to a curt general farewell, giving the chorus bare time to voice the town's admission that Mary has a wider future, by subdued but sonorous deep chording, with a solo-violin *in alt.* as a guiding star.

I have never heard (4), above, in its new setting, but it must be a strain on the dramatic powers of the two singers to make it the 'worthy climax' claimed for it by Howes. A similar problem arises over the ecstatic re-union duet between Leonora and Florestan in *Fidelio*, Act 2, after the signal of the arrival of the Minister. But such a duet has inevitably no precedent in the opera, and Beethoven relies on a single glowing impulse of mutual delight, good enough for so fast an aria. The more deliberate sequence and increasing plainness of the vocal line in the present *scena* are much more difficult to accomplish. There has always been a problem about rescue-opera after the rescue. Apart from this, the dramatic conclusion remains incredible: one can but picture a disconsolate but wiser Mary, back at her father's door. Hugh should have left the town alone, the lovers recognizing that if Mary's home ground was too confined for Hugh, his road was too long and hard for her.

It would have been difficult to press these criticisms in 1924! Nevertheless, the native qualities of the opera could not easily have impressed an audience that had barely had time to accept *Boris Godunov* (in 1913), no time at all for, say, *The Canterbury Pilgrims* and its period English, and slender memories of *The Wreckers*. The composer's manifest attempt to create a truly national opera, conserving the passions of normal urban living, rather than of operatic convention, and making vocal melody, new or old, paramount, involved an exclusion of other facets in the composer's appeal, not noticeable in the *London Symphony*. Vaughan Williams has been partly stimulated and partly hindered in this direction by his author, whose fresh and virile narrative commands many moods but is riddled with cliché, rural, idealist and amorous. Foss well compares the more spontaneous dialogue of Hardy's *Trumpet Major*, another Napoleonic tale. Here, 'Lean down your head upon my breast'—in the final scene—seems to spring straight from the heart of Alfred Bunn. The upshot is a cantabile of hazardous quality and a declamation that frequently borders on plain sentimentality, without the overriding symphonic developments that integrate Wagner's most extravagant and cloying situations.

The peculiar advantage of the work, as an appeal to a new public, is that its meaning, as emotionally balanced music for the stage moment, is clear throughout. 'The directness of an old English engraving' is Kobbé's summary in his synopsis of the plot. No grounding is necessary; and no single quotation would be generally informative, for, apart from the 'Hugh' motto, no theme or phrase acquires any marked degree of development or reminiscence. (A possible exception is the rising and falling figure, played after Hugh's first song and suggestive that he will upset Mary's equilibrium. Oddly enough, Howes does not refer to this in his analysis.) Hugh and Mary reveal their firm and tender moods in the song, not the line. It is not easy to explain why, apart from a nationally disinterested public, the opera has never taken root, like *The Bartered Bride* in Prague, as a refreshing and indigenous product, except that its operatic appeal is lacking in climaxes. The fight, for example, which so attracted the composer to the libretto, and has often been praised for its stage appeal, is not convincing operatic stuff, for its issue is presented as a Sports Result, rather than as of burning interest to a third party. In consequence the chorus part is fragmentary, plain and uncumulative, unlike the absorbing return, for example, to the tune and roulades of Beckmesser's serenade of Magdalena, in the riotous finish of *Meistersinger*, Act 2. Moreover, the failure of a divided Mary, in the rejected scene of Act 2, is more interesting and songworthy than her brave coolness in the following scene. Yet the proof of an operatic text lies in the music: Verdi's *Macbeth* might be, but actually is not to be, compared in sustained intensity with *Otello*. The blunt encounters of *Hugh* must not be forgotten.

SIR JOHN IN LOVE

The next full-sized opera to appear shows an obvious development of certain features of the first. Like the opera *Much Ado about Nothing*, *Sir John in Love* makes some preliminary capital out of an established play on its subject, though here this is less pronounced and, indeed, confused in style, so that the composer's reference to 'Shakespeare's genius' is well off the mark.[1] The new opera contained something more and something less than plot and character. It is a picture of English bourgeois living, at various levels of rank and psychological substance, framed round one character larger than life. This image of family existence, in which the true, father-opposed lover has only to be patient, while the rake earns a little passing discomfort and, lacking a shred of

[1] Any serious examination of *The Merry Wives of Windsor*, as found in the Folio text and the dubious Quarto of 1602, discloses cleavages of texture and many loose ends. A reasonably vigorous opening of anti-Falstaff factions is superseded by an amorous escapade, whose ulterior money motive scarcely makes it more credible for the white-haired gormandizer that Falstaff has been known to be previously. Moreover, suggestive details for the concealment of a 'lover' can be found in contemporary (or conceivably contemporary) Italian stories, one of them actually mentioning a clothes-basket. This derivative-sounding plot is thinly covered by the robustness of the characters and surrounding episodes. The large proportion of prose and the poverty of the verse, the weak finish and the excessive number of eccentrics and caricatures, such as Dr. Caius, altogether point to hasty composition and probable adaptation of an existing comedy of 'jealousy', spiced with topicalities.

The tradition, started by John Dennis in 1702 and expanded by Rowe and Gildon, that the play was written in a fortnight by royal command, has no known authority, but it would, of course, explain the circumstances in which Shakespeare might have been forced to adapt more than he wrote spontaneously. In any case, he left the play as he had thus worked it out, loose ends and all.

While, then, this farcical intrusion of Falstaff on the Windsor and Cotswold burghers shows some flickers of creative vitality, the play is barely Shakespearian and certainly not strongly so. Its plot is merely familiar. But ever since the romantic movement, Shakespeare has been a magnet for musicians, amongst other stage craftsmen; and earlier, the composer had arranged and conducted music for the production of Henry IV, Part 2 and two other Shakespeare plays at Stratford, which, no doubt, planted a seed. It is noteworthy that for material for an opera to be written in a year Britten went, in 1959, to *A Midsummer Night's Dream*, a play equally conspicuous not only for stimulating differences of level, but also, in judicious selection, for its constant sense of movement, not without a suggestion of family charades. Already, this dramatically whimsical translation promises wide international audiences. It remains to observe whether this hold is maintained. That will be the acid test of the music.

guilty feeling, can still mock his fill, is not opera as commonly experienced.

Certainly Boito, Verdi's librettist, went to some trouble to sharpen such outlines as he found in *The Merry Wives*, before searching for lyric opportunities.[1] He reduced the cast and simplified the plot, while keeping in mind the gently sententious Falstaff of *Henry IV*. ('Can honour set to a leg?' is the nearest thing to aria in the opera.) It is Caius, not Shallow, whom Falstaff robs, and Caius whom Anne's father, the irascible Ford (not Page), intends her to marry. Fenton thus joins the plot to inveigle Falstaff into Ford's house from interested motives. Hence the enraged Ford, after hearing suspicious sounds behind a screen in his house, receives a double blow when he finds, after much pomp of screen-removal, not, as he had assumed, Falstaff and his wife together but only a surprised and embarrassed Anne and Fenton kissing. Naturally this whets both his future opposition to them and his future support of Caius. (In the *Merry Wives*, Ford returns from one search only to pursue another.)

Anne and Fenton are thus the operatic, secret lovers *par excellence*, the misogynous Ford and cantankerous Caius little more than peppery schemers. Falstaff is a mass of greed for wine and women, revolting in proportion to the presumed age of his 'old body', and chiefly a mountain of flesh, but not without his moments of exultation at his own level; a distinct 'character-part', as Stabile has demonstrated. In the park scene, the fairy masquerade is merely accessory to the further humiliation of Falstaff and the defeat of Ford and Caius. Finally, seeing little sense and no curtain in the Shakespearian dénouement, Boito almost abandons the struggle. The actors all come to the footlights to share with the audience, in spirit, a concluding thought: 'All the world's a joke'. On the whole Boito has considerably tightened the threads, thrown out possible loose ends and filled gaps with aphorism, ceremonious politesse, lip-smacking and an occasional lyric, yet he has provided Verdi with material for comedy rather than the rollicking affair

---

[1] The Falstaff settings of Salieri (1799) and Balfe (Her Majesty's Theatre, 1838) are both in Italian, apart from Salieri's mock-German insertions. It is unlikely, however, that either the voluble farce of Salieri or the irrepressibly melodious Balfe influenced so doubly endowed a mind as Boito's, and still less that either was consulted, even for vocal qualities, by Verdi or Vaughan Williams. Verdi had known the *Merry Wives* for fifty years, but accepted without much question the 'lyrical comedy' that Boito handed him. Nicolai's ubiquitous German comedy (1849) seems to have had no influence, for all its sharp, humorous characterization, sensitive colour and balanced ensembles.

which *Falstaff* sometimes becomes. And if Verdi's humour contains a dash of Rossini's madcap temper, it also embraces Donizetti's sardonic quality (*L'Elisir d'Amore*) and the deeper, jealous passion of Verdi's own *Don Carlos*.

Holst's bland recovery, in *At the Boar's Head*, of the earlier Falstaff, trying to impose an heroic image of himself on his Tavern-companions and comforters, cannot now be regarded as happy or exemplary, although it was well received (at Manchester) and respectfully mentioned by Vaughan Williams in his preface. Ultimately irrelevant, it is only sifted here for the sake of its extraordinary but comparable methods of composition. In joining together Falstaff scenes from *Henry IV Part 2*, by fitting the dialogue, mainly, to the intonation or rhythmic measure of some forty selected folk or contemporary tunes, after finding by accident that it was technically possible, Holst was oddly attempting to force together two entities, neither of which needed the other, or, since musical expression is habitually slower than the spoken word, encouraged the other to a more than passing encounter; for even a short strophical tune calls for another and continuing verse and is inimical to dry wit. 'A task which might have daunted any one less obstinate', remarks Imogen Holst fairly of her father's curious confidence in his project. Indeed, the insertion of some tunes joined to their proper words, beginning with one verse blissfully free from setting, almost draws atttention to the string of marriages of convenience, in which one party or the other has the worst of it. Usually the tunes or their 'variants' are meant to enhance the declamation, but they frequently put a break on the verbal sense, or, if instrumental, are simply distracting. Quite apart from the lack of tension or serious action on the stage, there could be no opera here, only the impact of varied dance-mood and contingent accompaniment, nothing if not humorous. There is no characterization: only degrees of rhythmic élan in the folk-dance cycle.

Holst shared with Vaughan Williams a belief in folk-song as a kind of dateless tone for any rural occasion. He does not seem to have scared his friend off on this occasion, but he well might have. In general conception, *At the Boar's Head* is a structural solecism. It was also a bad influence on an opera composer forming his own style. Somehow, Holst's attitude to opera, as an art form, was dangerously near *olim in anno licet insanire*, in spite of the ubiquitous counterpoint and purposive ground-basses. It is so far refreshing to turn back for a moment to the Straussian panache with which Elgar delivered his orchestral portrait of Prince Hal's former boon companion, intriguer, dreamer and egotist, but human at many levels. Such a stratagem-ist might be oppressive, rather slimy company, but he would never dissolve into song and dance, least of all literally.

In *Sir John in Love* Vaughan Williams accepted most of the trappings of the *Merry Wives*. The action is a little too familiar to go easily on the stage. The lapse into folk-dance formation in Act 2 is a reminder of the total lack of operatic precedent, and almost of operatic style. Yet the composer arranged his plot well. Boito begins all three of his acts with Falstaff at the 'Garter' Inn, stretching his limbs luxuriously or, as in Act 3, painfully, and planning intrigue; a second scene lifts the action out of ponderous humour into fast-moving episodes, introducing the bemused wives, Ford and the lovers in developing situations: a little too much structural coincidence.

Vaughan Williams's first act leaves the spectator with all the main threads before him, ending with a glimpse of the two wives, mischievous but lyrical, and the awakening suspicions in Ford's mind. Act 2 leads from half-indignant wives (and a half-consoling Mrs. Quickly) to Falstaff's overt letter-writing and pompous exit—the only 'Garter' scene. Act 3 passes from a spectacular opening, added in the revision, that is more movement than action, to the Evans-Caius imbroglio and the crucial scene in Ford's house. Here, again, an operatic irate-husband cannot afford not to find someone in concealment, and this time it is that paragon of propriety, Mrs. Page. Act 4 contrives to begin serenely with a repentant Ford, before developing as a masque with a resounding epilogue at the end. The last, although intended to be addressed to the audience, is kept internal and expressive of 'the feeling of the meeting', with a popular dance-tune (half a century ahead of the Elizabethan period) to press the convivial turn home, for better or worse.

This fresh shaping of the action common to *Merry Wives* and *Falstaff*, with some reversions to the former, is curiously but considerably implemented by the addition of miscellaneous Elizabethen poems to the prosaic narrative, which may appear precious at first, from the perception of insets from another work or piece, but find their level with more acquaintance. On these lines, there is ample material for an intimate opera about these merry wives, half Elizabethan, half idyllic and pensive. The Falstaff of the French wars and English stews is past history.

Before considering the music as a whole, however, it is necessary to examine certain further statements in the composer's preface to the vocal score. The frequent mention of the titles of songs and dances in Shakespeare and elsewhere, with other evidence, indicates that such music was in the air, and generally known. For connoisseurs, many tunes were familiar through variation-sets. 'John, come kiss me now', for example, known as a dance-tune after 1600, is the subject of sixteen variations by Byrd for virginals. Accordingly, a verse of a 'period' tune or two might be expected, to add verisimilitude to the dialogue, if it can be absorbed in the general musical texture.

But Vaughan Williams goes a great deal further. Not only does he introduce, in the course of the opera, five folk tunes in three or more verses, and more isolated allusions to others, to enhance a dramatic point, but, as he says in his preface, 'When I could not find a suitable folk-tune, I have made shift to make up one of my own . . . If the result is successful I feel justified; if not no amount of "originality" will save the situation. However, the point is a small one, since out of a total of 120 minutes "music", the folk-tunes occupy less than 15.' These statements are quoted with approval by Howes and Young and, no doubt, will continue to be so quoted, but they are all most questionable. The introduction of a folk-tune in art-music, so far from being the best thing possible, is likely to be a raw moment in an otherwise original scene. This simple farrago is no ancient tale of distress, invoking some 'liberating' folk-song. Rather, nothing *but* 'originality' will save the situation. 'Making shift' with folky substitutes has a dubious Russian precedent. Finally, the impact of the folk-song incidents depends not so much on their relative duration (and 15 minutes is surely an under-statement) as on their structural and dramatic bearing. Howes's suggestion that the composer can '*cap his own music*' with a tune that belongs to the people, period and topicality of the play (my italics) needs musical demonstration in each context. *A priori* it sounds very improbable.

Once more, then, the 'pretty virginity' of the party enters to the incidental strain of a lilting folk-song, 'The sailor home from the sea', here played by the orchestra for the sake of the tune as harmonized. It is a lovely tune, but it has no meaning here ('My true love has come back, rich' is singularly irrelevant) except to shape formal conversation, and its further verses, as Anne's signature-tune, sound increasingly utilitarian. Nor, of course, are the six cumulative verses of the once popular dance tune 'John come kiss me' more acceptable now because their subject is more or less applicable, but only because the phrases develop later in a rather obvious way. In Act 2, Mrs. Quickly's odd verse of 'Sweet, lovely Joan' may pass muster, but the orchestra's later verses, the last with 'John' elements, make, with the recapitulation of

Mrs. Page's reactions to Falstaff's letter, a thin optional extension of the interlude between scenes.

In Act 3 one cannot reasonably question 'Greensleeves' being sung to its appropriate ballad of unfaithfulness by Mrs. Ford. One *may* question the corrupt version of this Dorian tune at the cadence—see Sharp's *Wyresdale Greensleeves Dance* for the true tune, or the version used in the composer's ballet, *On Christmas Night*—and the fervency of this celebration of the Other Woman seems strained. The orchestral verse in the interlude in Act 4 is both superfluous and out of place. (The curious may compare Busoni's elegy, *Turandots Frauengemacht*, with its racy pianism, improving on the song in *Turandot*, 2. 1.) And the numberless verses which the two-bar 'Peg-a-Ramsey', once a ballad of the over-*watched* husband but inversely appropriate, successively acquires in Act 3 (6, 6 and finally 8 on end) are a callous intrusion; the last bout (comparable to the end of *Hugh the Drover*, Act 1) making a very jejune curtain tune for the final romp round the humiliated Ford. Also, as in many a final ballet of Gluck, 'Half Hannikin', however resourcefully orchestrated, is in grave danger of reducing a climax to an anti-climax, with its perpetual measure of 8–8 bars, and harmonic burden based on a recurrent melodic curve of 1–2–1–7 round the tonic. In short, these extensive quotations rarely cap anything, or, if they have a dramatic point, they wear it to the bone more often than not. (I cannot agree with Howes that six variations on so simple and sophisticated a tune as 'John come kiss me now' are adequate to Falstaff's gesture of self-admiration. And surely Byrd's sixteen were enough.)

The 'shifts' to replace folk-songs consist of the usual amalgamation of old-time vocal movement, probably modal, and 'modern' figurative, harmonic development. The entry of Caius and of the thieves (laden) are thus furnished with quasi-popular matter, and so are the two wives at the end of Act 1. (The second half of the first phrase of the wives' refrain is hardly up to the first, with its laboured ascent to the tonic in bars 5–6.) In Act 2 Mrs. Quickly has her opportunity with the now bemused characters, after the letter-scene. Having sung her folk-song (off) she rouses their spirits with a vigorous air, at first pentatonic, yet much too harmonic, antiphonal and elaborate to be a folk tune, however racy. (It is quoted in Ex. 32a.) Her text, one of the inserted poems, is 'Sigh no more, ladies', and thus compares for a moment with the male-chorus opening and full choral close (with Sturgis's educational fourth line[1]) of Stanford's *Much Ado*. Stanford's setting is cosily spry

---

[1] (v.2) 'for fickle men may wiser grow'.

and imitational. Vaughan Williams's is blunter but a good deal more piquant. In the new scene of Act 3, May-dancers are given a fetching neo-Lydian refrain. The trite and irrepressible waltz tune that follows is one more evidence of the composer's 'frightening duality'.

A store of vernacular or quasi-vernacular melody takes these cues and fills in gaps, and thus enhances or promotes what has here been termed the family level of urban co-existence, in comparison with the much more tribal crowd-feeling of *Hugh the Drover*, riveted by war-conditions. This broader communication forms the background for the more distinctive revelations of character.

It is a packed stage, whose variety threatens to turn into masquerade. There are five main strata: Falstaff's gang; Anne Page and Fenton: Caius and party, with parson Evans; Falstaff pursuing Mrs. Page and Mrs. Ford, who enjoy their own slice of life; and Ford in changing relations to his wife and Falstaff, with room also for Mrs. Quickly, Slender, and the extended plots against Falstaff's comfort of mind and body. There are, further, intense lyrical moments induced by the stray poems that happen to fit or enrich a situation, for example, Jonson's 'Do but look upon her eyes'[1] and 'See the chariot at hand'. There are thus far more character types than in either *Hugh* or *Falstaff*. Fenton and Anne are now passing foils to Falstaff's excursions with love, except for the new scene of Act 3 (and one kiss-pause in Act 1); 'Doctor' Caius's party adds new zest to the exhibition of rural characters; the two wives are refreshing challenges to the duet-craft; and Ford more than replaces Butcher John; his pursuit of Falstaff in his own house, on top of the Evans-Caius preparation for a fight, balances the fight in the Cotswold village. The final curtain-tune is an 'extra', but a splendid one, and has the advantage of being less mannered than Verdi's fugue.

In matching this spreading train of characters and events with expanding music, Vaughan Williams relies less on recurring strophe than in *Hugh*. The exceptions are of interest. At his first entry Fenton, assisted by Anne and orchestra, has no difficulty in singing a spicier verse ('the bud of the briar') *on* the stage, holding Anne in his arms, than he has just sung off it. Caius's sudden, un-English plunge into sentiment, on the other hand, takes the form of a repetitive and florid French air, of which a single verse is enough to save his face emotionally. At the end of the act, the mischievous cuckoo song of the two wives spontaneously

---

[1] From *The Devil is an Ass*. One of the few music-worthy moments in the play which Elgar considered for an opera, rejecting Shaw's suggestion of another 'Falstaff'.

repeats itself (with some pantomime), in order to jar on Ford's disturbed state of mind, and rouse his unconscious awareness of trouble afoot.

In Act 2, 'Sigh no more ladies', added between first performance and publication, runs readily to a second verse without any change, with a conspiratorial *più lento* close, and in the next scene Falstaff's love-letter composition, with its mock vocal and structural rhetoric, inevitably repeats itself, on broad lines, in Ford's psychological hearing and with his own brooding thoughts. In Act 3, Scene 1 (as revised) resolves itself into a choral ballet. The maying dance, and to a wider extent the triumphant floral waltz for Anne and Fenton, promote their refrains on simple lines of rhythmic accumulation, dramatically static. In Scene 3, the ground prepared by correspondence, Falstaff's impulsive addresses to Mrs. Ford (in a whole verse of Philip Sidney, as Howes explains) naturally fall into the strophes and after-song of reputed minstrelsy. At each stage, alternating woodwind propel a phrase on to a fresh discord, either modern or *vieux jeu*.

In Act 4 (one score of which shows the replacement of 'The Fat Knight' by the present operatic title), the opening song, finely prepared by an impromptu and intimate orchestral prelude (distilling joy in heaven over one repentant mistrustful?) falls into two verses of simple but subtly knit phrases, the first sung by Ford, the second played by the strings (mainly) as a background to the inquisitorial dialogue of the Pages. After Ford's dark moods and the noisy tedium of 'Peg a' Ramsey', this clear flow of original melody on his behalf makes a most striking opening, and indicates the composer's reserve of matter outside the patent demands of the coming masque. The nearest precedent is Berlioz (e.g. *Les Troyens*, Act 5, *init.*: the nostalgic Hylas).

These effective amplifications of stanza, with the folk-tunes, form recurrent periods of phrase-rhythm, against which clue-themes have to contend to maintain their pervasive hold over the ear. In the first act, passing over the E flat–C minor progression which underlines Shallow's complaints, a forecast of later works (as well as of the last scene here), and the much more expressive phrase (viola solo) through which Anne laments her father's choice of Slender for her husband, we may halt at the Ford motives, as the point of greatest musical tension. 31*b* is an extension of the semitonal antinomy of *On Wenlock Edge*; while 31*c* shows an odd coincidence with *Sancta Civitas* (Ex. 29: 2*c*) and *In the Fen Country* (Ex. 14). Through these, it is made clear that the rich procession of types that has led up to Falstaff in pursuit of new conquests is challenged by a bitter and determined character.

Ex. 31a

Ex. 31b

Ex. 31c

Act 2 shows the further resistance of the wives, beginning with Mrs. Page's rage over the overtures that she has received, as displayed in oscillating chords on the degrees 1, ♭2, ♭3, repeated in the interlude that follows, and in a tortuous dactylic figure, descending in major sixths in the orchestra. Falstaff's subsequent lecherous conversation with Brook (Ford) naturally rouses Ford motives, but also a special mobilization of his self-defence in a fresh arioso, marked by Phrygian-minor colour. Act 3, Scene 1, begins with what proves to be a preparation for the final scene of all, but soon relaxes to an unhurried delivery of its swinging tunes of May-celebration and young love.

The following scenes are marked by growing orchestral movement for the Caius-Evans fight, and then for the alarms and excursions in Ford's house. One feature of the latter is an imperative rhythmic figure, demonstrative of the further trenchancy of the Phrygian minor, and the other an old sword-dance tune, whose regular and irrepressible recurring phrases, turning sturdy inquisitorial action into mime, seem odd matter to choose for so weighty a moment. (Ford may cut a grotesque figure, but his main facts were right.) It would seem to be a case of a desperate quest for an integral tune and *moto perpetuo*, after the desultory feeling of the corresponding, rather monotonous passage in the fight-music of *Hugh*. It does not add a line to Ford's character to be saddled with three strophes of 'The old wife of Dallowgill', any more than a similar measure of 'The sailor' brings Anne to life. On top of this come four verses of a naïve Mixolydian tune for Mrs. Page's unexpected appearance from behind the curtain, expanding from oboe to a quiet tutti, and then 'Peg-a'-Ramsey' once again. A noisy, tumultuous act, after the first scene. It is rather a strain on the ear, with its pertinent illustrations, from Evans's quaking before a fight that he never sought to the general mockery of Ford's exasperation.

In Act 4, after Ford's air of pacification already noted, the 'Hearne the hunter' legend at once promotes its tokens of mystery (declining bass in two-tone steps) and wayward movement in jig-rhythm, enhanced by the pantomime on the stage of main characters dressed and dancing fantastically, but breaking into a more settled mood for 'Round about in a fair ring-a'. In the second scene, a procession of motives (Ex. 32*b*, below, is for Caius's entry) converges in the confined 'Pinch him' figure, quaintly pentatonic and assisted by the entry of the xylophone, and the calmer mockery of a persistent figure in E major ('Nay, do not fly'). Further distraction over the bogus wives of Slender and Caius is swept aside by a striking setting of 'See the chariot' (Jonson). This lyrical outburst, absorbing all individual entanglements in its magic charm, steadies the ear in preparation for the simple but conclusive fresh tune to 'Whether men do laugh or weep' (32*c*) and its three swinging twelve-bar verses, supported (?) by a blunt version of 'Half Hannikin' (dance). So far Act 4 is the richest in original commentary. Elsewhere this is more spasmodic, or, as in Act 3, derivative. Seldom do individual episodes grip the senses in the Russian way.

Something, however, must now be said of the composer's use of colour. Vocally, the general range from Anne's high soprano to Ford's bass, via Fenton's tenor and Falstaff's baritone is a good deal more than a matter of mere amplification of register in the parts of Mrs. Page and the rest. Orchestrally, again, a routine list of the combinations habitually employed would convey little of the variety of uses; for example, (1) open-air strings (accompaniment to Ford's song in Act 4; in general, rarer than in, say, *Meistersinger*); (2) strings, wood and horns (Ex. 31*c* and *passim*); (3) wood and percussion, including plucked strings (entrance of Caius's party; the Host's reconciliation of Caius and Evans); (4) *tutti* of trumpet-tune and lofty string-wood harmony (climax of 'John come kiss me now'): (5) *tutti* composed of bustling figure in

Ex. 32a

cls. double v.II and v I (lower note)
d.b. doubles vc: lowest note (loco)

violins and wood against brass-string chords and percussion (sustained
chords with drum-roll, at midnight in Windsor Forest; short chords
reinforced by side-drum, for the dance of the fairies later); (6) piquant
semi-*tutti* such as the celebration of the innocence of the person behind
the curtain in Master Ford's house, in the third verse: light tune in
clarinet, trumpet and violin, and flute in three octaves, against percussive harmony (strings and triangle), supporting *soli* and chorus in
sustained harmony. My main example shall be of the composer's light
touch in the presentation of a tune already considered earlier (Ex. 6e)

Ex. 32*b*

for its hexatonic affiliations. The second, from the penultimate 'riot', shows Vaughan Williams emulating Strauss for the now doubly grotesque 'Doctor' (once, it seems, a recognized impostor figure at Windsor). The third example, introducing the tumultuous concluding

Ex. 32*c*

tune, is dynamic without pomp. If ever a study score were published, it might be as instructive in its own way as *Gerontius* is in extended music not connected with the theatre.

A remarkably diversified stage, then, is kept musically moving and at the same time consistent, section by section, by a blend of (1) extemporary vocal movement, harnessed to orchestral rhythm, (2) occasional development of significant themes, and (3) bursts of overt or underlying strophical expansion or mere insistence. On this basis, Act 2, which is eventually involved with the simple, jaunty quarrel-motive (Caius *v.* Evans), restlessly modulating and superseded by the triumphant motive of suitor John, has an interesting but fragmentary conclusion. Act 1 sinks down to an apparently serene strophical and satirical repeat (the wives), which enhances the fury of Ford's vivid interruption. Act 3 blandly lets 'Peg o' Ramsey' have its way on top of the simple recurrences of the ingenuous Mrs. Page theme, after the extended pursuit-dance led by Ford. Act 4 ends with a fresh tune with enough reserve strength to make the plain climax conclusive.

These differences illustrate the fragmentary and elusive features of the work, and its abiding appeal to the listener. One often longs for a more musically abandoned episode, as in that grand sequence of improbabilities, the finale of the second act of *Figaro*, motivated by another jealous husband, much more imperious than Ford. Nevertheless, *Sir John*, with all its raw spots, as now detailed, has an impressive and congenial breadth, which compensates for the lack of dramatic tension. It is a substantial and truly comic *Falstaff* setting, which lifts the intrigue and manœuvring to a plane of poetry and a growing Olympian resilience and mirth. It has not the consuming Vaughan Williams quality which marks the contemporary *Job*, but is much the most extended work so far. The opera must surely take its place in the English repertory from time to time. (There was a tremendous ovation at the Sadler's Wells performance in 1958 in the presence of the composer, almost his last public appearance, as it proved.) There seems no solid reason why this work should not alternate with Verdi in say, Germany, Hungary and Czechoslovakia, in a not too vast opera-house. Its slow speed and lack of passion would be a handicap in Italy, and one cannot imagine it at the Opéra Comique.

THE POISONED KISS

In *The Poisoned Kiss or The Empress and the Necromancer* (in the full score, *The Magic Kiss*) the composer let himself go in more ways than one. The opera, called 'a romantic Extravaganza' with characteristic mischief, tells a thoroughly sophisticated fairy-story with a plain and unconvincing moral: love is potent against every contingent acid. The poisoned first kiss of Tormentilla, prepared by her magician father, Dipsacus, on a diet of the most virulent acids, cannot harm Prince Amaryllus, similarly conditioned by his mother, the Empress, a former pupil of Dipsacus, against every sour event in his *affaires*. In three Acts disposed round the planning, execution and disintegration of the fatal spell attached to the first kiss, the steady progress, on well-trodden lines, of the respective attendants of the courting pair, of the assistants on each of the contending sides and finally of magician and empress themselves, converges with the fortunes of the prince and his girl, happily united, in a glow of science confronted by science and psychological forces stronger than either. Intermediately, there is a string of witty and industriously contrived numbers, some more and some less relevant; the main ploys being that Dipsacus's magic establishment is professional, the Empress's free-lance, and that between the rugged breast of Dipsacus and the stony heart of the Empress is something that, as she observes, breaks all rules.[1]

The text was compiled by Evelyn Sharp, Cecil Sharp's sister, from features in Richard Garnett's short story, 'The Poison Maid'—in *The Twilight of the Gods*—and in 'Rapaccini's Daughter', a precedent story found in Nathaniel Hawthorne's *Mosses from an Old Manse*. The librettist supplied the subsidiary characters, the topical setting and its fairly amusing satire, and presumably the dramatic scheme. The musical method is a complete reversion to ballad opera, with free resort to spoken dialogue. The indulgence in melody, *per se* or in a harmonic setting, ranges fantastically. There are recollections of Sullivan and of the sentimental ballad, of the now familiar slippery steps of mode patterned by harmonic interest and the equally trite transports of semitonal and tangential progression, and sometimes an almost nostalgic dig at the Vaughan Williams of the first and second decades, as well as a

---

[1] In 1956 the composer revised the work. He cut the following ten numbers or sections: in Act 1, nos. 9 (up to Tormentilla's lullaby to her pet snake), 11 (Amaryllus's tale of past dalliance), 13 (Dipsacus's ballad) and 14 (patter-trio); in Act 2, nos. 24 (patter-trio and chorus), 26 (Tormentilla's lament), and 30 (duet: three-beat section); in Act 3, nos. 36 (angry magicians and attendants), 40*a*, *b*, *c* (hobgoblins' chorus and melodrama) and 43 (patter-duet). Earlier (for some of the above numbers are included) he had replaced the dialogue by fresh material, in rhyming verse, in about thirty of the forty-six numbers. This pantomime style appears to be a distinct improvement on the too conscious humour of the original.

considerable amount of characteristic music, some vivacious to a fault
and some exalted.

Here then, is a provocative text, at once fanciful and arch in an
Edwardian way, liable to destroy any music which relies on its obvious
rhyming devices and the like, and so far precarious in a public opera-
house where realism predominates. This is set to a texture so eclectic,
and frequently so overtly satirical, that it takes a moment to realize just
when the composer is being serious. The overture is to be played with
the house lights up, and the audience is asked not to stop talking, lest
they know 'all the tunes before the opera begins'. A new way of inducing
silence? Actually the overture is such a medley as to be almost meaningless. Heard or unheard, it prepares for the mixture that follows, with
Tormentilla and Angelica her maid, soprano, Amaryllus tenor, his
servant Gallanthus baritone, Dipsacus bass, the Empress (Katisha
without her past) contralto, and the two trios of assistants spreading the
female and male registers.

Some cross-sections may be quoted as an interesting indication of the
manifold tradition in the depths of the composer's mind at any given
time of his maturity. There are no direct self-quotations, but rather
mimetic mannerisms, which may wear thin in strophical repetition,
unless the patter is sufficiently distracting. The examples are in the
order of appearance. 33a is an obvious pseudo-melisma plus typical

Ex. 33a

Ex. 33b

Ex. 33c

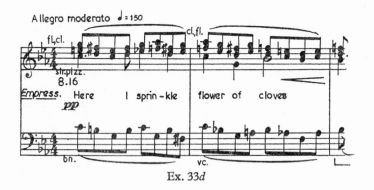

Ex. 33d

Ex. 33e

triplet; 33*b* may be described as mature but reflecting the composer's earlier seventh-less song-style; 33*c* is a neat setting of a neo-pentatonic line; 33*d* is the elaboration of a strophe previously set to plain 1 3 5 chords for each syllable, and is in the composer's serious impressionist style; this continues in the Empress's later invocation, sung at the critical moment of the whole opera and set to 33*e* with some awareness of an impulse that later became severe in *Dona nobis pacem.* Vaughan Williams never regarded modal melody as less natural than the major which inevitably also recurs and triumphs in this work.

I have not quoted the flowing carol-lullaby sung by Tormentilla to her pet snake, almost a tune for the lighter moments of *Songs of Praise,* and ultra-Mixolydian in its reluctant ascent to the seventh degree. Nor is there space to indicate the entrancing lure of the penultimate number of Act 2, in which Tormentilla and Amaryllus combine in slow coloratura style, accompanied by male trio and chorus. Mention may be made of the stalwart song of the Empress (and Tormentilla) in Purcell style; and the eminently singable final tune, set to an almost *English Hymnal* bass. There are tangos and waltzes, too, and other piquant topicalities, now mellowing to 'period' touches. A xylophone enlivens the trochaic flow for the entry of Dipsacus's hobgoblins. The subtle parodies, skilfully indicated, convey an acrobatic humour. (By comparison, the parody of Wagner in *The Perfect Fool* (Holst), a tale of a foiled magician whose love-compelling potion (for himself) got switched to the fool, is laboured; an odd adhesion of the Wagnerism which the composer thought that he had put out of his system in *Sita.*)

While, with some qualifications for the revised dialogue, the brand of verbal and dramatic wit in *The Poisoned Kiss* is too finicky for a general audience—however well the jokes went down with responsive audiences at Cambridge and elsewhere—the musical satire is constructive and versatile, and non-contemporary enough to be durable. In short, the general neglect of this operetta is to be deplored. Even if the degree of 'rehearsal' tone is extravagant, the plea for an over-riding wisdom in human relations is not frivolous, and with so many tunes at all levels of intensity some, certainly, will stay in the mind. Nor, of course, is there a lack of contrapuntal skill, whether grotesque, as in the trios, or serious, as in 'Blue larkspur', melodically cited in full by Howes. The concluding impression is that the composer enjoyed constructing this work, not least for its demands of a steady flow of strophical material near the rhythms of speech, and the more subtle call for some kind of act-structure on these broken-up lines. As Foss observes, here, in the right place, is the kind of tune that moves awkwardly in *Hugh*. Musical expression has broadened in keeping with an old-fashioned story and a perpetually diversionary setting.

RIDERS TO THE SEA

Riders to the Sea, a musical setting of Synge, without sub-title but virtually a chamber-opera, like Holst's *Savitri*, moves to the other extreme. No concessions are made to the listener. If anything, they are withdrawn. In few works is the human struggle so intensely sustained, almost to the end. Only when Maurya knows that her last son, Bartley, has been drowned and is lying before her, does she achieve her 'great rest'.

Synge's play, produced in 1904, was not, of course, an isolated manifestation, but in its own range a high point in a short but heartening piece of national stage history, conspicuous for the common sense of purpose amongst its leading personalities on and off the stage.[1] In 1899 Yeats joined forces with Edward Martyn and Lady Gregory in founding the Irish Literary Theatre in Dublin, on the model of the parallel organizations, the Théâtre Libre, the Freie Bühne and the Independent Theatre, London; an artistic revolt against the commercial theatre, with a promotional journal, *Samhain*, to explain the new aims. Yeats was interested in applying his fertile but somewhat exhausted lyrical gifts to the enactment of Irish legend, and also in hearing his verse recited on a public stage. Martyn was concerned to cultivate a more or less psychological drama, Ibsen without his sting. This collaboration soon broke up, officially, but in 1902 the Irish National Dramatic Company, vigorously assembled and directed by W. G. and F. J. Fay, produced Yeats's *Cathleen ni Houlihan*, a tragic tale of love and patriotism with a poignant universal appeal, and amongst other plays *The Racing-Lug* by James Cousins. (It was Cousins who brought the Fays into touch with 'A. E.' (George Russell), the chief promoter of the new company. A. E.'s prose-play *Deirdre* opened the first season.)

The Racing-Lug (published in *The United Irishman*) is a thin and elementary tale of human conflict, ending in a tragic loss and an ultimately cheerful restoration. Johnny, an old Ulster fisherman, is against the courting of his well-educated daughter, Bell, by Rob, a young dare-devil, having hopes that she will become the wife of a Presbyterian minister. Rob, desperate at being cold-shouldered by Bell,

---

[1] For a full account, see Ernest Boyd's *Ireland's Literary Renaissance*.

announces his intention of going off fishing in a racing-lug, and eventually goads Johnny into joining him. Johnny is drowned; Rob is picked up. He returns, conscience-stricken, to a chastened Bell. The minister, in an agony of disappointment, bows to providence. Meanwhile Johnny's wife has died from shock: she is at peace. Such was the sophisticated, somewhat didactic, precedent of *Riders to the Sea*, leaving Synge the idea of an unrelieved tragedy, uncomplicated by human motives; possibly also the idea of an unromantic Rob, no lover, but a hard-working son, and more pertinently, the calm of the closing line, '"And there was no more sea", no more separation'.

In 1903, the Irish National Theatre Society continued its progressive operations, with Yeats now as president. Besides two more Yeats plays, Synge's *In the Shadow of the Glen* was given, as well as Padraic Colum's *Broken Soil* (published, re-cast, as *The Fiddler's House*), a study of a restless vagabond temperament in a hostile environment. *Riders to the Sea* followed, and then an alternation of Synge comedy and tragedy, ending prematurely with *Deirdre*.

Yeats's hope of a revival of the poetic drama, preferably legendary or historic, and the as yet rough promise of psychological drama *per se*, had thus given place to folk-drama of two types: one, Colum's, chiefly concerned with the hard facts of an aspiring rural existence; the other, Synge's, with its more intense and symbolic vision of life. Both dramatists wrote in prose, but Synge in a peculiarly heightened prose, based on observed country speech, which is a literal translation of the native Gaelic. A theatre movement with a literary and artistic backing and a considered policy, first formulated in *Samhain*, had been fortunate enough to find, after two years of experiment, a genre, its working exponent and, in the brothers Fay, its infectious producers, with Yeats a stalwart and generous defender against any Gaelic mob reaction. No one who is familiar with the conditions of theatre production can doubt the importance of national feeling or the essential role of the patrons mentioned.

An Anglo-Irish style, then, had taken root: a mirror of contemporary peasant life. For any perceptive spectator of 1904, *Riders to the Sea*, sturdily objective and yet anything but prosaic, was a remarkable fusion of traditional speech, character-study in some measure, and heroic temper; the literary counterpart of a composer's accepted use of folk-idiom for some suggestion of lonely existence. Synge had pursued Wordsworth's aims ('to adopt the very language of men') with a Shakespearian ear for colour. He gained a mastery of a vernacular prose

277

with its own rhythmic power and to this he added a special acquaintance with peasant nature. (His later account of his human material, *The Aran Islands*, reveals the insight of this retiring individual into the troubles of the islanders whom he portrays, without the professional touch of 'field-work'.)

The widow's cottage is thus no 'Thunder Rock' but a typical dwelling of hard-pressed people, geared for the struggle with a cruel sea. The prolonged strain, enhanced by dramatic selection and compression, is thus of peculiarly strong and haunting quality. But there are limitations in this portrait of a much enduring mother. There must have been many others (since 1904) who have had to live out a bitter existence of which the last blow seems (to quote a letter from one) 'the end of everything'. Yet the wide statement of Professor Allardyce Nicoll, 'The figures in the cottage ... are titanic in their courage and grandeur,'[1] is a not untypical claim. Let it be admitted that the portraiture of character is singularly truthful and direct. But none of the chief characters makes any decision which vitally affects the course of the play. Bartley, for example, had made up his mind to take the boat long before he enters. Even Yeats once told Synge that he found Maurya too passive. The play might have been an ill-omened prologue or epilogue to a wider tragedy. In fact, it humanizes no more than a chapter of cumulative misfortune in one house.

Hence, outstanding as Synge's achievement was, in a rich and fresh soil of experiment and purpose, it can be understood that Vaughan Williams judged that it left more than a margin of fresh cultivation for the composer. For this purpose he was ready to take over the play almost as it stands, omitting only some practical and prosaic phrases that would come through in the spoken dialogue but would be distracting in a musical recitation. Actually, the omission of any indication that it is Michael's old stick that Nora hands her mother weakens the force of the latter's reference to young men leaving things. (Ex. 36*e* below.) Nor, in intimate opera, can I see any point in cutting Cathleen's spontaneous reference to the slippery '*big* stones', which she has already heard someone (Bartley) passing. But Nora's impulsive declaration, *without explanation*, that the clothes found are Michael's, is acceptable, and adds dramatic point to Cathleen's precise identification and no less fervent confirmation. The suppression of Nora's typical recollection of the assurance of the priest who was not prepared to oppose Bartley's progress, and of Maurya's retort of contempt, is interesting,

---

[1] *British Drama*, 1947 edition, p. 412.

since it removes a suggestion of religious cover for a spiritless nature. In his setting (*L'Appel de la mer*, see p. 289), Rabaud firmly underlines the disillusionment by thematic methods.[1]

The composer was thus furnished with a simple drama of a mother and her daughters, which it will be convenient to summarize at once. At the start, Michael, Maurya's fifth son, is assumed to be drowned, and it only remains to discover and identify his body, without which he cannot be given proper Christian burial. Cathleen and Nora hide a bundle of clothing taken off a body found in the sea in remote Donegal, which they later identify as Michael's. He can be buried in peace. Meanwhile, Bartley, the last son, most unromantic of drovers, has insisted on taking the boat for the mainland, to buy horses at Galway Fair, despite his mother's protest. She is sure that he is going to his death, and, having gone to wish him God-speed on his way, she returns to unfold a vision of Michael riding behind him. (This is the nearest that Synge comes to the other-worldliness of Maeterlinck's *L'Intruse*.) Her intuitions are confirmed. Bartley is brought in dead. The last man in the family has gone. But now she can be at peace, and stop worrying about the wind and the storm, as she used to do.

There is a slight distinction between the informative Nora and the dominant Cathleen. It is Cathleen who chides Maurya for not giving Bartley her blessing, and tells her to catch him as he passes with the bread that they had forgotten, so that the 'dark word will be broken' (and she will be out of the house for time enough to allow for the scrutiny of the clothes-bundle). Bartley is entirely concerned with ways and means of supporting his depleted family, and, never afraid of a risk, he hardly hears his mother's protests. He is the dauntless breadwinner, on the stage just long enough to be the living concern of the rest. In general, there is no firm sense of conflict between the women in the cottage, but only of one common grief augmented by the presage of another. All are equally obsessed with the menace of the elements, and the signs of even worse, until the end. In the spoken word, there are undertones and overtones of anxiety and suspense, and the deeper moans of Maurya breaking into sheer lament, but otherwise no relief. One may recall that Savitri, threatened by death, has at least death as a visitor.

---

[1] Maurya's exposure of priestly hypocrisy finds an unexpected echo towards the end of Graham Greene's *Heart of the Matter*: 'I know the Church "says". The Church knows all the rules. But it doesn't know what goes on in a single human heart'. There a suicide's widow is being addressed, and significantly the speaker is Father Rank himself.

The composer was left free here to find fresh intensity in the intonation and accompaniment, but it must be ingrained, not super-imposed in the vocal parts, and while the setting might show, apart from a working harmonic utility, some indication of clue-theme, it could scarcely embrace symphonic development. For this is no tale of a distracted sailor-man flying to or from the sea which he accepts as his element, or of any redeeming presence, or providential rescue, but only of a rising storm observed. Any pomp of departure or arrival would be fatal to the dramatic pitch. (Rabaud takes risks here, as will be noted later.) Hence, the vocal narrative relies for its incisiveness on the extension of the semitonal elasticity of early folk-music, as indicated in Chapter IV, with much swifter oscillations of mode, and no fixity of key. Each of the instrumental motives is a compact unit of a bar or two, and trenchantly atonal in most cases. One hardly knows which to admire more, the appropriateness of the rebarbative vocal inflections to the bitter narra-tive or the economy of thematic development. However, the composer allows himself forty bars of introduction and he has a part in the score for a 'sea-machine', to be employed off-stage, as a perpetual image of the demonic power with which the family are engaged. This seems tire-some, but is typical of the composer's later fondness for the *concrète*. Of the normal orchestra, the nine wind include bass but no other clarinet, a trumpet but no trombone. The absence of soprano clarinet, leaving agitation and lamentation to oboe, flute and the bassoon in its top register, will recall to some listeners how much Berlioz did with the clarinet in the orchestral lament for Andromache and Astyanax, as the bereaved wife and son of all Troy (*Les Troyens*, Act 2). This surrender added to the discipline of composition.

Six or seven distinct motives maintain the general movement and interest. A suggestion (mine) that they are all based either on a fall of one degree and then a leap of two or three, or on an ascent of three con-secutive notes in a scale, is suspect, but it points to a broad homogeneity of style. The prelude thus releases a network of trenchant paraphrases of the first type (bars 1, 5, 13), of which the first is the most incisive, but the last (Ex. 34) is later the most recurrent. One perceives indications of the terrors which any recollection of Synge's play brings to the memory, but also discords which, like the more substantive progressions in the opening of *Tristan*, convey some significance in themselves. (In one autograph score, the time-signature, and hence the tempo, has been altered from four crotchets to two minims, implying a more animated rendering.)

Ex. 34

The overt action falls into eight musical stages, roughly indicated by the leading or solo personalities concerned: (1) Cathleen and Nora; (2) Maurya and Bartley; (3) Cathleen and Maurya; (4) Cathleen and Nora; (5) Maurya's grief and her vision of Michael; (6) Maurya's retrospects; (7) entrance of Bartley's body; (8) Maurya's calm resignation.

(1) A plain pentatonic line (bassoon) falls into three stages 5 4 3 1, 5 7 5 and 5 4 3 1 again, all repeated at the higher octave (oboe). This introduces Cathleen busy and in command of the situation. (Young suggests 'spiritual hope'.) The same formula figures in sections 2 and 3, as Cathleen goes into action or has her attention drawn. A slower tempo prepares for the furtive entrance of Nora, wishing to avoid her mother. Her thoughts are on Michael. Her disclosure of the clothes brought from Donegal is marked by a falling intonation of one and then two degrees, pivotal later. For convenience, some 'variants' may be put together now:

Ex. 35a

Ex. 35b

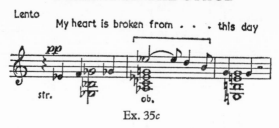

Ex. 35c

In contrast, the solemn fall and rise of a semitone in ritual style (triplet, three notes deep) underlines the concern for a 'clean burial' for Michael, to which Maurya and Cathleen allude in sections 2 and 5.

Mention of Bartley taking the boat for the mainland, raises for the first time the crucial question of the weather signs, and the use of Ex. 34 (first a compression of bars 1–2 into one, reiterated in the orchestra, and then a more shapely melodic line, with the original bar 4 lingering in an orchestral *tutti*, 36a) now associates the expansion of the falling semitone with the anxiety about Bartley, which occupies most of the drama.

Ex. 36a

(2) This rather faster tempo throws into relief a suggestion of the brooding Maurya, in Nora's mind as she listens for her approach:

Ex. 36b

Maurya is worrying about Bartley, but inevitably with Michael in mind. Hence, Ex. 35b, a piquant extension, is a suitable background for the painful question, 'Will he sail or not?' As an enhancement of this tense counterpoint of lines, the top line eventually broadens, in leaping fourths, to a blunt twist upwards (1 4 7 8) and back, in anticipation of Bartley's entrance. The suggestion may be that Bartley's unconcern is not going to help anyone. In any case there is increasing apprehension at his arrival (cf. the minatory clue-theme of leaping fourths for Satan (*Job*) and in the fourth symphony). Exx. 34, 36*a* and 36*b*, with a fresh development of the trochaic rhythm of 34 for the menacing sea-wind facing all sailors, keep the ensuing dialogue with Bartley vivid, ending in a summary *tutti*. Maurya responds with a fresh lament, 36*c* in main texture, with 35*a* as a link.

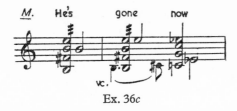

Ex. 36*c*

(3) It is now time for Cathleen to face her mother, while echoing her own anxiety. The downright pentatonic line of section 1 reacts nicely to the semitonal texture. This, however, is a mere prelude to her serious injunction to Maurya, at rather faster speed, to catch Bartley on his way out with bread and benediction. Ex. 36*d* seems to recall Michael, and through him the hazards of fishermen's relatives. Maurya is also thinking partly of Michael as she takes his stick (36*e*; 36*e*(*x*) being a hint of a ritual tone used in the final sprinkling of holy water).

(4) For the scrutiny of the clothes, the oboe develops 35*a* further. At the almost hysterical recognition of Michael's clothes, a plain ascending phrase leading to a variant of 36*c* emerges, first for Nora, then (more

Ex. 36*d*

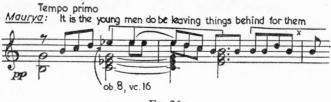

Ex. 36e

contrapuntally intense) for Cathleen, with 36a to follow; the identity-test being in absolutely plain recitative, depending on a rejoinder of B flat minor to A minor. An extension by Nora carries this essential turn in the psychological drama to its fulfilment. A line of practical recitative, for gestures of concealment of clothes and tears, relaxes the pitch before Maurya returns.

(5) Maurya's theme (36b), coloured by the high bassoon register and intensified by a fresh bass, leads to 36f. To describe this as a 'combina-

Ex. 36f

tion' of 35a and 36b would be naïve: themes cannot thus be added, and the essential curve here is the spontaneous rise to the top note. Yet it is significant that this moment of broken hope is the climax of much striving, of which 35a and 36b are components. Maurya's terrible vision is adumbrated through 36g. The connection of this with 35b may seem

Ex. 36g

far-fetched. It is, but formally it strikes the ear as a free extension of the original falling interval from diminished to augmented fourth (comparably from A–E sharp to the present A–E flat). This shadowy and very characteristic oscillation becomes the essential background of the new movement, in which Maurya relates her experience (36*h*, apparently owing its bass to 36*c*). The oboe-flute repartee after 'the grey pony behind him' (replacing Maurya's gesture of hiding something from her eyes) enables the two varied strophes of this very impressive episode, one of the justifications of the opera, to be carried to a high pitch of fearfulness (*tutti*).

va.8, hn.4, d.b.16

Ex. 36*h*

(6) Maurya's ensuing recollections start with a background of 36*f*, which continues with 35*b*. She touches a note of ritual calm at 'they're gone now', with intimate chords of E–C–E in slower tempo, but this is swallowed up by a plenary return to 34, last heard with Maurya's reproaches to Bartley and now dimly reinforced by women keening in the distance. (In *The Aran Islands*, Synge writes: 'In this cry of pain the inner consciousness of the people seems to lay itself bare for an instant'.)

(7) A perfunctory ascending motive in regular repetition, almost borrowed from one of Bach's 'grief' figures, prepares for the introduction of Bartley's body, with explanation.

(8) Maurya returns to her calmer mood in the same ascent of three notes, but now with a much more conventional D–G minor–D background. It is broken by 36*a*, but now set as a mere clue-theme (note the violins in lower-octaves with the oboe), to match a routine weather check that has ceased to carry any worry. After another gesture of calm, all the preludial themes similarly return as calm memories, achieving an almost joyous climax.

To make resignation positive, a new theme emerges, cast in one prevailing mode (Lydian major). Its string texture exhibits the properties of the violoncello A-string, and also of a solo quartet. Inevitably 35*a* returns, in the general texture and explicitly in the oboe. It will be clear to some listeners that if 36*g* is, in ethical terms, the Everlasting No,

Ex. 37

37 is the Everlasting Yea. It remains to reduce this Yea to its three essential chords, after a final reminder of the terrors of the past, in which a bass-drum roll is answered by a kettle-drum roll. These chords, picked out (in horns and violins, blended in a manner reminiscent of the close of *L'Après-midi d'un faune*), make a quiet, fading finish and darkened stage spells conclusion. Quiet, but for the insuppressible *mare ex machina* conveying its familiar concrete message of increasing and decreasing disturbance.

While, then, a strong aural grip of 34, 35*a*, 35*b*, 36*b*, 37 and the Cathleen motive will carry many listeners confidently through the network of pervasive theme, aware of its ruthless logic, not just of its intonation and harmony, narrower observation reveals many pertinent and creative variants, in harmonic texture especially, to which no reasonable person can refuse the terms development or originality. Further, any close comparison of text and music discloses numberless fine points of illustration and expression which a casual hearing would miss. The music is, indeed, such a powerful re-creation of what Synge put into his second piece of intimate vernacular drama that in time the play cannot easily be heard spoken or read, without calling to mind the trenchant intonations, masterly extensions and transcendent final calm, but also the incisive musical design, of the Vaughan Williams setting. The music is uncompromising, deliberate and, on the surface, monotonous. While a more alert observation than has been involved in this scrutiny may readily identify echoes of *Flos Campi*, in typical progression and method, much here has no precedent.

The foregoing attention to the musical material proceeds from the inference, not easily gained at the first impact, that here Vaughan Williams has wholly achieved *dramma per musica*; that the unity of mood suited him and roused his imagination and experience to find the necessary variety of means within the given limits; and that the few distinct themes in the drama gave him the freshness of reference that a symphony could not ensure. *Sir John* and parts of *The Poisoned Kiss* show some convincing stage moments, that could not possibly occur here, just as Synge put up a Playboy that could give Falstaff points in outrageous pretentiousness. *Riders to the Sea* is the only piece of coherent musical thought wound about its text. Apart from the practical difficulty of finding any venue for intimate opera, the subject will always limit audience response. Yet few half hours of drama are more rewarding in the end than this. It is surprising that it did not seem more rewarding to the composer, to the extent of pressing him to consider a tragic music-drama of wider dimensions, classical, documentary or imaginative.

In keeping close to the spoken drama, while allowing the orchestra some rein, Vaughan Williams had various precedents. Debussy's spacious and exquisite setting of Maeterlinck's *Pelléas et Mélisande* is often and glibly mentioned for comparison, as a thorough-going translation of an independent piece of spoken drama, which took the composer some ten years to achieve and remained his only complete essay in *drame lyrique*. But the differences of level are vital. The struggle of the Galway family for bare existence has no living contact with the mannered, and partly symbolist world, in which Mélisande, her husband and her lover become so irresistibly involved together, with the resigned and grieving King Arkel and the almost involuntary accessory, Yniold, as spectators. The cultivated simplicity of Maeterlinck's dialogue, from Mélisande's 'Je ne sais rien' (4. 4) down to Golaud's prurient 'Regarde!' injunction to his spying little son (a quaint analogue of Ford's equally wild determination to catch Falstaff and his wife together), is an entirely different medium from the poetic naturalism that Synge learnt to make his own. The music is correspondingly diverse and differently aimed. Debussy's characters distil a steady flow of speech-song, in subtle correspondence with the spoken word, but musically often so spare as to be fragmentary and lacking in total shape in itself. This proceeds, with occasional orchestral interludes, against a wayward and tenuous instrumental background of fleeting, memorable phrases, rarely pressed home. Some salient intonation-curves, referable to the main characters, may broadly be discerned, in an essentially oscillating rhythmic and harmonic context; for example, the rising tone and rhythmic summons that initiate the sundry but sparse appearances of the most recurrent Golaud motive. But these are no more than the bare threads of melodic consistency in an extremely variegated weave that extends to fifteen of the original nineteen scenes. The wonderfully pliant musical dialogue is fitted with typical passing illustrations which cohere almost involuntarily in five successive acts.

In *Riders to the Sea*, the underlying strain of the double dramatic situation focused round Michael and Bartley is matched by a plain and searing intensity in the tortuous intervals of the dialogue, and this is thrust into shape and consistency by the recurrent motives. For these, as has already been shown, a few general twists of melodic intonation suffice as the main basis of the miniature act. They are, as such, more trenchant than Debussy's, and their total impact is, after Debussy, monotonous and raw, but concentrated. At no essential point, then, does the dramatic tone, declamatory method or orchestral development of *Pelléas* provide any genuine precedent, apart from the exaltation of the free rhythm and pungent brevity of the spoken word.

Paradoxically, Holst's quasi-mythical *Savitri*, to his own text, is nearer the mark. In a restrained recitation over a slender choral-instrumental texture, an idiom derived, in part, from folk-song, but not from any particular song, somehow matches the plain anglicized vernacular of very early Indian legend, the *Mahabharata*. Moreover, the figure of death, proceeding firmly ahead in *canto fermo* style, while Savitri pours out her whispered fears, offers a dramatic and musical advantage, which seems to be echoed in manner in the growth of the Cathleen motive in the orchestra. Further, Savitri and Maurya alike are womankind confronting death. There the precedent almost ends. Savitri and her woodman husband are radiant, dedicated beings, above life's grim necessities. 'Welcome, Lord' (to death) is a natural fulfilment. Maurya's final passiveness is of another stuff; just as Beethoven's hazardously adventurous Leonora cannot very well be compared with fire-tested Pamina. Holst's music is correspondingly hieratic and undiscursive, moving rather from one chain of sonorities to another, some of these, as Imogen Holst observes, being trite and sentimental; the method of appeal is uncertain and transitional, as far as it goes, as well it might be in so early a work. Vaughan Williams never falters.

Vaughan Williams was not without predecessors in treating *Riders to the Sea* musically. Apart from a symphonic prologue by Henry Gilbert, using Celtic folk-elements (1915), a setting by Fritz Hart (once a fellow-student of Vaughan Williams and Holst) appeared in the same year, stimulated presumably by the opera group of the Melbourne Conservatory, and following Hart's setting of Yeats's *Land of Heart's Desire*. It is not published, nor did it reach Britain.[1]

---

[1] Miss Peggy Glanville-Hicks, who, herself a composer, was concerned, as a student, with the production of several of Hart's operas at Melbourne wrote to me of the work, 'I still recollect ... a sheer "theatre" and vocal-brilliance

Henri Rabaud's third opera, *L'Appel de la mer* (1923), a 'Drame lyrique' set to his own translation, appeared at the Opéra Comique, Paris (1924), in Brussels (1925) and, in German, in Leipzig (1927). Using a full orchestra, the work shows, in some respects, a more organized and methodical presentation than its successor's. Behind it lay, not only the conflict of the earlier orchestral *Poème sur le libre de Job* (1905), but the competence of the lightly fantastic opera *Mârouf, Savetier du Caire* (1914), an *Arabian Nights* tale. In the latter, dramatic control is matched by a shrewd blend of traditional harmonic idiom and judicious challenges to the ear.

A short prelude, marked by the superimposition of A major (and a 1–3–5– ♮7–9 chord on G) on a chord of G major, is securely, but hardly relevantly, revived at the end in a manner almost prophetic of the resumption of routine after tragic events in another seaside drama, *Peter Grimes*. The general dialogue is moulded into speech song after the model of *Pelléas*, if anything. Frequently the declamation moves lightly forward over a thin counterpoint, with impromptu after-phrases of richer colour to heighten the suspense ('Nous verrons si n'est pas à Michael . . .'); Rabaud can thus retain Catherine's analysis of the clothing and other prosaic details. But clue-themes, too, come and go with unmistakable pertinence. Nora's quotation of the pious curé's assurance, 'le Dieu Tout Puissant ne voudre point . . .', is given a clear melodic shape in F major. Its simple recollection at the end, omitted by Vaughan Williams, follows the same bland, decorative 3 6 5 1 outline, but the violoncellos have now a subversive semitonal figure, which continues under Maurya's dry rejoinder (anticipating the mockery of Father Rank's 'The Church *says* . . .'; see p. 279). A striking, surely mocking, cascade of tone follows. Bartley (or his horse?) has his pronounced identity card, a stoic, Dorian motive, steadily trochaic. This serves later to illustrate Maurya's narrative of her vision on the seashore. A pentatonic Michael-theme operates similarly from the sisters' talk to the mother's.

In the centre, a climax of tone is reached for Maurya's cry after Bartley's exit, leading to a passionate but contrived vocal cadenza. For her final tranquillity, Rabaud employs a melodic idiom and colour, of which isolated features are strangely reminiscent of Vaughan Williams: a vocal rise and fall in the Mixolydian mode (1–2–3–4|5 4–2–♮7|1);

ability that made his operas madly exciting . . . The lyric Celtic strain, too, was there'. Hart spent his last years at Honolulu, Hawaii, where his manuscripts are probably to be found in the university or in the keeping of Mrs. Hart.

oscillating 8–♮7 string chords in multiple texture, plus oboe holding 8; a 1–5 drone below, amplified by the sophisticated major-key (6 5–6) reiterations of keeners. The style is eclectic to the end.

Yet it would be interesting to have heard, as a near precedent, Rabaud's obviously intelligently 'expressive' setting, for its own sake, and as a measure of Vaughan Williams's apparently much less professional exposure of the ordeal of those much enduring peasant women, which Synge has translated with such artlessness from his observations in the Aran Islands. French listeners might not find a 'drame lyrique' in music so sparing of the passionate vocal line. They would certainly not find opera as they understand it.[1]

Opera or music drama, the genre did not, somehow, lead Vaughan Williams any further. Or at least his next stage work was in its own class of Morality with music, which places it in Chapter XII. Before he had completed this, he had produced his sixth symphony. One cannot be far wrong in assuming that, while appreciating the opportunities for idiomatic novelty offered by opera, he found most range for his expressive powers in the symphony, like Beethoven and Sibelius. To the symphonies, then, we return, speculative as to what could succeed the third besides another *Pastoral*.

---

[1] On the Italian reception of *Cavalcata a mare*, the reader is referred to a review by F. L. Lunghi. (*S. Cecilia*, 8 (February, 1959).)

Three More Symphonies

SYMPHONY NO. 4 IN F MINOR

One must not be misled by the 1788 record of the composition of three master-symphonies in six weeks. However quickly Mozart worked out the basic material of those twelve movements, relying now on original motives and now on formulae of the time, each had first to arise in his consciousness, with a potential yield, from the experience of the *Prague* and the fresh accumulating symphonies, of veins exhausted but new methods confirmed. The promptness of such outstanding renewals of symphonic stimulus is a personal matter, like the long silences between symphonies on the part of other composers. So much, then, for the ten-year gap that occurs in the present case.

In his third symphony, Vaughan Williams had mostly abandoned his previous blend of modern and vernacular textures in favour of impersonal and usually modal melodic lines, whose appeal lies in their being woven with other threads of independent mode, their manifold, impressionist harmony, their orchestral colour and their rare but characteristic cadences. There is correspondingly less development and recapitulation for its own sake, and a coda is conceivable, as in two movements here, but not essential. There was promise in the free polyphony, but not of another symphony in this rhapsodic style. Fresh melodic and rhythmic character must be found. Conceivably the third symphony of Arnold Bax, to whom Vaughan Williams's fourth symphony is dedicated, gave the older composer a jog, as the climax of a period of symphonic struggle in which the recurrent *feroce* of the early tuba theme is symptomatic.

So much sober conjecture on the impasse after 1922 may be permitted before surveying a selection of the new material. Some of it

291

Ex. 38a

Ex. 38b

Ex. 38c

Ex. 38d

may have occurred to the composer as shown, some has obviously been deliberately stiffened in detail, but these are the end-products in their context. It will be noticed that 38d, the only diatonic motive besides 38h (i.e. conforming to a single scale or mode), is at once pinioned by discord and clashing semitone (D flat); and 38*b* could not have figured in the *Tallis Fantasia*, with which it shares a Phrygian contact. The rest are all marked by some contradiction of semitone for a given degree. Ex. 38*c* is the most downright example of a double oscillation of thirds (two falling thirds, and an ambivalent third degree) that recurs in more florid or bravura contexts (38*e*, 38*f*, 39*a*), but 38*a* is a document in trenchancy of which 38*g* and 39*b* are typically wide variants. Nearly every salient line is thus notched melodically, so that it can reappear in the most transformed context and still be identifiable.

One such typical intonation persists throughout the symphony, a second does so less noticeably, and a third, not so recognized by the composer, is more recurrent than he realized. The feature X in 38*a* is established in the first movement as a curve of melodic definition compressed to the semitonal limit, and as a terse summary of the first subject. Just emergent in the second, it pervades the third movement in a deliriously repetitive style and dominates the coda of the finale. (The third and fourth movements are here considered as separate.) Such a cyclic process had marked earlier symphonies, notably Berlioz's *Fantastic*, Liszt's *Faust* and Mahler's eighth, but never before with so uncompromising a motive—for motive it certainly becomes.

Motive Y (38*b*), significantly terminating where Beethoven began his historical account of world-disorder (ninth symphony, finale), discloses an Olympian frown, and brusquely invokes re-statement as a propellent bass rhythm in the first movement. But it also figures initially and transitionally in the second, and finds an agile disguise at the opening and yet another in the interlude (cf. 38*h*) of the Scherzo—for a fantastic ascent of two fourths and a third (not to be compared with the unequivocal *octave*-spanning fourths—Ex. 17—of the *London Symphony*) is not easily identifiable in these recurrences of three or more fourths, one mercurial, the other ponderous. Finally, the curve, not rhythmically committed enough to qualify as a substantive motive, penetrates the Epilogue in kaleidoscopic style (39*b*) and ultimately with extreme bluntness, after a pale reflection of itself in the midway string interlude, which is a translation of the end of the first movement.[1]

The cadential motive Z (38*c*) and its impatient pair of thirds, soon

---

[1] An early piano score shows a rise to C♮ in 1.3 (as in 1.4) on the first beat, as *erased*. An odd truncation! The five-note swoop up to a flat twelfth freely persists in F.S. (i) 4.14; (iii) 1.2 etc.; (iv) 9.17, 23,7, 26.3, 9; the rise to a ninth elsewhere being more plausibly a reduction of effort than the 'optional' twelfth is an extension.

compressed to three notes to form another pivotal bass (38e), reappears in the second movement as a pathetic, stylistic mannerism (38f). It disguises itself in the third movement as an impressionist bravura whirl to accompany the second-subject theme (Ex. 7d), and is a noticeable figure of punctuation in the last movement (39a). All this adds to the ultimate riveting quality of the whole work, for only in the Epilogue can it be said that the clue-themes (X and Y) run at all counter to the main movement in which they recur. They do not otherwise exercise an over-ruling influence, as a motto theme is apt to do, down to the crudity of Tchaikovsky's fifth symphony. Finally, the opening bars of the symphony make a decisive close (38a with 38b).

In the due proportion of alert and integral listening, then, undisturbed by the parade of motto-themes in every programme-note from the composer's downwards, it may as well be recognized at once that certain features of the first movement are pungent enough to penetrate to the end of the work, as happened to the contemplative, non-committal but expansive motto in the *London Symphony*. The driving power of the basic material clearly affects the structure of the movements. Let us assume some sort of bi-focal imagery, in which the old term 'subject', for a group of distinct impressions complementary to one another, may serve, though the original balance of key-character has gone. In the first movement, then, 38a in downright two-part harmony, 38b and 38c make up a first subject, with a certain common recognition of F as tonic, for if 38a is naturally construable as in C (Phrygian minor), its repetition a fourth higher establishes F. It will be noted that motive X emerges almost accidentally, as a quick revision of the original sequence (bars 3–4), which maintains its integrity up to the closing bars of all.

It was not Bach who wrote whole fugues on B–A–C–H, but, since Schumann and others took the plunge, Vaughan Williams pointed out that his clue-theme was different. It approximates, in fact, to B–A–H–B by literal comparison (B being musical German for B flat and H for B natural, while actually C flat is required). It is a confined curve, where B–A C–H at least moves outwards. The latter type appears in bars 3–5, so that the compressed intervals of bars 6–8 are in the nature of a correction. Indeed, it might almost be suspected that in his spontaneous opening the composer found himself treading on and jumping off the 'Bach' wire, and then decided to outdo B–A–C–H with the discipline of the monotonous B–A–H–B variant.

The symphony thus starts with a clashing falling semitone and then formulates, canonically and agitatedly, its first melodic clue. If this stern stuff is first subject, what can be second without becoming a pathetic relaxation? This is where, as opposed to the corresponding major-but-modulating motive in Walton's first symphony, the modal austerity of 38d comes in, without any gesture of transition except *meno mosso*, and even that only amounting to a change from two to three equivalent beats (and from three to two subsidiary beats). If it were not for the harmony, we might be back in *Benedicite* (solo entry: 'him for ever'); the friendly triplets begin to multiply, and a warm

Ex. 38*e*

climax is achieved, followed by 38*e*, the bass of which is not far from the 'lightnings' and 'works' of the same respectable work. Some pristine vigour is perceptible. But if the comparable bass of *Benedicite* is a genial and eloquent suggestion of nature's moody energy, this bass is relentless. An impulsive attempt at a new theme, a florid version of 38*c* in E flat, is swept aside by 38*e* and its ubiquitous, and now also ponderous, bass, entering first in canon (a revision).

'Second subject' has been duly registered in a new version of D major. Over, then, to 38*a* in D minor, fully harmonized, but still with a pronounced fissure between top and bottom chording, with A, not D, in the bass. (The *London Symphony* is more ostentatious here.) It is incumbent to establish motive X as more than a variant, beginning with the bassoon against tremulous strings, as in Sibelius's fifth symphony (K3), except that here the violas support. A jaunty compression into single bars of alternate shrieks and growls, *tutti fortissimo e animato*, removes any illusions that this is a meditative theme or one of the persevering Sibelius type, and it prepares for later grim jests from the powers that be. Motive Y hastily closes the 'discussion', with its magisterial scowl and ready capacity for bass-propulsion, like the motto-theme of the *London Symphony*.

So back to 38*a* in F (1.7). It is in full blast, where the recapitulation of the ultra-semitonal subject in the *London Symphony* was so confined to the shadows as to be structurally ambivalent; but the harmonization of 38a is further stiffened,[1] and motive X runs into 38c, so that the whole subject is compressed from fifty bars to ten. Ex. 38b is not heard. Its time will presumably come later.

In the second subject, 38d is also stiffened and shortened by contrapuntal economy, losing its tunefulness in the process. The climax is soon reached. But now 38e and its rollicking or pompous bass would be a relaxation in the wrong place. So the theme is transfigured in key, tempo, dynamics and other features. The bass becomes four sustained notes, at first with what, in the same key as before, would be C sharp as pivot. The F sharp line on top continues. But the answering falling figure at the end of 38e is now at once (reflecting the E flat incident) conflated with 38c in the composite curve 8 (♯7) ♮7 5|5 ♯4 (♮4) ♯3 ♮3 1, and this antiphony assumes an automatic course of hieratic repetition, in varied rhythmic detail (the bracketed degrees above showing later additions and the vertical line an alternative start) and swinging, in actual pitch, from D flat to D and back. And all this to no loud and tumultuous bassoon and supporting wind, but for muted strings and consonant fragments of wind and muted horns, *lento*, converging cadentially in the subtle antiphony of wood and strings, dwelling, with a studied oscillation between minor and major harmony, on the final fall from 3 to 1. So to a breathless close. With better acquaintance this last section, 28 bars to the precedent 40, actually sounds much shorter, because it consists principally of two set bars, echoing and re-echoing along two adjacent paths which coalesce in formal movement along the first. Hence the whole recapitulation is at once spare and startlingly refreshing, while balancing the exposition. So serene a transformation needs no coda. The new material has found significance in a classical schedule that uses a key-system to distinguish the main sections but leaves the concluding section where it belongs, out of the main strife of the movement.

So far comment has been concerned with distinguishing (as against that of the third) the trenchant harmonic and melodic character of the new symphony as revealed in the inventive structure of one movement and productive of later encounters. But in fact, the emphasis with which these features are produced is exceptional in general intensity, volume and the hard dazzle which brass in particular is able to turn upon the ear. What, if anything, this portends, will be discussed later; but

---

[1] One two-piano score shows that the addition of the three-beat counterpoint in bars 2, 5–7 of this *a tempo* was an after-thought, pencilled into the score, unilinear at first. See Appendix C.

with loudness as the normal degree, rather than the peak of emphasis, here, the re-creation of 38e marks an extreme at the other end of the scale, that must either be revealingly corrective or in the nature of a pathetic escape from the main tumult. It remains to verify which. Meanwhile, as other-worldly music, it shows a peculiar, painful poignancy, anticipated only at the very end of *A Sea Symphony* and of the second movement of the third. No other first movement that I can recall ends with such meaningful restraint. And no other has so much to restrain. The Furies are seen to be the Kindly Ones. The naked truth is, for the moment, too overpowering.

The second movement runs smoothly along its balanced 'classical' course, in the tradition of the earliest symphonic slow movements, which tend to be the shapeliest, and in a texture of 'wandering counterpoints' to which the composer's third symphony may be said to have conditioned the exploring ear. 'Who are these coming to the sacrifice?' asked Richard Capell after the first performance. After an enigmatic but half-familiar start (Motive Y), the persistence of the detached, percussive, plucked-string figure promotes a strong sense of measured movement, against which the violins weave long threads of fugal entry in a strange mode, Lydian in one half (1–5), Aeolian in the other (6–7). It was first apparent in the ecstatic theme introduced for the 'Sanctus' in *Sancta Civitas*, with a strongly defined flattened sixth (♭6 1 3 5) which recurs here in a different way; there can be no careless talk about a 'lament'. (Another melodic precedent happens to be the languorous chorus of the slave-girls, and Konchakovna's cavatina, in the second act of *Prince Igor*.) The tempo here prompts a comparison, if anything, with the much more extended slow processional movement of Shostakovich's eleventh symphony, entitled 'The eternal memory', with its evocative plucked bass. The tune there, however, is square and strophical, and is, indeed, traditional in source.

The oboe initiates a fresh turn to the imitational counterpoint, and an oscillation of rising fourths here changes to an almost hieratic descent, semitone upon semitone, as a counterpoint to a solemn but passionate delivery of Y in the brass, now duly exposed as more than an inauguration. A cadential passage, $38f^1$ in C, provides poise, and echoes the refrain at the end of the first movement in its circling round 38c.

The slight development being concerned with the oboe line and Y,

---

[1] For the better guidance of orchestral players, the composer writes this harmony on the basis of C major (key-signature), but the observant reader will not miss the Lydian touch here.

these features are compressed in recapitulation, and the opening violin theme, now begun by viola, is shortened, a later adjustment shown in

Ex. 38*f*

one piano score. The coherence of the basic expression remains, ending this time in F, comfortably if it were not for the intrusion of motive X on the trombones (muted), in fifths, hinting at G flat. The pivotal flute takes care of this intrusion, though its ending is inconclusive. (Its last note is now E, not the F originally printed.) Young's comparison of *Magnificat* is interesting, as a hint of the emotional genre.

If one takes the slow movement of the *London Symphony* as a precedent, then here the single plucked-string line under a long-drawn descant replaces the chain of minor chords, rising densely under a pattern of melodic phrases, and the contrapuntal cadence (38*f*) compares with a richly harmonic progression. The present movement is not therefore better; the contrapuntal is not necessarily the good, any more than the harmonically progressive, or the harmonically impressionist. But this has a narrower melodic basis, and its subtle thinking takes time to apprehend. With familiarity, its 'pathos' recedes; indeed, the references to 'profound melancholy' by Downes and others reduce the emotional scope of the movement to a common trend of romantic music, noticeable since the minor scale developed as a kind of renunciation of the major, and associated in particular with Tchaikovsky. Not all burdened music is sad. The very Crucifixus of the *B Minor Mass*, the archetype of humanity's heaviest ground-bass, is no mere lamentation over what man has done to man. Yet in this Andante there is a feeling of restraint and restlessness in the semitonal contradictions, nagging bass and altogether inconclusive tone, which the grave reappearance of X confirms. This makes its full contribution to the impact of the whole symphony. It was possibly on this account that Richard Capell (of the *Daily Telegraph*) missed, at the first hearing, the composer's 'contemplative depth'. Something is renounced, consciously or unconsciously.

Capell was not slow, however, to recognize 'a wonderfully fantastic and uncanny Scherzo'; on which ground he was nearer the mark than his opposite number on *The Times*, who found the Scherzo 'easily enjoyed by all and sundry at a first hearing, because it has humour which is sensitive in the opening theme and becomes broad when the tuba begins to caper in the Trio'. The comparison of first impressions is made because now, when the symphony is in danger of becoming almost too familiar, one has to try to appraise the 'humour' in its true historical quality. Humour in music consists, amongst other things, of displaced accent, extended melodic tempo and compass, unexpected instrumentation and abrupt antiphony, each carried to such an abnormal degree as to be acceptable only as a kind of rehearsal of the proper expression. All these features are here. But what was fantastic a generation ago will probably become the established fashion later. The pioneer in this field, with the modern orchestra, was, of course, Richard Strauss. In *Till Eulenspiegel*, to go no further, the agility of the smallest clarinet spreads to the heaviest brass with the sure touch of an experiment becoming a *fait accompli*, under the stimulus of promoting the reincarnation of the hubristic spirit. Holst continued the process in his *Planets* suite, sorcerer-wise in 'Uranus' and with uproarious geniality in 'Jupiter'. In the latter, a motive of leaping fourths reaches in restatement some provocative stages in the brass.

The borderline between acrobatics and humour had thus narrowed by 1930. So far the outbreak of terse spasms of fresh rhythm, extending motive Y by a piquant descent of fifths, may pass as *jeu d'esprit*. The grimness lies in the degree in which that descent is hammered into the sound-track, up to the limit of sheer brass. Meanwhile motive X, brusquely compressed to the present metre (38*g*), has stamped its in-

Ex. 38*g*

cisive quality upon the texture, also the fresh tonality of D. A devastatingly acrobatic version of 38*c* similarly attends the B minor reverberations of a monotonous new figure (rising third)—here shown in D minor

—in a wickedly dispossessive manner, but a continuing repartee (in a new key) is forthcoming. Originally this figure began with two whole-beat notes.

[Ex. 7*d*]

The recovery of the foregoing matter, after considerable play with X for its own sake, rivets the association of ideas beyond any level of humorous experiment. But what of the fresh gambols of the scarcely *feroce* brass in a mock-fugue, far more whimsical than Beethoven's (in the fifth), in what may be taken to be A flat pentatonic major (not E

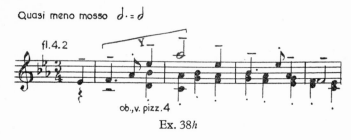

Ex. 38*h*

flat)? The observation of the fifth entry (38*h*), in a style remarkably reminiscent of Holst, supports the acceptance of this interlude in slower tempo as a moment of broad relaxation, maintained by considerable ingenuity in the handling of the three-part writing. It is sufficiently congenial to the common listener to make the return of the Scherzo, more or less as at its second hearing, effectively rebarbative.

A fresh attempt at the fugue is inevitably cut short, but the tonic or pivotal note, A flat, survives as G sharp, a bass to which the music becomes tied in relevant rhythmic tension (skeleton of vibratory 38*c* figure as already described). (This enharmonic correspondence between two notes of quite different scale associations—the single black note on the piano functioning as either, according to context, but tuned as neither—finds a curious parallel in *Sancta Civitas* in the transition from the bitter A flat of Babylon's degradation to the serene G sharp of the New Heaven.) A calm and subdued rendering of motive Y in restless tonality, with a nagging oscillation of bass (kettle-drums with strings), keeps up the suspense. Except that G sharp is not essential to D as a classical A flat, falling to G, can be considered pertinent to C minor or major—by long association—the listener can hardly refrain from recalling the suspended A flat at the end of the scherzo movement of Beethoven's fifth symphony, already a vague precedent for the corybantic interlude. The entrance, as into an increasing vacuum, of motive X, forcing home A in a desperately involuntary sequence, suggests that the G sharp pedal might resolve upwards and thus, from a now conventional A, as fifth degree, bring D back. In fact, the formalities are disregarded, and instead there is a leap to D tonality.

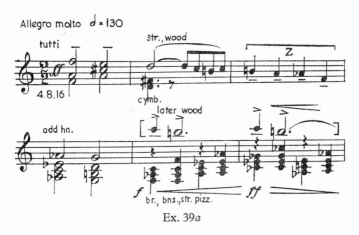

Ex. 39a

Thus out of an impasse, as in Beethoven, springs (specifically without alteration of the conductor's two beats) a fresh movement. In this context no sensitive listener could be as perverse as to regard so torturingly *postponed* a change of mood as a new episode of the Scherzo, which Howes suggests as a 'natural' confusion. All the same, any sophisticated reminder of the release of spirit in Beethoven's fifth symphony, Mahler's second or Sibelius's second, ceases abruptly. The fragmentary nature of this dynamic opening is all its own. The primary phrase (39a) is only four bars long, and its tonality contradictory. The first key implied is D minor-major; but the reverberation of 38c indicates F major-minor as the true issue, and the continuation is decisive.

The heavy strain of the opening of the symphony has thus been balanced by a strong theme with a clear feature of descent, workable in close canon at identical pitch, and a distinctive D–F twist in rejoinder to B-A-H-B. The entry of the full brass, piccolo and (less audible) double bassoon—as, historically, in Beethoven—makes it clear that that descent is meant seriously. The relation of the Scherzo to an independent but continuous sequel in the same two beats, but differently divided (two subordinate beats instead of three), has been established, provisionally, as the peculiarly complex nature of this third and last movement, in harmony with isolated but signal precedents. Let us not underestimate the burden of a symphonic mind which so requires this double-move-ment finish—for there is preparation but no punctuation here—by observing that the Scherzo could never settle down to a close. It is usually much simpler to end abruptly and make a fresh start.

Once begun, the new sub-movement proceeds with a certain brusque confidence. A wayward anacrusis, depending on a 'till ready' bass line, three notes deep, observes a capricious mode (the Locrian, as in the white-note scale, B to B). Its delivery in a 'jazzy' syncopation of brass and full string percussion has received inordinate attention in wayside comment from having been described by the composer as 'oompah'. As a rhetorical feature in a wider display of virtuosity, it has a precedent in the Saturday night disturbances at the Boar's Head in Elgar's *Falstaff*, in the delivery of the second theme in 'Jupiter' (Holst) and, nearer home, in the falling-tone motive of the Scherzo of the *London Symphony*. The secret of this *oompah* lies in its hubristic tone. The subsequent addition of a declamatory phrase that cannot intone further than one degree at a time augments the touch of uncanny impudence, and a more shapely phrase—a complete revision, as it happens—follows. After pronounced skirmishes with the primary theme, in imitational style, the minatory finish of the theme (Z with a grinning flourish) ensures a peremptory close.

There is no link. The music simply takes a fresh turn for the second subject. The audible theme (see Ex. 40: tenor) is another of the piquant melodic phrases that are composed for wear and tear. It gives little away at the first impact of its shapely neo-Lydian curve and clear fourth-degree key. An interruption by the brass (in six metre) initiates a general period of increasingly automatic, uncontrolled reverberation of each part of the first subject in turn, with motive Y as a steadying feature in the bass. Soon the music starts moving in a straight line, typified by F sharp (drum-roll). But now the basses move from a consonant C sharp to C natural, and so invoke 38e, not in its original blustering energy but as transformed at the end of the first movement. The pure string rendering of this leisurely and sustained echo provides an exquisite and unmistakable point of repose. As a means of expression the prevailing chord of D major over C is on the way to establishment as a *concord*, in readiness for more distinctive use in a later work. The analytical may recall 'Picked sparingly' (*Sea Symphony*) as a precedent.

Motive X, moving restlessly round one degree in serpentine fashion, and Y, equally restless in another way, are the obvious available stimuli for extricating the movement from its confinement in a groove of contemplation. Soon, against unceasing admonition by the horns with fragments of Y, an antimony of B-A-H-B in A and A flat, simultaneously but in different rhythmic senses, is the signal for the recapitulation. Here a mechanical entry of the first subject would be jejune after the intervening stiffening of its texture by contrapuntal weaving, and after the establishment of a metrical stride which has lost its freshness. Hence, the main theme is first halted on its controlling note (D) before it proceeds further. (A similar rhythmic vacuum of sheer tonic assertion is created at the stroke of the restatement in the first movement of Beethoven's fourth symphony. But this halting bar here was an afterthought.) The four primary bars of Ex. 39a are then consonantly compressed to three, and this variant repeated. The much-developed *oompah* follows, with its declamatory phrase attached at once, and then the shapely corrective, already mentioned as an afterthought. In the earliest piano score, this subsidiary theme of nine bars does not appear at all. Instead, there are fifteen bars of continued *oompahs*, with a free melodic line, followed by a recovery of the first subject, in canon as in the exposition (score: 4. 1–13). In the revision, the second subject presses on the heel of the briefer summary, in D, with a secondary sequence of close brass entries in an interval-pattern that reflects the leaps of Y in reverse order. (The treatment of the Khan theme in the coda of the *Prince Igor* overture offers some parallel.) Z is reserved to 'conclude' the restatement, in tumultuous reverberations of the first theme in toccata style, summarized in a new jingle of A–F and A♭–F in increasingly pressing repetition.

Thus peremptorily the set material of the new part-movement exhausts its quasi-classical pattern. There can be no coda or further development on these lines. As a melodic assertion, plain or canonic or bravura, the first theme has a limited power of return; the drifting *oompah* is out of the question; and the wiry second-subject motive has already been brilliantly dragooned, as the attaché of a Y scheme.

Back, then, to clue X. Not creeping out Fafner-wise, as before, but fiercely declamatory, and, in part, a symmetrical four-bar unit (not the six at first projected, as in the tenor trombones' second entry). Fugue is employed, too, to maintain a certain mechanical evenness and extent of expression. Procedure is extremely capricious as regards order and rhythmic shape of entries, but holds on to B-A-H-B tenaciously enough to be able to absorb in turn, in a wizardly variety of contexts—in which, I confess, I cannot identify the B-H-A-B variant cited by the composer— the 'treble' of *oompah* (with motive Y as in 39*b*), the second subject, the six-metre interruption in the second subject (triangle entry), and last, of course, the main theme—as the final projection of X, which at one moment is moving as prehistorically as Fafner and at the next as scientifically as Loge. One sensation remains: the beginning of the whole work. So here it comes, with a reduction of speed. In the com-

Ex. 39*b*

Con anima

Ex. 40

poser's stark parting word, to end all annotation, 'The work ends with a reference to the opening bars of the first movement'.

Compression can now claim its masterpiece. The key is, of course, F minor as in the original restatement (and in the twentieth bar of the symphony). B-A-C-H is restored, as in bars 3–4 of the work, now up a fourth. But the original sequel, B-A-H-B, the ragged, rugged trend traceable throughout the symphony and never more so than in the Epilogue, is a closed avenue. Hence this is the moment for a tense semitonal sequence, reserved from bar 10 of the symphony, leading to motive Y, similarly excluded from restatement in the first movement. The latter appears in the brass as at first (*plus* cymbal roll), but melodically with its kinked 1–4–♭7–♭9 ascent hammered, first, into a straight 5–1–5 (♭6) to add momentum to the piercing quality of the flat 9th, *tutti*. Into this last, shrill discord enter G flat and F at opposite ends of the towering gamut, and D flat–C, A–A flat in proximity in the middle of the harmony, the minor chord of the tonic crushed against that of its closest negative, the flattened second. The final F–C blast is, by comparison, a release. By the symphonic principle, a powerful exordium has reached fulfilment in a summary determined by a wider context on the scale of three full movements, the last comprising scherzo, finale and epilogue.

The Epilogue, then, which this coda is entitled, is not to be compared with the epilogue of the second symphony. There the pain and torment of the finale are, apart from some piquant touches, set aside in favour of fresh exploration of the broad motto-theme, which has not been noticeable as such since the first movement. This converges in a serene echo of the prologue, as the opening of the symphony proves to have been. In the present symphony, the material of the main movement after the Scherzo is displaced by the motto-themes already heard at the end of the development, but only to revitalize a temporarily exhausted structural pattern and relaxing texture, most of the finale-material recurring in fresh conjunction. The epilogue is thus far the movement's own coda. The foregoing material and the emergent cyclic motives achieve a rich conflation. The true epilogue to the symphony lies in the concluding and taut twelve bars, corresponding to the meditative thirty-two to which the epilogue of the *London Symphony* was finally reduced.

It remains to recognize that the texture of this third and composite movement is entirely consonant with that of the first in its brusque and ejaculatory tone, its hard brilliance, its acceptance of brass quality and intense scoring as paramount, its general rejection of conventional quietude on strings, and its uncompromising acceptance, where necessary, of the 'note which looks wrong and sounds wrong [harmonically] but is right'. (The early references to 'roystering finale—bitter jollity' (Capell), or to the finale as extending 'the new freedom of mood . . . supported by unexpected brilliance in orchestration' (*The Times*), seem to have missed something owing to a common assumption that speed and clarity spell gaiety, or they reflect a too whimsical rendering.) On these lines the rough road is pursued to the end, with cumulative signs that what has been projected, in the terms of Ex. 38, has found its complete form in a symphony, through an imaginative attack on the structural problems of the intransigent texture. This conviction will not come at once. Mrs. Pakenham is not the only listener who was on further acquaintance baffled by the noise and dissonance of the work which had accidentally converted her to a recognition of the composer's genius. Only alert listening, aided by the score, will translate the raw impressions and fragments into something organically necessary and significant in itself.

On such lines the evidence will accumulate of a masterpiece of construction in its chosen limits. Many listeners will be content to leave it at that, in view of the absence of any title; merely noting that three movements of Walton's first symphony (1934–5) show a rather similar assault on the ear. Once more, then, I quote Fox Strangways's admirable early summary in *The Observer* (November 24, 1935, notably antecedent to an entirely sceptical impression of Bax's sixth symphony, given in the same week). 'This man, we say, can drive a nail home as no other man alive can. The defects count for nothing against this, that the nail which he drives, holds. He happens to be an Englishman, but the music speaks the universal language. His pathos palpitates, his climax sears, because he is speaking the simple truth.'

This verdict of a critic thirteen years the composer's senior is penetrating and judicious. It may reasonably be inferred that the nails hurt, and that the enigmatic calm, as at the end of the first movement and throughout the second, and equally the humorous touches, are diversions that may continue to haunt the mind, as in the centre of the finale, but are indubitably subordinate to the main impact. But this gives no countenance to interpreting the 'truth' of the composer's experience as a mirror of events. A growing body of interpretation, nourished since the War, has assumed this to be a romantic symphony; as an exposure, that is, of the menacing features of certain European states in the thirties, and by implication of human (or at least totalitarian) wickedness, as the 1935 burden of men of good will. To these the symphony is addressed through a moving cartoon of uncontrolled violence in sound, with the Whitman *Drum Taps* movements, in *Dona nobis pacem*, not far off. The symphony has even been considered a grave warning of the outbreak of war in the near future, although a reference by Holst in April, 1932, to old and new versions of the symphony points to substantive construction in 1932, in which year the only certain calamity, the collapse of the disarmament conference, made war more likely but not inevitable. However re-cast, the work as a whole was obviously conceived as it is from the start, and could not have been seriously modified by any deepening sense of world-disaster.[1]

Foss, after admitting uneasily the absolute appeal, assents to a 'new truth of violent force' in a contemporary sense. Howes, after repudiating, in his original analysis (1937), any didactic message in the new note of sheer power, has now found 'a revelation of the essential nature

---

[1] Holst's letter to Vaughan Williams (*Heirs and Rebels*, 79–81) was written from Harvard University and dated April 15, to which an editorial '1932' is added from a positive knowledge of the year and circumstances of appointment. Holst, ill at the time, returned to England in June, 1932. A later letter from Vaughan Williams to Holst, now in hospital, is editorially, and doubtless incontrovertibly, dated December, 1933. The writer speaks of a replacement of the 'nice' tunes in the Finale [of the new symphony] 'by better ones (at all events they are *real* ones) . . . the others were made-up stuff and these are not'. This indicates both the general progress of the symphony before 1934 and its purely musical conception. Even if the revision of texture were drastic—of which there is little evidence in the piano scores, beyond the replacement of unsuitable transition (see p. 504)—one would not attribute this to gathering storms on the frontiers.

of violence' in the ruthless dialectic of the music, though 'rather logic than ethics'. Capell, writing as early as 1937, rejected the 'pure dialectic' theory, divining a 'furious outburst of scorn and indignation at the world's wickedness'. The most cogent essay in this kind of inter-pretation, however, was an article by Mr. N. G. Long (*Monthly Musical Record* (June, 1947)). This infers from the tightly bound struc-ture, the ruthless urgency and vehement irregularity of rhythm (in the third movement especially), the often closely contrapuntal texture, and the unnecessarily heavy and noisy orchestration, a 'story of inexorable brutality . . . a picture of contemporary ends-justify-the-means philo-sophy . . . the victory of force over ineffective, tortured tenderness. Yet humanity always appears'. In a more recent article in the same journal (March-April, 1960), Mr. David Brown re-opens the question in the context of all nine symphonies, and, while scouting any unduly dramatic reading of a symphony—the seventh, in particular—warns his readers not to disregard clear signs of a 'message' beyond the mere notes, if it illuminates otherwise unintelligible music.

All these projections of a reaction to menacing forces in the world draw attention to the defiant originality of the music, as heard in the concert hall. To many inexperienced observers, any very striking art must 'mean' something beyond itself. (References to *Job*, as a turning point in the same trend of expression, do not pass scrutiny. There are severe clashes there, but they are eloquently resolved. Nor is the piano concerto more than an augmentation of the somewhat Mephistophelian tradition of Stravinsky and others.) Performances of the work will continue to arouse similar images of organized battalions, barbarian hordes or key-men behind some trigger to be pressed, snapping out of control, while Walton's brilliant first symphony, for all its 'malicious' scherzo and searing climaxes, moves securely into its place as, briefly, 'after Sibelius'. But the composer of the F minor symphony, who was not one to cut himself off from the world, never said anything about war. He wrote 'Take it or leave it, for that is nearly all I can tell you about it' at the time, and his prosaic parting comment, obviously aimed at discouraging any extravagant interpretation, has been quoted. In 1952 he wrote to a friend at length on the absence of 'intended meaning'.

To regard a reflection on the state of Europe as a *necessary* explanation implies some degree of non-acceptance of the music for its own sake. It also suggests that the divining of the political exposure or denuncia-tion implied, bridges the gap, just as an understanding of the national determination of Russia to defeat Germany, in a remembered phase of the War, encourages a better response to the obsessions of the *Leningrad Symphony*. This is arguable, but hypothetical. Alternatively, the inference of political comment is declared, not as musically necessary, but as so unmistakably a corollary today (whatever the composer consciously meant but did not indicate) that it must be regarded as part of the appeal behind concert performance. This, too, is arguable, and may pass muster as a subjective interpretation. But it may also be deemed superfluous, without the slightest renunciation of political concern on the part of the listener involved. 'Nails that hurt' remains as good a summary as any.

Political or mythical images or concerns may supply a framework for music, but they cannot shape a symphony, a theme, or a progression.

SYMPHONY No. 5 IN D

With open ears, then, and without asking for psychological context, one may turn to the fifth symphony (1938–43).[1] Once more, the time lag is incidental; and any conjectures that total war would produce a Number Four *plus*, in character, were falsified. Nor, on the other hand, should the connection with *The Pilgrim's Progress* be overstated. Originally, the well-known reference to Christian's vision of the Cross appeared in the score, and figured in every announcement, before the third movement. This was confirmed when the 'House Beautiful' music was heard in its stage context. That quotation, and a reference to the use of themes 'from an unfinished Bunyan opera', were withdrawn, and the composer later claimed the symphonic movement as musically prior in a disarming dictum, 'If anyone [at the Morality] asks "Isn't that the fifth symphony?", say "Yes"'. One must also discount any conjecture that in this symphony lies an almost concluding, benedictory message from the depths, the composer having turned seventy. In whatever degree Bunyan's narrative was drawing him towards the contemplation of last things, a symphony does not develop from such meditations, but from

---

[1] First performed (and broadcast) under the composer at a Promenade Concert on Midsummer night, 1943, complete with Mendelssohn *Midsummer Night's Dream* overture at the start and, nearer the feeling of some of the audience, Ireland's *Epic March* at the finish. Three days earlier, Henry Wood had conducted Brahms's second symphony to resounding applause. In spite of everything, the musical life of the nation continued its familiar way. At this level, the only banner was of common culture, English or accepted-as-English. It was not so elsewhere.

themes and moods expressible in musical imagery. Finally, the dedication to Sibelius may safely be taken to be a personal compliment. Only in the penultimate stage of the Scherzo is there the slightest reminiscence—of Sibelius's similar string passage in his seventh symphony. The pervasiveness of the theme here is quite unlike the Sibelian conciseness.

Symphony 5 in D, then, measures itself in the first place against symphony 4 in F minor, considered as sheer symphony, and at once shows a fresh type of structure and texture. Hardly less concentrated than its predecessor, at its own pace, it suggests spacious treatment from the start. In the first movement, miscalled Preludio—for with the quick Scherzo it occupies half the symphonic time, and is in no way a mere prologue—homogeneous themes cohere as a Moderato that recurs freely, with a fresh and unforced conciseness, after a brief interlude at double speed. In the Scherzo to follow, a background harmonic figure, furthered by a tune that old-time carmen might have whistled, forms a plastic refrain that resourcefully embraces one capacious and one brief episode and still has ideas for a coda. The third movement, oddly entitled Romanza, releases a deeply meditative mood, in two motives in slow and not-so-slow tempi. The first, a brief progression, recurs freely in changing tonality and orchestration, and the other motive expands in leisurely balancing stages. The finale treats a bass figure, with counter-melody, first as a set measure for variations, then as matter for symphonic development. Creative reserve finds in a tranquil return of the basic combination a conclusion of the whole matter.

In short, there is none of the sharp compression of the fourth symphony. On the other hand, rhapsodic episodes are mainly restricted to the slow movement, and even these show a positive metre. Moreover, if the first movement is a four-beat Moderato at nominally the same speed as the Molto moderato of the third symphony (80 beats to the minute), the harmonic rhythm in the fifth symphony is simple and unencumbered by half-beats, besides being relieved by a brief Allegro. With the three-beat Scherzo (120 *bars* to the minute) to follow, there is no weakening of the deliberate effect of the Romanza, after which the final three beat Moderato (actually 120 beats to the minute) soon moves ahead. Thus the rhythmic solecisms and drag of the third symphony are not repeated here.

In texture, too, a reaction from the fourth symphony is at once noticeable. The listener is back on modal or pentatonic ground. (The last adjective appeared three times in Edwin Evans's sagacious note on the symphony for the first performance.) Semitonal acidities are exceptional or, as in the Romanza, strictly regulated to appear as substantive. On the other hand, while something of the typical impersonal touch recurs from the third symphony, the actual curves are rather more characteristic here. Moreover, the harmonic texture is inclined to be contrapuntal; that is, stimulated by cross-rhythm, not moving automatically with a given line in a manifold style. When such a manifold reveals itself, as in the accompaniment to the trumpet theme in the first movement, it is quite startling. On the whole, the contrasts of theme and mood within each movement are in low relief, and depend on mode, or a positive major, or, a here exceptional semitonal species, and similar subtleties, rather than on any sweeping differences of rhythm or texture. Few of the transformations or satiric touches of the fourth symphony are apparent here, apart from the last half of the finale. The swinging fourths of the Scherzo remain mercurial, never sinister, and the ritual chords of the Romanza retain their severity. The appeal of each movement is plainer, and sometimes even on the jejune side.

It remains to distinguish certain features of this more streamlined course. The orchestra is that of the *Unfinished Symphony*, with an occasional piccolo and a cor anglais for second oboe throughout. There is no harp or tuba or noisy percussion.

In the Preludio, the themes are mainly typical melodic curves from and to a fourth (4 ♮7 8 5, 8 ♮7 5) rather than characteristic intonations. They derive their interest from their woven texture, a veiled and oscillating tonality with some pivotal points, a plasticity of mode, and the underlying current of various rhythms, chiefly the trochaic figure suggested by the opening horn-call in the Moderato, and the flow of quarter-beat figures in the Allegro.

The opening chord, intimating that music has been going on unheard before it reaches our hearing, is bound to arouse some speculation. It is, literally, D major over C natural; an echo, it might be, of the prevailing colour of the string interlude in the 'finale' of the fourth symphony. To classical ears, this is a fifth-degree chord with a seventh (dominant seventh) in the key of G major and the dissonant C must fall one degree. (H. K. Andrews's audacious suggestion of a second-degree chord in C major, as prompted by the violin entry, has no confirmation.) But it might equally be a first-degree chord in D Mixolydian major (Ex. 4). (It is incidentally a good half-century since A. H. Sidgwick reported Flavia, the folk-song fanatic in *The Promenade Ticket*, as stating that chords which sounded strange were 'really all right if based on the

Mixo-Lydian scale'.) In that case the C is equally free to move up to D or down to A or B. (A reference to the trumpet cadenza in the 'slow' movement of the third symphony may make this free approach to or from the seventh degree clearer.) Soon it appears that D *is* the tonic, but of an oscillating mode; yet the C stays until the key changes. Hence, for those familiar with the composer's idiom, it will not come at all amiss, but rather as the obvious curtain, that the movement ends by banishing an alien key (F minor) with this somewhat neutral 'chopsticks' chord, so much more euphonious than the nihilist G sharp-A chord that grips in a vice the close of the Scherzo of the fourth symphony. Only when it recurs in the coda of the finale, as the typical chord of the reverberating Prelude, does the bass move down to G, from which a cadence is formed to a plenary D major.

These light equivocal contacts with D and other keys, however, are superseded by a hushed entry (*tranquillo* in the latest score) in E major of the wind, with drum-roll. (The accession of trumpets and drums here seals this incident as something special. How special, is not apparent till the end of the symphony. Dramatic confirmation came later in the admission of Pilgrim through the wicket-gate, with the present motive as clue-theme.) That such familiar circling round the fifth and sixth degrees sounds so much more than halting intonation, is readily experienced. This convergence of the main thought leaves the Moderato strong enough to accommodate a short Allegro interlude in fresh minor keys, beginning with C. The curve of the vibrating string figure here may recall *On Wenlock Edge* to some listeners, and the subsequent music could certainly be a fresh outburst of the angry elements. The return of the trumpet as leader in a close canon of elementary pentatonic character in D, while the string bass is heading for a Phrygian A, brings these restless weavings to a head before they collapse into the Moderato. This return, by compressing the opening sixty bars to a more tightly-packed twenty, loses no time in reaching its resounding climax of solemnity. The tonality leaps here to B flat and then sinks to G, major and pentatonic, the last delayed by a spontaneous sequence of sevenths. Hints of the Allegro and a collapsing tonality are cut off by a renewal of the initial chord, as firm limiting point. The horns are now muted.

Thus ends another unusual first movement. The modal subtleties may at first defy the listener's grasp of a tonal centre, but the resolutions in E and G major cannot miss their intention. The spaciousness of the orchestration adds to the general feeling of roominess in exposition and development. In this atmosphere the lack of decisive theme hardly matters. The rhythm, aided by the harmonic drive of a changing key colour, is the main appeal.

The rising-and-falling fourths motive of the Scherzo, announced in queer unison by muted strings, may recall the fourth symphony (motive Y), but to no purpose. This movement is even more modal than the first. An attention to the bass is sometimes at first necessary to steady one's grasp of an evasive tonic, but it is usually perceptible, defining the mode as Dorian, etc., or pentatonic, basing the melodic idiom on an early or even primitive period of vocal intonation. The opening, plain and typical E–A–D–A–E acknowledges no centre of gravity, but soon settles for A, when a harmonic bass is established. In this more settled relationship, the 'whistling' tune is insouciantly announced and re-iterated in A and D, with the first motive settling down to automatic impressionism, in two-bar periods or in close fugue. The ascending fourths of the latter, staggered over the metre, act as a link, unconsciously attaching to the main thread the string of incidents that follows, without making a substantive entry.

The first and most prevalent motive, started in C by the oboes, was first hinted at in the Moderato, at the approach to the Allegro. It depends on an ancient antinomy of major and minor third, such as is exploited in the fourth symphony (Ex. 38c). From this arises later a voluble descending figure. The accompaniment for this oboe motive, fifths circling a fall from the third degree (♭3 ♭2 1), shows a dry wit reminiscent of the Mephistophelian *oompah* in no. 4 (Ex. 39a). The next event, a phrase delivered in a jaunty three-octaves by the wood, with the lower strings in canon, would seem to top-line listeners to be one more variant of the curve, 5–7–5 4 5 1, noticeable in 'The captain's apprentice' and the like. Actually, as the harmony declares, it is 1–3–1 7 1 4 in the Phrygian mode—a rarer phrase, open at the end till the last note drops out. Its direct tunefulness catches the ear as it passes. The rising fourths of the refrain having spread themselves out to absorb manifold string volubility, the jaunty motive, too, is extended in notes of triple length. In this version it serves to introduce metrically a solemn trombone theme in E, whose second phrase acknowledges its source melodically. A resemblance to the 'solemn' theme in the Moderato would therefore be confusing and can be disregarded.

A sober tone having thus been imparted to these 200-odd bars of episode, a more extended fugal 'refrain', still monotonous in pitch, brings back the main tune, first re-set, staccato, and then piquantly involved with the fourths. This is just enough stimulus to suggest a further, broad and rather raw version of the oboe motive in C, which eventually the trombones start handing down the whole-tone scale (E♭, B, G, E♭). This threat of *oompah* is countered, after a final splutter of major and minor third in the now unmuted strings, by an austere string rendering of the fourths, still in C minor, slightly reminiscent of the texture of the early string melody in Sibelius's seventh symphony. Finally, the original theme burns itself out in the bassoon and flute, over a 1 3 5 7 chord of A, at first with 5 in the bass. (Young is misleading in describing this as a 1 3 5 6 chord—on C. The whole point is to restore A.) A flicker of close string imitation, carelessly recollecting what fugue there has been, leaves a final spark of A in the double bass (plucked), augmented, in the latest revision, by a drum. Originally, entries were solo, unmuted.

This Scherzo has something in common with that of the second symphony, in its subdued tones, stealthy structure, ceaseless wayward movement of string and wind figures, strong antique flavour and a certain bareness of expression. As in the earlier Scherzo, too, the rondo structure is unshapely; there is one large episode, of which the infectious first incident makes an isolated return in a rather blustering style. One inference might be that the main tune, good as it is, is a closed circuit. It can only be displaced. The fourths are also useful, chiefly for absorbing loose ends and final diversions, not as a conclusion. The second episode seems to be the drastic remedy for this dilemma.

Ever since Beethoven's scherzos superseded the robust but confined minuet that Haydn had grafted from the loose-limbed divertimento, it has always been a matter of personal craftsmanship to make an expressly capricious mood musically effective. A sweeping rhythm, broken by a contrasted interlude, according to the oldest tradition, is easier to maintain. Having produced such a Scherzo, in the ferocious-satirical vein of no. 4, the composer here sought something more elusive. If a struggle is at times apparent, the new synthesis is creative. It has been impossible to cite the many felicities of orchestral blend and humour, somewhat clarified in the late revision (see Appendix B). But the conventional demand for something more stable and immediately comprehensible remains until the following movement.

The planning of a harmonic progression, to impart preliminary compulsion and later extend spontaneously as the basis of a penetrating cantabile, is not a new idea for a slow movement. It can be observed in Franck's symphony, and partially in Dvořák's *New World*, as well as in the *London Symphony*. All use a solo oboe. In the last, the salient progression is of a single line rising in tones in an automatic multiple formation (1–♭3–5). There is no independent harmonic sting. In the present symphony the echoing and half-echoing four-bar progression is brief but harmonically evocative. It can be summarized as a melodic curve set to the primary chords of C major, A major, G minor, A major. Which is the tonic, the alto-oboe tune being drawn towards a non-committal E? The next section confirms A as the keynote, and we may assume that the second note is the cadential one in subsequent recurrences. In this sense, then, the rich, sixteen-part, muted string harmony begins its solemn step, joined by the oboe in a declamatory manner, beginning with the triplet noticeable at the outset of the last three movements of the third symphony. ('From far, from eve', in *On Wenlock Edge*, might be recollected, with its refrain of what would be here A–C–B flat–C–A.) Unexpectedly, the rising fourths of the Scherzo at once introduce and typify (1) a fresh, rather faster section of pentatonic string melody, establishing A; (2) a rhapsodic, imitational passage for the wood-wind. After confirming this association of mood, in E returning to A, in a more intense and altogether more ornate fashion, for whose close-woven thought 'the Great Exclamation' (cited by Goddard) seems a queer description, the music finds brief contrast in an animated version of the opening chords and of the oboe's G–F–E–D (bar 3), the latter translated from a shapely curve to increasingly blunt multiple sonorities.

The restoration of the two chief tempi, beginning in E flat, and with rhapsodic figures to replace the now overworked and indeed sharply satirized oboe theme, reaches a full orchestral climax, the drum entering here only. In an intense coda, the main progression gravitates from F sharp to A major. Through etherealized string chords sounds a veiled horn cantabile, less the introductory triplet, and fervent string antiphony admits sliding fifths in the ritual, celestial style of *Sancta Civitas* and *Flos Campi* (*fin.*), with a lingering penultimate chord (1 ♯3 5 ♯7 on the fourth degree) paralleled in the *Sea Symphony*. Thus a subtle synthesis of ideas and tempi develops freely but symmetrically into one of Vaughan Williams's most absorbed movements. The imaginative play of the Scherzo has given place to a fresh personal concentration, to which such picturesque wanderings as are found in the second symphony's Lento are no precedent.

So much for the purely musical appeal. Actually the quotation originally placed before the movement and since withdrawn showed that the composer had in mind the moment when Pilgrim (Christian), heavily burdened, finds comfort in a cross and sepulchre that he came upon; a moment of dedicated tranquillity. But, as the composer realized later, it was better not to start the listener pursuing the road to salvation in the middle of a normal symphony.[1] The connection with the Scherzo (which I find rather pointless) makes it clear the Lento is in some measure a transformation of the previous *jeu d'esprit*. For the rest, its place in the symphony is clear enough, and 'the House Beautiful' is a distraction. Similarly the reappearance of key-passages in that scene is a matter to be judged in its own context, not here.

After the concentrated end of the Lento, three sequels seem conceivable: (1) a drastic break (cf. Beethoven, no. 9, finale, *init.*); (2) a linking prelude to a new movement, thoughtful but non-committal, (3) an unpretentious beginning, which conveys the feeling of something rising to bare consciousness from previous unconscious thought (as in the second and constructive stage of thematic evolution in the same finale). In choosing the third alternative, Vaughan Williams hit upon a contrast to the transitional note which he had struck at the outset: ground-bass. Beethoven, with a crowning all-ness in mind and no misgivings about the strophic variation, made his theme rhythmically square and inevitably major, as a repudiation of all that had preceded in the minor. Vaughan Williams, concerned with building up an exposition with as few joins as possible, makes his melodious bass seven bars, with bars 5–7 a loose connection, any component of which may be freed to begin a new variation of eight bars or less. He also made it fully major as against the modal major of the Preludio, since a set modal harmony can never go far or smoothly, but he inclined chiefly to the older type of major scale, bearing chiefly on the degrees 8 6 5 4 2 1.[2] By this means, he secured a pentatonic bass that might be useful to amplify in a mode later, and by closing on 6 or 6 7 he avoided the conventional cadence on 5. By moving at twice the speed of the Lento, he placed out of court any comparison of the three beats in each movement. However, directly he has brought his variations to a climax, he changes to four

---

[1] In the latest autograph score, to the preliminary reference to the *Pilgrim's Progress* music, as the source of some themes, is added: 'But *except in the slow movement* the Symphony has no dramatic connection with Bunyan's allegory' (my italics). The composer started with a clear association between the present Lento and Christian's release of spirit beside the Cross, decided accordingly to attach the appropriate text, and reluctantly, perhaps, withheld it from the first and subsequent printed scores.

[2] Bar 5 first read 4 3–1 6; bar 12, bass, 5–4 3–1 6 (R.C.M.).

beats, and in that metre the movement remains stubbornly to the end. So far the substantive variation-set is preludial.

The first variation presents a balanced counter-melody of irreproachable character; assured enough, indeed, to continue in the sequel with a graceful descent down the scale in two stages that find a place in the closing bars of the work (Ex. 41 below). (It is pointless to refer such a spontaneous after-phrase to the hymn-tune *Lasst uns erfreuen* or one of its congeners; or later ascents to the Dresden *Amen*.) On these lines, nine variations accumulate readily, in a subtle blend of strings and wind, with an occasional dynamic repartee. The rise of the bass (henceforward the 'primary' theme) to the top in the fifth variation and, with impetuous and care-free sonority, in the ninth, punctuates the series, and invites the counter-melody to show its independence. Increased speed and contrapuntal eloquence promote a brief interlude and, after an animated excursion of key, a tonal climax at the original speed but of unmeasured elation (41*b*).

Confronted thus with a note of termination, the composer turns from more or less strophical variation to thematic enlargement, keeping the basic combination of theme in mind, but developing the opening contours in so florid a style that the connection may not be apparent. A trite variation of key is avoided in favour of the exploitation of modal variants of answering minor keys. The pentatonic main theme is thus exhibited in new aspects with almost brusque conciseness, but with inflections of the kind made familiar in earlier movements. From D Aeolian-minor (41*c*) the tonality reaches by circuitous means a typical F major-minor disagreement (in the brass, horizontal and unmistakable). This crux, and some overt manipulation of the D–C in the first bar of the theme, when in F, while the drum enters on C, evokes the Preludio. With it return the equivocal chord of its close, the sweeping trochaic rhythm, *moderato*, and the rising fourth.

The resolution of outstanding tension in an absolute D major, as explained at the outset, marks the beginning of what is clearly the coda. As in the *allegro* interlude, this chiefly relies on the counter-melody and its descending-scale aftermath, now attenuated by wayward distribution over extended phrases of four-metre. The primary theme just retains its connection, and one may take the opportunity to recall, as repeated hearings will certainly recall, some of the stages through which it has passed. For the rest, the inevitably closing descent to the keynote is kept moving by a string weave of plain ascents in an increasingly impressionist idiom. To some listeners a reference of the final,

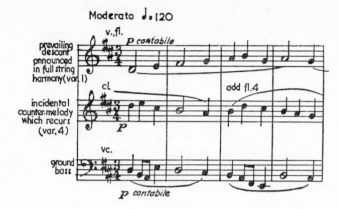

Ex. 41*a*

Ex. 41*b*

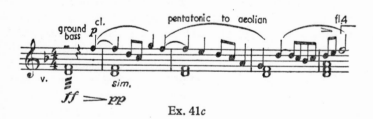

Ex. 41*c*

Ex. 41*d*

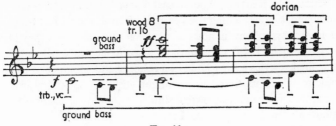

Ex. 41*e*

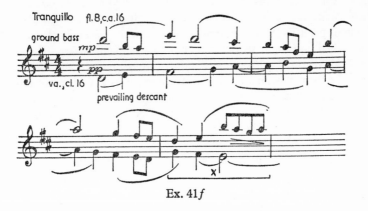

Ex. 41*f*

gracious descent from the sixth degree to the fifth (6 5–4 5) to the E major entry in the Moderato may seem far-fetched; but the later restatement of that theme twice stressed just that the drum, whose transcendent roll now muffles the string harmony, entered there in the first instance, and a final projection of the wind's ascetic intonation on to this last stir of melody at the top of the E string, where it is still fresh, is both symphonic and persuasive, as a signal of perpetual serenity after the (somewhat brief) disturbances midway. However apprehended, the simple appeal of these closing bars needs no promotion here.

This movement has thus an original construction of variation, symphonic development and coda, which, though it nearly splits the movement in two, keeps the old-fashioned major tonality fresh up to the coda. There the fervour of expression is in danger of being weakened by its anticipation at the end of the Lento; a problem which the conductor may solve by not thinking of the final *tranquillo* direction as a matter of reduced speed. In my experience, any undue lingering may wrap up the closing cantabile too preciously.

Alternatively, it may be thought that that cadence must be as pressing, emotionally, as the receding tone permits. This is the view of those who find in the symphony a note of personal summary and conclusion, related (even in 1943) to visions of a world at peace. Possibly this simple finale carries a suggestion of a restored and enlightened common round, to which its first hearers might wishfully look forward, to a point of transfiguration, somewhat similar to the closing changes of, say, Beethoven's late E flat quartet. Listeners in 1943 and after were prone to relate this sensation to the composer's honoured maturity of wisdom and experience. This, however, is going beyond musical criticism, and any conjecture of 'benediction' and farewell must now seem like the famous pianist's 'final appearance' (till the next). Traditional elements are called into ample service here, but the symphony makes a clear and individual appeal to the understanding through the ear, and the use of *Pilgrim* themes is no warrant for accepting it as anything but music. It does not grasp the ear as its predecessor does, but it achieves the universal quality of a true symphony by its unprecedented range and leisurely but compulsive logic.[1]

Symphony (No. 6) in E Minor

There was a time when the third symphony seemed to have been the work in which Vaughan Williams stood most alone; in which he was writing for himself, for others to overhear or not as they pleased. The fourth occupied this position for some time, but its penetrating message ended by breaking the barriers of what one may term regional prejudice, and to some extent of national prejudice abroad, too; more than any other work except *Job*. The fifth was probably too quietist for many foreigners, but its homely fervency was no mystery to English audiences. Of all the nine, the following symphony, 'in E minor' (1948, slightly revised in a fresh impression published in 1950, see p. 329), remains the most pronounced assertion of sheer individuality.

The first movement, 'establishing the key of E minor through that of F minor' (composer's description) seems at first also to have been conditioned as a whole by its opposite number in the earlier key. After that first movement of the F minor, so minatory at the start, so sensitive at the close, the psychological pattern of the new opening sounds half

[1] Some further details are suggested in an article in *The Music Review*, 6. 1 (February, 1945). A proof of this article was sent to the composer and returned by him 'unread', in accordance with his usual practice with all printed matter concerning himself.

familiar, although the intermediate sections are fresh in genre as well as in content. Yet the steady remoteness of this movement is its own. Once more, the modal touches are the chief contact, as regards creative method, with tradition; that is, with the composer's tradition.

The singular character of the slow movement needs no demonstration. The painfully compressed melodic curve of the main refrain, and of the declamatory phrase announced by the brass, are forbidding enough; but the reverberation of the matter so exposed against a 'background' of a rising and forbidding crescendo of anapaestic trumpet and drum reiterations, is quite beyond all known licence in ruthless tenacity. The historical first movement of Walton's first symphony carries violent repetition to startling proportions, but the organic use of rhythm there does not explain away the desiccating effect of the irrepressible mutter that grows to a point of explosion here. When the cor anglais and lower strings are left in possession, the latter significantly end by assuming the percussive role, with the drums, in a set pattern that pulverizes.

The Scherzo, too, is a ferocious fugal piece. In contrast with the sweeping vivacity of the F minor's Scherzo, one is confronted, in the main movement, with a sense of blustering and immoderate invective that carries with it all the searing effect of the 'self-conscious arithmetic' that music meant to Leibnitz; the fugal craftsmanship being partly of the calculating type, illustrated by the composer's observation on the restatement: 'so for a bit the two (the subject and the subject upside down) go on together, and to the delight of everyone including the composer the two versions fit.' In relief from this tireless dialectic, the interlude proves to be an extended, yet repressed and virtually satirical kind of saxophone tune in a neo-Phrygian mode, with restless accompaniment. Its loud appearance at half speed for a coda to the repeat of the Scherzo is quite devastating. Characteristically, the Scherzo closes with the now familiar feature of the subject 'upside down'; that is, in reversed direction, up or down, at each point of its curve (not in totally reversed order of intonation, which would be meaningless).

Finally, and most individually, comes the Epilogue, now occupying an entire movement, and that not as an appendage either to the third movement or to a hypothetical finale. Like the Scherzo, it is intermittently fugal; but its fugal subject is no capricious ascent, but a meticulously confined intonation, plastic in detail. Nor is its absorption of mood felt to be a matter of abandoning the Scherzo, exhausted anyhow, but of framing an independent association of ideas, with the support of harmonic episodes. The subdued tones in which this fresh stage of expression discloses its imagery implies, indeed, as the title indicates, a detachment from all three of the minatory movements that have preceded; not a convergence but an imaginative leap to a fresh focal centre. Apart from some very slight echoes, in the brass and oboe themes of the opening bars, there is no gesture of resuming the initial mood, as in all the preceding symphonies but the third. In these uncompromising terms, continuity with the first three movements is renounced in favour of the most contemplative, apparently least symphonic, movement ever written for a symphony. For although the mainly minor-key finale is an unexpected end, despite the initial ambiguity of key, Brahms's to third symphony, for example, yet its ample rondo structure and normal dynamic shape balance the first movement. On such grounds this symphony in E minor remains the most challenging succession of four movements. In comparison, the seventh is irregular throughout, and more suite than symphony, but rounds a circle.

It is thus necessary to appreciate what structural assertions underlie the succeeding movements. The first is, in the main, clear and arbitrary. The opening F–to–E phrase and a congenial hustle of brass chords,

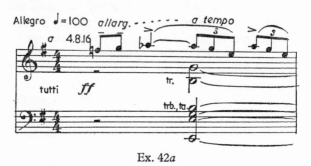

Ex. 42a

rising and falling semitonally, leads to a more shapely, but no less semitonal, descending string-wind motive, vaguely entangled with 'fussy semiquavers in the cognate key of C minor' (R. V. W.). All this makes a set of polytonal but compulsive appeals, coupled with which a quasi-vocal but wickedly over-scored trumpet-and-wood theme, moving against an oscillating pair of chords in a fresh twelve-beat rhythm, makes a positive contrast and captures the interest by its interplay of rhythms. But what, then, is the point of the elusive, but more serious tune that follows in a kind of Dorian B minor in three octaves (violins, flutes,

Ex. 42b

Ex. 42c

violas and cor anglais)? The twelve-beat figures continue their winking and blinking, yet the new tune is hardly complementary to the trumpet theme. One must wait to hear more. After a free version of the trumpet episode (so the composer assigns it, but the pitch-shape recalls the last tune), the Dorian tune reveals a higher potential dynamic in unmistakable terms, in a fresh key, G minor, the original key of the trumpet tune—a coincidence better ignored, for development has reared its head. But with the intrusion of the kettle-drum, rolling on E, not G, the first subject makes itself felt, and in about eight bars, indefinitely but positively, restatement is established, and the composer's cautionary *'reprise* only hinted at' proved misleading.

Ex. 42d

The first subject preserves its integrity, and incidentally its key, in half the previous space. But nothing is heard of the trumpet tune, or the twelve-beat rhythm. They are recognized as episodic and now unessential. The Dorian tune thus emerges arrestingly unencumbered, and prompted by a rather solemn background of ritual chords (harp and trombones). It has now become a tune in a neo-Lydian (neo-Mixolydian) major, of unquestionable breadth, and virtually transformed from an almost primitive encounter of phrases to the splendidly placed climax of the strings' strophe, and the rich sonority of the shortened repeat. The former is considerably enhanced by the assignment of the first violins to the fourth string—so that they play increasingly high and unusual notes on that string—while the second violins temper this

Ex. 42e

preciosity by using all the normal strings, thus covering any 'wolf' tone from the opposite desks.

But the tonal climax seems a grim reversal. It is the original motive, adapted. Thus instantaneously, without distortion, the beautiful closing melody is exposed as a temporary sublimation, as the corresponding close in the fourth symphony, too, proved to be, only later. This is quite in keeping with a tune which supersedes the first-subject rigours a little too glibly. Poetic justice confirms this reversal.

The composer has thus left his first movement with a compressed exposition which may be summarized as *a*, *b*1, *b*2, extended by the free continuation of *b*1 and *b*2 and brought to a head by the return of *a* and *b*2, with more than a hint of *a* again. The chief 'arbitrary' element lies in letting *b*1 rip and then dropping it. The obvious explanation is that the composer wishes to emphasize his transformation of *b*2 without distraction. This leaves *b*1 where it belongs: as an interesting but ultimately preliminary sortie, from which *b*2 comes into bare recognition. Yet the absorption of *b*2 into the vacuum thus created is startling: the listener is whisked homewards. (One may now contrast the spacious closing section of the Moderato maestoso of the ninth symphony.) This compression is in accordance with an intention to focus on E for the purpose of disturbing it with the trumpet B flat of the next movement. All in all, the blunt lack of transitions makes the movement a hectic experience, but the taut restatement is persuasive.

In this Allegro, then, a forcible impulse is set, via episodes and preliminaries, into relation with a calm lyrical conception, in which the scale-shaping of earlier centuries conditions the melodic line; and this convergence is achieved by symphonic means. By the same means, the closing melodic assertion, which is summarized in its key note, E, implying G sharp and B, is firmly renounced by the trumpets with the signal of B flat. Most discordant of the relationships to E, next to the contradictory semitone (F), B flat becomes the centre of a reluctant semitonal rise and fall, and later almost its own destructive centre. For it lies within the nature of pitch-valuation that there is a recognizable degree, beyond which to stress one primary note is to render it superfluous and ultimately discordant. The main theme acquires its shape falteringly, but it is driven on by a relentless reverberation of the anapaestic repetition on every third note of each component phrase and elsewhere, with full percussive accessories of skin and string, except that the side-drum is muffled. The brass fanfare round F minor, which halts the main momentum, is purely an oscillation of adjacent or related notes, in varying chordal disposition and antiphonal movement, spread out by a mysterious unison phrase. This constitutes a break, but not a substantive episode, and it does not return except to formulate an impressionist cadence.

The mounting insistence of the restatement is thus entirely reserved for the main refrain, as it probes and re-probes the nuances of the curve shown (43a), each note a multiple minor chord (1 ♭3 5), with the fifth in the bass, functional but unprogressive; the asterisks marking the

Ex. 43a

Ex. 43b

points of anapaestic ictus of trumpets and drums. Inevitably a shorter creep upwards (x), treated in canon and extended higher, varies the ominous march brinkwards, and the carefully prepared sense of a catastrophic summit rests on opposed G flat–G natural vibrations (43b), for semitonal movement up or down has lost any melodic meaning. This adds up to no more than twelve preparatory and thirty-two substantive bars. Yet it amounts to one of the most piercing passages in symphonic expression. As an emotional experience, it may appear an intolerable burden; and it is. Some interposition is necessary, and a rhapsodic cor anglais, with adumbrations of the brass fanfare on the strings, relaxes the tension to a cadential point, C flat pressing against B flat, with now insouciant stress.

These concrete observations may afford a clue to the kind of musical appeal that this movement makes. Plain and monotonous as it is in melodic and harmonic texture, it reaches a new level of terrific emphasis. It has been tempting, as the baffled 'forties have given place to the disillusioned 'fifties, to jump beyond mere aural impressions with declarations of a romantic, didactic, and therefore more bearable, intention: to frame an image of the violence which guilty dictators, or guilty democracies, from First Citizen to you and me, are promoting or failing to control; to produce a work which might, after Reger, be called another 'symphonic prologue to a tragedy'. The hurtling discords of the F minor finale, coming from the now exposed and explosive early 'thirties, support the idea. But once more it is dangerous to assume that what the loud street band had been to the composer of the *London Symphony*, the unheard explosions of 1947 were now. That quest for 'realistic', consciously motivated music, an obsession of communist states, is a desperate abandonment of musical responsibility. If the music here is justified, it needs no such interpretation and is, indeed, reduced in stature by a concrete basis. If the music is not justified—and it is provocatively confined in mood and orbit—political and ethical explanations will soon wear thin, and in time, as already suggested, dwindle to the level of an outworn scholastic gloss, along with Napoleonic footnotes to the *Eroica* symphony. Better a literal but musical reception! It will be more natural to maintain in the long run. The best way to influence national or world opinion on fundamental issues is, in fact, by joining actively the appropriate association, or (as in the case of Vaughan Williams's support of the Briand idea of a United States of Europe) by pertinent comment, rather than by symphonic expostulation. Righteous indignation at such symbolic levels is a common indulgence that feeds on itself. It is inconceivable that the composer was unaware of this; and he did not call this the Anarchist symphony.

The Scherzo also keeps to one main subject, apart from the interlude, but its problem lies, not in any conscious monotony, but rather in its irrepressible dialectic. The obvious precedent for fugal method is the sixth fugue of Bach's *Art of Fugue*, in which the main subject of the series is soon so interwoven with the subject at double speed that this new version subtly acquires the basic appeal, making the original subject a retarding factor. Inversion (reversing ascent and descent) varies the harmonic bearing of this interplay of metres. Here, the increasingly compressed subject not only at once supersedes its declared source, but soon amalgamates imitative entries in one single melodic line. This seems a truer outline of procedure than the composer's statement that the main subject appears initially only in 'bad shots at it' before it settles down definitely as *b*. The basic material thus sways between close polyphony, in which a decline from an ascending sharpened fourth (or flattened fifth) is the pivotal intonation at one speed or another, and a fantastic unilinear stretch of pitch, in which the same ascent is pursued cumulatively and then reduced to sliding chordal figures. What was annihilating in the transition from first to second movement is now a

327

Ex. 44a

Ex. 44b

figure of diabolical humour. (The Satan-entry in *Job* justifies this metaphor.)

'A trivial little tune' (i.e. a repetitious ornamentation of a prime interval, cf. 45), soon reinforced by a brass and xylophone figure in the revised version, provides the same sense of movement and distraction as in the first episode of the preceding Scherzo. An irrepressible antiphony or polyphony of higher and lower sonority, plain and bravura, normal and diminished, normal and syncopated rhythm, *forte* and *fortissimo*, reaches hubristic heights on the strength of the main theme. From all this the saxophone tune breaks away into a nominally melodic but actually rather artificial strain of two phrases, originally much more symmetrical and without the Phrygian flat second degree. The prickly harmony, thunderous repeats and, perhaps, the doubtful past of the saxophone as the symbol of the Wily Hypocrites in *Job*, enhance the sense of satire. In the return of the Scherzo, inversion of the amalgamated theme (44c)—oddly recalling *Elinor Rumming* in melodic curve—is extended so as to exercise the bassoon in all registers, and is

Ex. 44c

absorbed by the orchestra with malicious glee. This is challenged by the trombones with the normal, uninverted theme (top line of Ex. 44a, from bar 3), as described by the composer above, but itself emerges in a bass canon, with the initial curve. As a climax (cymbals), the normal subject appears in massive canon with the inversion, and re-asserts itself as a standing variant.

As in Bach, all these professional antics are merely the substantive changes in an ubiquitous and often sensational development. On top of this, the saxophone tune breaks out in full, in thirds, at half speed, in a whole-tonal A flat major, with the full power of the orchestra— another raw moment of *folie de grandeur* which baffles the listener. It is not enough to say that it is meant to be a grotesque and quasi-moronic dance-hall style. But soon the fabric collapses and the clarinets, normal and bass, readily take the bassoon version of the chief theme to a receding oscillation point, finally defined as F slipping to E. This means nothing except a context for the future. With the present theme, atonality is basic and inevitable.

The listener must acknowledge the resource and balance of the underlying close imitational treatment before making any critical pronouncement. Yet this daring reliance on a dissonant interval for the pith of the argument wears thin; and the saxophone tune is not strong enough for its *tutti* handling. However, by fresh means, the trenchant note has been struck, under the shadow of the Moderato and in pursuit of the prevailing mood of the Allegro.

This is the most revised movement of the four. The 1950 score shows a number of corrections of orchestral balance, such as the reinforcement of flutes and violins by trumpet and xylophone in a piece of repartee just after the climax of the restatement (33: bars 3–5 in the score), and of clarinets by flutes in the top octave, with an optional fourth trumpet below, for the returning saxophone tune (39). But there is also a new brass figure, derived from the main theme. This is to lend more body to the fussy semiquavers. It arises in the following bars in the score: 1.5–2.1, 4.4–5, 12.3–13.2, 25.1–2, 26.5–7. The not-so-fussy F sharp at 1.6 has been lowered to F natural to conform with the extra stoop down of the brass. Oddly enough, these additions, or variants of them,

Ex. 45

appear first in the later, non-autograph two-piano copy, added in red ink, like the pencilled accretions in the two-piano copy of the fourth symphony (first movement, restatement). Apparently, at some fresh play-through, pianistic or fully orchestral, the jejune texture struck the composer, and he inserted the new figure in various contexts, in the piano score nearest to hand, and incorporated this in the full score with some changes of detail (4.5 was at first augmented by A–A–E E♭, not C–C–G G♭, and the trombone note before 37 was originally E flat). The early autograph piano score shows no sign of all this.

Unlike the Scherzo of the F minor at its normal close, this Scherzo offers no still inflammable material to kindle to a burst of finale. On the contrary, the volcanic nature of the first three movements is abandoned in an enigmatic but characteristic aftermath that proves to be the entire finale. It is enigmatic in its suggestion of life not released but imprisoned in a narrow circle. It is characteristic in its relinquishment of a blunt token of anarchy in favour of a steady contemplation of a dispassionate loneliness in itself, appalling in its unrelieved restraint.

Once more, as in the fifth symphony, the composer has contrived to convey from the start the rare symphonic impression of movement that has already been going on, by means of an absorbed theme, obsessed with one figure, a specially subdued tone, which persists to the end, and a tonality which, while non-committal, seems to relate to F more than to the surviving E of the bass clarinet. This proves to be the extended subject of a further fugal piece. Stray entries in the strings against a

background of sliding chords are steadied and rendered accessory by
half-speed entries, as of a traditional tone, in the wood, and later harp;
these are punctuated periodically by a mysterious cadential phrase,
introduced by full muted brass. (If this echoes the brass harmony in
the fifth bar of the symphony, I do not understand the point.) All this
is very severe in its reduction to essentials. Thus an oboe solo, conspicuous by the rising and falling sixth round the peaknote of each
phrase, seems to strike a more human note, as at the end of the
Moderato. After a further simplification of the fugal theme, now presented in a quasi-ritual unison, a return to the start in tremulous strings
(the link with E now established), with a half-speed entry following in
ethereal harp harmonics, initiates a stage of restatement.

Ex. 46a

Ex. 46b

The oboe now has one long phrase, rising quickly and descending gradually to E. This point fixed as a bass, the plastic fugal theme is able, in the off-beat version it acquired in bar 28, to frame a cadence from what sounds as E flat major to E minor (Ex. 46b; *Riders to the Sea* moved from D sharp minor to E major.) It remains for the upper strings to press home the cadence *per se*. Although so marked, after over a hundred bars of express *pianissimo*, this is no *niente* finish in the ordinary Vaughan Williams sense, but rather the graceful acknowledgement that the imagery is exhausted in its harmonic summary, leaving further reflection to the listener, if he has any. At the beginning the approach to E was from F. Now it is from E flat. Comparably to the B-A-H-B of the fourth symphony, H-B finds a rejoinder in A-B. The common sensation, of intonation crushed to the limit, recurs, significantly perhaps, in the line followed by the derisive voice of the blizzard in *Scott of the Antarctic* and the derived symphony, and in the setting of Blake's piercing 'Cruelty has a Human Heart'.

A firm construction, then, lies behind this baffling and materially elusive music. Its nuances of 'variant readings' are more integral than in the Scherzo, and will take time to sort out in repeated hearings. Ultimately, however, the Epilogue is revealed as a masterly essay in its peculiar style. This plain renunciation of, or at least moving beyond, the earlier movements, needs no explanation of its own coherence. But what is it doing here?

The obvious explanation is that the composer judged the three movements to have sufficiently exploited the dark moods of existence along comparatively conventional lines, and that it remained to pursue an inner ring of purer musical thought, undisturbed by the emotional emphasis of loud and soft, in a hard contemplation of things in themselves. He was satisfied that this apparent dissociation was, in the long run, as symphonic as, say, the quite unpredictable elation of the finale of the ninth symphony (Beethoven). 'Genius does what it must and talent does what it can.' As a clue, the composer named the movement 'Epilogue'.[1]

There is nothing fantastic in this hypothesis, and the brilliant suggestions of 'Dead Sea fruit' (Howes) and the like, following three omens of 'war-making', seem to underestimate both the emotional quality of this reticent music, which increases rather than diminishes

[1] On the composer's typical use of symphonic epilogue, the reader may well consult a comprehensive article by Mr. Hugh Ottaway in *Musical Opinion*, 79, p. 145 (December, 1955).

as it continues, and its intense refinement of theme. The more serious problem is to assess the quality of the symphony as a whole, with the wayward course but wide range of the first movement, the narrow cast of the second, the laborious gusto of the Scherzo, and the penetrating but confined Epilogue. On the whole, the symphony may be said to have held its place, as distinctive enough to warrant its peculiar features, and as a departure from the fifth symphony without any serious regression to the fourth, with whose constructional virtuosity it cannot compete.

Something of the basic appeal of this symphony has been freshly exhibited by Mr. Deryck Cooke in his thorough functional analysis of the work in his recently published *The Language of Music*. Cooke refers the 'formal and expressive unity' of the symphony to the 'persistent use, transformation and interpenetration' of four basic symbols: the 1–♭3–1 curve; the clash of major and minor thirds; the ♭2–1 progression; and the sharpened fourth. All this is pertinently exhibited in citations of the main material and its environment, with a developed comparison between the Scherzo and the 'Rondo Burlesque' of Mahler's ninth symphony. But, as he has shown earlier by select examples from many periods and styles of music in the minor key, for Cooke the four symbols 'express something': distressful brooding, or 'a sense of inescapable doom' (p. 140), a destruction of the order of the universe (p. 84), and other painful and devastating experiences. They are this by established association. On these lines, Cooke rationalizes his sense of the powerful, but finally anything but loud, impact of the music, as cataclysmic and annihilating. This rendering follows a similarly romantic interpretation of Mozart's G minor symphony (K.550) in terms of a painful obsession with 'the darker side of things' (p. 239).

Like the present writer, Cooke overdoes the observation of interval— of which his book is, indeed, primarily a study—but he has integrated with considerable skill incidents that might otherwise pass unrelated. He has shown the concentration of the main melodic trends of the symphony in the Epilogue material, and he has some ground for summarizing the Epilogue as 'inactivity . . . in a basic minor context, fading into nothingness'. It is not at all necessary, however, to accept Cooke's thesis of fruitless struggle as the 'unambiguous emotional impact' of the symphony. That is, once more, to reduce its appeal to the *emotional tone* of an admonitory social document by refusing to recognize the validity, in their own right, of the themes and of their 'transformation' and 'interpenetration'. If the end of Tchaikovsky's *Pathétique* symphony is, unlike the formally confined finale of Brahms's E minor symphony, 'depressing', as Cooke declares, it is because the 'consolatory' major theme there sounds, transposed to the minor, too trivial to bear its orchestral burden of chording and figuration; not because the music symbolizes despair. Some listeners similarly find the end of Vaughan Williams's eighth symphony depressing because the basic melodic formula is, for them, inactive and nugatory. We shall similarly observe later that the composer replaced the affirmative, major Yea at the end of *Scott of the Antarctic* by the stoic ambiguity of the close of *Sinfonia antartica*. Evidently, he found a higher truth of expression that way, the Yea theme having been left in the first movement.

While, then, it would be idle to deny the enigmatic character of the substantive finish of this challenging symphony, psychological analogies will not solve problems. They can only condition the mind for solving them on musical lines, by supplying a fresh focus to one's listening.

In these middle symphonies, as they have numerically become, Vaughan Williams most consistently achieved symphonic status, and maintained his standards without relaxing his harmonic research or his control of structure. The sense of enlargement, which these works promote, is so much the tougher in quality, compared with the conservative harmonic idiom of Mahler, whose ample symphonic output has run close enough in time to be compared. Even Sibelius, concerned with new types of theme, movement and movement-relation, still resorts constantly to the tonic-dominant hierarchy of the major and minor scales.

On these lines, having exhausted impressionism in the *Pastoral Symphony*, Vaughan Williams discovered a fresh sense of compulsion in semitonal themes, some recurrent throughout, and in the F minor symphony secured an overwhelmingly riveting impact, relaxing only in a secondary or seemingly ironic sense. The pursuit of rhythm is here attended by so much orchestral virtuosity that some listeners continue to suspect an unacknowledged symphonic poem, which we may call *Europe*. The inner sense of disturbance, and yet of ruthless dialectic, remains. The fifth symphony, re-admitting impressionism, thrives on the spacious theme and the shapely theme. A reversion to mode is perceptible. Yet the movements strike a balance of thought and contemplation, which, once more, abides in the mind longer than any associations of conscience and redemption. The fourth symphony has been followed up by a reaction in method without betraying a weaker invention.

SYMPHONY (No. 6) IN E MINOR

The sixth symphony, significantly the first E minor of two, takes the impressionist method into the semitonal sphere. The trenchancy of the fourth symphony penetrates again, but the organization of movements is on the loose side, and there is little development beyond repetition, except in the imitational virtuosity of the Scherzo and, in a lesser degree, of the Epilogue. The cumulative passion of the slow movement is thus unprecedented, and so is its confined orbit. The Epilogue movement is also unprecedented. There is an enlargement of context, but it proceeds spasmodically rather than by any persuasive construction. It is significant that the last climax is based on the interlude tune of the Scherzo, delivered at half speed, almost detaching itself, as, a moment later, the Epilogue detaches itself from the rest. The struggle between pattern-making and material stimulus continues, but it is in control.

Between them, the three symphonies cover an outstandingly wide field. The first movements of the fourth and sixth symphonies have a certain likeness of structure in their subdued and organic endings, reflected, we know, in the ninth symphony. Otherwise, of no three other consecutive symphonies is it less true that they are 'one symphony written three times', as was once carelessly said of Bruckner. Each is a world, and a chain of relationships, in itself. One problem of method seems to have posed itself: how to organize diversions in stages, strophical in principle, but not in detail, and thus curb the spasmodic. This was to be solved creatively later.

Before turning to the other three symphonies it will be convenient to survey three non-symphonic works which have in common an unmistakable impulse of inner conviction, and so far, for all their differences of treatment, present a consistency of purpose on a varying scale.

XI

Affirmations (1) 'Job'

T. S. Eliot once observed that he considered the term 'religious drama' to be as bad for religion as it was for drama, and we know what he means. A concern for one type of predicament in a challenging world leads to the other. Music in itself is remote from such discussion. Yet a composer who was wont to stress that music was not a luxury commodity but a spiritual necessity, that 'all art is the imperfect human half-realization of that which is spiritually perfect', stood beside Eliot. Nor is it a coincidence that many of the choral works so far considered have been concerned with a religious message. There is a good case for trying to link three works that bear every sign of a resolution to bring into music the communication of a call from God to the modern world.

Job was first given in concert form at the Norwich Festival in 1930, but in 1931 received a stage performance by the Camargo Society which established it in its true conception, apart from a reduced orchestra. Subsequent concert and radio performances, and recordings, have demonstrated the independence of the musical interpretation without putting out of countenance the stage presentation as the real thing. Goddard has suggested that for some listeners the music should be heard away from the stage, with, instead, Blake's illustrations. The anomalies of this proposition will appear later. As a ballet, the work was not only a decisive feature in the establishment of an English ballet tradition, but has shown its reserve strength in the quarter-century since. Haskell has compared it with *Petrouchka* for 'inevitability' (*Ballet Decade*, 1956). Just how hazardous was this first step towards national ballet, Dame Ninette de Valois has recounted with candour in her memoirs (*Come Dance with Me*).[1] But the swan-song that she envisaged proved, after all, the harbinger of a new day.

A serious ballet art, combining a ballet-scheme, choreography, décor and music, in a skilled and experienced production, was not brought into general cultural life until the advent in Western Europe of Serge Diaghilev (1872–1929), with all the patrons, teachers, artists, composers and stage performers whose names his career celebrates. (See especially Arnold Haskell's vivid and painstaking life of Diaghilev.) Amongst the many names of stars and impresarios, it was Diaghilev who maintained in the most dynamic sense the prime and indispensable connecting link, and that link was ballet as it is now understood. The achievement of his successor, Colonel de Basil, was to make a single director less essential, and to make a travelling repertory confident of public support. The establishment of an unprecedentedly characteristic, yet ultimately impersonal art was Diaghilev's work in the Russian imperial theatres, with which he remained in contact for replacements of personnel. One result was the establishment of the male dancer, as a foil to the ballerina. The rise of Bolm, Nijinsky, Massine and their successors made possible the Polovtsian dances (*Prince Igor*), *L'Oiseau de feu*, *Petrouchka* and *Daphnis and Chloe*. These achievements paved the way for a ballet in which Satan is the chief soloist. Much more did the twenty-year association between Diaghilev and Stravinsky, with Fokine as first choreographer, establish a genre in which each component art must be worthy of the other, and realized as such. In *L'Oiseau de feu*, *Petrouchka* and *Le Sacre du printemps*, Stravinsky and Fokine worked in intimate collaboration, not in self-contained stages. *Le Sacre*, which may appear spasmodic and uneven in the concert-room, is saved by its appositeness in its full setting.

This cosmopolitan art remains fundamentally Russian, more than anything else, in its emotional plasticity and release, its vivid sense of colour and its uninhibited rhythms. Although Diaghilev saw the promise of an English ballet style in the accomplishment of certain native dancers, he did not, as will appear, make an opportunity to further it. Yet he, if any one, had made it possible, and when the Camargo Society was formed (in tribute to the dancer-reformer who had first dared to reveal the language of feet and legs), it was almost inevitable that the main influence working on a vernacular attempt should be Russian. This

---

[1] Appalled by the rough and ready state of preparation at a penultimate rehearsal, Holst secretly provided for an extra rehearsal.

emergent company, then, was the entourage which an English composer might expect at Sadler's Wells, London. He would be hard put to it to find a native provenance. The anti-Victorian satire of *The Triumph of Neptune* (Berners) could not be repeated. Vaughan Williams was offered an idea for a quasi-biblical scenario.

The subject of *Job* had a wayward musical tradition both behind it and ahead of it, as an image of personal trial in the ultimate degree, in which frustrated sexual longing and the threat of vengeance, the common motives of opera, have no place. When Handel transferred his dramatic work from opera to oratorio, he retained his cosmopolitan mode. The passion of his Samson Agonistes and other Old Testament figures is reduced to numbered and confined stages of declamation and meditation, and, as in a modern biblical film, the contrast of pagan and orthodox forces is more picturesque than pertinent. Even *Messiah* is curiously lacking in any sustained sense of injustice or mental stress, in its steady succession of heroic, deterrent and severe assertions. 'Thy rebuke' is a solitary moment, soon forgotten, and Job's cry from the depths (Part 3) is no challenge, wrested from doubt, but calm and spacious. In *Elijah*, again, the prophet's enemies may pass muster, but he himself is eloquent only in short bursts of fierce retribution and one extended period of despair. Handel had established the 'full and solemn kind of music' as English oratorio, and it remained more solemn than penetrating for another century and a half.

Parry's oratorio *Job* broke new ground in focusing its interest increasingly on Job's agony of mind, between desperate cursing and illumination, mediated by that poetic sense of hidden power in which Parry specialized. Dallapiccola's recent *Job* (1959)—a short and musically suppressed work, half song and half speech, in seven movements—covers similar poetic ground with its peculiar blend of a literally declamatory choralism, an advanced vocal line and a tumultuous, vibratory orchestra, in a style of tense compression. Satan is a true match for God, and the reproaches of the comforters, intensified by double and triple canon, prepare for Job's renunciation of life. But God remains didactic and transcendent, rather than a creative force. He is the enigmatic, catechizing Jahweh of the book, not the creator spirit of Blake's designs. In Parry, at least, the poetic mediation is the important thing, not the final, pious, all-too-cadential confession of loyalty, wrung by cross-examination.

A little later than Parry, the free vocal movement and astonishing orchestral eloquence of *Gerontius* carried an intense feeling of personal trial to celestial and infernal levels, and so to a powerful suggestion of the consuming quality of the divine judgement. But here, too, the sense of inner struggle is wayward. After the devils have jeered their damnedest, the 'salvation' music flows almost unimpeded. The later supreme crisis, too, though eloquently projected, is one of sensational suspense rather than of personal decision, almost betraying its late and seemingly casual construction (see Diana McVeagh's account in her book on Elgar).

Neither *The Apostles* nor *The Kingdom* reach the same intensity as *Gerontius*, unless it is in the character of Judas. The full and solemn music of world-conversion and united prayer emerges rather glibly, and sometimes just pompously, and the historical trial scene relaxes all too soon in homily, cold comfort for the resolute in adversity.

Vaughan Williams's noticeable entry in this field began with *Sancta Civitas*. Here he was concerned with the writer's sense of opening a door that is shut to most minds, especially in the repressive world of an imperial dictator. The door once opened, a sense of possession, far more probing than Parry's, prevails, augmented with a deterrent judicial mood which finds room for human sympathy over the Babylon stage of deterioration. But it all springs, like Holst's *Neptune*, from a tremendous receptiveness, not from personal choice. Possibly, some awareness of this guided the composer's hand in his selection of material for *Dona nobis pacem*, which poses a clear conflict of purposes. Meanwhile, he had written *Job*, which he insisted on miscalling a 'masque for dancing', presumably to avoid the common ballerina associations. There is no vocal part prescribed, only a ballet scenario and music; and while the work is no less a Morality in the broad sense, its future lies in ballet-seasons rather than in festivals of religious drama. With the spectacular pageantry of the Caroline Masque *Job* is not concerned at all, but Young shows some slight anticipation, in the masque and antimasque of that tradition, of the sharp contrasts between the celestial dances and the wily gambols of the hellish crew.

The choice of genre and subject is significant. Contemporary ballet fashion inclined to audacious novelty, whether the knockabout farce of *Les Matelots* (Auric) or *Le Pas d'acier* (Prokofiev), a glorification of the machine age and incidentally of the *constructiviste* scenery in vogue. Strauss had gone no further, biblically, than *The Legend of Joseph*, there collaborating with Hofmannsthal and Count Kessler. *Joseph* was sophisticated and (by making Joseph a boy) erotic enough, with young Massine as the 'wonder boy', to be produced by Diaghilev in Paris, before its appearance at Drury Lane (June, 1914). The whole conception of *Job* repudiates the glare and glitter, the virtuoso expressions of temptation and inner ecstasy, of *Joseph*, while asserting its own principles of artistic validity. It is an appeal to face issues, not with a competent egoism, or, on the other hand, with resounding declarations of righteousness in an evil world, but rather with the unspoken gestures of the spirit, and with the unconscious wisdom furnished by an alert and receptive mind. It is at once music for mime and a poetic warning in the quasi-oratorio tradition.

In *Job* converges the richest possible current of ideas, involving three entirely separate stages of thought and four media. The observant listener may at first respond to the simple harmony of mime and music, without further mental ado, and be satisfied by the assertions of melodic and orchestral contrast, as symbols of a human spirit transformed by a great and traditional ordeal, such as the dancers may seem to represent. But this response misses the true quality of the appeal which comes to the twentieth century from a clash of different minds, in a capricious evolution from the poetic conception of the fourth century before Christ, via the challenging theology of William Blake, and similarly from the written word to the musically accompanied mime constructed from Blake's engravings. 'Evolution', indeed, is a rash word to use of such a fortuitous combination of arts not demonstrably made to combine, and many problems and contradictions are commonly ignored. An informed response to each side of the total expression, though disintegrating at first, and not without its anomalies, produces the most far-reaching and illuminating vision of Job the man, as here revealed. It will not be shirked here, at the risk of seeming elementary to students of the Bible and of Blake.

First, there is the text of the most outspoken book in the Old Testament: a weave of introductory folk-tale and poetic dialogue between Job, his friends and God, with a later interpolation, the speeches of Elihu, not to mention an extraneous piece of wisdom, and disputable passages, such as God's second speech, and a blatantly adventitious epilogue. Textual controversy apart, the general intention is clear: to give a poetic answer, as the *Republic* of Plato gives a philosophic answer, to the rule of force and cruelty and disease in the world, by a vindication of the disciplined will. The good man can only advance to serious conviction from the simple piety of prayers and observances by facing his doubts at the highest level and with a clear conscience, which gives him a sense of intimate communion with God. This firm moral consciousness is proof against the intellectual dishonesty of the friends who, by their silence in the prologue and by their speeches later, embody the conventional didactic response to crushing calamity: it must be an intimation of the wrath of God reserved for the unjust. On the hypocrisy of this suggestion that the exploiter class never remains at the top but always goes down in the end, Job has plenty to say. God's forbidding assertion of his inscrutable nature puts the comforters in their place, leaving Job in dust and ashes, but with a fresh vision of life. In the truer Greek text of the Septuagint (40.8), replacing a verse of opposite tenor in the Hebrew as translated in the English Bible:

> 'Despise not my chastisement!
> Dost thou think I would have revealed myself to thee
> Were it not that thou mightst be proven righteous ?[1]

The dramatic dialogue marks the growth of experience broadly foreshadowed in the prologue. In the prologue, the adversary is not the Satan of later literature, but simply a figure of prosecuting cross-examination under divine orders. Consequently he does not appear in the dialogue. He has tightened the screw according to instructions. The rest is for Job to answer for, in the name of something more committal than either Promethean stoicism or the lonely 'sense of the absurd' of Camus's *homme revolté*.

Such is the now familiar background of tested belief on a moral foundation, whose realistic confrontation of the injustices of life makes it of perpetual interest to the modern, sceptic thinker on difficult problems. To a certain degree, God represents the champion (Authorized Version: redeemer) who bursts on Job's awareness earlier; that is, an exaltation of himself. On the whole, however, the writer sets Job's sights at a high angle, and, so far from being 'charged with presumption', as has commonly been stated, Job is utterly vindicated, pleading only for his friends.

We come to the next source. Except that he turned in principle to the 'consciously and professedly inspired' writers of the Bible, as opposed to the Classics, for an archetype of the Christian vision that he sought to expound in his poetry and art, Blake had little concern with the biblical Job, beyond the portrait, in his own particular imagery, of a man who found God through a testing experience. The twenty-one *Illustrations of the Book of Job*, developed from a set of water-colour

---

[1] Moses Buttenwieser, *The Book of Job*, p. 63.

drawings, made about 1820, into the engravings executed for John Linnell in 1825[1], are no mere amplification of the original dramatic lyric. On the contrary, they are a mature embodiment of the kind of expression which Blake had committed to paper throughout his career and which had ended with the two compressed and complementary epics of struggling man, *Milton* and *Jerusalem*. The biblical figures of the celestial and terrestrial groups, the whirlwind and even Leviathan, are all re-enlisted in the service of a fresh presentation of stages in the fall and rise of the man of vision, commonly termed by Blake, the poetic genius.

In *Milton* the personality of the elder poet, prodigal and heroic yet confined by many inhibitions, had similarly been invoked only to be rigorously corrected and liberalized, in a redeemed Albion, 'to justify the ways of God to men' (*sic*). More particularly, the illustrations of Robert Blair's *Grave* had traced a descent and ascent in scanty regard for the author's dreary piety. Moreover, the change from illustrated poem to ideographic illustrations, profusely packed with cited texts, was partly a matter of emphasis, not of an entirely fresh choice of medium. Accordingly, much of the symbolism of the *Job* illustrations is illuminated by the system of ideas which steadily emerges from the two-fold satire of the *Songs of Innocence* and the *Songs of Experience* to the major poems; and to that system must be related the series of pictures presented to the eye, not without certain purely visual symbols of spiritual distinctions.

Heaven and hell, then, are states of mind, choices between a living creative spirit and a fallen, body-bound, nature-bound existence. What human society needs is visionaries, not a master-race, whose will to conquer and dominate can only produce passive, non-creative good. The purpose of art is to stabilize such experience in a consistent imagery. Allegory is an acceptable approach, if its language reveals the archetypal genres of experience. Thus, as a tense summary of the final liberation from the disorder and contradictions of natural impulses in *Jerusalem*, the Job myth could be shown to reveal stages of decline, from the insecure religious confidence of a literal, law-abiding piety to the hellish depths of 'selfhood' or self-righteousness. But this would be followed

---

[1] Reproductions of the *Illustrations* in their various versions have been published in a very handsome edition edited by Sir Geoffrey Keynes. There is a copy of the engravings in the British Museum. Reproductions of these appear, on a slightly reduced scale, in Joseph H. Wicksteed, *Blake's Vision of the Book of Job* (1910; revised 1924), and also in *William Blake's Engravings*, ed. Keynes (Faber and Faber).

by stages of resurrection, through an almost innocent mood of enlightenment and physical experience, to the supreme vision. The *Illustrations* accordingly provide, not a literal presentation of any scene, but an allegorical series of clues, the allegory being remotely based on a cross-section of the original book, in the Blake version. The fall of Job is thus enacted and re-enacted, almost symphonically, to the second or third degree, and similarly his ascent. The familiar train of biblical narrative and poetic sequence becomes just a convenient link between each group in the series, just as the Shakespeare rendering of the Montague-Capulet legend bridges the gaps between the successive movements of Berlioz's *Roméo et Juliette* symphony.

In each group Job is subject to two influences, his latent creative spirit and his spirit-breaking doubts. That spirit is represented as like himself, at once transcendent and immanent, whether Jehovah, Eliphaz, or Christ. A steady indication of the transcendent element is the forward position of the right hand or foot, as the left signifies Job's human or corruptible nature. This discovery on the part of the pioneer interpreter of the *Illustrations*, Joseph Wicksteed, releases a constant train of accessory imagery and latent psychology, as he has shown in his book. Satan, it may be assumed, represents the death impulse of selfhood which reduces men to tyrants or their inert victims. He is the arch-accuser or principle of unbelief; the human counterpart of inert matter, of life imprisoned in its own cycle of natural decline. He does not usually resemble Job, but his flying figure is accompanied by reflections or emanations of Job and his wife. Mainly invisible after the first stage, his influence is apparent in the judicial attitude of the friends (hence Blake's provocative statement that Milton's Messiah is, in *Job*, called Satan), and blatant in the cloven-hoofed god of Job's evil dream, which marks the lowest depths of exposure. Blake's Satan is thus a blunt fusion of the biblical accuser and the diabolical influence of later tradition, but, equally with Jehovah, he is Job's emanation. Except in Job's nightmare, he appears as an almost Perseus-like figure, and his final personification of evil, in the fall from heaven, is a subtlety that has to be explained on partly external and literary evidence.

In the rescue of Job-man from this fell clutch, as a 'tiger of wrath', the adventitious Elihu (anticipated by the youth in the sixth of Blake's *Blair-Grave* illustrations) provides the first stimulus, and the Leviathan or spiral of nature offers a defiant pattern of flux, inexplicable but real. In the figure of Christ, Job's spirit burns for a moment with a 'tiger-eye' blaze. The remaining pictures provide homely assurances of his transformation. These include the final aural imagery of the sudden *tutti* of the instruments in use which, at the commencement, hang high above the heads of the family assembled for palpably formal worship.

This leaves a clear two-part scheme which, following Wicksteed's subdivisions, we may summarize as follows in conventional terms. In his more recent book (1924), Mr. A. Foster Damon has detected a recurring seven-fold state related to the 'seven eyes of God' in the Prophetic Books, in *Illustrations*, 1–14, 15–21, but 12 is manifestly the turning point in a balanced series.

A. *Descent* 1–3 } 4–6 }	A vulnerable, statute-abiding Job, in contact with a faltering God and an increasingly powerful Satanic emanation; comparable to the image-worshipping Aaron of *Moses and Aaron* (Schoenberg).
7–11	An isolated, stricken, and despairing Job, in touch with God only as visualized by Eliphaz, a cruel dispenser of justice; accused by his friends of false religion, yet still confident of right, but finally cast down to hell itself by the discovery, in a nightmare, that his moving spirit is Satanic, punitive, and earth-bound. (This theme has been treated in another quasi-biblical context in Pirandello's *Lazarus*.)
B. *Ascent* 12–15	The wrathful Elihu chides Job by pointing to the stars, whose evocative beauty begins the process of rescuing Job from the abyss of his pride. A vision of a partly cruciform God in the whirlwind, of the higher and lower creation.
16	A last judgement. Job repudiates (on his left) his past life, of which Satan is the key figure, and is thus purged of error.
17–21	A vision of Christ, drawing Job and his wife upwards and humbling his former critics. Formal worship and praise in a transformed context—somewhat prolonged, it seems, to make twenty-one. (God is present now only in his halo. The ideal stage is reached: *esse est percipi*.)

Such is the historic archetypal series that aroused the daring ambition of the Blake scholar and enthusiast, Sir Geoffrey Keynes, after reading Wicksteed, to reduce the inherent drama to a ballet scenario. One can but wonder at the formidable undertaking. If music was to be involved, it might at first be thought that some kind of 'symphonic poem' (Rabaud had supplied a precedent in 1905) would be more appropriate: the portrait of a new type of leader, visionary, fallible and worthy of redemption, but not overwhelmingly possessive. One can imagine Strauss, who was never at a loss for symbols of the overweening pride of youth or maturity, planning such an advance on *Death and Transfiguration*, or such a sharp rejoinder to the wayward outline of *Zarathustra* and Nietzsche, until it is recalled that he had covered similar enough ground in his portrait of the much tempted young visionary, Joseph, a kind of ambivalent Elihu, without his sting, yet by rejecting the advances of Potiphar's wife driving her to remorse and suicide, while he is vindicated.

Keynes also resolved on ballet. He evidently decided that, in spite of the symbolic and repetitive character of the *Illustrations*, their intense sense of inner drama called for choreography. With the co-operation of the late Mrs. Gwendolen Raverat, who devised and designed, he planned eight scenes, and sent a French scenario to Diaghilev, in London at the time. He rejected the idea as too English and old-fashioned. Perhaps he did not like his title-role to reek of misfortune, or to be the mere vehicle of doctrinal ideas, which to him were no more than pawns in a game, to gambit at will.[1] Actually, he kept the set of reproductions of the engravings which he had been sent, and in Diaghilev's production of *The Prodigal Son* (Prokoviev), which appeared rather surprisingly in 1929—'c'est tout ce que je déteste' was his later comment, but not on the music—Keynes was interested to discern signs of a Blake influence. Yet, pronounced experimentalist as he was, Diaghilev cannot be blamed for regarding a Blake ballet, tied up with a series of engravings as well as with music, as an awkward project.

The choreography of *Job* was eventually undertaken by Dame Ninette de Valois, a former *soliste* in Diaghilev's company, but now the bold director of her own school, with an almost pedantic grasp of musical construction. Her *Job* marked her new association with the Camargo Society, and also a distinct advance on her *Rout* (Bliss). It demonstrated that 'literary' involvement was not necessarily a handicap. Incidentally, Anton Dolin (Satan) had received his training, as a vigorous *premier danseur classique*, at Monte Carlo under Diaghilev. He had won his spurs in *Le Train Bleu*, a *ballet sportif* by Cocteau. Here athletic prowess was not enough, but Dolin used his Perseus-like figure to advantage. David Blair, however, was later considered to be the Satan most in harmony with the Blake portraiture, in his blend of 'fiendish ambition

---

[1] Diaghilev's literary-manifesto career had begun as editor of the Russian *World of Art*, in part an attack on the didactic, 'story-telling' aims of the well-meaning but limited *Ambulants*' movement. 'To force ideas is blasphemous.' See Arnold Haskell, *Diaghileff*, chapter 4.

and tarnished radiance'.[1] In any event, Satan dominates this ensemble ballet.

While the scenario was being sent around, Vaughan Williams had been asked to write the music, and naturally Diaghilev's indifference did not deter him from completing his full score. Hence the concert performance at Norwich. The enterprise of the just founded Camargo Society soon made stage presentation possible; but for the smaller orchestra engaged a reduced score was made by Constant Lambert. Even so, *Job* 'created a very powerful impression' (*The Times*) at such a performance at Oxford a little later. Thus the *Job* music became a pivotal element in this fresh translation of the universal legend. We may now consider its relation to the declared Blake source, and partly to the biblical source.

Vaughan Williams, working in touch with Keynes, compiled his own scenario in nine scenes, making two of Keynes's fifth scene, and attaching citations from the *Book of Job* to each scene. (Howes shows in full the two synopses, one for a ballet programme and the other permanently in the score.) The composer's scheme follows Keynes's closely in principle. Its relation to Blake's order is tabulated opposite. The subdivisions of scene are made for convenient comparison.

Certain changes will be noticed at once: Satan's dance of fiendish ecstasy is put forward, and Job's untranslatable dream is replaced by two separate events, the nightmare intrusion on Job's normal sleep of plague and his fellows—referred by Keynes to an engraving of 1783 and rather misleadingly called by him Satan's 'Trinity of Accusers' (*Blake Studies*, 152), who in most drawings are theft, adultery and murder—and the revelation of Satan on God's throne (a masterly intimation). There are also some signal omissions. In consequence, the cumulative symmetry of Blake's repeated patterns in Part A, and of his balance of transcendent demonstration and immanent revelation in Part B, is lost. But the major alteration is of perspective. In the music for Part A, Satan appears as the rebel angel, agent of destruction; the friends are near-grotesque mock sympathizers; and the final blasphemy comes rather suddenly. Even so, this crucial point of defeat comes late in the ballet; more than two-thirds of the way through. Part B is in consequence very compressed. There is no sign of the consuming invective of Elihu, or the whirlwind revelation, or, inevitably, the supreme vision. A prelude, pavane, and triumphal galliard cover the gaps in the ideographic

---

[1] *Ballet Annual*, 1960, ed. A. Haskell: article by Mary Clarke.

BLAKE ILLUSTRATIONS		RELATED VAUGHAN WILLIAMS SCENES	
A.1	Job and family ⎤	1a	Job
2	Satan and Job before the ⎬	1b	Saraband of the Sons of God
	throne of God ⎦	1c	Satan's entry
3	Satan's visitation on Job's	3a	Family dances
	family	3b	Destruction
4	Messengers of death to Job	5	Dance, procession; Job
5	Satan leaving the presence of God		
6	Satan overwhelms Job with disease	2	Satan's Dance of Triumph
7	The lament of the friends ⎤	6a	Dance of Comforters
8	Job's despair ⎦	6b	Job curses God
9	Eliphaz's vision		
10	The exposure of Job by his accusing friends	6a	Dance interlude
11	Job haunted by satanic figures of deity	4a	Job's quiet sleep disturbed
		4b	by visions of plague, famine and battle
		6c	Job invokes his vision of God: Satan revealed on God's throne
B.12	Wrath of Elihu	7a	Elihu's Dance of Youth
	Vision of the stars		
13	God in the whirlwind		
14	Vision of creation	7b	Pavane of the Heavenly Host
15	Leviathan		
16	Fall of Satan	8a	Satan driven down. Galliard
		8b	of the Sons of the Morning
17	Vision of Christ		
18	Job's sacrifice	8c	Altar Dance. Galliard
19	Receiving gifts		
20	Job and his daughters		
21	Job and his family	9	Job, again surrounded by his family

panorama. For the epilogue, Job is simply restored as he was. There is no element of transformation.

Blake's precisely poised structure has thus not only been shortened, but loosened in favour of a suite of movements, which reaches its crisis at the end of the sixth, and thereafter moves serenely along from one dance to another. While the essential correspondence between the figures of God and Job remains, the subtle immanence of Satan is considerably relaxed in favour of a more conventional and intrusive diabolism—in the interest, presumably, of clear and practical stage presentation. It falls largely to the music to shape the whole impact of this modified

Blake design, with its own emphasis, amplified or qualified by choreo-graphy. Meanwhile, a fundamental apotheosis of the disciplined will may be posited. For most listeners that will be rejoinder enough to the challenge of violence and cruelty, as demonstrated by immense pressure groups in the nations of the world today. But it will be clearer now why earlier reference was made to arts never meant to combine. It seems that while observing the Blake sequence, the composer was cultivating his own interest in the features of the legend, as aroused by his feeling for the possibility of characteristic dances. Satan has thus been processed down to a broad, more conventionally diabolical character, whose definition must be left to the impersonating soloist.

Whatever the precise relation to its sources, the music may be expected to distinguish three levels of being in the microcosm which the Job legend brings before the reader's imagination: Job the human, Job the spiritual, and Job the corruptible. These are apparent, from the first scene, in contrasts of melodic and harmonic character. Indeed, the sudden changes of mood, just palatable for the spectator, sometimes produce in the music a quite reckless sense of *non sequitur*, which threatens the cohesion of a movement. One may cite as examples: between the serene strophes of the Saraband come not only a potentially explosive Satan but suggestions of Job, Satan and divine decision in dubious juxtaposition; after all the disturbances of Job's unconscious and conscious mind by terrifying visions and visible messengers of deprivation, the return of his calm (end of Scene 5) is unconvincing; and paradoxically the curse-music, etc., that follows the despairing moan of saxophone and violoncello is too annihilating. These and other tears in the fabric should be reconsidered by those who declare too readily that the music is absolutely acceptable as an orchestral suite.

With this caution, one may observe the three general strains. For Job and his family, there is a neo-modal style in the minor key, with snatches of folk-song, sometimes in 'manifold' formation, but with frequent spasms of semitonal diversion, of a hectic quality apt, by a stretch of the imagination, for good-timers. For Satan and his associates, the texture is semitonal to an unmistakable degree of cynical contra-diction, or as subversively whole-tonal, or bluntly discordant. The three great dances of the creative spirit, the Saraband, Pavane and Galliard, are all early-major; the first Mixolydian, the other two hexatonic, but all without sharpened seventh, except for an occasional turn in the Galliard. The impact is stylized, but without being sophisticated. These tunes are old-fashioned, quite apart from their passing revival of bygone dance formalities. (There is no suggestion in the music of pairing the Pavane and Galliard; the Galliard would be, rather, a 'spirited digression' between the two Pavane strophes, if it were not so important.) But the dances are exceedingly positive in their ritual way. The music confirms the situation as 'a clear case of God-fixation' for the arch-cynic, but it is not burdened with a sense of omnipotence. Rather, the ecstasy of the creative life, in harmony with God.

These melodic differentia are reinforced by contrasts of timbre. The family music is for chamber orchestra, with strings for Job in solitude or separation (Scenes 4 *init.*, 5 *fin.*, 8, altar dance), wood cadenzas as a passing oriental feature of the bearers of grave tidings (Scene 5), and a freely moving solo violin, sobered by deep lower-string harmony, for Elihu's Dance of Youth. (Elihu here has thus no relation either to the wordy supernumerary of the book or to the subtle catalyst of the designs. Musically all too familiar, he cuts a somewhat whimsical figure, as it might be Ariel.) In contrast, the nemesis approaching Job's family is underlined by a buzz of string tremolo and percussion. The heavenly music is mainly for full orchestra, with a well-supported tune at one octave in strings and wind (Pavane and Galliard), or in three octaves in strings or *tutti* (Saraband, verses 1 and 2), but never for brass alone or uncovered. Apart from harps and kettledrums, the percussion is used sparingly, with cymbals and big drum for solemn punctuation, side-drum and triangle to add a sense of invincibility to Satan's expulsion, and chime-bells to give lustre to the Pavane's return.

In clear differentiation, wood and brass announce Satan, and brass hurl forth the *Gloria* tone of Satan's mock homage. His wild but highly contrived and, indeed, limited dance-tune (a slight reflection of the sinister Faustian Scherzo of Beethoven's ninth symphony, as the re-peated bass figure almost overtly derives from the same composer's quartet in F, op. 135) is in four octaves, and includes xylophone, plucked strings and later harp, besides brass. The intrusion of Battle, Murder and Sudden Death is marked by an impromptu, insistent and monotonous phrase in the trumpets, shrilly amplified by violins in the upper octave. This is accompanied by *oompah*-trombones (see p. 302) and syncopated string percussion, and answered by muted trumpet with wind and xylophone and side-drum. After a blaze of vibrating terrorist colour, a shrieking syncopation hovers, vulture-like, over the former trumpet phrase, now forced down into a nasal *tutti* of trumpet, wood and strings in unison; the rasp of the G string in the violins and violas being 'packed' with the more normal resonance of the A string at the top of the violoncello gamut, as one of many telling points of textural detail. The hubristic tone is patent, but it is precisely established, in the Meyerbeer style.

For 'intimate effect', his grotesque satanic friends comfort Job with Modern Music: soprano saxophone solo against percussive harmony, with a violoncello descant to implement the return of these three 'wily hypocrites' to gestures of pretended sympathy, after an ill-tempered brassy interlude to betray what it is worth. The medley of equivocal and contradictory degree-relationships in a glib atonality, and the oily tones of the all too familiar demotic voice, are commonly accepted for their probing portraiture, whether of the friends' anxiety to reassure a beaten man that with their support he can stand the unendurable, or of their equally hypocritical exposure of Job's pride, as in Blake. (Dallapiccola uses the vibraphone to reinforce his comforters' insidious canon.) But is so horrid a sound-relationship ever acceptable? In the concert-room it is meaningless and intolerable. If 'the joy of the hypocrite is for a moment', it is still too long. This single reed with a conical bore, steadily producing a strong fundamental and a piercing harmonic two octaves up, is somehow oppressive to the ear.

Between these three main strains of human activity and the idealized alternating exercise of convinced or doubting man crystallize moments of mixed being. In Scene 1, as a token of Job's false moral security as he blesses his children, the blend, in an extremely loose weave, of the central Job theme and the dance in progress, when continued, is haunted by a lofty, reluctantly descending violin counterpoint. This sense of impending trial, hovering over the normal routine of human observances, becomes explicit later. With this symbol, in Scene 3, Satan scatters death on a developed scene of quiet pleasure—no debt to Blake's third illustration here—first secretly and then in ponderous descent. By the same token, at the beginning and end of the nightmare of Scene 4, the significance of his unconscious experience violently rouses and finally comes home to him (wooden sticks for the kettle drums and a 'concluding' entry of the tam-tam or gong). In Scene 5, a funeral procession of flutes and drums similarly confirms his fears. Here, the implied melodic level (flutes) unobtrusively veers, over a persistent tonic bass (kettle-drum), from a descent from the seventh degree, to a descent from the third, before returning to the more formal and pivotal fifth degree, as the start of a top line which becomes three-deep (5–3–1) at the later stages. Meanwhile a viola ascending counterpoint, far below, similarly develops from a single line to three-deep muted-trumpet harmony, forming rich passing chords with the flutes above. Finally, when the comforters have broken Job's spirit, this motive suddenly breaks out with terrible potency (Ex. 47a below), sweeping the saxophonery aside and leading to the organ's supreme repudiation of spiritual essence, as physically revealed in the triumph of Satan in God's place. (The organ is used in a similar sense for 'earth torn apart' in the music of the Blake film, as a drastic prelude to the recitation of the redemptive 'And did those feet'. In Dallapiccola, on the other hand, the organ substantiates a flourish of power before the final divine pronouncement.) To the imaginative listener, the modern pertinence of this sense of an inexorably linked defeatism and nemesis is most overwhelming.

Ex. 47a

On the other side, the cultivation of an old melodic and textural vein in Scene 7 rests the mind from the horrors of misrule, and braces it, in the name of Elihu, towards the second signal of fresh ecstasy, free from diabolism, the Pavane. The reformative dream-music of *Joseph* makes an emotional precedent. Nevertheless, after the aural stress of Scene 6, this *Lark Ascending* touch is perplexing, since it is intelligible neither to the biblical student nor, on the whole, to the Blake student. The latter will recognize the starry vault (in the conventional sense: Mr. Damon suggests that the stars are, rather, the *illusory* material order, exposed); but he will find the rescue 'from the pit' missing, or at least very lightly acknowledged in this sudden transformation. This is no *Magic Flute*! Much involution is thus left to the solo-dancer here, for the music, once directed, moves in a straight line. However, the heavenly mood is established, with some melodic recollection of the *Pastoral Symphony* (finale).

The subsequent Altar Dance not only combines a sense of domestic occasion with signs (provocative to the Blake enthusiast) of a normal, aspiring Job, but rouses a perception of more than terrestrial proportions in the preliminary, towering, hushed string chord and subsequent spacing of tune and accompaniment. Once more and spontaneously, the common round is observed *sub specie aeternitatis*. By way of verification, the ritual movement on earth is at once woven, musically and visually, with the Pavane on its return. The solemn Pavane, now led by trumpets in a manner prophetic of their entry in the fifth symphony (and, in general harmonic progression, of the close of *Scott of the Antarctic*), achieves a brief, almost glittering culmination before reaching its cadence for general adoration, set as in Scene 1, but briefer.

The return to earlier motives in the epilogue must be taken as a last glance at a reformed Job, disciplined and ready for the future, and freed by hard experience, fearless and unperplexed. But there is no sign of any difference in the music. Blake's purpose is apparent in the merry noise of wind and harp genres that replaces, in the mind's ear, the initial and typically unmusical observance of the written religious code. This is entirely disregarded in the easy satisfactions of thematic recovery, here employed to place the drama in a final mood of pure, unprogressive contemplation. The composer drops back to the biblical Job, made wise the hard way, as his scenario reference to 'an old and humbled man' betrays. Similarly, the previous cadence of adoration, by equating this second homage with the first, entirely ignores Blake's contrast of Job's domination by a dubious, law-abiding spirit with the movements of a dedicated visionary who is freed of the need for the conscious consultation of his inner convictions. So grooved, stage movement is earthbound.

The music of *Job* shows these set moods of three distinguishable genres, whether in general dances, the more intimate and variegated dances of smaller groups, or solos; but between these are pointed and sometimes angular transitions, preludes and postludes. The latter have led to a false impression that the work is not a full ballet, but they are mainly indispensable links.

It remains to notice the impact of the music in its period. The most obviously new ground lies in the Satanic music in the broad sense. From a comparatively simple combination of slowly revolving chords of F, D flat and E flat with coursing ascending fourths from F to D flat (Satan's entry) to the bitonality and irregular scales of Satan's dance, the featuring of the discord that is no mere postponement of concord takes on, with a constant dynamic or other rhetorical emphasis, a fresh line of minatory music, only touched upon in the *London Symphony* (finale) and *Sancta Civitas*. But many phrases, like the second (*con fuoco*) in Satan's main dance, are forceful in their driving, probing incision. Once more, the means employed are basic enough in rhythm and melodic movement to stand the wear of repetition within the compass of each dance or episode. This portraiture of the mind's reckless abandonment to evil ways gains in impressiveness with the parallel visual impact, but it also establishes a constant validity in its own right. The music for the three 'wily hypocrites', a trio of accusers widely paralleled in Blake's literary works and art, falls within this paragraph, and has already been singled out as the exception which wears thin; but superlative ballet might well justify the obvious intentions of this display of the self-righteous character 'who only wants to help'—by arraignment.

The dances and casual miming on earth are not so progressive in content. One might have expected an oriental touch somewhere. The Minuet of Scene 3 is the most pronounced, being strong enough to absorb the satanic figurations in the last strophe. Yet the antiquity of these dances and link-pieces sounds fresh in their varied colouring. It begins with the subdued lights of revolving string chords, with violas on the top line, pricked out by harp somewhat perkily. It ends with the same music in a finer chording, headed by soaring violins.

The heavenly dances follow the simple pattern of a universal thought; auguries of experience. The first and last appear to be obvious analogues of Blake's best known illustration (14), a picture of the unification of all the faculties under divine imagination, intuitive rather than dialectic. The two strophes of the Saraband, though both sonorous, demonstrate the essential and the ampler implications. In its first strophe the Pavane, having a narrower melodic range, surveys masterfully a sequence of keys: G, E, D flat, B flat, E, G. The second strophe, separated from the first by the Galliard and part of the Altar Dance, is actually a steady compression of phrase, although the same key-orbit is maintained. Yet its constant weaving of subsidiary theme, together with the full scoring, including the all-embracing harps, leaves an impact of saturation about its pattern of 5–2–6–3–3 bars, which finds dynamic calm in the last phrase.

The approach to the so-called Galliard (160 beats to the minute) is by the music of Satan's dispatch (Scene 1). Identical, apart from a shriller first harp (for satanically pricked ears), it enhances expectation. 'Satan claims the victory.' God pronounces sentence of banishment. For

Blake, it was a plain matter of ultimate judgement; of identifying and so destroying error. In modern terms, the cynicism of accepting the worst that force can do as a law of nature must be recognized and expelled. For Vaughan Williams, this is one more moment for the decisive melody which he has made his peculiar concern. He constructs a hexatonic major tune of three beats in a plastic measure of 5–4 bars, a contrasted interlude of indeterminate units, and a brief but elate repeat, which finds the right key from a thundering cadence, and is then propelled by a trochaic, mainly two-beat bass. The key is inescapably D. Thus succinctly, the resolution of every good will, the conviction of all who call on God, and the conversion of the stiff-necked from their pride, aspire to the condition of music, while the dancers enact the agelong intention of the committed:

> And finally beat down Satan under our feet.

Here in repeat is the second phrase answering 47a, the motive for the stealthy, sinister influence which has haunted Job from the start. The melody asks no questions, and maintains a firm course. It is, indeed, a

Ex. 47b

little too predictable to be altogether persuasive. It will reverberate in the eighth symphony finale. While, then, these diatonic tunes cumulatively match the more striking diabolical inventiveness, they do so in the broadest terms. They counter the binding phrase with a gesture of release.

The *Job* ballet-music has now been reviewed against the disparate background of the original didactic lyric and of Blake's masterly series of paintings and engravings. It may seem unnecessary to have borne Blake so much in mind. But it was Keynes's initiative which, having dramatized Blake, invoked the composer, and the Blake conception certainly persists in certain essential respects, including the role of Satan. For the informed listener, it must be very apparent that Vaughan Williams goes his own way considerably. He is not interested in the inner workings of Job's conversion, but in the primary motives of human endeavour, creative, destructive, and utilitarian, and, we may conjecture, in the power of the individual or world-society to control the pressure of the destructive elements at man's disposal and to release the constructive, partly by exercising a receptive ear for the inner voices.

Within the orbit of the Job saga, this overwhelming struggle is maintained up to the end of the sixth scene in characteristic dances, during which Satan and his agents haunt the conscience of any spectator who is aware that he is contemplating no fantastic fable, but present issues that will face the world as far as can be predicted. The solo-virtuosity of Satan's dance, the family dances and Job's quiet dream, space out the greater impact of the prologue, the horrors of evil dreams and the increasing trenchancy of the Comforters scene. After that the tension is released. Satan returns for eight bars only to be expelled. There is thus a certain debilitating monotony in the last three scenes, which Blake's resourceful series (12–21) brings home to the critical listener. This need not be pressed, but must be allowed for. On the whole, the integrity of the work makes it one of the composer's most pronounced achievements. It recognized no category when it first appeared, as an original treatment of a familiar theme in the world's treasured experience, parallel with an earlier attempt in another medium. It recognizes no category now. Hence its reservation for this late chapter. On the stage, it should be saved for rare and special occasions.[1]

It will be interesting to note how well Dallapiccola's balanced setting of the biblical lyric, with its declamatory emphasis, orchestral virtuosity, and subservience to the text, stands up to revival.

By a coincidence whose significance deepens with examination, Blake's illustrative art constitutes a link with the more normal music-drama, by which Vaughan Williams revealed his didactic aims in a more pointed manner, taking his text from Bunyan's dream-journey. Blake executed twenty-eight water-colour drawings for *The Pilgrim's*

---

[1] This judgement is supported by Mary Clarke (*Ballet Annual*, 1954, ed. A. Haskell).

Progress.[1] The set of drawings is contemporary with the *Job* engravings. and loses no opportunity to contrast formalist and massively monumental (i.e. materialist) religion with the creative approach; and Christian's blooming youth enhances the sense of need. 'Christian meeting Evangelist' (3) strikingly suggests, and nos. 7 and 8 amplify, the comparison, although Evangelist personifies experience in a non-satirical sense, anticipating the musical portrait. 'Christian before the Cross' (14) is impressive. It is obviously influenced by the wonderful presentation of a cruciform Albion, standing in adoration before the Cross, in 'Jerusalem' (Plate 76). The illustration here conveys, with a suddenness that may recall the celestial outburst in *Gerontius*, the distant but no less penetrating vision of Christ that comes to Christian as he stands, in rags and semi-cruciform, with his burden of sin set down where it will roll into the sepulchre beside him. This is a distinctly more striking conception than the subdued musical features (apart from fourteen bars of desperation) of Pilgrim's entry upon the identical scene. Christian climbing the precipices of the hill of Difficulty by keeping a firm hold of solid rock above (16), skilfully portrays agonizing danger faced. 'Christian beaten down by Apollyon' (20) is rather blatantly horrific and draconic, but it stays in the mind more than the terse musical setting. The lurid showmen of 'Vanity Fair' (22) are intriguing glosses on the musical showmanship. Finally, the picture of Christian and Hopeful on the threshold of the celestial city, if one ignores the adventitious facial detail, is a serene finish, worth comparing with the musical one.

Having, then, necessarily set the *Job* music against the series of engravings that brought it into being, one can do worse than consider the same artist's representation of Bunyan's vision before confronting the same composer's stage setting of the perilous journey.

There is a twenty-ninth drawing in Lord Crewe's portfolio. Previously confused with the Bunyan set by Rossetti, it is evidently, as Keynes has stated, a representation of Christ dismissing a flying Satan

[1] Once more it was Sir Geoffrey Keynes's interest which brought these freshly to light. Having been given access to the set, he was inclined at first to agree with William Rossetti's depreciatory reference in his list of works in Alexander Gilchrist's *Life of Blake* (1863), but later he realized that the uneven quality and unfinished state concealed a magnificent series of designs and with the help of the owner, Lord Crewe, he arranged—the year was 1941—for a set of reproductions, for a new edition of Bunyan's book, by the Limited Editions Club of New York, in which city the originals can now be seen in the Frick Collection. Collotype reproductions of six (2, 9, 14, 17, 22, 25) can be found in Keynes's *Blake Studies* (1949).

after the first Temptation, and must have been a rejected draft for *Paradise Regained*. By combining the ideas of illustrations 16 and 17 of *Job*, it supplies a background for the implied doctrine of the expulsion in Scene 8 of the ballet. It provides an impressive image of self-discipline that is usually missing from the pomp of expulsion accompanying the swinging Galliard.[1] While the illustration of the Christ figure (17) remains out of the composer's scheme, as unsuitable for stage treatment, no thoughtful spectator of today would contemplate the victory over Satan, and all that it signifies in a disordered world or individual, in terms only of an enlightened Job. Indeed, Satan does not appear in the main biblical story: a prediction of the Temptation must be assumed. That the masque of *Job* is as Christian a conception as the *Illustrations*, it would be preposterous to deny. The commonly recognized link was riveted, textually, in *Messiah*, however fortuitously. It is left to the spectator to work out what the faith of the enlightened twentieth century means in terms of decisive struggles, whose issue is tinged with the release of Ex. 47*b*.

The Blake bicentenary, 1957, found the composer writing music for an admirable short film, *The Vision of William Blake*, introducing the *Job* Saraband and other matter, including a fresh setting of ten Blake poems. A notice of this will appear at the conclusion of Chapter XIV. A probably unconscious precedent was Rawsthorne's well-designed music for *The Drawings of Leonardo da Vinci* (1955) on a similar scale.

---

[1] The drawing may be regarded as the sublimation of a pencil drawing (*c*. 1815) of a new version of the Laocoön group. Here Laocoön, that is, Jehovah, and his sons, Satan and Adam, are struggling in the coils of Good and Evil. (*Blake's Pencil Drawings*, second series, ed. Keynes.) The human struggle is most realistic. This may so far be added profitably to the Blake background for the simple triumph of the Galliard, as a suggestion of what H. F. M. Prescott has, in her novel so entitled, called 'The unhurrying chase', God being the hunter who never tires.

XII

Affirmations (2) 'The Pilgrim's Progress' and 'Hodie'

THE PILGRIM'S PROGRESS

The crucial episode, of Pilgrim's departure from the Delectable Mountains for the deep waters which separate him from the Celestial City, was produced as a chamber-opera in 1922, in the obvious context of the *Pastoral Symphony*. This found a place as the penultimate scene of the nine in which the composer eventually disposed the action of *The Pilgrim's Progress*, with prologue and epilogue in the person of Bunyan himself. Thus strangely, once again, English stage music challenged other contemporary work, this time at Covent Garden in 1951 (revised for the performance on February 12, 1952, in the edition now published).

The four acts of the dream proper, three with two scenes and the last and longest with three, separate four chosen stages in the journey described in Bunyan's Part I, with an allusion or two from Part 2: (1) the preparation of Christian, here called Pilgrim, by the anonymous evangelist and by the mysterious beings in the House Beautiful that stands by a Cross, where he is relieved of his burden of sin; (2) the arming of Pilgrim for his journey on the King's highway, and the defeat of Apollyon in the valley of Humiliation, after a nominally tense, compressed struggle; (3) the spectacle and hustle of Vanity Fair, where Pilgrim is arrested and thrown into prison, from which he frees himself; (4) his further journey through the Delectable Mountains to the city of his quest. There are

358

thus five types of characterization: (1) Pilgrim, the aspiring, resolute, exhausted, frightened, and, most habitually, receptive visionary; (2) the Evangelist and other spiritual beings; (3) Apollyon; (4) Lord Lechery and other vivid characters of Vanity Fair; (5) episodic characters, of whom Mr. and Mrs. By-Ends are the chief.

In comparison with *Job*, one is soon aware of the absence of drama. The composer has frequently compressed different incidents into one episode or dialogue, and thus kept a certain consistency of mood in each scene, but, from the second scene onwards, he finds himself reduced to furnishing many singers with adapted scriptural quotations and accessory informative phrases such as 'Be thou arrayed in fine linen', 'A treasure of joy and gladness be given to thee', 'I am more than conqueror through him that loveth me' (after the fight with Apollyon). The Interpreter and the rest are personified images of goodness, whose utterance is usually second-hand; they lack any third dimension. The last quotation is cited by Bunyan himself, in the aphoristic method maintained throughout the book. A conceivable aside in a didactic narrative, it is utterly undramatic on the stage. The dying Fafner, a dragon with a human heart, warns his slayer, in whose identity he shows a proper interest, of trouble to come; leaving an introspective Siegfried behind. One could wish that Apollyon also had thought out one taunt to keep Pilgrim wondering before he disappears. No doubt the composer would have declared, if challenged, 'If the Bible won't satisfy, nothing else could save the situation.' It is enough to observe that in *Job* there is little time to sit and stare, except for Job himself, the Elihu scene, and the evocations of divine grace dancing. Here there is all too much time with the ritual of welcoming Pilgrim in the House Beautiful, arming him for his journey and consoling him after the fight, and then his own meditation in prison, his 'rambler' dialogue with the shepherds on the mountains, and the choruses celestial and terrestrial.

Every act thus ends quietly, the joyful final scene tapering into an epilogue which comprehends the convergent trend of all the previous acts. It is not much good citing E. J. Dent's declaration of the stage-worthiness of the work.[1] The situation must be faced that many scenes are tableaux rather than music-drama. These exalt the contemplative side of resolute experience, nearer oratorio than opera, and, as a pro-

---

[1] Dent's supporting comment, 'It would be a mistake to put the piece into a cathedral and call it oratorio. Bunyan stands for pure religion' (quoted by Mr. Michael Kennedy in a broadcast on the Morality), hardly improved his case.

gress, desperately near 'the illustrious ascent of the best boy in the school, with a dull passing-out ceremony' (D. Shawe-Taylor). The individuality of some ten solo-parts, other than Pilgrim or Evangelist, is negligible. Considerable accent therefore falls on the intrusion of Apollyon and the Vanity Fair crowd, and the By-Ends. It is established oratorio experience that a stage is not necessary for the delivery to a soul of a characteristic and dedicated 'Go forth!', but here, as in *Parsifal*, the flow of pious thought is somewhat overwhelming.

The composer's reply to the challenge of his own scenario is, one must admit, surprising. The prevailing texture is conservative and diatonic. (1) Pilgrim has no clue-theme at first except the trenchant semitonal progression, to utter his sense of guilt, with which he comes to life in the imagination of the visible Bunyan of the prologue. That clue is inevitably dropped as soon as he has been relieved of his burden; it is a perfunctory process, involving only six plain bars of vocal tension. But the salient and primitive falling and rising intonation round the tonic (1–2–5 1), for the Interpreter's 'Thus art thou sealed' (Scene 2), anticipated in the prelude as the title-theme, becomes, as a trumpet flourish, a mark of Pilgrim's identity, like Siegfried's equally brassy theme, but not so adaptable and, indeed, raw in repetition. It is prominent in the trumpet calls and recurrent strophe ('Who would true valour see') of the arming scene, unmistakable orchestrally in the Apollyon crisis, recalled in the escape from prison (by master-key) and in the first scene of Act 4, and the inevitable but weak link with the last scene of triumph, where it recovers a well-worn text (*Revelation*, 5. 13) somewhat mechanically. The growing resemblance to the Albert the Good tune, in *Albert Herring*, is unfortunate in so slender a setting. A more shapely phrase, the choral unison of 'Put on him the whole armour of light'—with a pentatonic-major rise from the tonic (1 2–4|5 ♯6|5)— is a fairly noticeable antiphonal feature in the arming scene, and re-appears significantly in Act 4 as the woodcutter's boy directs Pilgrim to the city.

Otherwise, Pilgrim's music is extemporized: declamatory in the Apollyon and Fair scenes; freely *arioso* in the melancholy meditation in prison (with salient chords as in *Sancta Civitas*, *init.*) and in the calmer and extended sequel, propelled by flowing three-deep lines in the orchestra, whose exploration of key is rather glib. In the last act, Pilgrim has no solo work of importance! He reaches the celestial heights a loyal but limited figure, as repressed, by common operatic standards, as one might expect from his secondhand theology.

6. Ralph Vaughan Williams, *c.* 1951

(2) The Evangelist seems, in the first scene, to live permanently in E flat minor, except when the orchestra are quoting the fifth symphony. He enters to the sound of a falling semitone in rich chordal apparel, which lends colour to his constant aid, but on his reappearance at the end of Act 2, using E flat (Lydian) major in plainsong style for his longest injunction, his initiative does not reach beyond a simple hexatonic D major, lingering on the sixth degree in readiness for the fifth (3–5 ♯6 5) to close the scene. One of the flattest finishes. The Shining Ones (Scene 2), the Watchman (optional nocturne, added to bridge the gap of scene-changing between Acts 1 and 2), the Interpreter and Bearers of Act 2, maintain an equally discreet modal or early-major style. The modal timbre of the later shepherds' dialogue (Dorian) and the more eloquent 'bird-voice' (Mixolydian), in what is actually the earliest part of the work, has more character, mannered as it is. The Messenger's song there is also penetrating, thanks to the chordal movement in the orchestra.

The chorus give out a solid, simple, hexatonic tune (no fourth) for the 'Pilgrim hymn' from Part 2, too long to quote, but wrapping the familiar text in a close-fitting rhythm that avoids any comparison with the well-known and looser folk-song adaptation. Three separated verses exhibit the tune in various styles of address: (i) in casual, spaced out phrases of block harmony, which are interrupted by other matter and key-changes and not perceptibly complementary; (ii) registering complete continuity in fresh harmony; (iii) as continuous bass (choral unison and orchestra) to plain orchestral harmony, with pulsating descant in triplets at the top. These emergent verses lend strength to their scene. Another version appears in the next interlude, and two 'verses' blandly open the last entracte in a simple voluntary style. The latter, a concession to the ecclesiastical ear? The space-filling is very patent. The choral part in the final scene leans first on the discordance of the chord of B flat against the overlapping E natural in the bass (cf. transition to the Moderato of the sixth symphony). The plainest antiphony follows, or descant to the hymn-tune, *York*, which began the work and now returns to the orchestra in shining tones. The reverberating phrase initially associated with 'eternal life' here motivates an increasing sense of a gravitation from the minor chord of the fourth degree in the romantic tradition.

The composer was evidently determined to keep this final encounter free from rhetoric. But it sounds as if *Sancta Civitas* had exhausted his command of means. Even *Benedicite* shows more elation. Apparently, for many spectators of religious (or semi-religious) profession, this visible scene encourages the faithful, and rouses displaced persons of all sorts to dream fresh dreams. 'Authentically celestial' was a leading critic's spoken comment, implying a detachment which many will reject, remembering Blake (see p. 342). That is a matter of private concern. But even for the most sympathetic, repeated hearing is likely to expose the slender material. Something more is needed to convey a sense of creative energy, whether of 'the hardest part' of a suffering God, or of an unfaltering exuberance of care for man; not a perpetual state of rest and cadence, if there is to be music at all for such an imaginative but visible occasion. The Pavane in *Job* communicates such a sense of inexhaustible activity, aided by the actual rhythm on the stage.

(3) In the valley of Humiliation, the wordless chorus of Dolefuls recalls the avenging angel in *Sancta Civitas*. They have no sustained utterance. Nor has Apollyon. His fearful appearance on the stage is barely sketched by the orchestra in its brief hint of dark colour and grotesque satanic majesty. This conflict of half a day is reduced to a perfunctory episode. One suspects that Apollyon's bluff has been called; his defeat and retreat are blacked out. Siegfried at least shattered Wotan's sword.

(4) The long Fair scene has been expanded to nearly twice its size in the original 1951 version, by two major additions and minor amplifications, totalling almost three hundred bars.[1] It now occupies, materially, a quarter of the score. Musically, it is the most arresting interlude. A close succession of incidents, choral and solo, matches the lurid sell-all atmosphere, leading to a judicial proscription of sales-resisters, with a fascinating variety of entertainment. Yet the unity of style is as potent as that of the mountains scene to follow later. One observes clear stages, after some acquaintance: (i) declamatory traders' chorus, in which an oscillation of semitones is resourcefully exhibited to suggest shady transactions, while keeping a firm grip on the tonality of G minor. (The opening unison statement—bars 3–33—is new.) (ii) A major addition (1952), an air with chorus for Lord Lechery (a somewhat romantic sketch of a ponce, text by Ursula Wood), extends in freely developing strophes in G and other keys, in neo-

---

[1] I based my early account of the Morality (*Monthly Musical Record* (February, 1952)) on the replicas of the vocal score put at my disposal in 1951. As the new version appeared shortly afterwards, the composer deplored to me the prematureness of my article. But I was quite unaware that a new version was in hand and would be used for publication.

Lydian style, with, however, a habitually flattened sixth, especially in the bass. (iii) A renewal of the traders' rough attack on reluctant purses is intensified by the arrival of Pilgrim. The key is again G minor, with more accent on its attendant A flat. (iv) In a grotesque but moderately repellent procession of men who sold imperishable things for money (Demas, Judas, and company), each has a verse of a new song, in a new mode (Phrygian minor, with the sharpened fourth of section 2), reminiscent of Varlaam's air in *Boris*. Here, the addition of a few bars (bars 5–9 of Simon's song, 4–5 and 8 of Glory's) has lent more shape to the money-lust of Simon Magus and Worldly Glory than in the original version. (v) A trio for Wanton, Bubble and Lechery acquires a comparatively seductive semitonal waltz-rhythm. (vi) After Pilgrim's defiance of Prince Beelzebub, a derisive-indignant chorus (with vacuously repeated figure in the bass, the equivalent of H-B-B-A as compared with the B-A-H-B of the fourth symphony) leads to the entry of Judge Hategood and accusers, whose exactly corresponding charges (precise canon) are demonstrably 'framed', as in Bach's *St. Matthew Passion*. This and the following section make the second major addition to the scene (106 bars). A trenchant orchestral motive, marked by the descent of a semitone and a third and at first confined to the announcement of the shady sheriff of modern pictorial legend, is now fully developed. (vii) An extended ensemble, led by Bubble, Wanton, and Hategood, piles on accusations in an increasingly insinuating manner, converging in a ferociously united demand for the lynching of Pilgrim. (viii) Crowd-demonstration, as in section 6, is now renewed, with Hategood formulae repeated and ironed out (the last revision), and a characteristic *à la lanterne* march, in which the falling semitone of the corrupt nature reaches a new depth of vindictive undertone.

The upshot is that, although Pilgrim's part here is musically negligible—hence his extended arioso in the next scene—he reaches the fourth act much the richer in experience of competing standards of living. The music ensures this by its adroit assembly of individual obsessions and general avowals of resistance to truth. Its exploitation of semitonally shaped melodic lines and harmony, and generally sensational texture, hazardously informal, whets the desire for diatonic material afresh. After it, the modal tinge of the mountain scene sounds pertinent, where in the episode of 1922 it seemed ecclesiastical and self-conscious.

(5) Of the minor characters who show more individuality than the celestial beings, the four obstreperous neighbours scarcely go beyond

agitated declamation. Wanton and Bubble, absorbed in wayward ensembles, are not enabled even to rival the Windsor Ladies in character-interest, much less Kundry. It seems queer that the creator of Elinor Rumming is at a loss here, but an opportunity for soprano diversion is missed in favour of the glib strophes, with crowd-rejoinders, of the tenor buffo, Lechery, and his too symbolic come-and-go followers. Hategood hardly achieves more than what Holst called Wagnerian bawling. The Usher's model seems, incidentally, to be Köthner, the Mastersingers' pompous M.C. All this comes surprisingly from one who found Elgar's demons 'too mildly respectable'. One cannot help contrasting what Smetana, Strauss and Britten can do with minor characters; but obviously it did not come into the composer's conception of a struggling soul in a cynical world, to make the sinister personages haunting memories like the legalist Hunding and the designing Count Almaviva and Monostatos. In that respect he was like Beethoven. But *Fidelio* at least has Leonora, as a wife of grit but also of compassion and melancholy moods, like Pamina. One never feels that Pilgrim, however fearless, has earned his security except by a kind of analgesia.

The solo soprano part, then, if there is not a boy-treble, is the woodcutters' boy, singer of the nine-bar pentatonic-major strophes (confined to the degrees 1 2 3 5 6 of the major scale) of 'He that is down'. The time-serving conversation of the By-ends has more character. As a persistent symbol of non-committal ethical accommodation, there is a playfully ceremonial motive, preferably in thirds, in an evasive hexatonic Aeolian minor (no sixth). Yet the fussy monotony with which By-ends thus insinuates that he is in with top people, of however doubtful reputation among honest men, is not musically effective; and the vocal declamation is not particularly interesting. Somehow, the inner nature of this crawler, so modern in type, has missed its true revelation. The use of the mode, too, in E minor, with a characteristic E modal minor to follow in the mountains scene, is unfortunate. The listener with an accurate sense of pitch-relations registers E modal minor, D and E major (mountain prospect), A flat (boy's strophe), F and D (entracte), E modal minor (shepherds)—and wonders what connection of character is being underlined.

In the mountain scene, the basic opening texture is Dorian, with an oscillating sixth and later third, and multiple whole-tone lapses (in the manner of the third symphony) for a hint of the dangers in Pilgrim's route to the City. On these traditional lines, an eloquent viola and the strophical phrases, arioso and speech-rhythm of the shepherds (middle-aged baritone, old bass and young tenor) establish a pastoral tone, in the missionary sense, developing to a visionary gleam. A short duet between Pilgrim and the young shepherd expands in a move to F Dorian-minor, brisk tempo, probing rhythmic figures in a faster section and then, still quickening, semitonal disturbances, but with an acute sense of vocal line. The ensuing pastoral movement in the conventional sense (middle shepherd, Pilgrim and soprano bird-off-stage), in F Mixolydian major—as against the rather similar conclusion of Act 3, which is Lydian major with a flattened seventh—achieves, in relief, a remarkable, uncloying serenity, aided by the soprano line for Psalm 23 and the open orchestral texture. Indeed, the disposal of the verse on death in a neat D Dorian minor seems a little casual.

From this point, the narrative may be taken to subsume the more familiar passing of Mr. Valiant-for-Truth (Part 2). Once again, the visionary harmony of the Messenger of Death (new rising and falling phrase, resolving a 1 3 5 7 chord at varied pitches, followed by a fixation on the same chord) is qualified by a comparatively perky modal section for the anointing of Pilgrim. So, with renewed intensity, to the crossing of the stream, as contemplated by the shepherds, now (1951) joined by newcomers, in a brief, closely-woven piece of imitation that eventually simplifies down to the salient phrase over an incompatible, persistent bass. In the original episode, this suspense was resolved in the sound of a kind of joyous *moto perpetuo* in the original key for trumpets and women's voices, off stage, conveying Pilgrim's arrival at the other side. This made a slender but imaginative close. In the full Morality, the scene changes to a veiled but positive view of the celestial citizens and their reception of Pilgrim. A problem for producers.

This mountain scene thus makes a firm pastoral episode in a combination of stoic and more rapt moods. It needs to be revived now and again for its own sake, with its own conclusion.

The use of features from the fifth symphony calls for comment. The E major theme of the first movement accompanies the Evangelist's direction of Pilgrim beyond the wicket-gate, in the first scene, and returns for the Interpreter's welcome in the next scene. The ground-bass of the last movement is recalled, melodically and freely, when Pilgrim is given his room for the night. Much more persuasively, the main progression and oboe motive of the third movement are drawn upon for the establishment of the redeeming atmosphere of the House Beautiful, there being no counterpart to Blake's vision of Christ here. The composer had apparently no misgivings about this kind of self-quotation, in spite of the awful example of the intrusion of 'Nimrod' in *The Music Makers*. I must admit that I find the slight allusions to known themes of established works as distracting as bits of folk-tune elsewhere. Quotations must be critical or fantastic.

The steady incursion of the slow-movement motive is a more serious cross-reference. It raises the question, is this theme intended for a symphony or for a stage scene? It cannot be both. If it is musically self-sufficient, it will suffer from being given an intense semantic setting. If it was composed for this scene, it will be somewhat enigmatic in a symphony. It was previously suggested that the symphonic movement should be heard free of the allusion to this scene, originally attached to it in the score. It is equally desirable that the scene should be received in its own context, and that the composer's advice, 'If you are asked, "Isn't this the fifth symphony?" say "Yes"', should be emended by the addition, 'But this is the House Beautiful.' Bach (cantatas 110, 146, 169) is no authority for such bland translations.

Nor can one accept at all literally the suggestion of Mr. Deryck Cooke (*The Listener*, April 7, 1960) that *Pilgrim's Progress* is a glossary of the emotional associations of melodic and other terms developed, not only in the fifth but also in the fourth and sixth symphonies, and partially confirmed in the *Sinfonia antartica*. A symphony is a communication in the concert-room, and its basic material is not made more significant to the listener from having acquired dramatic associations later. These need not last.

The pivotal use in the Prologue, final scene and Epilogue of the psalm-tune known in Hart's Psalter (Edinburgh, 1615, etc.) as 'the Stilt' and in the Psalters of Ravenscroft (1621) and Playford (1671, etc.) as 'York', merits separate discussion. One of the dozen short and general tunes devised for the common metre of psalm-versification in the Scottish psalter, it was assigned by Ravenscroft to five psalms, by Playford to seven more, by various modern hymnals to selected or conflated verses of six more. Each of these eighteen is different. While, then, the striding, incisive intonation, which earned the tune its first title and early popularity, and its common rejection in the nineteenth century, has the right persistence for the burning vision of the allegory, the tune has no generally accepted collocation of text, and, with such an ending, can hardly be described as an outstanding tune in itself. Its joyous orchestral return as Pilgrim joins the elect is thus arbitrary, and apt to sound pompous, and its echoing phrases in support of the closing appeal of Bunyan to the audience to heed his message do not ring pertinently. There is something so derivative about the whole conception of salvation through *York* as to weaken the finish.

Again one can hear the protest, 'If traditional melody will not do here, nothing else can save the situation', and disagree. Here what might have been an acceptable passing recollection of the opening scene (as in *Meistersinger*) is overwhelmed with more ceremony than it was ever meant to take. It might be added that the instrumental appearance of a chorale, *tutti*, as accessory to life-renouncing strings in the cantata, *Es ist nicht Gesundes*, is a solecism in Bach, and that there and elsewhere the doctrinal or emotional allusion is well pointed. *York* appears as the subject of *Laetatus sum* (Psalm 122), the second of John Gardner's *Cantiones sacrae* for soprano, chorus and orchestra (1952), following a fantasia on *Ein' feste Burg*. The dedication of the piece to Leonard Hancock, who conducted the first performances of the Morality, reflects a direct postscript. The phrase-by-phrase treatment for the new text acquires a florid polyphony and harmonic piquancy of its own. But *York* remains what it is, a common-measure-tune calling for a good hymn.

It remains to comment on the general structural impact of the four acts. The first moves from a provocatively documentary start to a state of tension for the beginning of the dream-journey, which the first scene maintains, but the second scene and the optional nocturne-interlude are entirely contemplative. In the first scene of Act 2, similarly, the boister-ously hymnal and otherwise cantabile arming of Pilgrim is ritual and mainly solemn. The terrors of the descent into the valley of Humiliation for Scene 2—the blackening shades of the precipices, the flaming pit besides the hardly discernible path, the bones of the giant's victims— are barely envisaged, still less amplified, and the struggle with Apollyon briefly despatched; after that, more serial contemplation, emotionally in a straight line. The Fair scene of Act 3, if scarcely the nightmare scherzo of the work, is a thorough jolt to this hieratic frame of mind; but appended to it is the introspective movement for Pilgrim, in and out of prison, in melancholy distraction and then once more jogging along, treading spiritual air. Act 4 is, apart from the wayward By-ends episode, meditative throughout Scene 1, the entracte, and the richer and more integrated Scene 2, up to the crisis of Pilgrim's passing; the anointing being, once more, sacramental. The crisis stirringly and briefly envisaged, the transcendent world is broadly but unexpansively revealed in glowing but not glittering music. It remains to make the return to documentary in the epilogue as uplifting as the missionary test is urgent; for which the opening of *York* carries the main impulse.

Despite the clarity of artistic intention, there is a struggle for expression, and too often the result is not only dramatically static but musically unadventurous to a degree. Coming to this work from the grip of the sixth symphony, at once appalling and, in the finale, rapt, one cannot but miss those qualities which hold the attention in one movement and in another add point to what has gone before. (In the article cited, Mr. Cooke stresses the flat handling of material previously developed more effectively in the symphonies—apparently from too long cerebration.) Here, arresting punctuation is confined to brief hints in the Apollyon and shepherds scenes, and to simple choral declamation and modal formulae in the last. To whatever degree one shares Bridges's rejection (Essay, 1904) of Bunyan's scheme of soul-saving and its correspondingly inhuman theology, or, alternatively, embraces for its own sake the reformatory message, it is left to the music to make it worth while; to conceal any suggestion that by this route the Christian warrior is so much surrounded by protectors that he has hardly a quality to call his own, and, positively, to match the allegory with a coherent musical symbolism. Apart from the Fair scene, an obvious foil to the work as a whole, the musical level cannot but be regarded as uneven, and marked by raw moments whose inadequacy deepens as the work proceeds. To try to maintain that this work of presumed high intention found its fulfilment at last is to assume that the long pondered must be the good, and to ignore the standard of contemporary efforts. The Morality must be set down as patchy, although worth an occasional revival for the wonderful serenity of certain moments of moral elation, not found elsewhere.

To some listeners these may mean more; but I am reluctant to admit that particular music is mystical or rouses a mystical state of being. Spiritual communion, rising to direct apprehension, may stir a composer to creation, but it cannot constitute the matter of his art. Music admits of degrees of intensity, and if the highest class puts the audience completely in tune with itself, in a dedicated situation, what more the listener gives to his experience is his concern. Some listeners are taken out of themselves by a certain type of jazz, others by incense-laden music of varying context—from *Parsifal* to *The Apostles* and the House Beautiful scene, others by the asceticism of a simple setting like *On Christmas Night* or 'Come, the way' (Herbert), or of a primitive-sounding progression, as in 'King of Kings' (*Sancta Civitas*) or the introduction to *Job*; others, again, by an overwhelming, uncensored accumulation of impressions in a broadly symphonic order, as in the concluding portions of the Creeds of the Bach and Beethoven Mass-music (in D and B flat respectively). Each of these phenomena have crystallized by an encounter of burning musical imagination with calm critical construction in face of a literary situation. To declare any particular example as mystical is arbitrary, and conveys no clear distinction.

The passing of Mr. Valiant-for-Truth (Part 2) is absorbed, we suggested, in that of Pilgrim. But around 1942 the composer wrote a short and specific setting for chorus of what has come to be the best remembered event in the double journey. By an experienced blend of solo-recitation and choral phrase for the main symbolic narrative, the composer reaches the supreme stage. A simple perpetual canon of tenor and treble establishes a continuum of steadily echoing phrases and pulsating metre, evoking a unanimous cadential phrase for 'sounded for him', declaimed three times. A turn of key, unexpected without being extreme (B flat to G major, echoed later at the opening of *Thanksgiving for Victory*), recognizes the transcendent note of the text. The spoken word is impressive enough here, but the intimacy of this choral intonation will always be valued on the right occasion, linked, perhaps, with a thought for the composer who probed thus far, together with the resolute of all classes and periods, remembered by nations or by the few.

HODIE

Job and *Pilgrim's Progress* pursue didactic routes in unusual directions. The cantata *Hodie* (a more convenient reference than the first title, *This Day*) is a straight choral work, using the now recurrent convention of a multiple text, as in *Dona nobis pacem*, but with several breaks in the sixteen numbered movements, so that the works falls into ten sections of prologue, interlude, and epilogue, and combinations of plain gospel narrative with reflective movements. They succeed as follows. (1) Choral prologue: *Hodie Christus natus est* (Vespers). (2) Narration (trebles, tenor, and chorus): a message for Mary and Joseph. Soprano solo (and S.A. chorus): Milton, *Nativity* hymn, verses 1, [3], 4, 5. (3) Narration: the birth in a Bethlehem manger. Chorale: Coverdale, 'Now blessed be thou' (see p. 221), verses 2, 5, 7. (4) Narration (trebles and chorus): a message for the shepherds. (5) Interlude (baritone solo): 'Christmas Eve' (Hardy). (6) Narration (trebles and S.S. chorus): the shepherds respond. Baritone solo: 'The shepherds sing' (Herbert). (7) Narration: Mary's response. Air for S.A. chorus: 'Sweet was the song' (W. Ballet). (8) Interlude (tenor solo): 'Bright portals of the sky' (Drummond). (9) Narration (trebles and chorus): wise men from the east. Chorus: 'From kingdoms of wisdom' (Ursula Wood). Chorale: 'No sad thought' (anonymous and Ursula Wood). (10) Epilogue (baritone, tenor, chorus): *John*, 1. 1–14 and Milton, *Nativity* hymn, verses 13, 12, 15. (My numbering, which will be observed below.)

The music thus alternates between close collocation, in direct contact or at one remove, with the familiar narrative and a more remote and independent evocation, to a text ranging from Hardy and Milton back to John. In spirit, then, this is oratorio, and in fact is clearly designed to frame the intermittent narrative, as Bach, much more loosely and expansively, and with the most insouciant transferences from 'homage' works, put together parts 1, 2, 3, 5 and 6 of what is known as his *Christmas Oratorio* round the same general text, with some additional verses on Herod's reactions. For this call to worship, or to a condition of worship in an active life, Bach relies on a well-placed chorale-verse, one supreme narrative-chorus ('Glory to God'), exuberant opening choruses of varying dignity, a sustained but derivative lullaby, and a didactic arioso or two. The rest is conventional and usually borrowed aria, bringing the 'cantata' for each day in the festival to its appointed length, as vernacular Gospel-music for the Lutheran Mass, without fuss but rarely with any sense of majestic instancy.

In *Hodie* one is soon aware of compressed utterance, of a somewhat fanciful literary variety. On the radio, without a text to point the fresh turns of thought, the work may even seem scrappy at first hearing. Only when the literary scheme is assimilated will the conciseness be appreciated as a judicious balance of the lightly lyrical or picturesque and of true concentration. There are, on the one hand, two plain chorale-type movements ('Choral' is ambiguous here), a choral lullaby and an equally soothing naturalistic piece (2), three songs of worship and praise (5, 6, 8), and a general salute to the wise men. Of these, the 'chorales' are in fact settings of carol-like, strophical tunes in a restrained major-key texture. The first is set to Coverdale's rendering of verses 2, 5, 7 of 'Gelobet seist du', of which verse 6 appears in Bach's first cantata with a similar intention of underlining Christ's humble birth. Vaughan Williams's plain tune, without any disturbing accidental, identifies the first two verses in melodic, rhythmic, and harmonic progression sufficiently to point to the third as more expansive, for alert ears. The second tune exploits an oscillation of third, fourth and seventh degree in the major scale to flattened, sharpened, and flattened variants, and then these lapses spread to other degrees, resulting in a piquantly characteristic style as Parry understood the term, rather precious and reminiscent of Warlock but a timely reaction from the Dorian mode collocated with the forward march of the wise men.

Of the airs, the soprano-setting of Milton's opening is an exquisite essay in a forgotten pastoral style, with the war-verse as a break between

Ex. 48

two free but flowing strophes, whose mettle is stronger than it might seem. The celesta is one of many links between this and the second movement of *Flos Campi*. The Hardy setting handles with a dignified economy an appalling piece of whimsy and might well be omitted. The next air, again for baritone, is a shapely expansion of Herbert's homely text, again in pastoral style. The choral lullaby has a salient major-key curve (8 6 1 2 3) which echoes the Kipling song in *Thanksgiving* but in favour of the present serene piece. The interplay of voices and instruments, and chorus and soloist, keeps the sense of progression fresh, and the sheer gratefulness of the writing grips the ear, homely as is the style. The tenor solo, actually an after-thought to encourage an otherwise inactive tenor, breaks away from this towards something more tense, sonorous (with full brass, chime-bells, cymbals and slithering harp tone at the climax) and unpredictable, not least in key. The salient feature is a revolving flow of chords, two to the beat, chiefly of asymmetrical fifths (perfect, sharpened, flattened). This establishes different keys in turn, in keeping with the opening doors of the poem. The free return of the first strophe for the third verse keeps the song from growing diffuse, but it is more an arioso than an aria, and it will take a fine singer (and trumpeter) to rise above Drummond's flamboyant phrases.

The ride of the wise men may at first recall the march of the veterans in *Dona nobis pacem*. Anyhow, the start is demonstrably based on a primitive rising intonation (1 4 5 7). The expansion of this into an orchestral refrain forms the main impulse for the opening and closing choral strophes, which are divided by a more coloured setting of the middle stanzas of Ursula Wood's extended text. There is something raw about these primitive and recurrent phrases (Ex. 49). When it comes to judging this as romantic art, no one can miss the message of the march, of the call for the toughest effort of mind for the basic needs of a bare, grey world. Yet the spontaneity of this return to a neo-modal idiom hardly survives the pomp of reprise.

Ex. 49*a*

These seven movements space out the narrative-pieces, most of which rely on plain intonation in a modal style that embraces frequent changes of key, while three grow into distinct movements. The prologue introduces the narrative with a short but pronounced chorus. This, without using the traditional plainsong as Britten does in the *Ceremony of Carols*, at once defines the character of the work and introduces, along with jubilant phrases—recalling the burst of *Noel* entries in G. M. Nanini's polyphonic *Hodie*—motives to convey the greater glory to be revealed; one for *Gloria*, two for *Alleluia*. All are marked by a sharpened

Ex. 49b

Ex. 49c

fourth. The *Gloria* motive consists of a plain Lydian major curve (5–3–5 ♯4), with the accent on the distinctive fourth degree. The first *Alleluia* curve has actually a flattened seventh, marking a scale anticipated

Ex. 50

in *Sancta Civitas* ('Therefore are they before the throne') but not here leaning on the seventh. The second *Alleluia*, similarly, includes a flattened sixth and so may recall 'Heaven and Earth' in the same work to sharp ears, but again this sixth is incidental, as it has been already in earlier *Hodie* phrases, and the melody is pure Lydian. The total effect of this detail, displayed in four metres (a lively six-beats, the three of a tedesca or waltz, the solemn three of *Alleluia*, the brisk two of *Alleluia*), is to contrive a special melodic and harmonic texture, pronouncedly unclassical but, like some folk-music, not rigidly bound to one formula. Thus unobtrusively *This Day* proclaims a fresh freedom of utterance in a movement totalling under 160 bars.

The first narrative-piece adds two more pivotal themes: one for the inner voice to strengthen Joseph's resolve, the other for the continuing revelation of the nature of the child to come. The first of these, subdued for the tenor solo, reappears as the semitonal bass formula for an ecstatic choral 'Emmanuel' (see Ex. 52 below). The second, preceded by a mysterious oscillation of semitones, is a nondescript Dorian curve (1 5–6|7 4–5|6) but recurs later. The soprano-solo number which follows adds a fifth and more extended motive, already cited (Ex. 48).

Thus the main narrative begins well equipped. For the announcement of the birth of Christ, Vaughan Williams has, as comment, his first carol-tune. (Bach has chorales before and after the narrative.) For the shepherds' scene, the repetition of the earlier suggestions of inner message correlate the shepherds' experience with Joseph's, and inevitably *Gloria* (now in English) follows. With it return the *Alleluia* themes, now set to the words of peace and goodwill and, for renewed

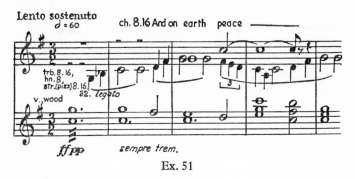

Ex. 51

and more dynamic impact, of the following sentences in the Communion Service. The *Gloria* music echoes in the shepherds' response, now subdued but ornamented with celesta support and clarinet coloratura. At the Wise Men's rejoicing, the organ starts up a flowing chordal figure to accompany an ornamental treble line to the end.

In the Epilogue, the composer returns to the two themes for the message to Joseph, the second (the modal one) appearing first, adding its grave tone to *John*. The remaining theme comes once more to a head, but instead of cadencing on C as before (A♭–E–C, in brief), turns to an exultant G major, already marked as the key of the angelic *Tedesca*, for the revival of the main tune of the earlier Milton setting. There are three more tremendous verses: 13, 12, 15. Verse 13 ('Ring out') comes inevitably first here, 12 follows reasonably, and 15 ('Yea, truth and justice then') frames the climax of this Christmas oratorio, as a present call to a tragically sundered and ill-assorted world to respond committally and resolutely to a vision of world-order, not in the heavens, but established by agreement among men. This, at least, is the most obvious interpretation of the tumultuous finish. Other listeners may dwell more on the condition of worship, to which the homely, jubilant, grave, joyous, philosophic phrases and sections aspire, as well as the Gospel narrative shared with Bach. Yet the composer's final return to Milton's lyrical and outspoken verses leaves it beyond doubt that for him the chain of evocations which began with the quasi-ritual celebration of Christmas (*allegro giocoso* in the first sketch) must lead performers and audience to come out of themselves and into the world and its discords, and to come spontaneously.

In some such communal context, the revived song, though recognizable in its stanzas, is reconditioned for massive and cumulative delivery.

Ex. 52

The first verse is in choral harmony, marked by a general note of reverberation in the attending voices. The second verse (whose reference to *Job*, 38. 7, links this work in spirit with the Pavane of the ballet) is straightened out in a broad outline with a tremulous, harmonically mysterious cadence. The third verse appears mainly in choral and orchestral unison, with a blunt, percussive counterpoint, many notes thick; each verse being given a tumultuous send-off of bells and other melodious noise-makers, to the tune of the salient pattern (D–B–E–D)

of the first and third verses, readily diverted into extraneous regions at
the penultimate stage.

What was a delicate lyric at the early, fanciful stage has become a
surge of enthusiastic melody, unanimous, a little more deliberate than
at first and increasingly emphatic. No amount of sympathy for the
message of this music can make the theme any stronger for the burden
of percussion that is now placed upon it. This is, indeed, a critical

Ex. 53

moment, which only fine phrasing and balance will save from a lack of
inner vitality. Granted these, the composer's purpose will be fulfilled.
The early association between the Emmanuel music and the serene
strophes of Milton's opening verses makes its confirmation a just
answer to the ecstasy of the prelude and its themes. After the directness of this translation of Milton's stanzas, thus selected and separated
by other matter, the setting of the same verses in the centre of C. B.
Rootham's choral rendering of the whole ode seems laboured for all its
fervent lines and glowing contrast of key.

A clear and coherent impact of evangelical music, then, is blended with miscellaneous reflections, two or three of which are on a different level from the rest, without impairing the general effect, since their function is episodic, picturesque or fanciful. In spite of its fresh text, the 'heavy' music for the homage of the wise men seems misplaced, so near the epilogue. The upshot is an obviously compact and not so obviously revealing work. It matches Bach's six-fold formula with an integrity of its own, while sharing with the German composer certain methods of concerted approach to the common text. Its wider outlook should carry it beyond the pious homes, where Christmas celebration is chiefly an intimate, ceremonial recollection, to re-animate the resolution of men and women devoted to the tasks of promoting settlement and other grave issues.

From the early carol fantasia, part introspective and part joyously extravert, to this late cantata, Vaughan Williams has shown a concern that music shall carry emblems of renewed hope and effort, but also of inner vision, among those who call themselves sons of God and brothers in Christ, and among those, too, who wait for enlightenment, uncommitted. As the fantasia handles plain country tunes with the skill of a trained musician, so *Hodie* blends plainsong and homely phrase with contemporary harmony and the waywardly archaic. *Sancta Civitas* had shown the need for new idioms to delineate strange states of being, not to be described. *Job*, much more worldly in spite of its rejection of ballet as a title, keeps a place for the all-sufficient melody, as well as for the music which proclaims rebellion from the depths of its nature. Such melody establishes itself as a valid rejoinder to, or triumphant replacement of, other matter; not as a concession to human weakness and assumed craving for serenity. The rejoinders of *Pilgrim's Progress* are less persuasive, or over-rehearsed: and the rebellions sound contrived or downright weak. It was left to *Hodie* to restore the sense of deep disturbance which unites *Joseph* and the rest with *Job*. No other composer has so firmly held in solution the divine and satanic elements.

Such has been the progress of Vaughan Williams on the difficult path of that affirmation which is not ultimately exposed as having been made at the expense of music. This progress does not display the recurrent pattern of a normal musical genre. There is nothing like Bach's familiar signals of revealing hymn-tune background (*York* has no background today) and suggestive texture; nor, as in Bach, a clear development of working methods of instrumental refrain and vocal fugue to meet difficult situations with established patterns. On the contrary, nothing could suggest more the unfathomable character of the world of the spirit, in tune with Blake the artist in one way, with Bunyan in another, and with Milton in another again. Yet an imaginative reception will always try to unite deliverances, so clearly referred to one tenor, despite their several levels of probing quality. In varying degrees of mental tautness, these three works together provide an illumination of the spirit's ceaseless shaping of intractable routes.

XIII

Three More Symphonies

SINFONIA ANTARTICA (NO. 7)

The sixth symphony showed that Vaughan Williams was not 'mellowing'. On the contrary, if difficult moods pressed on his awareness and prevailed, they must be entertained for their truth's sake. If discords rushed in, they were admitted in their own right, not 'that harmony should be prized'. The next symphonic stage was equally uncompromising. If it shows some relaxation, this lies chiefly in the concern for balanced structure. The seventh symphony—as *Sinfonia antartica* might just as well have been entitled, to save one more later effort of calculating the symphonic order by inference from the official four (4, 5, 8, 9)—shows structurally a wayward continuity in the five movements, all clearly referred to some aspect of Captain Scott's last expedition. A recurrent feeling that selected extracts, some a direct echo of the film *Scott of the Antarctic*, some an imaginative aftermath, have been pasted together, rather than having compelled their present sequence, raises the question of symphonic status, and indeed of formal status in general. The eighth symphony begins with 'variations without a theme'; that is, a series of loosely linked orchestral strophes. After that, there is no structural development more elaborate than that of contrast and reprise, and the vibraphone and other 'noises' are exploited. The ninth symphony similarly relaxes grip in the middle movements, the Scherzo being overwhelmed with episodic turns. The finale links two movements rather oddly. The composer continues to write without apparently troubling, so much as earlier, about the sum of his assembled motives and movements. There is no sign of his making earlier, structural innovations an integral principle, as in

380

SINFONIA ANTARTICA (No. 7)

Sibelius's seventh symphony, or an approach to a wider orbit, as in Beethoven's ninth. The tabulating mind has to be content with the heading of this chapter.

The seventh symphony is, for the informed listener, somewhat heavily documented at the outset. Not only is the development of the motto theme derived, with many other motives, from the music for the film *Scott of the Antarctic* (1948). The movements are furnished with texts which, ranging from *Prometheus Unbound* to Captain Scott's final diary, relate the whole work to the inflexible spirit of Scott's last journey, and particular movements to a medley of poetic evocations. The symphony has to be disentangled from these associations. It is epic in spirit and contains unmistakable biographical and geological references. Yet it remains, potentially at least, a symphony.

Let us consider for a moment the original film music, to which I shall return in the following chapter. In a review of a 'noble and, in parts, grandiose score' (*Music Review*, 10. 2 (May, 1949); substantially transferred to an entry in *Grove's Dictionary of Music and Musicians*, *s.v.* 'Film Music'), Hans Keller comments on two features: the excessive economy of the music, and the provocative juxtaposition of tragic pieces and others which border on triviality; of the significant and the negligible. Keller holds that the emphasis of the motto-theme was misconceived in relation to the film's obsession with the long and bitter journey, since monotony multiplied by monotony can only result in the exaltation of a formula that is not really needed. Finally, in texture, the *Scott* music shows an influence that can cause no surprise: that of the first and second movements of the sixth symphony.

This exposure of certain limitations in Vaughan Williams's finest film-music has a considerable bearing, with obvious modifications, on the listener's problems in the seventh symphony. Assuming that the work is concerned with the lasting triumphs of Scott's achievement, one can understand that, in the absence of the film, the 'titles'-theme which was used later for the attack on the glacier, was the obvious clue-theme to resume in the symphony; not the final transcendent major theme, a transformation of the basic motive that could only strike home once and is here confined to the end of the first movement; nor the magnificently evocative tramping theme of the return from the Pole, too tense and self-contained a strophe to be capable of symphonic use. Moreover, the studied variety of the middle three movements and, in part, the last, called for some sort of reprise. Yet there is something obstinate and strained about the manner in which the titles-music reappears, almost in full, at the penultimate stage, reaffirming the opening, but sounding much less relevant than the epilogues of the second and fourth symphonies.

Secondly, the juxtaposition of heroic and atmospheric music is disconcerting. Neither Beethoven nor Strauss made this confusion in their accounts of the superman. While there is not much borrowing from the purely descriptive film music—the penguin motive is the chief —the divertissement touch is apparent and embarrassing both to symphonically inclined ears and to listeners who recognize the film allusions. 'Sinfonia antartica' hardly warns the listener to expect a symphonic poem. The strength of the true symphony lies in its power to absorb incidents and encounters like 'storm' finales, minuets that are almost an actual dance, and odd movements that try more to describe than to express. But not even Beethoven's *Pastoral* tests the listener's musical adaptability beyond one movement, there the Scherzo. In the present symphony, the visual and psychological method pulls much more at the ear. Even Ernest Irving considered the work 'a symphonic poem rather than a symphony' (*Cue for Music*, p. 176).

The air of fancy is enhanced by the texts of each movement. In a current gramophone record these extracts, all the work of poets except for Scott, are recited with studied restraint by Sir John Gielgud, but, whether or not this had the approval or consent of the composer, it appears to me a most disturbing procedure, quite apart from the dissociation of the third and fourth movements (interrupting the trumpet's transition from a held F sharp to F natural) to make way for Donne; Pakenham anticipates my reaction. In any case, the harnessing of each of the five movements to these divergent scraps of verse is more provocative than directive.

The reader-listener is thus presented with the following scheme: (1) Prelude: Andante maestoso. 'To suffer woes which hope thinks infinite ... life, joy, empire, and victory' (seven lines). (2) Scherzo: Moderato. 'There go the ships and there is that Leviathan . . .' (*Psalm* 104. 26). (3) Landscape: Lento. 'Ye ice-falls! . . . Silent cataracts!' (five lines scraped from Coleridge's *Hymn before Sunrise, in the Vale of Chamouni*[1]). (4) Intermezzo: Andante sostenuto. 'Love all alike, no season knows nor clime . . .' (two lines from Donne, *The Sun Rising*). (5) Epilogue:

---

[1] A pretentious and derivative religious poem on the lines of *Job* 38; not at all a text for the challenge of the ruthless cycle of the ice-barrier, except by complete dissociation of the quoted lines from their later significance. Shelley's *Mont Blanc*, in the same field, would have been more apt, with its pattern of 'unknown omnipotence'.

Alla marcia moderato. 'I do not regret this journey ... things have come out against us, therefore we have no cause for complaint' (Captain Scott's last journal).[1]

Do the movements need these outside promptings ? If so, on the one hand the symphonic impact is somewhat weakened. On the other, the nagging question arises of the equally dubious relation between text and music, in so far as the basic film-music is not now common experience. If one accepts the symphony as a whole as a 'sinfonia eroica', as a translation or amplification of 'man's attempt to conquer nature' (J. S. Weissmann in *The Music Review*, 14. 2 (May, 1953)), this does not take in Prometheus or the psalmist's bland celebration of the divine creation, or Coleridge's, or Donne's aphorism. These must illuminate their music in some other way. To take only the first, one understands the appositeness of *Prometheus*, but what has Shelley's text to do with the vibraphone motive ? Nor does one wish to begin by limiting the motto-theme to resolutions to suffer, forgive and defy. Hence the listener's need for disentanglement. It is far better to forget Prometheus, Leviathan, and the rest and any pictorial and epic associations retained from the film.[2] It is sufficient to recollect that the motto-theme and its derivatives originated in the contemplation of the natural barrier, to conquer which was the historic resolution recognized, by scientists and laymen alike, in the title of the symphony.

The seventh symphony may thus appear, on the romantic level, as a continuation of the explorer ethos of the first, and equally of a Job-like trial, in which to regret decision is the last blasphemy, but it is equally unimaginative to underestimate the ghastly intransigence of opposed forces, or incidentally to miss the strange beauties of outlandish life. It is a poetic answer, as the Scott Polar Institute at Cambridge is the constructive scientific answer, to the despondency which, within living memory, spread from the supporting members of the expedition to the nation at large, at Dr. Atkinson's shattering announcement, 'The Polar Party has not returned'. It is also a musical expansion of Scott's 'No regrets'. But, once this contact has been recognized as the background of a new stress, of a new feeling for experiment and extension in the orchestral medium, the symphony may be apprehended as music, divertissements and all.

---

[1] This quotation significantly replaces the original citation of *Ecclesiasticus*, 44. 14, as the autograph score shows. The symphony ends on a sharp, stoic, philosophic note, not a soft commemorative one.

[2] For a tabulation of this contact, see p. 449.

So regarded, the symphony sets the listener some acute problems of construction. The prelude has to be recognized as in part a prologue to the whole symphony, to be balanced by the last section of the epilogue-finale. The motto-theme (Ex. 54*a*) is followed by a subdued and unanimous semitonal descent in five octaves, developed later by wordless

Ex. 54*a*

Ex. 54*b*

Ex. 54*c*

voices. There is also an ominous fall of fifths, resulting in a 'problem' chord of ♭7 1 ♭3 ♯4 in the middle of the movement. This recurs somewhat menacingly in the last two movements. Otherwise this 'prelude' embarks on a remarkably episodic course, in which the tempo changes slightly at least six times. A vibraphone progression starts up a 'middle section', and the return to the original triple metre for a fanfare incident (a rise of 1 2 5, etc., from the tonic) leads to the glowing presentation of

vibraph., va.,vc.8, v.4

Ex. 54d

trb.8 wood, str.8.16

Ex. 54e

the transcendental version of the main theme, previously used in *Coastal Command* as well as in the close of *Scott*, with its idealist citation of the *Ulysses* lines on the memorial cross on Observation Hill. This makes a reasonable finish for the first movement, though shortened by thirty-one bars (after fig. 15 in the score) from the original draft. It marks a transition from the original E♭–G ambiguity of the motto-theme to a G major never again touched. It remains a romantic structural turn without supporting text, for any thought of 'monument' is premature here, and it is alien to the defiant mood of *Prometheus*. The original ending, after 13. 1 (*niente*), looked to a G major finish later.

The experimental character of this exordium is enhanced by the pursuit of fresh timbres. The tuned percussion includes a vibraphone, a piano to reinforce harp harmony with its own sonority or with sweeping scales, a volatile xylophone, supporting rapidly oscillating chords on the piano, and later celesta arabesques and chime-bells, implementing vibraphone harmony. The extra wind (to a full assembly of twelve wood and eleven brass) includes female voices (soprano solo and small S.S.A. chorus). An invisible 'wind-machine' underlines a roll of drums, completing the first vocal entry. This invasion of the *concrète* style recalls the sea-machine of *Riders to the Sea*. In the symphony its intrusiveness takes some time to accept. A wind-machine may be all right in the comedy of Strauss's *Don Quixote*, but here the confusion of the actual and the imaginative strains the bounds of art. How is the sound produced? At the Edinburgh Festival, 1953, a 'secret device' was used: fifteen horn-players singing in a high falsetto through their instruments. This suggests that there is also a serious practical problem of not making the realism ludicrous. Unless this can be solved, its employment cannot be regarded as essential. In any case, this recurrent suggestion of blizzard is distracting and may defeat its object, like an overworked slogan.

The initial tempo having been *maestoso*, a scherzo sequel is inevitable. Here a lithe phrase, introduced by trumpets and flutes (and clarinets) in neat relays for smooth delivery, holds in its orbit, in turn, a musically negligible and rather grotesque 'whale' motive and a witty motive for the penguins. The Keller stricture does not entirely apply to this wayward but firmly constructed Scherzo, with a nice reminiscence of the trumpets on the violins and a piquant blend of celesta and muted brass to recall the horn opening. All the same, the exploitation of colour knows few limits, and, with such slender material, 'more painting than expression' is the trend. Not that the colouring is casual. In bars 2–4, 6–8 the harp excursions have replaced a roll on the side-drum. The slow movement uses a horn cantabile ('cuivré', i.e. brassy) to enclose an exciting series of incidents; various queer descents of a third in the bass; a mysterious rising unison motive (1 ♭2 5|♭6 5), announced by full strings and wood with the brass in canon, alternating with a noticeable oscillation of plain chords, rising substantively one tone;

Ex. 55

and a laboured lower-string theme. Weissmann stresses, not altogether persuasively, the importance of the unison theme, as prophetic of a new phase; a continuation of Holst's last period, perhaps influenced by the finale of the sixth symphony.

The oscillating chords are eventually released on the full organ (alone), as the outcome of the loud reappearance of the canonic passage. The intention is clearly to reflect the arrest of human effort by the ice barrier. A comparison with the similar use of the organ in *Job*, when Satan is shown enthroned, suggests that the acceptance of this arrest is, to the explorer, the last blasphemy. Instrumentally, the intrusion of the organ is peculiarly sensational. In any event, the return to the horn opening, now on muted trumpets, is a strain on one's sense of proportion. The whole construction is baffling. It is the romanticist's constant problem in a symphony; what to do with a dynamic episode. In the Scherzo of Elgar's second symphony, the solution is, to pack it into the centre of a sonata-rondo pattern (a b–a c b–a), so that the secondary theme follows close on its heels, leading in the inexhaustible principal motive. Here the early bass episode is not strong enough to support this function. The horn-motive, which must recur, is mannered and barely evocative. Its original label was, indeed, 'ice waste—Ross Island' before the composer re-headed it as 'Landscape' for the start of this movement. Hence the call on Coleridge. But in a structural frost poetry is not enough.

However, the music continues in the Intermezzo. Here, again, an oboe motive in the composer's *Flos Campi* style (or even earlier) holds in solution a series of heterogeneous episodes: a short allegretto with a violin solo; a solemn string cantabile, emerging from the ominous falling fifths of the first movement; and, antiphonally with this, a revival of the motto-theme (bars 6–7). A most conglomerate movement, designed apparently to lower the tension before the Epilogue, but too moody to leave more than an impression of restlessness. Lacking the flow of a scherzo, easy symmetry of a minuet or other divertimento type of pre-finale, or the coherent suggestiveness of a late episode in a symphonic poem, this Intermezzo betrays the derivative quality of matter saved from various film contexts, not chosen to connect one movement. The identification of the clue-themes from the film (or the film-score) makes, indeed, no sense of their juxtaposition here, and the musical sum is equally scrappy and spasmodic.

The Epilogue, a misnomer by every precedent, begins with a fresh fanfare, to introduce a resumption of the motto-theme, now in four-metre, expanding the bars (6–7) already recovered in the Intermezzo, with an aftermath of solemn brass in the likeness of the *London Symphony* march. A mysterious cantabile follows in the clarinets. After the bassoon and others have expanded this, and the motto has reissued its terse challenge repetitively, leading to a series of ominous 'noises' and anticipatory gestures, the serious reprise, in the original tempo and key, begins.

How far this ample return 'achieves formal unity' (Weissmann) is doubtful. Materially, it at once balances and resumes the opening strain of the symphony, but, as in the film-music, something more than that is needed to account for the ample recurrence of matter fully developed in its original place; some sense of vacuum, perhaps, which only a resort to the earlier movement will satisfy. In the *London Symphony*, the plenary but quickly exhausted recapitulation of the 'march' leaves just this sense, calling for the reserve power of the prologue of the symphony; and the prologue turned epilogue was twice shortened. It is difficult to account here for the grand reprise of matter so recently and sonorously developed. However, once this is embarked upon, the end is clear: not the unison theme that followed in the prelude, but its vocal projection, here freely expanded. Thus the symphony ends by conflating G with E flat to the last bar, an epitome of the end of a journey but not of resolution; not, incidentally, to be confused with the philosophic calm of E flat with G comfortably below it, as *third* degree, as in the *Sea Symphony*. The wind-machine lends its wails to this final rhapsody, a triumphant finish having been transferred to the prelude.

It would not have been surprising if Vaughan Williams had decided to make a more or less descriptive suite out of the *Scott* film-music, as had been done with *Coastal Command*. Here lay matter which called for some kind of permanent setting, beginning with the magnificent title-music. After the sheer vocalism of the third-symphony finale and of *Flos Campi*, audiences were prepared for the horrific soprano-and-chorus keening, both for its unusual effect and for its vivid suggestion of the pitiless cycles of an ice age that continues to hold dominion, or possibly of a maliciously triumphant Antartica. The composer's straightforward film-setting technique, of juxtaposed sections, precisely timed and yet extendible or compressible by means of a network of optional repeats, left him with a number of short but characteristic 'periods', *some* of which called for wider development or richer contexts of a symphonic order. Nevertheless, while much of this material is apt enough on the borderline of sight and sound, both as naturalistic suggestion and as an amplification of one of the nation's most treasured narratives, it is so much the less symphonic in itself.

The motto-theme is, in repetition, an intelligible and inevitable aural aid of the crucial advance up the glacier, even if its key and content remain fixed. It is less persuasive as a symphonic subject that is pursued outside its own movement. In Elgar's first symphony, the crisp sonata-rondo structure of the finale in D minor—A b A c A b—leaves the coda in just that state of disorganization and impromptu method, in which a third strophe of the motto-tune, totally abandoned since the first movement except for a passing allusion in the introduction to the present movement, and restoring A flat at last, is the only finish possible. Vaughan Williams's finale reaches the impromptu stage clearly enough, but the recurrence of the motto-tune strikes the ear as a ceremonial close, rather than a long awaited fulfilment. Only the vocal sequel, being more detached and ethereal, returns without any sense of satiety. To this extent the cyclic ending reaches a true convergence of mood, in 'epilogue' style—in the last twenty bars.

The second most impressive feature of the symphony is, as Weissmann hints, the canonic unison theme and the oscillating chords (Ex. 55), which, drawn from the grim ascent of the Beardmore glacier, form the memorable centre of the third movement. Yet these, too, though developed, or rather repeated, for their own sake are utterly episodic or non-generative by nature. The stark, full-organ version of the second seems to admit this. The parallel passage in *Job*, where evil is seen diabolically triumphant, is similarly no more than the terse and ponderous statement of an earlier and comparatively trite semitonal descent, associated with Satan's destructive power, but not structurally important.

This leaves, mainly, the Scherzo, the Intermezzo and the non-committal first section of the Epilogue, all film-based in material and all wayward structures, scantily parcelled up (even the last) by a final reprise. Their dubious symphonic impression confirms obvious apprehensions over this film-into-symphony. The epic programme contained in the preliminary texts may be a mask for certain anomalies in the structure, but no words can be a substitute for musical necessities. Defensive comments on the 'universal qualities' of the symphony, and so forth, do not face the music and its wayward course.

A conductor, then, who includes this work in a normal orchestral concert has a great deal to account for, however impeccable his command of orchestral balance, tempo-variation, and other necessities. No one can miss the nobility of the initial conception, or the passing fascinations of certain passages, but a symphony demands more than good intentions. The elaborate literary and historical trappings, which beguile the readily conditioned listener and will ensure regular performance, in the fortification of the morale of a nation prone to celebrate defeats as victories, have made a true estimate difficult to unravel in words. Nevertheless, the standard of the earlier symphonies forbids the classification of this *sinfonia* on the same level of sustained musicianship.

THREE MORE SYMPHONIES

Symphony No. 8 in D Minor

Symphony No. 8 in D minor (*sic*) has its eccentricities, but is a straight-forward four-movement appeal to the ear in its own terms. These terms may be summarized as a quiet confidence in the mood or texture of the moment, provided it leads to other encounters in some degree or other. The first movement, called Fantasia, is the longest and most developed. Its perky sub-title, 'Variazoni senza Tema', has been anticipated in Malipiero's light-hearted and elastic 'variation'-sequence, in seven tempi, for piano and orchestra (1923), a typical demonstration of association by contrast, not thematic variation; piquant but trifling. The present Variazoni amount to a miniature series of symphonic variations. The second movement, reserved for the wind, is a witty but rather slight *alla marcia* gambol, with an interlude and reprise of under thirty bars each. The sequel, assigned to strings, is a short but shapely movement that adds more than a revived interest in mode to its cantabile strains. The finale is a diversionary movement with a pattern of melodic assertion that is too blatantly pronounced for some ears, in D major.

Thus, the work has not the intense absorption in its themes, characteristic of the middle symphonic period. Yet the imagery is a good deal more comprehensive than might appear on the surface of one hearing, and with one's awareness crowded out by the oscillations and jingles of certain accessory instruments. Indeed, 'still a frightening sense of duality' is one passing comment at the head of a comprehensive article by Mr. Hugh Ottaway (*Music and Letters*, 38. 3 (July, 1957)), which can be recommended as the most perceptive review of a Vaughan Williams symphony in print, and will be the main source of critical reference here. A symphony so suggestive, in its chosen moments, cannot be lightly dismissed because it lent weight, but not superiority, to the final Saturnalia of London's 1957 Promenade Season.[1] It has its fixations, but never degenerates into a divertimento. Nor is it so lacking in a sense of continuity as to justify the half-approval of 'symphonic suite', assigned to it by one reviewer.

The orchestra may be summarized as Schubertian with unusually full percussion, including the normal untuned percussion, celesta, xylophone, vibraphone, six tubular bells and, an afterthought, three gongs *après Turandot*; almost *sinfonia orienta*.

---

[1] Those who have never attended these final Promenade Concerts should realize that the now customary 'demonstrations' are strictly confined to the moments between musical items.

The Fantasia is made up of eight separate sections, clearly defined by changes of tempo. The composer does not recognize the last as independent, but in its succinct style it re-establishes the opening tempo and theme in all its piquancy. The various sections shrink progressively and elusively from an average of fifty bars in the opening variations (1–3) to shorter interludes (4–5) and a still shorter concluding group (6–8), but they show broadly the common measure of a strophe, though not to be expressed in any simple terms of balancing phrases; less so than, for example, Schoenberg's *Variations for Orchestra*, at their initial stage. There is also a recurrent relation between, on the one hand, a

Ex. 56a

Ex. 56b

Ex. 56c

Ex. 56d

Ex. 56e

serial and casual ascent of rising fourths to a dominant note of reference (D, G, E, A, varied by D, G, E flat, A flat; *aliter* D, G, E flat, A natural by comparison, but now in a different key), and, on the other hand, a conjunct but semitonal descent, usually multiple in texture and con-

Ex. 56*f*

Ex. 56*g*

Ex. 56*h*

veying tension. To this extent the impression of a series, founded on the *aba* pattern sketched in the opening strophe, is conveyed, as in Elgar's *Enigma Variations*.

The order of procedure can thus be summarized and distinguished as (1) Moderato, (2) Presto, (3) Andante, (4) Allegretto, (5) Andante non troppo, (6) Allegro vivace, (7) Andante largamente, (8) Tempo primo. Six beats prevail in variations 1, 2, 4, 6, 8, four in 3, 5, 7. Var. 6–7 and 8 are thus readily identifiable as reverberations of 2–3 and 1. But there the strophical pull of the Fantasia stops. From the second sub-movement onwards, it becomes clear that the composer is concerned to develop each motive freely, not according to any established principle of repartee; and, by a suitable deceleration of the descending theme, he is able to maintain the fusion of the two motives in a loose weave of texture.

The third variation follows rather awkwardly after a rest of one-sixth of a beat plus one beat, each in a different tempo, so that the new rhythm is obscure. The predominance of the upper strand is now stabilized melodically and concentrated in the key of C major, and thus there is a suggestion of a 'second subject', which the composer, in his programme notes, identifies with a chuckle over his academic correctness of behaviour, as if there were magic in a pattern.

It is, however, downright confusion of substance to speak of 'sonata form' in connection with such homogeneous, cumulative material. There is no sense at this stage of that complementary, repeatable factor, which marks a true second subject. It is one more serial accretion. Whether the earlier descending phrase (8 ♭7 ♭6 5) can be said to lead to the new outline (♮3 2 1), is doubtful. Ottaway dismisses the idea; but the fall by conjunct steps prepares for it contrapuntally. In any event, the variation approximates to the absorbed type of harmonic progression, attached to a fall from the third degree of the major scale, noticeable in earlier slow-movement themes (symphonies 1 and 2) and episodes, especially a rejected episode of the finale of the original *London Symphony* (see p. 203). The escape to the major strikes me as facile rather than 'eloquent' (Ottaway), and it is scarcely 'chorale-like' (R. V. W.).

Its serenity serves, at least, to expose the next two variations as in the nature of a development, variation five (Ex. 56*d*, 56*h*) being more dreamy than the third, and marked by that circling round a pitch in multiple texture that dates from the *Tallis Fantasia*. Significantly, it begins in E major, but becomes distracted. The sixth variation thus makes an impression, described by the composer as a 'perversion' of the original descending phrase, of a more than terse revision of the second variation, and the sequel (after another jerky start) is indubitably an expansion 'on a larger and more grandiose scale' of the third, in two keys, B flat and D major. This solemn return achieves a characteristic dignity and poignancy, owing to the underlying and basic flattened fifth and sixth degrees, but its warmth of manner ('this great affirmative passage' to Ottaway) is apt to sound strained. After it, a brief recourse to the opening fourths, without any rejoinder, except on the part of a returning vibraphone, is a nice touch.

In this suite of separate miniature movements, then, whose general connection and echoing phrases no alert listener would deny, the composer has contrived to bring together a singularly rich succession of musical facets, for which symphonic is the only name. There are the wayward, neo-modal trends of the opening, fourth and last variations, the biting humour of the second and sixth, the earnest melody of the third and seventh, and the leisurely meditativeness of the fifth. Elgar's masterly *Variations* afford some parallel for the swift turns of mood on a common bi-thematic basis. Here the changes of texture are more subtle and elusive, but no less penetrating, once assimilated. Rawsthorne's *Symphonic Studies* (1938) are a demonstration, with two themes, of a freer method of transformation and extension.

The genetically minded might like to compare the early set of sixteen didactic variations on a flexible Dorian set-bass, called 'Pretty ways: for young beginners to look on' (from a well-known handwritten collection in the British Museum[1]). Here lies a precedent of an at first rigid six-bar measure which stretches nicely, by rhythmic reorganization, to eight bars for six variations (9–14) before snapping back to the cut-and-dried pattern. There is even a suggestion of melodic interest midway (var. 9). So much can be had of a plain bass-outline in search of varied readings, as a prelude to this enigma of a hidden strophe, part bass, part sequence, part fugal potential, part descant, part instrumental antiphony, yet integrally none of these.

This reference to a variation-work of seemingly early Tudor period points bluntly the listener's problem in co-ordinating the stages of alteration on the compressed scale of presentation. One can, for instance, recognize the chime-bells as necessary reinforcements of the flutes in the second variation, and the triangle and side-drum as expedient accessories to the vibratory, pivotal, virtual monotone of the strings in the sixth, but what has such persistence to do with the vibraphone and celesta concertante in the opening and close? Ottaway points out the essential character of the 'luminous and watery quality' of the vibraphone for the swaying chords, and the celesta fills in the gaps with its own special type of brittle but precisely toned arpeggio. It is as absurd to object to these instruments in their place, as it was for Gounod to condemn Franck's cor anglais as 'unsymphonic'. Or what about the drum-roll of Haydn's 103 in E flat? Vaughan Williams's first variation being exploratory, and the last dimly reminiscent, these preludial features are quite consistent with the probing piquancy of the sequel. It is just in this sense that the opening is not a 'theme' but an excursion; a development of intimations which proves to be the first of a series, rather than their ground-plan. A distinctly shaped series, it

---

[1] Additional MS. 29,996, transcribed by Hugh Miller in *Musical Quarterly*, 33, pp. 555–6.

allows of some repetition, as in the tremendous thirty of Brahms 4; but let us admit no ready allusions to 'sonata structure' in so strophical an appeal. This weakness for textbook classification belongs to the tourist class of criticism, and the composer's mock homage to it is one more jeu d'esprit at the expense of the doctrinaire analyst.

The course of the dapper little Scherzo in C modal-minor calls for little comment. There is a succession of four themes, announced by voluble bassoons, cantabile trumpet against a 'respectable' *oompah* background (there is a precedent in Bruckner's seventh symphony), didactic woodwind, and a more agile trumpet, brightened by clarinets. The second and third are sheer repartee and do not recur later; the fourth relates to the first. The first motive is incidentally framed on the rising fourths (56e) of the first movement, variation two, reversed, as the prankish flutes anticipate with their opening upward flourish. The interlude-tune comes blandly from the same tradition. In fact, it is the fourth motive that, prompted by the entry of the third in blunt close canon, takes charge with a lusty, unlettered *fughetta*, culminating in pronounced and quasi-didactic entries at half speed. This motive becomes also (by the insertion of six bars into the earliest version) mainly responsible for the reprise, such as it is. Its jaunty outline, swinging around a modal curve (1 3 2 1 ♭6 5) with a very unmodal spasm, stamps the tune as a confident 'absolute beginner'. (Bar 4 came later.)

The accessory humour of the short lugubrious interlude, which made the Manchester audience laugh at the first performance, and might almost be a parody of the usually omitted interlude to the march in the *Wasps* music, is thus a trifle embarrassing in its context. It also echoes the first motive melodically. The brevity of the return to the Scherzo, all coda in feeling, is very provocative. The textural hypothesis, of wind only, with strings for the next movement, may owe something to Respighi, but it certainly invites the audience to relax here, as to a band competition piece timed not to exceed four minutes. The pithiness of the Fantasia warns the listener not to take this march too lightly, but, as Ottaway candidly observes, its earthy humour amounts to 'almost a romp, beginning and ending with a musical snook.' The best bits are the transformation of the mock rusticity of the start of the interlude into the grace of flutes and clarinets, and, after all, the deft counterpoint that informs the final gruff humour. It may be admitted without further comment that this Scherzo has no precedent, though its dry pungency has been compared to Hindemith's. It rises above the mere brass-and-reed piece by the aptitude of its treatment to its material, and by that sense of musical values which marks a critical personality.

The apparently straightforward and familiar string movement in E, rather lightly termed Cavatina, requires some elucidation. Up to a point it is a recurrence of the kind of rhapsodic modal style which, emerging in the *Phantasy Quintet* and perceptible in the *Tallis Fantasia*, found its symphonic vocation in the development section of the finale of the *Pastoral Symphony*—there initiated by the violoncelli, as here—and added a concentration that many would style 'visionary', in the second stage of the slow movement of the fifth symphony. (There is no literary corroboration here: the motive in question does *not* follow the *cor anglais* theme anywhere in the House Beautiful scene of *Pilgrim's Progress*.) The title of Cavatina arose as a slight example of an instrument-digging process that is now associated with a succinct type of steady, emotionally rich cantabile, from Joachim Raff's once celebrated violin trifle to the absorbed movement of Beethoven's late B flat quartet. The movement accordingly explores intonations of long standing, on the traditional lines of circling round the fifth degree and other improvized centres of reference. For this are engaged, in turn, the top strings of violoncello and violin, *tutti* and later solo, with sonorous but precisedly spaced chordal but contrapuntal movement. Yet the open texture is fresh, and exquisite beside the packed sonorities of the earlier styles.

There is also a new astringency. First, a sense of the mode (E Aeolian-minor), in a free extension beyond the usual octave register, is soon distracted by variant degrees that amount to a change of tonic. In the *Pastoral Symphony* example, such a lapse of tonic, one tone down, occurs and recurs, and then the cantabile itself dissolves in hectic animation. A little later, a new tonic, which happens to be E, is seized upon for an emphatic restatement. It is pitted bluntly against the chord of B flat, and from that clash, again, B flat emerges as the prevailing tonic, E lapsing (Ex. 25*d*). In the present tune in E, B flat (bar 6) is the first and moving point of disturbance. It leads to C Dorian-minor, sliding into B flat minor (bar 11) and beyond, a steady repudiation of B, the dominant or controlling degree of E. But here E is regained for the second strophe (violins), and although it lapses again, it is recovered in the eleventh bar of the strophe. Thus, C minor and the rest have established themselves as pertinent to E minor, essential to the reprise.

Secondly, this modal motive is, at a literally more remote stage of control (bar 32), set against a more sophisticated cantabile in E flat major, beginning on the third degree (3|– 1 2|3 5 6|3). The interlocking string harmony is a poignant timbre and E minor is now a noticeable point of reference. (The tempo changes from four beats to three.) After this, a solo-violin and an oscillating key-sense can maintain interest before the restatement. (A brief episode in D major, replaced by the solo-violin link, was dropped in revision.) Surprisingly, E flat is again the emergent key. With E once more in the circle, it is comparatively effortless to slide back there via a basic C sharp and C natural. It is this second theme which, to my ears, seems too familiar; though it has clear structural purpose, it is raw for a symphony.

This reference to tonality is, once more, the only precise way of indicating the fresh turn which the otherwise not very characteristic principal theme takes. As O. W. Neighbour has observed (*Score*, 24 (November, 1958)), Vaughan Williams has always taken a tune and its phrases peculiarly seriously, with a correspondingly high consideration for variants of mode and key, echoing the more facile oscillations of mode in folk-song. Thus the Scherzo is balanced by something essentially sustained, and at the same time too unpredictable to be considered 'sloppy', except the reprise of the second theme. The diversions are in excellent accordance with those of the first movement.

The finale shows no attempt to be the crowning movement, except that it is in the equivocal major characteristic of the composer in certain moods of release. It is almost a reversion to the oldest type of symphonic finale, simple in order of appeal—here a plain rondo, with the main tune dinned into the ear by normal *tutti* and rollicking percussion—and, as in the 'storm' movements of some early symphonies, slightly fantastic. The composer's title 'Toccata', last used for the opening of the piano concerto, prepares the listener for solo-virtuosity, but scarcely for the reinforcement of the trumpet by chime-bells, pure bells and quasi-oriental gong, the bells subsequently *glissando*. Xylophone and vibraphone figure in the episodes. It is important not to lose one's balance, in either direction, over these accessories, which may prove expedient or necessary. The serious or even grave use of such tuned percussion has been observed in the seventh symphony and *Hodie*, and 'pentatonic jangle' at once begs the question at issue. The conflation of commonplaces of the old 'major' scale (8 6 5 3–5 3 2 1) calls for a redeeming brightness of some sort, and there is nothing unsymphonic about bells. On the other hand, a cheerful contrast of sound-devices does not make a theme a satisfactory refrain. It must be suggestive enough to call for as many episodes as there are (four), and to return freshly in itself; and the episodes must carry their own interest.

On these two counts, doubt must be expressed. The concourse of bells almost defeats its own object: the movement does not start too well. Further, the episodes are thin in melodic and harmonic content, especially the first, and rely too much on the xylophone and vibraphone and celesta. On the other hand, the refrain must not be taken too lightly. It is not clear why the composer regarded it as 'sinister', and no food for jollity. The juxtaposition of whole tones in opposite directions in the opening curve (1 ♯3 2|1 ♭6 ♭7|1) is hardly minatory now, though there is a progression of this kind in the Saraband of *Job*, and, more pertinently, in the music for the film *The Vision of William Blake*. The oscillation of major and minor third has been established usage since folk-song. It may thus be at the discretion of a conductor to keep the general *espièglerie* on the satirical or sophisticated side, to hold the episodes in picturesque but not too marked contrast, and to keep a reserve of creative energy for the finish. Otherwise this movement may sound fatally raw and hollow, and ultimately irrelevant. In due control, it can hardly miss a triumphant impact, though it is not the deeply conceived triumph of the first movement of the *London Symphony*, or the inner elation of the Galliard of the Sons of the Morning. Thus orderly and constructive Variations, a freshly elusive Scherzo, and a discreetly revivalist Lento come to a somewhat turbulent and capricious close with a sense of sustained and calculated contrast.

Symphony No. 9 in E Minor

Senectus non impedit. In Symphony No. 9 in E minor (April, 1958), numbered from its inception, the composer seems to have reacted somewhat from the economy and plain construction of no. 8 in the direction of amplitude, richness and a studied cumulative quality. In no. 8, there are barely ten salient and recurrent themes. In no. 9, there are over twenty. Further, the second movement, which serves as a 'slow' number, relies on a constant alternation of speed, and the last movement is even more temperamental. The structure is correspondingly involved. The opening theme is a momentary reminder of that of the seventh symphony. But whereas the latter's reappearance in the fifth movement at once determines the nature of the Epilogue, here the pivotal return of the first subject has the dimness of the second and third symphonies; 'hoping it doesn't intrude', as the composer remarks of its furtive entry. Meanwhile, there has been considerable development of other matter, perplexing to a retentive ear.

The two inner movements, by contrast, show a general symmetry of two balanced stages extended to a summary close, via an interlude in the Scherzo movement. Yet the composer's cheerful reference of the 'bitty' character of the Andante to a lost programme ('since apparently programme music need not be logical') conceals, in the music thus left to speak for itself ('whatever that may mean'), a certain inconsequence of phrase and theme; and the recurrences of the initial theme of barely ten bars sound functional rather than integrating. Further, even if in a scherzo the ear is more conditioned to subject and episode in mutual disregard, the waywardness is there. Finally, an oscillation between three tempi, and also between individual and more functional motives, acquires a certain cohesiveness in repetition, only to be attached, via a fresh episode, to a new movement, linked by the functional elements and by key-centre.

It need hardly be said that all this is not at once apparent in the grave, wistful and jaunty strains that meet the ear in this symphony. A first impression may well be that Vaughan Williams has found fresh and vigorous symphonic matter in a style partly experimental and partly episodic, with some pursuit of instrumental novelties in the cadential saxophones of the outer movements and the flügelhorn (or valved bugle) of the Andante. The last has a doubtful precedent in the luxuriant fanfaring of the triumphant bucinae in the finale of Respighi's symphonic poem, *Pines of Rome*, and scarcely justifies its ingratiating presence here. Yet some problems of structure cannot be charmed away by the voluble orchestral rhetoric, or by a spirit of cheerful acceptance of anything that the composer could produce so remarkably late in a symphonic career of half a century; still less by the mock admissions of the composer's annotations. There is something odd in the shape of the first and final movements, and the remainder are each crowded with ideas that contrast with, more than they fulfil, one another. And some of the ideas seem elementary for their situation, such as the *animato* incursions in the Andante, and much of the Scherzo. Also, in the last movement, the ascending theme of the *andante sostenuto* that follows the return to Tempo primo and recurs portentously later, can hardly be considered to have been derived from the opening motive of the symphony, but it is confusingly like it in shape. Once more, a certain bluntness attends this movement, conveying a determination to use all available material at any cost for the sake of an ample peroration. The jostling episodes of the seventh symphony have already been criticized. Here, too, there is conglomeration, in spite of the much more balanced arrangement of the designs for each movement. Moreover, the scoring is thick, and positively clotted at times.

It remains to consider the impact of the symphony more specifically. The form of the first movement is peculiar and obscure, and the composer's gleefully mock-modest citation of Haydn precedent ('what is good enough for the master is good enough for the man') for the exaltation of the second-subject theme does not in the least explain the resultant fixation, and furtive extrication, which ensue, if tonality means anything. The opening exposition is clear enough: (1) a pronounced quasi-vocal line, emerging fugally from the bass, against a reiterated tonic

Ex. 57a

—the main point of contact, besides the splendour of thought,[1] with the opening of Bach's *Matthew Passion*, to which the composer refers his initial jog—and acquiring a cadential feature for saxophones, and in a resumption (an addition to the earliest score), a counter-feature that confirms the strange degree-order of the Locrian mode, the melodic pattern that is almost a solecism up to the modern period, owing to its

[1] See p. 57.

avoidance of the usual pivotal fifth degree in favour of a diminished or flattened fifth, here E–B♭; (2) without any transitional feature, a quiet, rhapsodic leap to a typical inflection of equivocal third-degrees, (♭3 ♮3 ♭3 1), which at once leads to an extended descent, in canonic fashion, not cited by the composer, but the basis of later imagery. The

Ex. 57*b*

Ex. 57*c*

Ex. 57*d*

relation of this second group to the original motive is not clear, and up to this point may well be one of a transitional to an essential assertion. The return of *a*1 with *b*2 confirms this.

But *b*1 is now established, *dolce ma appassionato,* by the full orchestra in an oscillation between G major, the traditional second key here, and E flat minor; the characteristic leap having been stretched a semitone to arrive at once at B natural, falling through A sharp to G (♮3 ♯2 1).

A second focus has been recognized, without any relaxation of the strained mood. There is a close parallel for the dual key-relation at one of the most solemn moments in *Hodie* (see Ex. 52). Rhapsodic extension, aided by a brass phrase, whose compressed curve 7|1–♭3 1|7 recalls the Epilogue of the sixth symphony, adds another twenty bars, after which an almost violent return to *b*1 and *b*2, in G and the companion key, as before, is surprising. Free treatment of *b*2 similarly extends this stage under twenty bars. Unless, then, these fifty bars in and around G major are regarded as development, which would at least be a repudiation of all conventional key-values, there is no middle section to this movement. So far this section remains on the borderline of extension and positive development. For at once a brief restatement follows. Its initial line is veiled, and both *a*1 and the saxophone motive (adroitly transferred to wood horns and strings) are from the start haunted by a possessive *a*2; also, a startling version of *b*2 in C, recalling the appalling climax of the slow movement of the sixth symphony in texture and here also the dynamic peak, re-shapes the music, leaving an entire contrast in the quiet but absorbed return of *b*1 in E major, its contemplative character at last fully revealed.

Otherwise, the rough symmetry is apparent enough at the second hearing or if one is prepared for it, ignoring the composer's blandly misleading 'No sign of the first subject' here. A soft coda, as revised, adds *a*1 to *b*1 [bar 2] and the saxophone cadence, now back where it started, texturally. An association of themes in a common troubled mood and cumulative sonority is thus translated into a striking contrast of carefully prepared orchestral climax and intimate solo-violin. The latter is a kind of reflection of the string tune at the corresponding place in the sixth symphony, but not as an escape from a prevailing minatory mood. Rather, it is an attenuation of what has earlier been stated broadly. This tapers into a true Vaughan Williams coda, freshly coloured by the saxophones, for better or worse, but certainly balefully. The exuberance of the second subject, in the G major section, is somewhat overwhelming, as suggested, and the bluntly sectional trend of the movement, without any links, is disconcerting, but the symphonic touch is perceptible.

It is not possible to hear the restless sequel with the same confidence. Periods of varying tempi—andante (76 beats to the minute), animando (100) and, after a fresh start (bar 48), moderato (88) and animato (100)— are set in a capricious key-order: summarily, G minor; B flat minor to E flat major and minor. These are distributed in fitful succession, the animando occurring first in the eighth bar. Then, urged on by a menacing (but not 'sinister') bell, they claim a second hearing, now moving (Ex. 58) from a contrapuntal fusion of andante and moderato in B flat minor to a penultimate recovery of this key for a final andante, via G modal and E flat minor. The animato now drops out. The key-focus, as can be observed, oscillates between G and B flat. But the actual cadence is, capriciously, in C major. I quote the opening solo for flügelhorn, as it is adapted later, to combine with the moderato motive, but the original melodic line is preserved and can be followed here.

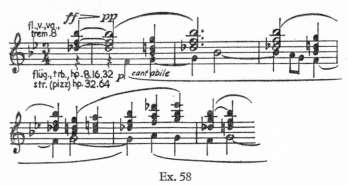

Ex. 58

The second note, G, seems to be the keynote. This would make the mode Locrian again. Alternatively, the third note, B flat, is the keynote, implied rather than stated, and the mode is Lydian with a declining third; and the main key-centre is clearer, in fluctuating modes and variants of modes.

The oscillating tonality in any case betrays a provocative experimentalism, to put it at its highest. The animando is artificial and almost commonplace. The haunting tune of the moderato, the fruit of meticulous shaping and re-shaping, wears better than might be thought from its pursuit of the third degree in a neo-major scale. Apart from the reprise, the basic structure almost suggests some extraneous balletic occasion rather than a constructed movement. Even if the 'lost' programme lightly mentioned by the composer were to be revealed, it could not make the music any more persuasive in its context. It is chiefly a diversionary interlude.

The Scherzo extends from a jaunty saxophone motive, Locrian in trend, to other matter: a quasi-Dipsacus incantation for full orchestra, not found at all in the earliest score, a swinging brassy interlude (marked 'Georgia' in one score) and a more vocal phrase, now descending Locrian, adding the pomp of brass and the glitter of xylophone to crown the saxophone roulades that specially introduce the tune, rhythmically. A canon later tightens the pressure. A compressed reprise finds fugue in the saxophone motive, but soon calls on the brassy phrase for counter-subject and the incantation for episode, with the stately fourth motive to follow as a trenchant canonic counter-theme to the fugue-subject. After a noisy demonstration, the saxophones furnish the impulse for an interlude in a cantabile style. The composer sketched this as a 'Cats' Choral', and persisted in calling it a chorale and in considering it an expedient interlude. Apparently pathetic, with its servile intonation and semitonal distortions, it gains in power as a pervasive Lydian melody. But to wind up the movement the orchestra give the original subject special treatment—at half speed in a mock Hindemith harmonic progression, grotesquely emphasized—and finally, after some pretence at fugue, one saxophone succeeds in recovering the original rhythm, only to yield the torch to a flickering side-drum. There seems no particular reason why the main theme should thus expire. There is a sharp line between the obvious and the inevitable, which critical listening will be inclined to draw here.

This is therefore an ampler scherzo than that of no. 8, but the trite-ness of the rhythm is somewhat exposed after so excursionary an andante. The saxophones are severely tested for symphonic worth, and if their querulous humour suits the fugue, their cantabile wears none too well in repetition. What one can but admire is the youthful abandon, as in *Façade*, in this otherwise taut and meditative work.

The sketches and preliminary drafts of the fourth movement show every possible evidence of meticulous shaping and deepening invention, but the conception of a detached 'second part' seems to have been present from the start. To the uninformed listener, the movement seems designed to compensate for any uniformity in the first, and for the loose construction of the inner movements, by the structural *tour de force* of a compound movement. This absorbs enough energy to create a vacuum that calls midway for a fresh theme and tempo, while yielding formal 'cyclic' material to link the two stages, and echoes of the first movement to ensure an all-embracing epilogue. There is, first, as in the second movement, but less spasmodically, a contrast of component moods: a leisurely andante (60 beats to the minute) with a soaring violin melody whose strange, doggedly imitational treatment almost recalls the sixth symphony finale; a poco animato (63) that by replacing a voluble six-beats by lilting pairs of three justifies its title; and, after the merest recollection of the opening tempo, an equally perfunctory andante sostenuto (104) of brief quasi-vocal imitation against a background of oscillating thirds (♮3 ♭3) in the tonic chord. (The rather confined Dorian motive in the last section is all that is left of an expansive 'harp tune' in the major in the sketches, reminiscent of the close of the first movement of the sixth symphony.) Meanwhile, the alert and informed ear may have become aware that the typical cadential formula (♭3–1) which strikes across the initial light scoring, in the brass and harps, has come to stay, like similar progressions in the third symphony (first two movements). This is confirmed by its use to recover the first tempo.

But fresh twists, cited by the composer as an accessory motive, render the cadential as a process, rather than a state (the basic ♭3 1 extending to ♭3 1=♭3 1 with a piquant second falling third). This halting step enhances the regular tread of the ascending theme of the short and enigmatic sostenuto. The relation of andante and animato is lightly reaffirmed in fresh colouring and key. This time the cadential turn is saved till after the animato, when it appears at reduced speed. The twist of key prepares for the sostenuto, which now seems to recollect the descending tones of Wotan's spear of 'resolution' only to regret them. A fresh intonation of long familiar and trenchant outline contrives to prepare the ear for fresh events without drawing attention to itself. Up to a late stage, this 'link' formed a full episode. It amounted to nearly thirty bars, where finally there are three. The composer's reluctance to sacrifice this intimate feature is reflected in the absence of one figure (15) in the score—obviously a late excision.

A slower movement (84) is thus established with a fresh motive, here shown at the second entry. Some listeners may be reminded, texturally, of the main theme of the slow movement of the fourth symphony, but there is a distinct touch of the composer of the *Tallis Fantasia*. Against this the ascent of the sostenuto is persistently and almost self-righteously urged. The cadential motive now finds its vocation as a break on the momentum, but the sostenuto theme persists. Its development seems

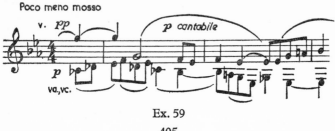

Ex. 59

to recall the opening struggle of the symphony, with whose motive it maintains an uneasy resemblance (its inflection being 1 2 ♯4 5 ♭6, as against the former 1 ♭2 4 ♭5 ♭6). The *meno mosso* theme returns to the attack in C major (a blunt entry, augmented by sixteen bars in revision), but so do sostenuto and a cadential figure; the latter pressing towards E major, the former (brass canon) making for E flat—as, at the end of the earlier E minor symphony (no. 6), E minor and E flat major oscillate before the close. A diminishing burst of E major harmony leaves a gap for one more wail from the saxophones, before the last chord recedes from a great sound, ruffled by harp cascades, past audibility. The sostenuto phrase, which emerged so waywardly at first from the cadential misgivings, has found symphonically its true match, and the cadential rejoinder has supplied a gesture of increasing assurance that the opening meander was flowing towards something conclusive. The troubled opening of the symphony has met its sober consequence after lighter, very much lighter, strains.

It is not necessary to specify what kind of trouble. In an article indicating the range of Vaughan Williams's nine symphonies, as in some sense the token of a wider and a more penetrating experience of life than Beethoven's (January 1, 1960), the music critic of *The Times* alluded to a defiant despair and cynical equivocation as prevailing underlying moods of the ninth symphony, exposing the moral bankruptcy of today. Certainly, the antimony of ♭3 and ♮3, of descending chords of E flat and C major, becomes an arresting focus of textual definition, and in the flavour of the inner movements there is, on the other hand, an occasional but decided taste of powdered substitute. Yet the nineteenth century, besides cultivating the bizarre and evil musically, from the trials of Florestan and Max and the culture-hero of the *Symphonie Fantastique* to the voluntary slide down and off the rails of *Till Eulenspiegel*, was also not lacking in harmonically deviationist trends, especially on the penultimate chord of a cadence; for example, in a major key the minor chord of the fourth degree (4 ♭6 8) (*Tristan, fin.*), or the major chord of a flattened second degree (♭2 4 ♭6). The chord of a flattened third degree (♭3 5 ♭7, or the typical variants, an ascending 5 ♭7 ♭3 or ♭5 ♭7 ♭3) extends the process in a context where a multiple melodic movement, of symmetrical chords regardless of harmonic consequences, has long been taken for granted. Thus the passion that lay in such degree-antinomy or diminished sonority, has been dimmed by the years. Hence, equivocation is a strong word for what is perceived simply as a multiple fall from ♭3 to 1, the scalic contradictions of which are no special concern of the receptive ear. Moreover, even if a consciousness of human failure informed the mood of the symphony, just as a sense of tragedy informed the opening of the *Matthew Passion*, cited as a source or influence, there is much, too, of a stimulating character as sheer sound-relationship, for example the pursuit of the Locrian mode, of the fugal saxophone, of a systematic change of tempo.

It is as repressive to tie this symphony down to the 'cold', psychological war and defeatism of the late 'fifties as it is to refer the fourth symphony directly to an awareness of organized battalions bursting beyond control in the 'thirties. An artist who spends his career in keeping up with the causes is in danger of cramping his range of expression. The strength of Camus's influence, for example, does not lie in his hard and quasi-documentary experience of poverty and oppression, but in a much more creative interpretation of misfortune and hopelessness. Here, too, the composer must be given credit for his own sustained perceptions and recollections of problematic relationships which might propel an opening, illuminate a transition or stamp a cadence. The problem is to keep the relationships an issue without forcing the premisses too patently, as Goethe's Faust, even at the moment of damnation, does not cease to be Faust, or Hell to be in the mind's eye along with salvation. It would be quite unbalanced to regard the slow movement of Beethoven's *Eroica* as a specific tribute to a particular person, or to interpret the episodes in terms of features of the superman conceived at first, as the score-history shows, in the mould of the ascending figure of the republican general Bonaparte. It is also fatal to *listen* to a work like Shostakovich's eleventh symphony as to an epic of the nation. What can be read in the titles can, as with Berlioz's four symphonies, be read, but nothing is sung.

Much more, in Vaughan Williams's last symphony all that can broadly be noted, beyond the assertions of sound-relationship, is some alternations of creative mood: differences such as Mr. P. Rahv (in *Image and Idea*, 1957) audaciously terms 'redskin' and 'paleface'—popular and realistic or individualistic and introspective; and a sense of release or repression, or a satiric concealment of either. The ninth symphony of Beethoven combines all these typical reactions in its initial portrait of a ruthless destiny, continuing in the sinister humour of the Scherzo, the startling absorption of the Adagio, and the sweeping strophical course of a liberationist finale. (The gradual and unprecedented move towards vocal expression and repeated 'joy' stanzas justify the '-ist'.) In the symphony of 1958, destiny is represented as more genial, in spite of the contradictions of mode; absorption finds no continuing focus; a wayward humour has a wider field; and the finale is enigmatic, or at least a struggle between elements. It is scarcely less ironic, even in its structural orthodoxy, than the first two movements of the immediately preceding symphony, but it has none of its later geniality. It is different, without calling for any emotional analysis in terms of waking life.

Beethoven's ninth is enigmatic in another sense. It is commonly assumed that, as a symphony on a great scale—combining a normal symphony in D with an 'adagio *cantique*' and a choral setting of many moods—and as a symphony with, ultimately, a text to be sung in an unmistakably prophetic spirit, Beethoven here found the consummation of the craft to which he had devoted his widest invention, confirmed by the more intimate research of the string quartets. But aurally it seems much more credible that at all these levels he was embarking on a new train of discovery of enlarged and, possibly, vocally interpreted designs for movements, to be duly resumed by Berlioz and later Mahler; or, again, on a new outburst of visionary experience. Conceivably, too, Schoenberg was right when he declared that Beethoven's tenth symphony, as crystallized, signified a range of perception for which the general ear of listeners was not ready, as Aaron, in Schoenberg's *Moses and Aaron*, found Moses' revelation too high a mood for popular understanding. Certainly, if the curtailment of Mozart's symphonic advance by death was a demonstration of genius cut short in its early and incomplete maturity, the knowledge that Beethoven completed no symphony after his ninth no less arouses grave speculations on what further expansions of territory the world has missed.

Vaughan Williams's ninth shows no such sense either of summary or of new departure, except on the Busoni doctrine of preventing art becoming a routine by letting each work 'constitute a principle'. The symphony breaks no fresh ground except in making variety of tempo a principle of communication. Yet it hardly resembles any of the other eight in genre. This symphonist remains unpredictable and unclassifiable to the end, in spite of his quasi-classical trends, and is the greater symphonist for that. Symphony is, once again, not a method of composition, but a resolution to amplify isolated experience in a fructifying context and ultimately homogeneous texture. Vaughan Williams leaves no keen sense of lost symphonies, but, rather, strong arguments from experience in favour of unforced production, waiting for fresh stimuli and working out fresh methods of thematic production, and then dealing with them symphonically. Thus, in contrast with his compatriots' earnest, Teutonic symphonies in the 'fifties, none of his numerous symphonies—a genuine symphonic record, with few parallels —is at all stereotyped. 'He remains as original and unpredictable as ever.'[1] He has practised what he preached in *The Making of Music*: his craft has kept pace with his art. He has not devised the instrumental effects first and the 'music' afterwards.

While some movements may be considered of decidedly less account, and the seventh symphony is a doubtful entry, there has been no sign that the nine lack their minority public, from the sociable first two symphonies to the stiffly contemplative third and fifth; from the terrific fourth to the otherwise minatory sixth, each absorbed in its own direction; from the epic and picturesque seventh to the otherwise capricious, but still affirmative, eighth and ninth.

Further hearings may bring home the expressive range of the symphonies. Quite ordinary common delights, stoic suffering and meditation have their counterpart in the revival of folk-song phrases and modes, trenchant harmonic progressions and the impromptu flow of textural impressionism, melodic, harmonic or instrumental. Yet these become no more than the stock repertory in the background of fresh impulses, many sketched casually on paper and then re-shaped to fit their context. Some of these may crystallize only to absorb a movement in a direct rhythm or other line of growth. Others create structural problems, and works are wider for meeting them. Other movements may leave problems, when all is done, and still give pleasure. Others, again, may inculcate an irresistible sense of logical development and conclusion, and still leave the listener resistant. Roughly, in the first six symphonies, the composer keeps pace with his ideas by constructional measures and adjustments. In the last three symphonies, he is more the explorer, consummating the sketches for these works, for the ninth especially.

Yet throughout, his *droiture d'esprit* can be felt, as a challenge to his successors, traditionalist, atonalist, dodecaphonist or whatever. That sense of personal responsibility to the listener is, briefly, the secret of the continuing satisfaction which Vaughan Williams the symphonist affords.

Towards the end of his career, Vaughan Williams took to consulting one or two others about his new works, especially in regard to orchestration.

---

[1] From a suggestive article by Colin Mason, 'Operatic high road, symphonic rut' (*The Saturday Review*, New York, May 7, 1955, 51); an appropriate sequel to the composer's article, 'Where craft ends, art begins' (March 26), which reappeared in his book, *The Making of Music*.

The first stage was to arrange a piano performance. Michael Mullinar excelled, 'turning an R.C.M. piano into a full orchestra' as he played the sixth symphony four times in one day. Then came Mr. Roy Douglas, in a similar role, up to the end. But in addition Mr. Douglas was steadily referred to on matters of balance, during the crucial first rehearsal of the seventh and eighth (and ninth?) symphonies, and occasionally in a preliminary consideration of the score. The composer's constant concern was, 'Will the tune come through?', and this raised practical questions. Should the brass be supported by strings in the opening of the ninth symphony? (Douglas thought not, and so it was not.) Should one add flute and oboe to the fiddle line in another place? (Answer, again, No, but the tune might still be added to the woodwind lines, each marked for two players, with piccolo.) Should second fiddles be added to a wind line? Are the brass too heavy? And so forth. These questions became more urgent as deafness increased, until, finally, they became unrealistic. Douglas did his best, and it was some embarrassment to him that the composer would sometimes give the idea that he had left the orchestration to his friend. This was quite untrue, and it may be necessary to repeat this out of the coadjutor's own mouth (*R.C.M. Magazine*, 55. 1, pp. 46–8).

It may also be expedient to state, on the same authority, that Vaughan Williams was an unconventional, but far from incompetent scorer, knowing what he wanted and finally concerned only about getting the details right, even if it meant printing a 'second version', with revisionary headaches for printers, conductors and others. These refinements do not preclude the possibility of over-scoring, any more than in the case of Meyerbeer, Strauss, Mahler and other masters of the orchestra. But the suggestion of faltering powers has no validity except in regard to the confirmation of the latest works in the concert-room, and that would take some proving. After all, Beethoven suffered from severe deafness in the latter part of his career.

In his treatment of individual instruments, Vaughan Williams was fastidious about discovering as much as possible about the best lie or register for a phrase. A statement that he decided the key of a section according to the lie of an instrument, transposing the whole section 'up or down a key'(?) if he found it awkward (*Ib.*, 52), cannot be taken literally, but it does show that he was as much concerned with breaks in instrumental intonation, including the erratic woodwind, as with vocal changes of *tessitura*, and usually familiar with their locations.

XIV

Miscellaneous Works

So far, apart from miscellaneous early works, of the music discussed only *Job* has been conspicuously in its own exclusive genre, the remainder being symphonic, operatic, or, briefly, choral-orchestral. It has been shown that the pattern of the operas has not reflected any substantial tradition but has, rather, been determined by the book; and the same may be said of the choral works, but at least an established advocacy can be presupposed. The works now to be reviewed fall outside this rough category of regular demand, and depend much more on special groups of performers. They comprise the various concertante works, the music for film, sound-broadcast and television, the piano and organ music, and odd choral-orchestral, chamber and solo-song works of the last two decades.

The concertos may be taken first. There are four; chronologically, for violin, piano, oboe and tuba as soloist. With these may be grouped the *Suite for Viola*, the *Romance for Harmonica and Strings*, and the *Concerto Grosso*, discussed later.

VIOLIN CONCERTO

The violin concerto, with string orchestra, dates from 1925, a period when the composer was enjoying the new freedom, gained in the *Pastoral Symphony*, to become absorbed in one direction or another texturally, without being concerned about a harmonic progression to the next point. On his choice of the violin no comment is needed, except that *The Lark Ascending* was a preliminary rehearsal. Of the official title, *Accademico*, it might jauntily be said that 'a name is better any day than a number' (Fox-Strangways), and that its first intention would appear to be to point to a model in what is usually called the baroque period—for example, Bach's A minor concerto—rather than to any indication that the work is written according to rules which are, or might have been, taught in colleges and conservatoires. But the ulterior motive is surely some jape, some desire to avoid the burden of a full-blown concerto, by a mock reference to the earlier type, on a 'What was good enough for the eighteenth century is good enough for me' plea. In any case, the problem of exploiting string solo against strings is assumed lightly; chiefly by keeping the violin in the high register, where possible, reducing the number of desks to a part to four, or two in some places, providing cadenzas, and spicing the texture with a little solo-chording here and there in the first movement. The work is a violin-and-strings concerto of divided rather than conflicting functions.

In the first movement, in D minor, the usual principle of classical concerto-movements, of an orchestral refrain of coherent but detachable phrases, alternating with solo-matter of cantabile or bravura quality, almost at once takes on a dialectical tone, owing to the constant impact of the rising fifth (1 5) of the opening phrase, and the falling fifth (4 7) of the fifth bar, the latter leading easily—before the orchestra have finished—to violin capers with revolving (i.e. consecutive) falling fifths and fourths, at the top of the E string, in the neo-academic style. The second and cantabile theme dwells affectionately on a similar 5–1–5 outline. A stiffly swinging theme, begun by low violins and high violoncelli, a curious blend, promotes enough development to call for recapitulation. The general refrain cuts in *after* the cantabile, and makes way in turn for the middle theme, now festooned with violin arpeggios, but a *presto* finish, piquant with falling fifths, supplies a ready exit. Even with the dashes of bitonality, specified by Young, the mode is mainly Dorian, and this adds to the dry formality of the pervading motive and bravura. The haunting animation of the Bach concerto in A minor, with its wide range, exposes the monotony and limited orbit of this opening.

An adagio (G minor), using a violoncello solo as a starting-point, releases two persistent orchestral figures to keep in motion the melismatic principal motive, sinking from the fifth degree, and a traditional rising scale feature. An exultant disturbance of key centre (C sharp minor) midway calls for an adjustment of theme, from transitional back to primary. The Dorian mode is again integral, and the rather glutinous modal harmony weighs heavily on the ear, behind the violin coloratura. A scherzo finale reveals a headlong descent (shaped as a multiple fall of 5 ♯4 1), taken nominally from the second act of *Hugh the Drover*, with concomitant creeping up again, to overhang a rather resolute ascending motive (1 ♯3 ♯4|5) in contrary rhythm, exhibited at once with the bass in canon, and a wayward jig-tune, inveterately modal. Other threads appear and combine with what has been heard. A resolute, almost didactic ending in the major dissolves into a solo-cadenza, strictly based on concomitant twists, with an almost prophetically equivocal third (♯3 ♮3) for cadence.

It would be idle to criticize so unpretentious a concerto for not being what it never sets out to be, but one is conscious of making allowances, if it comes to accepting this structural spryness and textural asceticism as the makings of a significant work. The slow movement is mannered but communicative; the others lack the motive-force which the solo-texture, or its relation to the *tutti*, should produce. Where are the sweeping phrases, the incisive cross-string rhythms, which the orchestra leads one to expect? Guido Pannain (*Modern Composers*, tr. M. R. Bonavia) notes the inner lyric feeling of the slow movement, only to be embarrassed by the absence of emotional equilibrium in the concerto as a whole. It seems very odd that a composer who was something of a violinist never strove with Sibelius, Walton, and the rest in seeking for a creative solution to the problem of a fully orchestral violin concerto, with its promise of cantabile as well as infinite nuance of solo and solo-ensemble. That he did not is no reason for treating this *jeu d'esprit* as a short cut to a contemporary level of symphonic attainment.

PIANO CONCERTO

The piano concerto of 1933, the solo part of which was later arranged for two pianos by Joseph Cooper 'in collaboration with the composer' (first performance, St. Cecilia's Day Concert, 1946, R.A.H.), is quite another matter. It broke new ground, never again covered by the composer; it is an interesting concerto in itself; and it abandoned tradition in its general pattern of movements.

Flos Campi, succeeding the *Pastoral Symphony*, had established the 'dynamic calm' of a fresh kind of harmonic progression, polyphonically contrived, and of a new degree of absorption in the phase of the moment, even if it was only a cadence or tapering-off, aided by a solo-instrument or other distinctive ensemble (viola and chorus). Such perceptions promote further systematizations, but they might end in a closed circle. Again, detachment from the prolific moodiness and jostling speech-absorptions of *Sir John in Love* might result in a quest for a more consistent, yet resourceful evocation of musical ideas, arising from some analogy with operatic repartee without depending on the stage event.

In such a mood of confidence early in his career, Brahms began work on a symphony. It was not till he had drafted a two-piano transcription that he discovered, in the latent presence of pianistic figurations and sonorities, that the true medium was a piano-concerto-symphony. Thus arose his first piano-concerto. The second, less abstract at the first intimation, had a piano in it from the beginning. It may be assumed that, on the premises outlined above, Vaughan Williams with a similar sense of fitness designed a piano concerto, in preference to a symphony, to hold any wayward progressions in a firm grip, for he wanted a dominating soloist. The solo-concerto associations favoured the interpolation of capricious fixations and dreamy interludes for the piano, when the orchestra relaxed its hold. Some of these might reverberate in orchestral analogies, less percussive or liquescent but relevant in their own right. Other features might arise in an atmosphere of orchestral riposte, but become 'automatic' in a later pianistic outburst. On the other side, the interplay of soloist, solo-ensemble and various grades of *tutti* could at once replace the coincidences of opera by a more orderly encounter, and promote an assembly of material tough enough to stand the boomerang sallies of a concerto.

Further, in a piano work, if the establishment or dissolution of a key-system is desired, there will be no difficulty in bringing home the fact. In most orchestral works up to 1920, the drums give a constant and final clue to the tonality. The piano, too, can assume the role of a chromatic, all-key drum. Another role, a more popular one, is to imitate the singer in positive melody, either in formal phrases or a freer but no less disciplined plainsong. The piano can also, of course, combine melody and dance-rhythm in a swinging refrain, when required. Finally, the piano is the fugal expositor *par excellence*, where there is no text. Where fugue abounds, whether in voluble answer, close combination of threads, alteration of the delivery-speed of the subject, in the contrary pull of an episode, or in a final exaltation of the subject, unthreaded, an even flow of tension is assured, as opposed to the hurly-burly of opera or kindred concert suite. On the other hand, the opportunity for being carried away by an impressionist effect is rigidly confined.

These speculations form one way of rationalizing the special impact of the concerto after the richness of a Falstaff opera, on the one hand, and the introspective tone of *Flos Campi* and *Riders to the Sea*, on the other. They explain, too, the orderly and tempered restlessness of the first movement, the more conventional but not unqualified absorption of the second, and the resort to monothematic fugue for a finale, with a recognized German dance (Tedesca) to follow, and then what is virtually an epilogue, though not so named. It is this blend of the V. W. of the 'twenties with a fresh vital force which, in a word, makes this concerto.

The shape of the first movement is original. It is, in miniature, classical with a difference. There is some suggestion of orchestral statement (in C, B and F) and counter-statement with piano (in C and E), waywardly continued, as if the movement were on a grand scale, in a fresh theme (orchestra and, later, soloist), with development and restatement to follow (in C–A♭, A♭ and C). But the piano is handing out material from the start; not only the opening pattern of revolving split

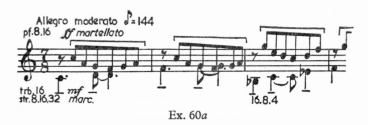

Ex. 60*a*

chords, spinning like two tops in perpetual contrary motion and untiring jingle, as counterpoint to the rising orchestral pentatone, but also the heavier outbursts of percussion hurled at the orchestra (bar 9) with a

Ex. 60*b*

triumphant bitonality (C–A♭) that recurs later, even when its original motive has been dropped. The next two themes, awkwardly alike, are nominally orchestral, but are soon captured by the piano, in the second case treading heavily on the heels of the tuba entry.

Ex. 60c

Ex. 60d

The piano continues to dominate the scene with the jingles in the development of the main motive, and the control of *a* (bass), *c* and *d* in the remainder. Its role is clear: opposition. In face of which, and in the total absence of a lyrical second focus, the only thing to do was to proclaim the technique in the title: Toccata! This does not prevent the motives from being modal: *a* (top) is hexatonal; *a* (bass), Dorian; *b* as in *Sancta Civitas* (Ex. 29: 2*a*); *c*, Aeolian; *d*, Mixolydian. It is a measure of the wider interest of the movement that these reversions are negligible as such. All the same, they may explain why this movement has a much more positive, established melodic grip on the ear than the comparable opening of Rawsthorne's first piano concerto (1939, strings and percussion; 1942, full orchestra), which he calls 'capriccio'. The later movement may be derived from the *Sancta Civitas* chord (bar 2 of motive *b* above), as a *donnée* of restless exploration. The main 'development', or rather free fantasy, takes the form there of an improvised fugal passage, thus securing momentary stability, as well as continuity of rejoinder, as the finale does here on a wider basis.

To return to the earlier concerto, the *tutti* having ended as *On Wenlock Edge* (bar 4) began, but here in a state of complete equilibrium, a mannered cadenza brings in the Lento, called Romanza, somewhat in the John Field tradition. The interest of the slight 'main' theme must lie in the fresh harmonic tint that it acquires as it passes from piano to flute and to a *tutti* of muted strings and horns, as later from oboe back to a shrilly sonorous piano. The middle tune, which enters in A flat and later in D flat, is mainly for a well-nourished orchestra, the piano

Ex. 61

later adding decorative figures prepared by earlier entries in D. Only in the last entry does the piano duplicate the melody; at oscillating levels in the original edition, to incorporate figuration below. It does not need much thought to realize that the piano's solo turn will come later, or to guess where, for ears conditioned by the composer's later epilogues. Meanwhile, it may as well be admitted that, in contrast to the violin concerto, this is the slightest movement. It begins in E, Phrygian and Mixolydian, but in restatement wanders to G Mixolydian, and thence to obscure tonality, involved with A flat. This is the opportunity for an entry by a new motive, in an irrelevant key (B), nullified by the persistence of a clear A flat bass. This proves to be the intimation of a fugue-subject.

In a second statement, trombones and mute-free strings declare the subject as dynamic in itself, and finally the piano launches the precise subject. In pitch, it seems to establish D as a pivotal note, violin vibrations confirming a reinforced pedal (held bass). Alert listeners will at once identify this as the keynote of an insistent Mixolydian descent in the subject of D–(C♯)–C♮–A–(G♯), sliding down to E. The answer, starting on G, favours the conventional rendering of D as the fifth-degree, assumed by Howes and Young. But actually the tonality is obscure and remains so. Hence the perky title, Fuga chromatica.

Ex. 62a

(Bach's tonality under the same colours, with its clearly terminating subject, is never obscure.) The ensuing weave is often tight and trenchant, but it must be understood that the strictly imitative side is not the hardest but the most mechanical part of the dialectic. Fugue, in fact, is a way of making quick progress from a given start. If threads combine, so much the smoother. However, the subject, after reacting to the stimulus of a recurring counterpoint that is almost a genuine and instantaneous counter-subject (a term commonly and rather absurdly used of an initial and inevitably ancillary accompaniment of the subject, if it is kept up), of close imitation of the freest, most equivocal kind ('false' is the official word), and liberal episodic interpolations and pianistic asides, eventually, after 122 bars of increasingly impressionist treatment, reaches a violent climax, marked by a broader rhythm (roughly trebling the length of the original, which now becomes a bustling counterpoint). This *canto fermo* style is eventually adopted by

Ex. 62*b*

the piano, to herald a cadenza, which absorbs the main topic (subject and counter-subject) in comfortable leisure, less contrapuntal and more strophical in texture.

However, from some fresh spark of counterpoint arises the next

Ex. 62c

movement, entitled Finale alla Tedesca—a German-dance finale in G. Here the apparently Mephistophelian subject assumes a gusty, earthy vitality of considerable power, propelled by the incessant mutual interplay of piano and orchestra. The broader rhythm, on the other hand, relaxes to the mood almost of *Sei mir gegrüsst* (Schubert), or some such affectionate vernacular. The infectiousness of this lurking nostalgia calls for a real coda. Here the two-piano version (MS) adds a pianistic interpolation of twenty-seven bars (at 50 in the published two-piano score of the original concerto) to enhance the orchestral entry. The dialectic is roughly as follows, *A* being the extended subject, *x* its continuation, *b* a C–D♭–C–G figure and *a* the original subject.

PF 1	*Ax*	*b*
PF 2	*b*	*Ax*
ORCH		
Key	G B♭ A♭ E♭ D♭	C A♭ G♭ E♭ F minor
Number of bars	4 1 1 1 1	4 1 1 1 1
PF 1	*A*	*a*
PF 2	*a*	*b*
ORCH		
Key	G→B♭ minor	G→C♯ minor→
Number of bars	4	4 3
PF 1	*b*	
PF 2	*b* *A*	
ORCH	*A x*	*A**⎫ *a* ⎭
Key	G B♭ A♭ B♭ B♭	→G→E♭
Number of bars	4 1 1 1 1	6

The effect of this addition is that the orchestra enters with its précis of 8 and 6 bars as the sub-climax of a pattern of 8–8 and 4–7 bars. In the process, *x* appears simplified orchestrally, but at the climax of the second entry A is screwed up by semitonal interpolations. Thus, instead of being

419

a sudden summary, the orchestral entry first appears as cumulative and confirmatory before clashing together the two versions of the subject. In both cases, the ultimate cadenza stage is reached in due course from an explosive *tutti*. The first bar of the subject having been pursued to a point of exhaustion, the opening of the Lento is suddenly recalled. (In the transitional matter after each phrase, the second piano adds a figure in contrary motion to the original ascent, both pianos being in octaves.)

That having brought the slow movement within call, the return of the middle tune from the same source will surprise no one. Whether this Solemn Melody, with its flowing and interweaving accompaniment of 1 4 6 chords and with the oscillation of octaves removed in the two-piano version, is a compulsive release, will depend on the pianist's powers of persuasion. It will not be easy. The key for this serenity is, correctively, B major. After that, originally, there was a final eighteen bars' spurt of close imitation, leading to the triumphal cadenza version of the subject (62c) in G, as in the printed version (1936). (A revision, of six bars of B flat minor reversed in the cadenza, perceptible in the hand-written score, was apparently rejected.) Now, in either version of the concerto, B major is inexplicably maintained in nine bars of quiet con-clusion, introducing the subject in a mutter of plucked strings against sustained pianistic chords of B in 1 4 6 position, finally absorbed by rich bowed-string chords. As Young observes, the substitution of B for G, in which the emergent Tedesca was clearly announced, means that key is no longer one of the unities that count. A suggestion of remote vistas proves, after all, to be the concluding point.

The arrangement for two pianos is sheer simplification or amplifi-cation. There is some elementary, barely audible antiphony, but no creative use of the enhanced resources.

In this manner a restless, pounding opening movement, followed by a meditative interlude, is balanced by a trenchant fugal outburst, com-bining probing counterpoint with an inner dynamic confidence, and broadening from scherzo repartee into a voluble Tedesca, from which cadenza and reminiscence supply a slow curtain-tune. An original sort of concerto, not without an obsession over the percussive and com-petitive sonority of the grand piano, but short enough not to suffer from the somewhat limited pianistic vocabulary. There is something diabolical and subversive about the later, post-Liszt tradition of piano with orchestra. Stravinsky apparently felt this in his piano concerto, as in the frantic struggle for pianistic life versus a menacing orchestra which led to *Petrouchka*. This, it seems to me, is how the fugue and its

420

sequel should be accepted; not as a quest for the unattainable or some such quasi-philosophic image. The subject is taken much too much out of its depth to make that credible. There is considerable confirmation of this use of fugue in the Scherzo of the sixth symphony. The obvious precedent is in the 'Mephistopheles' movement of the *Faust* symphony (Liszt), repeated phrase and all, but there the fugal pursuit of a frenzied version of the motto-theme (Margaret) makes a diversionary episode to the main movement. It remained to pursue an equally sinister imagery without the piano. For that, the brass would have to supply the opposition front. Whatever the inner relation, some spark from the concerto either kindled the start of the fourth symphony, or was already smouldering. Without invoking any contemporary thoughts of a re-armed nationalism, it may be observed that some explosive content remains common to the two works. At one stage, indeed, the composer conducted a two-piano version of the symphony at the R.C.M. (*R.C.M. Magazine*, 55. 31).

OBOE CONCERTO

The short concerto for oboe and strings (1944) may be regarded as a *pièce d'occasion*; the stimulus being the virtuosity of Leon Goossens. For better hearing of his 'tune', the orchestra are perpetually being reduced to eleven desks (3–3–2–2–1), leaving only fragments of *tutti*, totalling barely thirty bars in the first movement, and the rest in proportion. A paradox of tempo-marking is that although the first two movements are both marked *allegro moderato*, the first is, in fact, a slow four beats (96 in the printed version, 88 in the full score), while the three beats of the second movement go twice as fast. It may also be observed that the 'Finale (scherzo)', marked *presto* (86 for each three-beat bar in the printed version, but 76 in the score), is only a 'degree' faster than the minuet that it follows. The upshot is that the tempo of the unit-*bar* in each movement changes in the curious order of 22, 64, 76 to the minute.

In these proportions, the first movement (A minor) blends oboe and orchestral matter in a plastic rondo scheme, of which the recurrent feature is a jejune motive in the Dorian mode and the rest scarcely arises above a certain nimbleness. The second movement is a plain minuet (C minor), also Dorian, with a suitably drone-ish musette in an oscillating major mode. The Finale, in E Dorian lapsing into G, is more packed with different phrases, on the bi-focal basis of a sonata-pattern, but with stray episodes. There is a moment of contrived structural suspense, where the flowing third theme is decelerated into a coda-like episode, from which the original tempo has to be recovered. This seems to me quite unconvincing. The plain cantabile theme in E major, later in G, is almost negligible, and the penultimate resort to a new tune in G major, traditional in style if not in fact, desperate. Also, the abandonment of the original E modal minor is quite unpersuasive. Admittedly, not even Mozart could easily convert me to the idea of a concerto for so uncomprising a solo-element as one oboe. But for all his mastery of the lie of the instrument, and other rhetorical questions, the composer seems here not to have waited long enough before framing his ideas. After so slight a middle movement, scherzo virtuosity and facile cantabile do not add up to the absorbing finish needed.

It is interesting to compare the oboe concerto (1945) of Strauss, himself an octogenarian by then. The harmonic texture and immediate solo-domination are Schumannesque, the movements continuous but in clear patterns and in traditional order, except for a sort of appendix to the apparently final Vivace. A full orchestra being employed, the oboe has its proper *concertante* movements, in preparation for utterances of sheer oboe quality, such as the cadenza that neatly summarizes the Vivace and less persuasively invokes the final Allegro. Yet the abiding impact of the concerto is thin, and close examination of the solo part will discover more awkwardness than sympathy—even the concerto's warmest English admirer, Mr. John Boulton (*Music Review*, 9, p. 177 (May, 1948)) admits uncertainty as to why an oboe was chosen.

An altogether closer parallel appeared in Rawsthorne's short concerto for oboe and strings (1947), a witty work in the composer's most piquant semitonal style. The oboe dominates the central and brief final sections of the miniature French overture that forms the first movement; it shares the main subject of an 'allegretto con morbidezza' rondo with the orchestra, while each party contributes substantially an episode each; in the final Vivace, a more organized symphonic movement is strengthened in restatement by contrapuntal methods, including half-speed entries that call for a *bravura* finish, skilfully delayed by orchestral fixations and acrobatic display in the cadence. The pungent volubility and sad cantabile of the oboe are happily set in the string context.

TUBA CONCERTO

There can be no compromise in a tuba concerto. One may admire the craftsman's skill in creating a vacuum for a tuba, bravura, tenor and piquant, baritone and cantabile, or just itinerant, and in filling a gap with orchestral entries without too sharp a sense of returning to aural comfort. But the more amply these sallies are sharpened—bi-focally in the first movement, whose opening 'Gilbert the Filbert'[1] motive goes Phrygian, by complementary phrases in the second, by rondo and a more animated second subject in the finale—the more one is conscious that allowances are being made or must be made. We recognize the tuba in the orchestra as a roaming, efficient and reasonably co-operative Atlas, or as a draconic monster *par excellence*, but not as an acrobat, and grudgingly as a singer. One recalls with critical amusement Pasquarello's grotesque 'Cavatine', with tuba (ophicleide) concertante, in the carnival of *Benvenuto Cellini*, anticipating an episode in *Petrouchka*, and in the opera followed by the crowning of the tuba player by Midas, a hit at the critical capacities of the Rome Prize examiners from whose long ears Berlioz had suffered earlier.

Dr. Johnson's views on the paradox of a woman preaching have been quoted by at least one reviewer in the present context, and as the concerto moves from solo to orchestral entry, one can but wonder at the creative attempt. The shapely contours of the slow movement may, indeed, persuade a listener that the tuba has found its higher vocation—Mr. Oliver Neighbour goes so far as to single this out from its surroundings as a 'beautiful movement'—but the version of this movement for violoncello and piano, described in the tuba-piano score as 'also playable', exposes only too well the original compromise. The other alternatives mentioned are no less compromising. A euphonium could not be happy in the middle *coloratura* passages, and the bassoon would be thin in the tenor register. This is not absolutely to discourage such players from including this Romanza in their repertory, but they have been warned.

Romance for Harmonica

The *Romance* for mouth-organ, strings and piano is a curious trifle, using a light rondo pattern (*a b* (*a*) *c b a*) to expose a versatile but precarious solo-texture. Quicker tempi for the episodes enable the main *tranquillo* refrain to return easily when their rhythm relaxes, but 'refrain' is too definite a term for such liquescent harmonies, hovering round such a chord as Ex. 29: 2*a* in a siciliano style. If once more it be bluntly asked, 'What is the mouth-organ saying there?', the reply echoes

---

[1] A popular song of the past, which exploits the rhythm of its title.

jauntily from the dawn of the impressionist period, 'It is saying, madam, I am a mouth-organ'. While, then, this *Romance* will have its uses, its composition may be reckoned an act of grace to an accomplished soloist (Larry Adler). 'Romance' is a fanciful title, and 'harmonica' is mistaken politeness. There is a confusion with another instrument; and a mouth-organ by any name still sounds a mouth-organ. Should it not be left where it belongs, as the wandering minstrel's consolation, or, as in the *London Symphony* citation (Scherzo), let its idiom be heard obliquely as a flourish before a suitable tune?

VARIATIONS: DIVES AND LAZARUS

To turn from these strenuous exercises in craftsmanship to the first of the three miscellaneous variation-sets is to be aware once more of another Vaughan Williams. As the title declares, the *Five Variants of 'Dives and Lazarus'*, for a string orchestra in ultimately ten parts (2, 2, 3, 2, 1) and harp (doubled if possible), form a quasi-strophical set, not of articulate variations on a given version of the tune, but of successive variants, some spreading to two verses, of a common intonation. A note in the score explains that these variants 'are not exact replicas of traditional tunes, but rather reminiscences of various versions'; in other words, free adaptations. The fresh turns are assisted by the antiphony of opposing string groups, solo-violin for Variant 3 and lofty closely packed string texture for Variant 5, and also of key (D–F and G, to the prevailing B modal minor, in Variants 3 and 4) and mode, the last three variants changing the mode from Aeolian to Dorian. The familiar folk-tune turned hymn-tune is thus linked with five 'variations in search of a theme', except that the basic outline of 1 3 5 (lower) 7, etc., is clear enough to make one aware of its modification to 1 5 5 7 (i.e. browsing round 5) in Variants 1–3, and to 1 4–5 3 1 in Variant 5, along with changing rhythmic patterns and tempi. Collector's research is drawn upon without imparting a melodically corrective tone. The abandonment of the last phrase in the second verse of Variant 2, in favour of a miniature epilogue, the loosening of key-ties in Variant 3, and the development of diversionary figures in the more sophisticated Variant 4, break the sense of the predictable just enough, for sympathetic ears, to call for a solemn gesture of final recovery. This is clearly a matter of key and direct statement. The main tune, familiar as a bass interlude in the folk-song suite for band, was once 'The Red Barn' (*Journal of the Folk Song Society*, 7: Aeolian version, cited among several

424

other variants of 'Dives and Lazarus'). It has its own curve and its own Dorian touch. Instead of coming to a finish, the last phrase, borrowed from Variant 4, becomes involved in a half-close that calls for repetition (violoncello solo) and compensating full close. But this is conclusive enough.

On the surface, then, this unusual set of variations may appear to be wayward juggling with melodic shape. On its own premises, the modifications produce deft changes of pattern in a confined space. These are absorbed enough in a wider rhythm to bear their otherwise superfluous harmonic burden. The result is a searching meditation in a consistent imagery, whose traditional basis is general enough not to tie the music down, except to a strophical scheme. The set is one more example of the peculiarly liberating effect of folk-song on the composer's mind. It must have had rather a curious début as one of the English works conducted by Boult in the World Fair in the United States, 1939. This is a work for an intimate occasion.

Ten years later, variant strophes of 'Dives and Lazarus' (one later strophe had the first line ending on the fifth degree and the second spanning an octave descent from there, as in the 'Red Barn' setting) reappeared as the chief musical element in a short film, *Dim Little Island*. In this sketch Vaughan Williams is one of the four unseen speakers who are heard in a somewhat contrived elucidation of the creative future that lies ahead in this country for determined naturalists, ship-builders and musicians. As the declared foundation figure in the musical pyramid described by the composer, the folk-singer (first in solo-song, later in orchestral translation) provides the recurrent theme for the potential renascence of the imaginative life, or, as Vaughan Williams suggests, for the renascence that actually began with the reawakened national awareness in the War. Auxiliary fragments (?'Pretty Betsy of Ballahtown Brae' and 'Pretty Susan the pride of Kildare'[1]) introduce the dialogue, and a rather prim harmonic sequence (1 ♯3 5–♭7 2 4 ♭6–5 2 4 ♭7–1 ♯3 5) raises and draws the curtain.

The main tune was obviously selected as one of the earliest influences in the composer's response to the nation's musical potentialities. Most in the audience would have known it, if anything, as the hymn-tune *Kingsfold* for 'I heard the voice of Jesus', but, although the ballad title 'Dives and Lazarus' can be traced back to John Fletcher's *Monsieur Thomas* (3. 3), the proper collocation is undoubtedly the homiletic

---

[1] I have to thank Mrs. Noyes, the librarian of the English Folk Dance and Song Society, for identifying the second tune and conjecturing the first.

carol, 'Come, all you worthy Christian men' (*Oxford Book of Carols*, 60), which includes verses on Job and Lazarus, as models of the patient-deprived who made good, and thus comprehends 'Dives and Lazarus'. For the informed listener, indeed, the ascetic note is a little at variance with the promise of expansion in the spoken word. However, with this dialogue replacing the lilt of the folk-stanzas in a sort of melologue with illustration, the tune readily captures the musical stratum, as a forth-right, symmetrical appeal, more capable than 'Searching for lambs' or 'Bushes and Briars' of absorbing the jolt of the instrumental anti-phony in its own drive. Nor would it have been easy to pick a strain equally militant, antique, familiar and shapely. All the same, the com-poser might have made a fresh selection from his wide repertory, and the rejection from the shipyard scenes of any sea-song, even 'Spanish Ladies' or 'The Golden Vanity', seems odd. The sophisticated listener is too soon conscious of saturation and raw experience.

FANTASIA ON OLD 104TH

Free treatment of the dominating tune is discernible in some of the seven variations that go to make up the *Fantasia*, curiously subtitled 'for pianoforte solo accompanied by chorus and orchestra', on the tune *Old 104th*, arbitrarily named from its assignment to the 104th Psalm in Thomas Ravenscroft's music edition of the 'old' metrical version of the psalms; it replaced the original tune in English psalters. The now familiar hymn-tune recurs, complete, more often than not. But now and again one hears the tune as it might have been collected by or from Liszt, with separate phrases developing their own chain of variants. For the rest, all the standard methods are used to urge the music from one strophe or phrase to the next: the tune direct and the tune stretched out or interlaced; dynamic piano melody and choral unison, piano rhapsody and spacious choral polyphony and orchestral strophe; rivalry of key-centre, D minor being the centre of gravity but F minor the kick-off for the full theme and ensuing variations; changes from three beats to four, and alterations of the basic 4–4–5–5 bar pattern; and an occasional counterpoint on the broadest textural lines. But the vital repartee is from piano to chorus. The piano is concerned only with amplifying the component phrases of the tune, while in each of their verses the singers recall the listener to the radical purpose of the strophical progress.

For this realization of the proper setting, the original text, 'My soul praise the Lord', is revived here. It was first supplied with two dozen others by William Kethe, for the English congregation gathered at Geneva under Calvin.[1] The long tune there attached to it, covering a pair of verses, was lifted from the French psalter with disastrous accentual results. It was this which Ravenscroft replaced with an altogether more sweeping rhythm and coherent melody in the 'new tune' of his Psalter of 1621. Over, then, to the English refugees still in Geneva in 1561, stirred by their unprecedented encounters with congregational singing, so far as the formidable Calvin allowed it— rather than to the comfortable security of Gloucester Cathedral, 1950— for the true liberationist note of the five verses which together, for all their wooden phrases, sweep the piano rhetoric into the fervent atmosphere of the committed.

The *Fantasia* falls into three stages:

(1) *Prelude, Theme, and Two Variations.* D minor: Prelude (piano), trying out phrases. F minor: Theme, in a trenchant multiple texture (piano); verse 1 in choral polyphony, with piano bravura; an orchestral verse with choral extensions of each phrase, borrowing text from the first verse.

(2) *Three Variations.* A free and extended interlude for piano, beginning in B modal minor. D minor: a second verse, for choral unison in four-time, with the piano harping on the fourth phrase. A third verse absorbs 'How sundry, O Lord', etc., in fugued entries that do not go beyond the first melodic phrase and may be regarded as a fixation prompting a return to F minor, in which the piano leads the orchestral bass in a massive fourth verse.

(3) *Two Variations and Coda.* Another long piano interlude, emulating Busoni in style (or, more nearly, Liapunov's *Variations on a Russian Folk-song*), is sobered down to a choral unison verse in D minor, volubly but simply accompanied. This last verse overflows into a brief phrase of ecstatic polyphony, balancing the first with the fourth phrase in D major and minor, but inevitably, now, reaching the major for the close.

---

[1] Kethe's renderings first appeared in the *Fourscore and Seven Psalms of David in English Metre/by Thomas Sternhold and others* (1561), the second extension of the Anglo-Genevan Psalter (1556). Sternhold and Hopkins, who in the *Fantasia* short-score are credited with the text, were associate sponsors of the idea of congregational recital in English churches, with whose joint names the 'old' version of the English psalter in metre soon became associated, but they did not handle Psalm 104. Kethe's paraphrase became the basis of R. Grant's 'O worship the King'.

The new tune for *Old 104th*, then, has shown unexpected 'concerto' possibilities, while retaining its unmistakable essence. A brash echo of congregational fervour and stalwart rhythm at the start, it soon establishes its own imagery. There is no question that it was composed for harmonic setting, and if there is often little harmonization proper, there is no lack of impactive sonority; too much, indeed, for some listeners (*Music and Letters*, 32. 3 (July, 1951)), but its firm line can take it. While most of the variations are restricted in scope to features of textural interest, they gain by swift succession, and there are subtler, more wayward but more absorbed phrases, as well as the plain moments of personal declaration. Admittedly the solo at the beginning of the last stage is a blunt interpolation, but it is all relevant. The weakness of the musical design is that the work relaxes suddenly at the last stage (Variation 7 and coda), as if the tune had lost its sting. The end relies too much on personal delivery, to produce a substantial feeling of summary release. Yet in the right atmosphere, when expression is paramount, its directness will prove refreshing to join with in spirit. Not a major work, it is skilfully balanced. It should not be dismissed as a pompous chorale partita, laboured variations on an all too recognizable theme. That does not do justice to the craftsmanship with which the *mot juste*, that the composer finds in Ravenscroft's direct appeal, becomes eightfold, or to the sense of purpose which the choice of the original text clearly underlines. There is a time for energetic fervour.

VARIATIONS FOR BRASS BAND

The *Variations for Brass Band*[1] enjoy, paradoxically, the freedom of being entirely themselves, although they were written, undoubtedly, for the hard conditions of competitive wear and tear. (81 bands and 2,000 players in the Royal Albert Hall on October 26, 1957). The theme gives nothing away, except that it is clearly in the major, with a key-transition sharpward to the sixth degree which will be modifiable later. The pronounced variety of genre, ensured by the successive stimuli of a swinging waltz, a melting arabesque and a tumultuous polonaise, as recognizable features in a wider demonstration of mood, emerges later. What is revealing meanwhile is the degree to which the variations seem to give the theme what it needs, though the final fugue and 'chorale' are less successful. The treatment of the brass repudiates

---

[1] i.e. five cornets, flügelhorn, three horns, two baritones, three trombones, euphonium, two tubas and percussion.

sensationalism in an early instruction to cornets to play, 'like trumpets', with a straight non-vibrato, but it keeps the solo-instruments on their toes—as when the flügelhorn 'returns the service' of the cornet in the arabesque—and finds stimulating ground for the obvious group-rejoinders and cumulative leads, prompt or deliberate. Bands took to its exactions.

Gordon Jacob's arrangement for symphony orchestra (1960) rejoices in only eight wood and ten brass, but uses full percussion, including an active side-drum, chime-bells (supporting the wood in the first variation, waltz and chorale) and celesta (reinforcing the violins at the finish of the arabesque and the start of the chorale). He adds to the original score, which acknowledges the 'revision' of Mr. Frank Wright, a striking nimbleness of repartee. A smoother and more scintillating arabesque is followed by a polonaise in which strings keep the impact sharp by a ready incisiveness, or by their absence. This arrangement should widen the circulation of a work which, as a competition piece, is liable to be superseded once the competition is over. Schoenberg did the same for his wind-band variations.

Viola Suite

Three *concertante* works remain for consideration. The suite (1934), for viola and an orchestra of varying fullness, disposes eight plainly named pieces in three smaller groups (3, 2, 3), each of which, published separately, may be regarded as reasonably detachable. The playing time of under twenty-five minutes indicates the vignette style, and the constant resort to a contrasted interlude, usually of different tempo, in order to 'amplify' the opening mood or phrase, brings the sense of *multum in parvo* to a precarious level. However, the music should rather be taken in its three main stages, each working towards an obvious but distinct 'concert pitch' from or via a subdued colour. The reservation of one trumpet for the third, fifth, and seventh pieces, and of two, with piccolo, for the last, guides the ear, and a light percussion of harp, celesta or triangle adds incidental momentum. The first group assembles a developed prelude of slight listener interest, a simple tune, termed carol, which improves when the flute becomes leader to the viola in canon, and a kind of Galliard, mysteriously termed Christmas dance, whose salient phrases grow with contrast and later antiphonal touches for *tutti* and soloist, and key changes. The result is just positive enough in melodic appeal to call for stronger flavour. This is supplied by a solemn pentatonic tune, termed Ballad, intense enough to prompt some orchestral staggering of its phrases later, the viola justifying the gaps; and then a wild incisive dance, called Moto perpetuo from its nagging bravura, but precisely shaped in a two-theme scheme by a contrast of flute tune and viola chordal impressionism, which an accomplished player could redeem from ungainliness.

In overt reaction, the third miniature suite begins with another simple tune, as much a carol as the earlier one but here called Musette from its undertones. Vaughan Williams tunes that start on the third degree are apt to proceed according to form; and sure enough, this one ends by dwelling on a fourth-degree seventh (4–6–1–3), finally projected on to a film of solo-string texture, with celesta to give the last signal of completion. After the astringent Moto, its melismatic charm sounds hollow. The Polka following, marked 'melancholique' in the printed viola-piano score but not in the full score, is pungent and waywardly rhapsodic, with two episodes. Probably it is not meant to be conclusive. That is reserved for the final Hopak, called Galop, masterful, instant, and with the requisite energy to spare; something with Cossack devilment in it.

This suite was scarcely intended for such scrutiny, turn by turn. Nevertheless, it is easy to take a short symmetrical piece for granted, at its face value as this or that, and this octagonal suite clearly depends on the quick impact of different expressive features in prompt succession. No doubt, when a Tertis plays the solo, all sorts of unspecified overtones and shapely turns come to light and blend the frailer parts with the whole. But this cannot be guaranteed. While, then, many players will find many private uses for one component group or another, the limited scope of the entire suite is a strain on the ear of the symphonically minded. It is no substitute whatever for a viola concerto, now that Walton and others have shown that the viola is, after all, no exception among string soloists.

CONCERTO GROSSO

The short *Concerto Grosso* (1950), for a concertino of about twenty capable players, a *tutti* of third-position standard, and an optional body of elementary players, including some open-string contributors, is manifestly an occasional piece, more *concertante* suite than full-blown concerto, which will not lack opportunity for revival on one scale or another. Written for the twenty-first-birthday concert of the Royal Music Schools Association of Great Britain (which has grown from four classes in Hertfordshire to nine rural schools and one in South-East

London), it was performed accordingly in the Royal Albert Hall by massed orchestras (concertino and *tutti*), four hundred in all, under Sir Adrian Boult, in the presence of the Queen. This would be incentive enough for most composers to meet the special demands of the establishment, and it was certainly so for Vaughan Williams. The fact remains that it was he who was asked to comply by the executive, not of some fancy society, but of a teachers' association with some seven thousand weekly pupils on their lists. They were concerned to obtain, not a name, but a work that would be both feasible and stimulating in future to newcomers to the art and practice of music. For this Vaughan Williams was their man. Such was the special provenance of this *Concerto Grosso*; a 'Concerto Grosso for all comers', as Mr. Scott Goddard entitled it in his note for the souvenir programme, and by that very fact a solecism without any serious precedent.

Of the five movements, the Intrada, recovered at the very end, introduces the forces engaged, with hints of tough activity in the concertino and anything but a Handelian D major as the key-reference. Next, Burlesca ostinata contains two simple refrains in D minor, against a background of D–A–E and C–G (on open strings) which persists a little beyond this side of reason. The minor being variously modal, an intimate interlude in a rather modal D major, still with the *ostinata* around, readily establishes contrast, with an adroit use of the descending scale. But the continuation is anything but a formal *da capo*. A short Sarabande, with a melody rising from and returning to the G-string, echoes, with a difference, 'Tallis in G'—key, Phrygian second, solemn sadness and all.

The Scherzo is more for concertino and is from the same stock as its opposite number in the fifth symphony, with a concertino-led *da capo* in two beats, whose conversion to three in an eleven-bar presto would be at once entertaining and encouraging practice for *tutti* and optionals. The concluding March has a good tune, after the manner of the swinging phrase in *The Wasps* overture (complete with ♭3–1 progression) and could have been written by no one else, however Mixolydian in genre. The returning Intrada follows, as if the whole suite were a compendious overture, digressing to the Burlesca and the rest before recovering its essential *largo* solemnity. But this is a raw moment. It seems too much wanting in shape to be a satisfying close, however rarely the performers are aware of this.

A church committee report of 1922 (*Music in Worship*) expressed the sanguine hope that the old standing church orchestras might be revived.

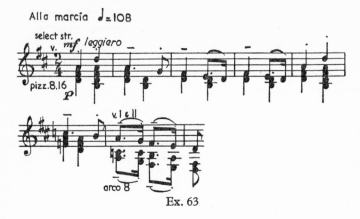

Ex. 63

This was not to be. But seven years later Mary Ibberson began her classes for rural music's sake, and in 1932 Sir Adrian Boult conducted a concert of Purcell, Gluck, etc. And so to the *Concerto* of 1950.

STRING PARTITA

Nevertheless, to listen to the *Partita* for double string orchestra (1948) is to be reminded of another Vaughan Williams. The work represents a fresh version of a work for double string trio (1939), now withdrawn, with a completely new finale. (Foss, confirmed by Miss Jean Stewart in *R.C.M. Magazine*, 55. 1.) The two independent three-part textures remain, with a double-bass part attached nominally to the second orchestra, but as often the bass of the whole harmony.

The composer's purpose, in altering the original, was to achieve greater clarity. He also, no doubt, wished to gain a more rounded tone for each of the antiphonal groups, less subject to the incidences of group performance, while retaining, as in the start of the Intermezzo, the option of anything up to three soloists, in contrast with a semi-*tutti*. Howes's suggestion of the working equilibrium of a concerto grosso, with the first orchestra as soloist section, is most misleading. The prescribed numbers in each orchestra are a minimum of 4–2–2 and 4–2–2–2, not the 1 : 2 relation which he reports. Further, the second orchestra's role could not possibly be described as *ripieno* or generalizing. From the start, it works in support of, or in an antiphony with, the first orchestra. The orchestras are thus habitually blended and conflated, just as the original trios were apt to become a sextet. The smooth, barely perceptible exchange of a typical *a–b* contrapuntal texture for *b–a*, for orchestras 1 and 2, in the Scherzo, bars 40–45, 112–115, would be noticeably laboured if the orchestras were unequal (*a–B, b–A*); and in the Intermezzo the solo and *tutti* of orchestra 1 equally pre-suppose a background throughout of light percussion tone (orchestra 2) which would be nonsensical as a generalizing effect. Again, the canons in bars 27–31, 97–105 of the Fantasia would be absurd if the follower part (second orchestra) were heavier than the leader (first orchestra); and even more the entry of the second orchestra in parallel motion with the first in bars 106–109.

Of the four movements, the second and the fourth are the most developed. The Prelude (i.e. first movement) contrasts the solo-viola's leisurely half-melodic, half-polyphonic curve, marked by falling fifths, with a more jaunty motive, multiple in texture, in two balanced stages, the second considerably more intense. D minor is established as the unobtrusive key-centre, sufficiently to contrast the second themes as first neighbouring but later remote (viz. involving the alteration of half the basic scale). The Scherzo, also in D minor, continues, now muted, the previous rhythmic texture at more than double speed, an unusual connection. The music at once reveals a primitive, very insistent background, derived, one may think, from the reiterations of a bamboo flute-player in the back streets of a town in Algeria, via Holst's quasi-oriental suite, *Beni Mora*.

Whether or not the sustained descending theme, soaring in the violins and moving imitatively to and from the basses, is accepted as an extension of this ritual preparation, the impact of its degree-pattern at its own tempo is absolutely distinctive, filling the melodic vacuum created by the repeated figures in the other orchestra, and at the same time promoting further rhythmic fixation later. A breakaway of key releases, unmuted, a medley of ideas, based on an impulsive, rather disturbing, rise of pitch. This cannot be regarded as the trio or interlude of the movement, for the new contrapuntal thread eventually qualifies a return to the 'Algerian' theme, now heard at half speed and made militant by opposition to it. This heated argument leaves the way clear for the recovery of the sustained theme, unimpeded but now more nearly exposed as the street-player's familiar chatter, sobered by diminished speed (four bars where there was one) into a sane intimacy, beginning with the violin's delivery in the G string. Flickers of the original rhythm re-appear later to fill the gaps in the spacious phrases.

The texture of this restatement may be compared with the coda of the

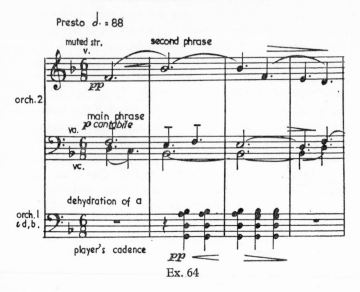

Ex. 64

Scherzo of the *London Symphony*. There the deliberate metre is an improvisation, being in fact the hint of a new episode, but the echoes of the prevailing *esprit de jeu* anticipate the present context. Here what begins as restatement develops into an increasingly absorbed period in a now familiar style, a passing slip into B flat minor being easily treated as a fresh link to D minor. While, then, it is unnecessary to stress so persistent a motive, beyond pointing out the difference between the gravity pull of 3 2 1 and the more poised descent of 8 7 5, the manifest quantitative and metrical relationships of the prevailing material call, at first, for close observation, and some ear-toe practice in identifying the same intonation, as a two-beat unit in a recurring series, and then as an expanding eight-beat phrase of woven texture. This relation is a rhythmic impact, not an intellectual conception. Certainly, it provides the main clue to the wide scope of the movement, vernacular to the point of *kitsch* without the forced realism of *Beni Mora*, yet reaching out in a wider circle to the archetypes of creative sanity. (See Ex. 64.)

It is surprising to pass to the Intermezzo. A new *pizzicato* movement, in simulation of the cross-rhythms of jazz—in tribute to Henry Hall, for reasons unknown—becomes the background of an extended *appassionato, molto vibrato* version of the motive of the Scherzo, treated polyphonically! However, the thematic reverberation is something of a formality, as far as it goes, and what catches the modern ear is the free, desiccated movement of the multiple harmonic texture, including the familiar fall of a middle third (A flat to F minor), and the apparently sad tune in the middle, which the composer has made shift to provide as a quasi-traditional ditty, enjoying his time off to try a sharpened seventh once again. Almost a tribute to Mr. Aaron Copland and his affection for the vernacular for its own sake. The Algerian flautist's challenge has been met by the sophisticated and equally melancholy *cri de cœur* of this new Cheyne Walk young man. An extended fancy portrait, but it might pass as a characteristic note for a gliding andante.

For the Fantasia, so named for want of a better title, has a clearly bi-focal pattern. It has nothing in common with the fugue and galli-maufry of a fantasia of 1600, or with the exploratory genre of 1800, and proceeds with some urgency and an unfaltering tempo. Its curious shape may be summarized thematically as A–B, C—C, a–b—(A), C; the small letters indicating incidental development of the basic material.

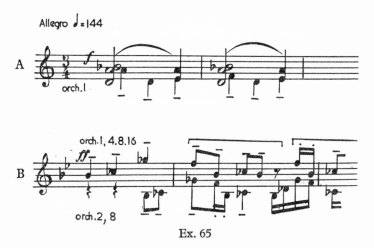

Ex. 65

It will be observed, and it may be aurally arguable, that, with more emphasis on the first re-appearance of A and B and less on the brief return of A, the pattern is symmetrical enough. It is just the absence of an impression of returning sequence that extends this bulge of develop-ment up to the restoration of C, now in D major. However, once gained, the 'dynamic calm' of this close, a slight reflection of the fifth symphony, confirms that this is a more set piece than any normal fantasia. The general restlessness of this finale, beginning with more than a suggestion of the Valley of Humiliation, is not at once convincing, and leaves an impression of artificiality, reflecting, perhaps, a search for a better finish than the original and apparently slighter movement.

The upshot is an interesting but uneven work, lacking in final shape.

A FOLK-DANCE SET

The Running Set is a quodlibet of folk-dance tunes, arranged for a moderate orchestra for an E.F.D.S.S. performance in the Royal Albert Hall, for a tune-less dance that Sharp had collected in the Appalachian Mountains in 1917. In introducing the dance into England, Sharp had chosen several traditional tunes, and, in their accepted collocation, these were combined to make one continuous movement. This set, fourteen verses in all, is thus no concert piece, though its rollicking tunes and infectious atmosphere made it, in spite of the repetitions, a pronounced success at its introduction at a semi-Vaughan Williams Promenade Concert in 1934. Two long dances culminate in the splendid swing of 'Cock o' the North', chosen to carry the dancers over a difficult new figure, and a fourth tune leads back to the first for the exit. The earlier two-piano version will interest those who wish to extend their folk-dance repertory. The sparkling arrangement calls for no further comment, nor does the composer's command of piquant orchestration. A distant precedent is Glinka's *Capriccio sopra alcune motivi russi* for piano duet. This development of three traditional tunes in varying tempi, with a bit of fugue and grand conflation of all three in the final Con moto, has no practical usefulness, except for duettists. The middle tune, later used as a descant in a garish chorus in *Ruslan* (Act 3), is in the minor, and the others major, and the harmonization is sophisticated throughout, with such turns as the second-degree major chord in the minor tune. After which, the hexatonic impact (no third whatever) of 'Barrack Hill' and the rest is a stimulating renunciation in itself.

FILM MUSIC: FORTY-NINTH PARALLEL

After travelling with his unit across Canada, going as far north as the 63rd parallel in order to obtain an 'authentic' sense of location, Mr. Michael Powell, film director, returned to the Denham Studios in England in 1940 to complete *Forty-ninth Parallel* (in the United States, *The Invaders*), a picture of the attempt of six Germans, stranded after the wreck of their submarine, to make their escape across Canada to the United States; the celebration of the longest undefended frontier in the world making a useful emergent background to the fierce encounter between hostile aliens and native citizens. It remained, amongst other things, to collect some unifying music.

This fell to Mr. Muir Mathieson, then at the start of his career as a film-music conductor. In sounding Vaughan Williams for this task, Mathieson had no difficulty in rousing the composer's enthusiasm for composition in a genre then unknown to him, or in persuading him that the subject proposed was relevant to his present desire to do something more than collecting 'salvage' to further the resolve of the British people in their greatest need. The score was soon written. It was not only successful but encouraging for the future. A film-music suite, since withdrawn, was produced (Prague, 1946), and the prelude recorded. The latter survives in *The New Commonwealth*, a unison-song of indifferent quality,[1] and the Scherzo of the late quartet is said to hinge on another motive from the film. But more was to follow; enough to raise the question of the film-composer's past attitude to film and sound track.

The first musical score, an introduction and five tableaux, written by Saint-Saëns for *L'Assassinat du Duc de Guise* in 1908, was soon followed by published strips and sets of music of different 'moods', and by the arrangement by Karl Breil of music by Grieg and Wagner, with more specific 'music cues', for the historical *Birth of a Nation* (1914), with a special preliminary screened appeal to viewers to adapt their sense of rhythm to the action of the film. But Milhaud's *L'Inhumaine* (1924) is probably the first film-score of any importance, and Max Steiner's score for *The Informers* (1935) remains a pioneer effort in the use of a plastic motto-theme, for What is Coming to Gypo, and of harmonic oscillations that might in time demand a vibraphone. The maturing of any film-music technique, to place besides the years of negligible experiment, has been slow. The establishment of synchronized dialogue and sound has naturally revolutionized the situation. It has also raised the problem of harmonizing the spoken word and music.[2]

To this modern situation there have been three types of solution and

---

[1] There are arrangements for male and for mixed voices, for an elastically reduced orchestra, for strings (Douglas), and for organ.

[2] See John Huntley, *British Film Music*, p. 55, and Roger Manvell and John Huntley, *The Technique of Film Music*, p. 53. Vaughan Williams's article on film music in *R.C.M. Magazine*, 40, 1 (1944), explains his early enthusiasm with his usual combination of shrewd comment and doctrinaire asides, not always to be taken literally. The fact remains that composers' names are not mentioned in catalogues of films, and are usually difficult to verify, except in the Central Film Library.

response. One is to compose down to the last detail, for the film as it is scheduled and revised. Such a synthesis of picture, dialogue and music has been the method of William Alwyn and on the whole of Walton. The second attitude has been to insist on the paramount claims of the composer, when he is 'on'. 'Film music is either heard, or it is not there'. To compromise is to surrender individuality. Viewers will tend all too readily to invest music with emotional qualities that it does not possess. That was the line taken by Sir Arthur Bliss; and, in reward, many of his film scores have become acceptable concert suites.

The third method is to compose to a known programme, but to leave open the degrees of repeat, optional phrases, etc., for a later *ad hoc* synchronization, which it is hopeless to try to anticipate. That has been Vaughan Williams's method. His music is not 'locked to the visuals', but runs its own parallel course, parallel enough to be relevant and at the same time justifying its own level of appeal. In the case of *Scott of the Antarctic*, he worked almost entirely to the script, and delivered his score, indeed, before he received (from Ernest Irving) a list of timings intended to 'help', with the usual note of optional cuts and extensions—before the picture itself had been completed. Freedom of expression was retained by adopting an elastic and cumulative method. The composer later observed, 'Never write a long tune in a film. It is sure to be interrupted, obscured or extirpated before you can state it'; advice cheerfully disregarded in Ex. 66 below.

COASTAL COMMAND

The fictional-documentary *Forty-ninth Parallel* was succeeded by music for the documentary *Coastal Command*, a Crown Film production, purporting to be an excerpt from the record of the crew of a flying-boat, protecting a convoy, shadowing a surface raider for attack by other aircraft and then running into trouble itself. Ken Cameron, who recorded the music, declared, in the name of his Unit colleagues, 'We knew that here was something great . . . nor did we waste . . . it was the visual material which suffered the mutilation. The music is, in fact, . . . the picture'. (Huntley, *op. cit.* p. 111). Fragments of the music were used later for a radio feature of unknown date, and Muir Mathieson soon arranged an orchestral suite of seven movements, of which he broadcast all but the sixth in 1943.[1] This suite is still current. Mathieson has

[1] The librarians of the B.B.C. music library and the Oxford University Press Hire Library allowed me to see their copies of the radio and film-into-suite precedents of the surviving suite.

followed the film order, apart from reversing what are now nos. 5 and 4. Nos. 3, 4, 5 and 7 are the most considerable movements, the last being much the most extended. The radio arrangement must have had its own script, and at one point (2*a*), the fresh title is of passing historical interest, which ex-airmen will appreciate.

The following table shows the apparent evolution of this action-music in its respective order, in terms of the suite numbers, which now constitute the only method of general reference. It must be understood that the radio music was only a selection from each number, and this is indicated.

Suite number	Film music: Headings	Suite number	Suite: Titles	Suite number	Radio feature: Titles
1	Titles, etc.	1	Prelude	—	—
2	Island Station (Hebrides)	2	Hebrides	2	Lonely station
2*a*	Taking off at night	2*a*	Taking off at night	3*b*	End of first day
3	Hudsons take off from Iceland	3	No title	4	Passage of time
5	Battle of Beauforts	4	Quiet determination	1*a*	Landing music
4	Sunderland goes in close (Quiet determination)	5	Battle of Beauforts	6	Uneasy
				2*a*	Wellingtons take off
6	No title (Later: J.U. [88] attacks)	6	No title	2	Lonely music
7	Title-page missing	7	No title	7*a* (1*b*)	Suspense We search and strike
				7*c*	The return
				7*b*	Finale

The suite begins with the titles-music, which, as a miniature overture, provides motives of resolution, aggression and visions of return. The latter anticipate the close of the *Scott* music—used again at the climax of the first movement of *Sinfonia antartica*. The radio music deals at once with action at base and has a brief triumph at the end. The tune of 'quiet determination', which appears once in the radio music and in several stages in no. 4 of film and suite, is in itself a striking example of the

439

Ex. 66

composer's plain kind of melodic affirmation, in an unfaltering major. In the radio version it appears with the unusual Elgarian *nobilmente*; in the suite, *cantabile*. The tune goes Phrygian later, and finally defiantly Locrian. (It was doubtless with such recollections in his head that the composer, asked after a lecture to look over an American student's latest exercise, rubbed his chin and remarked, 'If a tune comes into your head, I hope you will not hesitate to make a note of it.') But one wonders how it fitted the flying-boat's deadly struggle. In the battle-music of no. 5, the repetition of an eight-bar refrain in the Locrian mode (cf. Symphony 9, *init.* for the basic curve) fixes its shape on the mind, and then its circling round the keynote is made a point of insistence in fresh contexts; in sonorous and acrimonious attendance on a grim rising-fifth figure in trombones, in smoother accompaniment to the return of the opening resolution-motive from the Prelude, and in relentless arpeggio movement over the trombone ascents, whose minatory character recalls the rising fourths in the fourth symphony and leads, by way of rough finish, to a clash of semitones (♭3 5 ♮7 8) which does not differ in principle from ♭2 1 of the same work. A concentrated piece of imagery.

After the brief menace of no. 6, the finale draws the main threads together. The 'search and strike' motive from the Prelude (B flat) leads to the lilting 1–6–1 2–3 already expanded in no. 3. The contour of this second theme seems today to anticipate the first theme of the Scherzo of *Sinfonia antartica*. Originally in a light, provisional string texture in F, it is now in a militant and later pompous A major (brass, *tutti*), hinting at C sharp. After which, a return to resolution and vision (1 *fin.*) in D major is a foregone conclusion, though not the detail. The musical upshot is spasmodic and rather fragmentary, like life in 1942, but the place of this kind of committed music in the composer's output must be recognized by those who are inclined to place him permanently in a niche of other-worldly detachment. A vocal parallel was *England, My England* (Henley) for unison singing, and the orchestral texture here is accomplished and interesting, as may still be heard now and again. There is also a military band accompaniment, conveniently lowered a semitone, to D flat.

THE PEOPLE'S LAND

In 1943 the composer supplied music for two contrasted films: *The People's Land*, a brief display in colour of the work of the National Trust, and *The Story of a Flemish Farm*, a patriotic screen play by Jill and Jeffrey Dell. The former, still in the G.B. Film Library, is a purposive rural sketch with a smooth flow of scene and supporting dialogue for what may lightly be termed a miniature suite in the sometimes dim background, as the music moves adroitly from the grimness of stone circle and fortified castle to the expansive pattern of stately mansion and village and rolling national acres, and from the sheer activity of cyclists, scouts and children freely at play—a nostalgic touch in 1943— to the more special pursuits of fisherman, entomologist and mountaineer. So to a moment of vision and truth, strengthened by a return to the ageless white cliffs that confronted any continental spectator who might be concerned.

For this eminently pastoral sequence, a moment's breath of Blakian innocence before the grim return to experience, the composer has drawn upon tunes and fragments of folk-song. There are old favourites like 'John Barleycorn' (a queer choice for boy scouts, if one starts thinking about the corn spirit) and 'The spring time of the year' (for the butterfly-catcher, as formerly for the sad queen in *Richard II* at Stratford), 'Love will find out the way' and 'Chairs to mend' for Hall and village, a suggestion of 'Rakish Highland man' for the fisherman[1]

---

[1] With acknowledgements again to the E.F.D.S.S. librarian.

and two major-key clue-tunes, one for the Sussex cliffs (rising from the tonic to fifth and sixth degrees and back) and a more laboured ascent to the sixth degree for lakeland (cf. *Flos Campi*, 6).[1] The two last-named, in reverse order, coalesce with some intensity at the end, with a final slip from D major into F and back, and a melodic convergence on the sharpened or major-third degree, echoing *Coastal Command* and now familiar to *Scott* audiences.

Here, if anywhere, is the right place for reviving native tunes, and the often obscure bunches of fragments that link them are effectively unbiddable figures, refusing to conform and cohere. The fine and decorative liberationist setting, with the call to Everyman to inherit the land that is his, is the central appeal. For all its breezy contrasts, the music has no surprises, and is, indeed, almost too genial a monument to the tough perseverance that has maintained the National Trust for what it is, in the teeth of vested interests, legal obstructionism and national apathy. But this was planned for a release, not a summoning, of personality.

STORY OF A FLEMISH FARM

Story of a Flemish Farm, long since withdrawn, survives in an orchestral suite of seven short and eloquent movements, in an easier style than *Coastal Command*. The somewhat complicated plot was founded on the record of a daring stroke in occupied Belgium, compiled with the help of the Belgian Government and the British Air Ministry.

The titles of the suite refer reminiscently, and therefore obscurely, to the Flag, parting lovers, a dead man's kit, the Café, and the Major who 'meets his fate'. All the same, it is hardly necessary to ask what flag flutters (1) and wanders (7). In the context, this is the Flag above all the rest, as the returning motives of the opening declare, with a slight sense of mystery (G–B flat–G) at first, which deepens as, finally, an E flat picked out of the air (from A minor) leads into G in sonorous conclusion (7). In point of fact, it is the flag of the dispersed Belgian Air Force, buried in the Flemish farm, rescued despite enemy observation, and presented, in England, to the new Belgian squadron of the R.A.F. Melodically, the circling round the third degree may recall other occasions, such as the second movement of *Flos Campi*, but the signal is clear. Nor need one ask what lovers part at dawn (3), or in

[1] Has this sapphic tune (in the 11.6 metre of many French church melodies) been collected ? It is not shaped like 'The saviour's love' beyond a preliminary curve.

which Belgian café (4) there is light and sentimental music, perhaps a calypso for mouth organ, to judge by the thirds. The *Angst* is familiar; and the clarinet tune has a suggestion of Sibelius.

It might be more relevant to enquire the identity of the formal, rather gawky, modal figure that twice interrupts the café music and returns at the start of the finale as a kind of camouflage for the true finish. Presumably it is the returning Belgian pilot, who has to inform the farmer's daughter that her pilot husband has been killed.[1] As it is, without any such prompting the entry of this figure in the café number is defiant, and its final translation from B to A flat, the main key, forced. Nor is it easy to perceive its relevance, in the finale, to the flag theme. Once more, the restoration of 'dynamic calm' by the revival of the motto-theme is very sudden.

Other cyclic features are noticeable and enigmatic. 'Farewell to the flag' (2), originally the end, exposes three themes, of which the last is a pronounced rising and falling pentatonic phrase, delivered by trumpet and wood. Its due restatement now offers the extrinsic appeal, in

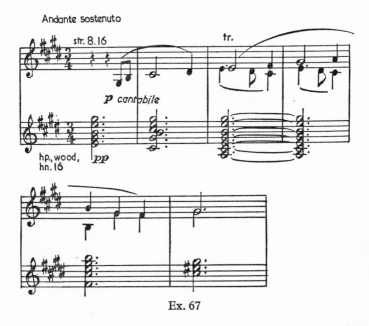

Ex. 67

[1] The original piano score of the film-music shows the suite-titles casually attached (in the order 5,1,4,3,6,7,2), but there is no surviving score of the film-sequences as such.

texture, of anticipating the close of the first movement of the sixth symphony in its blend of string line and harp-wind harmony. So far, so good. But the reappearance of the theme at the end of a persistent and minatory development, in no. 5 ('The Major meets his fate'—at the Belgian capitulation), is mystifying. On the other hand, the reverberation of the violoncello and violin phrases, and the muted horns, from no. 3, in the obviously reminiscent no. 6 ('The dead man's kit'), is sufficiently diversionary to be coherent, the main novelty being a fanfare for muted trumpet.

Inevitably a tense feeling hangs over most numbers of this suite. Only the café scene relaxes, and the final moment of objective hazardously achieved. Nevertheless every number has character, subject to the reservations made. On the whole, this suite, which was introduced to the Promenade Concerts in 1945, has been unjustly neglected since.

Flemish Farm has, hypothetically, a further genetic interest. According to Howes, the opening of the second and fourth movements of the sixth symphony drew thematically on motives originally conceived in connection with the film. Whether they were used eventually in the actual film the composer did not remember. There is no hint of that second movement in the suite. In 'Night by the sea' (2), there is a plucked string intonation, 1–2 ♭3|3–♭3 1, heard beneath a wind chord of F minor, whose relation to Ex. 46*b* could be tabulated; but it takes more than a melodic twist to make a motive. It is also unlikely that an odd phrase-intimation in 1942 would throw any sparks five years later. The ampler Ex. 67 is on the borderline here.

In 1945 appeared *Stricken Peninsula*, a short army film by the Ministry of Information, long since withdrawn and even in its time somewhat out-of-date and over-optimistic. It dealt with the problems of the Allied Armies in trying to restore an ordered and emancipated life in Southern Italy: food and water, transport, health services, schools, political expression. The music is lost. Apparently, it underlined some excellent photographs and made the film something more than a piece of once topical information.

JOANNA GODDEN

In 1947 *The Loves of Joanna Godden* followed. 'Involvements' would perhaps be a better description of all but the first of Joanna's associations with Martin, Arthur and Bert, in the more plainly titled novel by Sheila Kaye-Smith. Arthur is here debonair and dominating, later the almost heroic figure who loses all his sheep by foot-and-mouth disease. A recorded selection, long since withdrawn,[1] shows the composer's versatility in matching different features with brief music: the foot-and-mouth purge, village fair dancing, the death of Martin (keening and organ, both anticipating *Scott*), the attraction of Ellen, Joanna's more dashing sister, for Martin's father, and, chiefly, Joanna's buoyant spirit. The last, obviously an idealization but in keeping here, is motivated (5 6 1 2) by a forthright ascent to the second degree in early-major style. Joanna's starchy side, including her reaction to Ellen, is by-passed. This is not probing or enduring music and Keller refers slightingly to it in his review of *Scott*, but the call for variety obviously beguiled the composer, and there is no need to deprecate what was not written for perpetuity. The score of the film-music survives (see p. 448*n*)., but there is no suite.

SCOTT OF THE ANTARCTIC

These mainly documentary essays came to a head in the monumental *Scott of the Antarctic* (1948) which, as I write, is still current. There was one normal recording, apart from one made by the Rank organization (F.M. 43–44), of select material from the original score. The H.M.V. disc (C3834) includes the two Pony Marches and penguin music, and the heavy march from the Pole, besides the now familiar second stage of 'Climbing the Glacier', anticipated in the 'titles' sequence, and the visionary close. By 'now familiar' is meant, of course, the reverberation in *Sinfonia antartica* of the motto-theme (passim) and, at the climax of the first movement, the visionary theme. The Rank disc repeats the Pony Marches, distinguished below, but includes the inspiriting music for the departure of the *Terra Nova* from Ross Island, which somehow echoes the *Sea Symphony* opening in its evocative imagery.

Whether written to the rough initial script, or to a time figure (in seconds), or after precise discussion with producer and music director, the music is rarely tied precisely to any extended incident. It was thus assured in part of a certain independent quality, which made it a conceivable basis for a symphony. In a recent article, indeed, Mr. David Brown went so far as to maintain that the film-music proved to be a mere preliminary to the full creative intention realized in the *Sinfonia antartica* (*Monthly Musical Record*, 998 (March–April, 1960)). I have already suggested that the symphony should stand or fall as a symphony, not as a piece of glorified programme-music. So far I agree with Mr.

---

[1] Re-issue by Columbia (U.S.A.).

Brown, though with very different musical conclusions. But the film-music remains intact, and it should be assessed in its tremendous setting.

For in *Scott of the Antarctic* Ealing Studios' executive was embarking on a project quite out of the ordinary. The train of events has not only gone forcibly home to the nation in general but is remembered with indelible pride (and regrets) by those who participated and their successors. Script-writers, producers, actors and technicians alike took exceptional pains in learning the ropes. For verisimilitude, advice was sought from the Scott Polar Research Institute, Cambridge, whose foundation had marked an expanding scientific tribute to what Scott's last expedition stood for, just as the film itself now provided the dramatic answer to the nation's sense of honour in the most popular idiom of the day. Something of the extraordinary feeling of historical continuity which overtook the cast and unit, in their various typical locations, can be gathered from the short account of the film, written by one of the technical advisers, David James. An article by Professor Frank benham, who founded and became the first director of the Scott Institute, records a similar response on the part of members of the expedition, who attended the film with reserved anticipations and emerged quite overcome by the degree with which typical events had been re-enacted and the main personalities reflected in characteristic touches (*Polar Record*, 5. 37–8 (January–July, 1949)). For viewers in general, the first volume of *Scott's Last Expedition* (the second, for scientists) gives, in Scott's sober, steady and comprehensive diary, a vivid picture of the scientific side of the expedition and a profoundly personal sense of each stage of the crucial journey. Despite shattering reverses, failure seems so nearly inconceivable that one can read on hopefully in face of superior knowledge, and, if not dreaming of a happy issue, continue to regard Scott's real objective as valid. Many a 1914 volunteer saluted him as a forerunner *in extremis* (S. Gwynn, *Scott*).

The potential subject-matter, then, ranged (with whatever preliminaries might be thought necessary) from an immense, hazardous and often picturesque journey, to be made as typically comprehensive as possible, to the human background of organizing, setting out, approaching the Pole by stages, camping, manhauling and the final enforced encampment. Selection and compression became essential. First, there was a grand scheme for shooting (with technicolor camera) in different terrains to mark the principal stages of expeditionary effort: off Graham Land, within the antarctic circle, for a suggestion of the ice barrier and wild life; on the Aletsch Glacier and its crevasses—

alarmingly new experience for the distinguished guide who took Lashly's part—to match the Beardmore, the world's longest glacier, with Europe's best effort; and in Finse, Norway, for the low-lying plateau that contains the Pole; and there were polar, public and domestic scenes at Ealing. All this was matched by a drastic selection and conflation of pivotal features of the human story, in which, finally, every new turn augmented the mounting ordeal. The postponed announcement, for example, of Amundsen's telegram, 'Going South', in the wardroom of the *Terra Nova* after leaving New Zealand, serves an obvious presentational purpose and violates no vital order of procedure. On the other hand, the conception of the whole film as a flashback from Scott's last encampment was rejected, as giving a wrong slant to the epic.

With so much special scenery and light-effects, and so many brief incidents of assembly, despatch and leave-taking, characterization had no normal chance. Scott's romantic, controlling and single-minded figure, Wilson's genial and contemplative moods, Oates's blunt and sporting exterior, the differing self-control of a disappointed Lt. (Teddy) Evans and a physically distressed P.O. (Taff) Evans, and a hint of devoted wives, are typical cross-sections. But that does not mean that the journey as shown is monotonous for any perceptible length, except towards the end of the film. Besides natural phenomena of rare quality, there are, in turn, the Christmas party, the ponies, on which so much depends for a time, the threatening blizzard, the glacier climb, the somewhat over-dramatized choice of the polar party, the discovery of the Norwegian flag, the turn for the 'run home'; all threaded together by Scott's personal concern (soliloquy) over lost time, anxious comparisons with Shackleton's superior figures over the same ground, and growing worry over the physique of two of his companions. Only in the last third of the film, after the scene has closed in on the march from the Pole, is something lacking. Scott's dynamic alternations between hope and despair, the strain on the party of Evans's mental decline (following concussion) and Wilson's bad leg, the tension over Oates's final decision, all on top of the unspeakable conditions, go unsaid. Instead, the collapse of Evans and the self-sacrifice of Oates, and the 'inner voice' recital of the last letters of Bowers, Wilson and Scott, are reduced to a passive stoicism and religious resignation. The later shock of discovery, by the supporting party, is equally absorbed in the memorial close.

With so much self-significant action and sparse, terse dialogue, ending in action and monologue in sight of death, it is not easy to find room for music, and there is less on the tape than in the score. A strong film does not need a substantial amount of illustrative music, as, long ago, *Kameradschaft,* a film of near-disaster in a mine on the Franco-German frontier, demonstrated. Hence, Keller's criticism of the composer for 'interpreting monotony by monotony' (see p. 381) by using a motto-theme is based on a prejudiced view of the script, which few will endorse for the film as a whole.

Before considering the musical aspects of the criticism, it would be as well to glance at the main course of the film-music, as planned. It is summarized opposite, the thematic content being defined by reference to the only score published and recorded in continuity, that of the *Sinfonia antartica.* Numbers which do not appear in the film-music as finally taped are marked with an asterisk. The horizontal lines show the end of a reel, representing one-third of the 111 minutes of showing time.[1]

Let us consider, first, how far the motto-theme, in the deprecation of which Keller quotes didactic support, is worn threadbare.[2] For the

---

[1] Most of the music for *Scott of the Antarctic,* and all the music for *The Loves of Joanna Godden,* remains, as I write, in the archives of Associated British Picture Corporation Limited, which acquired the assets of Ealing Studios (later, Ealing Films) some years ago. In tracing these valuable scripts to their present home, which took me six months, I should like to acknowledge the help of Mr. Jack Worrow, now with Michael Balcon Productions. Mr. Stanley Black, music director of A.B.P.C., gave me all facilities for examining this music, which includes nearly three hundred pages of autograph. A notable appendix to the manuscript collection in the British Museum, were it more accessible.

The *Scott* music consists of the full score of some three dozen of the fifty-two numbers which at some stage made the total of the music sequences, together with the original piano score, in part (42 pages), and a piano score in numbered film sequences (another 42 pages) with copies of this piano score in some cases. For four numbers there is only a piano score, though two of these are in the British Museum in full score. For twelve numbers there is nothing, half of these being nos. 41, 43, 47–50. Nevertheless, should the film be ever withdrawn, there here remains both abundant evidence of the basic material of the *Sinfonia antartica,* and scores of no less distinguished numbers not so preserved and now calling urgently for some sort of assembly in an orchestral suite. The piano score, indeed, of 'Ice waste: Ross Island' has actually been re-entitled 'Sinfonia antartica 3/Landscape' in readiness.

I have to acknowledge the receipt of useful information about the film from Mr. Alan Gilham, of the schools department of the G.B. Film Library, which leases the film.

[2] In his article in *Grove's Dictionary of Music and Musicians, s.v.* Film Music, Keller adduces somewhat hastily, as repudiators of clue-theme technique, the American writers, H. Eisler (*Composing for the Films,* 1947) and F. W. Sternfeld (*Music Quarterly,* 33, p.517); for Sternfeld's main defence of Friedhofer in *The Best Years of our Lives* is that on the whole he employs his clue-themes with discrimination. Moreover, Keller demonstrates the 'mastery' of this technique in Walton's music for *Hamlet* (1948) and elsewhere, as proof that tautology can be avoided. His objection to indiscriminate reverberations remains.

Film-sequence number	Title and content	Place of development in *Sinfonia antartica* (number of movement or bar, and position)
1	Titles. Heroism.	1, init. Motto (finale version).
2	Titles.	1, Lento. Unison descent.
2a	Prologue. 'The terror and fascination of the South Pole' (R.V.W.).	1. Vocal motive (solo and ch.).
3*	Oriana [Wilson].	4, init. Oboe melody.
4*	Doom. First meeting [of Oriana] with Scott.	Cf. 1, 21. Bass (cymb. entry).
5 & 6*	Scott leaves Oriana.	Cf. 1, 21; 4, init.
7	Sculpture scene [Kathleen Scott and her husband.] (This scene now precedes the disturbed scene at the Wilsons'.)	4, Allegretto. B minor string m.
16	Departure of ship [from Ross Island]. (Record: FM 43: *b*.) (This comes after 21 in the film. The music for the departure from Britain, 'The Queen's Birthday March' (15), is not there. Nor is 'Will he no' come back again?')	Cf. 2, 20, Animando (trumpet m.) for theme in B flat.
18a	Ice floes.	2, 48, Second Moderato. Wood descent against repeated semitonal ascent (celesta, etc.).
18b	Iceberg (replaced by 18c).	3, 24, 44. Descents in bass.
18c	(Str./wood hn. chords plus motive in bass.)	3, 50, 24. Motives in reverse order.
19	(Opening pages missing.) Penguins. (Record: H.M.V.: *c*.) (This comes after 21 in the film.)	2, med., Scherzando. Wood descending motive and pernickety theme in close canon.
21	Ross Island.	3, init. Horn m.
24	Aurora (4 beats).	Cf. 2, init. Horn harmony.
25	Pony March [1]. (Record: H.M.V.: *b*; F.M. 43: *a*.)	
27	Parhelion.	
28*	Pony March [2], ending as in 25.	5, 52. Clarinet m. (fifths in wood and percussion).
29	Pony March [2], [preceded by] Blizzard. (Fierce *tutti*. Vocal oscillation. Oboe tune.) (Record: H.M.V.: *f*; F.M. 44.)	For Blizzard, cf. 5, init.; 1, Animato (vibraphone); 5, clarinet m.

Film-sequence number	Title and content	Place of development in *Sinfonia antartica* (number of movement, bar, and position)
30	Distant glacier (cf. 18c).	3, 24.
31	Climbing glacier. (Record: H.M.V.: d) (1, da capo.)	3, Lento (three beats). Unison and chordal motives (organ). Motto da capo.
33	Scott comes out . . . goes up [on top of the glacier].	Cf. 1, fin. Fanfare and tune, G major.
34	Snowy plain. Scott's decision [on personnel of Pole Party].	5, 68. Bassoon continuation of clarinet line.
36	Polar party moves off.	5, 19. Development of motto.
37	Amundsen. Black Flag. (Trombone descent from A to E flat.)	
39	The return. (Record: H.M.V.: e)	
42	Death of Evans.	(Motto).
44	Death of Oates. Oates lying awake . . . stands and goes out.	4, Poco più lento (string m. in F); 5, 19; 1 (vocal m.)
46*	Only eleven miles (replaced by wind-machine and voices in film).	1, med. Falling fifths (bell). Cf. 4, Pesante before Oates motive.
51 & 52	'To suffer woes . . . life, joy, empire, victory'. (In the autograph piano score, eight lines from Shelley's *Prometheus* appear at the top of the music, as in the score of the symphony, first movement.)	1, fin. Tune. Note: m. = melody

titles, distracting as they are to a listener, there is an impressive exposition of this magnificent motive, in the shorter version found in the finale of the symphony, and incidentally with the oboe and piano parts clearly *added* to the score. (The wind-machine part originally in the score was taken out at the request of the producer, as being redundant to a shot that showed wind visually. It was restored for the symphony.) This is followed by a second theme, soon ominously vocal. (The disembodied tone was obtained, by trial and error, by having the singers with their backs to the microphone.) In the first of the three combined reels, in which the original twelve are commonly conveyed, there is just a brief development (x), as a bass refrain, of bars 2–3 of Ex. 54a, stressing the

[Ex. 54a (motto-theme)]

[Ex. 54c]

curve 1 –♯3 – 4 –♭2, to mark, with 54b, the meeting of Scott and Oates.
An early entry, entitled 'doom', for the assumed and probably fictitious
exterior effect on Oriana of the arrival of Scott at the Wilsons' Scottish
bungalow, has been scrapped. In reel 2, the glacier-climbing music is
followed by a full repeat of the opening. This perfunctory *da capo*,
key and all, is a most illogical transition, and short shrift for a fine
theme. It is pointless and frustrating to any listener—and, after all,
only a listener would identify it after so much sound-material and vivid
incident.[1] The shot of the polar party, manhauling (reel 3), is set to an
extension of 54a (*x*), at first in three-time, on the G string, and then in
four-time, in the style of the symphony finale. This makes a brief but

---

[1] Mr. Charles Frend, the producer of *Scott*, has obliged me with a frank
recollection of the revisions at this stage. While he found the opening glacier
music (31), for the halt halfway up, admirable, he considered the remainder
lacking in the tension proper to the effort of gaining the top. That led him to
make the suggestion of replacing this with the title-music. 'Irving was under-
standably outraged . . . V. W. was quite undisturbed.' In his posthumously
published autobiography, *Cue for Music* (p. 162), however, Irving cited this
incursion of the title-music as an effective surprise-entry, typical of a deft clue-
theme in the sphere of film-music. (Cf. p. 458 here.)

It will be clear that while I would probably have agreed with Mr. Frend
over the music now omitted (which appears, from the autograph piano score,
to have been originally the clarinet tune now found in *Sinfonia Antartica*,

eloquent musical send-off for the five now chosen by a sanguine captain, and it makes a reasonable basis for a contrast in the return from the Pole, after Amundsen.

Further developments, then, for P.O. Evans's final collapse and for the desperate but resolute Oates, wriggling out of his sleeping-bag, seem to add an unfortunate fatalistic touch to a heroic motive. The final evolution of the motto in the major (cf. 54e), anticipated off 'Buckley Island' as Scott turns from a great vista of the glacier to look forward over the plateau, may seem to informed ears to be an echo of *Coastal Command*, quite as much as an offshoot of the present motto, but it is considerably expanded, with final entries in F, D, B flat and F, which seem to recall similar gestures of the spirit in the Pavane in *Job*. This music follows the catastrophic discovery, here reduced to a fleeting exposure of tent fabric and Scott diary, that 'the Pole party has not returned'; apparently Dr. E. L. Atkinson's stunning later announcement to this effect, on his return to the supporting party at Cape Evans —see Prof. Debenham's recollection—was judged too painful a memory to include. The cut accepted, the close, simple as it is in its blend of fanfare and conjunct movement, sounds the right note for the focusing on the monument on Observation Hill, moving from the inscribed 'To strive, to seek, to find and not to yield' to a view of the cross in its entirety, standing, significantly enough, on a cairn of rocks. Another 'thanksgiving for victory', implemented by the elementary connection with the original theme, emblem of unceasing mental fight.

The cyclic process, in short, is open to criticism in applied detail, but it is not an exaggerated translation of the long and wearing journey, cumulatively retarded by shocking adversity.

So much for the range of the heroic theme. Four other features make themselves felt musically: (1) the first sight of the ice-barrier; (2) the ponies; (3) climbing the glacier; (4) the return from the Pole. The first is based on a blunt, relentless alternation of D minor and B major,

---

5 (5. 6), lasting 1 minute 7 seconds), I do not endorse his insertion of the title music, literally, in place of this. However conveniently it may stop *for* Lashly's fall down the crevasse, it records only a cessation of movement.

Mr. Frend has also explained that it was owing to his intervention that the initial march-off of the five, at the end of the second reel, was left without music and almost complete silence, replaced 35a, 'The polar party departs' (Irving's manuscript), in content as in 36 but with the tune in the soprano register. (Inevitably the preceding echo of the Kathleen music, shadowing Scott's letter to his wife, goes out too.) In consequence, the momentum of the music for the march-forward (reel 3) is, perhaps, lightened, in comparison with the heavier return-music.

with a heavy falling phrase (5 ♯3 ♮3 1) in the bass, to make the music gravitate to D, and a tumultuous canon in the brass, with gong. The

Ex. 68*a*

ponies have first a rather trifling D major tune, helped out by a combination of xylophone, harp, celesta and percussive strings, to celebrate ardent hopes when pony transport catches up the ex-motorists, now forced to manhaul. When the animals are doomed, a more extensive and rather sinister tune, since familiar, is announced by the oboe, originally following a statement by clarinet, in low register, for an earlier sequence. The melody now emerges from horrific blizzard music, including the siren voices. An echo of Oates's 'despair' over conditions?

The glacier music, as it first appears, is, with its memorable combination of canonic and chordal themes, one of the strongest *episodes*. (You cannot add to the stature of the Beardmore, but you can turn it into an agendum, and categorize its wastefulness.) The first theme, with its piquant suggestion of a perpetual canon, and of a circular theme (cf. Exx. 5*b* and 5*c*), in a few bars, is an adroit token of the closed circle of the ice age's natural rhythm—Blake's Leviathan. Moreover, the second theme (cf. Ex. 55) has here a more fixed Lydian outline —3 2 3, 1 4, 3—which was altered in the symphony to a halt on an open 4. There is no organ to stress the defiance of evolutionary man. Both themes are rather overworked, ending with the first. They do not generate fresh energy, and the bare reverberation of the opening music on top of these reiterations is both provocative in itself and musically at a severe tangent. One needs either a fresh and homogeneous striving theme, moderato without pomposity, or an unpredictable new development of the motto, to match this crucial stage of progress.

The strophe which sets the heavy emotional pace for the return from the Pole, all daydreams gone, makes an impressive rejoinder to the hopeful march from the glacier, already discussed. The eloquent descent of

two semitones (*en effet*) in eight bars is masterly, and the repeat at the
higher octave, for a middle verse, intensifies this amplification of Scott's

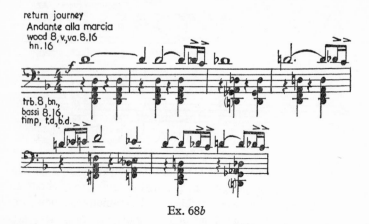

Ex. 68*b*

summary of the Pole as he found it: 'Great God! This is an awful
place'. But the closing repeat seems, again, perfunctory.

There remain a number of fragments, some passable, others so slight
as to be inadmissible in present company. The music for Kathleen
Scott is curiously inadequate. The wistful Oriana music has been
scrapped. Nansen's appearance, as the dog lover in a partly sinister
sense, has his piquant motive. The musically vernacular 'Queen's
Birthday March', for the ship's departure from England, roughly fills
a gap, with 'Will he no' come back again?' The returning sally forth

Ex. 68*c*

from Ross Island is a compressed but scintillating moment, recalling
the *Sea Symphony* by its broad vista. Scott's decision on final personnel
(34) invokes the alto oboe in a theme that survives in the symphony.
Amundsen, left without the music for his telegram, is briefly despatched
when it comes to the discovery of his precedence in the Antarctic. The
stoic deaths of Evans and Oates receive conventional treatment,

undistinguished in the latter case. The baleful chords and bell of 'Only eleven miles!' (to One Ton Depot), the notes of a triumphant blizzard, were in the end replaced by blizzard voices and human whispers (Wilson, Scott), and thus reserved for a later occasion. Keller's predication of 'negligible' has thus some force here and there.

It may be added that the idea of having a phonograph play *Abide with Me* (Liddle) as sung by Clara Butt, as Wilson used to do, seems now an excess of realism, which the remaining music shows up. Why could not the composer have produced, as Wilson's more articulate intimation, a little V. W. in the manner of the 'evening prayer' in the ballet, *On Christmas Night*?

The superfluous incidents (the luncheon party of the Royal Geographical Society, etc.) abandoned, the outline of the script progressively hardened, and the music could only remain subservient to it, entering as best it could. It became a question of unobtrusively augmenting the select unspoken thoughts of Captain Scott (mainly), as presented acoustically in his 'inner voice', with music's extra dimension. There was no chance of a musical design *per se*.

The composer was accordingly content to harness the unconquerable passion of a great, determined and heroic explorer to the trenchant harmonic rhythm of his opening imagery, with the briefer but heavy reluctance of the return, and the visionary gleam of the epilogue. He matched visual emblems of the ice age, its 'desert' challenge and its terrors with harmonic types of music, ruthlessly vibrating in a closed circle, emotionally restrained but no less tense. He relied on his film experience to deck out, as they pass, the penguins and ponies and parhelion, and on his deeper powers of composition to deal with weightier human episodes. He was prepared to turn on the title-music midway, in a nonchalant *da capo*, and extend its provenance later. Subsequently, in *Sinfonia antartica*, by adding the sinister vocal motive again, Vaughan Williams made this return of a musical clue conclusive in a fresh and more realistic direction. For the vicarious aspiration of a Tennysonian Ulysses, he substituted the unbowed head of the pioneer who knows that nature may be fiendishly victorious; that there are some questions without answers. The creation of the sixth symphony finale perhaps encouraged the composer thus to end his next symphony as confidently in a kind of stoic composure; a rejoinder to *Neptune* and *Egdon Heath*. In the film, he was content with the epilogue method that he had pursued in *Flemish Farm* and *Joanna Godden*, as well as *Coastal Command*.

While a certain proportion of stray musical episodes still, then, seem jejune accretions to the sound-track, and the conclusion is general rather than specific, earlier rather than contemporary Vaughan Williams, the outstanding impact of the music is that it is equal to its unique occasion. The same may have been said about much in the production.[1] But whereas this was mainly the result of intelligent research into the recorded events and phenomena, Vaughan Williams worked from his own convictions about music for the expedition, and without any concern for precise re-enactment, beginning with a simple plea for 'at least 60 seconds of mountains, which will finally merge into the [since scrapped] luncheon party'. The music thus seldom takes the course that could be expected. That is supplied at the quayside and Christmas party (G.K.W.) Yet the *Scott* music conveys its own assurance of 'sticking' qualities in the human spirit, along with lighter touches. It was doubtless owing to his confidence in the composer's mastery of the occasion that Ernest Irving, as he informed James later, had no hesitation in suggesting Vaughan Williams as the composer for *Scott*. (It may be added without comment, as a reflection of Vaughan Williams as others hear him, that Irving goes on to make the disarming observation, 'As everybody knows, Vaughan Williams's music is rooted in the folk-songs of Britain. He has forged for himself a style and technique which is intensely personal and strongly national. His five symphonies are all built on the same foundations'.)

Although open to some criticism for its hazardous organization, Scott's last expedition will not be forgotten, and if any documentary film is entitled to preservation, this is it. For it is inconceivable that any producer would launch out afresh. Yet, while the film personalities will continue to give satisfaction as being true to life, as the nature photography will be valued for being typically revealing of its period, the music will have the appeal of being not only right for the Scott story but also for its own pertinent and significant assertions.

We have now observed Vaughan Williams's art in contact with various almost self-contained imaginative or working projects and historical achievements: the Whitman message and *The Wasps*; *The Merry Wives* and *Riders to the Sea*; the visions of judgement and perfection in *Revelation*, 18–21, and the too often vulgarized lyrical appeal of *Magnificat mea anima*; the many-threaded protest of *Dona nobis pacem*

[1] Firm reservations on the final 'anti-climax' and 'elementary' handling appeared in the *Guardian*, *Daily Telegraph* (December 6) and *Time and Tide* (December 25), 1948. *The Times* (November 30) ignored the music.

and the restrained recognition of a rare opportunity in *Thanksgiving for Victory*; the war-documentary of *Coastal Command* and the subtle symbolism of Blake's *Job*; the inner drama of *Pilgrim's Progress* and the visible stress of the Scott expedition. Limitations and raw patches have been noted here and there. But seldom, if ever, has Vaughan Williams struck a false note, for those who are acquainted with the true situation. A peculiarly fine intelligence guides the composer's pen. The occasion has been transformed without a violation of its nature. How many other composers could claim a similar standard, or precedence at all, on such a wide scale ? And the listener's response must be worthily exercised to keep in tune. (I have quoted features of the film-music not known from the symphony.)

The musical commemoration of Captain Scott and his four redoubtable comrades, and of all for which they went out, first took place on Saturday, February 15, 1913, a year after their death. On that afternoon the funeral march from *Götterdämmerung* was inserted by Sir Henry Wood at the head of a normal symphony concert programme at the Queen's Hall. It voiced the national sentiment aroused by the frustration of a heroic exploit, whose unfaltering intentions had been made so clear in Scott's preserved diary and to whose material accomplishment and serious aims the recovered papers and instruments amply testified. Wagner's celebration of Siegfried's end was considered the best elegiac material available; a 'superhuman threnody', declared the programme. I remember being somehow aware at the time that such heroic pomp was not what Scott and Oates would have liked. It occurred to nobody, apparently, that Scott's contemporary, the composer of the *Sea Symphony* and *Tallis Fantasia* (not to mention the music for the three Shakespeare plays) might have been asked to provide music for this or for a later programme. In any case Vaughan Williams was always opposed to undertaking work to order. (He told me this in 1954.) Hence, Scott's memory had to wait indefinitely for any specific musical recognition. When the impulse to honour it came, three decades later, it arose from a rather unexpected quarter, but it reached a composer who had already achieved *Forty-ninth Parallel* and *Coastal Command* in the same genre, besides having faced the odds in modern war. *Scott of the Antarctic*, thus committed to matching those war-films with its own saga, strikes a plain but authentic epic note.

Here, indeed, is a variant of a previous critical refrain: what music but this could invigorate the great occasions of life, celebrating the few in the name of the many ? This is not the central purpose of music, one may think, but there is certainly a place for such a response to the remembered past and to the standing need of a community, gathered at random and spasmodically, yet linked by a sense of common purpose over the years, to find expression for its beliefs, when men have hazarded all in a cause of discovery, unique adventure and the minimum of self-aggrandisement. Only a true musician knows the secret of translating such inarticulate epic transport into a generally acceptable, perhaps universal, assertion of sound-relationship, in sequences that cannot be symphonic, since they are conditioned by pictured events, but are nevertheless coherent. There is a corollary. If this objective is fulfilled, there is no logical ground for trying to take the programme music thus evoked to a further stage of symphonic affirmation. However, some later awareness of a wider and more musical context drove the composer on, as we know, and took him to the end of a *Sinfonia*.

Symphony or no symphony, after this achievement no composer could regard film music as a minor problem of special technique, not worth one's creative energy, whatever the material awards. Vaughan Williams was so absorbed in its capricious discipline that he almost recommended it to wayward composers. 'Within limits, any music can be made to fit any situation', he wrote in 1944, with luminous illustrations of timely and wasted resource (*R.C.M. Magazine*, 40. 1). But he wanted a more thorough co-operation of author, producer and composer from the start, on Wagnerian lines. He also visualized a great film built up 'on the basis of the music', like Disney's *Fantasia* but not at all whimsical. A *St. Matthew Passion* film, to Bach's music, was his only suggestion at the time. He never considered, for example, writing his own music for the Stations of the Cross, a Haydnish idea applied to a film of some years ago but lacking the proper *ad hoc* music. The general idea of united art remains, and it falls to the composer to make it clearer to directors that when they engage the best musical talent available, there are special potentialities to exploit. At present, whatever may have been said in the Press and in honest indignation behind doors, the efforts of musicians and producers to secure the conditions for true composition have been less than herculean. One does not expect an artist of seventy-five years to be exerting himself in this direction. Yet *Scott of the Antarctic* leaves an impression that the composer, well past his first blush of excitement over a novel genre, might be establishing a new era in film-music, which, like *Fidelio*, might be the makings of a fresh national style. If Walton and Rawsthorne made their mark in the same decade, it is not at all clear that they have gone any further in the next.

The music for the subsequent film, *Dim Little Island,* has been discussed earlier (p. 425). The Blake film is mentioned on p. 482.

RICHARD II AGAIN

Besides his feature music for a broadcast version of *Coastal Command,* Vaughan Williams wrote incidental music for a broadcast of *Richard II.* It has not been possible to trace the date of this music, but it cannot be far from that of the sixth symphony, with the second movement of which it shares certain tokens of bitterness of soul ('Richard's night', Act 3. 2, *fin.,* etc.), while the hexatonic character of the viola solo for the music in the penultimate scene represents, on the other side, a phase which could break out at any period. The thirty-four precisely timed sections, covering fifteen scenes (all but 1.4; 2.2,4), vary from five seconds to over sixty. They contrive to add a musical dimension to the king's tragic decline from high estate, chiefly by melodic means. An ascending curve establishes itself sufficiently as a majestic 1 ♮3 ♯4 5, answered by 1 ♭3 2 1, to lend point to a return to the initial 1 ♭3 ♮4 5. There are also the mocking, accusing, bitter-sweet modal music (viola) of Act 5. 4, and a serenely major 1 ♮3 ♮4 5 turn, whose familiar outcome suggests the philosophic temper that may yet underlie an unruly nature. Similar broad and adaptable features outline kingly pomp, turned rather too easily into a dark minor for Richard's spiritual death (2.1: 4–17) and later for the final funereal entrance; and the noble John of Gaunt has his motive. There is an impressive semitonal ascent for Bolingbroke, etching his lively, unscrupulous ambition where the folk-tune of the earlier music (1913) is just débonnaire. A more striking ♭3–1 progression suggests the king's fatal oppressiveness. Familiar musical traits thus gain a fresh sense of contrast and dramatic context, projecting the equally familiar entrances and exits of *Richard II,* for the informed listener, on to a comparatively vernacular level of clue-theme appearance and transformation, without any attempt to do more than underline the text. In comparison with the medley of fanfare, folk-tune and functional numbers in the much earlier music for a visible *Richard II* (see p. 172), the personal touch and consistency of the writing, in this systematically introductory or reflective treatment of the spoken word, are refreshing. The former remains of purely genetic interest. The radio music might be used again, as long as music links continue to be expedient in sound broadcasting.

Also extant is music (thirty-eight numbers) for a four-episode serial broadcast of *The Pilgrim's Progress* (Bunyan), used in 1946 and 1954. This includes *York* and other now familiar features of the full musical setting, also some use of Tallis's third tune, second half (no. 3: 'What things are these?'). This collection of fragments may be regarded as a preliminary to the later work, and a foretaste for junior listeners of all ages. According to Young, round 1910 ('about forty years ago', nominally for 1952) Vaughan Williams wrote music for a pageant based on *The Pilgrim's Progress* 'using a psalm tune which was to become the basis of the *Tallis Fantasia*'. If this is so, there is no doubt of what he was thinking when he wrote the *Fantasia*.

MILITARY BAND: TOCCATA AND SUITE

We turn now to miscellaneous instrumental works. A *Toccata Marziale* for 'military' band (1934), voluble and ruminant, and martial only in its provenance and slightly 'bugle' idiom, remains the composer's original contribution to that repertory, although it relies on a folk-song feature midway. It can thus be grouped with Holst's first suite (1909), even if the latter begins with a steady Chaconne and ends with a March rigid enough for the Guards. Holst's second suite is a definite precedent for Vaughan Williams's *Folk-song Suite* and *Sea Songs*. The latter suite is a nonchalant assembly of three movements, in which 'Dives and Lazarus' cuts a queer caper in the bass in the centre of the first movement, and 'My bonny boy' is strained to supply melody for oboe and, fragmentarily, for trombone, as the main motive of a pathetic slow movement. Howes duly notes the common titles of all the songs (except 'Dives'), but these only show that, as in the *Norfolk Rhapsody*, the original texts are quite irrelevant. It is a pity that the composer did not go further with this medium than the late *Variations* and the *Prelude on Three Welsh Hymn-tunes* for brass. One conjectures that either he found the wind *tutti* and semi-*tutti* only good for whole melodies, or imitational figures whose immediate appeal would soon run out, or the Kneller Hall director, having asked for the suite, did not think it his role to press further. Gordon Jacob declares that he learnt how to write for military band from studying the score of this suite, which the composer had asked him to arrange for orchestra (*R.C.M. Magazine*, 55. 31).

CHORAL WORKS

A few choral works remain for discussion. *Pilgrim Pavement* (1934), for chorus and organ, a setting of the poem by Margaret Partridge read at the dedication of the Pavement in the nave of St. John's cathedral, New York, has been withdrawn. It may be described as a promising strophical conception on a declamatory basis that crumples up at the last stage, defeated by a text that slides into a pretentious, adoring close, too exotic to bear along summarily in the main stream or to translate into an epilogue. *Six Choral Songs*, for unison voices and piano (1940), has the queer sub-title, 'to be sung in time of war', implemented by so-called songs of 'courage', 'liberty', etc., as if these were wartime discoveries. Actually, the poems are short excerpts from *Prometheus Unbound, Hellas* and other poems by Shelley. The songs are straightforward readings of their text, all but the last making a single musical strophe, suitable for group-singing, propelled by a plain rhythmic figure in the piano, usually in the bass, and pressed to the final cadence via one break in the normal harmony, which is near *Songs of Travel* level. The fourth song celebrates the final victorious Prometheus in a change from E flat to C from which there is no return. The next song aims at a fervent vocal climax for 'A hundred nations swear that there shall be Pity and Peace and Love', but after a too protracted middle section. The end-chorus of *Hellas* (stanzas 1, 2, 5, 7)—a poem modelled on the *Persae* by Shelley in 1821, with an awareness that the issue of the Greek war was undecided, and hence a timely poem for 1940—is set to two strophes, the first contrasting the first stanza with the next two in the imagery of minor and major, the second placing the last stanza in the minor for a romantic repudiation of past hatreds but melting briefly into the major for a moment's vision of a world of freed and puissant nations, but at peace. In these songs, then, the composer, knowing that it was no time for artistic progress on an equalitarian level, turned back to an early period, while retaining his sense of vocal propulsion, for the sake of finding a general intonation of Shelley's liberationist poetry 'before we all lose our tempers'. The songs thus remain as possible school songs, or even as introductions to Shelley. They are a reminder of what the composer could do, in plain singing and a reasonable organization of phrase, to broaden or intensify a group perception of a poet's aphoristic intimations. They answered a need that is not likely to become out of date, for there is always a use for a unison song in institutions that cannot count on part-singing of a balanced kind.

SONG OF THANKSGIVING

The *Song of Thanksgiving*, originally entitled *Thanksgiving for Victory* (1945), for speaker, soprano, chorus and orchestra, was a short but spaciously conceived tribute to an occasion, the nature of which remained inscrutable in detail; eloquent but free from self-righteousness. The nationalist exaltation of the *Triumphlied* with which Brahms had followed up his *Requiem* in 1870 was warning enough in one direction. The dangers of celebrating a jostling co-conquest as a triumph of world-order were also apparent, and soon confirmed by the monumental atrocity of Hiroshima.[1] In such a context 'O God, thy arm was here . . .' might seem utter blasphemy. Yet there must be thanksgiving, promise of a less barren and self-destructive world and dedication to the future; unanimity and private devotion. Such was the difficult path which the composer trod in anticipation, at the turn of 1944–5. Accordingly, a fanfare of trumpets and soprano solo introduces an earnest period of thanksgiving, in which glibness is avoided by a spoken part, a device more practicable on the radio than in normal conditions and in any case controversial, as may be shown later. Then, a quiet vision of the recuperative work that must be undertaken after a war gradually gains militant expression, and fresh enlightenment follows a mood of resolution. Finally, in the spirit of those who are willing to learn from experience, the plain family thoughts of 'Land of our birth' (Kipling) gather in strength on a strophical basis, beginning with a special chorus of children's voices.

In such circumstances an intelligent and politically realist composer applied himself to the composition of a corporate act of thanksgiving in 1945, to be broadcast to the nation at a moment of high hope, but not without questions and conjectures. The work could be sung throughout the Commonwealth, as, at least, a spontaneous assent to a new life for the free peoples of the world, which was at last coming onto the horizon.

The texture is mainly conservative. Tonality is observed, in so far as a succession of key-basses, not related by any common chords, reveals some centre of gravity: B flat (Part 1); A minor and major, D flat (Part 2); D leaping to B flat for the last verse (Part 3). The salient trumpet motive is based on a 1–lower 5–1–2–5 curve, (anticipated in 'O clap your hands', as Young points out), and the harmonic bass moves calmly and independently down the major scale; the A major and D flat sections are similar in timbre, though the latter is more flowing; and the tune for Kipling, though not commonplace, as Young suggests, might have been from *Songs of Praise*. Only the beginning of what I have termed Part 2

[1] *Nagasaki*, oratorio by the young Soviet composer, A. Shnitke, may prove a substantive aftermath. (*Guardian*, January 4, 1962.)

shows a more recalcitrant harmony, incidentally anticipating Bunyan's evangelist in its chordal fall of a semitone.

Nevertheless, this was for many an inspiring piece at a difficult moment, and later on. The inflections of mood are more subtle than they look. The closing tune proves its quality in the final unison verse, with full orchestra and organ. And the epilogue for soprano solo and trumpet is sublime. Here the radio technique, in which a solo delivery can be made as sonorous as a tremendous *tutti*, and probably more incisive, guided the composer. It is not so simple in a cathedral. However, a climax of tone having been rejected as a means of reaching a genuine conclusion, and equally the mannerism of a fade-out, a solo was the only solution. The advantage of a melodic formula (1 2 5) is now apparent. It stiffens answering phrases with a sense of reverberation, and avoids the connection that might be made between a more tuneful finish and the Kipling tune.

This detailed account is rendered necessary because, paradoxically, the *Song*, too bound up with its occasion to be revived to a new text, may never again be called for. In its time it showed at last that at a critical moment this was the voice to which musical Britain turned for guidance and strength. Ireland had written his urgent prophecy in *These Things Shall Be* (1937), but his music had been rather too much burdened with the Symonds pomp to move freely from declamation and idealist refrain to a true trenchancy in the total impact. The *Song* proceeds, a little spasmodically but with unfaltering step, from an evocative start to the committed close, but, avoiding the conventional, almost impatient, finality of *Benedicite*, retains its innermost thought in reserve, where it belongs.

THE SONS OF LIGHT

The next choral-orchestral work, *The Sons of Light* (1951), to a long text by Ursula Wood, was composed for the Schools Music Association, celebrating their second 'festival' in the Royal Albert Hall under Boult. The orchestra may be full, reduced or strings and piano. The ideology of the verse is a mixture of astronomical documentary and legend, astrology and its whimsicalities, and a kind of modern appendix to *Genesis*. The three continuous and unequal movements do not ostensibly balance or cohere. The first and strongest moves waywardly from tempo to tempo in a mainly declamatory style that throws into relief the woven texture of the moonlit scene; the second movement is

463

committed inevitably to the serial implications of the twelve Zodiac signs; the third, after a brief recollection of the first, settles down, to the rhythm of a descending bass figure (1 6 5), to the short dance of the sons of light, choral and in G, turning briefly to E flat and E, only to end almost at once. The ending of *Hodie* is paced out without its strophical reverberation. The texture is piquantly varied and descriptive—the composer begged for advice on school potentialities—and school choirs seem to 'like' this work. Listeners, and in time performers, may still doubt what sort of integer it adds up to. It is scarcely an aesthetic whole. It will stand or fall, in the class-room and in the concert hall, by the appeal of the vivid moments, round which other events move in converging circles. Still, it is important for school teachers and county directors to have this piece of intelligible and singable modern music in store for a suitable year, at a reasonable cost per head and with not necessarily more than a string group accompaniment. For unaccompanied choirs, there is the brief, wry setting of 'Full fathom five' from the same period, the first of three Shakespeare settings.

AN OXFORD ELEGY

An Oxford Elegy, for speaker, small chorus and small orchestra (1952), is an advanced specimen of the composer's harmonic writing. In the term 'harmonic' I include both the deliberate chordal movement and the contingencies of linear counterpoint; that is, of the convergences and divergences of voices (or instruments) moving horizontally and regardlessly. The harmonic norm is thus set from the start for much pondering and symbolism, with a chorus who croon almost as much as they sing any lines and, on the other hand, a speaker who is responsible for most of the conflation of stanzas and fragments from Matthew Arnold's *Scholar Gipsy* and *Thyrsis*, which the composer has made his text.

'On the other hand' begs the question whether the spoken word can genuinely combine with music, a perpetual issue on the film-screen. Melodrama has had a capricious history. In modern times it was introduced (with the name) into stage plays as an exaggerated and tritely specified reinforcement of emotional turns ('I await my victim...' to Villain's Music, craftily softening when Maria Marten arrives). From the other side, melodrama thrust on opera a vivid blend of the spoken word with orchestral progressions, as in the dungeon scene of *Fidelio*. But these were incidents. Nor did the 'melologue' idea of soliloquy introducing music, adopted by Berlioz in *Lélio* from the precedent by Thomas Moore, involve any clash of media. The Edith Sitwell-Walton plan of rhythmic recital, geared to the accompaniment of an allusive sextet, made *Façade* a more notable experiment, but its success depended on the use of poetry as sound-sense, on a continuous stream of witty word-tone association, and a multitude of separate poems, and its method was not repeated.

The pioneer in the combination of 'spoken melody', or rather inflected speech, with music was Schoenberg, who in *Pierrot lunaire* and other early works and finally in *Moses and Aaron*, distinguishes spoken and sung pitch, the former starting a syllable at a definite level but then falling or rising; very like a wail in practice, whatever they may say. Apart from a tendency to make the words unintelligible and unmelodious, caught between two methods of inflection, the general purpose is illustrated declamation. There is amplification in the orchestra, but rarely sufficient contrary interest to divide the attention. The same is true of Dallapiccola's *Job*, in which the general purport of the dialogue is familiar. The words declaimed by soloist or chorus are a clue to, and are absorbed by, the music, uncomfortable as this process is for the ear.

In the *Oxford Elegy*, even with a loud-speaker system to assist the speaker, the interplay of poetic sense and instrumental rhythm constantly calls for the listener's compromise. The select lines of each of the two Arnold poems are mostly too 'spiky' to swallow undigested, if their sense is to be grasped. Meanwhile, instrumental or wordless vocal development, equally important to the listener, has taken place. Or take it in reverse order. Hence, one is perpetually conscious that speech and music do not go together, and that the music is staggered to admit speech. Any critical acceptance of the work must be prepared to ignore this jostle of method. With these rhetorical reservations, one can still find much to admire in the fragmentary impressions which wander past the ear, linked by the falling sixth of the opening alto-oboe motive[1] (e.g. Oxford, 'lovely all times') and other repeated clues, but proceeding with singular harmonic freedom, within final call of F major. It is not easy to sense the total impact, but this remains the last experience of the uncompromising Vaughan Williams 'in process' with a chorus.

[1] Clarinet at the Oxford première (Queen's College), to judge from the autograph in the Bodleian Library. The clarinet now doubles the alto-oboe at the upper octave.

CORONATION MUSIC

Silence and Music was the composer's contribution to *A Garland for the Queen*, a set of ten choral songs compiled in honour of the Coronation. This, to words by Ursula Wood, is austere and evasive, but Mr. Keller's description, 'painfully modal' (*Music Review*, 14, p. 219) is inexplicable, as there is not the slightest conformity to one mode or another. *O Taste and See*, the composer's motet for the Coronation service itself—following his *Credo* and *Sanctus*—has been happily compared by Pakenham to the boy's song in *Pilgrim's Progress*, Act 4. Unadventurous in scope, it makes a perfect *Bar* in miniature style. It was this sense of proportion and singable quality which made it, sung during the Queen's Communion, a 'moment of truth' in the ceremony.

MASQUE: THE BRIDAL DAY; EPITHALAMION

In the same year *The Bridal Day*, a masque devised by Ursula Wood on the basis of the recitation of about 120 lines from Spenser's *Epithalamion*, was produced on television (B.B.C.) to music by Vaughan Williams. In September, 1957, a performance of what is now named *Epithalamion*, a cantata version of the masque, inaugurated the eleventh season of the New Era Concert Society, in celebration of the composer's eighty-fifth birthday.

The masque is for speaker, dancers, mimers, baritone and chorus, strings, flute and piano, with the option of dispensing with the strings and, if necessary, flute. It consists of eleven numbers, of which only four (2, 6, 7, 11) have a pronounced vocal element, the rest being dances, with verse spoken between items. The cantata, also of eleven numbers, is based on selected lines of stanzas 2 and 3, 5, 7, 8, 9 and 10, 12 and 14, 15, 16, 18 and 20, 20, 22 and 7; all but 9 and 10 found in the masque but most of them spoken there. The adaptation thus consists in the main of choral additions in lieu of dancing, the omission of certain dances and two numbers (4 and 9), and the addition of one fresh chorus (6) and a short preludial chorus, and the omission of the speaker part. The changes are mainly in the first half. The music of the masque nos. 6, 7, 8, 10, 11 re-appears as the cantata, nos. 8, 9, 10, 11*a*, 11*b*.

The disturbance in the balance of the structure is therefore felt in the earlier part. The cumulative effect of the bridal dances leading to cries of 'Io Hymen!', diversionary dances of Bacchus and the Graces, and a general dance and triumphal exit (masque, 3–5), is lost in the three short numbers of the cantata (3–5). The extended additional chorus (6) makes some compensation, but the essential composition is ballet, linked by recitation and reinforced with singing. The cantata remains a useful compromise, more singable than the *Tudor Portraits*, and needing only a chamber orchestra, yet half a programme, worth the attention of enterprising choral societies who cannot undertake big works.

The comparative order of events is shown below. The general texture is in the composer's broad pastoral idiom, often modal in melodic trend and multiple in harmonic movement, but, as one reviewer remarked, abounding in *mots justes* and not straining at originality. In the masque, one may single out no. 6, the 'Dance of the Hours' with baritone *chant espressif* leading to the baritone strophe which is taken up by the chorus, and repeated for the final prayer to Juno. Bacchus' 'Grotesque dance' is thin music, leaving much to the dancer, and the following 'General dance', too, will need good dancing to succeed. The musicians' serenade (7) is, at its choral finish, reminiscent of the composer's own *Serenade* (see p. 233). Juno's entry (10) is a curious anticipation of the imagery of the most solemn number of *Hodie* (*John*, 1). In the cantata, the succession of the stylized tune of the 'Procession of the bride' for answering S.A. and T.B. groups, the many-coloured 'The temple gates' (the additional chorus), and the short but cumulative 'Bell-ringers' chorus', is grateful to the singers. The baritone is active from the second number onwards, but one wonders whether the steady *arioso* style is the best that could have been devised. The solo entry, for example, into 'The temple gates' suffers from being adapted to the halting 'General dance' (masque, 5, *init.*), and one cannot help comparing the studied Lydian invocation (to pour out) with the overwhelming congeniality of Iago's less disinterested call to Cassio and company to drink (*Otello*), good enough for more than one strophe.

The instrumentation, common to masque and cantata apart from some modifications of detail (e.g. flute anacrusis-patterns and pianistic figuration in the first number), is skilful, to say the least. The flute is a limited soloist, but it has a varied role. Its initial very Dorian 1 3 5 7 cadenza strikes a doubly ancient note. But a perky piccolo, supported by nimble violins and percussive strings, brings to life the musicians' pipe and tabor. Lazily and piquantly melodic, the flute in *Epithalamion* no. 3 appeals to the sun to be moderate, in consideration of the bride's complexion. Still melodic, in no. 5 it happily doubles the women's voices at the higher octave in the middle of their processional tune, enhancing the literal violin and violoncello support of later phrases.

MISCELLANEOUS WORKS

	BRIDAL DAY			EPITHALAMION
1			1	Prologue.
1a	Cadenza.		1a	Cadenza.
1b	Recitation.		1b	Chorus (17 bars).
1c	Dance of nymphs.		1c	Add S.A. chorus.
2	Entry of bridesmaids. ⎫ Song (baritone and chorus). ⎭		2	Song: 'Wake now'.
3	Entry of bridegroom.		3	The calling of the bride (chorus).
3a	Dances. Groomsmen.		3a	44 bars (29–33 new) ⎫ with
			3b	63 bars (1–49 new) ⎭ chorus.
3b	Bridesmaids.			
3c	Procession of priests.			
3d	Procession of relatives.			
3e	Recitation.			
3f	Crowd collect.		4	The minstrels.
			4a	19 bars with chorus.
3g	'Io Hymen!'			
3h	Enter Bacchus, Graces.			
3i	Enter minstrels.		4b	49 bars (17–49 new), with chorus.
3j	'Io Hymen!'		4c	'Io Hymen!'
			5	Procession of bride (chorus). (B.D.: 3d)
4	Dances of Bacchus and Graces.			
			6	The temple gates (chorus) (including references to Bacchus' entry and general dance: B.D., 3h and 5a).
5a	General dance.			
5b	Procession from church.			
5c	Recitation.			
5d	Dance of bellringers. Exeunt bride and bridegroom		7	The bellringers (chorus). 48 bars (30–40 new).

	BRIDAL DAY		EPITHALAMION
6a	Dances of the Hours and of the Evening Star. Song (baritone solo).	8	The lover's song (solo and chorus). Almost identical.
6b	Re-enter bridegroom and bride, attended. Song (solo and chorus). Exeunt lovers.		
7a	Musicians' serenade. Song (solo and chorus).	9	The minstrels' song (solo and chorus).
7b	Recitation.		
8a	The winged loves.	10	Song of the winged loves. Add S.A. chorus.
8b	Recitation.		
9	Juno's procession.		
10	Juno's blessing. 'Io Hymen!'	11a	Prayer to Juno (solo and chorus). Add baritone solo *init*.
11	Prayer to Juno (chorus) (as in 6b).	11b	Identical.

For the girls' carol at the end of no. 6, flute and violin in octaves, voluble second violins and variously percussive lower strings supply a fetching background for the two-part chorus, with the piano to cut in later. At the end of no. 10, flute amplifies the 'pretty stealths' as an imitational bass to a fluttering texture. A viola 'cadenza' to introduce the impatient lover of no. 8—strictly, a cadenza to no. 7, but establishing a new key-centre in neo-modal style—offers no surprise, after *Flos Campi* and many individual episodes, and it usefully changes the colour-scheme. The strings command a light springing texture in the rural dances of no. 3, a bright cantabile, somewhat blunted by the piano, in the climax of no. 8, repeated at the end, and an intricate sound for the musicians' song (no. 9). The piano part sounds like an appendix to Vaughan Williams's part for the *St. Matthew Passion*! It ranges from brisk, *continuo* gap-filling, or a rather pompous cantabile, to all kinds of passage work.

Such a comparison of elementary detail in the assembly of a miniature orchestra reminds the listener once more of Vaughan Williams's welcome of the rationed resources which, for some reason, he has accepted here. The economy could be readily illustrated elsewhere.

Let us place the cantata then, as an acceptable 'quiet' work, the relaxation of a composer who was moving towards *Hodie*.

PIANO SUITE

There remain works for piano, organ, chamber ensemble and voice, either solo or with various accompanying instruments. Of the piano works, the suite of 1921 may be described as a good plain introduction to the composer's modal leanings, well within the amateur's grasp, but the lilt of the middle Quick Dance has a more distinctive quality. The Slow Air following, recalling the slow movement of Bach's *Concerto in the Italian Style* in initial texture, though bi-focal in layout, sounds now like a brief rehearsal for the violin concerto's slow movement. The final Pezzo ostinato (persistent-figure piece) might similarly be regarded as a preliminary exercise for the Scherzo ostinato of the *Partita*. Anyhow, this ostinato is rather tiresome. The Slow Air would be more intense in the string version of the suite made by James Brown, 'in collaboration with the composer' and entitled the *Charterhouse Suite*; the right hand part being sustained by a viola solo. The Quick Air, however, would lose nearly all its resonant stamp on strings. *The Lake in the Mountains* (1947) may be cited as an example of the composer's gauche piano manner. The rhythmic impact of melody and accompaniment is almost entirely bare, refusing all temptation to treat it harp-wise, by projecting horizontal and vertical lines in a composite curve; and the ancient vocal idiom of the salient 5 4 7 1 curve here, apparently from *Forty-ninth Parallel* (Young, 222), is no matter for the piano. For comparison turn to Bax's *Hill Tune* for a piece whose affected harmony sounds good because the texture is sympathetic.

INTRODUCTION AND FUGUE

The texture of the contemporary *Introduction and Fugue* for two pianos is also burdened with thick chordal passages along with the expected interest of elaborate weave and economical thought. The fugal plan is, in fact, considerably helped out by the two motives of the

Introduction, each a single curve in multiple texture; one, from which the fugue-subject emerges, ascending the octave, the other falling a third from a much stressed pitch of uncertain degree. The illusion of double (i.e. two-subject) fugue is aroused, but there is no parity of fugal development for the Introduction matter. The latter thus figures as an accession to the main imagery, which ends by absorbing the rich polyphonic rhythm of the whole movement so as to embody, not what the title promises, but a rhapsodic piece in which fugal sections, and fugally contrived climaxes, are noticeable. This would sound frustrating if the subject was meant for fugue, and if the fugal weave were as tight as it is resourceful. In fact, the subject is non-committal in appeal, and the various fugal devices of treating the subject in counterpoint, at half-speed, cross-accentuation, half-entry, and so forth, chiefly determine the substance or background of a polyphony which becomes increasingly loose. At a certain point, for example—10 in the printed music—the first piano is engaged in treating in canon an extension of the re-accentuated subject. Meanwhile, the second piano's left hand is engaged in a busy private ostinato (cultivation of bass figure), and nine bars later passes to sheer tremolando octaves. When it spells out the subject with deliberation, it is acceptable that the first piano simply falls steadily down the scale at two levels before replying with the subject in double canon. Finally (12) canon has become so automatic, here between pianos, that almost at once it reaches a point of perpetual circular motion, leaving the way clear for the Introduction's second motive in a most arbitrary key. After that, procedure is that of a fantasia, and when the fugue attempts to start again seriously (after 21), the bass is committed to one paramount degree for long enough to exhibit the fugue as probationary.

The nearest precedent for all this is the fugue which concludes Brahms's *Variations on a theme of Handel*, op. 24, except that the imagery there is far more consistent, and more economical. The suspicion is aroused that this fugue was begun as the simplest way of constructing a schedule for two pianos. One is scarcely convinced that the fugue subject was inevitable, except that it knows its place. The upshot is a somewhat capricious work, twisted from the agility of its apparent fugal intentions into a mood of blunt sententiousness from which it appeared to have escaped. The piano writing is also inclined to be stiff and cumbersome, and to be obsessed with multiple 1–3–5 or 1–4–6 melodic movement, a reversion to the style of early Debussy, as if it were meaningful.

MISCELLANEOUS WORKS

Organ Hymn-tune Preludes

The two main organ works date from 1920–1, though the second was revised in 1930. The *Three Preludes on Welsh Hymn-tunes* 'are intended to be played as a series'; but they can also be performed separately, and the second, on *Rhosymedre,* is now one of the most familiar of modern voluntaries. The three do not, indeed, make any integer that can be specified, and can best be treated separately. The first is chiefly engaged with the first phrase of *Bryn Calfaria,* the resemblance of whose fugal answer to the subject of the two-piano fugue supplies some piquant anticipations here. The prelude is resourceful without being very communicative. The last phrase (*largamente*) can be made more pointed by withholding the pedal till the third beat of the second bar, entering then on two octave D's, answering the 'soprano' directly.[1] In the second prelude, the opening refrain takes charge of *Rhosymedre,* with flowing impromptu polyphony to make an interlude of the second verse. The texture enjoys the luxury of light parallel movement, so that when the second verse drops to the tenor, to repeat the last phrase, the upper parts are already in process. The serenity of this simply made piece remains indescribable, as the thousands who heard it in or from Westminster Abbey in September, 1958, must have observed. There can be no doubt that organists will go on playing it.

The third prelude makes a single verse of *Hyfrydol* by means of truculent polyphony and multiple lines moving in opposite directions, all, doubtless, enriched by Mixture Stops that give out 1 5 8, two octaves up, for every note played; a queer perfunctory finale, whether to the 'series' or to public devotions. However, the late *Two Preludes on Welsh Folk-songs* (1957) add little except matter. The two verses of the first, yet one more Romanza to add to the despair of the earnest Vaughan Williams etymologist, reverse the tenor-soprano pattern of *Rhosymedre.* The second prelude is called Toccata but is distinctly argumentative. There are some raw touches, such as a pedal part which just simplifies the tenor (p. 5, *fin.*), as a perceptive reviewer has pointed out.

Organ Prelude and Fugue

The chief organ work is thus the *Prelude and Fugue* in C minor. The *Prelude* is an interesting offshoot, one may think, of Bach in C minor

[1] Dr. Henry Ley gave me to understand that the composer endorsed this change.

(S. 546) and of what he did with a sonorous but also imitative refrain and a proliferating contrapuntal interlude. Vaughan Williams begins at once with multiple movement in each hand, harmonically coincident at first, only to proceed independently but still blockwise later. A voluble middle section serves an obvious purpose, but its pentatonic motive is jejune in repetition, and the return to the 'chords', with not unexpected surprise turns, is a relief, rather than, as in Bach, a positive climax of counterpoint and modulation. In the balanced and considerable fugue (139 bars), the subject, modal in its (1 ♭7 5) 1 2 4 2 1 outline, recalling *On Wenlock Edge*, and pastoral-mannered in its recurrent triplet, is exhibited in orthodox exposition and in widening contexts: extraneous keys (A and F sharp minor); the development of a plain but more rhythmic secondary subject, mainly without pedal; and the combination of the two themes, at first in general contribution to an affirmative C minor, and finally in a broad synchronization. Acute ears might identify this climax as a polyphony of (1) the second subject in the pedal; (2) its melodic reversal, three deep (left hand); (3) at the top, the first subject three deep; all marked by an oscillation of major and minor thirds, which enhances the major conclusion. Multiple texture, however, is rare here. The sense of woven sound is preserved. This is so far a more consistent fugue than the later two-piano work. It is, indeed, the composer's only true fugue in print. It has sterling quality, and the more trenchant prelude pricks the ears impressively in advance, on the whole. The corresponding Bach fugue here is a sprawling and rambling work, in spite of a thrustful subject, and offers no comparison.

QUARTET IN A MINOR

Two late chamber works call for review. The quartet published in 1947, described as 'in A minor', registers the establishment of that key at the end of the first movement and nowhere else. The second movement is in G minor, the third gravitates to F minor, and the last is half in F major (with hints of D Aeolian minor) and half in D major. In other words, while there are perceptible key-centres in the movements, their audible assertion varies from movement to movement, elusive in the first, more positive in the third, integral in the second, and simply two-pronged in the finale. The F major relates, of course, to the F minor of the Scherzo, but it gives place to an unspoken recollection of the fifth symphony. Incidentally, the composer seems also to have amused himself by writing an A flat (descending to G) whenever there is a G sharp (ascending to A) elsewhere, and even by writing A flat where G sharp would be the obvious notation in the context. So much for the key-title. The sub-title, 'For Jean on her birthday', signifies a compliment to Miss Jean Stewart, viola, and explains the viola bias of the work. The Menges Quartet gave the first performances (twice in the same concert) at one of the historic National Gallery Concerts, on the composer's seventieth birthday.

The quartet is light-weight on the whole. Almost a short suite, as one reviewer noted. The opening prelude barely maintains its bi-focal pattern, owing to a perfunctory second theme. The Romance (which, like the Prelude, shares its fancy title with the fifth symphony) is widely admired. Compared with the Romance of the early G minor quartet, in the same key, the spare measure of the material here is easily perceived, but the texture is again modal to a degree, not least in the middle section, and the second theme amounts to a few fragments in the *Tallis* mould, whose formal recurrence without change of key seems odd, as in the slow movement of the eighth symphony. The chordal secondary feature of the Scherzo is similarly improvisatory in character, though it reverberates more. The main impulse of the Scherzo, whose falling 2 1 ♭7 ♭6 is attributed (rather superfluously) in the score to *Forty-ninth Parallel*, but rightly referred by Young to an earlier source, is blustery and expends nearly all its force first time. A curious feature, difficult to justify throughout, is that, as in Brahms in B flat (op. 67), all instruments but the viola are muted so that the viola asserts its exclusive timbre, whatever its text. The so-called epilogue of sixty-four bars, the tune of which Miss Stewart (*R.C.M. Magazine*, 55.42) refers to music intended for a film on St. Joan which did not materialize, is a purely melodic statement in its two keys, and for all its indescribable peace almost negligible. A further hint of something less than a full quartet is the prominence of the viola. 'This invites seriousness', remarks Dr. Young.

The first movement attracts some interest in its juxtaposition of the chords of F minor and E minor, anticipating the approach of the sixth symphony, and incidentally Pilgrim's initial guilt-agitation. This preoccupation with a certain harmonic relation, indeed, places the quartet as a late work. But the range of expression shows no comparison with the composer of the symphonies. Around 1920 Vaughan Williams observed to me that a quartet was something to be written by a very young or by a very old composer. Either the Beethoven op. 18 in C minor, so to speak, or op. 132 in A minor. This A minor is obviously not a vintage quartet at all. It might be added that the op. 132 stage took for granted not only the youthful seriousness of op. 18 but the liberations of op. 59 and 95. The same may be said, *mutatis mutandis*, of the historical Bartók six quartets. Surprisingly, the string quartet never had a haunting interest for Vaughan Williams. Solo-violin or solo-viola were congenial accessories or dominants in a wider context, but the interplay of groups and textures left him unresponsive. One explanation is, perhaps, that he seldom thought in two parts, but, apart from solo-rhapsody, in three or four; with a corresponding fullness of harmonic texture. Hence, he did not feel a call for the euphonious two-part writing which finds its place in the quartets of the great Viennese period. Hence, too, perhaps, the deliberate embarking on a double trio. But this proved unrewarding as such, as we know.

VIOLIN PIECES

One might have supposed that behind the growing repertory of sonatas for violin and piano there could be found a respectable list of lighter pieces, exhibiting the violin, perhaps, as major soloist. Yet in an article in *Music and Letters*, October, 1925, Miss Marion Scott deplored the 'decay of violin solos', that is, of musical works in sympathy with the violin and concealing its limitations. Her exceptions include, for ingenious enterprise, such a piece as Szymanowski's *Nocturne*, and, for a true revival of a vulgarized feature, the top register of the E string, *The Lark Ascending*. Miss Scott might have mentioned a lyrical *Romance* and a neat *Pastoral* (1923) by the composer of the second work. The *Romance*, without any supporting text, exhibits tense E string altitudes and 'finger-board' restraint among other features in a shapely piece. The *Pastoral* is more conventional and modal. However, this pair did not lead the composer sonata-wards, as far as one knows, in spite of his personal understanding of the violin.

SONATA FOR VIOLIN AND PIANO

The sonata in A minor for violin and piano was first performed and broadcast on the composer's eighty-second birthday (1954). The first movement is unequivocally in A Aeolian minor, and the finale, though far less committed to any key, terminates in first-movement material. The middle movement is in D minor. It must be admitted at once that the composer's approach to the piano vis-à-vis the fiddle is provocative at many turns. Fistfuls of chordal 'movement', truculent

475

counterpoint, a too constant rhythmic unison of piano with violin, and the possibility that the piano part may be after all a reduction, are among the factors that will make it hard to establish this sonata, in competition with others which (like Bartók's) take the clash and anti-phony of bowed and struck strings as the creative problem, and have no inhibitions about an arpeggio or other decorative manner of displacing a chord. It may be added that, while the violin writing is studiously 'four-fingered', the violin chords are 'tough'.

This understood, the opening Fantasia seems the best-wearing move-ment. The contrast between the initial combination of plain violin intonation and lithe pianistic figure in 'gallop' rhythm and, on the other hand, the 'monolithic' motive announced later by the piano in a new tempo, is just far-reaching enough to make the second theme timely relief, and durable enough to reach in due course the proportions of a compressed sonata-movement, with the aid of some violin chording, bravura and gay, and a certain severity in the piano part. The Scherzo (four beats) has been widely acclaimed for its brilliant handling, though the frequent rhythmic coincidence of violin and piano is awkward, especially in the rising-fifth start of the second group (5 in score), a matter remedied in restatement. There is a vivid and exciting impres-sion of Vanity Fair up to the ending, which is at first ponderous (piano) and then resorts, once more, to violin chords, again reinforced far too literally by piano, pursuant to the last bar. A defiantly laboured con-clusion! The concluding theme-and-variations (Andante) is said to be based on a theme from a discarded work. Anyhow, the tune sounds Russian with its accent on the fourth degree (as the second note proves to be). The variations are extremely free, some (2 and 5) contrapuntal and canonic, some rumbustical (3 and, with added velocity, 6), one contemplative (4: the sole example of this vein in the work). They give place to an unacknowledged epilogue, a return to the prelude and A minor. I am unresponsive to variations, but these are certainly an acquired taste.

Most published notices leave a general critical impression that the 'grandeur' of the sonata comes through both the blunt instrumental handling and the antique mode. This may be true, though one must beware of supposing that there is necessarily hidden wisdom in the doubled chord or the Dorian mode. One must also, on the other hand, hesitate to dismiss this sonata as 'noble music', by the side of the Brahms D minor and the like. There is no mere aspiration behind the harmonic texture. The work remains, nevertheless, a problem of criticism, rather than a recognizable achievement. It is reasonably characteristic, as one would expect, but its inner dynamic is elusive, and 'three movements in search of a sonata' is, apart from the contrived epilogue, not an unfair estimate.

SOPRANO AND CLARINET

When there is no singer for a soprano part without words, the clarinet may deputize; in the *Pastoral Symphony*, for example. From that point a logical step, or at least experiment, might be to combine the two. Hence the Prelude, Scherzo and Quasi menuetto of the *Three Vocalises* for soprano and clarinet, published in 1960. The French title for *solfeggio*, or vocal exercise, and the cultivation of vocal tone *per se*, have been variously anticipated in Hettich's *Répertoire moderne de Vocalises-études*; in Fauré's succinct example (originally an oboe piece), Ravel's languorous and absorbed *Vocalise en forme d'habanera*, and Dukas's more extended and less rhythmic piece; in Rachmaninov's balance of vocal and piano cantabile, after an almost hostile attitude to the singer in earlier songs, in the last of his *Fourteen Songs* (op. 34); and in Copland's demonstration of a *tranquillo* that is nimble in more senses than one. But those are all for voice and piano, a ready contrast of pure and percussive legato. The present set implies parity of cantabile and coloratura for each part, as in an organ piece for two manuals. The figuration is almost identical. A corollary might be drawn. If one clarinet of two is missing, a soprano offers the nearest thing to subtle and close command of tonal inflections per reed; but a clarinet can replace a soprano in a wordless part much better, owing to its superior agility and wide variety of register, in persuasive amplification of the forms of song without the human content of words. In other words, the soprano has the rawer deal here; the contrast of media is not developed in the absence of words. Thus these slight pieces hardly justify the combination. Their basic material remains formal and unevocative.

SONGS

Some thirty-odd songs remain for discussion. They range from some earlier groups to some late ones; that is, from the third decade to the sixth. Nominally, a dozen earlier songs are balanced by nearly two dozen later ones, but the latter reveal a much sparer music, besides being for a singer and a mainly one-line instrument, as opposed to the normal piano accompaniment. The catalogue records, in fact, a short middle song-period, followed by a long silence, broken eventually by one special set and one published in 1960. Obviously, voice and piano soon ceased to interest the composer, as with Beethoven, though for complementary reasons, it may be guessed. Beethoven was unsympathetic to the sung word, Vaughan Williams to the piano; neither relished the piano as a genuine partner.

MERCILESS BEAUTY

The three settings of rondels ascribed to Chaucer, *Merciless Beauty* (1922), are for high voice and string trio or piano. They are all framed to the *aba¹ ca* pattern of the two verses in each, and thus constitute three symmetrical but contrasted readings, the first limpid, the second declamatory and disturbed, the third more shapely and more expansive. The first two are Dorian, the third Mixolydian in basis. The strings supply a plastic background, with more intensity in the second song, and more lilt in the third, than the piano could give. The upshot is 'not unpleasant music', but no more than a musical version of the rondels, none memorable.

WHITMAN AND SHOVE

Three sets were published in 1925. *Three Poems by Walt Whitman* are settings of poems drawn from the three groups, *Whispers of Heavenly Death, From Noon to Starry Night* and *Songs of Parting*: 'Whispers of heavenly death' (1868), 'A clear midnight' (1881) and 'Joy, shipmate, joy!' (1871). The first poem first appeared (in *Broadway Magazine*, London) with 'Darest thou now O soul?' (*Toward the Unknown Region*). The composer, as it happens, re-set the latter at this time, for unison singing, as a stalwart *Bar* in G hexatonic major, a revealing contrast to Stanford's solo-setting, in which a plain melodious tune is shaped into *aba* stages by key, and pointed by penultimate modulation and vocal leaps upward as in Vaughan Williams's choral setting of a year earlier. The second poem is the latest of the group that includes 'The mystic trumpeter', earlier celebrated by Holst and Hamilton Harty (1904, 1913). It was set by Frederick Converse, amongst other American composers. The third poem was set in a vigorous 'lead the line' style, with final *niente*, by Stanford, with 'Toward the unknown region' (*Songs of Faith*, set 2); and it was set by Delius, as the fourth of the *Songs of Farewell*. The recurrent theme is, as declared in the last poem, 'Our life is closed, our life begins'; heavenly death, the soul's midnight flight, the leaping ship.

Of the three musical readings, the first, called 'Nocturne', is the most developed, with a persistent bass figure, chordal refrain and stages of 'speaking', 'singing' and 'speaking' voice, all fully intoned; the last stage being more deliberate and leading the so far clear neo-Dorian tonality of D to an obscure, 'impressionist' blur from which there is no recovery. A trenchant start. 'A Clear Midnight' is a vigorous 'Evening Hymn' in G major, propelled by a five-bar ground-bass, whose seven-fold appearance supplies a metre for it, without intrusively punctuating the declamation. 'Joy, Shipmate, Joy!' is a salute to death, in a hexa-tonic G major, with a thirty-fold bass figure to match the weighing of anchors. In this series, the music thus becomes progressively and intelligibly fixated, and so it must be accepted. None of the settings would make good sense by itself. The whole composition is a gloss on Whitman in the composer's variable style.

Four Poems by Fredegond Shove merely brings under one cover four settings of scattered poems from *Dreams and Journeys* (1918). Nos. 1–2, 3 and 4 are now published separately. The series shows, indeed, no common motive or sense of continuity, the first and the last poem being descriptive in type, the second a lyric of the seasons, and the third a symbolic legend of the divine Lord. The first, 'Motion and Stillness', is a monotonous but communicative evocation of 'evanescent hopes' in terms of unrelated parallel harmonic movement in the pianist's two hands. The last, 'The Water Mill', is the most sung setting of all this period. Its simple Mixolydian oscillating figure, shapely *a a b b a c* pattern and felicitous declamation have reduced a poem of thirty-eight lines of close observation of detail to an economic and symmetrical statement, mill-wheel, house clock and all, with a parting glance at the young men who waste their time calling. Here is a notable document in the memorably unpretentious, which will always attract a text-mindful singer and his audience. Between these, 'Four Nights' is a plain strophi-cal handling of the mind's four seasons, with a change of texture for autumn visions and a reasonably tense recovery for winter's annihila-tion. In 'The New Ghost', the encounter between spirit and spirit alternates between recitative and *chant espressif*, in a style not far from the *Pilgrim's Progress* episode of 1922. In the right mouth, this can be an impressive song. Not only are there no false notes, but the somewhat precious imagery of the words is absorbed in the musical progressions. Of the two Seumas O'Sullivan settings, only *The Twilight People* survives. The texture of the prevailing intonation (verses 1 and 3) is Dorian, not only in the degree pattern but in the salient curves, which echo plainsong, and in its melodic independence. On that account it can hardly be 'the best song' (Foss). The middle verse is semitonal but not far-reaching. The song is catalogued, but not printed, as 'acc. ad lib . . .' The piano adds little till the end of the last verse; but its cadence is needed there.

A Return to Barnes

Fifty years after setting 'Linden Lea', for the benefit of the Barnes Society the composer returned to Barnes in *In the Spring*, from the third collection of *Poems of Rural Life in the Dorset Dialect*. The absence of seventh degree makes the tune sound early-major, but the harmonic texture is in the composer's automatic and multiple manner. He has fitted each complete pair of verses to one verse of music, with new music for the last verse. A retrospective tune for a retrospective society, which may be presumed to have expected some echo of *Linden Lea*; almost dateless.

A Return to Housman

Voice and piano, then, held no future for the composer in 1925. He embraced no greater absorption of the text than a vivid or shapely intonation, with typical bass and plain or figurated harmony. His pianist remained too downright, and limited in resource, to sweep a text into musical history in expanding strophe or grinding progression. Or it was not in his nature to give vent to his sense of loneliness in a characteristic portrait of the oppressed solitary individual, or, as in Stanford, of the quasi-lyrical escapist. He published no song-sets for another three decades, and when he came back to verse, it was not with the piano. His professed poets were now A. E. Housman (1954) and Blake; Housman as an old collaborator, however involuntary, and Blake in connection with the celebration of the bicentenary of his birth in 1757. The Housman set, written *c*. 1925, might now seem out of season; but, while a modal style prevails, the new trenchancy and horizontal methods point forward to the Blake set, not back to the Shove period. Of nine settings one, 'The Soldier', after no. 3, was discarded.

The eight poems in the Housman cycle, enigmatically called *Along the Field* from the *incipit*-title of the first poem after the prologue, are

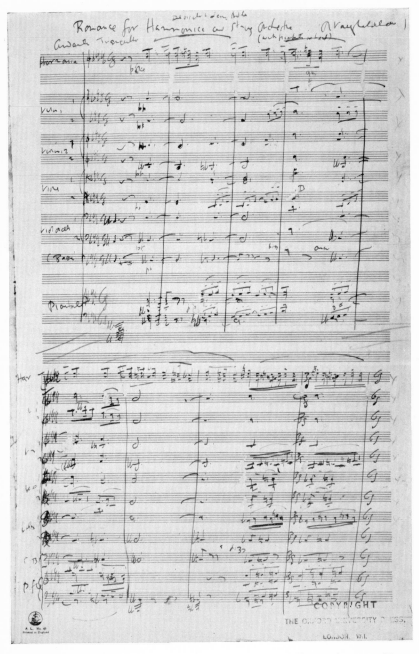

8. *Romance for Harmonica and Strings*: first page of full score (autograph)

9. Ninth symphony: first page of full score (autograph)

taken severally from the sixty-three poems of *A Shropshire Lad* and the forty-one of *Last Poems* as follows:

1. L.P. Prologue
2. S.L. 26, 'Along the field'
3. L.P. 26, 'The half-moon . . . '
4. L.P. 23, 'Good-bye'
5. L.P. 27, 'In the morning'
6. S.L. 5, 'The sigh . . . '
7. L.P. 41, 'Fancy's knell'
8. S.L. 54, 'With rue . . . '

There is no sense of planned succession, except that in each pair a compact setting-throughout is countered by a strophical and more extended setting, this order being reversed in the last pair. (It sounds, as well as looks, as if seven or less settings were planned within the framework of *Last Poems*, extended by *A Shropshire Lad*, and then 'With rue', capriciously added.) The accompanying instrument, the violin, reinforces the strophical appeal by its own figure in nos. 4 and 7, melodically replaces the voice in no. 2 (verse 2), dominates the non-strophical no. 5 with its flowing arpeggio and chordal sequence (*sempre pp*), and rises to parity in nos. 1 and 8. Elsewhere it is more purely functional, but maintains its own harmonic rhythm.

The prologue to the series, then, is a plain Dorian reading. In 'Along the field' the aspen's intimations are distinguished by the entry of the violin in drone style, a fresh vocal melody and a fresh mode. In the second verse, the violin plays the melody, enabling the singer to explain the message of the aspen, but then hands over to the singer for the pat repetition of the last phrase to recognize Housman's ironical jingle. A singing aspen! This, at least, the poet (who died in 1936) had not to know. 'The half-moon westers low' is a brief but trenchant monologue, exploiting the discordancies of the whole-tone scale to absorb the incalculable differences of speaker and addressee. In 'In the morning' the violin theme surely stresses too obviously the irony of the simple but not quite corresponding stanzas. 'The sigh that heaves the grasses', too, would take the most accomplished violinist to prevent a sense of oppressive commentary, searing as this is. 'O see how thick the goldcup flowers' (here 'Good-bye') is almost reactionary in its hexatonic texture, but its two similar and two different strophes make a spontaneous dialogue, with the girl's steadily dry and regardless reply to end each verse, incidentally echoing the clue-motive of 'Oh, when I was in love with you' (*Wenlock Edge*). 'Fancy's knell' carries out a similar pattern, with a pronounced violin refrain to represent the ubiquitous flute but a much more articulate vocal line. The broad rhythmic treatment compensates for the total loss of the original lightness. Indeed, after this the elementary reading of 'With rue' sounds rather misplaced and raw, and its oscillating upward leap distressing. Yet it exposes the passé Gurney rendering (1926).

The cycle cannot claim the devotion of out-and-out Housmanites, concentrated as it is. It will not at once appeal to the composer's followers either; it is too attentive to the verse! Nor does the instant appeal of any particular songs carry the listener past the more difficult renderings. It is a series of precise, generally sensitive readings, examination of which has shown the pattern and resource; a demonstration of methods to sample at pleasure, and a challenge to executant interpreters to reveal as something more, if they can, aided by the violin's haunting phrases across and on two strings.

The Vision of William Blake

The *Ten Blake Songs* for voice and oboe were written for a splendid commemorative film, *The Vision of William Blake*, arranged by the Blake Film Trust, produced in 1958 by Mr. Guy Benton, and still current. The music of the film shows none of the formal balance of Rawsthorne's music for *The Drawings of Leonardo da Vinci* (1955), which is an extension of a symphonic movement. But whereas in the earlier film the commentary is both nugatory and musically intrusive, in *Blake* the commentary is reduced to a link between Blake's poetry and art, deepened by a background or foreground of music. The film summarizes Blake's ideas and conditions of mind in representations of the poet speaking his own verse, and of his engravings, and in these fresh musical settings of the *Songs of Innocence and Experience*. Since the order of publication has no discernible meaning—to end with a pair of the 'gnomic' verses in any such recital seems extraordinarily naïve— the songs may best be taken in the order and context in which they appear in the film (they can be grouped according to source): 9, 1, 3 (*S.I.*), 10 (*Misc.*), 2,4,7,8 (*S.E.*), 5,6 (*S.I.*). First, 'The Divine Image', with a glance at Job, and other emblems of 'innocence' or unspoilt impulses, ending in the perception of a staircase to heaven, and then of Job with the halo of clear vision in which he appears in the concluding illustrations. Then, after the satirical conflation, 'He who binds to himself a joy . . . The look of love alarms . . .' (10), an admonitory reference to the creation of man and woman leads to the serpent, Satan (the Comforters motive from *Job*), the first murderer, a monstrous picture of the 'strange terrible place' beyond death, a forbidding demonstration of man overwhelmed (Satan's dance) and bound by papal authority, and, at the last stage of fallen man, the hellish prison of his very self. Four searing symbols of experience or corrupt nature punctuate this stage. Finally, after a life-giving process of torment and destruction (organ), on the cue 'energy is eternal delight' a return of innocence is conveyed by 'And did those feet' (recited), with the *Job* Sarabande and then Elihu's music, 'The Lamb' (5) (vision of three crosses, one cross) and, after a last 'stab' by Satan (rising-fourths motive), the Sarabande unconfined and 'The Shepherd' (6).

These Blake songs, then, are an assembly under one cover of contributory illustrations to an in every sense moving recovery of 'the end of a golden string' which Blake sought to give the world (a closely-packed twenty-five minutes). So understood, their succession makes sense. Sung in abstraction, they lose half their impact. They remain a series of austere projections of some of Blake's best-known poems, whose film-order shows some shape. As special but unexplained items of a vocal recital, they call fresh attention to their texts without showing more substance than trenchant intonation (8) or a well-turned *Bar* (see p. 152). 'Wonderful irradiations of the poems' may have been a first impression of such a recital in October, 1958, but it must be doubted whether it would survive the test of repetition. Once more, most Blake enthusiasts will not particularly need this colouring of the spoken word, and most of the composer's friends, somewhat frustrated by the reserve of the music, will find in the rest of the film-music and in the visual illustrations the prophetic appeal that they miss in certain songs.

As settings, most of the songs follow a two-verse pattern, with an after-song in two cases (9, 10). The first and last, and one other (9, 4, 6) are for voice alone. The familiar lines of 'To Mercy, Pity' (9) are thus exposed in a single Dorian strophe, which turns Lydian for the practical conclusion. A similar transformation to a more subtle scale (as in *Sancta Civitas*, Sanctus chorus) deepens the irony of 'He who binds' (10), thus incidentally demonstrating the fatuity of the printed order. Of the other strophical settings, 'Infant Joy' (1) needs no comment. In their supremely spare style, 'A Poison Tree' (2), 'London' (4) and the plainer but appallingly vegetative 'Ah! Sunflower' (7), the analogue of *Betelgeuse* (de la Mare, Holst), make a strong piece of self-accusation, leading up to the irony and penetration of 'Cruelty has a Human Heart' (8). In the last, the establishment of E as the keynote by way of F, by the oboe, rivets the final appeal of the close on that note, as approached from E flat and F by voice and oboe. The burden of Andromache in

Ex. 69

The Trojans is similarly intoned ($\flat$6–5). Of the answering songs, 'The Lamb' (5) is Aeolian and weak, whatever one's reaction to the poem; 'The Shepherd' (6), Lydian, has more shape, and is happier without the oboe. 'The Piper' (3), the longest song, is in free style; suitably wayward in phrase, as in mode and final key, but inconclusive. The *Experience* group is thus the most musically pronounced, but it would no more make sense by itself than Job's satanic self unanswered. In mere recital, the final *Innocence* songs would be unpersuasive, and the smooth sequence of 9, 10 after 8 would be hopelessly repetitive, as has been stated, while to end with the sneer at 'beauty' (i.e. the elaborate erotic apparatus of respectable females) would be just impish. It must be stressed that the printed order is liable to become a froward retention, which, it will be hoped, singers will firmly reject. To anyone who knows his Blake, it is grotesque.

Romantically, then, the *Ten Blake Songs* are likely to be remembered most for their bitter centre, as a piercing reminder of what lies under the surface of civilization—the 'marks of woe' of an oppressed, unrepresented class have changed in nothing but location—and as a postscript to the burden of the fourth and sixth symphonies which happened to be almost the latest finished product of the composer. This is salutary to the consciences of the sixties, but meagre tribute to the vision of William Blake. The spoken recital of 'Jerusalem' (with, for English hearers, a piece of Parry's sturdiness behind it) rouses expectation of a new song at the same level of divination. It does not come; only recollections of fine music of three decades back, and derivative miniatures. Admiration for the 'eternal delight' of our composer's sixth decade of creativeness must not award a sense of fulfilment where appearances are against it. To be frank, 'The Lamb' and 'The Shepherd' were a disarming choice to make for, or accept from, the producer. The pastoral convention, the conception of life as a simplified rural existence, has its traditional point as a satire on urban monstrosities. But the biblical shepherd imagery here is of softer stuff.

These songs record, nevertheless, a notable communion of spirit, of which the Job illustrations and music are the manifest artistic expression, while articulate comment provides confirmation. When, in a well-known letter to Thomas Butts—to whose faithful support (while it lasted) posterity owes the existence of many national treasures—Blake gave his simple answer to those who pressed him to pay more attention to popular demand, he was anticipating the loneliness of two decades later, when only the devotion of John Linnell made it possible for him to develop into engravings the set of water-colour illustrations for *Job* that he had made for the now wavering Butts. He was also sketching the integrity of a later artist, not constantly involved in making his art pay, but no less free to choose easier or harder courses of productivity.

If we refuse to do Spiritual Acts because of Natural Fears or Natural Desires! . . . I remember the Threats I heard!—'If you, who are organized by Divine Providence for spiritual communion, Refuse, and bury your Talent in the Earth . . .'

In 1908, Vaughan Williams, consoling Holst for his failure to win the Ricordi prize with the opera *Sita*, wrote, 'The real, important thing is that you have not been put in the awful position when 'all men speak well of you'.[1] More practically, he had remarked in the course of his historical preface to the *English Hymnal*, 'A tune has no more right to be dull than to be demoralizing'. The rest can be left to the imagination. It was poetically just that the composer's last main contact should have been with one of the most visionary of artists and one of those most concerned with a reformed, liberated society.

[1] *Heirs and Rebels*, 41.

MISCELLANEOUS WORKS

Four Last Songs

It is difficult to comment on the *Four Last Songs* published in 1960, to verses by Ursula Vaughan Williams (*sic*). These songs are offered, without any indication of grouping, as fragments of two song-cycles, planned but not completed. They are placed in reverse chronological order (1958–54). All except the second are readings of their text in the manner of *chant expressif*, stimulated by a harmonically active and a restless piano part in the first and last songs, 'Procris' and 'Menelaus'. The third song, 'Hands, eyes and heart', seems to rely on 1 3 5 7 chords for its elementary homogeneity as a ponderingly cadential strophe. The second song, 'Tired', in a clear major, shows the most patent shape, but its texture is limited. There is a melodic bias towards the third degree, and the usual concomitant 4 6 1 3 chord is now part of the rocking feature that propels the song. 'Menelaus' is the most developed setting. It remains a colourful reading, rather than an independent creation.

In the company of William Blake, then, let us take leave of the composer; a folk-singer, perhaps, in solitude of utterance, but not in acceptance of the received modes of the post-pentatonic periods, and hence able to match the terrifying ambivalence of human nature with just the right kind of trenchant or nonchalant lines; experienced, but neither crusty nor compromising. That has been his secret: his musicianship has not only kept up with his imaginative ideas but has also found its own provenance. It has not always been a smooth process of adjustment. For six ideas or plain phrases in the right place, there have been two or three that seem unduly to simplify their context; or, having let himself go in folk-song settings in cantata and opera, the composer may be prone to discover situations that call for melody, preferably strophical and, directly or subtly, repeatable. Again, for every fourth symphony, where what sounds wrong and discordant proves cumulatively coherent, there have been experimental works that seem too automatically directed towards fresh objectives; or there is a suspicion that the composer has challenged himself to be a devil (and not only in *Job*), or at least a terrifying deity, just as elsewhere he pursues a divine image of another kind.

But such sensations of raw expression must not be misinterpreted. They are only the accidents of a struggle to fulfil the conditions of music, where form and content are opposite aspects of one creative thought.

They leave much achieved that is strong in different ways: by direct rhythm or languorous cadenza, by trenchant progression or easy flow of fifths and fourths, by dynamic climax or fading finish, by structural compulsiveness or by inexplicable fitness to a text. The strength lies in the theme finding its moment and its movement. The sources of this power are always mysterious, but only applied intelligence can eke out intuition. Vaughan Williams's art calls for the exercise of the utmost powers of mind and sense in response.

APPENDIX A

A Concordance of Hymn-tune Books

The purpose of the table below is to indicate the musical influence of the *English Hymnal* on the choice of tune in subsequent editions of hymn-tune books in use in the various English, American and Canadian church bodies. In this context, *Songs of Praise* inevitably almost coincides. For comparisons with *Hymns Ancient and Modern*, only the earlier editions have been referred to. The selection of material may seem designed to under-estimate the influence of those historical productions by keeping mainly to tunes set to general hymns, but the beneficial work of *H.A.M.* in establishing certain hymn-tunes for Advent and the other seasons of the church's year, now in almost universal use, is taken for granted.

The main thing to observe is the considerable body of memorable tunes, commonly available in communities divided by doctrine or history or custom, by means of which all sorts of congregations may bring their professions, and their sense of unity with each other and with other dedicated bodies, to an infectious level, and with some steady extension of repertory to keep pace with a widening literary experience. I do not mind being told that the citation of a concordance for a given tune in a particular book is 'unrealistic', since it is well known that the tune is never heard in that context. If the tune is in the book, that is enough. By a deliberate decision, the *E.H.* has served since 1925, for congregational use. It is for the authorities concerned to provide ways for the expansion of congregational experience, as is done in most churches where the musical renderings are congregationally alive and progressive.

I wish to thank Dr. Erik Routley and Mr. Arthur Vallance, both church ministers, for information about concordances in certain books named below. I am similarly indebted to the late Dr. Maurice Frost.

The following are the abbreviations:

B.C.H.	Baptist Church Hymnal.	C.H.	Church Hymnary.
B.C.P.	Book of Common Praise	C.P.	Congregational Praise.
	(the hymn book of the	E.H./S.P.	Common to the first editions
	Church of England in		of both English Hymnal
	Canada).		and Songs of Praise

	where not otherwise stated by dates, 1933 denoting the second edition of E.H.
H.	Hymnal of the Protestant Episcopal Church of U.S.A.
H.A.M.	Hymns Ancient and Modern:
	O Original edition (1861, 1868).
	R Revised edition (1875, 1889).
	N New edition (1904).

H.B.	Hymn book of the Presbyterian Churches of U.S.A.
H.C.S.	Hymnal for Colleges and Schools (American).
H.W.	Hymns of Worship.
LU.S.B.H.	Service Book and Hymnal of the Lutheran Church in America.
M.H.B.	Methodist Hymn Book.
O.A.H.B.	Oxford American Hymn Book.

Name of Tune	1 H.A.M. 1861	2 E.H. S.P. 1906 1925	3 C.H. 1927	4 O.A.H.B. 1930	5 B.C.H. 1933	6 M.H.B. 1933	7 B.C.P. 1938	8 H.W. 1939	9 H. 1940	10 C.P. 1951	11 H.C.S. 1956	12 H.B. 1957	13 I.U. S.B.H. 1958
FRENCH GENEVAN PSALTER:													
Psalm 42		×	×						×		×		×
Psalm 68 (Old 113th)	O	×		×	(×)	×				×	×	×	
Donne secours	N	×	×				×	×		×	×		
ANGLO-GENEVAN PSALTER:													
Old 120th	N	×			×	×	×	×	×	×			
Old 124th		×	×	×		×	×	×	×	×	×	×	×
ENGLISH:													
16th-17th Century:													
Farley Castle		×	×	×			×	×		×	×		×
Martyrs		×	×	×					×	×	×		
Miserere mei		×	×	×						×			
Song 1		×	×	×		×	×	×	×	×	×		×
Song 46		×	×	×		×	×	×	×	×			
Late 17th & 18th Century:													
David's Harp		×	×	×		×			×	×			×
Epsom		×						×		×			

490

Tune	1	2	3	4	5	6	7	8	9	10	11	12	13
Folkingham	:	:	:	×	:	×	:	:	:	:	×	×	:
Illsley	×	:	×	×	:	×	×	:	×	×	:	×	O
Leicester (Bedford)	×	:	:	×	:	×	:	×	:	:	:	×	:
19th Century:													
Affection	:	:	:	:	:	×	:	:	:	:	×	×	:
Sandys	:	×	:	×	×	×	:	×	:	:	×	× 1925	:
Stracathro	:	:	:	×	×	×	×	×	×	×	×	1933	:
Folk-melody:													
Capel	:	:	:	×	×	:	×	×	×	:	:	×	:
Forest Green	:	×	×	×	×	×	×	×	×	×	×	×	:
Gosterwood	:	×	:	×	:	×	×	:	:	×	×	×	:
Kingsfold	:	×	:	×	×	×	×	×	×	×	×	×	:
King's Lynn	×	:	×	×	×	×	×	:	:	:	:	×	:
Monksgate	×	:	×	×	×	×	×	×	×	×	×	×	:
Sussex	:	×	:	×	:	×	×	×	:	:	×	×	:
WELSH:													
Ffigysbren	:	:	:	×	:	:	×	×	×	:	:	×	:
Gwalchmai	:	:	×	×	×	:	×	×	×	×	:	×	:
Hyfrydol	×	×	×	×	×	×	×	1904 ×	×	×	×	×	:
St. Denio	×	:	×	×	×	×	×	×	×	×	×	×	:
MODERN COMPOSERS:													
Holst:													
Cranham	×	:	×	×	×	×	×	×	×	:	×	×	:
Sheen	:	:	×	:	:	:	:	×	:	:	:	×	:
Ireland:													
Love Unknown	:	:	:	×	:	×	×	×	:	:	×	1925	:

Name of Tune	1 H.A.M. 1861	2 E.H./S.P. 1906/1925	3 C.H. 1927	4 O.A.H.B. 1930	5 B.C.H. 1933	6 M.H.B. 1933	7 B.C.P. 1938	8 H.W. 1939	9 H. 1940	10 C.P. 1951	11 H.C.S. 1956	12 H.B. 1957	13 L.U./S.H.B. 1958
MODERN COMPOSERS: (continued) *Somervell*:													
Kendal	⋮	×	⋮	⋮	⋮	⋮	⋮	×	1916	⋮	⋮	⋮	⋮
R.V.W.													
Down Ampney	⋮	× 1925	×	⋮	×	×	×	⋮	×	×	×	⋮	×
King's Weston	⋮	1933	⋮	⋮	⋮	⋮	×	×	⋮	⋮	×	×	⋮
Magda	⋮	„	×	⋮	⋮	⋮	×	×	×	⋮	⋮	⋮	⋮
Randolph	⋮	×	×	⋮	⋮	×	×	⋮	⋮	×	⋮	×	⋮
Salve festa dies	⋮	×	⋮	⋮	⋮	×	⋮	⋮	×	⋮	⋮	⋮	⋮
Sine nomine	⋮	×	×	×	×	×	×	×	×	×	×	×	×
PLAINSONG:													
Adoro te (late)	○	×	×	×	⋮	×	×	⋮	⋮	⋮	×	⋮	×
Aeterna Christi munera (late)	○	×	×	⋮	⋮	⋮	×	×	⋮	⋮	⋮	⋮	×
Pange lingua	○	×	×	⋮	⋮	⋮	×	⋮	⋮	⋮	×	⋮	×
Veni Creator	○	×	×	⋮	×	×	×	×	⋮	×	×	⋮	×
FRENCH FROM PLAINSONG: Christe sanctorum	⋮	×	×	×	⋮	⋮	×	×	×	×	×	⋮	×

Deus tuorum militum	…	×	×	×	×	…	×	×	×	×	×	×	×
Iste Confessor (Rouen)	…	×	…	…	…	…	×	…	×	×	×	…	…
Picardy (? folk)	…	×	×	…	…	…	×	×	×	×	×	×	×
GERMAN:													
Early:													
Laus tibi Christe	…	×	…	×	…	…	×	…	…	…	…	…	…
Lutheran:													
Das neugeborne Kindelein	…	1925 1933	×	…	×	…	…	…	…	×	…	…	×
Es ist kein Tag	…	×	×	…	×	×	×	×	…	×	…	…	×
Hast du denn Jesu } Lobe den Herrn }	N	×	×	×	×	×	×	…	…	×	…	×	×
Salzburg	O	×	×	…	×	×	×	×	×	×	…	…	×
Roman Catholic:													
Ave, virgo	N	×	…	×	…	…	×	×	…	×	…	…	…
Ellacombe	O	×	×	…	×	×	×	…	×	×	×	×	×
Omni die	…	×	×	…	…	×	×	…	…	…	…	…	×
Lasst uns erfreuen	…	×	×	×	×	×	×	×	×	×	×	×	×

Symphony 5 in D: Last Revision

The composer's final revisions of the full score around 1955, published in 1961, may be summarized as follows, in terms of numbered pages and bars. (R.=revision of.) They are incorporated in the Boult recording.

(1) *Alteration of texture*

(a) 2: 2–9 and 3: 1–2. R. woodwind. Fl. leave their trochaic figure to double the violins, which, with va. and vc. I in canon, are marked from *piano* or *mp* up to *mf*. Ob. drop out of 2–5. Cl., in place of shapely curves up and down, maintain 2:1 fixatedly for four more bars. Bns. in 5–7 confirm. The trochaic figure thus recedes in favour of the string 8758 formula.

(b) 4: 5–9 and 5: 1–2. R. fl., which double violins, cl. filling gap in 4: 6–8. Vn., vc. I, *mf* in 5, 7 and bn., hn., *pp* in 4, 7, but bn. *mp* in 5: 1. Again the stress is on the 8758 figure as thematic, on the trochaic rhythm as textural. In 4: 5–9, vc. parts have no lower C by double-stopping. Their contrapuntal weave is clarified.

(c) 22. V. II up to v. I level and both *mp*, not *piano*; the lead is now firmer but more ethereal than the opening.

(d) 23: 5. Hn. II reinforces trb. II, both half-accenting, as well as trb. I (*simile*) in 6–7; this the first bass entry of the returning motive calling for no less sonority than later.

(e) 26: 4–7. R. hn. II to double tr. I, not hn. I. In 6, tr. II doubles tr. I. A more subdued contrapuntal note.

(f) 69: 13. Add timp. (*pp*) to d.b. coup de grâce. For security in a large hall(?).

(g) 79–80. R. fl., cl. In 79: 4–7 and 80: 1–5, 8, fl. and cl. double ob. at 8′ and 16′. An expedient enhancement of this development of the c.a. motive (bars 11–12 of the Lento).

(h) 112: 4b–6. R. fl. to double v. I, as in (a) above.

(2) *Alteration of harmony*

61: 11. R., as 5, not 6(12). A symmetrical fresh start replaces the stylization of 6 as rejoinder.

(3) *Modification of dynamics and expression*

(a) 7: 7. Add *tranquillo* to new subject, which is in any case already marked *piano* after *pianissimo* in 6. Broader phrasing and longer bows and breaths(?)—for the preceding music has scarcely registered any sense of disturbance, beyond the *mf* noted in 1 (*a*) and 1 (*b*).

(*b*) 30. Add *misterioso* to *presto*. So, if the composer's command of the mysterious is in question, let us remember that it is prescribed in this *apprenti sorcier* movement, not the solemn and redemptive Lento.

(*c*) 36: 5. R. v. I, v. II, va. The four-octave resumption of the flute tune is to be *mf prominent*, not a continuing *piano*, making briefly for a more positive answering measure, with *piano* continuation before the oboes strike their dissonant note.

(*d*) 38: 1; 39: 8, 10. Violins and d.b. (*pizzicato*) and cl., h. II: *piano*, not *f* or *cresc.-dim.* 40: 2, 3: no *cresc.* in cl., hn., str. The 'expression' is left to the oboes, if they can find time.

(*e*) 71: 2. V. II: add *prominent*. Not to be submerged by va. I or vc. solo doubling, or lower-string turgidities.

(*f*) 98: 5. Tr. *p prominent*. Str. *pp* (2nd beat). Fl. and cl. *stacc.* up to 99: 2. A clearer melodic line, dominated by trumpet and not by oboe tone, and less encumbered by percussive string texture.

(*g*) 115: 7. Fl., c.a.: add *cantabile*, stressing the return of the original motive, vis-à-vis rising violins, which are apt to forego their *ppp* level when they reach their top position in safety.

(*h*) 116. Add *cresc.-dim.* 'hairpins' to desc. phrase in 2–3 (vc.), 3–4 (va.), 4–5 (v. II), 5–6 (v. I), underlining the thrust to the third note before the final lingering stress on the sixth degree of the now absolutely major scale.

(4) *Corrections of misprints not quite obvious to the listener*

(*a*) 12: 7. V. I, A *natural*.

(*b*) 42: 4 (ob., c.a. sound) and 6 (fl.), and 43: 8 (v. I): C *natural*, twice.

(*c*) 45: 1 (v. I), 46: 3 (v. II), 51: 3 (va.): *div.* (players divide for the chords). 51: 6 (va.) and 7 (v. II): *unis.* (players cease to divide).

(*d*) 50: 3. Cl. II plays e♮′, not the unplayable e♭, below compass. 62: 5. Picc. *sheds* unplayable low C similarly.

(*e*) 76: 9. Ob.: e′ a′ d″ e″. 107: 8. C.a. (written): b′ g′ f′ d′.

(*f*) 93: 10 to 94: 1. V.I G string texture continued, marking the anticipation of the close (cf. 3*h*).

In addition, many manifestly inconsistent notes, such as the bass C–B in 18: 3 and the tenor clef for bn. on the same page, and many failures to implement phrase and expression marks in one part or another, have been rectified, ensuring a steady definition of phrase throughout. Missing dots, ties, etc., have been corrected.

The Vaughan Williams Scripts

In 1960 a grant from the Vaughan Williams Trust enabled the manuscript department of the British Museum to add the corrected full score of the fourth symphony to that of the *Concerto accademico*, already in their possession; a third score, *Sinfonia antartica*, is included in the music collection of the Royal Philharmonic Society, and rests on indefinite loan in the keeping of the department. At the end of 1960 an outstanding accession to these was announced. Mrs. Vaughan Williams, with the happy co-operation of publishers who had long held certain autograph scores in their keeping, presented the Museum with sketches, piano scores and full scores, covering at least sixty sizeable works, and over twenty smaller pieces. These amount to a hundred and twenty-two numbers, as now catalogued and listed, with specifications of score-genre, by Miss Pamela Willetts, assistant keeper in the manuscript department.[1] These are summarized below. It is unnecessary to underline the superlative advantages of coherent assembly with which this magnificent gift has made available, in one centre for all time, a mass of evidence of the personal struggles for expression on the part of a composer whose finished art has been ringing in men's ears for anything from five to fifty years. In 1961 Sir Steuart Wilson added *Hugh the Drover*.

Many of the 'sketches' are much more than the experimental theme in process, familiar to students of Beethoven's method, to be appreciated by the knowing ear for its inferiority to the printed version. They mark a definite stage of ample creation, in which the hard core of persistent material may be as interesting as the total reconstruction of a given feature, or wider changes of shape, at a later stage, are illuminating. It is the sign of a major creative impulse that its successive manifestations can be traced in principle from the start, but, on the evidence of these preliminary versions, it is the mark of many truly satisfying works that sooner or later the one right phrase for its context proves to have been a late discovery, hard to come by, and frequently involving the sacrifice of what earlier seemed acceptable.

The importance of these intermittent stages, for the concert listener, is analogous to that of textual and other stimuli. They were indispen-

[1] *British Museum Quarterly*, 24, 1–2.

sable to the composer, and they explain to a responsive observer, if he can obtain access to the scripts in something like musical order, how much the music that he now hears was planned from the start, and how much it was determined by major or minor alteration of structure, texture, tempo or verbal instruction. Certain recurrent and successive methods of articulate expression may be mentioned, most demonstrable in the symphony-scripts but found elsewhere.

(1) Wayward drafts and revisions of trial themes, some at once recognizable as primary motives, others as conscious strivings, others as totally divergent paths, possibly recurrent in later scores but now past history.

(2) Piano version of a theme, section or, usually, the whole of a movement. This carries various roles. (*a*) It may be, in Wagnerian terms, the 'prose-drama' sketch, rough but complete, so far as it goes, as a statement of the harmonic rhythm that makes a movement distinctive. This is the commonest start. (*b*) A fair copy of an earlier version, embodying previous corrections and sometimes furnishing its own stage of revision. (*c*) A concomitant of a full score, either as a working reduction or as a revision, preliminary to a further score.

(3) Two-piano score. An alternative method to 2 (*a*), adopted in the middle three symphonies, promoting a more contrapuntal sense and admitting a more complicated weave, but not more than a penultimate statement, or even a demonstrably early one.

(4) Full score, occasionally with piano version at the foot. This, again, may be (*a*) an 'early' score, conspicuous for phrases since compressed or otherwise altered, but containing the clearest possible definition of intentions; (*b*) a later score, concealing traces of an old version in a significant paste-over. A corrected copy may be taken to be in the keeping of the publisher, presumably now a copyist's work, with possibly some autograph corrections. A once latest score may become obsolete, and, even if it is still in print, be replaced by another (on hire); (*c*) an uncompromisingly last score-script.

(5) The music examples for a programme-note, representing the latest stage at this level, are available for the last three symphonies.

The tabulated list below demonstrates the evolution of the symphonies and other works on these practical and adaptable lines, refining proportions, intensifying the harmonic pressure, and from time to time patently awakening to a greater concern for structural integrity, as opposed to variety of material. The plain pianistic beginning ensures a care for harmonic progression and phrase-shaping, but it also promotes a scrutiny of the impact of a chordal sequence, with some correction of bare texture by pencilled adumbrations of additional features. The later scoring brings home the quasi-melodic force of each phrase, prompting a check on 'sprawling' or, less commonly, on a too collected appeal, with all the spontaneous revisions that a master of the event finds necessary. Somehow these enigmatic paste-overs come to rouse a preliminary confidence in the composer's vitality of present conception or intimation, in his capacity to solve the problems of a new discovery effectively.

As this accession is so recent, only an interim statement can be given. I have so far been mainly concerned with the artistic history of the symphonies. But I have covered most of the extensive sets of 'sketches' and obsolete versions. For most other works a single and final version, in vocal or full score, survives in manuscript.

In this list, 1, 2, 3, 4, 5, refer to movements. A date in brackets refers a score to the nearest published version, where there has been more than one. 'Early' simply means a version appreciably precedent, as music, to the printed version. A name in brackets denotes the arranger. 'Incomplete' covers any gap from a missing outer page to a more serious hiatus. 'Fragmentary' denotes a sketchy score, not a break in the rhythm. 'F.O.' means the full orchestral score, of whatever dimensions for the work concerned. 'Vocal score' denotes voice-parts and piano reduction of the orchestral parts. An asterisk, or (A), follows the citation of the script of a movement or work already identified as primarily autograph. This may be taken to imply that other stated scores *of the same work* are chiefly in an arranger's script, with or without the composer's additions. Actually, the copyists' work is clear and trustworthy, and a rest to the eye, but many readers may wish to know which scripts are the composer's.

Apart from pardonable slips in the piano-reduction parts of the choral and stage works (for who would carp at a reducer's indispensable but laborious handiwork?), the printed scores are most trustworthy, except for works revised, like the piano concerto, only in the score and parts on hire. (Presumably the composer corrected the proofs in most cases.) The earlier scripts remain for the consideration of every serious student of this monumental surviving example of critical penmanship. Of the collection of over fifty bound notebooks that Beethoven kept till his death, much was quickly allowed to be dispersed beyond recall, and no full precedents survive for any of the Beethoven symphonies such as can be found for the Vaughan Williams nine, along with many less revealingly corrected vocal and full scores of other works.

THE VAUGHAN WILLIAMS SCRIPTS

SYMPHONIES

Sea Symphony (50361–6)
   (*a*) Sketches (23 books).
   (*b*) Vocal scores. 1, 3, 4: two versions.* (incomplete); 2: three versions.*
   Printed proofs of vocal score.
   (*c*) F.O.*
   (*d*) Printed score, corrected.

London Symphony (50367–8)
   (*a*) Sketches for 4 (mainly).
   (*b*) Piano. The 1914 score. The 1914 version, corrected as for the 1920
   edition.* (F.O. copy to follow from Liverpool.)

Pastoral Symphony (50369)
   (*a*) Piano (dated 1920). Second theme of 4.* Another copy, continuing
   further.* The first idea for the symphony.
   (*b*) F.O. (1922).*

Symphony 4 in F minor (50370, 50140)
   (*a*) Two pianos. 1 and 2: 'correct' copy and a rather earlier one. 3: an
   early copy. 4: 'correct' copy and a much earlier one.
   (*b*) F.O.*

Symphony 5 in D (50371–2)
   (*a*) Sketches for 1 and 4.
   (*b*) Two pianos (M. Mullinar). Two copies.
   (*c*) F.O. (1961). (R.C.M. Lib.: early copy.*)

Symphony 6 in E minor (50373–4)
   (*a*) Two pianos. Incomplete copies: 1 (early) and 3 (very early).*
   (*b*) Two pianos. 1, 2, 3, 4 (1948). Another copy of 2* and 4*.
   (*c*) One piano. 4*.

Sinfonia antartica (50375, Roy. Philh. Soc. Supp. 6)
   (*a*) Sketches for 1, 2, 3, 5.
   (*b*) Piano. 1, 3–5*: two versions (incomplete). 2: one version.*
   (*c*) F.O.*
   (*d*) Themes (programme).

Symphony 8 in D minor (50376–7)
   (*a*) Sketches. 1, 2, 3 (some in 50390, one (?) in 50482).
   (*b*) Piano. 3 (early).* 2 (incomplete)*.
   (*c*) F.O. and piano. 3 (earliest).*
   (*d*) F.O. 1 (incomplete); 2–4*.
   (*e*) Themes (programme).*

Symphony 9 in E minor (50378–384)
   (*a*) Sketches for 1, 2, 3, 4 (esp. 2, 4).
   (*b*) Piano. 1 (early)*, 1 (late)*; 2 (very early)*, 2 (early)*, 2 (fair copy, late)*;
   3 (very early, ends after 20)*, 3 (fairly late)*, 3 (late)*; 4 (very early)*,
   4 (fair copy but early)*, 4 (early)*. 1, 2, 3, 4 (late, corrected by Roy
   Douglas in connection with the composer).
   (*c*) F.O. 1 *(early); 2* (early and fragmentary); 3 (very early)*, 3 (late)*;
   4 (early)*. 1*, 2*, 3*, 4* (final version).
   (*d*) Themes (programme)*.

APPENDIX C

CONCERTANTE WORKS (50385–50392)

FULL SCORE:

Oboe Concerto (with some themes).
Piano Concerto (1936)* (cf. 50482 B).
Romance for Harmonica.
Suite for Viola.
Tuba Concerto. Two copies*, with piano also for 3* (cf. 50482, sketches).
Violin Concerto (*Concerto accademico*) (Eg. MS 3251).*

MISCELLANEOUS ORCHESTRAL WORKS (50393–50401)

FULL SCORE:

Household Music.
Hymn-tune Preludes, Two.
Prelude and Fugue in C minor.
Prelude on an Old Carol-tune.
Running Set, The (with two-piano score and parts).
Suite for Pipes.
(R.A.M. Lib.: *Fantasia on a Theme by Tallis*).

PIANO SCORE:

Folk Dance Medley (50427).*
March Suite founded on English Folk-tunes (*Ib.*).*

BRASS BAND

FULL SCORE:

Prelude on Three Welsh Hymn-tunes (50402).*
Variations (with sketches for Var. 10, 11) (50504–5).*

STAGE: OPERA, BALLET AND MASQUE (50406–50421)

F.O. or mainly F.O.

Bridal Day, The.
Hugh the Drover. Vocal score, 1914* (50843) and F.O. fragments.*
Job (sketches and two two-piano fragments).*
On Christmas Night.
Pilgrim's Progress, The (incidental music, two versions, and complete stage work. Cf. 'appendix' or extra number in 50482).
Poisoned Kiss, The (sketches, movements and whole work).
Riders to the Sea (two copies).*
Sir John in Love (Prologue, interludes and whole work).*

FILM AND RADIO (50422–50433)

Coastal Command. Sketches. F.O.: one film-number and suite (two copies).
Flemish Farm, The Story of a. Sketches. Piano: film music (suite titles). F.O.: suite (Muir Mathieson).*
Forty-ninth Parallel. Piano. F.O.
Mayor of Casterbridge, The. F.O. Incidental music (radio).
People's Land, The. Piano.* F.O.*
Richard II. F.O.: incidental music (radio).
Scott of the Antarctic. Piano: four sequences. F.O.: three sequences.

At Elstree Studios:

Joanna Godden, The Loves of. Piano.* F.O.* Piano: music for gramophone record.

Scott of the Antarctic. Piano: score*; score in numbered sequences*. F.O. a nearly complete set, complemented by the three sequences above.

CHORAL WORKS (50434–50480)

England, My England. Voice and piano.* F.O.* Full score for military band.*

VOCAL AND FULL SCORES:

Airmen's Hymn, The.
*Dona nobis pacem.**
Epithalamion.
Nothing is Here for Tears.
Old Hundredth.
*Oxford Elegy, An.** (Bodl.: original F.O.*)
Six Choral Songs.
Sons of Light, The (with sketches).*
Tudor Portraits, Five (with sketches, including v.s. of no. '2', 'Margery Wentworth').
*Willow Wood.**

FULL SCORES:

All Hail the Power.
*Benedicite.**
*Fantasia on Christmas Carols.**
Fantasia on Old 104th.
Festival Te Deum.
Flourish for a Coronation.
Folk-songs of the Four Seasons.
*Hodie** (with sketches, 50482).
Hundredth Psalm, The.
Magnificat (reduced and full).*
O Clap your Hands.
*Sancta Civitas** (with voice parts for Latin version*). (Bodl.: early v.s.*)
Silent Noon (cf. *The House of Life*).
Song of Thanksgiving (separate sketch, 50371).*
Songs of Travel (1–3).
Sound Sleep.
Sun, Moon, Stars and Man (adapted from *The Sons of Light*).
*Toward the Unknown Region.**
Voice out of the Whirlwind, The.
Windsor Forest, In.
(R.A.M. Lib.: *Serenade to Music.* Henry Wood's performance copy.)

VOCAL SCORES:

Five Mystical Songs (F.O. pages).
Mass (with organ part).
O vos omnes.
Te Deum and *Benedictus.*
Three Choral Hymns (1 and 3).

APPENDIX C

FULL SCORE:

'How can the Tree but Wither?'
Jolly Carter ((?) Moeran's setting).
Orpheus with his Lute.
New Commonwealth, The.

VOCAL SCORE

Blake Songs, Ten.
Carols.
English Folk-songs, Six.
German Songs, Three Old.
'God Bless the Master.'
Housman Songs, Nine (six, nos. 1–4, 7–8, 1954).
Hymn for St. Margaret.
'I have trod.'
Motion and Stillness (Shove setting).
Pilgrim's Progress, Seven Songs from.
Shakespeare Songs, Three.
Vagabond, The (male voices).
Vocalises for Soprano and Clarinet, Three.
Willow Whistle (voice and pipe).

Sketches Only

Bach, Fugue 33 in E, set to 'Mercy and truth' (50378). *St. Matthew Passion, continuo* for four numbers (*Ib.*).
Carol, 'A virgin most pure' (50379–80).
Folk songs, two notebooks (50361).
Helen ('Was this the face that launched') (50455).
Masque, introduction to (50378).
Old 100th in A flat, for Pageant Scene 4 (50455).
Praise the Lord (*Ps.* 104), tune (50371, 50427). Another setting (50455).
St. Joan (30387, title only).
Sonata for violin and piano (50482).
Vibraphone, 'Notes' for, (50378).
Wessex Prelude (*Ib.*).

It remains to mention certain features in the composition history here revealed. Inevitably the accent must fall on the Bismarckian improvisations of fresh policy, which the printed page now discloses, rather than on the solid core of musical thinking, which frequently persists from the start, as a train of ideas, embracing and promoting after-thought and refinement. But this stress on change will not be misunderstood.

Plain-figured references to the printed score of a movement will indicate the *rehearsal-numbers*, with or without complementary bar-citations from these points. '9. 5 to 11' means 'from the 5th bar after 9 to rehearsal-number 11'; but '9. 5–11' will mean 'from the 5th to the 11th bar after 9', where the context permits it.

Sea Symphony. The 'early sketches' (eight notebooks) are chiefly concerned with the last movement. Passing titles, like 'Walt Whitman Sea Songs' show how gradually the symphonic conception arrived. Of lines set and re-set, 'Down from the garden' recurs as an ethereal, other-worldly phrase for tenors, 'Yet soul be sure' is assumed to be a solemn, almost consoling moment in D major, in the Parry style, and 'O thou transcendent' is a rousing bass lead. Only in the 'final sketches' do we find the groping chords and primitive vocalization of the first text, each to be re-pointed later (1909), with 'Yet soul' echoing the revised tune. But the opening 'O vast rondure' shows a clear outline at once, rever-berating in 'Finally' in a repetitive style, and as a second-part motive 'O we can wait no longer' is a settled curve for imitational treatment.

Of the vocal scores, the first movement discloses a discarded orchestral close, the second a struggle to match the climax with the right key-change, and the last a long delayed exit from the ancestral haunts, as in the sketches, in quest of a true symphonic episode, but the way is found.

London Symphony. The 1914 version has been discussed in the main text, in terms of the early full score, corrected, like the second piano score here, to the 1920 version. The first piano score reveals the struggle with the final bars. Three stages may be observed for the processing of the cadence.

(*a*) chord of G major (1–4–6)—violin-solo, motto literally (d' : g' : a' d'' e'' : e'', etc.)—chords of E flat, B flat;

(*b*) a seventh on C, in the 'floating' position of an ascending 5–♭7–3–1–3)—violins as revised today—G major to E flat minor, twice, under soprano D–E♭, resolving on G major;

(*c*) a blue pencil alters the crucial chords to the more trenchant sharpened-fifth penultimate of G♭–B♭–D♮ E♭–G♮–B♮ under D–E♭, twice (once in the printed score), before reaching a profound G major. After this comes the laconic summary: '20 mins. Epilogue takes 5 minutes. Proposed cut, 1 *m* 15 *sec.*' It seems a trifling compression after 50 minutes of music, as it then was.

Symphony 4. 1. Later contrapuntal additions, not in a piano score, include the brass canon at half speed (9. 10), with a homogeneous finish (10. 7–12) replacing a ten-bar digression to C minor. In the initial canon of the restatement, the cross-rhythmic triplet now standing in four bars

(14. 5, 8, 9, 10) was at first no more than a unilinear ascent at these points, pencilled into the piano score. In the restatement of the second subject, the bravura anacrusis for the canonic entries at 16, and the C–E♭ (minor) bass rejoinder in bars 3–4, replacing a blunter E–G repartee, are fresh touches. At the last stage, the wood-string canonic extension of the wood-string antiphony (18. 5–6) appears as an insertion at the foot of the page, transforming a dull symmetry into an absorbed series in little.

In the full score, harp lines persist for five pages, all erased. This was no time for gently percussive sonorities.

2. In the second phrase (4 to 6), both piano copies show the reduction of an earlier draft by 7, 4, 2 bars after 4. 10, 5. 7, 5. 9. A tense climactic bar to the development (ta-a ta ta) sounds plausibly enough in the earlier score after 8. 7, but is pasted over in the other two scripts, presumably not to weaken the later impact of the motto (Ex. 38*b*). It is easier to understand why, at the start of the restatement, a 17-bar reflection of 1 to 3, with counter-melody extended to match, appearing in the earlier piano score, was compressed eventually to the 11 bars of 9. 5 to 11. 0 (by omitting bars 1, 6–9, 17 of the original draft); 3 to 5 (24 bars) being cut down to 8 bars (11. 1–8) in any case. A severe instancy marks even this more leisurely Andante.

3. The appearance of bar 1 of the second theme with the tune sounding only on the 1st and 4th beats (of six) at 5. 1, 4, 7; 6. 3; 12. 5 and 23. 1, 6, places the autograph piano score as early. The erasure at this level of the repeats of 12. 5–9 (lower octave) and 26. 5–8 are passing signs of rhythmic concern.

4. The 'early' piano copy shows at once a considerable degree of extraneous matter and, in 3 to 4, 5 to 6, 8 to 9. 12, the unilinear phases of a decisive but unaccomplished revision, pasted over the score.

At the end of the exposition, the hurtling unison rhythm is left to itself; the supporting motto-theme in the brass came later (9. 13–18). In the reverberation of the opening chords (16), there is no third bar of prolongation. This is added in the 'correct' copy.

Some 21 bars later, one scans the early copy for the recovery of the 8–9 bars of minatory unison which previously rounded off the *oompah*-interlude (3. 1–9), although, as stated, this figures only at the bare unilinear stage. But there is no sign of it here: recapitulation of so potential a theme has not yet been worked out. Instead, a plain C–B (17. 14) introduces 27 bars of other material, of which 15 appear under the paste-over at 3. These comprise (*a*) 15 bars of racy extension of the *oompah* course, wayward bass movement round F–A♭–F′–D′–B–A♭, directing or misdirecting a jaunty top line marked by the Scottish 'snap', ending on the lines of the expository 5. 7–9; (*b*) the imitational development of the second bar of the principal theme, anticipated in 4. 3–13. (Nearly all this is perfectly visible in the 'correct' copy, covered by a corrective sheet, providing 18 to 19.) These subversive 27 bars, then, were displaced by honouring briefly the unison motive at 3.

At the end of the restatement (21), the six-beat excursion of 8 *et seq.*, another after-thought left unilinear at first, is due. The early copy discloses not only different detail from 21. 1–8, but also, after 9–12 as printed, a perfunctory 6-bar continuation to link with 22. 18. The correct copy supplies the 24 bars from 21. 13, freer for the renunciation of what might be termed activist diversion at 18. *Oompah* has been checked by a succinct summary, and the second subject, compressed from 19 to 21, is geared for a more hurtling rhythm than before.

In the epilogue, the early copy discloses the abandonment of a fugue-subject of *six* bars, as in 23. 7–12 (trombones), and the contentious promotion of B A H B and the *oompah* tune, later to be superseded by the broader treatment, with a now canonic minatory motive, of 26 to 28. Finally, after 32. 12, a two-bar extension, no more, at first invoked the tempo primo. It became eight bars.

The evolution of this commanding symphony, especially in the finale, is one more testimony to the challenge of symphony to exact and relevant expression, and to the composer's concern for homogeneity but also for due proportions.

Symphony 5 in D. In the piano copies, the symphony is clearly entitled 'Symphony in G', corrected to D without change of key-signature. Otherwise, these scripts show little history, apart from revisionary phrases. The full score is the latest score, published in 1961, the special instrumental features of which have been cited in Appendix B. The correction of 17. 9 (as first printed) to a repeat of 17.3, in the Scherzo, proves to have been the restoration of a detail from the piano score. The R.C.M. score is more transitional (cf. p. 316*n*).

Symphony 6 in E minor. In the autograph, no. 3 follows 1 ('turn on for no. 2'), implying an earlier draft of the whole symphony. There are missing pages in the restatement in 1, and two gaps in the restatement in 3, when its four fragments are assembled; but the creative stage of either movement is clear enough. Various details (7. 7–9 missing) make this A version of 1 the earliest, while its continuing movement (3), with its symmetrical, Aeolian interlude-tune for saxophone, is a long way from the more sophisticated 'Trad' of the printed version, given in the non-A copy. The A version of 2 shows a 16-bar cut of thematic amplification at 7. 1, and a rhythmic reconstruction of the vital trumpet part in the restatement (11. 5 to 13. 6). The non-A copy is similar. There is like conformity in 4, replacing, for example, the repeat of 10. 1–2 after 10. 4 by 10. 5, and re-moulding the oboe line in 11. 2–3.

The non-A copy of 3 is peculiarly advanced. It shows, in red ink, those contrapuntal additions which distinguish the 1950 version from the 1948; namely, at 1. 5–8; 4. 4–7 (4. 6: A–A–E E♭); 12. 3–6; 25. 1–2; 26. 5–7; 36. 7 to 37. 2 (36, 7: D–D–E♭). It is surprising that these additions should have been made in this piano score, but their steady coincidence with the 1950 alterations precludes the supposition that they were all considered for the original version, rejected and then re-worked for 1950. (The other revisions, being purely instrumental, would not show in a piano score.) There is no trace of them in the autograph. Apparently, then, it was the piano score which induced the composer to stiffen the weave at these points, and the non-A copy is post-1948. The shape, however, of each movement has been clear from the start, as the A scripts show.

Sinfonia antartica. 1. The opening 25 bars were originally, as the piano score discloses, more quickly diversionary (comprising bars 1–7, 15–18, 19–21–22, 20–23–24, etc.). But at the climax (fig. 15) the full score reveals a surprising cut of 31 bars of extended celebration of the motto in extraneous keys. The earlier piano score stops at 13. 11.

2. The slithering harp replaces a side-drum roll (timpani sticks) in bars 2–4, 6–8. Hence, its doubling of the bass at the trumpet entry is cancelled.

3. In the organ interlude, at 10, the reverberating B is an afterthought, and then came B–A over G–A, now B♭–A over G♭–A.

4. The bell motive (6. 3) originally led to restatement via the bass motive of 7. 13 in three-metre. The 'Oates' interlude (7) was inserted over this transition.

5. The full score (title-page and movement-heading) shows that the original title-text was the *Ecclesiasticus* verse, 'Their bodies are buried in peace, but their name liveth for evermore'. But the Epilogue does not end, like the film, in an ecstatic commemoration, but in a dramatic recognition of nature's fiendish cycle, mocking human effort. Hence

Scott's plain and final 'No regrets', written as he looked death in the face, is a compelling correction, and a clue to so overwhelming a finish, adumbrated in symphony 1, steadily prepared in symphony 6, but never before so incisive at the primary melodic level. The original finish was after 17, as at 1. 5.

The succinct bell motive (11 to 12) replaces an extension of the 'expeditionary' theme (10. 1–2). The last ten bars have been revised in detail, and the whole score is punctuated by corrective insertions, examination of which might qualify the criticism of the cumulative structural appeal.

Symphony 8 in D minor. The scripts show all degrees of physical completion and artistic achievement.

1. The sketches display tentative ideas, and, in 50390, the crystallization of an 'opening string tune', the jaunty country-dance precedent, it may now seem, of 2. 11 to 3. 2; and a '2nd subject' in F major, whose ruminant 3–3–3–2–1–3 line and succulent 1–3–5–7 chord prepare the ear for the *sostenuto* variation (*lento* initially) and the harmonic addiction. The only continuous score is of var. 2–5, incomplete (6. 7 to 15. 0 only) and obviously early, but fully developed.

2. The full score at once declares itself as an early version: C F–D♭ C to start the first (bassoon) theme; a plainer second bassoon theme (6. 7) and its confined treatment up to 9. 5 in 23 bars, now 30; orchestrally, the answer of horn by trumpet-piccolo between these (5. 11), as now of trombones by trumpet-horn; and a barely recognizable restatement. Of the last 18 bars of today, 1–6 are missing, and 11–18 are a voluble finish, ending with a piquant flourish on the last half beat. The Tempo primo was thus even shorter and slighter than it is today. The piano score at the foot of this score shows a correction of some of these points. The separate piano score, truncated after three bars of Tempo primo, is a late copy.

3. Of the three scripts, the full score, without piano, shows a few minor variants: an extra sequential bar, rising from 6. 3; a 6-bar link from 9. 2 to 10, now extended by adding 9. 6–7; and G string marks for 1st violins at 3. 4, 11; 4. 1; 10. 1, since cancelled. The piano score, which ends at 8 with a 12-bar cut to follow, is similarly penultimate, though its earlier beginnings appear in the abandonment of a succinct six-beat version of the second subject, reaching 4. 6 in 11 bars (not 15) and then sliding nonchalantly into E major for 3 bars.

The other full score, with piano from 1. 4, reveals what must be the earliest stage. (*a*) After the extra bar after 6. 3, instead of the sequent 6. 4 to 8. 2 appear 10 bars in three-metre, in a tuneful neo-modal D major, not without G sharp, B flat and C natural. There is a hint of the Toccata here. But it proved too diversionary. (*b*) 9. 2 to 10 takes 6 bars. (*c*) In three of the last six bars, the strings are in close position before spreading out. (*d*) There are several drafts of the solo-violoncello's coloratura here.

4. The score is marked 'old copy—discarded'. Obsolete features include the doubling of the woodwind bravura by celesta, not violins, in 2. 8–10, a 13-bar version of 13. 1–9, and, more striking, two more bars before the final Largamente, modulating to D from E flat instead of jumping the points. The main impulse and structure are there, including the vibrations of the extra bar inserted after bar 7, and the pencilled-in B *double flat* at 10. 7. Stray pages of an older score show the tune without the minatory bars at 12 to 13.

Such 'variant readings', with the more distinct precedents, of movements so unlike as the wind Scherzo and string Cavatina, remind the thoughtful listener how much creative energy goes into the shaping of theme and context, as well as into deciding how much a mood can be consciously pursued, and how much it can yield to a sense of levitation in a chosen direction.

Symphony 9 in E minor. The most recent symphony yields, as might be expected, the richest procession of scripts. There are sketches for each movement, but especially for the second and fourth, whose second main theme and second-part theme, respectively, gave the composer much concern.

1. Of the two piano scores (50378), one is definitely on the early side. The repeat at 2 to 4 is envisaged but not worked out, and from 6 onwards the growth of the second subject has its own detail. The combination of strands at 6, the outburst at 8, are there, but from 9 the music follows an unfamiliar course, the saxophone motive (as in 10, brass) appearing in E, not B, and in reversed accentuation. The climax at 17. 5 is 'normal', with an extension of 18. 4–5 by repeating the E♭–C fall across a third bar. The erasure of this harmless bar is a determining feature of later scores. A mark of still later versions is the removal of the sequence of inner chords in a nervous cross-rhythm, which is at first found in 21 to 22. 2. These chords here follow a very sketchy unilinear version of the second subject from 19. 5. The adjoining score is virtually a fair copy, except for the chords at 21. Mr.

Douglas's score (50382) registers 18. 5 as final, and no cross-rhythm at 21, leaving the hieratic string-harp percussion unencumbered.

Of the two full scores, one is a rough and ready precedent, though completely scored, and, while at first corresponding with the early piano score, has its own ending. After covering the ground from 16 to 19, and from 19 to 21 (27 bars, now 13), the music reaches a dynamic climax (*ff appassionato*), maintained in the terms of 21 to 22. 5, but then giving place, not to the first subject, but to a continuation of the second as originally announced by the clarinets, confirmed by solo-violin. Finally, the saxophone motive, now on the horns, appears against the lofty string chords of the printed score. The other score begins the 'final version' of the symphony.

2. The sketches show contrasts of development. The first theme is an entire replacement of a jejune outline in a pentatonic D minor. The second and major theme, a rather mysterious waltz-tune, grows gradually from a swaying, trochaic motive in D, with almost Pre-Raphaelite colouring, to an increasingly absorbed melodic line in E flat (neo-Lydian). The combination of both themes, as at 14, appears in yet another notebook. It was worked out before composition began.

Of the three separate piano scores (50379–80), the 'fair copy' in the 5th notebook (of, at present, ten) is decidedly an early version. The 'recovery' at 14 is here in C sharp minor, not G minor. The rougher copy in the 3rd notebook is less early, but the Tempo primo at 6 is a tone higher (C minor) than now. The copy in the 6th notebook is virtually a fair copy and late. (The above numbering of notebooks is as they are now, disposed in a 'double-number'. But even if this is changed, the scripts should be readily identifiable by their description.)

In Mr. Douglas's score, the movement is titled and re-titled: Landscape, Pastoral, Andante sostenuto. A natural initial confusion with the icefalls of the deep South. The second theme (7) is re-directed from *and. sostenuto* to *più animato*. The trombones' rising sequence at 18 is the composer's addition, followed by the correction of two bars of further falling fifths to a stationary F, as now. At 12. 2 and 21 the melodic line is marked cantabile; and why not? Of the full scores, the fragmentary 'rough copy' has, *in toto*, more than half the pages missing, but it discloses longer stages of the present Animando, Tempo primo and Animando than 2, 2 and 2 bars, as printed, hence revision means economy. The appearance of 14 in C sharp minor relates this score to the first piano score. The 'final version' calls for no comment.

3. Sketches include a piece of the fugue and the 'Cats' Choral'

(saxophone entry at 26). Of the three piano scores (*Ib.*, notebooks 7–9) the first peters out halfway, but is evidently a very early draft. Detail is constantly unfamiliar, and it is interesting to note that the second theme (3) is not yet contemplated. The third score is comparatively late, but in the 4th bout of 'chorale' (30) the main theme is used as counterpoint; there are 20 extra bars of tune before 33; 33. 3 to 34 takes 3 bars (now 8); and the vibrant 36. 1–2 is missing. The second score is by no means penultimate. There are rough precedents of 3 to 5 and 7 to 11, and 38 to 39 has a counterpart but no precedent. At 6. 3 the third tune is headed 'Georgia'. Mr. Douglas's score thus amounts to more than an adjustment of detail. However, at 10 it modifies the saxophone roulades from six to four notes a beat, and inserts at last the 2 bars of sonorous envoy at 36. Of the two 'rough' full scores, one starts at 2 but continues to the end, unlike the first piano score above, on which it is clearly based. Hence this score shows not only the absence of the second theme and other vagaries of the earliest version, but the missing half of the movement. Here, with the tune in the bass round 30, one realizes that the composer wished at first to develop the misentitled 'chorale' as an almost folk-tune interlude, with the 4th theme (11). In the end, he compromised with 30 to 34. The other score is late, but for the absence of 36. 1–2. There remains the 'final' version.

4. Sketches stretch from an almost *nobilmente* 'harp tune' in three-metre (D E G|A|B A G|A), as a precedent for the Andante sostenuto theme (6), to a 'best version' of the new motive of Part 2 (16) in E, vague in rhythm but with a clear continuation that absolutely anticipates the bright confidence of 29. Another version of the latter theme, in E but in four-metre, is headed 'Introibo ad altarem Dei', hinting at a sense of transfiguration, however little the composer intended to *disclose* his personal intimations. It is clear that he regarded the theme as a touch of the sublime, which could only emerge from a studiously conditioned situation. Hence the attempt at a linking section after 14, whose late retention is betrayed in the absence of 15 in the score.

Of the three separate piano scores (381), the first is an early draft. The second, entitled 'Epilogue', reveals this preliminary stage. After 14. 3, appear 19 bars of extended development of the new motive, with a canonic treatment which is spontaneous enough to promote a sense of automatic writing. The spell is broken, however, by a change from three beats to four, and what is now 14. 4 follows easily as a pivotal point. Further, there is a jump from 29. 1 (erased) to 32. From there, the conclusion is left, more or less, in process. The third score is similar.

The late missing link (29 to 32) appears first at the end of the late piano score of the first movement. Mr. Douglas's score withdraws (*ad hoc*) the 19 bars after 14. 3, reconstructs the harmonic detail of 22. 5 to 23. 7, and determines the finish as we know it. The 'rough' and sketchy copy of the full score is an early version. The repeat of the second theme at 10, for example, is by violins in an ample score. The link 14. 1–3 is represented by 25 bars. The ending after 32 is hardly identifiable, there being no wind parts in the last five pages. The final score shows the reluctant removal of the link between 14. 3 and 14. 4, as well as an authentic finish, with 29 to 32 and also 33 to 34 as additional features in a subtle integration of the 'harp' tune, the plaintive saxophones and the lofty chording of the first-movement ending.

The remaining scores of vocal, dramatic and other works show, mainly, revisions of textural detail, not a radical reconstruction. There are no discarded versions. One 'vocal' or piano score and one full score (often with the printed voice parts), duly pasted over, usually see a work through to the final text.

Further details of script variant may be consulted in an article in *The Music Review*, 1962-3.

APPENDIX D

List of Works

The main object of this list is to give a conspectus of the order in which the composer's creative work came integrally into being, a conspectus distinguishing its various genres and recognizing, for purposes of sub-classification, primary differences of rhetorical method, setting, scale of treatment, and material, including the use of traditional melody as the basis of a composition. On the relative importance of such differences listeners may disagree, but each must exercise his judgment. As a rule, subsequent revisions of setting or material detail will be regarded as in the nature of postscripts to the principal act of composition, the chosen exceptions proving the rule.

Hence (1) my objective in deciding upon the most significant date for a work—which is frequently questionable in this narrative—has been to find the year of *main completion*. It will in most cases be the year either of first performance, or of publication, whichever is the earlier; both of these are sometimes much later than the main finishing date, and the publication date constantly so. Occasionally another and much earlier date is available, and, in its sometimes legendary style, more authoritative. This is an attempt to tabulate a creative record, not to compile a precise bibliographical note, which would frequently read as woefully dilatory promotion and would be musically misleading.

(2) Compositions that make use of several folk-tunes in a wider context will be described accordingly but classed with the wholly original works, but pieces which are demonstrably settings of a particular tune will be placed in a separate section of arrangements.

(3) It is unnecessary to specify excerpts or arrangements published. These are all in the comprehensive list published by the Oxford University Press Music Department, or transcriptions by other hands.

(4) Works since scrapped are shown in square brackets.

LIST OF WORKS

I. LARGER-SCALE INSTRUMENTAL WORKS

A. WORKS FOR ORCHESTRA

(i) SYMPHONIES

1909   *A Sea Symphony* [1]: *see* III, 'Works for Chorus and Orchestra'
1914   *A London Symphony* [2] (revd. 1920, 1936)
1921   *Pastoral Symphony* [3] (revd. *c.* 1930)

1935   Symphony 4 in F minor

1943   Symphony 5 in D (revd. 1955)
1947   Symphony [6] in E minor (revd. 1950)
1952   *Sinfonia antartica* [7]
1956   Symphony 8 in D minor
1958   Symphony 9 in E minor

(ii) SOLO INSTRUMENTS AND ORCHESTRA

1914   *The Lark Ascending*, a Romance for violin and small orchestra

1925   *Concerto accademico*, in D minor, for violin and strings
       Flos Campi, a suite for viola, small wordless chorus, and small orchestra
1930   [*Fantasia on Sussex Folk-tunes*, for violoncello and orchestra]
1933   Concerto for piano and orchestra (revd. for two pianos and orchestra, 1946)
1934   *Suite* for viola and small orchestra

1944   Concerto for oboe and strings
1950   *Fantasia on the Old 104th*: *see* III, 'Works for Chorus and Orchestra'
1952   *Romance* for harmonica, strings and piano
1954   Concerto in F minor for bass tuba and orchestra

(iii) MISCELLANEOUS

1898   [*Serenade* (small orchestra)]
1901   [*Heroic Elegy*]
1902   [*Bucolic Suite*]
1904   [*Two Orchestral Impressions*: 'Harnham Down' and 'Boldre Wood']
       Norfolk Rhapsody 1 in E minor (re-orchestrated 1925)
       In the Fen Country (revd. 1905, 1907; re-orchestrated 1935)
1906   [*Norfolk Rhapsodies* 2 and 3]

1910 *Fantasia on a Theme by Thomas Tallis* for string quartet and double string orchestra (revd. 1923)

c. 1910 [*Fantasia on English Folk-songs*]

1930 *Job*: see IIB, 'Ballets'

Prelude and Fugue in C minor: *see* VIIIB, 'Organ'

1936 *The Running Set*: *see* IIB, 'Ballets'

Two Hymn-tune Preludes for small orchestra

1939 *Five Variants of 'Dives and Lazarus'* for string orchestra and harps

Partita [for double string trio; re-written] for double string orchestra (1948)

1940 *Prelude* from *Forty-ninth Parallel*: *see* IID, 'Music for Films'

1945 *Story of a Flemish Farm*, suite: *see* IID, 'Music for Films'

1948 *Partita*: *see above*

1950 *Concerto Grosso* for strings

1953 *Prelude on an Old Carol-tune*: *see* IIE, 'Music for Radio Programmes'

B. WORKS FOR MILITARY AND BRASS BAND

(i) MILITARY BAND

1923 *English Folk-song Suite* (orchestral version arr. G. Jacob)

1924 *Toccata Marziale*

Sea Songs, Quick March

(ii) BRASS BAND

1955 *Prelude on Three Welsh Hymn-tunes*

1957 *Variations for Brass Band* (orchestral version arr. G. Jacob)

II. WORKS FOR THE STAGE, ETC.

A. OPERAS, ETC.

1914 *Hugh the Drover*, a Ballad Opera (unfinished; completed and produced 1924; revd. 1933, 1956)

1922 *The Shepherds of the Delectable Mountains*, a Pastoral Episode (later incorporated in *The Pilgrim's Progress*)

1929 *Sir John in Love* (short cantata version, *In Windsor Forest*, 1931)

1931 *Riders to the Sea*

1936 *The Poisoned Kiss*

1951 *The Pilgrim's Progress*, a Morality (revd. 1952)

B. BALLETS

1921 *On Christmas Night*, a Masque, with music devised as a quodlibet of folk tunes and country dances

1923 *Old King Cole*, a folk-dance ballet

1930 *Job: a Masque for Dancing* (version for theatre orchestra arr.
Constant Lambert, 1931)

1936 *The Running Set*, a Dance founded on traditional dance tunes
(version also for two pianos)

1953 *The Bridal Day*, a Masque (cantata version, *Epithalamion*, 1957)

C. MUSIC FOR PLAYS (THEATRE AND RADIO)

1905 *Pan's Anniversary*

1909 *The Wasps*

1913 *King Richard II*, *King Henry IV: Part 2*, *King Richard III*,
King Henry V, *The Devil's Disciple*: MSS

c. 1944 *King Richard II* (B.B.C. performance untraceable; no connection with the 1913 music)

1958 *The First Nowell*, a Nativity Play, with music arranged from
traditional tunes (completed by Roy Douglas)

D. MUSIC FOR FILMS

1940 *Forty-ninth Parallel* ('Prelude': *see* IA, iii; *see also* VIIIA,
'Piano', *The Lake in the Mountains*)

1942 *Coastal Command* (selection used in radio feature in IIE below;
orchestral suite (1942) arr. Muir Mathieson)

1943 *The People's Land* (National Trust), founded on folk-tunes: MS
The Story of a Flemish Farm (orchestral suite, 1945): MS

1945 *Stricken Peninsula* (lost)

1947 *The Loves of Joanna Godden*: MS

1948 *Scott of the Antarctic* (partly transferred to *Sinfonia antartica*):
MS

1949 *Dim Little Island*

1958 *The Vision of William Blake* (including *Ten Blake Songs*: *see*
VI, 'Solo Songs')

E. MUSIC FOR RADIO PROGRAMMES

c. 1942 *Coastal Command* (adapted from film-music): MS

1948–9 *The Pilgrim's Progress* (series of programmes): MS

1951   *The Mayor of Casterbridge* (series) ('Prelude' separately, as *Prelude on an Old Carol-tune*, 1953)

III. WORKS FOR CHORUS AND ORCHESTRA

(mixed chorus and symphony orchestra where not otherwise stated; soloists will not be specified)

1894   *Vexilla Regis*, for chorus, string orchestra and organ (exercise for B. Mus. degree, Cambridge): MS

1899   *Credo, Offertorium* (for orchestra), *Sanctus, Osanna* and *Benedictus* (for double chorus) (exercise for D. Mus. degree, Cambridge): MS

1903   *Willow Wood*, for women's chorus (revd. 1908)

1905   *Toward the Unknown Region* (revd. 1918; reset as unison song, *c.* 1925)

1909   *A Sea Symphony*

1910   *Five Mystical Songs*, for baritone, chorus (optional) and orchestra (version with piano accompaniment also; no. 5, 'Let all the world': version for chorus and organ)

1912   *Fantasia on Christmas Carols*

1925   *Sancta Civitas*

Flos Campi: see IA, ii, 'Solo Instruments and Orchestra'

1929   *The Hundredth Psalm*

Benedicite

Three Choral Hymns

1931   *In Windsor Forest*: see IIA, *Sir John in Love*

1932   *Magnificat*

1935   *Five Tudor Portraits*

1936   *Dona nobis pacem*

1937   *Flourish for a Coronation*

1938   *Serenade to Music* (originally for 16 solo voices and orchestra; orchestral version, 1940)

1945   *Song of Thanksgiving* (formerly *Thanksgiving for Victory*)

1950   *Fantasia on the Old 104th*, for piano, chorus and orchestra

Folk-songs of the Four Seasons, for women's chorus

1951   *The Sons of Light* (unison adaptation *Sun, Moon, Stars and Man*)

1952   *An Oxford Elegy*

1954   *Hodie* (*This Day*)

1957   *Epithalamion*: see IIB, *The Bridal Day*

LIST OF WORKS

IV. WORKS FOR CHORUS
(unaccompanied S.A.T.B. voices where not otherwise stated)

A. WORKS FOR CONCERT USE

(i) ORIGINAL PIECES

c. 1895   *Three Elizabethan Part-songs* (revd. 1912)

1903   *Sound Sleep*, for S.S.A. and piano (also orchestral accompaniment, 1903)

1905   *Rest*, for S.S.A.T.B.
       Ring out, Ye Bells, for S.S.A.T.B.

1907   *Fain would I Change that Note* (T.T.B.B., 1927)

1909   *Come Away, Death*, for S.S.

1913   *Love is a Sickness*

1921   *It was a Lover and his Lass*, for S.A. and piano
       Where is the Home for Me, for two parts and piano
       Dirge for Fidele, for two parts and piano

1936   *Nothing is Here for Tears* (unison version also) (written after the death of King George V)

1941   *England, My England*: *see* V, 'Unison Songs'

1951   *Three Shakespeare Songs*: 1. 'Full Fathom Five', 2. 'The Cloud-capped Towers', 3. 'Over Hill, over Dale'

1952   *The Vagabond*, for T.T.B.B., arr. by the composer (*see* VI)

1953   *Silence and Music* (for *A Garland for the Queen*)

1955   *Heart's Music*

(ii) ARRANGEMENTS OF FOLK AND NATIONAL SONGS, ETC.

(a) Mixed Voices

1913   *Mannin Veen*
       Five English Folk-songs
       Full Fathom Five (Purcell)

1919   *Motherland Song Book*, vols. 3 and 4: *Sea Songs*, for chorus and piano

1920   *Our Love Goes Out* (Purcell) (T.T.B.B. version, 1921)

1921   *The Lass that Loves a Sailor*
       Heart of Oak
       The Mermaid (sop. solo)
       Loch Lomond, for S.S.A.T.B.

1923 *A Farmer's Son so Sweet*, for S.S.A.T.bar. B.
1924 *Bushes and Briars*
  Alister McAlpine's Lament
  Ca' the Yowes
  The Turtle Dove

1934 *An Acre of Land*
  I'll Never Love thee More
  John Dory

  (b) Male Voices (T.T.B.B.)
1908 *Bushes and Briars*
  The Jolly Ploughboy
1912 *Down Among the Dead Men*
  The Turtle Dove
  Ward the Pirate
  The Winter is Gone

1921 *Heart of Oak*
  The Farmer's Boy
  Loch Lomond (bar. solo)
  The Old Folks at Home (bar. solo)
1923 *A Farmer's Son so Sweet* (T. bar. B.)
  The Seeds of Love (T.B.B.)
  High Germany (T.B.B. and T.B. soli)
1925 *Ca' the Yowes*

1934 *An Acre of Land* (optional accompaniment)
  The Ploughman (optional accompaniment)
  The World it Went Well with Me Then (optional accompaniment)

B. WORKS TO BE USED FOR WORSHIP

(Official or unofficial worship. Many of the component works of Section III are most frequently given in the concert room, but were written for, or would grace, a dedicated building. Likewise, some of the items below are sometimes brought into the concert hall; but they may be judged none the less to be—as the remaining works certainly are—distinct in their pronounced affirmatory or liturgical character, rejecting as they do conventional rhetorical aids without claiming any right to be dull for the sheer listener. They may so far be placed in this exclusive sub-section without arousing prejudice on either side about their quality.)

(S.A.T.B. chorus, and organ, where not otherwise stated)

(i) ORIGINAL PIECES

1913 *O Praise the Lord of Heaven* (triple chorus unaccompanied)

1921 *O Clap your Hands*, for chorus, brass, percussion, and organ
Lord, Thou hast been our Refuge, for chorus, semichorus, and orchestra or organ

1922 *Mass* in G minor, for soli, double chorus, and optional organ (Anglican version, adaptation by Maurice Jacobson, 1923)
O vos omnes, for alto and 8-part chorus, unaccompanied (English version, *Is it nothing to you?*, adaptation by Maurice Jacobson)

1925 *Magnificat and Nunc Dimittis* in C

1928 *Te Deum* in G, for double chorus and organ or orchestra

1934 [*The Pilgrim Pavement*]
Te Deum in E minor, and *Benedictus* in F, set to well-known metrical psalm tunes
O How Amiable

1937 *Festival Te Deum* in F, for chorus and organ or orchestra (Coronation)

1939 *Morning, Communion, and Evening Service* in D minor, for unison voices, chorus and organ

1941 *Valiant for Truth*, for unaccompanied chorus

1947 *The Souls of the Righteous*, for S. T. bar. soli and unaccompanied chorus
The Voice out of the Whirlwind, adapted from 'Galliard of the Sons of the Morning' (*Job*)
My Soul, Praise the Lord (version also for unison voices with descant, and for strings and organ accompaniment)

1948 *Prayer to the Father of Heaven*, for unaccompanied chorus

1953 *O Taste and See*, for unaccompanied chorus with organ introduction (Coronation) (version also for S.S.A. choir)

1956 *A Choral Flourish*, for unaccompanied chorus with introduction for organ or two trumpets
A Vision of Aeroplanes

1958 *The First Nowell*: see IIc, 'Music for Plays'

519

APPENDIX D

(ii) ARRANGEMENTS

(a) Separate Pieces and Small Collections

(congregation, choir, and organ, where not otherwise stated)

1919   *Eight Traditional English Carols*, for unaccompanied chorus

1920   *Twelve Traditional Carols from Herefordshire*, for unaccompanied chorus

1927   *At the Name of Jesus* (tune: *King's Weston*)

1938   *All Hail the Power* (tune: *Miles Lane*) (also with orchestral accompaniment)

1942   *Nine Carols*, for unaccompanied T.T.B.B.

1945   *Two Carols*, for unaccompanied chorus

1953   *The Old Hundredth*, with orchestra (Coronation)

1956   *God Bless the Master of this House*, for unaccompanied chorus

(b) Large Collections of which Vaughan Williams was Music Editor

1906   *The English Hymnal* (second edition, 1933)

1925   *Songs of Praise* (with Martin Shaw) (enlarged edition, 1931)

1928   *The Oxford Book of Carols* (with Martin Shaw)

(These contain many creative 'arrangements' of traditional melodies (e.g. 'Monksgate',' Lasst uns erfreuen', 'Laus tibi Christe'), and settings of the following original hymn and carol tunes by Vaughan Williams (each is set to one hymn, whose collocation is preserved, where his tune is used, in the various nonconformist hymn-books):

> *The English Hymnal*: 'Down Ampney', 'King's Weston', 'Magda', 'Randolph', 'Salve Festa Dies', 'Sine Nomine', 'White Gates'
>
> *Songs of Praise*: 'Abinger', 'Cumnor', 'Famous Men', 'Guildford', 'Mantegna', 'Marathon', 'Oakley', with all the above tunes in the *Hymnal*
>
> *The Oxford Book of Carols*: 'The Golden Carol' (173), 'Wither's Rocking Hymn' (185), 'Snow in the Street' (186), 'Blake's Cradle Song' (196))

V. UNISON SONGS
(with accompaniment)

(i) ORIGINAL PIECES

1923   *Let us Now Praise Famous Men* (later in *Songs of Praise*)

LIST OF WORKS

1925   *Darest Thou Now, O Soul (Toward the Unknown Region)*
      Three Songs from Shakespeare: 1. 'Take, O take', 2. 'When icicles hang', 3. 'Orpheus with his lute' (second setting)
1930   *Three Children's Songs for a Spring Festival*
1936   *Nothing is Here for Tears* (S.A.T.B. setting also)
1939   *A Hymn of Freedom*
1940   *Six Choral Songs*
1941   *England, My England* (with optional chorus part; versions with accompaniment of orchestra or military band)
1942   *The Airmen's Hymn*
1943   *The New Commonwealth* (adapted from *Forty-ninth Parallel* film-music)

(ii) ARRANGEMENTS

(Some of these were originally for solo voice, but they are suitable or conceivably usable for unison singing, and they are in most cases typical or collective rather than soloist in tone.)

1906   Songs collected from Essex, Norfolk, Sussex, Wiltshire, Yorkshire, London (tune only) (*Journal of the Folk-Song Society*, 8)
1907   *L'Amour de Moy*
      Réveillez-vous, Piccarz
1908   *Folk-songs from the Eastern Counties*
1910   *The Spanish Ladies*
1912   *Folk-songs from Sussex*
      Folk-songs for Schools, set 6 (Novello's *School Songs*)
1919   *Motherland Song Book*, vols. 3 and 4: *Sea Songs* (optional choral part)
      The Dark-eyed Sailor
      Just as the Tide was Flowing
      The Turtle Dove
      And All in the Morning
      Dives and Lazarus
      Down in Yon Forest
      On Christmas Night
      The Angel Gabriel
1920   *Our Love Goes Out* (Purcell) (also for mixed and male chorus)
1921   *The Lass that Loves a Sailor*
      Heart of Oak

The Mermaid

1934 *She's like the Swallow*
1935 *Six English Folk-songs*
1936 *Two English Folk-songs*, for voice and violin
1937 *Two French Folk-songs*
       Two Old German Folk-songs (a third remains in manuscript)

(1959) *The Penguin Book of English Folk Songs* (with A. L. Lloyd)
(1961) *A Yacre of Land*: sixteen folk-songs from Vaughan Williams's
         MS collection, ed. Imogen Holst and Ursula Vaughan
         Williams, arr. for unison voices and piano, or unaccom-
         panied chorus, by Imogen Holst

VI. SOLO SONGS

(The early dates are based on the 'only approximate' dates supplied
by the composer to the late Miss Katherine E. Eggar for an article in
the *Music Student*, June, 1920, and other dates given in an article by
Edwin Evans in the *Musical Times*, June, 1920.)

(with piano, where not otherwise stated)

1896 *Claribel*
       How can the Tree but Wither? (also with orchestral accom-
       paniment)
1902 *Whither Must I Wander?*
1903 *The House of Life*, song-cycle of six sonnets ('Silent Noon'
       also with orchestral accompaniment)
       Orpheus with his Lute, first setting (also with orchestral accom-
       paniment)
       Tears, Idle Tears
       When I am Dead
       The Winter's Willow
       Adieu
c. 1903 *Boy Johnny*
       If I were Queen
       The Splendour Falls
       Blackmore by the Stour
       Linden Lea
c. 1904 *Songs of Travel* (seven songs in two sets as published, and
       'I have Trod the Upward and the Downward Slope', the
       long lost epilogue, published 1960; with perhaps *Whither
       must I wander?* from above) (orchestral version of songs 1–3,
       1905; 'The Vagabond' for T.T.B.B. unaccompanied, 1952)

1905 *Cradle Song*
     Dreamland
1909 *Buonaparty*
     The Sky above the Roof
     On Wenlock Edge, song-cycle for tenor, string quartet and
        piano (or piano accompaniment; orchestral accompaniment,
        1924)
1914 *Four Hymns*, for tenor, piano and viola (accompaniment for
        strings also)

1922 *Merciless Beauty*, three rondels for voice and string trio
        (violin, viola, 'cello)
1925 *Three Poems by Walt Whitman*
     Four Poems by Fredegond Shove
     Two Poems by Seumas O'Sullivan (only 'The Twilight People'
        survives)
c. 1925 *Along the Field*: eight [A. E.] Housman songs for voice and
        violin (a ninth remains in manuscript)

1952 *In the Spring*
1958 *Ten Blake Songs*: *see* IID, *The Vision of William Blake*
(1960) *Three Vocalises*, for soprano and clarinet
     Four Last Songs: 1. 'Procris', 2. 'Tired', 3. 'Hands, eyes
        and heart', 4. 'Menelaus'

VII. CHAMBER MUSIC

1904 [Quintet in C minor, for violin, viola, 'cello, double-bass, and
        piano]
?1905 [Quintet, for violin, viola, 'cello, horn, and piano]
1908 String quartet [1] in G minor (revd. 1921)
1913 *Phantasy Quintet*, for strings (W. W. Cobbett competition)

1923 *Romance*, for violin and piano
     Pastoral, for violin and piano
c. 1924 *Suite de Ballet*, for flute and piano (published 1962)
1927 *Six Studies in English Folk-song*, for 'cello (or violin, or viola,
        or clarinet) and piano

1942 *Household Music: Three Preludes on Welsh Hymn Tunes*, for
        string quartet, or other instruments

APPENDIX D

1945 String quartet [2] in A minor
1947 Suite for pipes

1957 Sonata for violin and piano in A minor

VIII. WORKS FOR PIANO AND ORGAN

A. PIANO

1921 Suite of six short pieces
Twelve Traditional Country Dances (with Maud Karpeles)

1930 *Hymn-tune Prelude on Gibbons's 'Song* 13'
1931 *Job,* arr. Vally Lasker
1934 *Six Teaching Pieces* (three books): 1 and 2, Two Two-part Inventions, in G and E flat; 3 and 4, Valse Lente and Nocturne; 5 and 6, Canon and Two-part Invention in F
1936 *The Running Set,* for two pianos: *see* IIB, 'Ballets'

1946 *Introduction and Fugue* for two pianos
1947 *The Lake in the Mountains* (from *Forty-ninth Parallel* music: *see* IID, 'Music for Films')

B. ORGAN

1920 *Three Preludes on Welsh Hymn-tunes*
?1921 *Prelude and Fugue* in C minor (also for orchestra, 1930) published in 1930. (Whatever the date, the organ version published in 1930 is not an arrangement.)

1956 *Two Preludes on Welsh Folk-songs*

IX. EDITIONS

1905, 1910 Purcell: *Welcome Songs;* for Purcell Society edition (vols. 15 and 18)

X. LITERARY WORKS

N.D. *English Folk Songs,* an abridgment of a lecture given in 1912, written for the English Folk Dance and Song Society reprinted in Dr. Young's *Vaughan Williams*
1912 *R.C.M. Magazine,* 9:1, article, 'Who wants the English composer?'

LIST OF WORKS

1920   *Music and Letters*, 1:2, article, 'The letter and the spirit' (and many other articles and reviews)

1934   *National Music*, the Mary Flexner Lectures at Bryn Mawr College, Pennsylvania

1953   *Some Thoughts on Beethoven's Choral Symphony and Other* [reprinted] *Writings*

1955   *The Making of Music*, lectures at Cornell University.

See also *Heirs and Rebels*, edited by Ursula Vaughan Williams and Imogen Holst (1959), containing essays and correspondence between Vaughan Williams and his close colleague, Holst.

Index

This index divided into four parts, has various aims. Part I ('Works of Vaughan Williams') indicates the point of main discussion of each of Vaughan Williams's works, and assembles some points of anticipation or reverberation. Part II ('Miscellaneous Cross-references to Composers') lists works by other composers which relate to a Vaughan Williams work owing to similarity of subject or genre, or of a particular incident, despite a difference of method. Part III ('Vaughan Williams's Working Methods') defines, where they admit of tabulation, the recurrence of certain concrete features of composition—as opposed to broad types of technical handling such as harmonic treatment or counterpoint (i.e. contrapuntally contrived harmony); it is a measure of a deficient English vocabulary that there is no entry here for any rhythmic trait except strophical development. Part IV ('General References to Individual Performers, Critics, Promoters and Organizations') lists the individuals and organizations whose work has been associated with Vaughan Williams's art in a responsive way.

Inevitably some references will be of only indirect interest (references, for instance, to perhaps arbitrary comparisons). However, every important reference will be in distinctive type (often references of this kind will be to the first page of several concerned with an item); and the respective extent of other references will provide some estimate as to which of Vaughan Williams's works, or features of Vaughan Williams's works, are considered here to range most widely, or recur most noticeably, and which of the works of other composers suggest themselves most constantly as a standard of comparison or as an imaginative parallel.

PART I

WORKS OF VAUGHAN WILLIAMS

LARGER-SCALE INSTRUMENTAL WORKS
WORKS FOR THE STAGE, ETC.
CHORAL WORKS
SONGS
CHAMBER MUSIC
WORKS FOR PIANO AND ORGAN
COLLECTIONS

WORKS OF VAUGHAN WILLIAMS

529

WORKS OF VAUGHAN WILLIAMS

531

PART II

MISCELLANEOUS CROSS-REFERENCES
TO COMPOSERS (AND WORKS)

Alwyn, William, film-music
method, 438
Arne, Thomas:
Alfred, 75
Artaxerxes, 75
Auric, *Les Matelots,* 339

Bach, C. P. E., *Magnificat,* 222
Bach, J. S., 91
Art of Fugue (fugue 6), 327
Christmas Oratorio, **370**
Christus der ist mein Leben
(cantata 95), 121
Concerto in A minor, for violin
and strings, 412
Es ist nicht gesundes (cantata 25),
chorus, 367
Gott soll allein mein Herze haben
(cantata 169), air (from key-
board concerto in E), 366
Herr Gott, dich loben alle wir
(cantata 130), 222
Magnificat in D, 222
Mass in B minor, 298, 369
Passion, St. Matthew, **57**, 252,
363, 400
Prelude in C minor, for organ
(S. 546), **472**
Schauet doch und sehet (cantata
46), chorus, **220**
Unser Mund sei voll Lachens
(cantata 110), chorus (from
overture 4), 366
Wir müssen durch viel Trübsal
(cantata 146), chorus (from
keyboard concerto in D minor)
366
Balakirev:
*Overture on Three Russian
Themes,* **167***n.*
Russia, **167***n.*

Balfe, *Falstaff,* **259***n.*
Bantock, overture to *The Frogs,* 171
Barley, William, lute-song, **145**
Bax:
Hill-tune for piano, 470
Symphony 3, 291
Symphony 6, 306
Beethoven, **35, 95,** 97, 314
Coriolan, overture to, 201
Fidelio, 256, 288, 364, 406, 464
Mass in D, 186, 369
String quartets:
op. 59. 2, in E minor, 250
op. 127, in E flat, 320
op. 130, in B flat, 396
op. 132, in A minor, 117
op. 135, in F, 349
Symphonies:
3 in E flat (*Eroica*), 407
4 in B flat, 303
5 in C minor, 301
6 in F (*Pastoral*), 191, 208, 382
9 in D minor, 181, 316, 349,
407
Wellington's Victory, 97
Berg, *Lulu,* 226
Berlioz, **95**
Benvenuto Cellini, 423
Damnation de Faust, La, **182,** 225
Herminie, 169
Lélio, 465
*Symphonie dramatique, Roméo et
Juliette,* **71**, 169, **181,** 343
Troyens, Les, **73**, 160, 265, 280,
484
Berners, *Triumph of Neptune, The,*
338
Bliss:
Film-music, 438
Morning Heroes, 231
Pastoral Elegy, 229

PART III

VAUGHAN WILLIAMS'S WORKING METHODS

PART IV

GENERAL REFERENCES TO INDIVIDUAL PERFORMERS, CRITICS, PROMOTERS AND ORGANIZATIONS

DATE DUE